International
Economic
Indicators

INTERNATIONAL ECONOMIC INDICATORS

A Sourcebook

Geoffrey H. Moore
and
Melita H. Moore

Greenwood Press
Westport, Connecticut • London, England

Library of Congress Cataloging in Publication Data

Moore, Geoffrey Hoyt.
  International economic indicators.

  1. Economic indicators.   I. Moore, Melita H.
II. Title.
HC59.M62   1985   330.9   84-19194
ISBN 0-313-21989-3 (lib. bdg.)

Library of Congress Catalog Card Number: 84-19194
ISBN: 0-313-21989-3

First published in 1985

Greenwood Press
A division of Congressional Information Service, Inc.
88 Post Road West, Westport, Connecticut 06881

Printed in the United States of America

10 9 8 7 6 5 4 3 2 1

Contents

Preface

This volume provides detailed information on the international economic indicators that have been selected and compiled by the Center for International Business Cycle Research (CIBCR). The seven largest industrial countries are included: the United States, United Kingdom, Canada, West Germany, France, Italy, and Japan. The indicators are in three categories: those that lead movements in the business cycle and give advance warning of both recession and recovery, the coincident indicators that provide measures of current economic performance, and the lagging indicators that move more slowly but warn of developing imbalances or their correction.

Chapter 1 outlines the development of the study of business-cycle indicators in the United States, the extension of this study to other major industrial countries, and the more important uses of these data. Preliminary studies have been made of economic indicators in the smaller countries of Europe and in the Pacific area but these materials are not included except for some limited information in Appendix B. Similar systems of indicators have been developed by government agencies in a few other countries, but because of differences in content or methodology they are not comparable from country to country. The Organization for Economic Cooperation and Development in Paris has also recently begun to publish leading indexes for eighteen countries (see *Main Economic Indicators*, March 1983). The information in this volume will facilitate comparison with these other economic indexes.

Chapter 2 describes the content and coverage of each economic indicator. Also included is the published source of each series, the title used in this source, references to additional information, and the years covered by the data printed in Chapter 3. No data are published prior to 1948 although earlier figures are sometimes available in the original source. Units are listed as they appear in Chapter 3 and are not necessarily the same as those in the original source.

Chapter 3 sets out the time series for each indicator as well as the composite-leading, coincident, and lagging indexes for each country. Indexes for the four European countries taken together are shown, as well as those for six countries excluding the United States, and finally all seven countries. Growth rates for each of the composite indexes are also shown.

Appendix A lists the most important statistical publications in which the original data for these series appear. Appendix B presents growth-cycle chronologies for thirteen countries from 1948 to 1983 and discusses their meaning and uses. Appendix C presents tables showing the lengths of leads and lags of the individual indicators at growth-cycle peaks and troughs for seven countries. Appendix D describes the method of construction of the composite indexes. A sample printout from the monthly *International Economic Indicators*, published by the CIBCR, is shown. This publication contains revised and up-to-date figures for all the leading and coincident indicators and composite indexes shown in this book. A program to update the lagging indicators and maintain them on a current basis also is planned. Computer tapes for all the data in this book are available from the CIBCR and current data are available on-line from Citicorp Information Services in New York.

The Indicator Series Finding Guide gives a listing of the series by title and shows where the information about each series can be found in Chapters 2 and 3.

ACKNOWLEDGMENTS

The Center for International Business Cycle Research (CIBCR) has been fortunate to have the expert assistance of the statistical staff of the Organization for Economic Cooperation and Development (OECD) in developing and maintaining on a current basis the indicator series for European countries. Statistics Canada and the Japanese Planning Agency have likewise been most helpful in providing current and historical data for their countries. In addition to national statistics source materials, we have obtained much additional information on the indicators from publications of the OECD and the United Nations. We are grateful to the following statisticians for reviewing our descriptions of the series: M. J. G. Lockyer, Central Statistical Office, London; M. Devilliers, Institut National de la Statistique et des Etudes Economiques, Paris; Eugenio De Nicola, Istituto Nazionale per lo Studio della Congiuntura, Rome; Hermann Pieper, Bundesministerium fur Wirtschaft, Bonn; Darryl Rhoades, Statistics Canada, Ottawa; and Katsutoshi Hosobuchi, Japanese Planning Agency,

Tokyo. We alone, however, are responsible for any omissions or inaccuracies in the text.

Philip Klein of Pennsylvania State University has been associated with the international-indicators project ever since work on it began at the National Bureau of Economic Research in 1973, and we are indebted to him for his continuing efforts in assembling and analyzing the basic data presented in this book. We have benefited, also, from the work of John P. Cullity of Rutgers University on the development of the lagging indicators. Jean Maltz has been most diligent and meticulous in maintaining the entire data base. Elizabeth Wehle, Chantal Dubrin, and many other associates at the National Bureau and the CIBCR have contributed in various ways to the development of the series. We are indebted, also, to Dorothy Holly for assistance in translation, and to Lynn Hodges, Blanche Winikoff, and Stuart D'Ver for preparation of the manuscript.

The research underlying this book has been supported by grants and contributions from many sources, including the Olin Foundation, the Scaife Foundation, the Earhart Foundation, and the Conference Board.

International
Economic
Indicators

1

An Introduction to International Economic Indicators

For many years a system of leading, coincident, and lagging economic indicators, first developed in the 1930s by the National Bureau of Economic Research (NBER), has been widely used in the United States to appraise the state of business cycles. Since 1961 the current monthly figures for these indicators have been published by the U.S. Department of Commerce in *Business Conditions Digest*. Similar systems have been developed by government or private agencies in Canada, Japan, the United Kingdom, and more recently in many other countries. Because of differences in content or methodology, however, these independent efforts do not provide comparable materials. In 1973 the NBER began to develop an international economic indicator system (IEI) that would provide comparable data, organized and analyzed in a comparable manner, for a number of industrial countries. The Center for International Business Cycle Research (CIBCR) has continued this work since 1979.

The research has demonstrated that such a system can be helpful in tracking an international recovery or recession, in revealing factors that are holding back recovery or leading to recession, in anticipating changes in foreign trade flows, and in providing early warning of new inflationary trends. The Organization for Economic Cooperation and Development (OECD) and statistical agencies in Canada, the United Kingdom, West Germany, France, Italy, Japan, and the United States have cooperated with the NBER and with the CIBCR in compiling and analyzing the current data for this system of indicators. The practical results of this research program are made available through monthly publications of CIBCR and of the Conference Board in New York.[1]

This chapter explains the functions of the indicator system, summarizes the evidence concerning its strengths and weaknesses, and demonstrates how it can be used to forecast business cycles, exports and imports, and inflation rates. A comprehensive report on these matters is given in Philip

A. Klein and Geoffrey H. Moore, *Monitoring Business Cycles in Market-Oriented Economies*, Ballinger Publishing Co., 1985.

FUNCTIONS OF THE IEI SYSTEM

The NBER's first study of business-cycle indicators, conducted in 1937 by Wesley C. Mitchell and Arthur F. Burns, had as its immediate objective the use of indicators to signal a cyclical revival—that is, the ending of a recession, specifically the ending of the severe recession in the United States that began in the spring of 1937. When the work was taken up again after World War II, the objective was broadened to include signals of a cyclical downturn; and NBER studies completed in 1950, 1960, and 1966 as well as a Commerce Department study conducted in 1975 focused on both the beginning and the end of recessions. An international system designed along similar lines should signal both peaks and troughs in each of the countries covered as well as in several countries taken together. In short, an important function of the IEI system is to promptly detect a worldwide recession or recovery. The importance of this function is underlined by the fact that international recessions—those in which many countries participate more or less simultaneously—have been more serious than localized recessions. One need only point to 1973-75 and 1980-82 to find recent examples of recessions that were both serious and international.

A second, and closely related, function of the IEI system is to measure the scope, severity, and unusual features of an international recession or recovery while it is in progress. For example, during the 1975-76 recovery in the United States it became common practice, in reports devoted to the economic outlook, to compare the current recovery with previous recovery periods in this country. Similar comparisons were made during subsequent recessions and recoveries. News magazines, business journals, corporate annual reports, government reports, and newspapers used this device as a method of appraisal. But few of the publications made such comparisons for other countries, despite their relevance from a world point of view or their value in the diagnosis of specific problems pertaining to other countries. One of the reasons is that the necessary information is not widely known. An international economic indicator system permits comparisons of this type to be made routinely and kept up to date.

A third function of the IEI system is to help appraise prospects for foreign trade. The leading indicators are sensitive measures of the general state of demand. Although many other factors affect the volume of exports and imports, demand is surely fundamental. A trade deficit can come about because of sluggish demand for exports from a country's trading partners while its own demand for imports is growing. Since the leading indicators include such demand-related factors as new orders, inventory change, hiring rates, and profitability, one can expect that they would relate to the demand not only for domestic goods but also for foreign products. Leading indicators for an importing country, therefore, should tell us something about how much it is likely to import, or how much its trading partners may be able to export to it. The IEI system should therefore help us anticipate changes in the flow of trade among the countries for which leading indicators are available as well as changes in their trade balances.

Fourth, a system of international indicators can provide early warning signals of an acceleration or deceleration in the rate of inflation. Inflation is in part a demand phenomenon, and, as noted above, many of the indicators are demand oriented. Inflation is also an international phenomenon. All countries experience it, and waves of inflation often occur at about the same time in many countries. An appropriate set of international indicators should show how the price system responds to and feeds back upon the rest of the economy, including, of course, those variables that are under some degree of policy control, such as the money supply, the flow of credit, or the fiscal deficit.

LEADS AND LAGS IN RECOVERY AND RECESSION

The international economic indicator system described in this book consists of groups of leading, coincident, and lagging indicators covering a wide variety of economic processes that have been found to be important in business cycles. The leading indicators are for the most part measures of anticipations or new commitments. They have a "look-ahead" quality and are highly sensitive to changes in the economic climate as perceived in the marketplace. The coincident indicators are comprehensive measures of economic performance: real gross national product (GNP), industrial production, employment, unemployment, income, and trade. They are the measures to which everyone looks to determine whether a nation is prosperous or depressed. The lagging indicators are more sluggish in their reactions to the economic climate, but they serve a useful purpose by smoothing out and confirming changes in trend that are first reflected in the leading and coincident indicators. Moreover, their very sluggishness can be an asset in cyclical analysis, because when they do begin to move, or when they move rapidly, they may show that excesses or imbalances in the economy are developing or subsiding. Hence the lagging indicators can (and often do) provide the earliest warnings of all, as when rapid increases in costs of production outstrip price increases and threaten profit margins, thus inhibiting new commitments to invest, which are among the leading indicators.

A conspectus of the U.S. indicators arranged according to the type of economic process they represent and the cyclical timing they exhibit is in table 1. The compilation for other industrial countries is designed to represent substantially the same processes arranged in a similar manner. The degree of success in accomplishing this varies from one country to another, as shown in table 2.

Table 1
Cross-Classification of U.S. Indicators by Economic Process and Cyclical Timing

Economic Process	Cyclical Timing		
	Leading	Roughly coincident	Lagging
Employment and unemployment	Average work week, manufacturing New unemployment insurance claims, inverted	Nonfarm employment Unemployment, inverted	Long-duration unemployment, inverted
Production, income, consumption, and trade	New orders, consumer goods and materials*	Gross national product* Industrial production Personal income* Manufacturing and trade sales*	
Fixed capital Investment	Formation of business enterprises Contracts and orders, plant and equipment* Building permits, housing		Investment expenditures, plant and equipment*

Inventories and inventory investment	Change in business inventories*	Business inventories*
Prices, costs, and profits	Industrial materials price index, change Stock price index Profits* Ratio, price to unit labor cost, nonfarm	Change in output per man-hour, manufacturing, inverted
Money and credit	Change, consumer installment debt*	Commercial and industrial loans outstanding* Bank interest rates, business loans

* In constant prices.

Note: The list and classification is substantially the same as that prepared in 1966 and published in Geoffrey H. Moore and Julius Shiskin, *Indicators of Business Expansions and Contractions* (New York: National Bureau of Economic Research, 1967). The chief modification is that those series marked with * are converted to constant prices. The timing classification for each series is the same as shown in *Business Conditions Digest* for all turns (see Table 1, column 1, in any recent issue), except as follows: Unemployment is unclassified (U) at all turns in *BCD* because it leads at peaks and lags at troughs, but here it is classified roughly coincident, as in the 1966 list. Four series that here are in constant prices are shown in *BCD* only in current prices: change in consumer installment debt, investment expenditures for plant and equipment, commercial and industrial loans outstanding, and change in output per man-hour, manufacturing, inverted, which is the constant price equivalent of labor cost per unit of output. The constant price series are assigned the same classification as the current price series.

Although the indicators listed here share a common ancestry and rationale with those currently used in the composite indexes published in *Business Conditions Digest*, only about half the series are identical. A number of series in the two lists are closely related but some are quite different. Despite these differences, the movements in the U.S. indexes shown below are broadly similar to those in *BCD*.

7

Table 2
A Classification and List of International Economic Indicators

United States	Canada	France
Leading	*Leading*	*Leading*
1.0 Average workweek, mfg.	1.0 Average workweek, mfg.	1.0 Average workweek, mfg.
2.0 New unemployment claims[b]	2.0 New unemployment claims[b]	2.0 New unemployment claims[b]
3.0 New orders, consumer goods[a]	3.1 New orders, consumer goods[a]	3.1 Change in unfilled orders[c]
4.0 Formation of bus. enterprises	NA	NA
5.0 Contracts & orders, plant & equipment[a]	5.1 New orders, equipment[a]	
	5.2 Nonresidential bldg. permits[a]	
6.0 Building permits, housing, no.	6.0 Residential building permits, no.	6.0 Residential building permits, no.
7.0 Change in bus. inventories[a]	7.0 Change in bus. inventories[a]	7.0 Change in stocks[a]
8.0 Industrial materials prices, change	8.0 Industrial materials prices, change	8.0 Raw materials prices, change
9.0 Stock price index	9.0 Stock price index	9.0 Stock price index
10.0 Profits[a]	10.0 Profits[a]	NA
11.0 Ratio, price to labor cost	11.0 Ratio, price to labor cost	11.0 Ratio, price to labor cost
12.0 Change in consumer debt[a]	12.0 Change in consumer debt[a]	NA
Coincident	*Coincident*	*Coincident*
13.0 Nonfarm employment	13.0 Nonfarm employment	13.0 Nonfarm employment
14.0 Unemployment rate[b]	14.0 Unemployment rate[b]	14.1 Registered unemployed, no.[b]
15.0 Gross national product[a]	15.0 Gross national expenditures[a]	15.0 Gross domestic production[a]
16.0 Industrial production	16.0 Industrial production	16.0 Industrial production
17.0 Personal income[a]	17.0 Personal income[a]	NA
18.0 Mfg. & trade sales[a]	18.1 Retail trade[a]	18.1 Retail sales[a]

United States

Leading
1.0 Average workweek, mfg.
2.0 New unemployment claims[b]
3.0 New orders, consumer goods[a]
4.0 Formation of bus. enterprises
5.0 Contracts & orders, plant & equipment[a]
6.0 Building permits, housing, no.
7.0 Change in bus. inventories[a]
8.0 Industrial materials prices, change
9.0 Stock price index
10.0 Profits[a]
11.0 Ratio, price to labor cost
12.0 Change in consumer debt[a]

Lagging
19.0 Long duration unemployment[b]
20.0 Plant & equipment investment[a]
21.0 Business inventories[a]
22.0 Productivity change, nonfarm[b]
23.0 Business loans, outstanding[a]
24.0 Interest rates, bus. loans

United Kingdom

Leading
1.0 Average workweek, mfg.
NA
NA
4.1 New companies registered
4.2 Business failures
5.1 New orders, engineering indus.[a]
5.2 New orders, construction[a]
6.1 Housing starts, no.
7.0 Change in stocks[a]
8.0 Basic materials prices, change
9.0 Stock price index
10.0 Profits[a]
11.0 Ratio, price to labor cost
12.0 Increase in hire purchase debt[a]

Lagging
19.0 Long duration unemployment[b]
20.0 Plant & equipment investment[a]
21.0 Business inventories[a]
22.1 Productivity change, manufacturing[b]
23.0 Business loans, outstanding[a]
24.0 Interest rates, bus. loans

West Germany

Leading
1.1 Short-hour workers[b]
2.0 Unemployment applicants[b]
NA
4.1 Insolvent enterprises[b]
5.1 New orders, investment goods[a]
6.1 Residential constr. orders[a]
7.0 Inventory change[a]
8.0 Basic materials prices, change[c]
9.0 Stock price index
10.1 Income from enterprise[a]
11.0 Ratio, price to labor cost
12.0 Change in consumer debt[a]

Lagging
19.0 Long duration unemployment[b]
20.0 Plant & equipment investment[a]
21.0 Business inventories[a]
22.0 Productivity change, nonfarm[b]
23.0 Business loans, outstanding[a]
24.0 Interest rates, bus. loans

Table 2 (*continued*)

United States	United Kingdom	West Germany
Coincident	*Coincident*	*Coincident*
13.0 Nonfarm employment	13.1 Employment, industry	13.1 Employment, mining & mfg.
14.0 Unemployment rate[b]	14.1 Registered unemployed, no.[b]	14.1 Registered unemployment rate[b]
15.0 Gross national product[a]	15.0 Gross domestic product[a]	15.0 Gross national product[a]
16.0 Industrial production	16.0 Industrial production	16.0 Industrial production
17.0 Personal income[a]	17.0 Personal income[a]	17.0 Disposable income[a]
18.0 Mfg. & trade sales[a]	18.1 Retail sales[a]	18.1 Manufacturing sales[a]
		18.2 Retail trade[a]
Lagging	*Lagging*	*Lagging*
19.0 Long duration unemployment[b]	19.0 Long duration unemployment[b]	NA
20.0 Plant & equipment investment[a]	20.0 Plant & equipment expenditure[a]	20.0 Plant & equipment expenditure[a]
21.0 Business inventories[a]	21.0 Business inventories[a]	21.0 Business inventories[a]
22.0 Productivity change, nonfarm[b]	22.1 Productivity change, industry[b]	22.1 Productivity change, industry[b]
23.0 Business loans outstanding[a]	23.1 Indus. & agr. loans outstanding[a]	23.1 Bank loans outstanding[a]
24.0 Interest rates, bus. loans	24.0 Interest rates, bus. loans	24.1 Interest rates, large loans

United States	Italy	Japan
Leading	*Leading*	*Leading*
1.0 Average workweek, mfg.	1.1 Monthly hours, industry	1.1 Overtime worked, mfg.
2.0 New unemployment claims[b]	NA	NA
3.0 New orders, consumer goods[a]	3.1 Change in unfilled orders[c]	NA
4.0 Formation of bus. enterprises	4.1 Declared bankruptcies[b]	4.1 Business failures[b]
5.0 Contracts & orders, plant & equipment[a]	NA	5.0 New orders, machinery and construction[a]
6.0 Building permits, housing, no.	6.0 Residential building permits	6.1 Dwelling units started, no.

10

7.0 Change in bus. inventories[a]	7.0 Change in inventories[a]	7.0 Change in inventories[a]
8.0 Industrial materials prices, change	8.0 Producers' materials prices, change	8.0 Raw materials prices, change
9.0 Stock price index	9.0 Stock price index	9.0 Stock price index
10.0 Profits[a]	NA	10.0 Profits[a]
11.0 Ratio, price to labor cost	11.0 Ratio, price to labor cost	11.0 Ratio, price to labor cost
12.0 Change in consumer debt[a]	NA	12.1 Change in consumer and housing debt[a]
Coincident	*Coincident*	*Coincident*
13.0 Nonfarm employment	13.0 Nonfarm employment	13.0 Nonfarm employment, regular workers
14.0 Unemployment rate[b]	14.0 Unemployment rate[b]	14.0 Unemployment rate[b]
15.0 Gross national product[a]	15.0 Gross domestic product[a]	15.0 Gross national expenditures[a]
16.0 Industrial production	16.0 Industrial production	16.0 Industrial production
17.0 Personal income[a]	NA	17.1 Wage & salary income[a]
18.0 Mfg. & trade sales[a]	18.1 Retail sales[a]	18.1 Retail sales[a]
Lagging	*Lagging*	*Lagging*
19.0 Long duration unemployment[b]	NA	NA
20.0 Plant & equipment investment[a]	20.1 Plant & equipment investment[a]	20.0 Plant & equipment expenditure[a]
21.0 Business inventories[a]	21.0 Business inventories[a]	21.0 Business inventories[a]
22.0 Productivity change, nonfarm[b]	NA	22.1 Productivity change, industry[b]
23.0 Business loans outstanding[a]	NA	23.1 Total loans outstanding[a]
24.0 Interest rates, bus. loans	24.0 Interest rates, bus. loans	24.1 Interest rates, bank loans

Source: Center for International Business Cycle Research.

Note: Series numbers are based on the U.S. list. The digits after the decimal indicate whether the series is virtually the same as the U.S. series (0), or differs somewhat (1 or 2).

[a]In constant prices.
[b]Treated invertedly in the composite indexes.
[c]Change in net balance of survey responses.

11

The attempt to duplicate the U.S. system abroad does not mean that all countries are thought to be alike or that other indicators could not be found that would serve equally well or better. Duplicating the U.S. system is not an ultimate goal but merely a practicable interim target. The U.S. indicator system has the advantage of being familiar to many users, and both its empirical properties and the economic logic on which it was based have been thoroughly investigated by many scholars over a long period.[2] This logic seems applicable to many countries where free enterprise prevails. Orders placed for those types of machinery that are made to order are likely to lead machinery production in any market-oriented economy, and are likely also to lead the production of the goods the machinery helps to produce. Similarly, in any enterprise economy, changes in the relations between prices and costs influence incentives to expand future output and to make capital investments. In countries where there are markets for common stock, one can expect stock prices to be especially sensitive to changes in profit prospects, as well as to changes in interest rates, and hence to anticipate the effects of these changes on output, investment, and employment.

The selection of the U.S. indicator list as a target also advances the objective of providing sets of indicators as comparable as possible across countries. Unless some attention is paid to this, comparisons of cyclical movements in different countries are likely to become hopelessly confused. To cite one example, the index of leading indicators published by the British Central Statistical Office includes a series on interest rates treated invertedly—that is, a rise in rates is counted as a depressing factor, and vice versa. This is not an unreasonable position to take, but in the U.S. classification, interest rates are treated on a positive basis and are included among the lagging indicators (see table 1). It is recognized that at times, as noted above, a rapid rise in such indicators can be interpreted as an adverse development. A straightforward comparison of the U.S. and U.K. leading indexes as published in each country would run afoul of this difference in procedure.

Nevertheless, it is obvious that the system should not be held in a straitjacket, and that adaptations to the way business is done in each country and to the particular statistical data available should be made as more experience with the system accumulates and additional research is conducted. Perhaps two systems will evolve, one in which international comparability is strictly maintained, and one in which each country's own data and cyclical response mechanisms are used to best advantage—always avoiding, as far as possible, arbitrary differences in methodology.

The acid test of the plan to assemble comparable sets of indicators for each country according to the U.S. system lies in whether such data behave in the way U.S. experience has led one to expect. To perform this test long-run trends were fitted to each indicator, including those for the United States, cyclical turning points in the deviations from trend were identified, a chronology of growth-cycle turns for each country was set up to represent the peaks and troughs in aggregate economic activity (after allowance for trend), and the leads and lags of each trend-adjusted indicator were measured with respect to these growth-cycle turns. The trend-adjustment procedure, although subject to difficulties of its own, was essential to the identification of cyclical movements in countries that had experienced almost continuous rapid growth through the period from 1948 to 1973. Computer programs, carefully monitored to rule out dubious results, helped to enhance the objectivity of the data processing. A summary of the findings on cyclical timing, based on composite indexes constructed from each group of indicators, is given in table 3.

The leading indexes, constructed from indicators corresponding to those classified as leading on the basis of U.S. data, lead in each of the other countries. The coincident indexes, of course, show virtually no lead or lag, because they and their components are used to determine the growth-cycle chronologies themselves. The lagging indexes lag. Significantly, because the grouping of the indicators is based on U.S. experience only, and not on experience in the country itself, the sequence of turns among the leading, coincident, and lagging groups in each country corresponds roughly to the sequence in the United States. The detailed results show that this sequence has been repeated at virtually every turn in each country. Moreover, this consistency includes the tendency for the turns in the lagging indexes to precede opposite turns in the leading indexes, corresponding to the economic logic noted above (compare the top line with the second line in each panel of table 3). The sequences do not appear to differ systematically from one country to another; hence it is appropriate to average them (see the last two columns of table 3). The average sequence is set forth schematically in figure 1. Since the growth-cycle chronologies and the recorded leads and lags are based on trend-adjusted data, the rising and falling phases are roughly symmetrical, as are the intervals into which they are subdivided by the turns in the indexes.

Nevertheless, it is true that there are wide variations in the lengths of lead or lag from one cycle to another or from one indicator to another. The system is neither simple nor mechanical. But the historical record is available to help guide current interpretations, and it appears to support the basic hypothesis underlying the scheme, namely, that the U.S. indicator system is broadly applicable overseas.

The composite indexes referred to in table 3 have been computed using a method employed for some years by the U.S. Department of Commerce. The indexes are constructed so that their trend rate of growth during 1969-79 is equal to that of real GNP for the country concerned during the same period. The procedure corrects for the rather haphazard long-run trends that are likely to result from combinations of indicators that, despite efforts to obtain comparability, are not precisely the same in the several

Table 3

Cyclical Timing of Composite Indexes During Growth Cycles, Seven Countries

(Median lead (−) or lag (+), in months)

	United States 1948-78	Canada 1951-80	United Kingdom 1951-79	West Germany 1951-80	France 1957-79	Italy 1956-80	Japan 1953-80	Averages: Six Countries ex. U.S.	Seven Countries
At growth-cycle peaks									
Lagging index trough	−15	−15	−24	−12	−18	−14	−14	−16	−16
Leading index peak	−2	−2	−10	−7	−3	−9	−4	−6	−5
Coincident index peak	0	0	0	0	0	0	0	0	0
Lagging index peak	+6	+5	+6	+3	+5	+8	+4	+5	+5
At growth-cycle troughs									
Lagging index peak	−11	−16	−19	−18	−14	−7	−14	−15	−14
Leading index trough	−2	−4	−9	−2	−4	−6	−4	−5	−4
Coincident index trough	0	0	0	0	0	+3	0	0	0
Lagging index trough	+6	+4	+8	+4	+6	+10	+8	+4	+7

Source: Center for International Business Cycle Research.

14

Figure 1
Average Sequence of Cyclical Turns in Three Composite
Indexes during Growth Cycles, Seven Countries

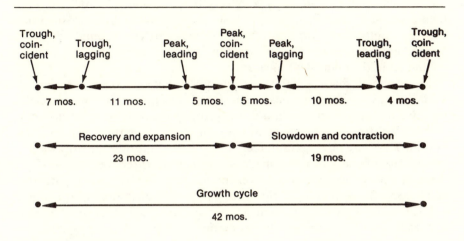

Source: Table 3.

countries. In addition to the indexes with trend equal to the trend in GNP, indexes are available with the long-run trend eliminated. These depict the growth cycles discussed above. The trend rates of growth in the individual indicators are of interest in themselves for the purposes of analyzing each country's long-run rate of growth.[3] Finally, short-run rates of growth in the indexes have been compiled, based on changes over successive intervals of 6 months or 12 months. These rates also depict the growth cycles, but they do not depend upon any trend-fitting procedure and hence avoid the uncertainty that is inevitably attached to bringing such trends up to date.

Although the procedure insures that the long-run trend in the indexes will be approximately the same as the trend in real GNP, the fluctuations in the indexes are larger than those in GNP, partly because most of the components are more sensitive than GNP, and partly because most of them are monthly rather than quarterly. Another reason is that the average month-to-month change (without regard to sign) in each country's industrial production index is used as a standard with which to equate the month-to-month change in the index, and industrial production usually undergoes wider swings than GNP. The indexes thus provide measures of economic performance based not on a single indicator but on a group of significant indicators that are relatively homogeneous with respect to cyclical timing. As a consequence of both the cyclical homogeneity and the variety of economic data included, the indexes are relatively free of the month-to-month irregularities that beset most economic time series.

Figure 2 compares the leading and coincident indexes for the United States and for six other countries combined (Canada, United Kingdom, West Germany, France, Italy, and Japan) during 1972-83. In the combined index each country's index is weighted by the country's GNP in 1980 (expressed in U.S. dollars). Figure 3 shows the growth rates for the same indexes.[4] Both charts demonstrate the capacity of the leading indexes to keep a few months ahead of the broad measures of economic performance contained in the coincident indexes.

The economic basis for this relationship is that the components of the leading index represent actions of an anticipatory nature that are especially sensitive to changes in cost and profit prospects and the state of demand. New orders for equipment, contracts placed for construction work, and housing starts are obvious examples. The length of the average workweek is one of the first adjustments made when manufacturers detect a shift in demand and reduce or increase overtime work or the number of part-time employees. By combining a dozen or so of such measures into a single index, the idiosyncrasies of any single one of them are muted, and the result is a leading index possessing the properties described. These properties do not make it an infallible instrument for appraising the outlook in any country. But when a businessman judges the future of his company, he does not regard the current state of his order-books as an infallible guide either. That does not stop him from wanting to know what state they are in. It is the same with the leading indexes. They reflect actions that are likely to affect production a few months hence, and consequently are useful guides to the state of the market.

RECESSION-RECOVERY PATTERNS

Once a historical chronology of business cycles or growth cycles has been established and a collection of indicators assembled, it becomes possible to compare the current behavior of the indicators with their patterns of change during the corresponding stages of previous cycles. Although no two business cycles are exactly alike, there are family resemblances, and they can be employed systematically to evaluate the current situation and glimpse what lies ahead.

Methods of making such comparisons have been employed for many years in the United States. The Commerce Department's *Business Conditions Digest* regularly carries charts of this type, and the CIBCR issues periodic reports utilizing the technique.[5] The comparisons help one to anticipate what is typical business-cycle performance and to observe whether current performance is in line with it or not. Although every business cycle has its own surprises, partly because of policy actions taken, many developments are not surprising, having occurred many times before. Hence a look at what has happened during the later stages of past business cycles is also a look ahead.

Figure 2
Leading and Coincident Indexes,
United States and Six Other Countries, 1972–83

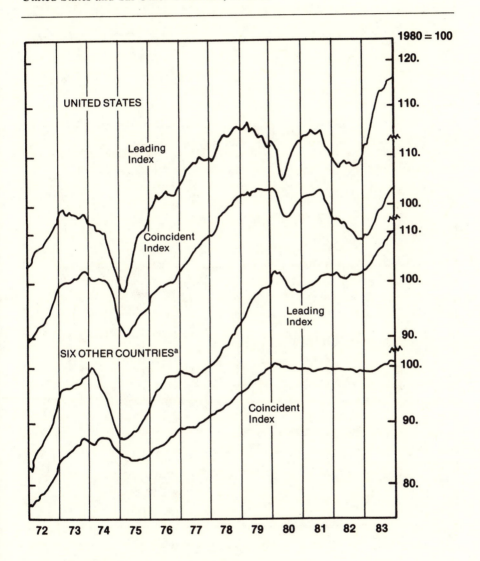

aCanada, United Kingdom, West Germany, France, Italy, Japan.
  Source: Center for International Business Cycle Research.

Figure 3
Growth Rates in Leading and Coincident Indexes, United States and Six Other Countries, 1972–83 (6-month smoothed percentage change)

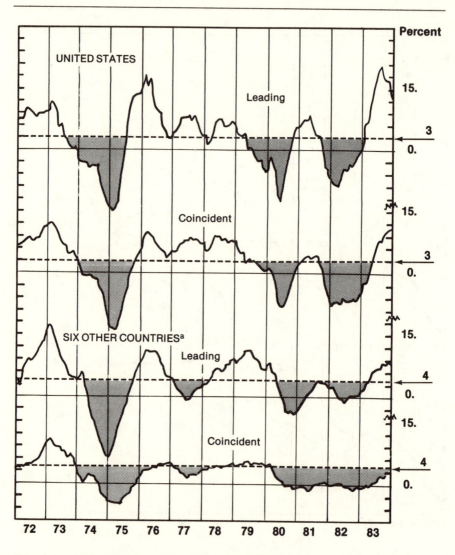

Note: Arrows indicate rate of change, 1969-79, in the indexes and in real GNP.

[a]Canada, United Kingdom, West Germany, France, Italy, Japan.

Source: Center for International Business Cycle Research.

An example of how this works in practice is provided by figure 4. The behavior of the U.S. leading and coincident indexes shortly before and during the recovery that started from the business-cycle trough of November 1982 is compared with their average pattern during six of the preceding recoveries. Such charts give one a quick grasp of how vigorous a current recovery is, whether it is slowing in the usual manner, whether signs of recession are developing, and so on.

IMPLICATIONS FOR FOREIGN TRADE

The effect upon the economy of one country of a slowdown in economic growth in other countries is likely to be most visible in that country's exports. The volume of exports depends upon the trend of economic activity in the country to which the exports go. Ordinarily this is measured by gross national product or industrial production, both of which are among the coincident indicators. Since the leading indicators, as we have seen, usually anticipate the movement of the coincident by several months, the leading indexes for the trading partners may also anticipate the movements in exports to them. A number of tests of this hypothesis have been made, using the leading indexes to forecast the rate of change in the volume of trade to and from particular countries or groups of countries, and for trade as a whole as well as for various commodity groupings. The results of this research show that a substantial proportion of the year-to-year changes in trade flows can usually be accounted for in this manner. Figure 5 displays the results of one such test, where the percentage rates of growth in U.S. manufactured goods exported to all countries, after allowance for changes in prices, are forecast by the prior changes in the leading index for the six countries outside the United States as well as by prior changes in exchange rates. Despite the fact that exports are affected by many other factors not explicitly taken into account in this simple model, the method tracks the major swings well.

The same method can be employed to forecast the exports of any country, developed or developing, that trades with the industrial countries for which we have leading indexes. We have already obtained similar results for the exports of the United Kingdom, West Germany, Japan, the European Economic Community (EEC) countries as a group, and for a major group of developing countries. Naturally this method by itself has serious limitations, since it ignores other factors that influence the quantities of goods exported. Changes in tariffs and other barriers or incentives to trade, supply conditions, and pricing policies are taken into account only insofar as they affect the leading indicators for the importing countries. Yet, in view of the importance of trade flows and trade balances in the economic relations among nations, even a modest contribution to our economic intelligence in appraising trade prospects is worthwhile.

Figure 4
Patterns of Current and Previous Recoveries, United States

U.S. LEADING INDEX (IEI)

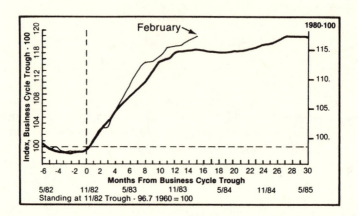

U.S. LEADING INDEX GROWTH RATE (IEI)

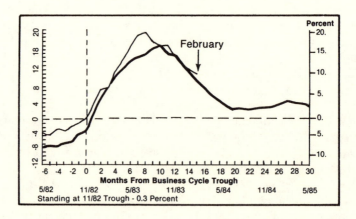

U.S. COINCIDENT INDEX (IEI)

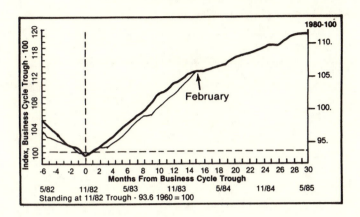

U.S. COINCIDENT INDEX GROWTH RATE (IEI)

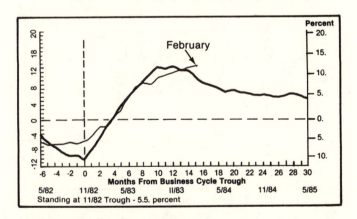

——— **Current recovery, from Nov. 1982**
——— **Average, 6 previous recoveries, 1949-80**

The vertical lines at zero represent business cycle trough dates. The current and six previous business cycles (1948-1975) are aligned so that their troughs fall on this line. The horizontal lines in the charts for the indexes (top) represent the level of the indexes at business cycle troughs, with the historical data adjusted so that the level at each trough is equal to the November 1982 trough level. The growth rates (bottom) are six-month smoothed rates, plotted at their actual levels, at annual rate.

Source: Center for International Business Cycle Research.

21

Figure 5
Forecast and Actual Percentage Change in Volume of U.S.
Exports of Manufactured Goods to All Countries

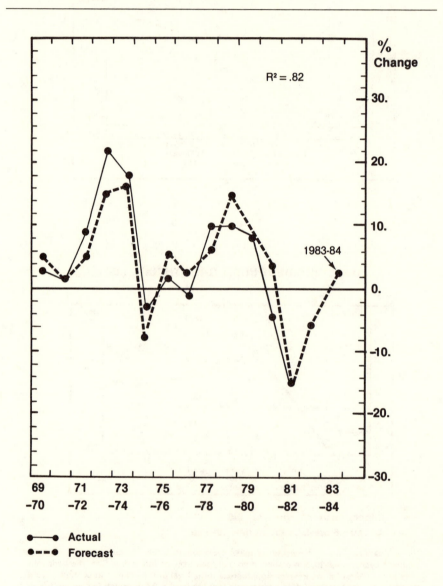

Note: The forecasts are based upon (a) the growth rate in the leading index for six major
industrial countries other than the U.S. as of the preceding December, and (b) the
growth rate in the dollar exchange rate for ten countries as of the preceding July.

Center for International Business Cycle Research

IMPLICATIONS FOR INFLATION

Growth cycles are closely associated with the rate of inflation. Indeed, as far as the U.S. experience is concerned, declines in the rate of inflation have been associated with virtually every slowdown or contraction in real economic growth and have not occurred at other times. Both parts of this proposition are important. Declines in the rate of inflation have not been as rare as commonly believed, but they have occurred only at times of slower economic growth, never at times of rapid growth. The proposition appears to be true in other countries as well as in the United States.

The international economic indicator system is helpful in examining the evidence and so is the concept of the growth cycle described earlier. This distinguishes periods of rapid growth from periods of slow growth by reference to a long-run trend. Trend-adjusted data rise as long as the short-run rate of growth exceeds the long-run rate. They decline as long as the short-run rate is less than the long-run rate. The peaks and troughs in trend-adjusted data, therefore, delineate periods of rapid and slow growth relative to the trend rate.

For the United States, a chronology of growth cycles based on trend-adjusted data for the physical volume of aggregate economic activity is used in figure 6 as a backdrop against which to examine the movements in the rate of change in two price indexes. The index of industrial materials prices—that is, prices of metals, textiles, rubber, and the like—shows an especially close relation to the growth cycle. Downswings in the rate of change in these prices occurred in every period of slow growth or recession, and upswings occurred in every period of rapid growth. Often, as in 1956 and 1959, the downswings began before the onset of the slow growth periods. The rate of change in this price index is one of the leading indicators in table 1; here it leads not only the growth cycle but also the rate of change in the consumer price index (CPI), the bottom line in figure 6. The CPI, which of course includes the prices of services as well as commodities, responds to the growth cycle as well, but often with a lag of a year or more. The lags have been so long, especially in recent years, that sometimes the rate of inflation in the CPI has risen almost throughout the period of slow growth or recession, giving the erroneous impression that slow growth had no influence on inflation.

Watching both price indexes together, and bearing in mind their differences in sensitivity and tendency to lag, enables one to see that growth cycles have pervasive influences upon the price structure. The change one sees in the consumer price index (as, for example, the decline in its rate of increase from autumn 1974 to spring 1976) is a lagged response to or reflection of similar developments in commodity markets that react far more promptly to changes in demand pressures or supply conditions.

Corresponding data and growth-cycle chronologies for the six other countries covered in the IEI system suggest that similar relations are to be

Figure 6
Rates of Change in Two Price Indexes during Growth Cycles, United States, 1948–84
(6-month smoothed percentage change)

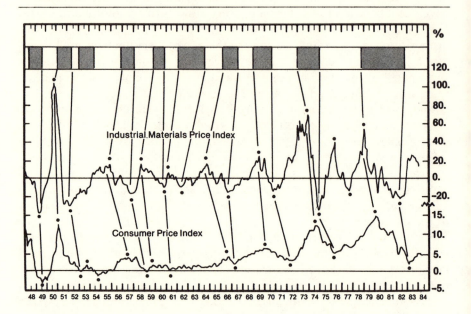

Note: Shaded areas represent slowdowns in economic growth as determined from trend-adjusted measures
of aggregate output, income, sales, and employment. Lines connect corresponding peaks and troughs
in the rate of change.

Source: Industrial Materials Price Index: 1948-61, Bureau of Labor Statistics; 1962 on, Journal of Commerce.
Consumer Price Index: Bureau of Labor Statistics.

found in these countries. Conditions that produce rates of economic growth
greatly in excess of long-run trend are conductive to an acceleration of
inflation, while conditions that make for slow growth or recession are
conducive to a reduced rate of inflation or even to deflation. When ordering
is brisk and order backlogs accumulate, sellers have opportunities and
incentives to raise prices, and buyers are less averse to paying them. Costs of
production tend to creep up, labor turnover increases, control over
efficiency and waste tends to decline. New commitments for investment are
made in an optimistic environment, building up demand for limited supplies
of skilled labor and construction equipment. Credit to build inventories is
more readily available and is in greater demand, even if higher interest rates
must be paid for it, thereby raising costs. Labor unions see better
opportunities to obtain favorable contract settlements, and their members
are more willing to strike to get them. All these conditions apply to more
and more firms and industries and produce upward pressure on more and
more prices. Indeed, one of the principal factors underlying a rising rate of

inflation in the general price level is not just that some prices rise in big jumps but that more prices rise at more frequent intervals.

During periods of slow growth or actual decline in aggregate economic activity, the opposite conditions prevail. Firms and industries cut back their output, reduce or eliminate overtime, shave costs, give bigger discounts off list prices, reduce inventories, repay bank debt, and postpone new investment projects or stretch out existing ones. Unemployment rises, reducing earnings and spending. Quit rates decline, indicating that workers feel they must hang on to their jobs, and labor demands for pay raises become more conservative. Interest rates drop. As price increases become less widespread and less frequent, and as more price cutting takes place, the rate of inflation declines.

Since many of the processes sketched above are represented among the leading and lagging indicators, they can also be employed to monitor inflation, evaluate its twists and turns, and judge its prospects. In 1983 the CIBCR constructed a leading index of inflation for the United States, specifically designed to capture forces in the commodity markets, labor markets, and financial markets that lead to inflation. Similar studies for other countries are also being conducted.

FURTHER RESEARCH AND DEVELOPMENT

A continuing research and development program is essential if the system of international economic indicators described above is to be used effectively and improved. Coverage of the indicator system has already been extended by the CIBCR to many additional countries, including Sweden, the Netherlands, Belgium, Switzerland, Australia, South Korea, and Taiwan. Attention is being given to speedier access to data, new types of graphic displays, and other analytical tools. Methods of trend-adjusting current data are being tested, as well as methods of defining early warning signals of recession and recovery. Detecting an international recession promptly and measuring its scope and severity, appraising trade prospects, and getting early warning signals of new inflationary trends are matters of vast consequence to the peoples of the world. If the contents of this book contributes to these tasks, it will have served its end.

NOTES

1. For further information, address inquiries to the Center for International Business Cycle Research, Columbia Business School, 808 Uris Hall, New York, New York 10027.

2. For a list of NBER publications that explain the behavior of and relationships among particular indicators, see Geoffrey H. Moore, *Business Cycles, Inflation, and Forecasting*, National Bureau of Economic Research Studies in Business Cycles, no. 24, (2d ed.), Ballinger Publishing Co., 1983, chapter 21.

3. The method of trend-fitting is described in Boschan, C., and Ebanks, W. "The Phase-Average Trend: A New Way of Measuring Economic Growth," *Proceedings of the Business and Economics Statistics Section*, American Statistical Association, 1978.

4. The growth rates are calculated by taking the ratio of the current month's index to the average index for the 12 preceding months and expressing this as a compound annual rate. This method produces a rate of growth (or decline) that is similar to but smoother than the percentage change in the index from 6 months ago. The 12-month average smooths away erratic factors, such as a strike or unusual weather, that may have affected the 6-months-ago figure. The method does not, of course, smooth out any erratic influences affecting the current month. The rate is called a 6-month smoothed growth rate.

5. *Recession-Recovery Watch* has been a bimonthly publication of the CIBCR since 1979.

2

Descriptions of Economic Indicator Series

UNITED STATES

1.0 AVERAGE WORKWEEK, MANUFACTURING, United States

Monthly, beginning 1948

Unit: Hours per week

Title in source: Average Weekly Hours of Production or Nonsupervisory Workers on Private Nonagricultural Payrolls, Manufacturing

Source: *Employment and Earnings*, Department of Labor, Bureau of Labor Statistics (BLS). Seasonally adjusted by source. Also published in *Business Conditions Digest* (series 1), U.S. Department of Commerce.

Description: The figures represent average hours paid for per week and cover not only hours actually worked (including overtime) in the reporting week, but also hours paid for but not worked, such as annual vacation, public holidays, sick leave, and other paid leave. They relate to full-time and part-time production or nonsupervisory workers (but include working supervisors) who worked during or received pay for any part of the pay period including the twelfth of the month.

The data are based upon payroll reports from a sample of establishments. In March 1983, approximately 9,951,000 production and related workers were covered by the series, representing about 55 percent of all employees in manufacturing. The average workweek is derived by dividing total man-hours paid for per week by the corresponding number of production workers. Such factors as unpaid absenteeism, labor turnover, part-time work, and stoppages cause average weekly hours to be lower than scheduled hours of a week for an establishment. However, over-time hours cause the average to be higher. In recent years the figures have, to an increasing degree, exceeded the number of hours actually worked because of the increasing amount of paid sick-leave, holidays, and vacation.

More information on the establishment surveys and adjustment of sample data to complete coverage (benchmarks) may be found in the description for series 13.0 below. Monthly data beginning in 1932 are given in the October 1978 issue of *Employment and Earnings*.

For further methodological details, see *BLS Handbook of Methods,* Bulletin No. 1910, 1976, and *Employment and Earnings*, Explanatory Notes, Department of Labor, Bureau of Labor Statistics, Washington, D.C. For a comprehensive discussion of weekly hours and related economic activities see Gerhard Bry, *The Average Workweek as an Economic Indicator*, Occasional Paper 69, National Bureau of Economic Research, New York (1959); Hazel M. Willacy, "Changes in the Factory Workweek as an Economic Indicator," *Monthly Labor Review*, Bureau of Labor Statistics, October 1970, pp. 25-32; and Philip L. Rones, "Response to Recession: Reduce Hours or Jobs?" *Monthly Labor Review*, October 1981, pp. 3-11.

2.0 INITIAL CLAIMS, UNEMPLOYMENT INSURANCE, United States

Monthly, beginning 1948

Unit: Thousands of claims per week

Title in source: Average Weekly Initial Claims, State Unemployment Insurance

Source: *Business Conditions Digest* (series 5), U.S. Department of Commerce. Seasonally adjusted by source. Basic data are weekly figures published by the Employment and Training Administration of the U.S. Department of Labor in *Unemployment Insurance Claims* with a slightly different coverage (see below).

Description: Insured unemployment represents the number of persons reporting at least 1 week of unemployment under a state unemployment insurance program. It includes some persons who are working part-time and thus would be counted as employed in payroll and household surveys. Excluded are persons who have not earned rights to unemployment insurance. At present, persons engaged in agriculture, domestic service, unpaid family work, selected non-profit organizations, some state and local government activities, and self-employment generally are excluded.

A covered worker, upon becoming unemployed, files an initial claim to establish the starting date for unemployment compensation. Although there is a 1-week noncompensable waiting period, the figures are adjusted to the week in which unemployment actually occurred. The initial claims represent first claims filed by workers for unemployment compensation upon becoming newly unemployed or for a second or subsequent period of unemployment in the same benefit year. A benefit year is a 12-month period during which an eligible worker's annual benefits may be received. Since July 1949, transitional claims (claims filed by persons already in a claimant status for determination of benefit rights in a new benefit year) have been excluded.

The data are collected by the Employment and Training Administration in weekly reports from the State Employment Security Agencies in the 50 states, Puerto Rico, the Virgin Islands and the District of Columbia. Data from Puerto Rico are not included in the series although Puerto Rico is included in the figures published by the source agency. The monthly averages of weekly data are adjusted for split weeks on the basis of a 5-day week.

For an extensive description of these data see Saul J. Blaustein, "Insured Unemployment Data," National Commission on Employment and Unemployment Statistics, Background Paper No. 24, 1979 (U.S. Government Printing Office).

3.0 NEW ORDERS, CONSUMER GOODS AND MATERIALS, in constant prices, United States

Monthly, beginning 1948

Unit: Billions of 1972 dollars

Title in source: Value of Manufacturers' New Orders for Consumer Goods and Materials in 1972 Dollars

Source: *Business Conditions Digest* (series 8), Department of Commerce. Seasonally adjusted by source.

Description: This series measures new orders for durable goods (excluding capital goods and defense products) and for the four nondurable goods industries which have unfilled orders: textile mill products; paper and allied products; printing, publishing, and allied products; and leather and leather products. New orders are defined as commitments to buy, supported by binding legal documents, involving either the immediate or future delivery of goods. The series includes all new orders placed during the month less cancellations.

Basic data for the series are the reports on sales and unfilled orders collected from individual firms by the Bureau of the Census. Since the change in unfilled orders during the month is equivalent to new orders less sales and cancellations, net new orders are computed by adding shipments to the change in unfilled orders during the month.

Each of the component indexes is adjusted to constant 1972 dollars by means of an appropriate producer price index. These indexes are sectors of the U.S. Producer Price Index (formerly the Wholesale Price Index) computed by the U.S. Bureau of Labor Statistics and measure price changes for goods sold in the primary markets compared with prices prevailing in 1972.

Further information may be found in *Handbook of Cyclical Indicators*, the supplement to *Business Conditions Digest*. A description of the Producer Price Index may be found in *BLS Handbook of Methods*, BLS Bulletin 2134-1, 1982, Chapter 7. See also John F. Early, "Improving the measurement of producer price changes," *Monthly Labor Review*, Bureau of Labor Statistics, April 1978, pp. 7-15. The series is published regularly in the *Monthly Labor Review*.

4.0 NET BUSINESS FORMATION, United States

Monthly, beginning 1948

Unit: Index, base 1967 = 100

Title in source: Index of Net Business Formation

Source: *Business Conditions Digest* (series 12), Department of Commerce, Bureau of Economic Analysis (BEA). Seasonally adjusted by the BEA and National Bureau of Economic Research.

Description: This series provides an estimate of the net formation of business enterprises. There are no direct measures of the monthly change in the total business population but it is believed that these estimates adequately represent the short-term movements of new entries into, and departures from, the total business population.

The estimate is based upon three component series:

1. New business incorporations measure the number of stock companies receiving charters each month under the general business incorporation laws of the 50 states and the District of Columbia. Figures prior to 1958 do not include Hawaii, those prior to 1960 do not include Alaska, and those prior to 1963 do not include the District of Columbia. The figures include new businesses that are incorporated, existing businesses that are changed from a noncorporate to a corporate form of organization, existing corporations that have been given certificates of authority to operate also in another State, and existing corporations transferred to a new State. Data for each State are collected from the Secretaries of State for the State government. They are compiled by Dun and Bradstreet, Inc.

2. Dun & Bradstreet also compiles the weekly number of business failures. A business failure is defined as a concern that is involved in a court proceeding or a voluntary action that is likely to result in loss to creditors. Firms that are liquidated, merged, sold, or otherwise discontinued without loss to creditors are not considered failures. The data cover 48 states and the District of Columbia (Alaska and Hawaii are not included).

3. The third component prior to 1979 is based on confidential data pertaining to telephones installed and, after 1979, to other public utility information.

The composite index is computed by BEA from these three components with the composite business failures data inverted.

A quarterly series, 1945-58, showing the net change in the number of operating businesses is described in Geoffrey H. Moore, *Business Cycle Indicators*, vol. II (NBER), 1961.

5.0 CONTRACTS AND ORDERS, PLANT AND EQUIPMENT, in constant prices, United States

Monthly, beginning 1948

Unit: Billions of 1972 dollars

Title in source: Contracts and Orders for Plant and Equipment, Constant Dollars

Source: *Business Conditions Digest* (series 20), U.S. Department of Commerce, Bureau of Economic Analysis. Seasonally adjusted by source.

Description: This series measures the value in constant prices of new contract awards to building contractors and to public works and utilities contractors and of new orders received by manufacturers in the capital goods, nondefense industries. It is the sum of three series:

1. The value of contracts for work about to get underway on commercial buildings (banks, offices and lofts, stores, warehouses, garages, service stations), and manufacturing buildings.

2. The value of contracts for privately owned nonbuilding construction such as electric light and power plants, gas plants and mains, pipelines (oil and gas wells), railroad construction, water supply systems, airports (excluding buildings), and so on.

3. The value of manufacturers' new orders received by capital goods, nondefense industries. Industries included are nonelectrical and electrical machinery and the nondefense portion of communications equipment, shipbuilding, and aircraft and parts.

Data for the first two series are compiled by the F.W. Dodge Division, McGraw-Hill Information Systems Company, and cover new construction, additions, and major alterations but exclude maintenance. Valuations represent actual construction costs and exclude land, architects' fees, and in the case of manufacturing buildings, the cost of equipment which is not an integral part of the structure. Since January 1969, data cover construction in the 50 states and the District of Columbia. In 1956-68, Alaska and Hawaii are not included and prior to 1956, the data cover only the 37 states east of the Rocky Mountains and the District of Columbia.

To adjust the two construction contracts series to 1972-dollar values, the current-dollar data are divided by an implicit price deflator that is obtained by dividing the current-dollar value of nonresidential construction put in place by the constant-dollar value for this type of construction. The manufacturers' new orders compiled by the Census Bureau are deflated by appropriate combinations of sectors of the Producer Price Index compiled by the U.S. Bureau of Labor Statistics, and published in the *Monthly Labor Review*, U.S. Bureau of Labor Statistics (see series 3.0 for references).

6.0 NEW BUILDING PERMITS, PRIVATE HOUSING UNITS, United States

Monthly, beginning 1948

Unit: Index, base 1967 = 100

Title in source: Index of New Private Housing Units Authorized by Local Building Permits

Source: *Business Conditions Digest* (series 29), U.S. Department of Commerce. Basic data, seasonally adjusted, from Bureau of the Census.

Description: This series measures changes in the number of housing units authorized by local permit-issuing places. Frequently, several months may pass between the issuance of a permit and the start of construction and a small number of permits are not used at all.

A housing unit has been defined as a single room or group of rooms intended for occupancy as separate living quarters by a family, by a group of unrelated persons living to together, or by a person living alone. Transient accommodations and group quarters such as dormitories are excluded.

The original data for the period 1948-53 are based upon an estimate of the number of new, privately owned dwelling units authorized in urban areas as defined in the 1940 Census of Population. From 1954 to 1958, the data are based on reports from approximately 6,600 identical permit-issuing places; for 1959-62 on 10,000 places; for 1963-67 on 12,000 places; for 1968-71 on 13,000 places; for 1972-77 on 14,000 places; and from 1978 to date, from 16,000 permit-issuing places. Permits issued by these 16,000 places account for approximately 88 percent of all new residential construction. The data have been spliced together with overlapping data and converted into an index, but, because of the difference in coverage, the figures for the intervals noted above are not strictly comparable.

Further details may be found in the *Handbook of Cyclical Indicators, 1984*, the supplement to *Business Conditions Digest.*

7.0 CHANGE IN BUSINESS INVENTORIES, in constant prices, United States

Quarterly series, beginning 1948

Unit: Billions of 1972 dollars, annual rate

Title in source: Gross Private Domestic Investment, Change in Business Inventories, All Industries, in 1972 dollars

Source: *Survey of Current Business* and *Business Conditions Digest* (series 30), U.S. Department of Commerce. Seasonally adjusted by source.

Description: This series, a component of the national income and product accounts compiled by the Bureau of Economic Analysis of the Department of Commerce, measures the change in the physical volume of inventories valued at 1972 average prices. Estimates are obtained separately for farm and nonfarm sectors of the economy. Nonfarm inventories include purchased materials, supplies, goods in process, finished goods, and goods purchased for resale; farm inventories include livestock and harvested crops.

The book value of nonfarm inventories are based on data reported to the Census Bureau and business income tax returns tabulated by the Internal Revenue Service. For manufacturing and trade inventories, which comprise about nine-tenths of the nonfarm total, the censuses of business provide benchmarks for selected years. Annual and quarterly estimates are derived from the Census Bureau current business reports: *Manufacturers' Shipments, Inventories & Orders; Wholesale Trade*; and *Annual Retail Trade*. The extrapolation of retail trade inventories within the year is derived mainly from a subsample of the annual retail trade survey. For other nonfarm industries, annual inventories are obtained from Internal Revenue Service data and quarterly estimates are based on unpublished data from the Federal Reserve System, the Department of Energy, and from trade associations. Book values are deflated to 1972 values by means of composite price indexes for about 60 industries, constructed from components of the Producer Price Index computed by the Bureau of Labor Statistics.

The value of farm inventories, in current and constant prices, is estimated by the Department of Agriculture.

Beginning with 1960, data include estimates for Alaska and Hawaii. For further information and data, see *Handbook of Cyclical Indicators*, U.S. Department of Commerce, and the references listed under series 15.0. See series 3.0 for reference to information on the Producer Price Index of the Bureau of Labor Statistics.

A quarterly series in current dollars 1921-38 is given in Harold Barger, *Outlay and Income in the United States, 1921-38*, table 11 (National Bureau of Economic Research). The data cover manufacturing and distribution only.

8.0 CHANGE IN INDUSTRIAL MATERIALS PRICE INDEX,
United States

Monthly, beginning 1948

Unit: Percentages, annual rate

Title in source: Daily Price Index of Industrial Materials

Source: *The Journal of Commerce.* Not seasonally adjusted. Percentage changes in the index are computed by the CIBCR.

Description: This index measures the prices of 15 raw materials on commodity markets and organized exchanges. The commodities included are: burlap, cotton, printcloth, polyester, silk, copper, lead, tin, zinc, steel scrap, hides, linseed oil, rubber, tallow, and turpentine. The index is a weighted arithmetic average and published with three subgroups (textiles, metals, and other). Prior to November 1982, the index is based upon monthly averages of Tuesday prices; subsequently they are averages of all daily figures (excluding week ends and holidays). All averages are computed by the Center for International Business Cycle Research (CIBCR).

Figures prior to January 1962 relate to the Index of Spot Market Prices of Industrial Materials compiled by the U.S. Bureau of Labor Statistics (BLS). This series was discontinued by the BLS in May 1981, but is available from the Commodity Research Bureau, Inc., and is published as series 23 in *Business Conditions Digest*. Nine of the 13 commodities included are the same as those in the index described above. The spot market index includes wool tops rather than polyester and silk, copper scrap and lead scrap rather than copper and lead, and rosin rather than linseed oil and turpentine. Indexes of spot market prices for each Tuesday are computed as unweighted geometric averages of the individual commodity prices relatives, and the monthly index is a geometric average of the Tuesday indexes during the month.

The rate of change computed by the CIBCR is a 6-month smoothed annual rate, based upon the ratio of the current month's index to the average index for the preceding 12 months. Since the interval between midpoints of the current month and the preceding 12 is 6.5 months, the ratio is raised to the 12/6.5 power to derive a compound annual rate.

9.0 STOCK PRICE INDEX, S & P 500 Common, United States

Unit: Index, base 1941-43 = 10

Title in source: Index of Stock Prices, 500 Common Stocks

Source: *Business Conditions Digest* (series 19), U.S. Department of Commerce. No seasonal adjustment. Basic data from Standard and Poor's Corporation.

Description: This index of 500 stocks closely approximates the average movement of all stocks on the New York Stock Exchange. The series is based on daily closing prices for the month. The price of each stock is weighted by the number of shares outstanding and the aggregate current market value is divided by the aggregate market value in the base period, and the quotient multiplied by 10. The index formula is modified to offset unusual price changes caused by the issuance of rights, stock dividends, split ups, and mergers. Selection of stocks for addition to or removal from the index is the responsibility of the 500 Index Committee at Standard and Poor's.

The index was introduced in 1957 but revised in July 1976 to include some over-the-counter stocks, mainly bank and insurance stocks. Formerly, three groups were represented: 425 industrials, 60 utilities, and 15 railroads. The revised index has four groups: 400 industrials, 40 public utilities, 20 transportation, and 40 financial. A total of 45 stocks in the old index were replaced in the new index.

Earlier indexes, beginning in 1871 were compiled by the Cowles Commission and the Standard and Poor's Corporation. These data on a 1935-39 base may be found in Standard and Poor's Corporation, *Security Price Index Record*, 1955 edition.

10.0 CORPORATE PROFITS AFTER TAXES, in constant prices, United States

Quarterly, beginning 1948

Unit: Billions of 1972 dollars, annual rate

Title in source: Corporate Profits after Taxes in 1972 dollars

Source: *Survey of Current Business* and *Business Conditions Digest* (series 18), U.S. Department of Commerce. Seasonally adjusted and adjusted to 1972 dollars by the Bureau of Economic Analysis.

Description: Corporate profits is the income of corporations organized for profit and of mutual financial institutions that accrues to residents, before deduction of depletion charges, after exclusion of capital gains or losses, and net of dividends received from domestic corporations. In addition to profits earned in domestic operations, corporate profits include net inflows of dividends from abroad, reinvested earnings of incorporated foreign affiliates, and earnings of unincorporated foreign affiliates. Profit taxes include federal, state, and local taxes on corporate income.

To adjust the figures to 1972 dollars, the current dollar series is divided into two components: dividends after taxes and undistributed corporate profits after taxes. The net corporate dividends component is deflated by dividing by the implicit price deflator for personal consumption expenditures. The undistributed profits component is deflated by dividing the current-dollar estimates by the implicit price deflator for nonresidential fixed investment.

For a statement of the methods and sources of data used in preparing profit estimates and also the implicit price deflators, see the references listed under series 15.0 for the gross national product compiled by the Bureau of Economic Analysis, Department of Commerce. Data beginning 1939, seasonally adjusted by the National Bureau of Economic Research, may be found in Geoffrey H. Moore, *Business Cycle Indicators*, vol. II (NBER, 1961). A series compiled by Harold Barger for the years 1920-38 is published in the same source.

11.0 RATIO, PRICE TO UNIT LABOR COST, NONFARM BUSINESS, United States

Quarterly, beginning 1948

Unit: Index, base 1977 = 100

Title in soure: Ratio, Implicit Price Deflator to Unit Labor Cost, Nonfarm Business Sector

Source: *Business Conditions Digest* (series 26), U.S. Department of Commerce, Bureau of Economic Analysis (BEA). Seasonally adjusted by source.

Description: The basic data used to construct this ratio relate to the gross domestic output of the nonfarm business sector of the national accounts, compiled by the BEA, which excludes the output of farms, households, institutions, and government.

The numerator is the implicit price deflator of this sector—derived by dividing the current dollar value of output by the constant dollar value of output. The denominator is unit labor cost; this is computed by the U.S. Bureau of Labor Statistics by dividing an index of compensation per hour by an index of output per hour.

Compensation per hour includes wages and salaries of employees plus employers' contributions for social insurance and private benefit plans. The data also include an estimate of net income and supplements of the self-employed. The index of output per hour is the ratio of constant-dollar gross product originating in the nonfarm business sector to the corresponding hours worked.

The ratio is computed by the Bureau of Economic Analysis. Further details may be found in *Handbook of Cyclical Indicators*, 1984, Department of Commerce.

12.0 CHANGE IN CONSUMER INSTALLMENT CREDIT, in constant prices, United States

Monthly, beginning 1948

Unit: Billions of 1972 dollars, annual rate

Title in source: Consumer Installment Credit, Net Change

Source: *Federal Reserve Bulletin* (series at monthly rates in current dollars), Federal Reserve Board. Seasonally adjusted by source. Series in current dollars also published in *Business Conditions Digest* (BCD) (series 113), U.S. Department of Commerce. Figures adjusted to 1972 dollars by CIBCR by means of the implicit price deflator of retail sales.

Description: This series measures the change during a month in the seasonally adjusted amount of consumer installment debt outstanding. The basic data include all short- and intermediate-term credit used to finance the purchases of commodities and services for personal consumption or to refinance debts originally incurred for such purposes. Credit extended to government agencies and nonprofit or charitable organizations, as well as credit extended to businesses, farmers, or individuals exclusively for business purposes, is excluded.

Installment credit includes all consumer credit held by financial institutions and retail outlets that is scheduled to be repaid in two or more installments. Financial institutions hold nearly 90 percent of all consumer credit outstanding, with retail outlets and gasoline companies holding the remainder. Specific categories of consumer credit include automobile paper, including both direct and indirect loans; revolving credit; mobile home credit; and other installment loans (including loans for home improvement, other consumer goods, and personal cash loans). Home mortgage financing is excluded.

The monthly estimates are extrapolated from comprehensive benchmark data which become available periodically. Sample data are obtained through the voluntary cooperation of lenders and other credit grantors. Federal Reserve banks, the National Association of Mutual Savings Bank, the Federal Home Loan Bank Board, and reports of finance companies provide a major portion of the financial institution data. Retail outlet data are obtained from Bureau of the Census surveys on sales and accounts receivable.

The published current-dollar data are adjusted to 1972 dollars by the Center for International Business Cycle Research (CIBCR) by dividing by an implicit price deflator that is obtained by dividing a series of current-dollar sales in retail stores by the series expressed in 1972 dollars (series 54 and 59 in BCD). Both series are seasonally adjusted. They are described in *Handbook of Cyclical Indicators*, U.S. Department of Commerce.

13.0 EMPLOYEES ON NONFARM PAYROLLS, United States

Monthly, beginning 1948

Unit: Thousands of Persons

Title in source: Employees on Nonagricultural Payrolls

Source: *Employment and Earnings,* U.S. Department of Labor, Bureau of Labor Statistics (BLS); Seasonally adjusted by the BLS. Also published in *Business Conditions Digest* (series 41), U.S. Department of Commerce.

Description: Data are obtained from the establishment survey conducted each month by the Bureau of Labor Statistics (BLS). An establishment is defined as an economic unit which produces goods and services such as a factory, mine, or store. It is generally at a single physical location and is engaged predominantly in one type of economic activity.

The industries included in the data are mining; construction; manufacturing; wholesale and retail trade; government; finance; insurance, and real estate; electric and gas utilities; transportation; other services.

The primary sources of data are state employment security agencies which collect data from cooperating employers. Data relate to the payroll period which includes the twelfth of the month. For federal government establishments, data represent positions occupied on the last day of the calendar month.

Data cover the 50 states and the District of Columbia and include full-time, part-time, temporary, and permanent workers; workers who are on paid leave (sick, holiday, vacation); and persons who worked only part of the specified pay period. Persons on the payroll of more than one establishment are counted each time they are reported. Excluded are proprietors, self-employed, military personnel, domestic workers, unpaid family workers, and persons in a nonpay status for the entire period due to layoff, strike, leave without pay, and so on.

The monthly sample of establishments included in the BLS survey of March 1983 covered 195,100 establishments with about 35 million employees —about 40 percent of total employees. Comprehensive counts of employment (benchmarks) are normally made annually and appropriate revisions are made to reflect these data as well as changes in industry classifications.

Historical statistics are published in *Employment, Hours and Earnings, United States, 1909-84*, Bureau of Labor Statistics. For further methodological details, see *BLS Handbook of Methods*, Bulletin No. 1910, 1976, and *Employment and Earnings*, Explanatory Notes.

14.0 UNEMPLOYMENT RATE, United States

Monthly, beginning 1948

Unit: Percentages

Title in source: Unemployment Rate

Source: *Employment and Earnings*, U.S. Department of Labor, Bureau of Labor Statistics (BLS). Seasonally adjusted by the BLS.

Description: Unemployed persons comprise all persons aged 16 years and over who did not work during the survey week but made specific efforts to find a job within the past four weeks and were available for work during the survey week (except for temporary illness). Also classified as unemployed are persons who, though available for work, did not work at all, and who were either waiting to be called back to a job from which they had been laid off or waiting to report to a new job within 30 days.

The series is based upon data obtained in monthly labor force sample surveys, conducted by the Bureau of the Census. The survey sample includes about 60,000 households representing 629 areas in 1148 counties and independent cities in the 50 states and the District of Columbia (prior to 1960 Alaska and Hawaii were not included). The data relate to employment activity during the survey week which includes the twelfth of each month.

Unemployment percentages are computed by dividing the number of unemployed by the estimated total labor force (employed and unemployed) obtained from the monthly surveys. Labor force data relate to the total noninstitutional population age 16 and over including members of the Armed Forces stationed in the United States but excluding inmates of penal and mental institutions, tuberculosis sanitariums, and homes for the aged, infirm, and needy.

For more complete methodological details and historical data see *Concepts and Methods Used in Labor Force Statistics Derived from the Current Population Survey*, BLS Report 463; and *Labor Force Statistics Derived from the Current Population Survey: A Databook*, vols. I and II, BLS Bulletin 2096, September 1982.

15.0 GROSS NATIONAL PRODUCT, in constant prices, United States

Quarterly, beginning 1948

Unit: Billions of 1972 dollars, annual rate

Title in source: Gross National Product in 1972 Dollars

Source: *Survey of Current Business,* and *Business Conditions Digest* (series 50), U.S. Department of Commerce, Bureau of Economic Analysis. Seasonally adjusted by source.

Description: This series represents the value of all finished commodities and services resulting from economic pursuits, that is, the value of the nation's output before deduction of depreciation charges and other allowances for business and institutional consumption of fixed capital goods. The figures include only the value of final products, excluding intermediate products except those added to inventory during the period. Certain items of production "in kind" are included, such as the value of food, clothing, and financial services that may be received by persons, and the estimated value of owner-occupied houses. The chief components of gross national product are: personal consumption expenditures on goods and services, gross private domestic investment (including changes in business inventories), net exports of goods and services, and government purchases of goods and services.

Gross national product measures the output resulting from the labor and property supplied by the nation's residents (including Alaska and Hawaii, beginning with 1960). In addition to domestic production, the figures also include profits repatriated from foreign branches of U.S. businesses, earnings of U.S. employees of foreign governments and international agencies stationed in the United States, and interest and dividends received from foreigners. They exclude profits repatriated from U.S. branches of foreign business, and interest and dividends paid to foreigners.

The constant dollar estimates are derived by dividing the current dollar components by appropriate price indexes (base 1972 = 100).

Further information may be found in *Business Statistics,* the biennial supplement to the *Survey of Current Business.* Also see Carol S. Carson and George Jaszi, "The National Income and Product Accounts of the United States: An Overview," *Survey of Current Business*, vol. 61, no. 2, February 1981. Quarterly estimates beginning in 1921 may be found in Geoffrey Moore, *Business Cycle Indicators*, vol. II, (NBER), 1961.

16.0 INDUSTRIAL PRODUCTION, United States

Monthly, beginning 1948

Unit: Index, base 1967 = 100

Title in source: Industrial Production, Total Index

Source: *Federal Reserve Bulletin*, Board of Governors of the Federal Reserve System. Seasonally adjusted by source. Also published in *Business Conditions Digest* (series 47), U.S. Department of Commerce.

Description: The movements of this index reflect the changes in production in the manufacturing, mining, and gas and electric utility industries. Production at government-owned-and-operated plants and shipyards is included.

Currently the index includes 235 series based on individual commodities produced or shipped, quantities of electricity adjusted for changes in output per KWH, and production-worker man-hours adjusted for changes in output per man-hour. Adjustments are sometimes made in the individual series when annual inquiries furnish more appropriate or complete data than are available on a monthly basis. Adjustments are also made to the physical product indexes for differences in the number of working days. The basic data are supplied by government agencies and by various trade organizations.

The index is calculated as a base-weighted arithmetic average of relatives of the indicators of output. The weights used are based on value-added data for manufactures, minerals, and utilities. The 1967 percentage weights for the major groups are: mining 6, durable manufactures 52, nondurable manufactures 36, electricity and gas 6. The percentage shares of the types of indicators in 1976 were: physical output 45, quantities of electricity consumed 31, man-hours adjusted for productivity 19, the last two indicators combined 5. Prior to 1967 the weights from quinquennial censuses of manufactures are used for periods beginning with January of the census year until the next census year. The overlapping indexes are linked at the January dates except in 1963 where the annual average is used.

Monthly data for this series are available beginning in 1919. For earlier data and further details on the construction and composition of the index, see *Industrial Production*, 1971 edition, Board of Governors of the Federal Reserve System.

17.0 PERSONAL INCOME, in constant prices, United States

Monthly, beginning 1948

Unit: Billions of 1972 dollars, annual rate

Title in source: Personal Income (Total) in Constant (1972) Dollars

Sources: *Survey of Current Business* and *Business Conditions Digest* (BCD) (series 52), U.S. Department of Commerce, Bureau of Economic Analysis. Seasonally adjusted by source.

Description: This series represents the income received by persons from all sources including transfer payments from government and from business enterprises. "Persons" cover not only individuals (including owners of unincorporated enterprises), but also nonprofit institutions, private trust funds, and private health and welfare funds. Most of the income is in monetary form but it also comprises income in kind—such as food and housing to employees—and it includes imputed income—such as the net rent of owner-occupied homes, the value of food produced and consumed on farms, and the value of services rendered by financial institutions for which explicit monetary charges are not made.

Personal income is the sum of wage and salary disbursements, other labor income (employer contributions to private pension, health, unemployment, welfare, and workman's compensation funds, plus director's fees), proprietors' income, rental income of persons, dividends, personal interest income, and transfer payments less personal contributions for social insurance. Transfer payments consist of income received by persons from government and business for which no services are currently rendered. Government transfer payments include payments under social security (including medicare), state unemployment insurance, railroad retirement and unemployment insurance, and government retirement programs; direct relief; payments to nonprofit institutions other than for work done under research and development contracts; and several other items. Business transfer payments consist of corporate gifts to nonprofit institutions, consumer bad debts, liability payments to persons, and minor items.

This series is compiled by the Bureau of Economic Analysis. To adjust the current value data to 1972 dollars, they are divided by the implicit price deflator for personal consumption expenditures. Additional information on this series and the deflator may be found in *Business Statistics*, 1982, and in *Handbook of Cyclical Indicators*, 1984, both issued by the Department of Commerce.

18.0 MANUFACTURING AND TRADE SALES, in constant prices, United States

Monthly, beginning 1948

Unit: Millions of 1972 dollars

Title in source: Manufacturing and Trade Sales in 1972 Dollars

Source: *Business Conditions Digest* (series 57), U.S. Department of Commerce, Bureau of Economic Analysis. Seasonally adjusted by source.

Description: This series measures the monthly volume of sales of manufacturing, merchant wholesalers, and retail establishments in constant dollars.

Manufacturers' sales are equal to the value of their shipments and include receipts, billings, or the value of products shipped, less discounts, returns, and allowances. Shipments for export as well as for domestic use are included, as are shipments by domestic firms to foreign subsidiaries. Shipments from one establishment to another within the same company are included, but shipments by foreign subsidiaries are excluded.

Merchant wholesalers' sales include: 1. sales of merchandise and receipts from repairs and other services to customers after deducting returns, allowances, and other discounts; 2. sales of merchandise for others on a commission basis. Federal excise taxes and sales taxes are excluded.

Retail sales include total receipts from customers after deductions of refunds and allowances for merchandise returned. Receipts from rental or leasing of merchandise and from repairs and other services to customers are included also. Since 1967, finance charges and excise taxes collected from customers are excluded.

The series are compiled from data collected each month by the Bureau of the Census in the manufacturers, merchant wholesalers, and retail trade surveys. They are adjusted to benchmarks from the five-year census of manufacturers, wholesale trade, and retail trade and to interim annual surveys.

Data for sales in all sectors are adjusted for holiday and working day differences. The Bureau of Economic Analysis deflates the current dollar series as follows: manufacturers' and wholesale sales are deflated by appropriate Producer Price Indexes; retail sales are deflated by kind of business using components of the Consumer Price Index for all Urban Consumers. Both price indexes are computed by the Bureau of Labor Statistics. The selection of price data and the weights for the component price indexes are based on sales by product line from the 1972 or 1977 censuses.

For further details, see *Handbook of Cylical Indicators*, 1984, Department of Commerce.

19.0 LONG DURATION UNEMPLOYMENT, United States

Monthly, beginning 1948

Unit: Percentages

Title in source: Unemployment Rate, 15 Weeks and Over

Source: *Employment and Earnings,* Department of Labor, Bureau of Labor Statistics. Seasonally adjusted by source. Also published in *Business Conditions Digest* (series 44), U.S. Department of Commerce.

Description: The figures are based on data collected in a household survey of the labor force (see series 14.0). Measurements are taken of the average length of time, in weeks, during which persons classified as unemployed had been continuously looking for work or, in the case of persons on layoff, since the termination of the most recent employment. A period of two or more weeks during which a person was employed or ceased looking for work is considered to break the continuity of the present period of looking for work.

This series measures the total number of persons who have been unemployed for 15 weeks or more as a percentage of the civilian labor force (civilian noninstitutional population 16 years of age and over who are classified as employed or unemployed).

20.0 INVESTMENT EXPENDITURES, PLANT AND EQUIPMENT, in constant prices, United States

Quarterly, beginning 1948

Unit: Billions of 1972 dollars, annual rate

Title in source: Expenditures for New Plant and Equipment by U.S. Nonfarm Business

Source: *Survey of Current Business,* U.S. Department of Commerce. Seasonally adjusted and adjusted to 1972 dollars by Bureau of Economic Analysis (BEA).

Description: The figures represent expenditures for new plant and equipment by all nonfarm business. The expenditures refer to all costs, both for replacement and expansion, that are chargeable to fixed asset accounts and for which depreciation accounts are ordinarily maintained. They include expenditures for new construction, machinery, and equipment such as computers, automobiles, trucks, and other transportation equipment. The figures do not include expenditures for land and mineral rights, maintenance and repair, residential construction, used plant and equipment, nor expenditures made in foreign countries.

Comprehensive data have been collected for certain benchmark years:

1948, 1958, 1963, 1967, and 1972. The quarterly data interpolated and extrapolated from these benchmarks are estimates based upon reports submitted by a sample of about 15,000 companies to the Bureau of Economic Analysis of the Department of Commerce. The expenditures of the companies in the sample accounted for 53 percent in 1972 of the estimated universe expenditures. The results of the quarterly survey provide estimates for actual spending in the previous quarter and anticipated spending for the following three quarters.

The current-dollar figures are adjusted to 1972 dollars using implicit price deflators for each major industry group based on unpublished data in the national income and product accounts.

For more information, see *Survey of Current Business*, October 1980 and September 1981.

21.0 BUSINESS INVENTORIES, in constant prices, United States

Monthly, beginning 1948

Unit: Billions of 1972 dollars

Title in source: Manufacturing and Trade Inventories, 1972 dollars

Source: *Business Conditions Digest* (series 70), U.S. Department of Commerce. Seasonally adjusted by source.

Description: The figures measure the dollar value, at constant prices, of inventories held by manufacturing, merchant wholesalers, and retail trade establishments. Inventories of nonmerchant wholesalers, contract construction, mining, transportation, communications, public utilities, services, finance, insurance and real estate, and farms are excluded.

The series are compiled from inventory data collected each month by the Bureau of the Census in the manufacturers, merchant wholesalers, and retail trade surveys. They are adjusted to benchmarks from the five-year censuses of manufacturers, wholesale trade, and retail trade and to interim annual surveys.

Manufacturers' inventories are book values of stocks-on-hand at the end of the month, and include materials and supplies, work in process, and finished goods. Inventories associated with nonmanufacturing activities of manufacturing companies are excluded.

Merchant wholesalers' and retailers' inventories are also book values of merchandise-on-hand at the end of the month. Goods held on consignment by wholesalers and retailers are excluded.

The current dollar figures are deflated by the Bureau of Economic Analysis using appropriate Producer Price Indexes. Manufacturers' inventories are deflated at the two-digit SIC level, and wholesalers' and retailers' inventories are deflated by kinds of business. The deflators are weighted averages of Producer Price Indexes with appropriate lag structures based on information on inventory turnover periods developed from stock/sales ratios and survey data on inventory accounting practices. The book-value inventory estimates and the deflators are seasonally adjusted prior to the deflation.

For further details of this series see *Handbook of Cyclical Indicators*, 1984, Department of Commerce. References for the Producer Price Index of the Bureau of Labor Statistics are listed in series 3.0.

22.0 CHANGE IN HOURS PER UNIT OF OUTPUT, NONFARM BUSINESS, United States

Quarterly, beginning 1948

Unit: Percentage of change from one year ago

Title in Source: Index of Output per Hour, All Persons, Nonfarm Business Sector

Source: *Productivity and Costs: Private Business, Nonfarm Business, and Manufacturing Sectors*, Bureau of Labor Statistics. Also in *Business Conditions Digest* (series 358), U.S. Department of Commerce. Seasonally adjusted by source.

Description: The Center for International Business Cycle Research (CIBCR) computes the percentage change over four-quarter intervals in the number of employee hours required to produce a unit of output, which is the reciprocal of output per manhour. It therefore measures, in physical terms (hours), the change in labor costs per unit of output.

Output per manhour is published as an index, base 1977 = 100. It is the ratio of the value in constant (1972) prices of final goods and services produced to the hours paid for, including hours paid for holidays, vacation, and sick leave, of all persons—employees, proprietors, and unpaid family workers. The output concept is real gross domestic product of the nonfarm business sector, compiled by the Bureau of Economic Analysis, which is the 1972 dollar market value of the goods and services produced by labor and property located in the United States.

Labor input data are based primarily on the hours and employment series compiled by the Bureau of Labor Statistics from monthly reports submitted by nonagricultural establishments to state employment security agencies (see series 13.0 for details of the coverage and methods of the establishment survey). For proprietors and unpaid family workers, where establishment data are not available, data from the national income and product accounts compiled by the BEA, and data from the current population survey compiled by the Bureau of the Census are used to develop hours and employment estimates.

23.0 COMMERCIAL AND INDUSTRIAL LOANS OUTSTANDING, in constant prices, United States

Monthly, beginning 1948

Unit: Millions of 1967 dollars

Title in source: Commercial and Industrial Loans Outstanding, Weekly Reporting, Large Commercial Banks

Source: *Business Conditions Digest* (Series 72), U.S. Department of Commerce, Seasonally adjusted by source. Adjusted to 1967 dollars by the Index of Producer Prices of Industrial Commodities (series 335 in source).

Description: The figures measure the average dollar amount of business loans outstanding each month. Included are data on all loans for commercial and industrial purposes except those secured by real estate. Loans to financial institutions and loans for the purpose of purchasing or carrying securities are also excluded. Commercial paper issued by nonfinancial companies is included.

The data are based on reports to the Federal Reserve System by approximately 170 banks. The reports include the amount of commercial and industrial loans outstanding as of each Wednesday and the amount of loans sold outright during each week to the banks' own foreign branches, nonconsolidated nonbank affiliates of the banks, the banks' holding companies (if not a bank), and nonconsolidated nonbank subsidiaries of the holding companies. The monthly series is the arithmetic mean of weekly data compiled by the Bureau of Economic Analysis.

To take care of a discontinuity in January 1972, figures prior to that date have been multiplied by a factor (.91118), the ratio of the two January 1972 figures. Prior to 1972 the data cover about 320 banks.

The current dollar figures are deflated by the Center for International Business Cycle Research (CIBCR) by dividing by the Index of Producer Prices of Industrial Commodities (base, 1967 = 100). This is a major sector (77.2 percent in December 1975) of the index for all commodities, compiled by the Bureau of Labor Statistics. The weights represent the total net selling value of commodities produced and processed in the United States and those imported for sale that flow into the primary markets. Prices relate to the Tuesday of the week in which the thirteenth of the month falls. See series 3.0 for references of this index.

For further information on this series, see *Handbook of Cyclical Indicators*, 1984, Department of Commerce. A similar series in constant 1972 dollars, deflated by the All Commodities Index of Producer Prices, is published in the source above (series 101).

24.0 BANK INTEREST RATES ON BUSINESS LOANS, United States

Monthly, beginning 1948

Unit: Percentages

Title in source: Average Prime Interest Rate Charged by Banks on Short-term Business Loans

Source: *Federal Reserve Bulletin*, Board of Governors of the Federal Reserve System, and *Business Conditions Digest* (series 109), U.S. Department of Commerce, not seasonally adjusted.

Description: The figures represent the interest rate that banks charge their most credit worthy customers on short-term loans. The prime rate is the base from which rates charged on loans to other customers are usually scaled upward. It is not as sensitive as rates on money-market instruments which fluctuate daily in response to short-term supply and demand conditions. Instead, its movements tend to be infrequent, changing only by increments of at least one quarter of a percentage point.

The data are monthly averages computed by multiplying the "predominant" prime rate (the rate charged by the majority of 30 large money market banks) in effect each day during a month by the number of days it was in effect, summing these products, and dividing by the total number of days. The series is not seasonally adjusted.

CANADA

1.0 AVERAGE WORKWEEK, MANUFACTURING, Canada

Monthly, beginning 1948

Unit: Hours per week

Title in source: Average Weekly Hours, Total Manufacturing (series D4870)

Sources: *Employment, Earnings and Hours* (catalogue 72-002), and *Canadian Statistical Review*, Statistics Canada. Seasonally adjusted by source.

Description: The figures represent the average weekly hours paid in the manufacture of durable and nondurable goods. They cover not only hours actually worked (including overtime) in the reporting week, but also hours paid for but not worked—such as annual vacation, public holidays, sick leave, and other paid leave. They relate to production and nonsupervisory workers (but include foremen performing functions similar to those of the employees they supervise) who worked during or received pay in the last pay period of the month. Casuals who worked less than seven hours in the pay period are excluded but regular part-time workers are included regardless of the number of hours they worked.

The data are based upon reports from firms employing 20 persons or more in any month of the year. Participation in the survey is compulsory and the response rate is about 88 percent. The sample covers about 90 percent of employees in manufacturing. Average weekly hours are derived by dividing the total weekly man-hours by the number of wage earners who were paid for those hours. The number of wage earners who received pay for only part of the reference week is included in the denominator and the number of hours for which they were paid is included in the numerator. Monthly data beginning in 1934 are available. Further methodological details are given in the source publication.

2.0 INITIAL CLAIMS, UNEMPLOYMENT INSURANCE, Canada

Monthly, beginning 1948

Unit: Thousands of claims

Title in source: Unemployment Insurance, Initial and Renewal Claims Received (series D1232)

Sources: *Statistical Report on the Operations of the Unemployment Insurance Act,* Statistics Canada (catalogue 73-001); also *Canadian Statistical Review.* Seasonally adjusted by CIBCR.

Description: Beginning in 1972, unemployment insurance has been extended to virtually all paid workers in the labor force and members of the Armed Forces. The main exceptions are salaried and hourly paid workers who work less than 20 hours a week, those on piece work and commission earning less than 30 percent of the maximum weekly insurable earning (87 dollars in 1980), and persons 65 years and over. It is estimated that almost 90 percent of the persons in the labor force were covered in January 1980.

In order to qualify, the claimant must be available and searching for work. From 1972 until the end of 1977, 8 insurable weeks were needed to qualify but this was changed to a variable 10-14 weeks depending on the rate of unemployment in the claimant's region. Claimants not in the labor force for 14 of the 52 preceding weeks required 20 insurable weeks to qualify and repeaters required up to 6 weeks more than the 10-14 needed (except in areas where the unemployment rate was greater than 11.5 percent). The maximum benefit period is 50 weeks. A tripartite system of premiums has been established where the employers, employees, and federal government contribute to pay for the cost of the program. Employers and employees absorb the cost of administration and initial benefits; the federal government is responsible for regionally extended benefits.

Prior to 1972, unemployment insurance had more limited coverage, excluding federal, provincial, and municipal workers, the Armed Forces, and several other categories. However, all persons paid by the day, hour, or piece rate were insured regardless of the amount of earnings. The requirements regarding prior contributions in order to qualify for benefits were more stringent than in 1972-77.

For further information, see the Technical Notes of the July-Sept. 1980 issue of the first publication noted above in source.

3.0 NEW ORDERS, CONSUMER GOODS, in constant prices, Canada

Monthly, beginning 1952

Unit: Millions of 1971 Canadian dollars

Titles in source: Estimated Value of Shipments of Consumer Goods, Nondurable (series D310462) and Durable (series D310463). Estimated Value of Unfilled Orders at End of Month, Consumer Goods, Nondurable (series D310478) and Durable (series D310479)

Sources: *Canadian Statistical Review* and *Inventories, Shipments and Orders in Manufacturing Industries* (catalogue 31-001), Statistics Canada. Seasonally adjusted by source. Deflated by the CIBCR by appropriate price indexes described below.

Description: This series is derived by the Center for International Business Cycle Research (CIBCR) from statistics on shipments and unfilled orders. New orders are computed from total shipments within any month plus the change in unfilled orders from the end of the previous month to the end of the month under review.

Monthly data are projections of annual Census of Manufactures values based on returns from a stratified systematic sample of manufacturing establishments. The totals are subject to adjustment when more recent census data become available. The sample is revised annually in accordance with the census base. The population is divided into groups of large, medium, and small establishments according to the total value of shipments for the census year. Monthly values are sought for all large establishments and a sample is chosen separately for each of the other two groups. There are about 10,000 establishments in the reporting panel. A more detailed description may be found in the January 1973 issue of the second source noted above.

Prior to 1961, the figures are published in the *Canadian Statistical Review* as New Orders, Total Consumer Goods Industries.

From 1952 through 1955, this series is deflated by the CIBCR using the price index for fully and chiefly manufactured goods, a component of the General Wholesale Price Index, original base 1935-39 = 100. This index is a base-weighted aggregate with weights derived from the average values of domestic production marketed or exported plus imports during the base period. Prices usually refer to actual sale prices of producers on ex-factory bases. This series was published in *Industry Price Indexes* (catalogue 62-011) and *Canadian Statistical Review,* Statistics Canada. It is not seasonally adjusted. For further details, see *Wholesale Price Indexes* 1913-1950, Reference Paper No. 24, Statistics Canada.

Beginning in 1956, the series has been deflated by the Industry Selling Price Index: Manufacturing (D500000), original base 1971 = 100, which has been linked to the Wholesale Price Index. Prices are collected for new orders placed on the fifteenth of the month or a near transaction date. The index measures the movements of prices of gross shipments of manufacturing industries, including inter-industry shipments between individual industries within manufacturing, and hence duplicates the movements of some prices. It is also published in *Industry Price Indexes* and is not seasonally adjusted. A more complete description may be found in *Industry Selling Price Indexes: Manufacturing 1956-77* (catalogue 62-543), Statistics Canada.

5.1 NEW ORDERS, MACHINERY AND EQUIPMENT, in constant prices, Canada

Monthly, beginning 1953

Unit: Millions of 1971 Canadian dollars

Titles in source: Estimated Value of Shipments and Unfilled Orders, Machinery and Equipment Industries (series D310464 and D310480)

Sources: *Canadian Statistical Review* and *Inventories, Shipments and Orders in Manufacturing Industries* (catalogue 31-001), Statistics Canada. Seasonally adjusted by source. Figures converted to 1971 dollars by the CIBCR using the price indexes listed below.

Description: This series is derived by the Center for International Business Cycle Research (CIBCR) from statistics on shipments and unfilled orders. Figures are computed from total shipments within any month plus the change in unfilled orders from the end of the previous month to the end of the month under review. Monthly data are projections of annual census of manufacturing values based on returns from a stratified sample of manufacturing establishments. All figures are subject to revision each year when more recent census of manufactures data become available.

Data prior to 1961 relate to a series New Orders, Total Capital Goods Industries that has been linked to the current series.

Figures for 1953-70 have been deflated by the Wholesale Price Index for fully and chiefly manufactured goods which has been linked in January 1971 to the Industry Selling Price Index, Machinery Industries (except electrical), original base 1971 = 100 (series D532900). Both are published in *Industry Price Indexes* (catalogue 62-011), and the *Canadian Statistical Review*, Statistics Canada, until 1979 when the Wholesale Price Index was discontinued.

For further information on this series and both indexes used as deflators, see the description for series 3.0 above.

5.2 NONRESIDENTIAL BUILDING PERMITS, in constant prices, Canada

Monthly, beginning 1949

Unit: Thousands of 1971 Canadian dollars

Title in source: Nonresidential Building Permits (series D4898)

Source: *Building Permits* (catalogue 64-001), Statistics Canada. Seasonally adjusted by source. This series is deflated by "Input Price Index for Nonresidential Construction" (series D476601) published in *Construction Price Statistics* (catalogue 62-007), Statistics Canada. Both series are also published in *Canadian Statistical Review*, Statistics Canada.

Description: Data are collected on permits issued by 2,000 municipalities and cover industrial, commercial, institutional, and government structures. Industrial buildings are those used for manufacturing and processing; transportation, communication, and other utilities; and agriculture, forestry, mine, and mine mill buildings. Commercial buildings include stores, warehouses, garages, office buildings, theatres, hotels, and a miscellaneous group of smaller structures. Expenditures made by the community, public, and government for buildings and structures include schools, universities, hospitals, churches, government office, and administration buildings, and so on, together with ancillary buildings such as dormitories, residences, gymnasiums, heating plants.

A building permit may be issued by municipalities for: construction of new buildings; alterations, additions, or conversions to existing buildings; installation of heating, plumbing, and other facilities; erection of signs, posters, canopies, and other improvements to property.

At present, not all municipalities are covered in the Building Permits Survey. According to the 1976 population census, the population of the municipalities reporting is about 88 percent of the total, being 98 percent in urban areas but only 58 percent in rural areas. Frequently large industrial plants are constructed outside the boundaries of a building permit municipality. Further details may be found in the December 1980 issue of *Building Permits*.

This series is adjusted to 1971 dollars by CIBCR by dividing by an input price index for labor and materials used in nonresidential building construction (original base 1971 = 100). Fixed weights relating to 1971 costs are used to combine the component indexes. Indexes for the materials group and labor input are also published separately in the source. Figures prior to 1952 were deflated by "Nonresidential Building Materials Price Index," original base 1961 = 100.

6.0 RESIDENTIAL BUILDING PERMITS, Canada

Monthly, beginning 1960

Unit: Number of permits

Title in source: Building Permits, Dwelling Units (series D849088)

Source: *Building Permits* (catalogue 64-001), Statistics Canada. Seasonally adjusted by source.

Description: the figures represent the number of permits issued for the construction of self-contained dwelling units. For example, if an apartment building is constructed that contains six apartments, it will be shown as six dwelling units. In addition to single residential units, the figures include seasonal dwellings (cottages), duplexes, row houses, and apartments—including those that are part of a nonresidential structure. Permits for the conversion of existing structures into dwelling units are also added.

See the description for series 5.2 for indications of the coverage of the monthly Building Permits Survey conducted by Statistics Canada.

7.0 CHANGE IN NONFARM BUSINESS INVENTORIES, in constant prices, Canada

Quarterly, beginning 1948

Unit: Millions of 1971 Canadian dollars, at annual rate

Title in source: Value of Physical Change in Nonfarm Business Inventories (series D40615)

Source: *National Income and Expenditure Accounts* (catalogue 13-001), Statistics Canada. Also published quarterly in *Canadian Statistical Review*, Statistics Canada. Seasonally adjusted by source.

Description: This series is a component of estimates of gross national expenditure. The book value of inventories is deflated to remove the effect of price change and the derived "physical" change is then valued at average 1971 prices.

Business, nonfarm inventory stocks include all inventories of raw materials, goods-in-process, and finished products held by corporations, nonfarm unincorporated businesses, and government business enterprises. About 90 percent of inventory book value holdings in Canada are held by the manufacturing, wholesale, and retail trade industries. In these industries, regular monthly sample surveys are conducted by Statistics Canada, and the information on book values of inventories held at the end of each quarter are available from the monthly published report. In these areas, the quality of the quarterly inventory estimates is considered quite good but for other industries it is generally less satisfactory. The information obtained monthly from sample surveys is adjusted to annual benchmarks derived from annual censuses.

Price data for the deflation of the inventory book values in manufacturing and wholesale trade are based upon components of the wholesale price index, and for retail trade upon components of the consumer price index. Other series are deflated with information from the wholesale price index or the industry selling price indexes. For more details on the inventory revaluation procedures and for further information, see *National Income and Expenditure Accounts*, Vol. 3 (catalogue 13-549E), Statistics Canada.

8.0 CHANGE IN INDUSTRIAL MATERIALS PRICE INDEX, Canada

Monthly, beginning 1948

Unit: Percentages, annual rate

Titles in source: 1948-78, Wholesale Price Index of Thirty Industrial Materials (series D601017); 1979-, Industry Selling Price Index: Manufacturing-Basic Industries (series D634404)

Source: *Industry Price Indexes* (catalogue 62-011), Statistics Canada. Not seasonally adjusted. The percent changes are computed by the CIBCR.

Description: The wholesale price index of 30 industrial materials was calculated as an unweighted geometric average on the base 1935-39 = 100. The materials included related to groups such as "stable" prices (12 commodities), "sensitive" prices (13), and food prices (5). The index was discontinued since it contained prices for some materials that no longer constitute important industrial inputs and in December 1978 was linked to the Industry Selling Price Index for Basic Industries. This index is a special aggregate of the Industry Selling Price Index: Manufacturing, and covers prices in the wood, paper and allied industries, and the primary metal and nonmetallic mineral products industries. It is a Laspeyres index computed on the base 1971 = 100, with weights derived from shipments values in that year. See series 3.0 above for further details of the Industry Selling Price Index and reference to a published description.

More information on the earlier Wholesale Price Index may be found in *Prices and Price Indexes, 1949-52*, Vol. 23 (catalogue 62-501), Statistics Canada.

The rate of change computed by the Center for International Business Cycle Research (CIBCR) is a 6-month smoothed annual rate, based upon the ratio of the current month's index to the average index for the preceding 12 months. Since the interval between the midpoints of the current month and the preceding 12 is 6.5 months, the ratio is raised to the 12/6.5 power to derive a compound annual rate.

9.0 STOCK PRICE INDEX, Canada

Monthly, beginning 1948

Unit: Index, base 1975 = 100

Title in source: Canadian Stock Price Index, Toronto Stock Exchange (series B4237)

Source: *Bank of Canada Review*, Statistics Canada. Not seasonally adjusted.

Description: The Toronto Stock Exchange 300 Composite Index System is grouped to conform as closely as possible to the Standard Industrial Classification system used by Statistics Canada. However, to qualify for inclusion in the index, each issue was subjected to certain eligibility requirements such as turnover volume, ownership principally by Canadian investors, and so on, so that the 300 largest stocks chosen in terms of the float-weighted average quoted market value may not include certain industry groups.

Stock prices are weighted by the outstanding shares, producing the current aggregate market value of the stocks which is compared to the aggregate market value in the base period, 1975. Indexes are computed each quarter-hour by the Exchange. Adjustments are made for mergers, increases or decreases in capital, and new industries within the Index System. If more than 50 percent of outstanding shares of a company are held as a controlling block, they are not included in the index calculations which are based only on publicly available shares.

From 1968-75, the Toronto Stock Exchange Index covered 208 stocks: 150 Industrials, 28 Base Metals, 19 Oils and 11 Golds. From 1956 to 1968, 108 stocks were included. Prior to 1956, the data relate to the Industrial Share Price Index compiled by Statistics Canada, a component of the Investors Index, and published on the base 1971 = 100 in *Industry Price Indexes* until 1979.

The figures are representative of closing quotations at the end of the month.

See the *Toronto Stock Exchange Review* of January 1977 for more information.

10.0 CORPORATE PROFITS AFTER TAXES, in constant prices, Canada

Quarterly, beginning 1948

Unit: Millions of 1971 Canadian dollars, at annual rate

Title in source: Corporation Profits After Taxes (series D31515)

Source: *National Income and Expenditure Accounts* (catalogue 13-001), Statistics Canada. Seasonally adjusted by source. Deflated by Gross National Expenditure Implicit Price Index (series D40625), from same source.

Description: This series is derived from the Gross National Product accounts. Federal and provincial taxes have been deducted.

Information on corporation profits is collected by Statistics Canada through regular quarterly surveys. The estimates are made for three separate groups of corporations: industrial (nonfinancial) corporations;

financial corporations (except banks and insurance companies); and banks and insurance companies. For the period 1948-50, before the quarterly survey became available, data are based upon the average quarterly pattern for the years 1950-56 to distribute the annual profits by quarters. A number of adjustments in the book profits as reported by corporations are made to make the profits figures compatible with the definitions used in the national accounts.

The figures have been deflated by the Center for International Business Cycle Research (CIBCR) by dividing by the index of Gross National Expenditure Implicit Price Index, base 1971 = 100. This index is derived by dividing the current value series of Gross National Expenditure by the deflated constant dollar series. The result is a current weighted Paasche-type price index which reflects not only changes in prices but also change in expenditure patterns.

Further information may be found in *National Income and Expenditure Accounts,* Vol. 3 (catalogue 13-549E), Statistics Canada.

11.0 RATIO, PRICE TO UNIT LABOR COST, MANUFACTURING, Canada

Monthly, beginning 1961

Unit: Index, base 1971 = 100

Title in source: See description below for titles of component series

Sources: Price Index: *Industry Price Indexes* (catalogue 62-011) and *Canadian Statistical Review,* both Statistics Canada. Source for first three series used in constructing Unit Labor Cost: *Employment, Earnings and Hours* (catalogue 72,002), Statistics Canada. Source of fourth series is noted below.

Description: The series is obtained by dividing the Industry Selling Price Index for total manufacturing industries (series D500000) by a unit labor cost index, base 1971 = 100, constructed from the following series: a product is obtained of (1) the employment index in manufacturing (series D1330), (2) the average weekly hours in manufacturing (series D4870), and (3) average hourly earnings in manufacturing (series D4867); this product is then divided by the index of real domestic product in manufacturing (series D144179). This calculation is carried out by the Center for International Business Cycle Research (CIBCR).

The Industry Selling Price Index for manufacturing, base 1971 = 100, covers data for approximately 110 industries. Responding firms and the selection of commodities to be priced were derived from the annual Census of Manufactures. The index measures the movements of prices of gross shipments of manufacturing industries, including inter-industry shipments between individual industries within manufacturing. See series 3.0 for further details; a complete description may be found in *Industry Selling Price Indexes: Manufacturing 1956-76* (catalogue 62-543), Statistics Canada.

The index of employment in manufacturing and the series for average weekly hours and average hourly earnings are compiled from reports of firms employing 20 persons or more in any month of the year. Data relate to the last pay period in the month. The series on average weekly hours is the series 1.0 above whose coverage also applies to the series on average hourly earnings. The index of real domestic product in manufacturing industries, base 1971 = 100, is published in *Indexes of Real Domestic Product by Industry* (catalogue 61005), Statistics Canada.

12.0 CHANGE IN CONSUMER CREDIT OUTSTANDING, in constant prices, Canada

Monthly, beginning 1956

Unit: Millions of 1981 Canadian dollars

Title in source: Consumer Credit: Outstanding Balances of Selected Holders (series B115)

Source: *Bank of Canada Review*. Seasonally adjusted by source. Deflated by Consumer Price Index, base 1981 = 100 (series D484000) published in *Canadian Statistical Review,* Statistics Canada.

Description: The series shows the month-to-month change in estimated amounts of consumer credit outstanding on the books of selected lenders. The basic data relate mainly to credit extended to individuals, but also include unidentifiable amounts of credit extended for nonconsumer purposes. Credit extended through the use of all-purpose credit cards is included with the balances of the selected lender responsible for their issuance. The data do not represent total consumer indebtedness since they do not include credit on the books of: furniture, T.V., and appliance stores; other retail outlets; motor vehicle dealers; public utilities; other credit card issuers not elsewhere included in the data; and credit card accounts of oil companies. Data on consumer credit on the books of these lenders are available until December 1978 in the Statistics Canada publication *Consumer Credit (61-004).* In addition, data on fully secured loans, long-term indebtedness (such as residential mortgage and home improvement loans), loans between individuals, or balances on bills owed to professional practitioners, clubs, hospitals, or other personal service establishments are not included.

The basic figures are a total of the following subgroups published in the source: chartered bank ordinary personal loans; sales finance and consumer loan companies; life insurance company policy loans, Quebec savings banks unsecured personal loans; department stores; and trust and mortgage loan companies.

Changes in the balances outstanding are computed by the Center for International Business Cycle Research (CIBCR) and then adjusted to constant 1981 dollars by dividing by the Consumer Price Index, base 1981 = 100. This index is described in the notes for series 17.0 below.

13.0 NONFARM EMPLOYMENT, Canada

Monthly, beginning 1953

Unit: Thousands of persons

Title in source: Employment in Nonagriculture (series D772021)

Source: 1953-75, *Canadian Statistical Review*, Statistics Canada; subsequently, *The Labour Force* (catalogue 71-001), Statistics Canada. Seasonally adjusted by Statistics Canada; entire series revised annually in light of the most recent information on changes in seasonality. Revisions published each year in *Historical Labour Force Characteristics* (catalogue 71-201), Statistics Canada.

Description: The series covers the civilian, noninstitutional population 15 years of age and over who were employed in the reference week. It includes all persons who: (1) did any work at all, as employees or self-employed; (2) had a job but were not at work due to illness or disability, personal or family responsibilities, bad weather, labour disputes, or vacation. Excluded are persons who expect to return to a job from which they have been laid off and those who have a job to start at a future date.

Data are obtained from a sample survey of about 56,000 households during the week containing the fifteenth of the month. The sample has been designed to represent all persons in the population 15 years and over residing in Canada except: residents of the Yukon and Northwest Territories, persons living on Indian reserves, inmates of institutions, and full-time members of the Armed Forces. Beginning 1971, the series has been revised to the 1976 census base. Prior to 1966 the surveys covered persons 14 years or over and the sample comprised about 30,000 households.

Labor force surveys were undertaken quarterly from November, 1945, until November, 1952, and have subsequently been carried out monthly. Substantial revisions were made in the surveys beginning January, 1976. A comprehensive description of the design of the labor force survey can be found in *Methodology of the Canadian Labour Force Survey* (catalogue 71-526), Statistics Canada, 1976.

14.0 UNEMPLOYMENT RATE, Canada

Monthly, beginning 1953

Unit: Percentage

Title in source: Unemployment Rate, 15 Years of Age and Over (series D767611)

Sources: *Canadian Statistical Review*, Statistics Canada; also, *The Labour Force* (catalogue 71,001), Statistics Canada. Seasonally adjusted by Statistics Canada; entire series revised annually in light of the most recent information on changes in seasonality. Revisions published each year in *Historical Labour Force Characteristics* (catalogue 71-201), Statistics Canada.

Description: The unemployment rate represents the number of unemployed persons as a percentage of the labor force (that portion of the civilian, noninstitutional population 15 years of age or over who were employed or unemployed during the week containing the fifteenth of the month). For details on the labor force surveys, see notes on the preceding series, 13.0. Prior to 1966, the surveys included also 14 year olds.

The unemployed category includes those persons available for work during the reference week who: (1) were without work and had actively looked for work in the past 4 weeks; (2) had not actively looked for work in the past 4 weeks but had been laid off from a job for less than 27 weeks to which they expect to return; (3) had not actively looked for work in the past 4 weeks but had a new job starting in 4 weeks or less. Full-time students seeking part-time work are considered to be available, but not those looking for full-time work. For further methodological details see *The Labour Force* noted above and *Canadian Labour Force Survey* (catalogue 71-526), Statistics Canada, 1976.

15.0 GROSS NATIONAL EXPENDITURES, in constant prices, Canada

Quarterly, beginning 1948

Unit: Millions of Canadian 1971 dollars, annual rate

Title in source: Gross National Expenditures (series D40593)

Sources: *National Income and Expenditure Accounts* (catalogue 13-001), and *Canadian Statistical Review*, Statistics Canada. Seasonally adjusted by source.

Description: This series is published by Statistics Canada in constant (1971) dollars. The components are: personal expenditure on consumer goods and services, government current expenditure on goods and services; gross fixed capital formation consisting of expenditures by government and business; value of physical change in inventories; exports of goods and services from which are deducted imports of goods and services.

In order to avoid duplication, only final output is included in the expenditure categories, intermediate production being excluded. Personal expenditures include imputation for free board and lodging and other income in kind as well as imputed space rent for owner-occupied houses. In addition, the operating costs and profits of life insurance companies are included to reflect the value of services rendered by such companies, as well as the value of services rendered by banks and other financial intermediaries for which there is no charge. Farm products consumed directly in households are also imputed.

In addition to domestic production, the figures include returns on investments by Canadians in other countries as well as earnings by Canadians living abroad. Excluded are the investment returns and earnings of nonresidents arising out of activities in Canada.

Deflation to 1971 prices of almost 300 individual series involve the use of a wide range of price information. The Consumer Price Index and its components constitutes a very important source of price information for the deflation of personal expenditure on goods and services, a category that accounts for well over half of gross national expenditure. For further information on these details and all other information, see *National Income and Expenditure Accounts, vol. 3* (catalogue 13-549E), Statistics Canada.

16.0 INDUSTRIAL PRODUCTION, Canada

Monthly, beginning 1948

Unit: Index, base 1971 = 100

Title in source: Index of Industrial Production (series D144312)

Sources: *Indexes of Real Domestic Product by Industry* (catalogue 61-005), and *Canadian Statistical Review*, Statistics Canada. Seasonally adjusted by source.

Description: This index covers the following industries: mining; manufacturing; and electricity, gas, and water. The industries surveyed accounted for about 30 percent of gross domestic product at factor cost in 1971.

The index is calculated as a base-weighted arithmetic average, the weights being derived from the gross domestic product at factor cost in 1971. The index is adjusted for differences in the number of working days in each month as well as seasonal variation.

Data used in calculating monthly indexes, and their percentage share in total weight are: quantity of gross output of individual products 60 percent, employee-hours worked 36 percent, quantity of individual raw materials consumed 3 percent, and value of gross production of individual commodities adjusted for price changes 1 percent. These indicators are compiled mainly from the results of official inquiries and are revised in the light of commodity surveys and other definitive data. Annual indexes are calculated separately, based upon more complete information, and the monthly indexes are adjusted to the level of the annual index.

This index is linked at 1971 to an index on original base 1961 = 100, and at 1961 to an index on original base 1949 = 100. An earlier index was based on 1935 = 100.

See *Index of Real Domestic Product by Industry, 1971 = 100* (catalogue 61-213), Statistics Canada, for additional information.

17.0 PERSONAL INCOME, in constant prices, Canada

Quarterly, beginning 1948

Unit: Millions of 1981 Canadian dollars, annual rate

Title in source: Person Income (series D40282)

Sources: *National Income and Expenditure Accounts* (quarterly catalogue 13-001), and *Canadian Statistical Review*, Statistics Canada. Seasonally adjusted by source. Deflated by Consumer Price Index (series D484000) published in *Canadian Statistical Review.*

Description: The sources of personal income are: wages; salaries and supplementary labor income; military pay and allowances; net income received by farm operators from farm production; net income of nonfarm, unincorporated business (including rent); interest, dividends, and miscellaneous investment income; and current transfers from government, from corporations, and from nonresidents.

The figures are deflated by the Center for International Business Cycle Research (CIBCR) by using the Consumer Price Index, base 1981 = 100. The index is computed as a weighted arithmetic average with fixed weights. Subsequent to March 1982, the series is based upon 1978 expenditure patterns. From September 1978 to March 1982 weights relate to 1974; from May 1973 to September 1978 they relate to 1967 expenditures; and prior to May 1973, 1957 expenditure weights were used. The major components and their relative importance in 1978 are: food 21.1 percent, housing 35.4 percent, clothing 9.6 percent, transportation 16.2 percent, health and personal care 3.7 percent, recreation 8.6 percent, and tobacco and alcohol 5.4 percent. For further details, see *Consumer Price Index, Concepts and Procedures* (catalogue 62-553), Statistics Canada.

18.1 RETAIL TRADE, in constant prices, Canada

Monthly, beginning 1948

Unit: Millions of 1981 Canadian dollars

Title in source: Value of Retail Trade (series D650087)

Sources: *Retail Trade* (catalogue 63-005) and *Canadian Statistical Review*, both Statistics Canada. Seasonally adjusted by source. Adjusted to 1981 dollars by dividing by the Consumer Price Index, also published in *Canadian Statistical Review* (series D484000).

Description: Figures are the aggregate sales made through retail locations, defined as places whose principal activity is the sale of merchandise and related services to the general public. They do not include direct selling except mail order and catalogue sales. In addition to sales of merchandise, the figures also include receipts from related services such as repairs, equipment rental, and so forth.

The monthly estimates cover: food, clothing, and shoe stores; department, general merchandise, general, and variety stores; motor vehicle dealers; service stations and garages; automotive parts and accessories stores; hardware, furniture, and appliance stores; pharmacies; book and stationery stores; florists; jewelry stores; sporting goods and accessories; other retail stores.

Beginning in 1975, new sampling and imputation techniques have been used. Earlier figures were derived from a sample of 12,000 firms selected from the 1961 census. The monthly estimates were made from ratios derived by linking sales of firms within a cell to sales in the corresponding month of the previous year. But since 1975 the figures have been obtained from a stratified sample of the 16,000 firms chosen from the taxation list. To obtain the monthly estimate, each unit is inflated to universe levels by multiplying by the inverse of the probability of selection for the unit.

The series is adjusted for both seasonal and trading-day variations. More detailed information may be found in the first source noted above.

Figures are adjusted to constant 1981 dollars by the Center for International Business Cycle Research (CIBCR) by dividing by the Consumer Price Index, base 1981 = 100. Information on this index is given in detail for series 17.0 above, and a more complete description may be found in *Consumer Price Index, Concepts and Procedures* (catalogue 62-553), Statistics Canada.

19.0 LONG DURATION UNEMPLOYMENT, Canada

Monthly, beginning 1953

Unit: Thousands of persons

Title in source: Unemployment, Duration 14 Weeks and Over

Source: *The Labour Force* (catalogue 71-001), Statistics Canada. Seasonally adjusted by CIBCR.

Description: See series 13.0 and 14.0 above for descriptions of the unemployment and labor force figures.

Prior to 1976, the labor force surveys covered the civilian population aged 14 years and over while later surveys covered those aged 15 and over. However, the unemployment of long duration of 14 year olds is not significant. From 1953-65, the figures include those unemployed for 4 months or more (series D755478). From 1966 through 1975, they are the sum of two series: those seeking work for 4-6 months (D775894) and those seeking work for more than 6 months (DD775895). From 1976, they relate to those seeking work 14 weeks and over (series 770285).

Further methodological details are presented in *Methodology of the Canadian Labor Force, Survey* (catalogue 71-526), Statistics Canada.

20.0 PLANT AND EQUIPMENT, INVESTMENT EXPENDITURES, in constant prices, Canada

Quarterly, beginning 1948

Unit: Millions of 1971 Canadian dollars, annual rate

Titles in source: Business Gross Fixed Capital Formation: Nonresidential Construction (series D40609) and Machinery and Equipment (series D40610)

Source: *Canadian Statistical Review*, Statistics Canada, seasonally adjusted by source.

Description: This series is a component of the quarterly estimates of gross national expenditures (see series 15.0 above). Business gross fixed capital outlays for nonresidential construction and machinery and equipment cover investment in all forms of productive assets by business which are used to produce a future flow of goods and services. Included are all plant and equipment expenditures of corporations, unincorporated business enterprises (including farm operators), and government business enterprises. The capital outlays of noncommercial institutions such as universities, churches, and charitable and welfare agencies are also included in the estimates.

Figures for the period 1948 to 1973 were in 1961 dollars; a conversion to 1971 dollars was effected by using a conversion ratio of 1.38.

21.0 BUSINESS INVENTORIES, in constant prices, Canada

Monthly, beginning 1949

Unit: Millions of 1971 Canadian dollars

Title in source: Value of Inventories Owned, Manufacturing (series D310359)

Sources: *Canadian Statistical Review*, and *Inventories, Shipments, and Orders in Manufacturing Industries* (catalogue 31-001), Statistics Canada. Seasonally adjusted by source.

Description: The figures are monthly projections of annual census of manufacturers' values based on returns from a stratified systematic sample of manufacturing establishments. The figures are adjusted to 1971 dollars by the Center for International Business Cycle Research (CIBCR), by dividing by the Industry Selling Price Index in Manufacturing (series D500000). Prior to 1956 the index used as a deflator was the wholesale price index for fully and chiefly manufactured goods.

The estimates for December may differ from year-end census totals to the extent that census totals include establishment reports for fiscal years that may end on dates other than December 31. In addition, some components of inventory are included in the monthly survey's benchmark value that may not be included in census inventories. Respondents are asked to report their book values of raw materials, work in progress, finished products, and progress payments separately in order to provide aggregate values of inventory by level of fabrication. The inventory levels are calculated on a Canada-wide basis, not by province.

Further information on the selection of the sample of about 10,000 establishments and also about the indexes used to adjust the series to 1971 dollars may be found in the description for series 3.0 above.

More detailed description of the concepts and survey methods is found in *Inventories, Shipments, and Orders in Manufacturing Industries*, January 1973.

22.1 CHANGE IN HOURS PER UNIT OF OUTPUT, MANUFACTURING, Canada

Monthly, beginning 1962

Unit: Percentage change from a year ago

Title in source: See description below for titles of component series

Source: Statistics Canada

Description: The Center for International Business Cycle Research (CIBCR) computes percent changes over a 12-month span in the reciprocal of the series for output per man-hour in manufacturing. The index of output per hour, computed by Statistics Canada on the base 1971 = 100, is obtained by dividing the series for gross domestic product in manufacturing (series D144179) by the product of (1) employment in manufacturing (series D1330); and (2) average weekly hours in manufacturing (series D4870). All series are seasonally adjusted by Statistics Canada. The two series in the denominator are each put into index form on base 1971 = 100 before the final calculation.

The index of gross domestic product is published in *Gross Domestic Product by Industry* (catalogue 61-005) and the two series in the denominator are published in *Employment, Earnings and Hours* (catalogue 72-002), Statistics Canada. See the last paragraph of the description for series 11.0 and also 1.0 for details of these series.

Statistics Canada publishes more comprehensive monthly labor productivity series on output per person employed in its *Current Economic Analysis*. Output is defined as total gross domestic product and employment is defined on a labor force survey basis. It is an index, base 1971 = 100, seasonally adjusted.

23.0 BUSINESS LOANS OUTSTANDING, in constant prices, Canada

Quarterly, 1948-55, monthly, beginning 1956

Unit: Millions of 1971 Canadian dollars

Title in source: Chartered Banks, Business Loans Outstanding (series B1623)

Source: *Bank of Canada Review*. Seasonally adjusted by Bank of Canada; the CIBCR converts the series to 1971 dollars.

Description: Canada's commercial banking system is comprised of privately owned banks which have been chartered by Parliament or have received letters patent by Order-in-Council as provided for in the 1980 Bank Act. Under this act, the banks are required to submit reports on their operations to the Minister of Finance and the Bank of Canada.

The data are averages of the four or five Wednesdays in the month. They cover loans to private businesses: agriculture; fishing and trapping; logging and forestry; mines, quarries, and oil wells; food, beverage, and tobacco products; leather, textile, and apparel products; metal products; transportation equipment; petroleum products; other manufactures; the construction industry; transportation, communication, and other public utilities; wholesale and retail trade, the service industries, and conglomerates.

It has been the practice to revise the Bank Act at approximately ten-year intervals. The most recent revision was in 1980. As a result of these revisions, as well as periodic changes in regulations and changes in the structure of the industry due to mergers, earlier data are not always strictly comparable. Beginning in December 1971, the figures include loans of majority-owned subsidiaries of chartered banks and of foreign-owned banks. Beginning in November 1981, the data include loans to farmers, to institutions, to grain dealers, and sales finance dealers, none of which were included in earlier figures. They now exclude nonresidential mortgages, which had been included before.

The 1948-55 quarterly data relate to end-of-period.

This series has been deflated by the Industry Selling Price Index for manufacturing (1971 = 100), by the Center for International Business Cycle Research (CIBCR). See series 3.0 for information on this index. The 1948-55 quarterly data were deflated by the Wholesale Price Index of fully and chiefly manufactured goods (1935-39 = 100), linked to the Industry Selling Price Index at 1956, also described in series 3.0.

24.0 BANK INTEREST RATES, BUSINESS LOANS, Canada

Monthly, beginning 1948

Unit: Percentages

Title in source: Chartered Banks' Rate on Prime Business Loans (series B14020)

Source: *Bank of Canada Review*. Not seasonally adjusted.

Description: This is the interest rate charged to the most credit-worthy borrowers and applies only to large business loans. The rate shown is of the last Wednesday of the month. When there are differences in the rate charged by individual banks, the most typical rate is taken. Since May 1973, the chartered banks from time to time have had in effect a lower base rate for small business loans under authorizations of $200,000 or less. For the definition of chartered banks, see the description above for series 23.0.

UNITED KINGDOM

1.0 AVERAGE WORKWEEK, MANUFACTURING, United Kingdom

Monthly, beginning 1956 (1956-60 figures only available for 6 months; 1961 for 9 months)

Unit: Index, 1980 = 100

Title in source: Index of Average Weekly Hours Worked per Operative in Manufacturing Industries

Source: *Department of Employment Gazette*, Department of Employment. Seasonally adjusted by source; 1956-61 data seasonally adjusted by the CIBCR.

Description: The series is an index (original base 1962 = 100) of average weekly hours worked per operative in Great Britain. All manufacturing industries are included. The industry groups published in the source are: engineering, shipbuilding, electrical and metal goods; vehicles; textiles, leather, and clothing; food, drink, and tobacco.

The figures cover wage earners including apprentices, maintenance workers, storekeepers, cleaners, and some foremen and supervisors. They do not include administrative, technical, or clerical personnel. They cover wage earners engaged in outside work such as erecting or fitting but not home workers.

Information about the average weekly hours actually worked by operatives is available for a selected week in October from an earnings survey. By taking into account monthly variations in the incidence of sickness, overtime, and short-time working, in conjunction with changes in normal hours, estimates are made for other months. Provisional estimates are prepared for months subsequent to the latest available October survey figures and these are subject to revision when the following survey is published.

Normal weekly hours are obtained from centrally determined collective agreements. Overtime and short-time working are obtained from the answers of a sample of industrial establishments to a monthly labour survey conducted by the Department of Employment. Short-time working relates to arrangements made by the employer for working less than normal hours. The effects of sickness are estimated from administrative records of the Department of Health and Social Security.

4.1 NEW COMPANIES REGISTERED, United Kingdom

Monthly, beginning 1949

Unit: Number of enterprises

Title in source: New Companies Registered in Great Britain

Source: *British Business* (formerly *Trade and Industry*), Department of Industry. Not seasonally adjusted since 1968; prior to that adjusted by source.

Description: The figures cover new companies registered for the first time in Great Britain only, excluding unlimited companies and companies limited by guarantee. Companies must register with the Registrar of Companies and satisfy certain statutory requirements before they can commence trading with the liability of their members limited in the event of liquidation. (The device of limiting by guarantee is generally restricted to nonprofit bodies such as charities or clubs, which have no shareholders in the usual sense but which wish to limit their members' liability.)

The statutory provisions governing registration have not changed materially since 1949, and the method of compiling the data has been consistent. However, there were sharp declines in new registrations between 1964 and 1966, between 1967 and 1968, and between 1973 and 1974. The first of these declines followed a change in the system of company taxation, which probably made incorporation less attractive, and the others followed increases in the fees charged for registration. Whether these factors caused the declines is not known.

A point which should be borne in mind, when using the registrations figures as an indicator of economic activity, is the fact that company agents regularly arrange for incorporation of what are called "shelf" companies. These companies are not formed to operate immediately as trading organizations, but are intended for sale to parties who subsequently alter the company's name and constitution to suit their purposes before commencing trading, thereby avoiding some of the paperwork and time involved in the incorporation of a company. It is thought that some 35-40 percent of all new companies are at first "shelf" companies, but this proportion may of course vary over time in response to the agents' assessment of the likely demand.

4.2 BUSINESS FAILURES, United Kingdom

Quarterly, 1960-78; monthly, beginning 1979

Unit: Number of failures

Title in source: Insolvencies in England and Wales: Bankruptcies

Source: *British Business* (formerly *Trade and Industry*), Department of Industry. Seasonally adjusted by source.

Description: The figures refer to individuals and partnerships who are dealt with under the Bankruptcy Acts or who made arrangement with their creditors, and include receiving orders, administration orders, and deeds of arrangements. Annual data for all of the United Kingdom are published in the source.

A receiving order is made by the court on the petition of a creditor if it is satisfied that the debtor has committed an act of bankruptcy, or on the petition of the debtor himself. The order makes the official receiver, who is an officer of the court, receiver of the debtor's estate and deprives the debtor of the right to deal with it. In 1976, the minimum debt to support a creditor's petition of bankruptcy was changed from 50 pounds to 200 pounds. Combined with increases in the deposits required on petitions, this led to a substantial drop in the number of bankruptcies after 1976. Administration orders relate to deceased insolvents. Deeds of arrangement relate to arrangements between debtors and creditors that are reached without recourse to the courts.

The figures are obtained from the Department of Trade's Insolvency Service which has Official Receivers attached to all bankruptcy courts. Deeds of arrangement must be reported to the Insolvency Service.

The monthly figures beginning in 1979 published in the source are a three-month average (current month and two preceding) of seasonally adjusted data, an attempt to smooth out sharp fluctuations.

For further details, see *Economic Trends*, March 1975, and *British Business*, August 22, 1980.

5.1 NEW ORDERS, ENGINEERING INDUSTRIES, volume, United Kingdom

Monthly, beginning 1958

Unit: Index, base 1980 = 100

Title in source: Volume Index Numbers for the Combined Engineering Industries: Orders

Source: *British Business* (formerly *Trade and Industry*), Department of Industry, London. Also published in *Monthly Digest of Statistics*, Central Statistical Office. Seasonally adjusted by source.

Description: The index figures are derived from new orders (net of cancellations) of the mechanical, instrument, and electrical engineering industries. Since 1963, transport equipment has been excluded but prior figures include locomotives, commercial vehicles, and wheeled tractors. The industries now covered account for about one quarter of value added in manufacturing.

Orders are valued at actual selling prices, net of discounts and excluding the value added tax and other indirect taxes. Orders placed by other establishments of the same enterprise are included as are orders for repair on contract work, renting of own goods, and goods purchased for resale without further processing. The volume figures are obtained from value figures adjusted by price indexes especially constructed using components of the Wholesale Price Index and taking into account the time lag between order and delivery dates. New orders in a given month are computed by adding deliveries made that month to the change in unfilled orders from the previous month, all expressed in constant prices.

Beginning in 1972, data have been obtained in a monthly inquiry of establishments with over 100 employees in mechanical and instrument engineering and over 200 employees in electrical engineering, conducted by the Business Statistics Office. Before this the main inquiry was quarterly (and attempted to cover all establishments employing 25 or more), but was supplemented by a monthly sample. There are discontinuities in this series between June and July 1965 and between 1971 and 1972 due to changes in method of inquiry.

The original base of the series is average monthly sales in 1980 = 100 (the 1980 annual figure for this series on this sales base is 93 and the published data are adjusted by this factor). The original base of the index is 1958 (through 1962); 1963 (through 1968); 1970 (through 1972); and 1975 (through 1980). They are linked on 1963, 1970, 1975, and 1980. The weighting pattern is derived from the base year value of deliveries. Further details may be found in *Economic Trends*, April 1972, Central Statistical Office.

5.2 NEW ORDERS, CONSTRUCTION, PRIVATE INDUSTRY, in constant prices, United Kingdom

Quarterly, 1957-63, monthly, beginning 1964

Unit: Millions of 1980 pounds

Title in source: Value of New Orders Obtained by Contractors at 1980 Prices, Great Britain, Private, Industrial

Source: *Housing and Construction Statistics*, Department of the Environment. Seasonally adjusted by source. Also published in current prices in *Monthly Digest of Statistics,* Central Statistical Office.

Description: The data, published quarterly in the source but also available monthly, are current value figures revalued at constant prices by means of a tender (offering) price index. The series relates to contracts awarded for new construction work by clients in the private sector (excluding subcontracts from other contractors), including extensions to existing contracts, construction work in "package deals," and serial contracts. Also included is speculative work undertaken on the initiative of firms (without a contract).

The figures include the cost of site preparation (not site value), demolition, and the cost of materials supplied by the contractor. Extensions and alterations to existing structures are included, but not repair and maintenance.

The value of the order is taken to be the gross value of the contract, and is entirely attributed to the period when the order is placed; for serial contracts, where the total value of the work may not be determined at the time the contract is let, an estimate of the total value of work to be done during the period is included. No deductions are made for cancelled orders.

The Department of Environment maintains a statistical register of private contracting firms from which samples are drawn for enquiries. In mid-1981 the register contained about 125,000 firms.

Information on the tender price index used to deflate the value figure may be found in the July 1978 issue of *Economic Trends*. The data in 1980 prices have been linked to the series formerly published in 1975 prices. Prior to 1979, the deflator used was an index of the cost of construction described in *Housing and Construction Statistics, Notes and Definitions Supplement*, 1977.

6.1 HOUSING STARTS, United Kingdom

Monthly, beginning 1948

Unit: Thousands of dwellings

Title in source: Housebuilding Performance, Great Britain, Starts, Private Sector

Source: *Housing and Construction Statistics*, quarterly, Department of the Environment. Seasonally adjusted by source.

Description: The series relates to new permanent dwellings only, those that may be expected to last 60 years or more. The private sector includes private landlords (persons or companies), and owner-occupiers.

A dwelling is a building or any part of a building which forms a separate and self-contained set of premises designed to be occupied by a single family.

A house or flat is counted as started on the date that work begins on laying foundations but not including site preparation. Thus when foundation work commences on a pair of semi-detached houses two houses are started, and when work begins on a block of flats all the dwellings which that block will contain are started.

7.0 CHANGE IN STOCKS AND WORK IN PROGRESS, in constant prices, United Kingdom

Quarterly, beginning 1955

Unit: Millions of 1980 pounds

Title in source: Value of Physical Increase in Stocks and Work in Progress; all Industries; Revalued at 1980 prices

Sources: *Monthly Digest of Statistics,* and *Economic Trends Annual Supplement*, 1981 edition, pages 17-19, Central Statistical Office. Seasonally adjusted by source.

Description: The quarterly estimates for manufacturing, wholesaling, and retailing are based on information about the book value or the standard cost valuation of stocks supplied by a sample of companies to the Department of Industry. The figures for recent quarters are based at first on quarterly returns from panels of companies which cover about half of all manufacturers' stocks (including most of the larger companies), but a smaller proportion of stocks held by wholesalers and retailers. These figures are revised in the light of the results of the annual censuses of production and the annual inquiries into the distributive and service industries when these become available. Prior to 1970, the census of production was carried out at five year intervals.

The volume figures, expressed in constant 1980 prices, are derived from the basic book value figures at a detailed industry level by use of a wide range of price index numbers and other information, but where information about stocks at standard costs is supplied, the reported changes are considered to represent the value of physical change. Seasonal adjustment is carried out at the level of broad industry groups. The value of stocks and work in progress at the end of December 1982 was 64,840 million pounds at 1980 prices (seasonally unadjusted).

The basic data are described in detail in Chapter XIII of *National Accounts Statistics: Sources and Methods.*

8.0 CHANGE IN BASIC MATERIALS PRICE INDEX, United Kingdom

Monthly, beginning 1958

Unit: Percentage, annual rate

Title in source: Producer Price Index of Materials Purchased by the Manufacturing Industry

Sources: *British Business* (formerly *Trade and Industry*), Department of Trade and Industry, not seasonally adjusted; *Monthly Digest of Statistics*, Central Statistical Office. Percentage changes in the index are computed by the CIBCR.

Description: The index numbers are calculated from the price movements of materials and products representative of goods purchased by U.K. industry. Crude oil and coal for carbonizing are included. The weights used have been derived from a 1974 purchases inquiry, supplemented by overseas trade statistics, and information supplied by trade associations and other sources. The value of purchases used for weighting are net, that is, transactions between undertakings within manufacturing are excluded.

Prices are obtained by mail surveys, from the specialized press, or reported by importers or trade associations. Prices of imported goods are measured as closely as practical to a delivered basis. The prices collected are those that are quoted for current orders placed, which are not necessarily the same as those at which current deliveries are being received.

The Laspeyre's index, base 1980 = 100 (weight base 1979), has been linked to previous indexes: the original base is 1954 through 1962; 1963 from 1963 to 1969; 1970 (weight base 1968) from 1969 to 1975. They are linked at 1963, 1969, 1975, and 1980. The index is based on the Standard Industrial Classification (SIC) to 1962, on the 1968 SIC to 1980, and on that of 1980 subsequently.

A more complete description is given in *Wholesale Price Index: Principles and Procedures*, Studies in Official Statistics No. 32, Central Statistical Office. Details of changes from the former Wholesale Price Index to the current Producer Price Index may be found in the April 15, 1983, issue of *British Business*, Department of Trade and Industry.

The rate of change computed by the CIBCR is a 6 month smoothed annual rate, based upon the ratio of the current month's index to the average index for the preceding 12 months. Since the interval between midpoints of the current month and the preceding 12 is 6.5 months, the ratio is raised to the 12/6.5 power to derive a compound annual rate.

9.0 COMMON STOCK PRICE INDEX, United Kingdom

Monthly, beginning 1948

Unit: Index, base 1980 = 100

Title in source: Financial Times—Actuaries Share Indices; 500 Share Index

Source: *Financial Times*; also published in *Financial Statistics*, Central Statistical Office. Not seasonally adjusted.

Description: The index is a weighted arithmetic average of the percentage price changes of 500 industrial shares actively traded on the London exchange. Weights for each constituent are the total market value of the shares issued at the base date but are modified to maintain continuity when capital changes occur, for example, rights issues, or when constituents change as when companies disappear owing to takeovers or new companies become large enough to qualify for the index. The sample of shares was originally chosen from companies with a market capitalization greater than four million pounds except those operating mainly outside the United Kingdom.

The daily quotation used for each stock of the index is middle market price at the close of business. Prices are collected by Financial Times representatives. Monthly and annual figures are arithmetic averages of those for working days.

Further details of this index, original base 10 April 1962 = 100, may be found in *Guide to the FT-Actuaries Share Indices*, The Financial Times Limited. This index has been linked to earlier indexes: on April 1962 to the Actuaries Investment index based on 31 December 1957 for which monthly figures relate to the last Tuesday of each month. Prior to December 1957 the original base was 29 December 1950 and linked in December 1957.

10.0 COMPANIES' PROFITS LESS U.K. TAXES, in constant prices, United Kingdom

Quarterly, beginning 1955

Unit: Millions of 1980 pounds

Titles in source: Appropriation Accounts of Industrial and Commercial Companies, Income Arising in the United Kingdom: Gross Trading Profits, Total less U.K. Taxes on Income (Payments)

Source: *Economic Trends*, Central Statistical Office. Seasonally adjusted by source. The figures are converted to 1980 prices by the OECD by dividing by the Gross Domestic Product implicit price deflator as described below.

Description: The figures represent profits before providing for depreciation and stock appreciation. Annual estimates are ultimately based on Inland Revenue data obtained during the assessment of companies for tax. Because of delays in availability of assessment data, these estimates have to be projected forward by the use of sample data—a large sample for which special reports are made by tax offices, and a small sample of company groups reporting directly on quarterly profits. The latter source provides the quarterly interpolation of the final annual figures. All sources are subject to deficiencies and frequent revisions.

United Kingdom taxes on company income comprise corporation tax (which replaced profits tax and income tax under the Finance Act 1965) and petroleum revenue tax.

The gross domestic product implicit price deflator is the ratio of two series: (1) gross domestic product at factor cost, seasonally adjusted; and (2) gross domestic product at factor cost, seasonally adjusted, revalued at 1980 prices.

The ratio is shown as the implied index of total home costs in *Economic Trends*, and on pages 6, 7, and 8 of the *Economic Trends Annual Supplement*, 1981 Edition, Central Statistical Office.

11.0 RATIO, PRICE TO UNIT LABOR COST, MANUFACTURING, United Kingdom

Monthly, beginning 1963

Unit: Index, base 1980 = 100

Titles in source: Price series: Producer Price Index Numbers of Output (home sales); Output of Manufactured Products. Unit Labor Cost Series: Wages and Salaries per Unit of Output in Manufacturing Industries

Sources: The price index is published in *British Business* (formerly *Trade and Industry*), Department of Trade and Industry. It is not seasonally adjusted. The unit labor cost series is published in the *Department of Employment Gazette*, Department of Employment. It is seasonally adjusted by source. Both series are also published in the *Monthly Digest of Statistics*, Central Statistical Office.

Description: The numerator of this ratio is the producer price index for total home sales of manufactured goods. It is compiled in a broadly similar way to the producer price index for materials purchased by the manufacturing industry, described in series 8.0 above (see this series for further details and the linking to previous indexes). The value of sales used for weighting are net: for example, steel is included in the index only to the extent it is sold outside of manufacturing. However, sales of capital goods are all treated as sales outside of manufacturing in accordance with national income accounting practice. Prices may be on an ex-works or delivered basis, according to the practice in the trade concerned.

To obtain the labor cost per unit of output, annual benchmarks are obtained by dividing the index for wages and salaries by the income-based gross domestic product at current prices deflated by the series for total home costs. Total home costs is the ratio of the expenditure-based gross domestic product at current and constant prices. The monthly index is formed by interpolating and extrapolating from these benchmarks by a series that is the product of the series of employees in employment in manufacturing times average earnings divided by the index of manufacturing production. Before use for interpolation, this monthly index is seasonally adjusted and "smoothed." For further details, see the *Department of Employment Gazette* of April 1971 and pages 261-63 of June 1982.

The ratio is computed by the Organization for Economic Cooperation and Development (OECD). Both series are published on the base 1980 = 100.

12.0 INCREASE IN HIRE PURCHASE DEBT, in constant prices, United Kingdom

Monthly, beginning 1958

Unit: Millions of 1980 pounds

Title in source: Hire Purchase and other Credit Business; Implied Change in Debt Outstanding

Sources: *British Business* (formerly *Trade and Industry*), Department of Trade and Industry and *Monthly Digest of Statistics*, Central Statistical Office. Seasonally adjusted by source. This series is converted to 1980 prices by the OECD by dividing by the General Index of Retail Prices, also published in the *Monthly Digest of Statistics*, not seasonally adjusted.

Description: The data relate to hire purchase and other installment credit advanced by finance houses, other specialist consumer credit grantors (check traders, moneylenders, and so on), and selected kinds of retail business in Great Britain. The businesses comprise durable goods shops (that is, furniture shops; cycle and perambulator shops; radio, TV, and electrical goods shops; and showrooms of gas and electricity boards); department stores (including cooperative society stores); other general stores and general mail order houses. They do not include the installment credit business of other kinds of retailers.

The figures cover credit advanced in hire purchase and other installment credit agreements, budget account agreements, and personal loans repayable by installments. From second quarter 1977 onwards, noninstallment credit agreements are also included. Trading checks issued by retailers and exchangeable only in their own shops are included throughout, but credit advanced by check traders is only included from second quarter 1977 onwards. The figures exclude monthly account credit and sales on bank credit cards such as Access and Barclaycard.

The estimates of debt outstanding at the end of each month are derived by projecting the results of benchmark inquiries forward by means of monthly returns from stratified panels of finance houses, retailers, and, from second quarter 1977 onwards, other specialist consumer credit grantors. At the end of 1982 debt outstanding was 9,694 million pounds (current prices).

The General Index of Retail Prices (original base 15 January 1974 = 100), is a chain index with links, the weights being changed at the beginning of each calendar year. Weights are obtained from a continuing family-expenditure survey (covering 3,500 households a year for 1957-67 and 7,000 from 1967) for the 12 months ending the previous June, revalued at the prices ruling at the date of revision. The index covers the great majority of households in the United Kingdom, including practically all wage earners and most salary earners. The major groups and the 1983 percentage weights are: Food, drink, and tobacco 32 percent; Housing (rent, owner-occupiers' mortgage interest payments and insurance, repairs, rates and water charges) 14 percent; Fuel and light 7 percent; Clothing 7 percent; Durable household goods 6 percent; Transport and vehicles 16 percent; Miscellaneous goods 8 percent; Services 6 percent; and Meals outside home 4 percent. Further details may be found in *Method of Construction and Calculation of the Index of Retail Prices*, Studies in Official Statistics No. 6, Department of Employment.

13.1 EMPLOYMENT IN PRODUCTION INDUSTRIES, United Kingdom

Monthly, beginning 1952

Unit: Thousands of persons

Title in source: Employees in Employment in Index of Production Industries

Sources: *Department of Employment Gazette*, Department of Employment and *Monthly Digest of Statistics*, Central Statistical Office. Seasonally adjusted by source, except for figures prior to June 1962 that have been seasonally adjusted by the CIBCR.

Description: The figures relate to Great Britain and cover wage and salary earners but exclude self-employed persons (whether or not they have any employees). They include part-time and seasonal workers and those temporarily absent because of holidays, illnesses, strikes, and lay-offs. Part-time workers are counted as full units. Production industries consist of mining and quarrying, manufacturing, construction, gas, electricity, and water.

Since June 1971, the estimates have been based on a census of employment as a benchmark. The census was conducted annually from June 1971 to June 1978 and in September 1981. The estimates for other months are obtained by applying percentage changes in the numbers employed, derived from returns rendered by a sample of employers, government authorities, and others, to the benchmark figures. The figures are provisional until subsequent census results are available after which they are revised.

Until June 1971, the benchmark figures were obtained from mid-year counts of national insurance cards. However, in order to avoid discontinuities and to facilitate comparisons over time, the Department of Employment has prepared series of continuous monthly estimates back to June 1962. These have placed all employees in employment figures from that date on a Census of Employment basis and have allowed for other discontinuities which appeared in previously published series.

Discontinuities remain, however, at May 1959 and June 1962. Figures from May 1959 to June 1962 have been multiplied by a factor of .95878 and figures prior to May 1959 by a factor of .90817 to provide comparability.

All figures relate the middle of the month.

Further information on the construction of this series may be found in "New Quarterly Estimates of Employees in Employment," pages 891-93 of the September 1975 issue of the *Department of Labor Gazette*.

14.1 UNEMPLOYED, United Kingdom

Monthly, beginning 1949

Unit: Thousands of persons

Title in source: United Kingdom Unemployed, Excluding School-leavers

Sources: *Department of Employment Gazette*, Department of Employment, and *Monthly Digest of Statistics*, Central Statistical Office. Seasonally adjusted by source.

Description: The figures are derived from returns from local employment offices, professional and executive recruitment offices, and careers offices of the numbers registered for employment and available for work on the day of the count. The figures exclude persons seeking work who do not register. Also excluded are adult students registered for vacation work, temporarily stopped workers, certain disabled people who are unlikely to obtain work other than under sheltered conditions, and people registered for part-time work who are not claiming benefit. Before seasonal adjustment, unemployed persons under 18 years of age who have not entered employment since finishing full-time education (described as school-leavers) are deducted from the total.

Since October 1975, the count of unemployed persons on the registers has usually been made on the second Thursday in the month. Previously, counts were made on the second Monday of the month. Figures for December 1974 and November 1976 are estimated since no data are available because of industrial action. Adult students seeking vacation work were included up to March 1976.

The introduction, in September 1979, of a new national scheme for claiming and paying unemployment benefit every two weeks rather than every week had the effect of artificially raising the level of the unemployment figure for Great Britain. To allow for this effect the seasonally adjusted figures have been reduced by 20,000.

Earlier figures for this series may be found in *British Labour Statistics*

Historical Abstract, 1886-1968, and more information in "A review of unemployment and vacancy statistics," pages 497-508 of the May 1980 issue of the *Department of Employment Gazette*.

15.0 GROSS DOMESTIC PRODUCT, in constant prices, United Kingdom

Quarterly, beginning 1955

Unit: Millions of 1980 pounds

Title in source: Gross Domestic Product at Factor Cost, Revalued at 1980 Market Prices, Based on Expenditure Data

Sources: *Economic Trends*, and *Monthly Digest of Statistics*, Central Statistical Office. Also, pages 12 and 13 of *Economic Trends Annual Supplement*, 1981, give entire series in current prices. Seasonally adjusted by source.

Description: The gross domestic product is a measure of the value of the goods and services produced by United Kingdom residents before providing for depreciation (or capital consumption). The expenditure measure of gross domestic product at market prices is the value of total final expenditure on goods and services, less imports. Total final expenditure comprises consumers' expenditure, general government consumption, gross domestic fixed capital formation, the value of the physical increase in stocks and work in progress, and exports of goods and services.

Gross domestic product at factor cost is obtained by deducting taxes on expenditure, less subsidies, from gross domestic product at market prices.

Some individual series used in the aggregate are true volume indicators but most series are basically in terms of current prices and have been adjusted to 1980 prices by appropriate price indexes.

The estimates are in accordance with the classifications and definitions recommended in the United Nations System of National Accounts. The series have been linked to figures previously published at 1958, 1963, 1970, and 1975 prices. The current series has been linked to the former series in 1973.

Estimates of gross domestic product are also built up from independent data on incomes and on output and an average of the aggregates from the three estimates is published.

A detailed description of the sources, methods, and definitions used in making the estimates is given in *National Accounts Statistics: Sources and Methods* (1968) and brought up to date in the notes to *National Income and Expenditure*, 1980 edition. See also *Economic Trends,* March 1983.

16.0 INDUSTRIAL PRODUCTION, United Kingdom

Monthly, beginning 1948

Unit: Index, base 1980 = 100

Title in source: Output of the Production Industries, All Industries Other Than Construction

Source: *Monthly Digest of Statistics*, Central Statistical Office. Seasonally adjusted by source.

Description: The index covers industries in two major categories: energy and water supply, and total manufacturing industries. It is grouped according to the United Kingdom's Standard Industrial Classification 1980 edition whose coverage differs from the earlier 1968 edition. It is calculated as a base-weighted arithmetic average of 329 component series, each representing the output of an individual industry or part of an industry. The weight assigned to each industry is proportional to its estimated contribution to gross domestic product in 1980 calculated mainly from the results of the 1980 Census of Production. Energy and water supply has a weight of 26.4 percent and manufacturing 73.6 percent.

Although some series are quarterly, the majority are computed for weeks or months. The percentage share of the types of indicators are: deflated value of sales 47 percent, physical output 39 percent, quantities sold 7 percent; the remainder are based on a mixture of these, employment, unit values, work done, or materials used.

The original base of the index is 1954 from 1948 to 1957; 1958 from 1958 to 1962; 1963 from 1963 to 1967; 1970 from 1968 to 1972; 1975 from 1973 to 1977; and 1980 from 1978. The indexes are linked on 1958, 1963, 1968, 1973, and 1978.

For further details, see *The Measurement of Changes in Production, 1976; Series and Weights Used in the Index of Industrial Production*, Occasional Paper 8, December 1980 (revised), Central Statistical Office; *Economic Trends*, October 1983.

17.0 PERSONAL DISPOSABLE INCOME, in constant prices, United Kingdom

Quarterly, beginning 1955

Unit: Millions of 1980 pounds

Title in source: Real Personal Disposable Income at 1980 Prices

Sources: *Economic Trends* and *Monthly Digest of Statistics*, Central Statistical Office. Seasonally adjusted by source.

Description: The personal sector of the national accounts includes unincorporated enterprises, non-profit-making bodies, life assurance funds, and private trusts. Total personal income includes income from employment, self-employment income, rent, dividends and net interest, and government grants to persons. Total personal income less U.K. taxes on income and national insurance contributions equals total personal disposable income. Real personal disposable income is personal disposable income revalued by the implied consumers' expenditure deflator (1980 = 100).

The series has been linked to figures previously published at 1958, 1963, 1970, and 1975 prices. The current series has been linked to the former series in 1973.

See series 15.0 above for references.

18.1 RETAIL SALES, volume, United Kingdom

Monthly, beginning 1957

Unit: Index, base 1980 = 100

Title in source: Index Numbers of Volume of Retail Sales in Great Britain, All Retailers

Sources: *British Business* (formerly *Trade and Industry*), Department of Trade and Industry, and *Monthly Digest of Statistics*, Central Statistical Office. Seasonally adjusted by original source.

Description: The index figures (original base 1980 = 100) cover the whole field of retail trade in Great Britain and are based on the results of the Retailing Inquiry in 1980. All sizes and types of retailers are represented including those trading by mail order.

The statistics are based on voluntary returns from a sample of contributors chosen to be representative, as far as possible, of the different sizes of retailers and the different parts of the country. The panel at present comprises about 2,100 small retailers (with turnover less than 1 million pounds in 1978) and about 350 large retailers who account for about 70 percent of the total sales of large retailers.

The basic estimates of sales for each month are compared with those for the same month of the preceding year and chained back to the base year. This volume series is not affected by the changes in the value added tax since the retail price series used in the conversion have the same tax as the sales figures. Data are benchmarked on the 1957 Census of Distribution to 1960; on the 1961 Census of Distribution from 1961 to 1965; on the 1966 Census of Distribution from 1966 to 1970; on the 1971 Census beginning 1971; on the 1976 Retailing Inquiry beginning 1976; and on the 1978 and 1980 Inquiries beginning in 1978 and 1980, respectively. Estimated sales in 1980 were 57,406 million pounds.

Descriptions of this series were given in the *Board of Trade Journal*, November 10, 1961 and in *Economic Trends*, May 1962; also see *British Business* of 2 and 9 March 1984.

19.0 LONG-DURATION UNEMPLOYMENT, United Kingdom

Quarterly (March, June, Sept., Dec.), 1949-61; (Jan., Apr., July, Oct.) beginning 1962

Unit: Thousands of persons

Title in source: Unemployment by Duration, over 26 and up to 52 Weeks

Source: *Department of Employment Gazette*, Department of Employment. Seasonally adjusted by the CIBCR.

Description: This series represents the number of persons registered as unemployed for over 26 weeks and up to 52 weeks in Great Britain. See series 14.0 for a description of unemployment statistics. Unlike series 14.0 however, this series includes school-leavers.

Figures for January 1974 were not available because of the energy crises and for January 1975 because of industrial action at local offices of the Employment Service Agency. In both cases, figures were estimated as the mean of the preceding and subsequent quarter. Since 1975, the figures have excluded adult students. Since the final quarter of 1979, the figures may have been affected by a fortnightly rather than a weekly payment of unemployment benefits.

20.0 PLANT AND EQUIPMENT INVESTMENT, in constant prices, United Kingdom

Quarterly, beginning in 1955

Unit: Millions of 1975 pounds

Title in source: Fixed Capital Expenditure in Manufacturing Industry, Plant and Equipment

Sources: *Monthly Digest of Statistics*, Central Statistical Office. Also pages 57 and 58 of the *Economic Trends Annual Supplement*, 1981 edition. Seasonally adjusted by source.

Description: These figures are a component of the quarterly estimates of national income and expenditure. They are based at first on information supplied to the Department of Industry by panels of companies which account for about two-thirds of all capital expenditures by manufacturing industry. The figures for recent quarters are at first based entirely on this quarterly inquiry, but are later revised in the light of information from the annual censuses of production. The figures are net of receipts from the sale of assets. From 1973 onwards the figures supplied at current prices are revalued at constant 1975 prices, using separate deflators for 13 subgroups of industries. These deflators combine wholesale price indices for various capital goods with weights reflecting the estimated commodity pattern of expenditure in 1975 in each subgroup. For earlier years the constant price estimates were originally compiled using deflators reflecting expenditure patterns in 1970 or 1963. Estimates at 1975 prices were then obtained by scaling, thus preserving the weighting pattern within each industry. Finally, the figures for total manufacturing were obtained by aggregation.

For further information see Chapter XII of *National Accounts Statistics:*

Sources and Methods, and *Monthly Digest of Statistics Supplement,* 1981 edition.

21.0 BUSINESS INVENTORIES, in constant prices, United Kingdom

Quarterly, beginning 1955

Unit: Millions of 1980 pounds

Title in source: Value of Physical Increase in Stocks and Work in Progress, Revalued at 1975 Prices

Sources: *Monthly Digest of Statistics,* and *Economic Trends Annual Supplement,* 1981 edition, Central Statistical Office. Seasonally adjusted by source.

Description: This series is described in series 7.0, the change in stocks and work in progress. To obtain the level of inventories, the changes have been cumulated backwards and forwards from the level of 64,840 million pounds (at 1980 prices) at 31 December 1982. This calculation has been made by the Center for International Business Cycle Research (CIBCR).

22.1 CHANGES IN EMPLOYMENT PER UNIT OF OUTPUT, PRO-DUCTION INDUSTRIES, United Kingdom

Quarterly, beginning 1961

Unit: Percentage of change from a year ago

Title in source: Output per Person Employed, Production Industries

Source: *Department of Employment Gazette,* Department of Employment; *Economic Trends* and *Economic Trends Annual Supplement,* 1981, Central Statistical Office. Seasonally adjusted by source.

Description: This series is computed by the Center for International Business Cycle Research (CIBCR) by taking the change over a four-quarter span in the reciprocal of output per person employed. The numerator of output per person employed is the index of production in the production industries. Production industries include mining and quarrying, manufacturing, construction, and gas and electricity. The denominator covers employees in employment and the self-employed (with or without employees) in production industries, including both full-time and part-time workers as full units. The figures have been adjusted to reflect estimated employment levels for the quarter as a whole. The original base of the index of output per person employed is 1980 = 100.

23.1 INDUSTRIAL AND AGRICULTURAL LOANS OUTSTANDING, in constant prices, United Kingdom

Quarterly (end of Feb., May, Aug., and Nov.), beginning 1948

Unit: Millions of 1975 pounds

Title in source: Bank Lending to Industry, Private Sector

Source: *Financial Statistics*, Central Statistical Office. Seasonally adjusted and converted to 1975 prices by the CIBCR.

Description: The figures cover bank lending to manufacturing industries plus other production, including agriculture and construction. They measure the sums outstanding of lending to industry in both sterling and foreign currencies by all banks in the United Kingdom that observe the common reserve ratio. The Banking Department of the Bank of England and the five money trading departments of the banks are excluded but beginning in November 1978 the National Girobank is included.

Prior to February 1968 the figures covered only Great Britain and were linked to the subsequent data for the United Kingdom. There was a discontinuity in the series in November 1973 when six finance houses were confirmed as banks, and in May 1975 when export credit began to be treated as lending to overseas and not to industry as before. A further minor discrepancy occurred in November 1975 following a change in status of some banks. To adjust for these differences, the basic data for May and August 1975 have been multiplied by a factor of .98199; November 1973-February 1975 by .77379; February 1968-August 1973 by .81516; and February 1948-November 1967 by .82487.

The series has been adjusted to 1975 prices by means of the producer price index of finished goods (output of manufactured products) described in series 11.0.

24.0 COMMERCIAL BANK LENDING RATE TO PRIME BORROW-ERS, United Kingdom

Monthly, beginning 1966

Unit: Percentage

Title in source: Commercial Bank Lending Rate to Prime Borrowers

Source: *World Financial Markets*, Morgan Guaranty Trust Company of New York. Not seasonally adjusted.

Description: This is the clearing bank base lending rate. The rate is linked to the minimum lending rate established by the Bank of England and usually the premium is about one percentage point above the rate. The published rate is that charged at or near the end of the month.

WEST GERMANY

1.1 NUMBER WORKING SHORT HOURS, West Germany

Monthly, beginning 1951

Unit: Thousands of persons

Title in source: Kurzarbeiter

Sources: *Wirtschaft und Statistik*, Statistisches Bundesamt, Wiesbaden; also, *Statistische Beihefte zu den Monatsberichten der Deutschen Bundesbank, Reihe 4*, Deutsche Bundesbank, Frankfurt am Main. Figures seasonally adjusted by OECD.

Description: These statistics refer to the number of persons working less than their normal work hours, reported by business enterprises who meet certain government regulations regarding the definition "short hours." To be included in the statistics, one of the reporting requirements is that at least one-third of the employees in an establishment work more than 10 percent of normal hours in a four-week period. Seasonal industries are excluded as well as businesses that have no scheduled work hours.

   The figures relate to the middle of the month.

2.0 APPLICATIONS FOR UNEMPLOYMENT COMPENSATION, West Germany

Monthly, beginning 1957

Unit: Thousands of persons

Title in source: Anträge auf Arbeitslosengeld; Neu und Wiederbewilligungs-anträge Arbeitslosengeld; Gestellt im Laufe des Monats

Source: *Amtliche Nachrichten der Bundesanstalt für Arbeit,* Bundesanstallt für Arbeit, Nuremburg. Seasonally adjusted by OECD.

Description: The series covers both new and former applicants, who are making initial claims during the course of the month. To be eligible for unemployment compensation, an applicant must have worked at least 26 weeks in the last 3 years. After unemployment compensation has expired, a minimum of 26 weeks of employment is required before the worker is eligible to apply again.

   The source noted above periodically publishes both categories: (1) new applicants, and (2) those who have applied before. An alternate series on new entrants into unemployment (Zugang an Arbeitslosen) is available in the same source.

4.1 INSOLVENT ENTERPRISES, West Germany

Quarterly, 1962-74; monthly, beginning 1975

Unit: Number of enterprises

Title in source: Unternehmen und Arbeitsstätten; Insolvenzen, Zusammen

Source: *Wirtschaft und Statistik*, Statistisches Bundesamt, Wiesbaden. Seasonal adjustment by OECD.

Description: The figures cover agriculture, forestry and fishing; handicrafts; producing industries including construction; wholesale and retail trade; communications; banks and insurance companies; and service industries.

Courts in each state report cases to the statistical office in each state which in turn submit the data to the Federal Statistical Office. Information on an insolvency must be turned over to the court within three months after the first statement of termination. The court makes this information known after its decision has been reached.

West Berlin and the Saarland data are included in the figures. Further details may be found in *Unternehmen und Arbeitsstätten: Insolvenzverfahren (Fachserie 2, Reihe 4.1)*, Statistische Bundesamt, Wiesbaden.

5.1 NEW ORDERS, INVESTMENT GOODS INDUSTRIES, Volume Index, West Germany

Monthly, beginning 1962

Unit: Index, base 1980 = 100

Title in source: Auftragseingang im Verarbeitenden Gewerbe, Volumen, Investitionsgütergewerbe

Source: *Statistische Beihefte zu den Monatsberichten der Deutschen Bundesbank, Reihe 4*, Deutsche Bundesbank, Frankfurt am Main. Seasonally adjusted by source. Original data from Statistisches Bundesamt, Wiesbaden.

Description: The series is based upon a value series of new orders, at constant (1980) prices, for capital goods for which there has been a firm acceptance (verbal or in writing) but exclude orders placed by other establishments of the same enterprise. The orders figures are reported by the enterprises accepting the orders. Orders for repair or contract work and orders for renting of own goods are covered, but orders for goods purchased for resale without further processing are not included. However, export orders include those effected through resident firms which export the goods without further processing.

New orders are recorded at the date of acceptance, and include those filled from stock or current production of that month. Orders with open delivery dates are recorded when the delivery date is fixed. A monthly survey of gross new orders accepted during the month is conducted by statistical offices of individual states in collaboration with the Statistisches Bundesamt. Since 1977, all establishments employing 20 or more wage and salary earners are covered (the minimum size is 10 employees in some manufacturing industries). The survey is carried out by mail on a compulsory basis. There is a slight discontinuity beginning with the figures for 1978 owing to differences in data collection and the inclusion of handicraft enterprises.

The value index is computed from the ratio of the current monthly totals to the corresponding base year monthly totals of domestic and export orders received.

To obtain the volume indexes, the value indexes are deflated by specially constructed price indexes. These indexes are combinations of appropriate components of producer price indexes for domestic orders and of export price indexes for export orders.

For further details see *Wirtschaft und Statistik*, Statistisches Bundesamt, Wiesbaden, August 1983.

6.1 RESIDENTIAL CONSTRUCTION ORDERS, in constant prices, West Germany

Monthly, beginning 1971

Unit: Index, base 1980 = 100

Title in source: Auftragseingang im Bauhauptgewerbe; Volumen, Hochbau, Wohnungsbau

Source: *Statistische Beihefte zu den Monatsberichten der Deutschen Bundesbank, Reihe 4,* Frankfurt am Main. Seasonally adjusted by source. Original data from Statistisches Bundesamt, Wiesbaden.

Description: The index is obtained from value figures of residential construction that have been revalued at 1980 prices.

Data are obtained by statistical agencies of each state from 18,000 building contractors who have 20 or more employees, and from labor associations. The value figures relate to prices quoted in contracts at the time of acceptance.

The Federal Office of Statistics computes a value index from the ratio of the aggregate of current values to those in the base period, 1971, and this index is deflated by a price index to obtain the volume figures.

More information may be found in "Indices der Auftagseingänge und Auftragsbestände im Bauhauptgewerbe auf Basis 1971," *Wirtschaft und Statistik*, pages 534-37, Statistisches Bundesamt, Wiesbaden, 1973.

7.0 INVENTORY CHANGE, in constant prices, West Germany

Quarterly, beginning 1955

Unit: 10 million 1976 DM

Title in source: Vorratsveränderung

Source: *Wochenbericht* (Ergebnisse der Vierteljährlichen Volkswirtschaftlichen Gesamtrechnung) published weekly by the Deutsches Institut für Wirtschaftsforschung, Berlin. Seasonally adjusted by source. Basic data compiled by Statistisches Bundesamt and published, not seasonally adjusted, in *Volkswirtschaftliche Gesamtrechnung* (Fachserie 18, Reihe 1) and in *Wirtschaft und Statistik*.

Description: The data cover goods awaiting sale, intermediate materials and fuel to be used in production, and work in progress. The series measures the change in stocks owned by the enterprise sector and stocks of mineral oil and nuclear fuels held by the government. Agricultural stocks are covered but construction work in progress is excluded. Stocks ready for export are included but not those held only for re-export.

Only the annual data are computed directly. Opening and closing book values are extracted from the accounts of enterprises and government and converted to 1976 prices. Various price indexes such as sectors of the index of producer prices, of raw materials prices, and export prices are used to convert the data to constant prices. Earlier figures were published in 1970 and 1962 DM.

This series is a component of the quarterly estimates of expenditure on gross domestic product. The preliminary quarterly figures actually published are based upon the differences between the sums of all other components and the total gross national product on the production side.

Further details may be found in *Wirtschaft und Statistik*, pages 487-94, Statistisches Bundesamt, Wiesbaden, 1958.

8.0 CHANGE IN PRICE INDEX OF BASIC MATERIALS, West Germany

Monthly, beginning 1956

Unit: Percentage, annual rate

Title in source: Index der Grundstoffpreise; Grundstoffe aus dem Produzierenden Gewerbe

Source: *Wirtschaft und Statistik*, Statistisches Bundesamt, Wiesbaden. Seasonally adjusted by OECD. Percentage changes in the index are computed by the CIBCR.

Description: The index covers prices of domestic and imported fuel, raw materials, and semi-manufactured goods purchased by the industry and construction sectors. Domestic prices are actual selling prices for immediate delivery and exclude the value added tax since January 1968 (earlier prices included indirect taxes). Beginning 1968, the prices of imported goods are c.i.f. plus import duties, but from 1962 to 1967 they also included an import turnover compensation tax. Both this tax and customs duties are not included in the prices prior to 1962.

Prices are obtained in conjunction with the collection of prices for the Producer Price Index of Industrial Goods by means of a compulsory mail survey conducted by the statistical offices of individual states and to a small extent by the Statistisches Bundesamt. Import prices are those reported by importers. Monthly averages are calculated separately for domestic prices and import prices.

The index, base 1976 = 100, is a base-weighted arithmetic average of price relatives calculated by the Federal Statistical Office. The weighting pattern was derived from data on gross output, turnover values, import values, and excluding export values in the base year 1976. This index has been linked to an index with base 1970 covering the years 1968 to 1976. From 1962-67, the base was 1962; from 1958-62 the base was 1958; from 1956-58 the base was 1954.

More information on this index may be found in the July 1982 issue of *Wirtschaft und Statistik*.

The rate of change computed by the CIBCR is a 6 month smoothed annual rate, based upon the ratio of the current month's index to the average index for the preceding 12 months. Since the interval between the midpoints of the current month and the preceding 12 is 6.5 months, the ratio is raised to the 12/6.5 power to derive a compound annual rate.

9.0 STOCK PRICE INDEX, West Germany

Monthly, beginning 1955

Unit: Index, base 1980 = 100

Title in source: Index der Aktienkurse, Produzierendes Gewerbe

Source: *Wochendienst*, Statistisches Bundesamt, Wiesbaden. Not seasonally adjusted.

Description: The index shows changes in the price of a portfolio made up of ordinary shares of all German companies engaged in industry and construction and listed on a domestic stock exchange. The selection is based upon authorized capital with adjustment to include some small companies. Stocks of 217 companies were selected in December 1980 (the base period of the index) from the total list of 321, covering 95.1 percent of ordinary share capital. Between revisions, a company which disappears is replaced by another belonging to the same industry group whose share capital and share price are approximately equal to that being replaced.

For the companies included in the sample, spot prices fixed at the stock exchange nearest their main office are used. Quotations are taken from the *Börsenzeitung*, a stock exchange newspaper. Prices are adjusted for share dividends and rights but not for cash dividends.

Price relatives for each group are weighted by authorized capital of all companies as of December 30, 1980. From 1955-65, the original base of the series was December 31, 1965. From 1966-80 the original base was December 29, 1972, and included stocks of 245 companies selected from a list of 379, covering 96.4 percent of ordinary share capital. Monthly figures relate to the last business day of the month.

For further details, see "Neuberechnung des Index der Aktienkurse," *Wirtschaft und Statistik*, pages 43-56, January 1984, Statistisches Bundesamt.

10.1 GROSS ENTREPRENEURIAL AND PROPERTY INCOME, in constant prices, West Germany

Quarterly, beginning 1960

Unit: Millions of 1980 DM

Title in source: Bruttoeinkommen aus Unternehmertätigkeit und Vermögen

Source: *Statistische Beihefte zu den Monatsberichte der Deutschen Bundesbank, Reihe 4*, Deutsche Bundesbank. Frankfurt am Main. Seasonally adjusted by source. Converted to constant dollars by the OECD.

Description: This series of gross entrepreneurial and property income is a sector of national income estimates equal to national income minus gross wage and salary income. Included are total corporate profits (distributed and undistributed), income from owner-operated enterprises, interest, rental income, and income from intangible assets such as patents and copyrights. Published data do not show what part of this total is represented by corporate profits.

The figures are adjusted to 1980 dollars by the Organization for Economic Cooperation and Development (OECD) by dividing by the implicit price deflator of the gross national product, also published in the source noted above under the title Preisindex des Bruttosocialprodukts.

Further information may be found in *Volkswirtschaftliche Gesamtrechnung: Konten und Standardtabellen* (*Fachserie 18, Reihe 1*), Statistisches Bundesamt, Wiesbaden.

11.0 RATIO, PRICE TO UNIT LABOR COST, ENTIRE ECONOMY, West Germany

Quarterly, beginning 1958

Unit: Index, base 1980 = 100

Titles in source: Price series, Preisindex des Bruttosozialprodukts; Unit Labor Cost, Lohnkosten je Produkteinheit in der Gesamtwirtschaft

Source: Both series are published in *Statistische Beihefte zu den Monatsberichten der Deutschen Bundesbank, Reihe 4*, Deutsche Bundesbank, Frankfurt am Main. Seasonally adjusted by source.

Description: Both series are calculated by the Bundesbank based on information from the Federal Statistical Office. The ratio of the two series is computed by the Organization for Economic Cooperation and Development (OECD).

The price index is the implicit deflator of the gross national product.

The unit labor cost series is the quotient of an index of the gross wage and salary income per employee and an index of the real gross national product per employed person.

The indexes are given in the source on the base 1976 = 100 beginning in 1962, and prior to that on the base 1962 = 100.

A monthly index of unit labor cost in mining and manufacturing is also published in the source noted above.

12.0 CHANGE IN CONSUMER CREDIT, in constant prices, West Germany

Quarterly, beginning 1969

Unit: Millions of 1980 DM

Title in source: Lending to Individuals (Employees and Others) Except Lending for Housing Construction

Source: *Monthly Report of the Deutsche Bundesbank*, Frankfurt am Main. The published figures refer to credit outstanding at end of quarter. Changes during the quarter are calculated and seasonally adjusted by the OECD. The series is converted to 1980 DM by dividing by the Cost of Living Index all goods less food, published in *Main Economic Indicators*, part four, OECD.

Description: Data represent changes in short, medium, and long-term bank loans (excluding those relating to housing construction) to employees and other individuals not classified as "self employed." The basic figures cover installment sales credit, various kinds of personal loans, and book credit to holders of salary accounts and other accounts. Beginning in 1981, mortgage loans to individuals other than those secured by residential real estate are included (5,431 DM million in December 1980). Data are based upon returns at end of quarter from all banks showing a break-down of credit by type of borrower. The financial institutions covered are: commercial banks, savings banks, mortgage banks, credit cooperatives, installment sales financing institutions, banks with special functions, and postal giro and postal savings bank offices. Credit cooperatives are only partially covered since small credit cooperatives whose balance sheet is less than a given minimum (10 million DM since 1973) are not included.

Further details may be found in *Monthly Report of the Deutsche Bundesbank*, vol. 22, no. 10, October 1970, pages 34 and 35.

The Cost of Living Index, original base 1976 = 100, for all private households that is used to convert the series to 1980 DM is described in the December 1973 *Wirtschaft und Statistik* of the Statistiches Bundesamt. See series 17.0 for further details of this index. The conversion is made by the OECD.

13.1 EMPLOYMENT IN MINING AND MANUFACTURING, West Germany

Monthly, beginning 1951

Unit: Thousands of persons

Title in source: Produzierendes Gewerbe; Industrie; Beschaftigte; Bergbau und Verarbeitenden Gewerbe

Source: *Industrie und Handwerk, Reihe 1*, Statistisches Bundesamt, Wies-Baden. Seasonally adjusted by OECD.

Description: The figures cover wage earners, salaried employees, and active proprietors. They include persons on paid or unpaid leave and persons temporarily laid off or prevented from working because of industrial disputes, illness, or injury. Included also are seasonal and part-time workers, those in job training, and unpaid family members who work at least one-third of normal hours. Not included are people who work in their own home. In mid-1977, foreigners constituted 13.5 percent of workers in manufacturing.

All establishments or enterprises with 20 or more employees are covered although in a few industries, small establishments with 10 or more employees are included. Producing craft enterprises are included. Figures refer to the end of the month.

Further information may be found in *Produzierendes Gewerbe, Fachserie 4, Reihe 4.1.1*, October 1980, Statistisches Bundesamt.

14.1 UNEMPLOYMENT RATE, West Germany

Monthly series, beginning 1950

Unit: Percentage

Title in source: Arbeitslosenquote Gemessen an den Abhängigen Erwerbspersonen

Source: *Statistische Beihefte zu den Monatsberichten der Deutschen Bundesbank, Reihe 4*, Deutsche Bundesbank, Frankfurt am Main. Seasonally adjusted by source (figures prior to 1962, seasonally adjusted by OECD). Source of original data, Federal Labor Office.

Description: These percentages are computed by dividing the number of registered unemployed by the estimated number in the civilian "dependent" labor force as derived from the latest microcensus. The civilian "dependent" labor force includes wage and salary earners, civil servants and trainees, plus the unemployed. The data refer to the last day of the month.

The registered unemployed are defined as persons 15 to 65 years of age who are able to work and registered at employment offices as being out of work and seeking paid employment of more than 3 months. The figures include persons looking for their first job, those who have a minor occupation or who work for a short period (not exceeding 3 months), self-employed who have given up their work, and housewives looking only for part-time employment. They do not include people unable to work because of illness, persons still working but who wish to change their job and are therefore registered at employment offices, and foreigners who cannot obtain a work permit. A person who will accept only one type of work is not included. Registration is not compulsory, but is an essential condition for receiving unemployment benefits. Statistics for West Berlin are included and for the Saarland beginning in December 1958.

Microcensuses are carried out annually with a sampling ratio of 1 percent, covering a reference period of one week. The self-employed are excluded from the civilian "dependent" labor force. An alternative unemployment rate series is also available using the total civilian labor force.

For further details see *Arbeitsförderungsgesetz*, 25 June 1969, Bundesgesetzblatt Teil I, 1969.

15.0 GROSS NATIONAL PRODUCT, in constant prices, West Germany

Quarterly, beginning 1950

Unit: Billions of DM at 1976 prices

Title in source: Bruttosozialprodukt in Preisen von 1976

Source: *Statistische Beihefte zu den Monatsberichten der Deutschen Bundesbank, Reihe 4*, Deutsche Bundesbank, Frankfurt am Main. Seasonally adjusted by source. Basic figures, not seasonally adjusted, published by the Statistisches Bundesamt in *Wirtschaft und Statistik*.

Description: The preparation of national accounts statistics in the Federal Republic of Germany is undertaken by the Federal Statistical Office, Wiesbaden. Detailed data as well as description of the sources and methods used for the national accounts estimates are published annually in *Volkswirtschaftliche Gesamtrechnungen*. Estimates are in close accordance with the classification and definitions recommended in the United Nations System of National Accounts. Figures include relevant data for West Berlin.

The estimates of gross domestic product are based on the expenditure approach, in which each component is estimated by expenditure type except gross fixed capital formation which is calculated mainly by the commodity-flow approach.

The expenditure aggregates cover consumers' expenditures, government final consumption expenditure, gross fixed investment, change in stocks, and net exports of goods and services. Consumers' expenditures are defined as the value of all goods and services, except land and dwellings, purchased for consumption by the household sector and private nonprofit institutions. In addition, imputations are made for consumption from own production and for the rental value of owner-occupied dwellings, but not for services provided free of charge. Benchmark data are derived mainly from the trade census, craft census, and industrial production census and are updated principally from suppliers' reports to surveys such as those used to compile statistics on wholesale and retail sales, handicraft turnover, and the hotel and restaurant industry. Government final consumption expenditure is defined as the value of new goods and services other than land and fixed assets purchased by federal, state, and local governments for the production of services put at the disposal of the general public without direct charge.

Gross fixed investment is defined as the expenditure by enterprises, government, and nonprofit institutions on new and second-hand fixed assets, whether for replacing or for adding to those in use. The estimates are based on quarterly production reports, monthly construction reports, statistics on building activity and the censuses mentioned above. The component series, change in stocks, is described in series 7.0 above. Exports and imports of goods are based on foreign trade statistics while exports and imports of services are obtained mainly from the Central Bank.

For calculation of the constant price series, deflation by price indexes appropriate to the respective activities is usually done at a relatively high level of aggregation. An exception is the component series change in stocks (see 7.0 above).

16.0 INDUSTRIAL PRODUCTION, West Germany

Monthly, beginning 1948

Unit: Index, base 1980 = 100

Title in source: Produzierendes Gewerbe ohne Bauhauptgewerbe

Source: *Statistische Beihefte zu den Monatsberichten der Deutschen Bundesbank, Reihe 4*, Deutsche Bundesbank, Frankfurt am Main. Seasonally adjusted by source.

Description: This index reflects monthly changes in the physical volume of production in mining, manufacturing, and electricity and gas. It is compiled by the Federal Statistical Office on the base 1980 = 100 and it is computed as a base-weighted arithmetic average of relatives. Weights used to combine industry and group indexes are based on census-value-added quotas (including depreciation allowances, consumption taxes without value-added tax) in 1980. Weighting coefficients of the major groups are: mining 3.4 percent, manufacturing 90.8 percent, and electricity and gas 5.7 percent. The types of indicators (including 2 in the construction index) used are: quantum of output 356, deflated value of output 664, deflated value of sales 28, and man-hours worked 5.

Beginning in 1962, the monthly indexes have been adjusted for calendar irregularities (varying length of months, differing number of Saturdays, Sundays, and holidays in each month). The different production procedures in the various branches have also been taken into account. Monthly figures are based upon enterprises with 20 or more employees although all production industries are included in the weights. The indicators for mining and manufacturing cover 80.2 percent of the gross production value in 1980 for these two divisions.

Beginning in 1977, a new method of collection was introduced, and handicraft industries were included. The index has been linked to an earlier index on base 1976 = 100, which in turn was linked to a previous index on base 1970 = 100 and in 1962 to an earlier index with 1962 = 100. Prior to 1958, the index base was 1950 = 100.

For further details, see "Zur Neuberechnung der Produktions-und Productivitätsindizes im Produzierenden Gewerbe auf Basis 1980," *Wirtschaft und Statistik*, pages 931-46, December 1983, Statistisches Bundesamt.

17.0 DISPOSABLE INCOME, in constant prices, West Germany

Quarterly, beginning 1950

Unit: Billions of 1980 DM

Title in source: Einkommen der Privaten Haushalte, Verfügbares Einkommen

Source: *Statistische Beihefte zu den Monatsberichten der Deutschen Bundesbank, Reihe 4*, Deutsche Bundesbank, Frankfurt am Main. Seasonally adjusted by source. Figures are converted by the OECD to 1980 prices by dividing by the cost of living index for all households (Preisindex für die Lebenshaltung aller privaten Haushalte) published in the *Statistischer Wochendienst*.

Description: This series represents the disposable income of private households that have permanent homeownership in the Federal Republic of Germany. The figures cover not only individuals but also nonprofit organizations. Income from inside and outside the Federal Republic is included.

The figure for disposable income include wages and salaries net of taxes on wages and of the employee share of social security payments. They also include voluntary welfare payments by enterprises (especially net payments to company pension funds), withdrawals from entrepreneurial income, interest income, rental income, and transfer payments from government. Transfer payments include payments under social security, health insurance, unemployment insurance, direct welfare, household insurance, and government retirement programs. The figures are calculated by the Bundesbank based upon information from the Federal Statistical Office and other agencies.

To obtain the series in constant prices, the value aggregates in current prices are divided by the Cost of Living Index for all households. This index is computed as a weighted arithmetic average with fixed base, the weights corresponding to the base period (at present 1976 = 100). The 1976 weights were computed from a 1973 survey of 48,900 households and adjusted to 1976 levels by means of continuous small-scale enquiries addressed to 1,100 households. The major groups and their percentage weights are: food, beverages, and tobacco 26.6 percent, clothing 8.8 percent, rent (including imputed rent of owner-occupied dwellings) 13.3 percent, fuel and light 4.9 percent, household operations 10.0 percent, transport and communications 14.8 percent, health and personal care 4.3 percent, education and recreation 7.9 percent, and other goods and services 9.4 percent. Prices are obtained in 118 urban areas with 5,000 inhabitants or more. This index has been linked to an earlier index, base 1970 = 100. From 1961 to 1968 the base was 1962 = 100, from 1957 to 1961 the base was 1958 = 100, and for 1950 to 1957 it was 1950 = 100.

18.1 MANUFACTURING SALES, Volume, West Germany

Monthly, beginning 1957

Unit: Index, base 1980 = 100

Title in soure: Umsatz im Verarbeitenden Gewerbe, Volumindex; Insgesamt

Source: *Produzierendes Gewerbe, Fachserie 4, Reihe 2.2*, Statistisches Bundesamt, Wiesbaden. Seasonal adjustment by OECD.

Description: The figures are based upon a monthly survey conducted by statistical offices of individual states in collaboration with the Statistisches Bundesamt. All manufacturing industries other than food, beverages, and tobacco are surveyed. Since January 1977 establishments employing 20 or more wage earners are covered, with a minimum size of 10 employees in a few manufacturing industries. Handicraft enterprises are included since January 1978. Surveys are carried out by mail on a compulsory basis.

Basic data are the values of products invoiced during each month, excluding transfers to other establishments of the same enterprise. Products made elsewhere under contract for the reporting establishment are included at full value. Also included are receipts from repairs and contract work done on materials supplied by customers as well as rentals received for goods of own manufacture such as machinery and appliances. Direct exports by the producer are covered. The value of goods purchased and resold without further processing is not included.

The weights of the index are based upon estimated amounts invoiced during the base year 1976. The value indexes are deflated by specially constructed price indexes that are combinations of appropriate components of producer price indexes or export price indexes. Survey and calculation procedures were modified in January 1977 and from January 1978 the data are not strictly comparable with those of previous years.

This index on base 1980 = 100 has been linked to a former index on base 1976 = 100 which in turn was linked in 1962 to an index with base 1954 = 100. All figures include the Saar and West Berlin.

Further details may be found in *Produzierendes Gewerbe, Fachserie 4, Reihe 2.2*, January 1977.

18.2 RETAIL TRADE, Volume, West Germany

Monthly, beginning 1955

Unit: Index, base 1980 = 100

Title in source: Umsätze des Einzelhandels, Gesamt, in Preisen von 1980

Source: *Statistische Beihefte zu den Monatsberichten der Deutschen Bundesbank, Reihe 4*, Deutsche Bundesbank, Frankfurt am Main. Seasonally adjusted by source. Source of original data, Federal Statistical Office.

Description: The index measures direct sales to households of goods which were purchased for resale without further processing. Sales to enterprises of certain goods such as office machines, sewing machines, and agricultural equipment are also included if effected through usual retail channels and in only small quantities.

Total turnover from retail sales are reported including the value of own-consumption, with discounts deducted and indirect taxes (value added tax since 1968) included.

All forms of retail organizations are represented: department stores, chain stores, cooperative societies, specialty shops, and mail order houses. However, an enterprise is considered as conducting retail sales only if it operates in its own name. Retailers such as petrol stations which sell in the name and account of others are not included. A monthly postal survey is conducted by statistical offices of individual states in collaboration with the Federal Statistical Office of a random stratified sample of about 25,000 retail establishments based on a 1979 census (prior to 1981 about 40,000 were surveyed based on the 1968 Census of Distribution).

The monthly estimates are computed by multiplying the reported turnover of each enterprise in the sample with the reciprocal of that enterprise's probability of selection. The value index number is computed as the ratio of the current month total to the corresponding base year figures.

To obtain the volume index, the value index is divided by a retail price index. The prices used are those collected for the Cost of Living Index (see series 17.0 above) plus additional prices intended to represent goods sold at retail to local authorities and enterprises such as office machines, trucks and medical instruments. It is a Laspeyres-type index with base 1980 = 100.

The original base of the index was 1954 through 1964; 1962 from 1965 to 1969; and 1970 from 1970 to 1980. Indexes are linked at 1965, 1970 and 1980. The Saar is excluded from the series prior to 1961 and West Berlin prior to 1965.

For further information see "Neues Statistisches Berichssystem im Handel und Gastgewerbe," *Wirtschaft und Statistik*, pages 679-89, Statistisches Bundesamt, Frankfurt am Main, 1978.

20.0 INVESTMENT EXPENDITURE, PLANT AND EQUIPMENT, in constant prices, West Germany

Quarterly, beginning 1962

Unit: Billions of 1970 DM

Title in source: Ausrüstungsinvestitionen und Bauinvestitionen in Preisen von 1976

Source: *Statistisches Beihefte zu den Monatsberichten der Deutschen Bundesbank, Reihe 4*, Deutsche Bundesbank, Frankfurt am Main. Seasonally adjusted by source.

Description: This series is the sum of two components of gross national product: (1) investment in machinery and equipment, and (2) construction investment. Preparation of national accounts statistics is undertaken by the Federal Statistical Office.

As noted in series 15.0 above, the figures represent expenditures by enterprises, general government, and nonprofit institutions on new and second-hand fixed assets, whether for replacing or adding to those in use. In 1979, 84.2 percent was by the enterprise sector and 15.8 percent by general government.

The machinery and equipment figures cover domestically produced and imported goods including motor vehicles. The quarterly estimates are basically production plus imports less exports, and the main sources of data are the quarterly survey of manufactures and monthly foreign trade statistics.

The construction figures cover building (including residential construction) and civil engineering, and cover also major alterations and additions to existing structures. About half the estimates are based upon hours actually worked in building construction and the other half calculated on the basis of turnover data reported in the survey of handicrafts.

The 1962-67 figures, originally presented in 1962 prices, were converted to 1970 prices, by multiplying 1.25, the 1967 ratio of the two series.

21.0 BUSINESS INVENTORIES, in constant prices, West Germany

Quarterly, beginning 1955

Unit: Ten million 1976 DM

Title in source: Vorratsveränderung

Source: *Wochenbericht (Ergebnisse der Vierteljahrlichen Volkswirtschaftlichen Gesamtrechnung)*, Deutsches Institut für Wirtschaftsforschung, Berlin. Seasonally adjusted by source.

Description: This series, which measures the level of inventories at the end of each quarter, is derived by the Center for International Business Cycle Research (CIBCR) by cumulating changes in inventories in constant prices, the basic data published in the source noted above. Changes are cumulated starting with the first quarter of 1955. Hence the entire series understates the actual level of inventories by an undetermined amount, namely, the level of inventories at the end of 1954.

The data were earlier expressed in terms of 1970 and 1962 DM. See series 7.0 above for a description of the basic data.

22.1 CHANGE IN HOURS PER UNIT OF OUTPUT, MINING AND MANUFACTURING, West Germany

Monthly, beginning 1965

Unit: Percentage change from a year ago

Title in Source: Produktionsergebnis; je Beschäftigtenstunde (Produzierenden Gewerbe)

Source: *Statistische Beihefte zu den Monatsberichten der Deutschen Bundesbank, Reihe 4*, Deutsche Bundesbank, Frankfurt am Main. Seasonally adjusted by source.

Description: The Center for International Business Cycle Research (CIBCR) computes percent changes over a 12-month span in the reciprocal of the basic figures for output per man-hour in mining and manufacturing. This series on output per man-hour is in the form of a seasonally adjusted index based on 1980 = 100. It is derived by dividing the Index of Industrial Production excluding electricity and gas by total hours worked by wage earners during the month. The figures on hours include overtime but exclude hours paid for but not worked because of public holidays or any type of leave with pay. The hours worked series is published by the Federal Office of Statistics in *Beschäftigung, Umsatz und Energieversorgung der Unternehmen und Betriebe im Bergbau und im Verarbeitenden Gewerbe (Fachserie 4, Reihe 4.1.1)*.

23.1 BANK LOANS OUTSTANDING, in constant prices, West Germany

Monthly, beginning 1960

Unit: Billions of 1975 DM

Title in source: Kredite an Unternehmen und Privatpersonen

Source: *Statistische Beihefte zu den Monatsberichten der Deutschen Bundesbank, Reihe 4*, Deutsche Bundesbank, Frankfurt am Main. Seasonally adjusted by source.

Description: The series represents the level at the end of the month of bank lending to enterprises and individuals. Financial institutions covered are listed in series 12.0 above. The figures were deflated by the Center for International Business Cycle Research (CIBCR) by the producer price index for industrial products 1980 = 100 (Erzeugerpreise für gewerbliche Produkte), published in the same source.

The producer price index is based on actual selling prices, net of discounts, used by manufacturers in contracts signed on the nearest transaction date to the twenty-first of each month. Since January 1968, they exclude the value added tax but include excise taxes. It is a Laspeyres index compiled by the Federal Office of Statistics. Further details may be found in *Wirtschaft und Statistik*, March 1983, Statistisches Bundesamt.

An alternative series, including only loans to enterprises and self employed persons but excluding other individuals, is available quarterly in the *Monthly Report of the Deutsche Bundesbank*.

24.1 BANK RATES ON LARGE LOANS, West Germany

Monthly, beginning 1975; occasional months beginning 1968

Unit: Percentage per annum

Title in source: Lending Rates, Credits in Current Account, 1 Million DM and Over but less than 5 Million DM, Average Interest Rate

Source: *Monthly Report of the Deutsche Bundesbank*, Deutsche Bundesbank, Frankfurt am Main. Not seasonally adjusted.

Description: Average rates are calculated as unweighted arithmetic means of interest rates "within the spread." The spread is determined by eliminating the highest 5 percent and the lowest 5 percent of the interest rates reported in the survey. For method of data collection, see *Monthly Report of the Deutsche Bundesbank*, vol. 19, no. 10, October 1967, p. 45ff.

Prior to February 1975 the surveys were conducted for only four or five months each year. Prior to November 1973 the rates are for loans under 1 million DM, adjusted to the level of the later series by subtracting 0.44 percentage points, the difference in November 1973.

FRANCE

1.0 AVERAGE WORKWEEK, INDUSTRY, France

Quarterly: Jan., April, July, and Oct. beginning 1960

Unit: Hours per week

Title in source: Durée Hebdomadaire du travail (Ouvriers + Employés) dans l'Industrie sans Batiment et Génie Civil

Source: *Informations Rapides E*, Institut National de la Statistique et des Études Économiques (INSEE). Seasonally adjusted by source. Basic data in *Supplément au Bulletin mensuel des statistiques du Travail*, Ministère du Travail.

Description: The data represent average weekly hours usually worked by full-time wage earners in industry (but excluding construction and civil engineering) including any overtime hours offered to all workers. If different work hours apply to different services, an average—weighted by employment—is reported. The figures relate to the first week without public holidays of each quarter (the last of the preceding quarter before 1972).

Wage earners of both sexes over 18 years of age are covered but foremen and apprentices are not included. Beginning in April, 1972, the series is based on a survey of a stratified sample of establishments (Enquete sur l'activite et les conditions de l'emploi de la main d'oeuvre). Questionnaires are sent quarterly by the Ministère du Travail to all establishments employing 50 or more employees, and to one third of the establishments employing 10 to 49 employees. The mining and manufacturing sample includes 78,500 establishments with 5.3 million employees. Further information on the sample may be found below in the description of series 13.0.

The average weekly number of hours of work by activity is computed for each size class of establishment with the number of hours for each establishment weighted by the number of wage earners on its payroll on the last day of the quarter. Persons who, during the inquiry week, have not worked or who have worked only part of the week, as well as persons temporarily absent from work because of vacation, illness, industrial dispute, or other reasons are not included. Averages for the different size classes of establishments are then aggregated using 1975 employment weights. Annual figures are computed from data interpolated for intervening months and differ slightly from those in the source interpolated by a different method.

For further methodological details, see *Supplément au Bulletin mensuel des statistiques du Travail*, no. 28, 1975, Ministère du Travail (Paris).

2.0 NEW UNEMPLOYMENT CLAIMS, France

Monthly, beginning 1975

Unit: Thousands of registrants

Title in source: Demandes Enregistrées dans le Mois

Source: *Tendances de la Conjoncture*, Institut National de la Statistique et des Études Économiques (INSEE). Seasonally adjusted by source. Data compiled by the Ministère du Travail.

Description: The figures represent the number of new registrants for employment during the month at the offices of the National Employment Agency. See series 14.1 for a description of unemployment data.

3.1 CHANGE IN UNFILLED ORDERS, TOTAL, France

Monthly, beginning 1968

Unit: Percentage

Title in source: Monthly Survey of Manufacturing Industry—Net Balances on Order-books

Source: *European Economy, Supplement-Series B*, Commission of the European Communities, Luxembourg. Seasonally adjusted by source.

Description: Data are derived from an inquiry conducted each month by the Institut National de la Statistique et des Études Économiques of a sample of 2,200 firms. All manufacturing industries are covered except food, beverages, and tobacco. Industrialists are questioned whether the orders on their books are above normal, normal, or below normal.

Data are collected on a questionnaire provided by the Commission of European Communities and are returned to the commission for processing. The results are published as net balances of the percentage of firms reporting above normal orders on the books minus the percentage reporting below normal orders. Since these balances reflect the level of unfilled orders, the Center for International Business Cycle Research (CIBCR) computes the change in the balance, which then represents the change in unfilled orders. Changes are computed over a two-month span in order to reduce the erratic fluctuations in the series. Surveys are not conducted in August, hence August data are an interpolation between July and September figures.

Related data may be found in *Tendances de la Conjoncture*, Institut National de la Statistique et des Etudes Économiques.

6.0 BUILDING PERMITS, RESIDENTIAL, France

Monthly, beginning 1955

Unit: Thousands of permits

Title in source: Logements Autorisés, Situations Mensuelles Cumulées par Annees, France Entière

Source: *Statistiques de la Construction*, Ministère de l'Equipment. Seasonally adjusted by OECD.

Description: The series measures the number of dwellings authorized (some low-rent dwellings do not require permits). The permits refer to the date of application, whether the project is carried out subsequently or not. A permit is valid for 12 months and no new registration is required for an extension after this period. However, changes in a project, whether before or after the start of operations, cannot be undertaken without official endorsement, which counts as a new permit if the original permit dates back more than a year.

Only dwellings comprising at least one room and a kitchen are counted. The figures cover individual houses, communal buildings intended solely or primarily as residences, together with buildings not primarily used as residences. They cover not only new buildings but also dwellings created either by extending or adding further stories to existing buildings. Repair, conversions, or enlarging of existing buildings is not taken into account, even if a permit has been issued for such work.

7.0 CHANGE IN STOCKS, in constant prices, France

Quarterly, beginning 1963

Unit: Billions of 1970 francs

Title in source: Variations des Stocks aux Prix de 1970

Sources: *Les Comptes Nationaux Trimestriels en base 1971* and *Tendances de la Conjoncture, Cahier 2*, both published by Institut National de la Statistique et des Études Économiques (INSEE). Seasonally adjusted by source.

Description: This sector of Gross Domestic Product is estimated for three categories: producers, users, and trade. For certain products, principally petroleum products and products of the iron and steel industry, specific sources are available on the changes in quantity and value for each of the three categories of stocks. The rest is valued on the basis of tax returns for 40 products.

   To obtain the series in constant prices, current estimates of commodity stocks held by enterprises are deflated by using appropriate price indexes.

   See series 15.0 for further information on the estimates of Gross Domestic Product.

8.0 CHANGE IN WHOLESALE PRICE INDEX, RAW MATERIALS, France

Monthly, beginning 1955

Unit: Percentage, annual rate

Title in source: Indices des Prix de Gros, Matières Premières Industrielles, Taxes Comprises

Sources: *Bulletin Mensuel de Statistique*, Institut National de la Statistique et des Études Économiques (INSEE). Also published in *Tendances de la Conjoncture*, INSEE. Not seasonally adjusted. Percent changes in the index are computed by the CIBCR.

Description: This index of wholesale prices of domestic and imported industrial raw materials is a major subgroup of the wholesale price index of industrial products, original base 1962 = 100. Prices relate to the first wholesale transaction by producers or importers in France. Most domestic prices are list prices before deduction of discounts and include indirect taxes. Prices for imported goods correspond to c.i.f. prices plus customs duties, indirect taxes, and importers' margins. Indirect taxes have progressively taken the form of value added tax. Most of the prices are collected from professional organizations; otherwise they are obtained from direct surveys or from administrative records. All quotations refer to the period from the twenty-fifth to the end of the month.

Domestic raw materials, which constitute 50 percent of the index, include: iron (including scrap), aluminum, quarry products, synthetic rubber, colza, and flax. Imported materials include: nonferrous metals (copper, lead, tin and others), fats (oilseeds and nonprocessed oils), textiles (wool, cotton, burlap, sisal and others), rubber (smoked leaf), and others.

The index is computed as a base-weighted arithmetic average of price relatives. The weights are proportional to the value of the last wholesale transaction in 1962 and were derived from the 1962 industrial census. The index is linked at 1962 to an earlier index on the base 1949 = 100.

For further details, see *Bulletin Mensuel de Statistique*, no. 11, November 1970, INSEE, Paris.

The rate of change computed by the CIBCR is a 6 month smoothed annual rate, based upon the ratio of the current month's index to the average index for the preceding 12 months. Since the interval between midpoints of the current month and the preceding 12 is 6.5 months, the ratio is raised to the 12/6.5 power to derive a compound annual rate.

9.0 INDEX OF STOCK PRICES (INDUSTRIALS), France

Monthly, beginning 1948

Unit: Index, base 1980 = 100

Title in source: Indices Boursiers, Indice des Valeurs Industrielles

Source: *Bulletin Mensuel de Statistique*, Institut National de la Statistique et des Etudes Economiques (INSEE). Not seasonally adjusted.

Description: The index measures monthly changes in the spot price of a portfolio of all variable-yield industrial shares on the Paris Exchange. The sample of approximately 180 shares is updated each year, with selection based on the market value of share capital and the volume of transactions. Basic data are the opening spot quotations for the averages of last working days of each week.

The index is calculated by computing industry group indexes of unweighted averages of price relatives (adjusted for share dividends and rights), weighting these by market values of shares of all companies in each classification as of the end of the preceding year, and chaining the links to the original base December 29, 1972 = 100.

The original base of the index is December 1949 (to 1957), December 1958 (to 1960), December 1960 (to 1961), and December 1961 (through 1972). Each index was linked on its base period to the previous index.

11.0 RATIO, PRICE TO UNIT LABOR COST, MANUFACTURING, France

Quarterly, beginning 1955

Unit: Index, base 1980 = 100

Titles in source: Price Series: Indices des Prix de Gros, Produits Industriels Semi-transformés, Taxes Comprises; Unit Labor Cost Series: Cout Salarial par Unité Produite en France

Sources: Price series—*Bulletin Mensuel de la Statistique* and *Tendances de la Conjoncture*, Institut National de la Statistique et des Études Économiques (INSEE). Not seasonally adjusted. Unit Labor Cost series—*Indicateurs du VIIeme plan*, INSEE. Seasonally adjusted by source.

Description: The wholesale price index of semi-manufactured goods in the numerator is a major subgroup of the wholesale price index of industrial products. The other major subgroup has been described in series 8.0 where details of these indexes may be found. Industrial goods exclude investment goods and final consumer goods. Items in this sector are products that result from the first stage of manufacture of raw materials: ordinary and special steels, nonferrous metal semi-products, chemical products, thread and materials, cement and ceramic products, glass, tanned leather, simple wood products, paper and cardboard. Semi-manufactured products represent 77 percent of the weights of the Wholesale Price Index of Industrial Products. The original base of the index is 1962 = 100.

The index of salary cost per unit produced is the denominator of the ratio. This index is computed by dividing the hourly rate for wage and salary workers by the product of the index of employment times the weekly hours of work. These three series are obtained from data collected in the quarterly surveys conducted by the Ministère du Travail. The original base of the index is 1970 = 100.

The ratio of the two indexes is computed by the OECD.

13.0 EMPLOYMENT, NONFARM, France

Data relate to Jan., April, July, and Oct., beginning 1951

Unit: Index, base 1980 = 100

Title in source: Indices des Effectifs Occupés; Ensembles des Activités

Source: *Statistiques du Travail, Supplement au Bulletin Mensuel*, Ministère du Travail. Seasonally adjusted by OECD.

Description: The figures are derived from establishment surveys covering almost all nonagricultural activities except public administration. They cover wage and salary earners, excluding the self-employed, unpaid family workers and home workers. The wage earners are employees directly engaged in production and related operations and include apprentices, storekeepers and delivery staff but exclude foremen. The figures reflect the number on payrolls on the last day of the preceding quarter (first day of the quarter under review before 1968) including those absent without pay or on strike. Full-time and part-time workers are covered, both permanent and temporary, and whether paid at time rate or piece rate.

A quarterly survey is conducted by the Ministère du Travail addressed to a sample of establishments which was revised in 1956, 1970, and 1975. The latest revision covers 72,000 establishments with 10.8 million employees. The sample is stratified by industry, and, within each industry, by size of establishment in employment terms. All establishments having 50 or more employees are selected together with one-third of those with 10 to 49 employees. Participation in the sample is compulsory.

The index is computed as a fixed-weight chain index. Link relatives are computed from the quarterly percentage changes in employment. The present weighting pattern reflects the structure of employment at the end of 1975. It is based on employment data derived from tax returns and the percentage distribution of employment by skill as shown by a survey carried out in 1975 by the Ministère du Travail. From 1956 to 1972, the weight base was 1954, and from 1973 to 1975 it was 1970.

Annual averages are computed from interpolated monthly figures and may differ slightly from annual data in the source interpolated by a different method.

Further details may be found in *Supplements au Bulletin mensuel de Statistiques Sociales*, no. 28, 1975, and no. C8, January 1971, Ministère du Travail, Paris.

14.1 REGISTERED UNEMPLOYED, France

Monthly, beginning 1955

Unit: Thousands of registrants

Title in source: Demandes d'Emploi en fin de Mois

Sources: *Bulletin mensuel des Statistiques du Travail*, Ministère du Travail. Seasonally adjusted by source. Also published in *Bulletin mensuel de Statistique*, Institut National de la Statistique et des Études Économiques (INSEE).

Description: The figures represent the number of applications for work on file at offices of the National Employment Agency (Agence nationale pour l'emploi) at the end of each month. Applicants are persons without a job who are immediately available for work and looking for stable, full-time employment. Any person over 16 years of age who is seeking work may register. Registration is not compulsory, but is an essential condition for receiving social security benefits and unemployment benefits. Beginning in June 1972, the series excludes certain unemployed over 60 years of age who are recipients of "income maintenance benefits."

From October 1962 to December 1967, the figures exclude people repatriated from North Africa. The progressive implementation of administrative changes induced an upward movement in the figures from 1968 to 1973; data in October 1977 and in each subsequent autumn as well as in January 1978 were lowered because of administrative changes.

15.0 GROSS DOMESTIC PRODUCT, in constant prices, France

Quarterly, beginning 1963

Unit: Billions of 1970 francs

Title in source: Produit Interieur Brut aux Prix de 1970

Sources: *Les Comptes Nationaux Trimestriels en Base 1971* and *Informations Rapides* (rate of change only), both published by Institut National de la Statistique et des Études Économiques (INSEE). Seasonally adjusted by source.

Description: The figures represent the aggregate value in the market of all goods and services produced including work-in-progress and products for use on own account. The official estimates prepared by Institut National de la Statistique et des Études Économiques (INSEE) conform to the United Nations System of National Accounts so far as existing data permit.

Expenditure on the gross domestic product is shown in the following categories: private final consumption expenditure, government final consumption expenditure, gross fixed capital formation, increase in stocks, and exports and imports of goods and services. The commodity-flow approach is used in conjunction with the expenditure approach to estimate private, final consumption expenditure. In addition to data from the annual input-output tables, estimates are also based on the results of expenditure surveys conducted by INSEE, estimates of fiscal revenues, and statistics of retail sales derived from periodic surveys of large retail stores. The figures include expenditures by foreigners in France and exclude expenditures by residents abroad. The imputed rent of owner-occupied dwellings is included.

In estimating government final consumption expenditure, the budgetary accounts of the central government and accounting plans of local governments and enterprises are used. In estimating gross fixed capital formation in enterprises, data are available from the accounts of large national enterprises but the main sources are the annual surveys carried out by the Ministère de l'industrie et de la recherche; for general government agencies, estimates are obtained from the public accounts. Estimates for the increase in stocks have been described above in series 7.0. The figures for exports and imports of goods and services are estimated from customs returns and the official balance-of-payment statements.

The constant-price estimates are obtained from quantum indexes or by the use of appropriate price indexes. External trade data are deflated by unit value indexes built up from some 400 commodity groups.

The concepts are described in *Le Système élargi de comptabilité nationale-méthodes* and the official estimates published annually in *Rapport sur les comptes de la nation*, INSEE.

16.0 INDUSTRIAL PRODUCTION, France

Monthly, beginning 1951

Unit: Index, base 1980 = 100

Title in source: Indice Mensuel de la Production Industrielle; Indice Corrigés des Variations Saisonnières; Indice Général BTP Exclus

Source: *Bulletin Mensuel de Statistique* and *Tendances de la Conjoncture*, Institut National de la Statistique et des Études Économiques (INSEE). Seasonally adjusted by source.

Description: This index measures changes in the physical volume of production in mining, manufacturing, electricity, and gas, excluding activity in building and public works ("batiment et travaux publics" noted as BTP in the title above). The only major industry not covered is the clothing industry, but the wool industry is taken into account only in the annual index. Data are collected by INSEE through ministries and trade associations by means of questionnaires (completion is compulsory). Three different surveys—monthly, quarterly, and annual—each with a different coverage, are carried out. The monthly survey is partly on a sample basis and does not cover investment goods taking more than one month to produce. Hence the survey is confined to intermediate goods which cover about 53 percent of total production. The quarterly surveys provide considerable additional information, while the annual survey covers 78 percent of production. Among areas not fully covered are the production of machinery and mechanical equipment.

The index is computed as a base-weighted arithmetic average (1970 = 100). In most cases the data relate to actual quantities produced and adjustments are made for the number of working days in each month. However, when these cannot be measured directly, use is made of other types of indicators such as the value of production adjusted by a price index especially computed for that purpose (electrical and precision engineering), consumption of raw materials or metals (metal processing), and hours worked (aircraft industry). Index weights are proportional to 1970 value-added at factor cost derived from the national accounts data.

The index is linked at 1962 to a previous index, base 1959 = 100 although it should be noted that considerable differences exist between the two indexes. Data prior to 1956 are linked to an index based on 1938 = 100. For further details, see *Les collections de l'I.N.S.E.E.*, no. E35, February 1976, INSEE.

18.1 RETAIL SALES, Volume, France

Monthly, beginning 1955

Unit: Index, base 1980 = 100

Title in source: Indice Synthétique des Ventes du Grand Commerce (Grands Magasins, Magasins Populaires, Hypermarchés, Ventes par Correspondance)

Source: *Indicateurs et Indices C,* Chambre de Commerce et d'Industrie de Paris. Seasonally adjusted by source.

Description: This series measures the volume of total sales of department and chain stores, mail order houses, and hypermarkets in the country as a whole. Sales relate to food, household equipment, miscellaneous goods and services, textiles, and clothing.

An index of the value of sales is computed by the chain method with monthly links. The aggregate figures for a given month are compared with those for the same month in the previous year using only the same outlets in both periods. The ratio of the change is then applied to the index level of the month in the previous year. The volume index is obtained, at all levels of aggregation, by dividing the value index (adjusted for the number of working days and for sales intensity) by components of the consumer price index. Group indexes are combined according to their relative turnover in the base period, 1975 = 100.

Prior to 1971, the index covered only department and chain stores. From 1963 to 1971, the original base of the volume index was 1970 = 100. Figures for earlier periods are derived from an index of the value of sales covering Paris department stores only, calculated by the Bureau Central de Statistique Commerciale, Paris, on the base 1950 = 100 beginning 1958 and on the base 1938 = 100 for previous years. The value index was seasonally adjusted by the (Organization for Economic Cooperation and Development (OECD) and then divided by the consumer price index (indice mensuel des prix à la consommation serie France entière). This index is published in the *Bulletin mensuel de Statistique,* Institut National de la Statistique et des Études Économiques, and is based upon urban households whose heads are employees or working men.

19.0 LONG-DURATION UNEMPLOYMENT, France

Monthly, beginning 1979

Unit: Thousands of persons

Title in source: Demandes d'Emploi; Ancienneté des Demands, Moins de Trois Mois

Source: *Tendances de la Conjoncture, Cahier 1,* Institut National de la Statistique et des Etudes Economiques (INSEE). Seasonally adjusted by source.

Description: This series represents the number of unemployed whose registration for work has been on file for more than three months at the offices of the Agence nationale pour l'emploi. The Center for International Business Cycle Research (CIBCR) computes the figures by using the percentage figures in the series noted above (unemployed for less than three months), computing the complement (unemployed for more than three months), and multiplying the result by the number of applications for work on file at offices of the National Employment Agency. See series 14.1 for a description of the unemployment figures issued by the Ministère du Travail.

20.0 INVESTMENT EXPENDITURES, PLANT AND EQUIPMENT, in constant prices, France

Quarterly, beginning 1963

Unit: Millions of 1970 francs

Title in source: Formation Brute de Capital Fixe des Enterprises

Sources: *Tendances de la Conjoncture, Cahier 2*, and *Les Comptes Nationaux Trimestriels en base 1971*, both published by Institut National de la Statistique et des Études Économiques (INSEE). Seasonally adjusted by source.

Description: This series, a component of the estimates of gross domestic product, covers the expenditures on gross fixed capital by nonfinancial business firms (societes et quasi-societes nonfinancieres) as well as individual enterprises such as doctors, traders, and artisans, (enterprises individuelles). Data are available for the accounts of large national companies but the main sources are the annual surveys carried out by the Ministere de l'Industrie et de la Recherche. Other sources include surveys of business conditions, obtained from the heads of enterprises and statistics based on income-tax returns from the Direction Generale des Impots.

The figures cover durable goods purchases (buildings and equipment) that will be used in production for more than a year. Also included is work to extend the life of equipment (large repairs) and to increase output. See the description of series 15.0 for further details on estimates of gross domestic product.

21.0 BUSINESS INVENTORIES, in constant prices, France

Quarterly, beginning 1963

Unit: Billions of 1970 francs

Title in source: Variations des Stocks aux Prix de 1970

Source: *Les Comptes Nationaux Trimestriels en base 1971* and *Tendances de la Conjoncture, Cahier 2*, both published by the Institut National de la Statistique et des Études Économiques (INSEE). Seasonally adjusted by source.

Description: This series, which measures the level of inventories at the end of each quarter, is derived by the Center for International Business Cycle Research (CIBCR) by cumulating the change in inventories in constant prices, as published in the source noted above. Changes are cumulated beginning with the first quarter of 1963: hence the entire series understates the actual level of inventories by an undetermined amount, namely, the level of inventories at the end of ·1962.

The basic series, change in inventories, is a component of the estimates of gross domestic product. See series 7.0 and 15.0 above.

22.0 CHANGE IN HOURS PER UNIT OF OUTPUT, NONFARM BUSINESS, France

Quarterly, beginning 1964

Unit: Percentage of change from one year ago

Title in source: Productivité Horaire

Sources: *Tendances de la Conjoncture, Cahier 2* and *Les Comptes Nationaux Trimestriels en base 1971*, both published by the Institut National de la Statistique et des Études Économiques (INSEE). Seasonally adjusted by source.

Description: The Center for International Business Cycle Research computes the percentage change over a four-quarter interval in the number of hours required to produce a unit of output, the reciprocal of output per manhour given in the source. Output per manhour is obtained by dividing the value of production (expressed in 1970 francs) by the number of hours worked (hours per week).

23.0 BUSINESS LOANS OUTSTANDING, in constant prices, France

Quarterly, beginning 1979

Unit: Billions of 1970 francs

Source: *Tendances de la Conjoncture, Cahier 1*, Institut National de la Statistique et des Études Économiques (INSEE). Original source, Banque de France: *Conseil national du crédit*. Seasonally adjusted by source.

Description: The series covers credits to companies and to individual entrepreneurs. The figures include credits for current operations, investment, exporting, and so forth. Loans for investment include loans for the purchase of equipment as well as for industrial, commercial and agricultural buildings. Loans for export include credit both to exporters and foreign purchasers.

The figures are deflated to 1970 francs by the Center for International Business Cycle Research (CIBR) by dividing by the price index of production derived from the national income statistics (base 1970 = 100).

This index of prices of goods and services (prix de la production marchande) is published in *Tendances de la Conjoncture, Cahier 2*.

24.0 COMMERCIAL BANK LENDING RATE TO PRIME BORROW-ERS, France

Monthly, beginning 1966

Unit: Percentage

Title in source: Commercial Bank Lending Rate to Prime Borrowers

Source: *World Financial Markets*, Morgan Guaranty Trust Company of New York. Not seasonally adjusted.

Description: This is the base lending rate, excluding a commission of .05 percent per month on the highest debit balance during the month.

ITALY

1.1 HOURS PER MONTH PER WORKER IN INDUSTRY, Italy

Monthly, beginning 1972

Unit: Index, base 1980 = 100

Title in source: Indici delle Ore Effettivamente Lavorate Mensilmente per Operaio, Complesso Industria

Source: *Bollettino Mensile di Statistica*, Istituto Centrale di Statistica (ISTAT). Seasonally adjusted by OECD. Also published in *Congiuntura Italiana*, Istituto Nazionale per lo Studio della Congiuntura.

Description: This index, original base 1980 = 100, measures monthly changes in the number of hours worked in industrial plants. Included are workers in energy production and in manufacturing.

Basic data are obtained by ISTAT from a monthly survey of 1,000 plants that employed about 1,424,000 at the end of 1979. The survey does not include construction and public works, repair workshops for consumer goods, and tobacco manufacturing.

The index measures the actual number of hours worked during each month and excludes absence from work due to sickness, holidays, labor strikes, and so on. It is computed as a weighted arithmetic average, the weights relating to the number of workers in each classification.

3.1 CHANGE IN UNFILLED ORDERS, TOTAL, Italy

Monthly, beginning 1963

Unit: Percentage

Title in source: Monthly Survey of Manufacturing Industry—Net Balances on Order-books

Source: *European Economy, Supplement-Series B*, Commission of the

European Communities, Luxembourg. Seasonally adjusted by source.

Description: Data are derived from an inquiry conducted each month by the Istituto Nazionale per lo Studio della Congiuntura (ISCO) of a sample covering all manufacturing industries except food, beverages, and tobacco. Industrialists are questioned whether the orders on their books are above normal, normal, or below normal.

Data are collected on a questionnaire provided by the Commission of European Communities and are returned to the commission for processing. The results are published as net balances of the percentage of firms reporting above normal orders on the books minus the percentage reporting below normal orders. Since these balances reflect the level of unfilled orders, the Center for International Business Cycle Research (CIBCR) computes the change in the balance, which then represents the change in unfilled orders, or new orders minus shipments. Changes are computed over a two-month span in order to reduce the erratic fluctuations in the series.

Related data from the survey are also published in the *Congiuntura Italiana*, ISCO, under the title: Guidizi, Livello degli ordini e della domanda, in generale.

An index of the value of new orders in manufacturing industries is available monthly in the *Bollettino Mensile di Statistica*, Istituto Centrale di Statistica (ISTAT), under the title: Numeri indici degli ordinativi; indici totale.

4.1 DECLARED BANKRUPTCIES, Italy

Monthly, beginning 1952

Unit: Number

Title in source: Fallimenti Dichiarati, Totale

Source: *Bollettino Mensile di Statistica*, Istituto Centrale di Statistica (ISTAT). Seasonally adjusted by OECD.

Description: This series represents bankruptcies declared final at the end of judicial processes. Industrial, commercial, service businesses, and other activities are covered.

6.0 BUILDING PERMITS, RESIDENTIAL, Italy

Monthly, beginning 1955

Unit: Millions of cubic meters

Title in source: Attivita Edilizia e Opere Pubbliche; Volume dei Fabbricati Residenziali, Progettati

Source: *Indicatori Mensile*, Istituto Centrale di Statistica (ISTAT). Also published in *Bollettino Mensile di Statistica* (ISTAT) under the title Costruzioni e opere pubbliche, Fabbricati progettati, Volume, Residenziali. Seasonally adjusted by OECD.

Description: The series covers construction activity in the country as a whole beginning 1965 and prior to that the chief town of each province and for communes of over 20,000 inhabitants. The figures cover not only new construction but also buildings or parts of buildings created by reconstruction after demolition on earlier foundations or by enlargement of existing buildings. Virtually all construction activity is covered since all communes require a building permit. A building permit is valid for 12 months. Once this period has elapsed, an extension is necessary and this counts as a new permit, although cases of this kind are rather rare.

The volume of a building is the space contained between the outer surface of the outside walls, the outer surface of the roof and the lowest floor level. It includes both attic and basement rooms. A building is defined as a covered structure either isolated or separated from other structures by a common wall reaching from the foundations to the roof, and having its own entrance. Buildings are classified as residential if they are solely or mainly intended to serve as a dwelling for households.

Beginning in January 1980, ISTAT introduced substantial changes in the data collection of construction activity.

7.0 CHANGE IN INVENTORIES, in constant prices, Italy*

Quarterly, beginning 1970

Unit: Billions of 1970 lire

Title in source: Variazione delle Scorte

Source: *Quaderni Analitici: Conti Economici Trimestrali,* Istituto Nazionale per lo Studio della Congiuntura (ISCO). Seasonally adjusted by source.

Description: This series is a component in the estimates of gross domestic product compiled by ISCO. See the description for series 15.0 for further details.

*Not included in leading index for Italy

8.0 CHANGE IN PRICE INDEX OF PRODUCERS' MATERIALS, Italy

Monthly, beginning 1977

Unit: Percentage, annual rate

Title in source: Prezzi all'Ingrosso, Beni Intermedi e Materie Ausiliarie

Source: *Bollettino Mensile de Statistica,* Istituto Centrale di Statistica (ISTAT) and *Congiuntura Italiana,* Istituto Nazionale per lo Studio della Congiuntura (ISCO). Not seasonally adjusted. Percentage changes in the index are computed by the CIBCR.

Description: This index, a major group of the wholesale price index, covers intermediate goods and auxiliary materials. The total index comprises 5,800 price quotations relating to 375 commodities which are obtained monthly from the Chamber of Commerce, Industry, and Agriculture, by the Provincial Offices of Statistics, and by certain industrial firms. This group of intermediate goods is 51.06 percent of the total index and has the following subgroups: intermediate goods for consumers' goods 16.75 percent, intermediate goods for capital goods 7.86 percent and intermediate goods for consumers' and capital goods and auxiliary materials 26.45 percent.

The index is a base-weighted arithmetic average of elementary indexes. The weights were obtained from the gross value of production in 1979, less the producers' own consumption plus the value of imports. The original base is 1980 = 100 and the index has been linked to the former index, base 1976 = 100.

For further information, see *Numeri indici dei prezzi-base 1980 = 100, Metodi e Norme*, serie A, n. 20, Dicembre 1981, ISTAT.

The rate of change computed by the CIBCR is a 6 month smoothed annual rate, based upon the ratio of the current month's index to the average index for the preceding 12 months. Since the interval between the midpoints of the current month and the preceding 12 is 6.5 months, the ratio is raised to the 12/6.5 power to derive a compound annual rate.

9.0 STOCK PRICE INDEX, Italy

Monthly, beginning 1949

Unit: Index, base 1980 = 100

Title in source: Indice dei Valori Mobiliari, Valori Azionari Medii

Source: *Bollettino*, Banca d'Italia, Rome. Not seasonally adjusted.

Description: The index measures the monthly average of daily changes in the market value of closing quotations on the Milan stock exchange, of a portfolio made up of ordinary variable-yield shares of 40 major Italian companies. Prices are published in the *Listino ufficiale* of the Milan stock exchange.

The sample of shares used to calculate the index is changed as little as possible. It is computed as a weighted aggregative index with the original base 1958 = 100. The index is weighted by the value of all common shares included and adjusted for new capital and share dividends. From 1953 to 1963 the original base of the index was 1953 = 100 and was linked to the present index in 1964. Prior to 1953 the original index was based on 1938 = 100.

11.0 RATIO, PRICE TO UNIT LABOR COST, MANUFACTURING, Italy

Quarterly, beginning 1961

Unit: Index, base 1980 = 100

Titles in source: Relative Value Added Deflator; Relative Unit Labor Cost

Source: *International Financial Statistics,* International Monetary Fund, Washington, D.C. Seasonally adjusted and ratio computed by the CIBCR.

Description: The value-added deflator is the quotient of the current and constant price estimates of value added in manufacturing and is adjusted for changes in indirect taxes. It is a composite indicator of the cost (per unit of real value added) of all primary factors of production, including capital and "entrepreneurship" as well as labor. Cost of goods at intermediate stages are subtracted so that the prices represent only value added. The extrapolation beyond the most recent benchmark year is based on wholesale prices for manufactures adjusted to exclude the influence of changes in raw materials prices.

The unit labor cost series represents the compensation of employees per unit of real output (in the value added sense) in the manufacturing sector. Account is taken of employer-paid social insurance premiums and other employment taxes as well as wages and salaries. For the most recent quarters, however, it more narrowly reflects wages or wages and salaries per unit of total output of manufactured products rather than of value added in the manufacturing sector.

Both series are published on the base 1980 = 100 and are seasonally adjusted separately by the Center for International Business Cycle Research (CIBCR) before the ratio is computed.

13.0 NONFARM EMPLOYMENT, Italy

Data for Jan., Apr., July, and Oct., beginning 1959

Unit: 100-thousand persons

Titles in source: Rilevazione Forze di Lavoro, Cifre Assolute; "Occupati Totale" less "Occupati Agricoltura"

Source: *Bollettino Mensile de Statistica*, Istituto Centrale di Statistica (ISTAT). Seasonally adjusted by OECD.

Description: Data are derived from labor force sample surveys of the population aged 14 years and over. Classified as employed are those who have worked for pay or profit during the reference week or who were temporarily absent from their work as a result of sickness, holidays, or for other reasons. Beginning January 1977, students, housewives, pensioners, and others who have worked at least one hour during the reference week are also included. All civilian employment as well as regular members of the armed forces are covered.

Estimates are made from data obtained during one week in the first month of each quarter utilizing a sample of private households. The stratified two-stage sample comprises about 124,000 households residing in some 1,900 towns including the capitals of provinces and those with a population of at least 20,000. In 1977, the sample covered 85,000 families in 1,500 communities.

Annual figures are computed from data interpolated for intervening months and differ slightly from those in the source interpolated by a different method.

Further methodological details may be found in *Rilevazioni compionarie delle forze di lavoro, Metodi e Norme*, serie A, no. 10, 1969, Istituto Centrale di Statistica, Rome.

14.0 UNEMPLOYMENT RATE, Italy

Data refer to Jan., Apr., July, and Oct., beginning 1959

Unit: Percentage

Title in source: Rilevazione Forze di Lavoro, Cifre Assolute; Persone in Cerca di Occupazione, Totale, % Forze di Lavoro

Source: *Bollettino Mensile di Statistica*, Istituto Centrale di Statistica (ISTAT). Seasonally adjusted by the OECD.

Description: Data are derived from a labor force sample survey of the population aged 14 or over taken in the first week without public holidays in the first month of each quarter.

Classified as unemployed are those who had not worked and who were looking for work during the reference week including persons seeking their first job and those laid off without definite instructions to return to work. Persons who had made arrangements to start a new job at a subsequent date are not included. Beginning in January 1977, housewives, students, pensioners, and others who stated they were actively seeking work, are included.

Information on the sample surveys and reference to a published description may be found under 13.0 above. Prior to the November 1980 issue of the *Bollettino Mensile di Statistica*, the percentage figures are derived by dividing the series "persone in cerca di occupazione" by the series "persone appartenenti alle forze di lavoro."

15.0 GROSS DOMESTIC PRODUCT, in constant prices, Italy

Quarterly, beginning 1952

Unit: Billions of 1970 lire

Title in source: Conto Economico delle Risorse e Degli Impieghi: Prodotto Interno Lordo ai Prezzi di Mercato

Sources: *Congiuntura Italiana* and *Quaderni Analitici: Conti Economici Trimestrali*, Istituto Nazionale per lo Studio della Congiuntura (ISCO). Seasonally adjusted by source.

Description: The chief components of gross domestic product in purchasers' values are: private final consumption expenditures, government final consumption expenditures, gross fixed capital formation, increase in stocks, exports of goods and services less imports of goods and services. The figures include consumption by nonresidents. Each series is deflated to 1970 prices by an appropriate price index.

Prior to 1960, the data relate to gross national product in 1963 prices and were converted to 1970 prices by multiplying by 1.31212, the increase in the implicit price deflator between 1963 and 1970. No correction was made to take into account the difference between national and domestic product since the "net property income from abroad" was negligible.

Further information may be found in the supplement to *Congiuntura Italiana*, no. 1, 1975, in *Rassegna dei lavori dell'Istituto*, no. 14, 1968, and *Quadorni Analitici*, Dec. 1980 and April 1981, ISCO.

Annual and quarterly series for gross domestic product are also compiled by the Istituto Centrale di Statistica (ISTAT) and published in the *Bollettino Mensile di Statistica*.

16.0 INDUSTRIAL PRODUCTION, Italy

Monthly, beginning 1948

Unit: Index, base 1980 = 100

Title in source: Indici Generale della Produzione Industriale; Depurati della Stagionalità

Source: *Congiuntura Italiana*, Istituto Nazionale per lo Studio della Congiuntura, Rome. Also published under the subtitle "Indici destagionalizzato" in *Bollettino Mensile di Statistica*, Istituto Centrale di Statistica (ISTAT). Seasonally adjusted by source.

Description: The index measures monthly changes in the physical volume of production in mining, manufacturing, electricity, and gas. In principle, all establishments are covered except handicrafts. These establishments accounted for approximately 82 percent of the total value added in industrial production in 1970, the base year of the index.

Data on manufacturing are collected by ISTAT on a compulsory postal questionnaire from a sample of 8,000 enterprises. Exhaustive surveys provide data for the other sectors. A total of 607 commodity indicators are included in the monthly index. The indicators and their percentage share in the total weight are: physical output 77 percent, number of units produced 11 percent, quantities of materials used 6 percent, man-hours adjusted for productivity 4 percent, deflated values of output 2 percent.

The index is calculated as a base-weighted arithmetic average of relatives of the indicators of output. The weights used in combining the indicators into subgroup indexes are based on gross value of production, after eliminating duplications of values which occur in the combining of products.

Weights used to combine subgroup indexes into the indexes of major groups are based on the value added at factor cost in 1970. The weighting coefficients of the major groups are: mining 2.2 percent, manufacturing 90.7 percent, electricity and gas 7.1 percent. Metal products excluding transport equipment represent 22 percent of the manufacturing index. The index is adjusted for the number of working days.

The original base of the index is 1948 to 1954; 1953 from 1954 to 1966; 1966 from 1966 to 1971; and 1970 from 1971. The coverage of the series was considerably extended from 1966 and caution should be used in comparing the series before and after that date.

For further details, see *Bollettino Mensile di Statistica*, April 1973, ISTAT.

18.1 RETAIL SALES, in constant prices, Italy

Monthly, beginning 1956

Unit: Index, base 1980 = 100

Title in source: Commercio Interno—Numeri Indici delle Vendite del Commercio al Minuto delle Imprese della Grande Distribuzione; Ammontare Complessivo delle Vendite, Complesso

Source: *Bollettino Mensile de Statistica*, Istituto Centrale di Statistica (ISTAT). Seasonally adjusted and converted to constant prices (by dividing by the consumer price index) by OECD. The consumer price index is also published in the source.

Description: This index measures monthly changes in the volume of sales made by virtually all department stores, popular price stores, retail chains with more than 5 outlets, and by the largest of the consumers' cooperatives. At the end of 1980, the base year of the index, the establishments covered by the survey were: 16 department and popular priced stores (with 588 outlets, of which 272 were supermarkets), 180 retail chains (with 2,767 outlets, of which 456 were supermarkets), and 128 consumers' cooperatives (with 1066 outlets of which 187 were supermarkets).

Monthly sales figures obtained in the survey represent the total amount billed to customers, whatever methods of payments are used. They include indirect taxes, interest on credit sales, and additional charges for delivery or for alterations, and are net of any discounts granted by the retailer.

Basic data are obtained by ISTAT in a monthly survey by means of a postal questionnaire. The department and popular priced stores included in the sample cover about 90 percent of total turnover of these businesses and 85 percent for the retail chains. Indexes are computed for four groups of products (food, textiles and clothing, home furnishings, and other products) by comparing aggregate sales for the month with the average monthly sales in the base year.

This index is linked to an index on base 1970 = 100 which in turn is linked in 1970 to an index on base 1966 = 100 that covered only department stores and cooperatives.

The series is adjusted to 1980 prices by dividing by the Consumer Price Index, of wage and salary earners, original base 1980 = 100. The index is computed as a weighted arithmetic average on fixed base with weights derived from national accounts data. The index has been linked to previous indexes with original bases 1976, 1970, 1966, and 1953. For further details, see *Numeri indici dei prezzi-base 1980 = 100, Metodi e Norme*, serie A, n. 20, December 1981, ISTAT.

20.1 INVESTMENT EXPENDITURES, PLANT AND EQUIPMENT, in constant prices, Italy

Quarterly, beginning 1970

Unit: Billions of 1970 lire

Titles in source: Attivita Industriali: Costruzioni e Opere Pubbliche. Investimenti Fissi Lordi: Attrezzature e Mezzi di Trasporto

Sources: *Congiuntura Italiana* and *Quaderni Analitici: Conti Economici Trimestrali*, Istituto Nazionale per lo Studio della Congiuntura (ISCO). Seasonally adjusted by source.

Description: This series combines two components of gross domestic product: value added in construction, and investment in equipment and means of transport. The construction series is a component of value added by industry. Investment in equipment and means of transport is a component of fixed capital formation. Both series are published in prices of 1970.

The summation is done by the Center for International Business Cycle Research (CIBCR).

See the description of series 15.0 for further details on the estimates of gross domestic product.

21.0 BUSINESS INVENTORIES, in constant prices, Italy

Quarterly, beginning 1970

Unit: Billions of 1970 lire

Title in source: Variazione delle Scorte

Source: *Quaderni Analitici: Conti Economici Trimestrali,* Istituto Nazionale per lo Studio della Congiuntura (ISCO). Seasonally adjusted by source.

Description: This series, which measures the level of inventories at the end of each quarter, is derived by the Center for International Business Cycle Research (CIBCR) by cumulating the change in inventories in constant prices, as published in the source noted above. Changes are cumulated beginning with the first quarter of 1970. Hence the entire series understates the actual level of inventories by an undetermined amount, namely, the level of inventories at the end of 1969.

The base series, change in inventories, is a component of the estimates of gross domestic product. See series 7.0 and 15.0 above.

24.0 COMMERCIAL BANK LENDING RATE TO PRIME BORROWERS, Italy

Monthly, beginning 1966

Unit: Percentage

Title in source: Commercial Bank Lending Rates to Prime Borrowers

Source: *World Financial Markets*, Morgan Guaranty Trust Company of New York. Not seasonally adjusted.

Description: This is the unsecured overdraft rate for prime borrowers. It is the rate charged at or near the end of the month.

JAPAN

1.1 INDEX OF OVERTIME WORKED, MANUFACTURING, Japan

Monthly, beginning 1954

Unit: Index, base 1980 = 100

Title in source: Index of Overtime Worked, Manufacturing

Source: *Japanese Economic Indicators* (series 401), Economic Planning Agency. Seasonally adjusted by source, the Ministry of Labor.

Description: The basic data for the index are derived from establishment data. They cover average monthly overtime hours worked in manufacturing. Data relate to regular full-time and part-time workers, permanent and temporary, whether paid at time rate or at piece rate (self-employed and unpaid family workers are excluded). Regular workers are defined as wage and salary earners who have an appointment of indefinite duration or are employed under contract for a period longer than one month. Also included are those hired on a daily basis for less than one month but who were employed for at least 18 days in each of the last 2 months.

A survey is conducted each month by the Ministry of Labor of a sample of establishments engaged in all nonagricultural activities. Information on the design and coverage of the sample are given in series 13.0 below. Participation in the survey is compulsory and the response rate is almost 100 percent. Questionnaire forms are returned by mail.

The calculation is done separately for each of the cells in which the universe of establishments was divided for the purpose of drawing the sample of respondents. The weights used to compute the average for a given month are ratios of universe employment of regular workers in the preceding month to corresponding sample figures. The base of the index is moved forward every five years (original base at present, 1980 = 100).

For further information, see *Yearbook of Labor Statistics*, Ministry of Labor (Tokyo).

4.1 BUSINESS FAILURES, Japan

Monthly, beginning 1956

Unit: Number of failures

Title in source: Number of Failures

Source: 1956-October 1964, *1975 Annual Report on Business Cycle Indicators*; beginning October 1964, *Japanese Economic Indicators* (series 170), Economic Planning Agency. Seasonally adjusted by source.

Description: The figures represent the number of businesses that have suspended transactions with banks or have made application under the Corporate Reorganization Law. However, business failures do not necessarily indicate cessation of production and business activities.

The basic data are compiled by the Tokyo Shoko Research Organization and the Teikoku Data Bank. The Federation of Bankers Associations of Japan also publishes the number of enterprises whose transactions with banks have been suspended, and the amount of liabilities of these enterprises. The figures cover both incorporated and unincorporated enterprises with liabilities more than 10 million yen.

Data beginning October 1964 as published in *Japanese Economic Indicators* have been spliced by the Center for International Business Cycle Research (CIBCR) to the earlier figures by multiplying the earlier data by .5945, the ratio of average figures for October 1964-September 1965 of the later figures to the corresponding average of the earlier data.

5.0 NEW ORDERS, MACHINERY AND CONSTRUCTION WORKS, in constant prices, Japan

Monthly, beginning 1960

Unit: 100-million 1980 yen

Titles in source: New Orders for Machinery, Private, Excluding Vessels, and New Orders for Construction Works, Private

Source: *Japanese Economic Indicators* (series 337 and 325), Japanese Planning Agency. Seasonally adjusted by source. Adjusted to 1980 prices by the Wholesale Price Index of Manufacturing Industry Products (series 487), same source.

Description: The two series for new orders for machinery and for construction are combined by the Center for International Business Cycle Research (CIBCR) and divided by the Wholesale Price Index of Manufacturing Products, base 1980 = 100.

The basic series of the value of new orders for machinery and equipment, net of cancellations, represents orders received during the month from domestic private sources, as reported by a sample of major manufacturing enterprises. Those placed by other establishments of the same enterprise and those partly or entirely subcontracted are included. Orders for repairs and improvements are also included. Vessels are excluded. New orders and increases in quantities previously ordered are recorded in the month they are received and include those met from stock or current production. Cancellations and reductions in quantities are deducted from the data for the period when they are announced rather than when the order was placed. The prices are selling prices on an ex-works basis and exclude indirect taxes. Orders received from government, purchasing agencies, and foreign sources are not included here but are reported separately.

To obtain the value of new orders for machinery and equipment, the Economic Planning Agency conducts a monthly survey of the most important enterprises. The original series for 1960 through March 1969 covered 127 enterprises but when the coverage was expanded to 178 companies, the earlier figures were raised to the level of the new survey by multiplying by a factor 1.3355 (the ratio of the April 1969 figures for the two series). This adjustment was made by the CIBCR.

The series of new orders for construction works is based upon data received by the Ministry of Construction from 43 construction companies representing about 18 percent of total construction since 1975. The series includes only orders from private concerns, about half of all new orders placed. The ministry also obtains information on new orders placed with 40 other large construction companies and 465 medium and small companies.

6.1 DWELLING UNITS STARTED, Japan

Monthly, beginning 1953

Unit: Number of dwellings

Title in source: Dwellings, New Construction Started

Source: *Japanese Economic Indicators* (series 317), Economic Planning Agency. Seasonally adjusted by source.

Description: The data refer to permits for new construction, conversion, and restoration. They cover buildings with a total floor area of 10 square meters or more, for which the law requires a report to prefectural governors. The figures are compiled by the Ministry of Construction and exclude the Okinawa Prefecture prior to 1973.

7.0 CHANGE IN INVENTORIES, in constant prices, Japan

Quarterly, beginning 1952

Unit: 100-million 1975 yen

Title in source: Financial Statements of Incorporated Businesses, Inventory

Sources: *Annual Report on Business Cycle Indicators* (series 116) and *Japanese Economic Indicators* (series 186), Economic Planning Agency. Seasonally adjusted by source. Adjustment to 1975 prices described below.

Description: The basic data for 1952 through 1960 relate to enterprises with a share capital of 2 million yen and over and have been spliced at the beginning of 1961 by the Center for International Business Cycle Research (CIBCR) to the series with share capital of 10 million yen and over. The earlier figures are multipled by .8561, the ratio in the first quarter of 1961 of the present series to the 1952-60 data. The series is compiled by the Ministry of Finance.

The quarterly changes are computed by the Center and then deflated to 1975 yen. The series used to convert the figures to 1975 prices is the Gross National Product implicit price deflator obtained by dividing Gross National Expenditure at current prices (series 1) by Gross National Expenditure at 1975 prices (series 16) as published in the source noted above.

A series showing the increase in total stocks at 1975 prices, as a sector of Gross National Expenditure is also published in *Japanese Economic Indicators*, series 24.

8.0 CHANGE IN RAW MATERIALS PRICE INDEX, Japan

Monthly, beginning 1953

Unit: Percentage, annual rate

Title in source: 1952-60, Wholesale Price Index of Raw Materials; beginning in 1960, index combining four subgroups of the Wholesale Price Index (see below)

Source: *Economics Statistics Monthly*, Bank of Japan, Tokyo. Not seasonally adjusted. Also published in *Japanese Economic Indicators* (series 480, 481, 488, and 489), Japanese Planning Agency. The percentage changes in the index are computed by the CIBCR.

Description: The index, beginning in 1960, has been computed by the Center for International Business Cycle Research (CIBCR) by combining four series in the Bank of Japan Wholesale Price Index. The series and their percentage weights in this index are: mining products 37 percent, iron and steel 36 percent, nonferrous metals 18 percent, and inedible agricultural and forest products 9 percent. The weights are proportional to their relative importance in the total index but aggregate only 19 percent of the total index. The base period is 1980 = 100.

From 1952-60, the series used is the Wholesale Price Index of Raw Materials, linked to the index described above in January 1960. This index also includes foodstuffs; petroleum, coal, and related products; and miscellaneous products.

The materials included are produced by primary industries and not processed by manufacturing. Scrap materials and wastepaper are included. The prices are mainly the representative selling contract prices of wholesalers nearest to the producers.

The Bank of Japan computes the indexes as base-weighted arithmetic averages of price relatives. Weights are based on the transaction value of domestic products.

The rate of change computed by the CIBCR is a 6-month smoothed annual rate based upon the ratio of the current month's index to the average index for the preceding 12 months. Since the interval between midpoints of the current month and the preceding 12 is 6.5 months, the ratio is raised to the 12/6.5 power to derive a compound annual rate.

9.0 STOCK PRICE INDEX, Japan

Monthly, beginning 1953

Unit: Index, base January 4, 1968 = 100

Title in source: Index of Stock Prices

Source: *Japanese Economic Indicators* (series 181), Japanese Planning Agency. Not seasonally adjusted. Compiled by Tokyo Stock Exchange and published in the Exchange's *Monthly Statistics*.

Description: This series measures changes in the selling price of 690 shares quoted on the Tokyo Stock Exchange. The monthly index is the simple average of daily indexes. Selling quotations at the close of the afternoon session are weighted by the current number of shares listed. Adjustments are made to the base figure when shares are added to or deleted from the list and for new issues. No adjustments are made for stock dividends.

10.0 OPERATING PROFITS, ALL INDUSTRIES, in constant prices, Japan

Quarterly, beginning 1954

Unit: 100-million 1975 yen

Title in source: Financial Statements of Incorporated Business, All Industries, Operating Profits

Sources: *Japanese Economic Indicators* (series 193) and *Annual Report on Business Cycle Indicators*, Japanese Planning Agency. Seasonally adjusted

by source. Deflated by GNP Implicit Price deflator computed from series described below, published in same source.

Description: Beginning in the second quarter of 1960, the figures cover operating profits, before taxes, of all enterprises with share capital of 10 million yen and over, compiled by the Ministry of Finance. Earlier figures are the sum of two series; operating profits of manufacturing enterprises with a share capital of 2 million yen and over, and profits in wholesale and retail trade. The Center for International Business Cycle Research (CIBCR) has combined these two and spliced the earlier figures to the later series by multiplying the earlier figures by 1.0117 (the ratio of the later to earlier data over the period second quarter 1960 through first quarter 1961).

The figures in current value are adjusted to 1975 values by the CIBCR by dividing them by the implicit price deflator for Gross National Expenditures. This is obtained by dividing the series for Gross National Expenditure by the same series at 1975 prices (series 1 and 16 in *Japanese Economic Indicators*).

11.0 RATIO, PRICE TO UNIT LABOR COST, MANUFACTURING, Japan

Monthly, beginning 1953

Unit: Index, base 1980 = 100

Titles in source: (Numerator) Wholesale Price Index, Manufacturing Industry Products; (Denominator) Unit Labor Cost, Manufacturing

Source: *Japanese Economic Indicators* (series 487 and 421), Japanese Planning Agency. Numerator not seasonally adjusted, denominator seasonally adjusted by source.

Description: The Wholesale Price Index is a base-weighted arithmetic average of price relatives, computed by the Bank of Japan. Weights are based on the 1980 transaction value of domestic products (including export goods) and import goods. Included are domestic commodities with a transaction value of at least 18.3 billion yen, export commodities with at least 13.6 billion yen and imported commodities with at least 14.9 billion yen. The percentage weights of the major categories and the number of items are: domestic products 76.3 percent (819 items), export goods 11.3 percent (212 items), and imported goods 12.4 percent (154 items). Prices are mainly the selling contract prices of wholesalers nearest to the producers. For further details see *Price Statistics Monthly*, Bank of Japan.

Unit Labor Cost data are compiled by the Japanese Productivity Center. The index is computed by dividing the index of nominal wages (calculated by the Ministry of Labor) by the labor productivity index, both relating to manufacturing only. The Japan Productivity Center calculates the labor productivity index by dividing the index of the quantity of industrial output by an index of labor input, in man-days. Weights in the industrial output index are based on value added determined from the 1975 Census of Manufacturers. Weights of the labor input index are based upon the number of workers determined from this same Census.

Figures prior to 1968 that were originally on the base 1970 = 100 have been linked by the Center for International Business Cycle Research (CIBCR) to the current data on base 1980 = 100, based upon the ratio of the two series in January 1968. The CIBCR also computes the ratio of price to unit labor cost.

12.1 CHANGE IN CONSUMER AND HOUSING CREDIT, in constant prices, Japan

Quarterly, beginning 1966

Unit: 100-million 1980 yen

Title in source: Consumer Credit Outstanding

Source: *Japanese Economic Indicators* (series 184), Economic Planning Agency. The published figures refer to credit outstanding at end of quarter. Changes from quarter to quarter are computed by the Center for International Business Cycle Research (CIBCR), seasonally adjusted and then deflated to 1980 prices by dividing by the seasonally adjusted Consumer Price Index.

Description: The basic series, compiled by the Bank of Japan, represents consumer and housing credit outstanding at the end of each quarter in the banking and trust accounts of all banks. The term "all banks" includes 13 city banks, 63 regional banks, 7 trust banks, and 3 long-term credit banks. Outstanding loans by small specialized agencies, which play an important role in consumer credit, are not included. The figures cover only loans for installment sales where repayments are made in more than three installments in a period covering more than two months.

In recent years housing credit outstanding, shown separately in the source, is 93-95 percent of the total.

The Consumer Price Index used as a deflator, is computed as a weighted arithmetic average on a 1980 fixed base. The weights were derived from a family expenditure survey conducted in 1980 among a random sample of about 8,000 urban and rural households in 168 localities selected so as to represent the whole country. The major groups and percentage weights are: food 38 percent, housing 5 percent, fuel, light, and water 6 percent, furniture 5 percent, clothing 10 percent, medical care 3 percent, transportation and communications 11 percent, education 4 percent, reading and recreation 12 percent, and miscellaneous 6 percent. Prices are collected from about 30,000 retail stores and rent quotations are obtained from about 22,000 households. Seasonal fluctuations in the prices of fruit, vegetables, and fish are accounted for by varying monthly item weights within constant group weights. For further methodological details, see *Outline of the Consumer Price Indexes*, Bureau of Statistics, Tokyo. The index on base 1980 = 100 has been linked to previous indexes on the bases 1975, 1970, and 1965.

13.0 REGULAR WORKERS' EMPLOYMENT, ALL INDUSTRIES, Japan

Monthly, beginning 1954

Unit: Index, base 1980 = 100

Title in source: Regular Workers Employment, all Industries

Source: *Japanese Economic Indicators* (series 380), Economic Planning Agency. Seasonally adjusted by source. Basic source of data is the Ministry of Labor.

Description: "Regular workers" are wage and salary earners who have an appointment of indefinite duration or are employed under contract for a period longer than one month. The term also includes those hired on a daily basis for less than one month but who were employed for at least 18 days in each of the last two months. Regular, full-time and part-time workers are covered, permanent and temporary, whether paid at a time rate or piece rate. Excluded are self-employed and unpaid family workers.

The figures reflect the number of employees on payrolls at the end of each month. They include persons on leave without pay or on strike during a part of the month but not for the entire month. Persons temporarily laid off receive pay and are included but those laid off for an indefinite period are excluded. Persons on payrolls of more than one establishment are counted as many times as reported.

The basic data are obtained from a monthly survey by the Ministry of Labor of a sample of establishments engaged in all nonagricultural activities in the private sector as well as government-owned enterprises. The sample of establishments employing thirty or more regular workers is drawn every three years on the basis of results of the triennial census of establishments carried out by the Bureau of Statistics. The sample is adjusted twice a year to allow for changes in the size of establishments and creation of new ones. It covers about 16,700 establishments which account for about 12 percent of employment in the industries surveyed.

The calculation is done separately for each of the cells in which the universe of establishments was divided for drawing the sample. Projections from the triennial census figures are computed by link relatives of month to month changes in employment in each cell.

The index is published in the source on the base 1980 = 100. Figures prior to 1970 relate to employment in all industries excluding services and have been linked to the present series on the basis of 1970 annual figures by the Center for International Business Cycle Research (CIBCR). From 1970 to

1975, this series increased 1.8 percent while the series excluding services decreased 1.4 percent. The share in total employment of the service sector was 52.1 percent in 1975.

For further information see *Year Book of Labor Statistics*, Ministry of Labor.

14.0 UNEMPLOYMENT RATE, Japan

Monthly, beginning 1953

Unit: Percentage of unemployed

Title in source: Labor Force, Rate of Wholly Unemployed

Sources: *Monthly Report on the Labor Force Survey*, Bureau of Statistics, Office of the Prime Minister, and *Japanese Economic Indicators* (series 379), Economic Planning Agency. Seasonally adjusted by source.

Description: Data are obtained from monthly labor force sample surveys conducted during the week ending on the last day of the month. The unemployment figures represent all persons aged 15 years and over who did not work during the survey week and who actively sought work or were awaiting results of previous applications for work.

The sample covers about 76,000 persons in some 33,000 households selected from the entire country, with over-all sampling ratios of 1/920, 1/1380, and 1/1840 by a stratified two-stage sampling method using the enumeration districts of the population census as the first-stage unit and dwelling units as the second-stage sampling unit. Prior to 1973 the figures exclude Okinawa.

The unemployment percentages are computed by dividing the number of unemployed (x 100) by the estimated civilian labor force (employed plus unemployed).

For further methodological details, see *Year Book of Labor Statistics—Explanation*, Ministry of Labor.

15.0 GROSS NATIONAL EXPENDITURES, at constant prices, Japan

Quarterly, beginning 1952

Unit: Billions of 1975 yen

Title in source: Gross National Expenditure (at 1975 Prices)

Source: *Japanese Economic Indicators* (series 16), Economic Planning Agency. Seasonally adjusted by source.

Description: The estimates of expenditure on gross national product (GNP), compiled by the Economic Planning Agency, measure the value of the output of goods and services produced by residents of the nation, gross of depreciation and other allowances for consumption of capital goods, but after deduction of other business products used up by business during the accounting period in the process of production. The estimates are in close accordance with the classifications and definitions recommended by the United Nations System of National Accounts. The major components and their relative importance in 1978 were: purchase of goods and services by consumers 57.9 percent, current and capital expenditure by government 9.6 percent, gross private fixed investment 30.2 percent, change in stocks 0.6 percent, exports of goods and services 11.1 percent less imports of goods and services, 9.4 percent.

The series not only includes goods and services purchased for cash, but also includes the value of income-in-kind, the value of consumption of their own production by farm households, the imputed rent of owner-occupied dwellings, the purchase of imputed services from banking institutions, and the total value at the time of purchase of durables purchased on time payment. In addition to the estimate of gross private fixed investment based on expenditure data, an alternative estimate is made by the commodity flow method. In this method, the value of the domestic output of the relevant commodities is obtained from production records, and exports of the same goods are subtracted and imports added.

For revaluing the figures at constant prices, each type of expenditure is divided by a price index. The total is obtained by summing up the various items of expenditure at constant prices, less imports at constant prices. For further information, see the Annual Report on *National Income Statistics*, Economic Planning Agency.

16.0 INDUSTRIAL PRODUCTION, Japan

Monthly, beginning 1953

Unit: Index base 1980 = 100

Title in source: Industrial Production; Mining and Manufacturing

Source: *Japanese Economic Indicators* (series 212), Economic Planning Agency. Seasonally adjusted by source.

Description: This index of mining and manufacturing (excluding printing and publishing) covers, in principle, all privately owned establishments irrespective of size. It is calculated as a base-weighted arithmetic average on the base 1980 = 100, starting from elementary series of relatives based on quantities of individual commodities produced. The weights used are value added at factor cost in the base year, and are derived from the Statistics of Mining Trend and Census of Manufactures. Manufacturing has a weighting coefficient of 99 percent. The base of the index is changed at five year intervals. The index is computed by the Ministry of International Trade and Industry. This index on the base 1980 = 100 has been linked in 1968 to the former index on base 1975 = 100 by the Center for International Business Cycle Research (CIBCR).

Monthly data are obtained on the production of 532 commodities. Data on the production of about 93 percent of these commodities are obtained by the Ministry of International Trade and Industry; the other data are gathered chiefly from trade associations and other government agencies. The monthly data gathered covered approximately 60 percent of the total value added in production in 1980.

For further details, see *Industrial Statistics Monthly*, no. 3, 1978, Ministry of International Trade and Industry (Tokyo).

17.1 WAGE AND SALARY INCOME, in constant prices, Japan

Monthly, beginning 1954

Unit: Index, base 1980 = 100

Titles in source: Index of Regular Wages and Salaries, all Industries, at fixed prices; Index of Regular Workers Employment, all Industries

Source: *Japanese Economic Indicators* (series 410 and 380), Economic Planning Agency. Seasonally adjusted by source, the Ministry of Labor.

Description: This series, computed by the Center for International Business Cycle Research (CIBCR), is the product of two indexes, real wages per worker and employment.

The wage and salary index is based upon total cash payments per worker made in the month, including those applying to other periods. The payments include basic wages and salaries, overtime pay, family allowances, all other cash payments whether regularly recurring or not, and also those made for normal hours not worked. Retrospective payments following back-dated wage settlements are recorded in the month when they are paid rather than the months when they are earned. No additions are made for benefits of any kind. Earnings are measured on a gross basis before any deductions are made, such as income taxes and social insurance contributions.

The calculation of earnings is done separately for each of the cells in which the universe of establishments was divided for the purpose of drawing the sample of respondents. The sum of the earnings reported by the establishments sampled in the cell are divided by the number of regular workers employed in these establishments. The weights used to compute the aggregates for a given month are ratios of universe employment of regular workers in the preceding month to corresponding sample figures. The wage and salary index is converted to fixed prices by dividing by the consumer price index described in series 12.1.

The index of regular workers employment is series 13.0. Both the wage and employment series are based on the monthly survey of establishments conducted by the Ministry of Labor. See the description of series 13.0 for the definition of "regular workers" and for details on the linking of both series in 1970 to an earlier series that excluded services.

18.1 RETAIL SALES, in constant prices, Japan

Monthly, beginning 1954

Unit: Index base 1980 = 100

Title in source: Index of Retail Sales

Sources: *Economic Statistics Monthly*, Bank of Japan and *Japanese Economic Indicators* (series 303), Economic Planning Agency. Seasonally adjusted by Bank of Japan. Basic data are published in *Industrial Statistics Monthly*, Ministry of International Trade and Industry, Tokyo. Adjusted to constant 1980 prices by the CIBCR by means of the Consumer Price Index.

Description: The indexes are based upon monthly data obtained in the Current Survey of Commerce, conducted by the Research and Statistics Department of the Minister's Secretariat, Ministry of International Trade and Industry. The sample used in this inquiry covers retail trade establishments throughout Japan. Prior to 1973, sales of department stores in which a separate inquiry was conducted by the same ministry were not included in this index. Indirect taxes are included in the value of sales.

The sample is based upon the census of commerce conducted every three years and in computing the index, necessary adjustments are made taking into account the difference caused by alteration in the sample.

The articles covered are: food and beverages, apparel and accessories, dry goods and textiles products, household articles, pharmaceuticals, and items of personal care. For further details, see *Japan Statistical Yearbook*, Bureau of Statistics, Office of the Prime Minister, Tokyo.

The index is published in the source on the base 1980 = 100 and is linked in 1977 to the former index on base 1975 = 100. Figures prior to 1973 (index excluding department stores) have been linked to the former index in January 1973 by the Center for International Business Cycle Research (CIBCR). 1954-69 data were originally published on the base 1965 = 100. The index has been adjusted to 1980 prices by the CIBCR by dividing by the seasonally adjusted Consumer Price Index, base 1980 = 100, described in series 12.1.

20.0 NEW PLANT AND EQUIPMENT EXPENDITURE, in constant prices, Japan

Quarterly, beginning 1952

Units: Billions of 1975 yen

Title in source: Gross Fixed Capital Formation: Private Enterprises Plant and Equipment Investment at Constant Prices

Source: *Japanese Economic Indicators* (series 22), Economic Planning Agency. Seasonally adjusted by source.

Description: This series, a sector of the estimates of gross national product

(GNP), represents the market value of net acquisitions of fixed capital goods of more than one year's durability by private business and nonprofit institutions. For major items of construction and equipment such as vessels and heavy machinery, the investment is the value of work done during the period. Only those repair expenses incurred in the process of reconstruction or improvement are included, simple repair expenses being excluded. The main estimating method followed is the commodity flow method, where the value of domestic output of the relevant commodities is obtained from production records, and exports of the same goods are subtracted and imports added. The resulting aggregates are valued at producer prices. To convert these values to market values at which final sales are made, it is necessary to trace through the various stages of the distribution and installation process, making allowance for the costs incurred at each stage.

Expenditure on machinery and equipment is deflated by a price index built up from the components of the Bank of Japan wholesale price index. The works expense index of the Construction Ministry is used to deflate expenditure on construction work. The weights for the different types of structure are derived from input-output tables.

21.0 BUSINESS INVENTORIES, in constant prices, Japan

End of quarter, beginning 1952

Unit: Billions of 1975 yen

Title in source: Financial Statements of Incorporated Businesses (with Share Capital of 10 million yen and over): Inventory

Source: *Japanese Economic Indicators* (series 186), Economic Planning Agency. Seasonally adjusted by source.

Description: The figures in current prices are the basic data used in compiling series 7.0. The constant prices series has been estimated by the Center for International Business Cycle Research (CIBCR) by cumulating series 7.0 (change in inventories in 1975 yen), backward as well as forward from the level of inventories at the end of the first quarter of 1961 in the later series (8,832.2 billion 1975 yen). See series 7.0 above for a description and conversion of the change in inventories to 1975 yen.

22.1 CHANGE IN HOURS PER UNIT OF OUTPUT, INDUSTRY, Japan

Monthly, beginning 1961

Unit: Percentage of change from one year ago

Title in source: Index of Labor Productivity, All Industries

Source: *Japanese Economic Indicators* (series 412), Japanese Planning Agency. Not seasonally adjusted.

Description: The basic index of labor productivity is compiled by the Japan Productivity Center. It is obtained by dividing the index of the quantity of industrial output by an index of labor input in man-days. See series 11.0 above for further details.

The Center for International Business Cycle Research (CIBCR) computes the percent changes of the reciprocal of the index numbers over a 12-month span to obtain this series. The figures represent specifically the change in man-days, not man-hours, per unit of output, since no allowance is made for changes in the number of hours worked per day.

23.1 TOTAL LOANS OUTSTANDING, in constant prices, Japan

Monthly, beginning 1953

Unit: 100 billion 1975 yen

Title in source: Banking Accounts of All Banks: Loans and Discounts

Source: *Japanese Economic Indicators* (series 133), Japanese Planning Agency. Seasonally adjusted by source. Primary source is the Federation of Bankers' Association of Japan. Adjustment to constant prices by CIBCR.

Description: The figures represent the total of loans and discounts made by all banks in yen and other currencies. The four types of banks involved are city banks, regional banks, long-term credit banks, and trust banks. At the end of 1974, these banks accounted for 75 percent of loans and discounts of the banking system and 47 percent of loans and discounts by all financial institutions.

At the end of 1981, loans and discounts by these banks to various sectors were: manufacturing 32 percent; construction 5 percent; wholesale and retail trade 25 percent; real estate 6 percent; transport and communications 3 percent; electricity, gas, thermal, and water supplies 3 percent; services 7 percent; local government 1 percent; individuals 11 percent; and other industries 7 percent.

The figures have been adjusted to 1975 yen by the Center for International Business Cycle Research (CIBCR) by dividing by the Consumer Price Index which has been described above in series 12.1.

24.1 BANK RATES ON LOANS, Japan

Monthly, beginning 1955

Unit: Percentage

Title in source: Money Rates, Contracted Rate on Loans

Source: *Japanese Economic Indicators* (series 177), Japanese Planning Agency. Not seasonally adjusted.

Description: This series represents the average interest rates on loans and discounts of all banks. Rates are for both short-term and long-term loans. Loans to individuals as well as to enterprises are covered. Source of the data is the Bank of Japan.

3

Monthly and Quarterly Data, 1948–82

Note: The six-month smoothed growth rates shown after each composite index are compound annual rates based upon the ratio of the current month's index to the average index for the preceding twelve months.

UNITED STATES

LEADING INDEX, UNITED STATES (1980=100)

YEAR	JAN	FEB	MAR	APR	MAY	JUN	JUL	AUG	SEP	OCT	NOV	DEC	AVGE
1948	37.4	36.7	37.0	37.5	37.4	37.7	37.5	37.1	36.7	36.9	36.6	36.2	37.1
1949	35.4	35.0	34.5	34.0	34.0	34.1	34.6	35.2	35.8	35.5	35.8	36.4	35.0
1950	37.0	37.6	38.1	38.9	39.8	40.5	41.9	43.3	43.1	43.3	43.4	43.5	40.9
1951	44.1	43.1	42.6	41.8	41.6	40.9	40.3	40.0	40.3	40.4	40.5	40.7	41.4
1952	40.7	41.0	40.9	40.5	40.4	41.0	40.6	41.3	42.3	42.1	42.3	42.7	41.3
1953	42.9	42.9	43.0	42.9	42.7	42.2	42.3	41.7	40.7	40.5	39.8	40.0	41.8
1954	40.2	40.6	40.6	41.1	41.5	42.0	42.6	42.6	43.2	43.9	44.8	45.5	42.4
1955	46.4	47.3	47.7	47.8	48.0	48.3	48.6	48.6	49.0	48.7	49.1	49.0	48.2
1956	48.6	48.2	48.4	48.5	48.0	47.8	47.7	47.9	47.8	48.2	48.4	48.2	48.1
1957	47.7	47.6	47.8	47.6	47.8	48.1	47.9	48.0	47.2	46.7	46.1	45.5	47.3
1958	45.3	44.6	44.8	45.0	45.8	46.6	47.5	48.3	49.2	49.9	51.0	51.1	47.4
1959	51.9	52.5	53.5	53.8	54.2	53.6	53.1	52.3	52.6	52.4	52.1	53.2	52.9
1960	53.5	53.4	52.5	52.4	52.0	51.9	51.9	51.7	51.4	51.0	50.5	50.3	51.9
1961	50.7	50.9	51.8	52.5	53.1	53.8	54.1	54.9	54.7	55.5	56.2	56.5	53.7
1962	56.4	57.1	56.9	56.5	56.3	56.1	56.5	56.9	57.3	57.3	57.9	58.0	57.0
1963	58.3	58.6	58.9	59.4	60.1	60.1	60.2	60.5	60.9	61.2	61.2	61.7	60.1
1964	62.2	62.7	63.1	63.4	63.8	63.8	64.2	64.5	64.8	64.8	65.0	65.9	64.0
1965	66.8	67.4	67.5	67.5	67.9	67.9	68.1	68.1	68.5	69.1	69.7	70.3	68.2
1966	70.7	71.1	71.4	71.0	70.3	70.1	70.0	69.4	69.2	69.3	69.4	69.1	70.1
1967	69.6	68.9	68.9	69.0	69.5	70.4	70.8	71.8	72.1	72.2	73.1	73.5	70.8
1968	72.9	73.3	74.4	73.7	74.4	74.8	75.2	75.1	75.8	76.8	76.5	76.9	75.0
1969	77.3	77.6	77.0	77.5	77.4	76.9	76.6	76.5	76.6	76.0	75.1	74.6	76.6
1970	74.0	73.4	73.1	72.7	72.7	73.0	73.1	73.0	72.8	72.4	72.3	74.3	73.1
1971	76.2	76.2	76.7	77.2	77.7	78.2	78.5	78.5	78.8	79.3	79.9	80.8	78.2
1972	81.3	81.7	83.2	83.8	84.0	84.2	84.5	85.4	86.1	86.7	87.5	88.4	84.7
1973	90.0	90.4	90.4	89.3	90.1	89.4	89.3	89.0	88.9	89.4	89.8	88.1	89.5
1974	88.0	87.7	87.6	86.8	86.8	86.4	86.3	84.6	83.0	81.7	80.4	78.9	84.8
1975	77.6	77.2	77.1	79.3	80.7	82.6	85.0	86.2	86.5	86.9	87.4	88.7	82.9
1976	90.8	91.0	93.0	92.1	92.4	93.1	93.7	92.8	92.8	92.7	93.1	94.4	92.7
1977	95.0	96.0	97.4	97.1	98.3	99.0	98.9	100.0	99.5	99.2	99.8	99.8	98.3
1978	99.0	99.8	101.3	103.0	103.9	104.3	103.8	104.1	104.8	105.7	105.9	105.3	103.4
1979	105.3	105.8	106.7	104.7	105.3	104.8	104.0	103.6	103.9	102.5	101.7	101.8	104.2
1980	103.6	101.9	101.0	96.9	95.3	96.1	98.0	99.5	100.7	101.8	102.8	103.0	100.0
1981	103.6	104.0	104.2	105.0	104.5	104.1	104.6	105.1	103.5	101.5	101.0	99.7	103.4
1982	98.7	98.1	97.5	98.5	98.9	98.3	98.6	97.9	98.0	97.9	98.3	100.0	98.4

SIX MONTH SMOOTHED CHANGE IN LEADING INDEX, UNITED STATES (ANNUAL RATE, PERCENT)

YEAR	JAN	FEB	MAR	APR	MAY	JUN	JUL	AUG	SEP	OCT	NOV	DEC	AVGE
1949	-8.0	-9.3	-10.8	-12.4	-11.3	-9.3	-5.6	-1.0	3.0	1.7	3.9	7.3	-4.3
1950	10.6	12.9	14.5	17.2	19.6	20.6	25.2	29.3	24.0	21.2	18.4	15.2	19.1
1951	15.0	7.6	3.2	-2.1	-3.8	-7.8	-10.3	-10.9	-8.5	-7.2	-5.7	-4.1	-2.9
1952	-2.8	-0.6	0.1	-1.0	-1.1	1.8	0.3	3.1	7.6	5.8	6.1	6.9	2.2
1953	7.3	6.3	5.8	4.7	2.9	-0.1	-0.1	-3.3	-7.5	-8.2	-10.5	-8.5	-0.9
1954	-7.0	-4.4	-3.3	-0.3	2.0	4.8	6.6	7.9	10.2	12.4	15.0	16.3	5.0
1955	18.4	19.9	18.7	16.3	14.6	13.2	12.2	10.0	9.5	6.1	6.2	4.2	12.4
1956	1.5	-0.5	-0.4	0.0	-2.1	-3.1	-3.1	-2.3	-2.2	-0.4	0.4	0.0	-1.0
1957	-1.8	-1.7	-0.9	-1.3	-0.2	0.7	0.0	0.5	-2.7	-4.7	-6.2	-7.9	-2.2
1958	-7.7	-9.9	-8.1	-6.4	-2.6	1.3	5.6	9.2	12.9	14.9	18.4	16.7	3.7
1959	18.2	18.1	19.2	17.2	15.7	10.4	6.2	1.8	1.5	-0.3	-1.8	1.6	9.0
1960	1.9	1.3	-2.3	-2.3	-3.1	-2.9	-2.6	-2.9	-3.7	-4.8	-6.1	-6.3	-2.8
1961	-4.3	-2.6	1.3	4.1	6.4	8.4	8.9	11.1	9.4	11.3	12.6	11.7	6.5
1962	9.4	10.0	7.4	6.0	2.8	1.0	2.0	2.5	3.2	2.4	4.1	3.8	4.5
1963	4.4	4.7	5.5	6.5	8.0	7.0	6.3	6.0	6.3	6.5	5.4	5.9	6.0
1964	6.4	7.1	7.1	7.1	7.3	6.3	6.6	6.2	6.1	5.2	4.7	6.7	6.4
1965	8.2	8.8	8.0	6.8	6.9	5.8	5.4	4.4	4.7	5.4	6.1	6.6	6.4
1966	6.7	7.0	6.8	4.8	2.3	1.1	0.3	-1.6	-2.3	-2.4	-2.1	-2.8	1.5
1967	-1.2	-2.7	-2.4	-1.6	0.2	2.8	3.8	6.5	6.6	6.1	7.8	8.1	2.8
1968	5.5	5.8	7.6	4.5	5.4	5.2	5.4	4.2	5.3	7.0	5.2	5.5	5.5
1969	5.7	5.5	3.3	4.0	2.9	1.1	-0.2	-0.6	-0.8	-2.4	-4.2	-5.2	0.8
1970	-6.1	-6.9	-6.8	-7.1	-6.2	-4.6	-3.5	-3.1	-2.8	-3.1	-2.6	3.1	-4.1
1971	8.0	7.6	8.2	8.7	9.1	9.3	8.8	7.7	7.1	7.0	6.9	7.7	8.0
1972	7.5	7.3	10.0	9.9	9.2	8.3	7.7	8.7	8.8	8.7	9.1	9.5	8.7
1973	11.7	10.9	9.3	5.4	6.1	3.5	2.5	0.8	0.1	0.5	1.0	-2.9	4.1
1974	-3.1	-3.3	-3.2	-4.3	-3.8	-4.2	-3.8	-6.9	-9.4	-10.9	-12.4	-14.1	-6.6
1975	-15.1	-14.5	-13.0	-6.4	-2.1	3.5	9.9	13.0	13.4	13.6	13.7	15.4	2.6
1976	18.3	15.7	17.5	12.2	10.4	9.6	9.0	5.4	4.3	3.0	2.8	4.4	9.4
1977	4.8	6.1	8.0	8.0	8.0	8.5	7.2	8.5	6.2	4.5	3.4	3.5	6.4
1978	1.2	2.2	4.4	7.0	7.7	7.7	5.8	5.7	6.2	7.1	6.4	4.3	5.5
1979	3.4	3.3	4.0	-0.2	0.8	-0.7	-2.0	-2.8	-2.2	-4.5	-5.4	-4.7	-0.9
1980	-1.9	-3.7	-4.8	-11.0	-12.7	-10.0	-5.4	-1.8	1.1	3.6	5.6	5.7	-2.9
1981	6.7	7.5	7.5	8.5	6.2	3.9	3.6	3.6	-0.3	-4.2	-4.9	-7.0	-2.6
1982	-8.2	-8.6	-8.9	-6.1	-4.5	-4.8	-3.3	-3.8	-2.6	-1.8	-0.6	3.2	-4.2

UNITED STATES LEADING, COINCIDENT AND LAGGING INTERNATIONAL ECONOMIC INDICATORS

1.0 AVERAGE WORKWEEK, MANUFACTURING, UNITED STATES (HOURS PER WEEK)

YEAR	JAN	FEB	MAR	APR	MAY	JUN	JUL	AUG	SEP	OCT	NOV	DEC	AVGE
1948	40.4	40.2	40.4	40.4	40.2	40.2	40.1	40.0	39.6	39.7	39.7	39.5	40.0
1949	39.4	39.4	39.1	38.8	38.9	38.9	39.1	39.0	39.4	39.4	39.0	39.3	39.1
1950	39.6	39.7	39.7	40.1	40.9	40.5	40.8	41.1	40.8	40.9	40.9	40.8	40.4
1951	40.8	40.8	41.0	41.2	40.9	40.7	40.5	40.2	40.4	40.2	40.3	40.6	40.6
1952	40.7	40.7	40.6	40.1	40.4	40.5	40.1	40.5	41.0	41.1	41.0	41.1	40.6
1953	41.0	41.0	41.1	41.1	40.9	40.7	40.6	40.4	39.8	40.0	39.8	39.6	40.5
1954	39.5	39.7	39.5	39.4	39.5	39.6	39.6	39.7	39.5	39.6	40.1	40.0	39.6
1955	40.3	40.5	40.7	40.6	40.9	40.6	40.6	40.6	40.7	40.9	41.0	40.8	40.7
1956	40.8	40.6	40.4	40.6	40.2	40.1	40.2	40.2	40.4	40.5	40.4	40.5	40.4
1957	40.3	40.4	40.2	40.1	39.8	39.9	39.9	39.8	39.7	39.5	39.2	39.8	39.8
1958	38.8	38.6	38.7	38.6	38.8	39.0	39.2	39.4	39.6	39.5	39.8	39.8	39.1
1959	40.1	40.2	40.4	40.5	40.6	40.5	40.2	40.3	40.1	40.1	39.8	40.2	40.2
1960	40.5	40.1	39.9	39.7	40.0	39.8	39.8	39.7	39.4	39.6	39.2	38.4	39.7
1961	39.2	39.3	39.4	39.6	39.6	39.9	40.0	40.1	39.5	40.2	40.5	40.3	39.8
1962	40.0	40.3	40.5	40.7	40.5	40.4	40.4	40.3	40.5	40.2	40.3	40.2	40.4
1963	40.4	40.3	40.4	40.2	40.5	40.6	40.5	40.4	40.6	40.6	40.8	40.6	40.5
1964	40.1	40.6	40.6	40.8	40.7	40.7	40.8	40.9	40.5	40.6	40.8	41.1	40.7
1965	41.2	41.2	41.4	41.0	41.2	41.1	41.1	41.0	40.8	41.2	41.3	41.4	41.2
1966	41.4	41.6	41.5	41.5	41.4	41.4	41.2	41.4	41.3	41.3	41.2	40.9	41.3
1967	41.0	40.4	40.4	40.5	40.4	40.4	40.5	40.6	40.7	40.6	40.8	40.7	40.6
1968	40.3	40.4	40.7	40.7	40.9	40.9	40.8	40.7	40.9	40.9	40.8	40.7	40.7
1969	40.7	40.9	40.8	40.7	40.7	40.7	40.6	40.6	40.7	40.6	40.4	40.7	40.6
1970	40.4	40.2	40.1	39.9	39.8	39.9	40.0	39.8	39.3	39.5	39.5	39.5	39.8
1971	39.9	39.7	39.8	39.7	39.9	40.0	39.9	39.8	39.4	39.9	40.8	40.2	39.8
1972	40.2	40.4	40.8	40.9	40.5	40.6	40.5	40.6	40.6	40.7	40.8	40.5	40.5
1973	40.4	40.9	40.8	40.9	40.7	40.6	40.7	40.5	40.7	40.6	40.7	40.6	40.7
1974	40.5	40.4	40.4	39.3	40.3	40.2	40.2	40.2	40.0	40.0	39.5	39.3	40.0
1975	39.2	38.9	38.8	39.2	39.0	39.2	39.4	39.7	39.9	39.8	39.9	40.2	39.4
1976	40.5	40.3	40.2	39.6	40.3	40.5	40.3	40.1	39.8	40.0	40.1	40.0	40.1
1977	39.7	40.3	40.2	40.4	40.4	40.5	40.3	40.4	40.4	40.5	40.4	40.4	40.3
1978	39.7	39.9	40.4	40.8	40.4	40.5	40.6	40.5	40.5	40.5	40.6	40.6	40.4
1979	40.7	40.5	40.5	39.2	40.2	40.2	40.3	40.1	40.2	40.1	40.0	40.1	40.2
1980	40.3	40.0	39.8	39.3	39.4	39.2	39.2	39.4	39.6	39.6	39.8	40.0	39.7
1981	40.4	39.7	39.9	40.1	40.2	40.1	40.0	39.9	39.4	39.5	39.3	39.1	39.8
1982	39.2	39.4	39.0	39.0	39.1	39.2	39.2	39.0	38.8	38.8	38.9	38.9	39.0

2.0 INITIAL CLAIMS, UNEMPLOYMENT INSURANCE, UNITED STATES (THOUSANDS PER WEEK)

YEAR	JAN	FEB	MAR	APR	MAY	JUN	JUL	AUG	SEP	OCT	NOV	DEC	AVGE
1948	166.	206.	201.	210.	239.	219.	194.	202.	218.	203.	211.	234.	209.
1949	285.	305.	333.	379.	377.	359.	340.	385.	320.	386.	344.	298.	343.
1950	294.	288.	276.	263.	250.	252.	223.	170.	182.	194.	200.	197.	232.
1951	174.	181.	166.	199.	199.	209.	236.	254.	242.	234.	210.	213.	210.
1952	221.	201.	209.	219.	213.	242.	315.	207.	168.	175.	169.	190.	211.
1953	175.	177.	188.	179.	198.	195.	207.	229.	238.	251.	298.	280.	218.
1954	303.	318.	320.	313.	313.	314.	294.	319.	322.	315.	276.	253.	305.
1955	256.	240.	228.	228.	222.	222.	223.	233.	204.	224.	215.	214.	226.
1956	218.	226.	221.	223.	236.	227.	245.	224.	236.	214.	223.	230.	227.
1957	242.	225.	219.	239.	244.	246.	267.	235.	305.	302.	320.	355.	267.
1958	354.	407.	436.	438.	400.	410.	350.	363.	338.	314.	311.	320.	370.
1959	292.	284.	258.	244.	246.	258.	264.	291.	271.	311.	351.	275.	279.
1960	281.	271.	303.	294.	316.	322.	335.	363.	351.	373.	385.	381.	331.
1961	393.	429.	379.	381.	358.	334.	348.	316.	329.	304.	305.	296.	348.
1962	301.	295.	287.	283.	301.	304.	303.	305.	300.	304.	299.	310.	299.
1963	310.	301.	288.	293.	288.	284.	282.	290.	285.	282.	276.	301.	290.
1964	283.	270.	277.	265.	262.	257.	260.	244.	245.	249.	262.	251.	260.
1965	243.	248.	237.	237.	224.	224.	231.	248.	218.	209.	212.	206.	228.
1966	222.	219.	182.	179.	192.	194.	199.	195.	197.	203.	208.	219.	201.
1967	196.	231.	256.	259.	236.	231.	231.	212.	217.	220.	209.	204.	225.
1968	206.	196.	194.	193.	195.	194.	192.	199.	194.	188.	190.	190.	194.
1969	179.	186.	185.	181.	182.	197.	195.	196.	195.	202.	211.	210.	193.
1970	240.	256.	262.	326.	302.	291.	273.	287.	319.	329.	322.	299.	292.
1971	292.	286.	294.	281.	290.	289.	285.	325.	307.	294.	283.	265.	291.
1972	264.	262.	258.	260.	262.	286.	272.	246.	245.	250.	241.	236.	257.
1973	226.	223.	227.	238.	234.	233.	232.	247.	241.	244.	251.	284.	240.
1974	294.	315.	302.	289.	294.	314.	294.	350.	374.	419.	473.	494.	351.
1975	522.	532.	536.	521.	496.	491.	442.	449.	447.	420.	393.	364.	468.
1976	360.	340.	358.	371.	392.	394.	393.	389.	410.	409.	390.	361.	381.
1977	394.	427.	346.	371.	378.	358.	370.	368.	363.	357.	347.	342.	368.
1978	343.	381.	335.	322.	324.	331.	347.	339.	321.	326.	340.	347.	338.
1979	353.	352.	346.	411.	341.	358.	377.	383.	378.	400.	420.	428.	379.
1980	416.	397.	438.	532.	616.	581.	510.	495.	488.	447.	422.	420.	480.
1981	424.	410.	413.	395.	401.	405.	395.	421.	483.	517.	539.	551.	446.
1982	563.	514.	566.	566.	585.	551.	515.	597.	671.	670.	615.	538.	579.

137

3.0 NEW ORDERS, CONSUMER GOODS AND MATERIALS, IN CONSTANT PRICES, UNITED STATES (BILLION 1972 DOLLARS)

YEAR	JAN	FEB	MAR	APR	MAY	JUN	JUL	AUG	SEP	OCT	NOV	DEC	AVGE
1948	12.33	12.22	12.87	12.52	12.90	13.88	13.65	13.46	12.71	12.30	11.91	11.40	12.68
1949	11.01	10.66	10.44	9.98	10.03	9.57	10.24	11.86	11.96	11.17	11.66	11.45	10.84
1950	12.34	12.39	12.31	12.88	14.37	14.49	18.05	20.21	15.96	16.11	14.68	15.55	14.94
1951	20.27	18.13	18.62	16.95	16.28	15.76	15.67	14.31	13.73	15.21	14.66	14.19	16.15
1952	14.43	14.52	16.22	16.74	14.74	17.12	16.09	15.71	16.58	15.72	15.78	17.05	15.89
1953	18.53	17.75	18.00	18.62	18.13	17.80	17.62	15.39	13.77	13.32	13.56	13.68	16.35
1954	13.67	14.39	14.44	14.50	14.50	15.24	14.57	15.00	15.78	15.97	16.92	18.14	15.26
1955	19.03	18.88	20.21	19.67	19.52	19.91	20.28	19.67	19.35	19.13	19.85	19.46	19.58
1956	18.88	18.33	18.21	18.48	17.90	17.48	17.59	17.84	17.38	17.95	18.02	18.19	18.02
1957	17.78	18.52	18.14	17.56	17.48	17.63	16.93	17.13	17.19	16.46	15.81	14.91	17.13
1958	15.68	14.91	14.69	14.60	15.06	15.96	16.42	16.79	17.26	17.21	18.11	18.05	16.23
1959	18.94	20.79	20.17	19.70	19.09	19.24	18.91	17.84	18.60	17.97	17.44	18.79	18.96
1960	18.61	18.68	17.61	17.52	17.62	17.91	18.06	18.03	18.30	17.66	17.44	17.37	17.90
1961	16.74	16.80	17.82	18.23	18.75	19.28	18.62	19.40	19.22	19.29	20.32	20.97	18.79
1962	20.61	20.46	20.08	18.98	19.76	19.36	20.01	20.22	20.42	20.58	20.55	20.12	20.10
1963	20.72	21.60	21.73	21.99	21.54	20.99	21.80	21.13	21.28	22.09	22.06	22.07	21.58
1964	22.88	22.62	22.44	23.27	22.97	23.06	23.94	23.20	24.40	23.03	23.74	24.84	23.37
1965	25.21	25.44	25.50	25.07	25.19	25.39	26.01	25.48	25.21	25.66	26.74	27.38	25.69
1966	27.07	27.56	28.60	27.61	27.41	27.59	27.08	27.18	27.09	27.36	26.83	26.55	27.33
1967	26.50	26.27	26.02	26.22	26.45	26.75	26.76	27.96	26.81	26.40	27.54	29.46	26.93
1968	28.59	28.55	28.53	28.04	28.64	28.72	28.22	27.53	29.38	29.97	30.46	29.73	28.86
1969	30.20	30.06	30.02	29.87	29.55	29.73	30.36	29.66	30.18	30.28	29.30	29.02	29.85
1970	28.18	27.60	27.46	27.35	27.60	28.20	27.30	27.02	27.40	25.51	25.52	27.99	27.26
1971	29.16	28.87	28.06	28.26	27.96	27.72	28.52	28.21	28.32	28.70	29.55	29.82	28.60
1972	30.62	31.13	30.97	31.05	31.26	31.89	31.62	32.76	33.32	33.70	34.55	35.06	32.33
1973	36.56	36.90	37.21	36.00	36.34	36.09	35.89	35.75	35.69	36.24	36.83	34.71	36.18
1974	35.34	34.83	34.27	34.20	35.30	34.98	33.94	33.30	32.11	31.15	30.06	26.86	33.03
1975	26.88	26.75	25.84	27.17	27.48	27.94	29.60	29.58	29.94	30.16	30.01	30.18	28.46
1976	30.97	31.66	32.35	32.38	32.84	33.04	33.29	32.71	32.37	31.75	33.47	34.41	32.60
1977	34.78	35.05	36.27	35.73	35.78	36.39	35.89	36.40	36.52	36.17	36.71	37.30	36.08
1978	36.04	36.92	37.28	39.04	38.64	38.25	37.85	38.76	38.22	38.93	39.19	39.68	38.23
1979	39.71	38.94	39.28	37.83	38.88	38.12	37.03	36.82	36.79	36.15	35.57	35.03	37.51
1980	36.64	36.35	33.85	31.20	30.27	30.17	31.99	32.37	33.78	34.80	34.49	33.98	33.32
1981	33.08	34.36	33.88	34.54	35.07	35.01	34.66	33.11	32.83	30.75	30.05	30.05	33.12
1982	28.82	29.24	30.23	29.10	30.53	30.07	30.74	29.68	29.67	27.71	28.11	28.21	29.34

4.0 NET BUSINESS FORMATION, UNITED STATES (INDEX, 1967=100)

YEAR	JAN	FEB	MAR	APR	MAY	JUN	JUL	AUG	SEP	OCT	NOV	DEC	AVGE
1948	112.6	107.9	105.1	105.4	104.8	103.8	101.0	98.6	97.3	97.5	93.9	95.3	101.9
1949	91.6	89.0	86.9	86.0	84.6	84.2	82.8	83.9	85.5	85.9	87.2	89.4	86.4
1950	87.3	89.9	90.8	93.1	91.3	92.9	92.1	91.1	89.3	89.6	90.1	89.4	90.6
1951	89.3	89.7	90.1	88.8	88.6	88.7	88.9	88.9	89.6	90.1	91.2	90.4	89.5
1952	91.4	92.2	93.1	91.3	93.0	93.6	92.3	94.6	95.0	94.5	94.0	94.2	93.3
1953	95.1	94.2	93.7	93.1	92.3	91.6	91.5	91.8	89.4	89.9	88.6	89.5	91.7
1954	88.6	88.0	87.8	89.1	89.7	90.1	90.8	91.2	92.3	94.2	95.1	95.1	91.0
1955	97.7	98.5	98.6	98.2	98.1	99.4	98.9	98.5	98.6	97.8	98.2	98.2	98.4
1956	97.7	98.5	97.5	98.2	98.7	96.9	96.3	95.4	95.2	96.4	94.6	94.2	96.6
1957	93.5	93.5	93.8	93.6	92.6	93.6	93.2	92.6	91.7	91.3	90.4	89.2	92.4
1958	88.3	88.5	88.3	88.2	90.0	91.8	92.3	94.1	95.3	95.2	96.1	96.6	92.2
1959	98.3	98.6	100.1	99.8	100.0	98.4	98.4	98.5	97.8	97.4	98.7	98.8	98.7
1960	99.6	98.3	97.3	97.4	96.1	96.1	96.0	94.6	94.1	93.9	91.7	90.9	95.5
1961	88.9	90.8	91.4	92.4	92.3	92.8	93.2	91.7	91.8	92.8	93.8	93.8	92.1
1962	93.2	94.0	94.5	94.0	93.7	93.1	93.3	93.6	94.4	94.1	93.3	93.1	93.7
1963	94.0	94.8	95.2	94.1	94.5	95.2	95.2	96.0	95.8	96.1	95.4	96.0	95.2
1964	96.8	97.8	97.4	98.2	99.7	97.8	97.8	98.2	100.2	100.8	98.9	100.2	98.6
1965	100.4	100.8	100.0	99.2	99.4	100.5	100.5	100.1	99.9	99.5	100.6	100.9	100.1
1966	102.0	102.8	102.0	100.6	99.9	99.8	99.3	98.2	97.4	98.2	95.4	96.1	99.4
1967	97.0	96.7	97.4	96.9	98.2	100.0	100.4	102.3	101.7	101.6	103.8	103.8	100.0
1968	104.1	104.8	105.2	103.2	102.1	103.7	106.2	107.7	109.0	112.8	110.5	112.7	106.8
1969	112.9	113.7	112.8	113.7	113.6	113.3	113.2	112.6	111.5	113.5	111.5	112.8	112.9
1970	112.1	111.5	109.0	108.2	106.1	104.9	104.0	103.4	103.9	104.3	105.3	104.4	106.4
1971	104.5	103.7	106.0	106.3	107.7	109.9	110.4	109.9	109.0	110.6	111.4	112.3	108.5
1972	113.5	113.2	114.2	115.4	114.6	114.6	115.8	116.1	117.7	118.9	118.5	118.1	115.9
1973	116.1	117.1	117.7	116.0	115.9	115.5	115.4	114.7	112.4	112.2	114.1	110.7	114.9
1974	109.5	110.0	109.9	112.7	112.6	113.4	114.5	112.7	108.5	103.0	101.7	101.8	109.2
1975	99.7	99.4	100.2	101.3	103.3	108.7	112.3	111.4	111.2	110.5	111.1	114.3	106.9
1976	114.2	114.1	114.3	114.5	113.3	116.1	115.7	113.9	115.5	117.2	119.7	119.0	115.6
1977	120.1	120.7	122.1	120.2	120.8	123.5	122.8	125.3	124.0	126.4	126.2	126.3	123.2
1978	125.2	127.3	128.5	128.5	127.7	129.3	129.3	127.3	127.6	130.3	129.9	127.5	128.2
1979	128.3	128.1	129.1	127.9	129.1	126.7	128.4	127.9	130.0	127.0	127.9	129.7	128.3
1980	128.1	127.9	124.6	121.9	121.1	118.9	119.1	120.6	121.1	121.6	121.1	122.7	122.4
1981	121.6	120.7	120.8	121.9	119.1	117.3	118.2	118.7	117.6	114.8	117.4	115.2	118.6
1982	113.2	115.6	113.5	115.6	115.2	113.1	112.7	112.1	110.5	111.6	113.0	111.1	113.1

5.0 CONTRACTS AND ORDERS, PLANT AND EQUIPMENT, IN CONSTANT PRICES, UNITED STATES (BILLION 1972 DOLLARS)

YEAR	JAN	FEB	MAR	APR	MAY	JUN	JUL	AUG	SEP	OCT	NOV	DEC	AVGE
1948	3.17	3.64	3.47	3.84	3.30	3.80	3.42	3.19	3.13	3.17	3.11	3.09	3.36
1949	2.54	2.76	2.73	2.35	2.43	2.68	2.46	2.67	2.93	2.83	3.19	2.89	2.70
1950	3.16	3.14	3.42	3.41	4.20	4.05	4.85	5.98	5.55	4.92	4.90	5.21	4.40
1951	5.85	5.97	5.40	5.42	7.52	5.02	4.79	4.61	3.97	4.41	4.42	4.77	5.18
1952	4.22	4.28	4.34	4.30	4.01	4.53	4.65	4.18	5.71	4.23	3.99	4.80	4.44
1953	4.78	4.87	4.42	4.80	4.59	3.54	4.38	3.64	4.21	4.49	3.84	3.49	4.25
1954	3.60	3.66	3.12	3.19	3.27	3.36	3.51	3.52	3.78	4.00	3.69	3.92	3.55
1955	4.07	4.41	5.09	4.76	4.52	4.78	4.73	4.98	5.22	4.96	5.34	5.29	4.85
1956	5.11	4.95	4.94	5.08	5.26	5.32	5.06	4.98	4.78	4.76	5.35	5.04	5.05
1957	5.14	4.96	4.92	4.37	4.57	4.34	4.22	4.30	3.85	3.95	3.94	3.75	4.36
1958	3.81	3.67	3.65	3.68	3.72	3.92	3.76	4.33	4.31	4.18	4.07	3.94	3.92
1959	4.19	4.31	5.08	4.55	4.66	4.75	4.84	4.29	4.87	4.70	4.42	4.66	4.61
1960	4.37	4.47	4.35	4.72	4.72	4.56	4.60	4.59	4.66	4.52	4.33	4.71	4.55
1961	4.74	4.59	4.33	4.40	4.34	4.59	4.67	4.92	4.59	4.70	5.02	4.60	4.62
1962	4.85	5.30	4.94	5.15	4.94	4.84	4.90	4.92	4.87	4.97	5.34	5.52	5.04
1963	5.06	5.21	5.16	5.30	5.86	5.32	5.25	5.40	5.56	5.68	6.05	6.10	5.50
1964	6.22	5.61	5.83	5.89	6.34	6.52	6.12	6.18	6.26	6.31	6.76	6.85	6.24
1965	6.40	6.46	6.81	6.86	6.78	6.60	6.83	6.56	7.12	7.12	6.99	7.46	6.83
1966	7.49	8.04	7.83	8.14	7.98	7.78	8.31	7.77	8.51	7.66	7.58	7.54	7.89
1967	6.51	6.99	7.15	6.97	7.18	7.46	7.34	7.59	7.40	7.50	7.49	7.65	7.27
1968	9.17	9.24	11.34	9.29	8.63	8.52	9.73	9.89	9.07	10.81	9.22	10.12	9.59
1969	10.46	10.69	9.93	11.25	10.68	10.02	9.95	9.82	11.04	9.85	9.74	9.88	10.28
1970	10.14	9.71	9.15	8.70	8.72	8.39	8.68	8.22	8.42	7.40	8.50	9.29	8.78
1971	8.58	9.28	9.27	9.20	8.90	9.99	8.22	9.05	9.59	8.66	9.43	9.70	9.16
1972	8.86	9.34	10.04	9.89	10.86	9.41	10.47	9.67	10.98	10.57	10.84	11.00	10.16
1973	11.10	11.72	11.69	11.72	12.38	12.27	12.55	12.59	12.48	13.68	13.76	13.05	12.42
1974	12.84	13.07	13.12	12.45	13.27	12.08	13.82	12.36	12.49	11.73	10.55	11.23	12.42
1975	10.13	9.39	9.03	10.23	10.64	10.46	9.77	10.78	9.25	9.16	9.27	8.78	9.74
1976	10.48	10.30	10.58	10.77	9.77	11.26	12.13	10.84	11.56	11.84	11.25	11.43	11.02
1977	11.45	11.34	10.96	11.85	12.92	12.61	11.27	12.69	13.36	12.15	12.26	13.54	12.20
1978	12.98	14.31	13.18	13.12	14.57	13.32	14.30	15.03	15.40	17.29	15.30	13.75	14.38
1979	15.36	16.15	18.70	16.01	14.32	15.21	14.90	14.19	14.74	14.85	16.07	15.59	15.51
1980	16.20	13.68	14.00	13.89	12.64	13.96	15.20	14.04	14.41	13.94	14.32	15.66	14.33
1981	14.91	12.76	12.20	15.03	14.29	14.02	13.65	14.30	14.29	13.58	14.31	13.91	13.94
1982	13.40	12.05	13.03	13.76	11.56	11.08	10.96	11.30	12.25	11.99	11.40	13.00	12.15

6.0 NEW BUILDING PERMITS, PRIVATE HOUSING UNITS, UNITED STATES (INDEX, 1967=100)

YEAR	JAN	FEB	MAR	APR	MAY	JUN	JUL	AUG	SEP	OCT	NOV	DEC	AVGE
1948	109.4	100.4	104.0	116.5	106.7	103.1	102.2	94.8	84.8	89.4	86.2	82.8	98.4
1949	80.4	81.9	86.8	96.6	104.2	106.4	110.2	112.3	136.2	135.6	141.9	146.6	111.6
1950	157.4	159.2	159.1	161.9	161.3	160.7	182.8	158.2	133.7	126.2	123.6	158.6	153.6
1951	146.3	114.8	104.5	96.9	99.3	96.9	92.9	94.8	122.2	93.2	90.9	94.1	103.9
1952	99.6	115.3	105.5	103.5	101.2	101.6	107.9	107.6	115.5	116.8	117.2	108.3	108.3
1953	104.9	110.7	111.6	106.2	106.4	103.5	99.9	98.4	94.6	99.6	100.1	102.4	103.2
1954	101.9	100.4	105.8	106.9	108.8	116.9	119.9	118.9	121.9	126.2	135.9	132.1	116.3
1955	136.4	151.0	129.3	132.9	133.6	126.2	126.7	122.2	120.4	117.9	107.5	107.0	125.9
1956	109.8	106.8	109.8	109.5	101.9	100.1	99.4	97.0	94.5	93.1	93.7	92.8	100.7
1957	86.5	90.9	91.7	86.7	90.5	92.5	86.2	92.1	92.4	91.1	88.5	89.3	89.9
1958	91.5	78.7	87.2	91.9	96.2	102.7	111.9	111.7	114.5	118.2	134.1	115.8	104.5
1959	114.7	119.6	125.0	119.4	117.4	115.5	112.6	113.7	109.5	105.3	100.7	108.2	113.5
1960	102.7	102.3	89.8	95.6	98.9	90.1	93.9	93.5	92.6	91.4	92.1	89.3	94.3
1961	91.2	90.4	94.0	94.2	96.6	100.6	101.9	109.0	103.2	105.6	108.3	109.2	100.3
1962	105.5	112.3	106.7	116.2	107.4	108.5	111.9	112.8	114.9	111.1	116.2	116.2	111.6
1963	113.0	109.7	113.9	116.6	122.2	121.8	119.6	118.6	127.9	128.1	122.9	128.8	120.3
1964	117.4	130.6	118.8	114.5	117.6	115.8	118.1	118.3	114.5	111.5	113.5	105.3	116.3
1965	114.5	107.3	109.6	105.2	109.3	112.4	112.0	113.1	111.1	111.8	118.3	119.1	112.3
1966	120.0	104.9	111.8	103.7	97.7	86.6	84.4	79.4	70.2	66.9	66.6	67.2	88.3
1967	87.2	79.5	83.7	90.8	94.3	102.5	103.2	107.8	112.1	112.2	113.7	115.3	100.0
1968	103.3	117.6	120.0	112.8	113.7	114.0	117.9	118.9	128.4	124.6	125.8	121.8	118.2
1969	127.9	131.0	126.0	126.3	116.5	118.3	112.0	115.4	110.7	106.6	104.4	101.3	118.4
1970	93.1	98.0	99.2	107.3	116.5	115.8	116.1	122.2	125.0	137.2	131.7	154.8	118.1
1971	144.0	139.2	154.2	153.0	172.9	166.8	181.3	175.7	175.0	177.5	182.2	186.9	167.4
1972	192.9	186.9	181.4	184.3	178.1	188.1	189.2	195.1	206.2	202.9	192.6	208.5	192.2
1973	195.7	191.8	177.7	164.5	166.4	176.7	156.8	155.9	146.8	121.6	120.8	111.0	157.1
1974	114.7	117.2	124.1	108.1	98.1	93.6	86.3	79.0	72.4	71.0	67.4	74.9	92.2
1975	62.6	62.8	61.1	74.6	78.8	81.5	87.9	85.7	91.7	94.4	95.6	94.0	80.9
1976	103.0	102.6	100.3	97.6	102.9	102.4	107.3	112.8	127.6	122.8	132.0	130.2	111.8
1977	124.6	134.5	143.1	143.1	143.8	151.0	145.4	153.4	144.3	151.5	152.7	151.2	144.9
1978	140.5	140.2	145.3	157.4	142.6	160.2	144.3	136.6	141.4	143.9	145.0	146.8	145.3
1979	118.0	120.5	138.9	129.0	136.0	132.5	123.9	128.5	132.3	119.6	103.1	101.3	123.6
1980	103.4	96.8	79.8	65.3	69.5	90.3	101.7	110.4	120.0	110.3	111.7	100.9	96.7
1981	99.8	96.6	94.7	95.8	95.2	79.6	76.0	70.9	67.4	59.6	60.0	64.4	80.0
1982	64.9	64.0	68.7	71.0	76.3	75.0	85.8	71.7	81.0	94.7	96.3	105.4	79.6

7.0 CHANGE IN BUSINESS INVENTORIES, IN CONSTANT PRICES, UNITED STATES (ANNUAL RATE, BILLION 1972 DOLLARS)

YEAR	IQ	IIQ	IIIQ	IVQ	AVGE
1948	4.1	5.6	6.9	5.3	5.5
1949	-0.3	-7.1	-2.5	-7.7	-4.4
1950	4.4	7.7	8.0	22.1	10.5
1951	13.4	19.9	14.6	7.0	13.7
1952	7.3	-2.7	5.4	7.2	4.3
1953	3.9	5.1	1.9	-5.0	1.5
1954	-3.4	-4.1	-2.7	1.5	-2.2
1955	5.9	8.0	7.8	9.2	7.7
1956	7.5	5.5	4.9	5.4	5.8
1957	2.5	2.9	3.7	-3.0	1.5
1958	-6.8	-6.2	0.3	5.3	-1.8
1959	5.5	12.6	1.4	8.7	7.0
1960	12.7	3.3	3.4	-5.3	3.5
1961	-4.1	1.8	6.5	7.7	3.0
1962	10.4	8.1	7.5	5.3	7.8
1963	7.4	7.9	8.0	6.7	7.5
1964	6.9	7.4	5.5	8.6	7.1
1965	14.8	11.3	11.0	10.0	11.8
1966	15.6	17.1	13.6	20.8	16.8
1967	14.5	7.3	11.8	15.2	12.2
1968	5.4	12.2	9.8	8.6	9.0
1969	11.7	11.8	13.7	7.0	11.0
1970	2.1	5.0	6.5	1.4	3.8
1971	11.2	10.4	7.0	3.6	8.0
1972	6.3	12.1	12.8	9.7	10.2
1973	16.0	15.2	13.8	23.7	17.2
1974	13.2	12.6	7.7	12.9	11.6
1975	-14.3	-11.3	1.0	-2.3	-6.7
1976	10.0	11.3	7.3	2.4	7.7
1977	10.5	13.8	18.7	10.1	13.3
1978	17.3	18.4	13.3	15.2	16.0
1979	12.9	13.7	4.8	-2.3	7.3
1980	-2.6	-2.5	-8.5	-6.2	-4.9
1981	2.4	12.1	16.5	4.8	8.9
1982	-15.4	-4.4	3.4	-17.7	-8.5

8.0 INDUSTRIAL MATERIALS PRICE INDEX, SIX MONTH SMOOTHED CHANGE, UNITED STATES
(ANNUAL RATE, PERCENT)

YEAR	JAN	FEB	MAR	APR	MAY	JUN	JUL	AUG	SEP	OCT	NOV	DEC	AVGE
1948	18.9	8.4	-0.6	2.3	0.8	1.8	-0.2	-0.5	-3.7	-7.5	-2.0	-4.2	1.1
1949	-7.2	-14.8	-25.3	-37.6	-36.7	-38.0	-32.9	-22.2	-16.5	-19.9	-11.9	-9.8	-22.7
1950	-3.6	-1.6	0.6	4.2	12.4	18.5	39.8	69.1	96.5	95.8	104.5	98.5	44.6
1951	99.3	83.1	57.7	41.1	26.8	8.1	-18.1	-25.4	-27.4	-23.7	-24.8	-23.1	14.5
1952	-23.9	-28.2	-29.7	-29.6	-27.3	-26.4	-24.1	-22.0	-18.9	-20.8	-17.7	-15.9	-23.7
1953	-16.7	-14.4	-10.0	-15.7	-14.7	-13.5	-12.8	-12.0	-13.8	-16.8	-10.6	-8.9	-13.3
1954	-9.3	-8.9	-4.8	3.7	5.8	7.5	5.0	4.3	6.9	9.6	9.1	7.6	3.0
1955	11.3	12.9	6.8	8.3	4.7	6.5	12.6	13.7	14.2	10.7	11.8	15.9	10.8
1956	11.2	6.4	5.8	5.2	-2.6	-8.3	-7.6	-2.4	0.9	-0.5	4.4	4.4	1.4
1957	-0.5	-5.7	-5.6	-6.5	-7.0	-5.7	-6.4	-7.4	-11.9	-15.7	-17.4	-16.3	-8.8
1958	-15.8	-13.3	-13.1	-15.4	-12.8	-8.2	-1.4	3.5	4.6	11.0	15.9	11.5	-2.8
1959	8.9	7.6	9.8	10.2	9.7	8.3	6.5	6.0	7.6	7.5	6.5	3.8	7.7
1960	4.7	1.3	-2.8	-0.4	-0.2	-2.9	4.6	-3.7	-4.9	-7.1	-4.0	-10.3	-3.3
1961	-8.2	-3.6	-4.2	6.2	6.4	0.2	1.7	4.1	3.9	2.5	-4.0	-0.4	1.1
1962	2.5	-0.9	-3.4	-4.7	-7.6	-9.3	-9.9	-9.6	-8.2	-6.7	-3.5	-1.6	-5.2
1963	1.2	-0.4	-2.8	-0.6	1.2	-4.6	-8.3	-5.4	-6.8	-2.6	-1.0	-2.0	-2.7
1964	1.8	1.4	2.5	7.9	6.2	7.5	9.4	11.6	10.0	14.4	15.7	12.2	8.4
1965	8.1	5.8	3.6	5.9	7.5	2.3	-0.4	-0.4	-5.3	-6.2	-6.0	-3.7	0.9
1966	1.5	5.1	5.9	0.2	-3.3	-3.2	-1.3	-8.3	-13.2	-15.5	-14.7	-14.1	-5.1
1967	-12.7	-12.7	-11.9	-12.8	-10.5	-6.3	-6.1	-6.8	-5.2	-7.5	-5.1	-1.3	-8.2
1968	0.9	0.9	-0.4	-1.3	-1.1	0.7	-1.7	-1.3	0.0	2.4	5.0	7.9	1.0
1969	11.7	13.9	14.7	15.5	18.7	18.1	16.5	22.3	23.6	14.5	8.5	7.0	15.4
1970	14.6	21.9	14.8	8.7	3.6	2.9	-3.2	-4.7	-4.2	-6.0	-11.8	-14.0	1.9
1971	-11.3	-10.9	-12.6	-8.3	-5.9	-9.2	-11.1	-8.8	-3.8	-0.6	0.0	-1.4	-7.0
1972	8.0	10.4	13.5	19.8	22.4	21.9	19.4	19.5	15.5	21.7	23.3	24.8	18.3
1973	34.1	43.5	58.4	40.2	63.1	47.9	50.7	60.0	47.9	45.1	47.4	58.1	49.7
1974	61.2	68.9	57.5	47.9	21.3	22.3	23.7	7.0	1.6	-5.4	-19.8	-31.0	21.3
1975	-34.7	-32.3	-29.0	-22.2	-18.9	-22.8	-20.4	-7.6	3.1	-1.0	0.4	4.7	-15.1
1976	11.8	15.7	23.4	26.1	29.1	31.7	38.9	23.4	12.7	7.6	4.0	0.4	18.7
1977	-0.6	2.2	6.7	6.2	0.1	-8.7	-10.2	-12.1	-12.1	-13.4	-13.4	-7.3	-5.2
1978	2.0	4.5	5.3	8.1	7.8	11.1	13.6	15.9	15.7	23.7	29.1	24.7	13.5
1979	25.0	37.3	53.5	44.4	31.8	32.2	19.1	12.2	8.4	6.9	3.4	6.5	23.4
1980	11.3	16.2	11.4	1.8	-7.7	-16.7	-8.3	0.5	8.3	11.0	12.5	-0.8	3.3
1981	-6.0	-8.8	-4.6	-3.4	-7.5	-11.8	-13.1	-11.3	-14.5	-19.3	-21.8	-18.9	-11.7
1982	-13.8	-14.1	-17.9	-19.0	-18.9	-23.0	-19.5	-20.7	-18.8	-18.9	-19.5	-15.2	-18.3

9.0 STOCK PRICE INDEX, S&P 500 COMMON, UNITED STATES (1941-43=10)

YEAR	JAN	FEB	MAR	APR	MAY	JUN	JUL	AUG	SEP	OCT	NOV	DEC	AVGE
1948	14.8	14.1	14.3	15.4	16.1	16.8	16.4	15.9	15.8	16.2	15.3	15.2	15.5
1949	15.4	14.8	14.9	14.9	14.8	14.0	14.8	15.3	15.5	15.9	16.1	16.5	15.2
1950	16.9	17.2	17.4	17.8	18.4	18.7	17.4	18.4	19.1	19.9	19.8	19.8	18.4
1951	21.2	22.0	21.6	21.9	21.9	21.6	21.9	22.9	23.5	23.4	22.7	23.4	22.3
1952	24.2	23.8	23.8	23.7	23.7	24.4	25.1	25.2	24.8	24.3	25.0	26.0	24.5
1953	26.2	25.9	26.0	24.7	24.8	23.9	24.3	24.4	23.3	24.0	24.5	24.8	24.7
1954	25.5	26.0	26.6	27.6	28.7	29.0	30.1	30.7	31.4	32.2	33.4	35.0	29.7
1955	35.6	36.8	36.5	37.8	37.6	39.8	42.7	42.4	44.3	42.1	44.9	45.4	40.5
1956	44.1	44.4	47.5	48.1	46.5	46.3	48.8	48.5	46.8	46.2	45.8	46.4	46.6
1957	45.4	43.5	44.0	45.1	46.8	47.6	48.5	45.8	44.0	41.2	40.4	40.3	44.4
1958	41.1	41.3	42.1	42.3	43.7	44.8	46.0	47.7	49.0	50.9	52.5	53.5	46.2
1959	55.6	54.8	56.1	57.1	58.0	57.3	59.7	59.4	57.1	57.0	57.2	59.1	57.4
1960	58.0	55.8	55.0	55.7	55.2	57.3	55.8	56.5	54.8	53.7	55.5	56.8	55.8
1961	59.7	62.2	64.1	65.8	66.5	65.6	65.4	67.8	67.3	68.0	71.1	71.7	66.3
1962	69.1	70.2	70.3	68.1	63.0	55.6	57.0	58.5	58.0	56.2	60.0	62.6	62.4
1963	65.1	65.9	65.7	68.8	70.1	70.1	69.1	71.0	72.9	73.0	72.6	74.2	69.9
1964	76.4	77.4	78.8	79.9	80.7	80.2	83.2	82.0	83.4	84.9	85.4	84.0	81.4
1965	86.1	86.8	86.8	88.0	89.3	85.0	84.9	86.5	89.4	91.4	92.1	91.7	88.2
1966	93.3	92.7	88.9	91.6	86.8	86.1	85.8	80.6	77.8	77.1	81.0	81.3	85.3
1967	84.4	87.4	89.4	91.0	92.6	91.4	93.0	94.5	95.8	95.7	92.7	95.3	91.9
1968	95.0	90.8	89.1	95.7	97.9	100.5	100.3	98.1	101.3	103.8	105.4	106.5	98.7
1969	102.0	101.5	99.3	101.3	104.6	99.1	94.7	94.2	94.5	95.5	96.2	91.1	97.8
1970	90.3	87.2	88.6	85.9	76.1	75.6	75.7	77.9	82.6	84.4	84.3	90.1	83.2
1971	93.5	97.1	99.6	103.0	101.6	99.7	99.0	97.2	99.4	97.3	92.8	99.2	98.3
1972	103.3	105.2	107.7	108.8	107.6	108.0	107.2	111.0	109.4	109.6	115.1	117.5	109.2
1973	118.4	114.2	112.4	110.3	107.2	104.8	105.8	103.8	105.6	109.8	102.0	94.8	107.4
1974	96.1	93.4	97.4	92.5	89.7	89.8	82.8	76.0	68.1	69.4	71.7	67.1	82.8
1975	72.6	80.1	83.8	84.7	90.1	92.4	92.5	85.7	84.7	88.6	90.1	88.7	86.2
1976	96.9	100.6	101.1	101.9	101.2	101.8	104.2	103.3	105.4	101.9	101.2	104.7	102.0
1977	103.8	101.0	100.6	99.1	98.8	99.3	100.2	97.8	96.2	93.7	94.3	93.8	98.2
1978	90.3	89.0	88.8	92.7	97.4	97.7	97.2	103.9	103.9	100.6	94.7	96.1	96.0
1979	99.7	98.2	100.1	102.1	99.7	101.7	102.7	107.4	108.6	104.5	103.7	107.8	103.0
1980	110.9	115.3	104.7	103.0	107.7	114.6	119.8	123.5	126.5	130.2	135.6	133.5	118.8
1981	133.0	128.4	133.2	134.4	131.7	132.3	129.1	129.6	118.3	119.8	122.9	123.8	128.0
1982	117.3	114.5	110.8	116.3	116.4	109.7	109.4	109.6	122.4	132.7	138.1	139.4	119.7

144

10.0 CORPORATE PROFITS AFTER TAXES, IN CONSTANT PRICES, UNITED STATES (ANNUAL RATE, BILLION 1972 DOLLARS)

YEAR	IQ	IIQ	IIIQ	IVQ	AVGE
1948	44.3	45.9	43.8	41.9	44.0
1949	38.4	33.5	34.9	34.2	35.2
1950	35.0	41.8	49.7	53.4	45.0
1951	42.8	36.3	33.0	34.9	36.8
1952	34.2	32.1	32.1	34.9	33.3
1953	36.4	36.1	35.0	27.4	33.7
1954	31.3	32.2	34.2	36.7	33.6
1955	42.0	42.5	43.1	44.3	43.0
1956	42.1	42.6	39.6	41.2	41.4
1957	34.0	39.3	38.3	34.8	36.6
1958	29.5	29.9	33.3	37.8	32.6
1959	40.6	43.8	39.1	38.2	40.4
1960	41.0	37.9	36.5	35.0	37.6
1961	34.3	36.0	37.9	40.8	37.3
1962	41.8	41.6	42.8	43.8	42.5
1963	42.8	45.0	46.0	47.0	45.2
1964	51.3	51.1	52.3	51.7	51.6
1965	58.7	60.8	61.1	64.2	61.2
1966	64.8	64.2	63.3	61.4	63.4
1967	58.0	57.7	58.6	60.7	58.8
1968	58.5	59.2	58.9	59.7	59.1
1969	57.8	55.2	52.5	50.5	54.0
1970	46.3	45.5	45.5	42.3	44.9
1971	48.3	49.3	52.4	53.5	50.9
1972	56.9	57.0	58.8	63.6	59.1
1973	72.4	74.1	72.8	73.8	73.3
1974	75.2	74.9	77.2	67.0	73.6
1975	55.1	57.0	67.5	71.7	62.8
1976	75.1	75.8	75.7	74.8	75.3
1977	81.9	85.1	87.3	84.9	84.8
1978	86.5	94.2	96.2	100.7	94.4
1979	99.3	99.0	99.8	95.0	98.3
1980	93.3	76.9	79.3	77.6	81.8
1981	79.1	70.2	72.0	69.4	72.7
1982	55.3	56.8	56.0	54.2	55.6

11.0 RATIO, PRICE TO UNIT LABOR COST, NONFARM BUSINESS, UNITED STATES
(INDEX, 1977=100)

YEAR	IQ	IIQ	IIIQ	IVQ	AVGE
1948	100.8	101.6	101.3	102.1	101.4
1949	101.3	101.0	102.3	101.0	101.4
1950	101.6	102.6	104.7	104.6	103.4
1951	103.9	102.4	103.1	103.6	103.2
1952	102.4	102.1	101.4	101.4	101.8
1953	100.9	100.5	100.4	98.2	100.0
1954	98.5	99.3	99.8	100.9	99.6
1955	102.0	102.5	102.4	101.7	102.1
1956	100.4	99.8	99.4	99.6	99.8
1957	100.2	99.6	99.6	99.0	99.6
1958	97.8	98.8	99.0	100.4	99.0
1959	101.2	102.0	100.2	100.0	100.8
1960	100.2	98.9	98.5	97.9	98.9
1961	97.7	99.0	99.6	100.2	99.1
1962	100.2	99.4	100.4	101.0	100.2
1963	100.4	101.3	101.7	101.3	101.2
1964	101.9	101.9	102.1	101.5	101.8
1965	103.0	102.8	103.0	103.6	103.1
1966	103.0	102.4	101.8	102.5	102.4
1967	101.8	101.8	102.1	102.6	102.1
1968	102.1	102.4	102.0	101.3	101.9
1969	101.1	100.5	99.7	98.8	100.0
1970	97.5	98.5	98.4	98.1	98.1
1971	99.1	99.1	99.7	99.7	99.4
1972	99.2	99.4	99.4	100.0	99.5
1973	99.5	98.5	97.5	97.8	98.3
1974	96.8	96.8	96.3	96.6	96.6
1975	97.2	98.9	100.4	99.9	99.1
1976	100.1	99.6	99.2	98.9	99.4
1977	99.6	100.2	100.6	99.7	100.0
1978	98.4	99.6	99.4	99.3	99.2
1979	98.3	97.8	97.1	96.5	97.4
1980	96.7	96.0	96.4	97.0	96.5
1981	98.2	97.9	98.1	97.7	98.0
1982	96.7	96.5	96.8	97.3	96.8

12.0 CHANGE IN CONSUMER INSTALLMENT CREDIT, IN CONSTANT PRICES, UNITED STATES (ANNUAL RATE, BILLION 1972 DOLLARS)

YEAR	JAN	FEB	MAR	APR	MAY	JUN	JUL	AUG	SEP	OCT	NOV	DEC	AVGE
1948	4.93	3.24	6.99	4.93	3.82	3.27	3.69	3.65	4.32	0.84	1.69	2.02	3.62
1949	1.71	2.74	2.71	3.77	4.83	4.78	3.71	4.30	4.79	6.07	5.87	4.98	4.19
1950	5.44	5.98	4.86	4.28	5.97	7.96	9.91	6.46	7.16	2.56	-0.61	0.37	5.03
1951	3.84	2.24	0.25	-1.73	-0.75	-0.48	-2.30	1.79	2.23	1.55	2.63	2.49	0.98
1952	1.58	1.57	2.08	2.96	9.21	10.64	6.82	4.96	6.54	9.83	6.65	8.89	5.98
1953	7.44	7.10	9.88	6.33	6.58	4.57	5.85	4.23	3.79	3.82	3.23	0.41	5.27
1954	-1.03	0.20	-1.30	-0.01	-0.31	0.76	1.14	0.70	1.81	2.00	2.09	4.23	0.86
1955	5.26	6.42	9.96	8.77	9.12	9.73	7.23	9.40	9.22	5.02	5.53	6.17	7.65
1956	4.90	5.28	6.88	4.30	4.11	2.64	0.76	4.27	2.78	3.36	4.90	3.03	3.93
1957	2.58	3.98	-2.98	2.42	4.38	2.84	4.52	3.20	3.17	2.90	2.47	1.80	3.10
1958	0.31	-1.40	-2.66	-2.21	-1.34	-2.11	-0.11	-0.64	1.39	-0.86	2.01	4.76	-0.24
1959	6.44	5.87	6.31	6.84	7.80	8.30	9.11	10.16	9.55	9.07	6.76	4.79	7.58
1960	7.04	6.23	9.08	8.31	5.46	5.79	4.30	3.58	4.39	2.70	3.66	1.72	5.19
1961	4.13	0.95	-2.44	-2.84	-0.84	0.63	0.66	1.94	3.05	2.91	4.17	5.03	1.45
1962	2.39	6.54	2.76	7.83	7.04	7.02	6.88	6.77	6.27	6.68	8.77	7.97	6.41
1963	7.80	9.63	5.55	9.44	7.87	8.58	9.40	9.13	8.73	10.29	8.20	8.33	8.58
1964	11.07	3.28	17.54	8.10	10.98	9.52	9.68	8.83	11.29	8.86	6.13	10.73	9.67
1965	11.06	13.22	7.23	13.84	11.76	9.35	10.49	9.97	9.99	7.42	9.14	8.98	10.20
1966	9.76	10.79	6.05	5.15	5.00	5.42	7.75	6.16	4.99	4.64	6.13	6.86	6.56
1967	5.01	6.18	0.57	-0.02	0.97	4.81	3.16	5.57	5.99	2.50	8.01	9.16	4.33
1968	-0.13	1.83	19.95	9.76	9.64	9.95	10.07	8.43	9.03	12.38	11.45	12.53	9.57
1969	11.84	19.67	6.12	12.35	12.67	11.03	9.66	7.60	10.63	8.65	9.14	3.97	10.28
1970	7.67	6.39	0.60	-0.54	3.13	8.05	10.64	6.82	7.72	1.71	-2.39	7.97	4.81
1971	35.14	8.83	5.92	7.17	7.72	8.85	11.61	12.88	13.91	11.38	15.39	15.73	12.88
1972	5.30	-1.44	26.59	16.92	16.24	19.94	12.44	18.11	14.69	14.38	15.96	18.60	14.81
1973	43.85	23.45	18.69	18.13	23.13	19.99	21.83	16.69	15.37	18.51	16.80	9.68	20.51
1974	12.33	12.58	2.82	10.24	14.23	12.04	11.81	12.22	7.99	2.51	-1.22	-1.68	7.99
1975	4.31	10.70	-12.68	-2.11	-1.27	3.11	13.46	9.60	7.91	11.17	10.20	12.48	5.57
1976	13.72	-11.66	37.24	17.46	14.04	16.19	15.52	16.33	17.78	18.70	13.56	22.87	15.98
1977	30.18	25.39	24.85	26.96	26.08	23.66	23.52	24.93	24.84	24.12	28.41	25.12	25.67
1978	25.81	28.56	28.07	27.75	36.66	37.00	26.64	26.29	25.59	22.51	28.75	30.61	28.69
1979	33.26	36.76	18.46	28.41	23.43	17.41	21.36	21.35	24.92	21.63	21.60	10.70	23.27
1980	23.62	-12.73	32.52	-13.64	-22.81	-19.85	-4.40	7.79	-1.33	7.03	7.63	-3.15	0.58
1981	10.43	18.91	12.19	13.41	12.54	6.65	9.97	11.16	17.26	4.80	-2.22	-1.40	9.47
1982	10.80	4.38	1.33	9.92	9.12	10.43	2.34	0.40	4.98	2.45	7.74	14.39	6.52

COINCIDENT INDEX, UNITED STATES (1980=100)

YEAR	JAN	FEB	MAR	APR	MAY	JUN	JUL	AUG	SEP	OCT	NOV	DEC	AVGE
1948	32.3	32.0	32.3	32.2	32.5	32.9	33.0	33.0	33.0	33.1	33.0	32.7	32.7
1949	32.1	31.8	31.5	31.2	30.8	30.7	30.3	30.6	30.9	29.8	30.4	30.8	30.9
1950	31.5	31.8	32.6	33.0	33.5	34.2	35.2	36.2	36.0	36.3	36.3	36.9	34.5
1951	37.5	37.6	37.7	38.1	38.3	38.3	38.2	38.4	38.2	38.3	38.3	38.5	38.1
1952	38.7	39.1	39.2	39.1	39.2	39.1	38.5	39.6	40.6	41.2	41.6	42.0	39.8
1953	42.1	42.6	42.9	42.9	43.0	42.8	42.9	42.5	41.9	41.7	40.9	39.9	42.2
1954	39.4	39.2	38.8	38.6	38.5	38.7	38.6	38.6	38.9	39.2	39.9	40.4	39.1
1955	40.9	41.4	42.0	42.3	43.0	43.2	43.7	43.6	44.0	44.2	44.5	44.7	43.1
1956	44.7	44.7	44.6	44.9	44.7	44.7	43.6	44.8	45.2	45.5	45.3	45.6	44.9
1957	45.6	46.0	46.1	45.7	45.5	45.5	45.6	45.6	45.1	44.8	43.9	43.3	45.2
1958	42.6	41.7	41.3	40.8	40.9	41.4	41.9	42.3	42.8	43.2	44.1	44.1	42.3
1959	44.7	45.2	45.8	46.5	47.0	47.1	46.7	45.8	45.6	45.6	45.8	47.2	46.1
1960	47.7	47.9	47.4	47.6	47.4	47.2	46.9	46.7	46.6	46.3	45.8	45.4	46.9
1961	45.3	45.2	45.5	45.7	46.1	46.7	46.8	47.3	47.4	48.0	48.7	49.0	46.8
1962	49.0	49.5	49.8	50.1	50.2	50.2	50.2	50.5	50.6	50.8	50.8	50.8	50.2
1963	50.9	51.0	51.4	51.8	51.9	52.3	52.4	52.7	52.9	53.2	53.1	53.6	52.3
1964	53.9	54.3	54.5	55.0	55.4	55.5	56.1	56.3	56.6	56.2	57.0	57.8	55.7
1965	58.2	58.4	59.1	59.4	59.4	60.2	60.9	61.1	61.9	62.3	63.0	63.6	60.7
1966	64.0	64.7	65.2	65.2	65.4	66.0	66.2	66.4	66.6	67.0	67.2	67.2	65.9
1967	67.4	67.3	67.4	67.5	67.6	67.6	68.0	68.5	68.6	68.5	69.4	70.1	68.2
1968	70.1	70.4	71.0	71.5	72.0	72.3	72.8	73.0	73.3	73.6	74.0	74.3	72.4
1969	74.5	75.0	75.1	75.5	75.5	75.7	75.9	76.2	76.0	76.1	75.8	75.8	75.6
1970	74.9	74.6	74.5	74.5	74.2	74.0	74.0	73.9	73.6	72.5	71.8	72.7	73.8
1971	73.4	73.7	73.9	74.1	74.3	74.9	74.6	74.5	75.0	75.2	75.6	76.2	74.6
1972	77.3	77.8	78.4	79.0	79.5	79.6	80.1	80.9	81.4	82.6	83.7	84.5	80.4
1973	85.6	86.4	86.6	86.5	86.7	86.9	87.3	87.1	87.5	88.3	88.5	88.0	87.1
1974	87.4	86.9	86.9	87.0	87.2	86.9	86.8	86.4	85.6	84.9	83.1	81.1	85.8
1975	79.5	78.7	78.0	78.2	78.6	79.7	80.1	81.0	81.5	81.8	82.1	82.6	80.1
1976	83.8	84.8	85.2	85.5	85.9	86.9	86.2	86.6	86.6	86.4	87.2	88.0	86.0
1977	88.3	89.0	90.0	90.5	91.2	91.7	92.5	92.9	93.5	93.8	94.1	94.9	91.9
1978	94.5	95.2	96.2	98.0	98.5	99.1	99.4	100.1	100.3	101.2	101.7	102.1	98.9
1979	102.1	102.1	102.9	102.0	102.8	102.8	103.3	103.1	103.1	103.0	103.0	103.1	102.8
1980	103.3	102.9	102.0	100.1	98.4	97.8	97.7	98.0	98.8	99.7	100.2	101.0	100.0
1981	101.5	101.8	102.0	102.1	101.9	102.4	103.0	103.0	102.1	100.9	99.8	98.4	101.6
1982	97.2	97.5	97.1	96.5	96.7	95.9	95.4	94.9	94.4	93.6	93.5	93.5	95.5

148

SIX MONTH SMOOTHED CHANGE IN COINCIDENT INDEX, UNITED STATES (ANNUAL RATE, PERCENT)

YEAR	JAN	FEB	MAR	APR	MAY	JUN	JUL	AUG	SEP	OCT	NOV	DEC	AVGE
1949	-3.0	-4.9	-6.3	-7.5	-9.6	-9.2	-10.1	-7.6	-4.7	-10.3	-5.3	-1.7	-6.7
1950	3.5	5.5	10.6	12.5	14.9	17.7	22.3	25.8	21.1	20.1	16.4	16.8	15.6
1951	16.7	14.2	12.2	11.8	10.3	8.3	5.8	5.7	3.7	2.9	2.4	2.7	8.1
1952	2.7	4.2	4.0	3.1	3.0	2.1	-0.7	4.5	8.6	10.4	11.1	11.7	5.4
1953	10.6	11.8	11.7	10.0	9.1	6.9	5.7	2.0	-1.3	-2.9	-6.5	-10.4	3.9
1954	-11.8	-11.5	-12.2	-11.8	-10.8	-8.4	-7.2	-5.8	-3.3	-0.3	3.7	6.8	-6.0
1955	8.8	10.4	12.6	12.7	14.4	13.6	13.8	11.5	11.1	10.0	9.3	8.4	11.4
1956	6.9	5.4	4.4	4.4	2.3	1.6	-3.2	1.5	2.9	3.9	2.6	3.5	2.9
1957	2.9	4.3	4.2	2.2	1.2	0.9	1.0	0.5	-1.9	-3.4	-6.4	-8.3	-0.2
1958	-10.5	-12.9	-13.2	-13.9	-11.9	-8.4	-5.0	-2.0	1.2	4.0	8.6	8.3	-4.6
1959	10.9	12.1	13.7	15.0	14.8	12.8	9.3	3.3	1.6	0.3	0.5	5.6	8.3
1960	6.8	6.4	3.4	3.5	2.6	1.3	0.3	-0.4	-1.2	-2.9	-4.9	-6.6	0.7
1961	-6.2	-5.7	-3.7	-2.5	-0.1	2.6	3.1	5.0	5.6	7.7	10.1	10.2	2.2
1962	8.9	9.6	9.2	8.7	7.7	6.4	6.1	5.2	4.3	4.2	3.4	2.6	6.4
1963	2.6	2.4	3.2	4.1	4.0	4.9	4.9	5.1	5.4	5.8	4.5	5.6	4.4
1964	5.9	6.5	5.9	6.9	7.5	6.7	7.5	7.2	7.2	4.9	6.8	8.3	6.8
1965	8.5	7.9	8.9	8.4	8.7	8.9	9.5	8.8	10.2	10.0	10.5	10.7	9.2
1966	10.5	10.9	10.8	9.3	8.2	8.5	7.5	6.9	6.4	6.2	5.6	4.4	7.9
1967	4.1	3.0	2.7	2.6	2.1	1.8	2.4	3.4	3.1	2.4	4.7	6.1	3.2
1968	5.4	5.6	6.3	7.0	7.5	7.1	7.4	6.9	6.6	6.4	6.2	5.9	6.5
1969	5.6	5.8	5.6	5.0	4.3	4.0	3.7	3.9	2.7	2.4	1.1	0.9	3.7
1970	-1.8	-2.5	-2.8	-2.4	-3.1	-3.3	-2.9	-2.8	-3.1	-5.3	-6.2	-3.2	-3.3
1971	-0.8	0.3	0.7	1.3	2.1	3.6	2.5	2.2	3.5	3.5	3.9	4.8	2.3
1972	6.7	7.1	7.8	8.4	8.5	7.7	7.9	8.6	8.6	10.0	11.3	11.4	8.7
1973	12.2	12.3	11.0	9.1	8.0	7.0	6.7	4.9	4.6	5.2	4.6	2.6	7.3
1974	0.6	-0.7	-0.9	-0.8	-0.4	-1.0	-1.3	-2.2	-3.7	-4.8	-7.8	-11.1	-2.8
1975	-13.1	-13.6	-13.8	-11.9	-9.6	-5.8	-3.7	-0.2	1.8	3.3	4.6	6.0	-4.7
1976	8.7	10.1	9.7	9.0	8.3	7.0	6.4	5.6	5.0	3.7	4.5	5.3	6.9
1977	5.1	5.6	7.0	7.4	8.0	7.9	8.7	8.2	8.3	7.8	7.1	7.3	7.4
1978	5.3	5.7	6.7	9.2	8.8	8.8	8.1	8.4	7.5	8.1	7.8	7.5	7.7
1979	6.1	4.9	5.4	2.6	3.4	2.7	3.1	2.1	1.0	1.1	0.7	0.6	2.9
1980	0.9	0.1	-1.7	-4.9	-7.7	-8.1	-7.5	-6.2	-4.0	-1.8	-0.3	1.6	-3.3
1981	2.9	3.7	4.2	4.4	3.7	4.0	4.4	3.6	1.2	-1.5	-3.7	-6.1	1.7
1982	-7.8	-6.7	-6.8	-7.1	-5.9	-6.7	-6.5	-6.4	-6.1	-6.4	-5.6	-4.6	-6.4

149

13.0 EMPLOYEES ON NONFARM PAYROLLS, UNITED STATES (THOUSANDS)

YEAR	JAN	FEB	MAR	APR	MAY	JUN	JUL	AUG	SEP	OCT	NOV	DEC	AVGE
1948	44680.	44492.	44615.	44334.	44615.	44863.	45059.	45052.	45167.	45084.	45083.	45032.	44840.
1949	44631.	44399.	44169.	44057.	43806.	43582.	43415.	43490.	43708.	42823.	43148.	43497.	43727.
1950	43472.	43175.	43816.	44238.	44589.	44953.	45361.	46035.	46304.	46530.	46654.	46756.	45157.
1951	47227.	47519.	47700.	47849.	47803.	47915.	47923.	47806.	47743.	47833.	48026.	48119.	47789.
1952	48229.	48491.	48450.	48476.	48478.	48130.	47992.	48687.	49076.	49436.	49710.	49933.	48757.
1953	50043.	50271.	50360.	50367.	50343.	50386.	50385.	50216.	50216.	50114.	49824.	49627.	50184.
1954	49340.	49270.	49081.	48984.	48857.	48810.	48689.	48644.	48752.	48828.	49102.	49242.	48967.
1955	49363.	49523.	49867.	50106.	50414.	50705.	50823.	50905.	51085.	51308.	51491.	51721.	50609.
1956	51880.	52096.	52141.	52302.	52387.	52454.	51764.	52396.	52446.	52667.	52722.	52865.	52343.
1957	52808.	53000.	53052.	53029.	52999.	52961.	52970.	52918.	52825.	52673.	52458.	52281.	52831.
1958	52002.	51448.	51131.	50787.	50760.	50822.	50915.	51118.	51359.	51379.	51831.	51968.	51293.
1959	52410.	52558.	52863.	53190.	53382.	53603.	53683.	53230.	53265.	53203.	53503.	54033.	53244.
1960	54184.	54406.	54348.	54561.	54366.	54292.	54230.	54198.	54069.	53982.	53843.	53571.	54171.
1961	53524.	53373.	53462.	53485.	53664.	53922.	54052.	54232.	54303.	54375.	54636.	54739.	53981.
1962	54703.	54996.	55109.	55384.	55514.	55563.	55663.	55796.	55860.	55919.	55943.	55915.	55530.
1963	55927.	56039.	56157.	56398.	56534.	56571.	56705.	56832.	56971.	57148.	57125.	57251.	56638.
1964	57281.	57621.	57686.	57846.	57974.	58128.	58309.	58510.	58777.	58658.	59080.	59320.	58266.
1965	59419.	59710.	59921.	60080.	60389.	60590.	60868.	61072.	61333.	61538.	61859.	62209.	60749.
1966	62415.	62766.	63129.	63318.	63595.	63989.	64166.	64306.	64367.	64614.	64839.	65042.	63879.
1967	65240.	65224.	65305.	65373.	65478.	65642.	65816.	65933.	66074.	66091.	66570.	66767.	65793.
1968	66656.	67026.	67156.	67422.	67519.	67779.	67979.	68189.	68333.	68569.	68837.	69151.	67885.
1969	69297.	69575.	69803.	69980.	70197.	70478.	70629.	70742.	70800.	70957.	70921.	71119.	70375.
1970	71059.	71201.	71363.	71283.	70998.	70888.	70927.	70750.	70815.	70383.	70264.	70661.	70883.
1971	70752.	70689.	70766.	70969.	71129.	71136.	71169.	71168.	71499.	71485.	71723.	71977.	71205.
1972	72357.	72542.	72850.	73079.	73346.	73639.	73576.	73908.	74107.	74537.	74904.	75164.	73667.
1973	75521.	75923.	76168.	76308.	76473.	76743.	76713.	77009.	77170.	77506.	77867.	77933.	76778.
1974	78020.	78181.	78184.	78239.	78381.	78443.	78492.	78511.	78542.	78599.	78234.	77531.	78280.
1975	77153.	76743.	76429.	76333.	76470.	76400.	76640.	77034.	77216.	77479.	77582.	77878.	76946.
1976	78317.	78614.	78828.	79142.	79188.	79264.	79469.	79591.	79857.	79847.	80122.	80310.	79379.
1977	80527.	80783.	81228.	81615.	81984.	82392.	82743.	82954.	83460.	83659.	84012.	84260.	82468.
1978	84478.	84782.	85325.	86071.	86409.	86845.	87071.	87332.	87487.	87775.	88214.	88518.	86692.
1979	88724.	88927.	89367.	89329.	89694.	90010.	90099.	90169.	90232.	90344.	90432.	90556.	89824.
1980	90801.	90846.	90929.	90723.	90308.	89976.	89692.	89955.	90126.	90320.	90560.	90725.	90413.
1981	90909.	90913.	91014.	91099.	91131.	91286.	91396.	91322.	91363.	91224.	90996.	90642.	91108.
1982	90460.	90459.	90304.	90083.	90166.	89839.	89535.	89312.	89267.	88860.	88750.	88535.	89631.

14.0 UNEMPLOYMENT RATE, UNITED STATES (PERCENT)

YEAR	JAN	FEB	MAR	APR	MAY	JUN	JUL	AUG	SEP	OCT	NOV	DEC	AVGE
1948	3.4	3.8	4.0	3.9	3.5	3.6	3.6	3.9	3.8	3.7	3.8	4.0	3.7
1949	4.3	4.7	5.0	5.3	6.1	6.2	6.7	6.8	6.6	7.9	6.4	6.6	6.0
1950	6.5	6.4	6.3	5.8	5.5	5.4	5.0	4.5	4.4	4.2	4.2	4.3	5.2
1951	3.7	3.4	3.4	3.1	3.0	3.2	3.1	3.1	3.3	3.5	3.5	3.1	3.3
1952	3.2	3.1	2.9	2.9	3.0	3.0	3.2	3.4	3.1	3.0	2.8	2.7	3.0
1953	2.9	2.6	2.6	2.7	2.5	2.5	2.6	2.7	2.9	3.1	3.5	4.5	2.9
1954	4.9	5.2	5.7	5.9	5.9	5.6	5.8	6.0	6.1	5.7	5.3	5.0	5.6
1955	4.9	4.7	4.6	4.7	4.3	4.2	4.0	4.2	4.1	4.3	4.2	4.2	4.4
1956	4.0	3.9	4.2	4.0	4.3	4.3	4.4	4.1	3.9	3.9	4.3	4.2	4.1
1957	4.2	3.9	3.7	3.9	4.1	4.3	4.2	4.1	4.4	4.5	5.1	5.2	4.3
1958	5.8	6.4	6.7	7.4	7.4	7.3	7.5	7.4	7.1	6.7	6.2	6.2	6.8
1959	6.0	5.9	5.6	5.2	5.1	5.0	5.1	5.2	5.5	5.7	5.8	5.3	5.4
1960	5.2	4.8	5.4	5.2	5.1	5.4	5.5	5.6	5.5	6.1	6.1	6.6	5.5
1961	6.6	6.9	6.9	7.0	7.1	6.9	7.0	6.6	6.7	6.5	6.1	6.0	6.7
1962	5.8	5.5	5.6	5.6	5.5	5.5	5.4	5.7	5.6	5.4	5.7	5.5	5.6
1963	5.7	5.9	5.7	5.7	5.9	5.6	5.6	5.4	5.5	5.5	5.7	5.5	5.6
1964	5.6	5.4	5.4	5.3	5.1	5.2	4.9	5.0	5.1	5.1	5.4	5.0	5.2
1965	4.9	5.1	4.7	4.8	4.6	4.6	4.4	4.4	4.3	4.2	4.1	4.0	4.5
1966	4.0	3.8	3.8	3.8	3.9	3.8	3.8	3.8	3.7	3.7	3.6	3.8	3.8
1967	3.9	3.8	3.8	3.8	3.8	3.9	3.8	3.8	3.8	4.0	3.9	3.8	3.8
1968	3.7	3.8	3.7	3.5	3.5	3.7	3.7	3.5	3.4	3.4	3.4	3.4	3.6
1969	3.4	3.4	3.4	3.4	3.4	3.5	3.5	3.5	3.7	3.7	3.5	3.5	3.5
1970	3.9	4.2	4.4	4.6	4.8	4.9	5.0	5.1	5.4	5.5	5.9	6.1	5.0
1971	5.9	5.9	6.0	5.9	5.7	5.9	6.0	6.1	6.0	5.8	6.0	6.0	5.9
1972	5.8	5.7	5.8	5.7	5.7	5.7	5.6	5.6	5.5	5.6	5.3	5.2	5.6
1973	4.9	5.0	4.9	5.0	4.9	4.9	4.8	4.8	4.8	4.6	4.8	4.9	4.9
1974	5.1	5.2	5.1	5.1	5.1	5.4	5.5	5.5	5.9	6.0	6.6	7.2	5.6
1975	8.1	8.1	8.6	8.8	9.0	8.8	8.6	8.4	8.4	8.4	8.3	8.2	8.5
1976	7.9	7.7	7.6	7.7	7.4	7.2	7.8	7.8	7.6	7.7	7.8	7.8	7.7
1977	7.5	7.6	7.4	7.2	7.0	7.2	6.9	7.0	6.8	6.8	6.8	6.4	7.0
1978	6.4	6.3	6.3	6.1	6.0	5.9	6.2	5.9	6.0	5.8	5.9	6.0	6.1
1979	5.9	5.9	5.8	5.8	5.6	5.7	5.7	6.0	5.9	6.0	5.9	6.0	5.8
1980	6.3	6.3	6.3	6.9	7.5	7.5	7.8	7.7	7.6	7.5	7.5	7.3	7.2
1981	7.5	7.4	7.3	7.2	7.5	7.5	7.2	7.4	7.6	8.0	8.3	8.6	7.6
1982	8.6	8.8	9.0	9.3	9.4	9.5	9.8	9.9	10.2	10.5	10.7	10.8	9.7

15.0 GROSS NATIONAL PRODUCT, IN CONSTANT PRICES, UNITED STATES
(ANNUAL RATE, BILLION 1972 DOLLARS)

YEAR	IQ	IIQ	IIIQ	IVQ	AVGE
1948	479.4	488.3	492.9	497.9	489.6
1949	492.6	490.3	494.8	490.8	492.1
1950	512.6	526.4	543.8	556.3	534.8
1951	564.4	575.9	587.9	589.1	579.3
1952	593.7	594.3	600.5	614.6	600.8
1953	623.2	628.3	624.4	618.2	623.5
1954	610.5	608.1	616.9	628.4	616.0
1955	644.1	653.2	663.2	669.5	657.5
1956	666.8	670.2	670.7	678.4	671.5
1957	683.5	684.1	688.5	679.1	683.8
1958	665.5	669.9	685.9	702.5	680.9
1959	711.5	726.2	721.2	727.9	721.7
1960	740.7	738.4	737.7	732.1	737.2
1961	737.7	750.1	759.6	779.0	756.6
1962	789.2	798.4	805.5	808.0	800.3
1963	815.0	826.7	839.8	848.6	832.5
1964	864.2	873.7	880.9	886.8	876.4
1965	906.7	919.7	934.1	956.8	929.3
1966	975.4	979.3	987.9	996.6	984.8
1967	997.8	1004.2	1016.2	1027.3	1011.4
1968	1036.6	1055.7	1068.2	1071.8	1058.1
1969	1084.2	1088.8	1092.0	1085.6	1087.6
1970	1081.4	1083.0	1093.3	1084.7	1085.6
1971	1111.5	1116.9	1125.7	1135.4	1122.4
1972	1157.2	1178.5	1193.1	1214.8	1185.9
1973	1246.8	1248.3	1255.8	1266.1	1254.2
1974	1253.3	1254.7	1246.8	1230.3	1246.3
1975	1204.3	1218.9	1246.1	1257.3	1231.6
1976	1285.0	1293.7	1301.1	1313.1	1298.2
1977	1341.3	1363.3	1385.8	1388.4	1369.7
1978	1400.0	1437.0	1448.8	1468.4	1438.5
1979	1472.6	1469.2	1486.6	1489.3	1479.4
1980	1494.9	1457.8	1463.8	1479.4	1474.0
1981	1507.8	1502.2	1510.4	1490.1	1502.6
1982	1470.7	1478.4	1481.1	1471.7	1475.5

16.0 INDUSTRIAL PRODUCTION, UNITED STATES (INDEX, 1967=100)

YEAR	JAN	FEB	MAR	APR	MAY	JUN	JUL	AUG	SEP	OCT	NOV	DEC	AVGE
1948	40.8	40.9	40.4	40.5	41.2	41.7	41.7	41.6	41.2	41.6	41.0	40.6	41.1
1949	40.3	39.9	39.1	38.9	38.3	38.3	38.2	38.6	38.9	37.5	38.5	39.2	38.8
1950	39.9	40.0	41.3	42.7	43.7	45.0	46.4	47.9	47.6	47.9	47.8	48.7	44.9
1951	48.8	49.1	49.4	49.4	49.3	49.0	48.3	47.8	48.1	48.1	48.4	48.7	48.7
1952	49.3	49.6	49.7	49.3	48.8	48.4	47.6	50.7	52.5	53.0	54.1	54.4	50.6
1953	54.6	54.9	55.3	55.6	55.9	55.6	56.3	56.0	54.9	54.4	53.0	51.8	54.9
1954	51.4	51.6	51.3	51.0	51.3	51.4	51.5	51.4	51.5	52.1	53.0	53.6	51.8
1955	54.9	55.6	56.9	57.5	58.5	58.9	59.0	58.9	59.3	60.3	60.5	60.7	58.4
1956	61.1	60.5	60.5	61.0	60.5	59.9	58.1	60.5	61.8	62.4	61.8	62.7	60.9
1957	62.5	63.1	63.1	62.2	62.0	62.1	62.5	62.5	62.0	61.1	59.6	58.5	61.8
1958	57.4	56.2	55.5	54.6	55.1	56.5	57.4	58.5	59.1	59.8	61.5	61.6	57.8
1959	62.5	63.7	64.7	66.0	67.0	67.1	65.5	63.3	63.2	62.7	63.1	67.0	64.6
1960	68.5	68.2	67.6	67.0	67.0	66.1	65.9	65.8	65.1	65.0	64.1	62.9	66.1
1961	63.0	62.9	63.3	64.6	65.6	66.5	67.3	67.9	67.8	69.1	70.2	70.8	66.6
1962	70.2	71.3	71.7	71.9	71.8	71.6	72.3	72.4	72.8	72.9	73.2	73.2	72.1
1963	73.8	74.6	75.1	75.8	76.7	76.9	76.6	76.8	77.5	78.1	78.4	78.3	76.5
1964	79.0	79.5	79.5	80.8	81.3	81.5	82.0	82.6	82.9	81.7	84.2	85.2	81.7
1965	86.2	86.7	87.8	88.2	88.9	89.6	90.4	90.8	91.1	92.0	92.4	93.5	89.8
1966	94.4	95.0	96.3	96.5	97.4	97.9	98.4	98.5	99.4	100.1	99.4	99.6	97.7
1967	99.8	99.0	98.5	99.2	98.7	98.4	98.7	100.0	100.3	101.2	102.6	103.5	100.0
1968	103.7	104.3	104.7	104.9	106.2	106.6	106.5	107.1	107.1	107.4	108.6	108.8	106.3
1969	109.5	110.2	110.8	110.6	110.3	111.2	111.8	112.3	112.3	112.5	111.4	111.2	111.2
1970	109.1	108.8	108.8	108.6	108.3	108.1	108.4	108.3	107.6	105.4	104.8	107.2	107.8
1971	108.1	108.0	108.0	108.5	109.1	109.6	109.8	108.9	110.3	110.9	111.3	112.3	109.6
1972	114.6	115.3	116.5	117.7	118.1	118.7	119.3	120.7	121.8	123.4	124.4	125.8	119.7
1973	126.3	127.8	128.5	128.5	129.6	129.9	130.4	130.4	131.1	131.4	131.6	131.3	129.7
1974	129.9	129.6	130.0	129.9	131.3	131.9	131.8	131.7	131.8	129.5	124.9	119.3	129.3
1975	115.2	112.7	111.7	112.6	113.7	116.4	118.4	121.0	122.1	122.2	123.5	124.4	117.8
1976	126.1	128.1	128.7	129.0	130.1	130.7	131.2	132.0	131.3	131.3	132.6	133.6	130.4
1977	133.7	134.5	136.3	137.1	138.0	138.9	139.0	139.3	139.6	140.1	140.3	140.5	138.1
1978	140.0	140.3	142.1	144.4	144.8	146.1	147.1	148.0	148.6	149.7	150.6	151.8	146.1
1979	152.0	152.5	153.5	151.1	152.7	153.0	153.0	152.1	152.7	152.5	152.3	152.5	152.5
1980	153.0	152.8	152.1	148.2	143.8	141.4	140.3	142.2	144.4	146.6	149.2	150.4	147.0
1981	151.4	151.8	152.1	151.9	152.7	152.9	153.9	153.6	151.6	149.1	146.3	143.4	150.9
1982	140.7	142.9	141.7	140.2	139.2	138.7	138.8	138.4	137.3	135.8	134.8	134.7	138.6

17.0 PERSONAL INCOME. IN CONSTANT PRICES, UNITED STATES (ANNUAL RATE, BILLION 1972 DOLLARS)

YEAR	JAN	FEB	MAR	APR	MAY	JUN	JUL	AUG	SEP	OCT	NOV	DEC	AVGE
1948	356.1	357.9	367.4	364.7	363.7	370.5	368.6	371.5	371.9	373.4	372.6	369.2	367.3
1949	364.1	364.4	367.0	365.4	365.8	362.9	362.2	365.2	369.6	363.9	366.8	370.9	365.7
1950	385.7	389.7	398.8	390.4	389.9	390.5	393.2	399.5	399.7	403.6	405.8	409.4	396.3
1951	406.7	403.8	407.2	414.0	414.9	419.2	417.7	422.6	420.0	423.3	422.7	422.3	416.2
1952	419.3	426.0	427.7	425.7	431.2	432.9	429.2	440.5	445.7	445.3	443.5	445.4	434.4
1953	448.1	449.7	454.1	454.6	456.6	457.8	456.3	453.8	452.4	456.0	455.4	453.2	454.0
1954	449.6	449.8	448.0	446.2	448.3	448.6	449.4	453.1	456.7	459.7	462.3	465.1	453.1
1955	466.0	467.2	471.7	475.7	480.5	482.9	488.8	489.2	491.3	495.3	497.5	500.6	483.9
1956	500.0	501.4	501.2	506.8	505.2	506.7	501.5	508.6	512.3	516.0	515.9	516.4	507.7
1957	514.9	517.3	518.8	519.6	519.6	521.9	522.7	523.6	522.1	522.9	520.9	517.9	520.2
1958	514.2	514.4	514.9	512.1	514.6	517.2	526.8	525.7	528.6	529.8	535.2	536.3	522.5
1959	534.3	536.7	541.8	544.9	547.1	548.3	548.5	542.7	542.5	543.5	549.4	557.2	544.7
1960	558.9	556.9	555.7	559.2	562.1	562.5	561.6	561.2	560.7	561.7	559.4	556.9	559.7
1961	562.4	564.5	566.3	567.3	571.4	576.6	577.4	577.9	578.4	583.5	589.1	591.9	575.6
1962	590.0	593.4	596.9	599.7	600.3	602.0	604.3	605.2	605.0	607.3	608.8	610.6	602.0
1963	615.3	611.8	614.1	616.5	618.9	622.1	622.6	624.8	628.7	631.8	631.7	636.2	622.9
1964	639.4	642.5	645.9	650.5	654.0	656.6	659.4	664.6	667.4	667.3	672.0	678.9	658.2
1965	683.6	682.4	683.5	687.5	693.1	696.6	699.4	701.2	719.4	714.7	719.0	723.3	700.4
1966	724.4	728.7	730.7	731.9	734.9	739.1	741.8	744.5	748.1	751.2	755.4	756.5	740.6
1967	763.1	764.2	767.4	768.0	769.3	771.9	775.8	779.3	780.1	779.3	785.1	790.8	774.5
1968	789.8	795.8	801.9	805.8	811.3	816.1	821.6	825.2	827.2	829.2	832.3	835.7	816.0
1969	836.8	841.9	845.4	848.1	849.8	852.0	856.7	860.6	861.7	863.1	861.3	863.9	853.4
1970	862.7	865.1	868.9	886.4	879.0	878.2	880.3	882.8	884.5	878.1	876.7	879.6	876.9
1971	886.5	888.2	892.0	892.6	895.0	910.9	898.1	902.1	904.0	905.6	909.5	917.4	900.2
1972	924.9	932.9	936.8	940.7	943.6	933.8	948.3	955.8	956.5	972.8	983.3	987.3	951.4
1973	990.9	998.9	999.0	1000.0	1001.8	1004.3	1011.4	1006.9	1015.0	1018.4	1020.5	1017.2	1007.1
1974	1009.4	1003.2	998.8	1001.8	1005.3	1008.3	1012.8	1007.2	1002.3	1003.4	996.0	995.0	1003.7
1975	989.9	991.3	991.6	994.3	1003.3	1021.1	1009.1	1017.1	1021.7	1025.1	1026.7	1025.4	1009.7
1976	1035.3	1044.7	1047.3	1050.6	1052.8	1052.0	1058.7	1061.0	1062.0	1062.4	1071.8	1075.6	1056.2
1977	1075.4	1080.5	1089.1	1091.2	1095.6	1097.7	1109.1	1110.9	1118.8	1126.9	1130.6	1137.2	1105.2
1978	1133.3	1137.7	1145.6	1153.8	1150.8	1155.2	1167.8	1171.3	1172.7	1179.6	1183.8	1195.4	1162.2
1979	1189.6	1190.5	1197.3	1194.1	1193.6	1194.0	1206.4	1208.5	1206.9	1207.7	1210.8	1212.2	1201.0
1980	1215.8	1206.3	1201.6	1192.7	1190.1	1190.0	1204.7	1204.2	1208.3	1214.3	1217.8	1222.2	1205.7
1981	1227.1	1232.2	1234.5	1234.7	1234.0	1239.5	1248.1	1253.6	1253.1	1251.1	1250.1	1245.7	1242.0
1982	1236.0	1243.8	1245.0	1249.6	1256.7	1248.8	1251.0	1248.6	1245.1	1243.6	1247.6	1253.8	1247.5

18.0 MANUFACTURING AND TRADE SALES, IN CONSTANT PRICES, UNITED STATES (MILLION 1972 DOLLARS)

YEAR	JAN	FEB	MAR	APR	MAY	JUN	JUL	AUG	SEP	OCT	NOV	DEC	AVGE
1948	52474.	52498.	52894.	53129.	52455.	53121.	53583.	53694.	53657.	53715.	53491.	53918.	53219.
1949	53344.	53297.	53140.	52938.	52148.	53527.	51963.	53072.	54110.	52142.	52827.	52367.	52906.
1950	53378.	54487.	55208.	55853.	57205.	59549.	63996.	64897.	60894.	59609.	57766.	61016.	58655.
1951	62759.	61114.	60017.	58978.	59494.	59060.	57893.	59351.	59313.	59731.	59579.	58975.	59689.
1952	59929.	60593.	60220.	60987.	61683.	61821.	60499.	61728.	63820.	65902.	65554.	66862.	62475.
1953	67237.	68165.	68894.	68879.	68575.	67769.	68684.	67302.	66729.	66422.	64806.	63706.	67264.
1954	64027.	64786.	64435.	64958.	63869.	64713.	64486.	64096.	64431.	64675.	66600.	68159.	64936.
1955	69147.	69727.	71106.	71869.	72173.	72160.	72436.	72152.	73336.	73048.	73631.	73719.	72042.
1956	73309.	72733.	73047.	73213.	73009.	73331.	70206.	72478.	73135.	73726.	74094.	74799.	73090.
1957	75021.	75306.	74774.	73636.	73375.	73824.	73525.	74020.	73046.	72696.	71739.	70167.	73427.
1958	70035.	68806.	67788.	67509.	67766.	68991.	69715.	70912.	71275.	72388.	73512.	71670.	70031.
1959	74544.	75741.	76624.	77758.	78627.	78686.	78403.	75954.	75679.	75911.	75858.	77973.	76813.
1960	79391.	78992.	78497.	78900.	77831.	77768.	77406.	76990.	77846.	77448.	76432.	76472.	77831.
1961	74928.	75144.	76446.	75878.	77047.	78412.	77520.	79314.	79631.	80707.	81464.	81788.	78190.
1962	81905.	81915.	83031.	83107.	83096.	82657.	83032.	83609.	83389.	84204.	85382.	83942.	83272.
1963	84339.	85591.	85692.	86508.	85880.	86673.	87967.	87344.	87396.	88464.	87382.	89304.	86878.
1964	89833.	89916.	89653.	91129.	92155.	91854.	93317.	93086.	94014.	92311.	93336.	96520.	92260.
1965	96251.	96579.	98491.	98749.	97863.	98149.	99908.	99345.	99389.	100419.	101807.	102186.	99095.
1966	103228.	103401.	105038.	104157.	103668.	104928.	104306.	104970.	104786.	105032.	104659.	105074.	104437.
1967	105276.	104807.	105333.	105603.	105730.	105612.	105612.	107242.	106606.	105993.	108632.	111123.	106470.
1968	110642.	110169.	110781.	110918.	111393.	112226.	113689.	111986.	112615.	114201.	114882.	114176.	112307.
1969	114412.	114799.	115388.	115929.	115552.	115820.	116319.	116902.	117435.	118558.	116841.	116838.	116233.
1970	115395.	115688.	114637.	113809.	115060.	115520.	115497.	115117.	114984.	112985.	111314.	114727.	114561.
1971	116141.	117713.	117780.	118178.	119010.	120510.	119624.	119355.	120471.	120307.	122580.	123611.	119557.
1972	125345.	124342.	126127.	127177.	128175.	128418.	128656.	130745.	131980.	134308.	136194.	137923.	129949.
1973	140437.	141109.	140651.	140276.	139417.	139059.	141031.	138564.	138644.	141917.	143785.	141555.	140537.
1974	142051.	141419.	142020.	142246.	142188.	141776.	141683.	139976.	138289.	136219.	134143.	130002.	139334.
1975	130465.	130401.	126653.	128321.	128688.	130030.	131127.	131590.	132541.	132533.	132486.	133721.	130713.
1976	136722.	137466.	138305.	139169.	139015.	140575.	140920.	140863.	141045.	139880.	142600.	145334.	140158.
1977	145246.	146803.	148045.	148176.	148666.	149543.	150128.	150907.	151270.	151999.	152665.	153890.	149778.
1978	150071.	153613.	154429.	159026.	159275.	159414.	158948.	160651.	160368.	161955.	162215.	162446.	158534.
1979	161593.	160410.	164055.	160040.	164344.	162257.	163168.	163143.	162393.	162173.	160883.	161323.	162165.
1980	163811.	162219.	158439.	155401.	154013.	154163.	155888.	155681.	158725.	161009.	160388.	160680.	158368.
1981	162132.	161645.	161661.	162252.	161594.	162371.	161262.	160902.	159032.	156389.	155558.	153354.	159846.
1982	150871.	153723.	154188.	152619.	155866.	153409.	152957.	151770.	151184.	148456.	149877.	149959.	152073.

LAGGING INDEX, UNITED STATES (1970=100)

YEAR	JAN	FEB	MAR	APR	MAY	JUN	JUL	AUG	SEP	OCT	NOV	DEC	AVGE
1948	28.8	28.9	28.9	28.9	29.1	29.3	29.5	30.1	30.1	30.1	30.1	30.0	29.5
1949	30.2	30.1	29.9	29.7	29.5	29.1	28.7	28.4	28.5	28.5	28.4	28.1	29.1
1950	28.1	28.0	28.1	28.2	28.4	28.8	29.0	29.7	30.2	31.0	31.4	31.8	29.4
1951	33.0	33.9	34.5	35.3	36.3	36.5	36.7	37.0	37.1	37.5	37.7	38.4	36.2
1952	38.7	39.1	39.0	39.0	38.9	39.4	39.6	39.6	39.6	40.0	40.7	40.6	39.5
1953	41.1	41.6	41.8	42.2	42.9	42.8	42.9	42.9	43.0	42.9	42.5	42.0	42.4
1954	41.7	41.4	40.6	40.2	39.9	39.7	39.5	38.9	38.8	38.6	38.7	39.0	39.7
1955	38.9	39.0	39.3	39.5	40.1	40.8	41.3	42.6	42.7	43.5	44.1	44.6	41.4
1956	45.2	45.8	46.2	47.2	47.7	48.0	48.3	48.7	49.0	49.1	49.1	49.1	47.8
1957	49.3	49.3	49.6	49.8	50.0	50.1	50.2	51.1	51.2	50.5	50.2	50.0	50.1
1958	49.0	48.0	47.3	46.2	44.9	44.6	44.5	44.2	45.0	45.4	45.5	45.7	45.9
1959	45.8	46.0	46.4	47.1	48.0	49.2	49.8	50.3	51.4	51.7	51.8	52.4	49.2
1960	52.7	53.3	53.6	54.1	55.0	54.8	54.5	53.8	53.3	53.1	53.3	53.2	53.7
1961	52.9	52.8	52.4	52.0	51.8	51.9	51.7	52.1	52.2	52.3	52.5	52.7	52.3
1962	53.0	53.3	53.9	54.5	55.0	55.5	55.7	56.0	56.2	56.5	56.5	56.5	55.2
1963	56.5	56.6	56.8	57.0	57.0	57.4	57.7	58.0	58.6	59.1	59.6	60.0	57.9
1964	60.0	60.4	60.7	61.3	61.7	61.9	62.2	62.7	63.3	63.6	63.9	64.6	62.2
1965	65.4	65.9	66.0	67.4	68.3	68.6	69.5	69.9	70.4	71.0	71.4	73.1	69.0
1966	74.1	74.8	76.3	77.3	78.4	79.7	80.9	82.0	82.9	83.6	84.3	84.6	79.9
1967	85.0	84.7	84.7	84.2	84.5	84.6	84.8	84.4	84.5	84.6	85.4	86.6	84.8
1968	86.9	87.0	87.1	88.5	89.5	89.8	90.1	90.5	90.8	90.5	91.5	94.1	89.7
1969	95.1	95.9	96.6	96.9	97.7	99.0	99.1	100.6	101.1	101.5	101.7	102.0	99.0
1970	101.9	101.9	101.7	101.0	100.8	100.2	100.1	99.7	99.5	98.7	98.1	96.5	100.0
1971	95.5	95.0	95.0	94.9	95.6	95.8	95.8	96.2	96.7	96.6	96.3	96.5	95.8
1972	96.5	96.6	96.8	97.0	97.4	97.7	98.1	98.7	99.4	100.5	101.4	102.1	98.5
1973	102.9	104.3	105.7	107.2	108.3	109.5	111.3	112.2	112.8	113.2	113.5	114.8	109.6
1974	115.1	115.4	115.5	116.2	117.0	117.1	117.3	117.1	117.1	116.5	116.1	115.0	116.3
1975	113.2	110.9	108.4	106.3	104.4	103.0	102.2	101.9	101.7	101.9	101.3	100.9	104.7
1976	102.0	102.2	102.3	102.6	103.2	104.0	104.3	104.4	105.0	104.9	105.1	105.7	103.8
1977	106.1	106.6	107.1	107.6	108.1	109.1	109.4	110.3	110.4	110.9	111.3	112.3	109.1
1978	113.4	114.2	115.6	116.5	117.9	119.0	119.5	120.4	120.8	121.5	123.0	123.6	118.8
1979	124.6	125.1	125.2	126.5	127.3	128.2	128.8	129.2	129.9	130.1	130.4	129.9	127.9
1980	129.3	129.3	129.8	129.8	128.4	126.2	124.8	124.1	124.5	125.0	125.7	126.9	127.0
1981	126.4	126.1	124.9	124.8	125.9	126.7	128.1	129.1	129.6	129.7	129.5	129.4	127.5
1982	129.7	130.2	129.6	129.9	129.4	129.3	128.8	127.7	127.8	126.7	125.0	124.0	128.2

SIX MONTH SMOOTHED CHANGE IN LAGGING INDEX, UNITED STATES (ANNUAL RATE, PERCENT)

YEAR	JAN	FEB	MAR	APR	MAY	JUN	JUL	AUG	SEP	OCT	NOV	DEC	AVGE
1949	4.4	3.1	1.2	-0.6	-1.9	-4.9	-7.3	-8.5	-7.3	-6.2	-6.2	-6.8	-3.4
1950	-6.3	-5.7	-3.8	-2.6	-0.6	-2.6	4.6	8.6	11.3	16.0	17.3	17.8	4.9
1951	23.8	26.9	27.1	28.6	30.7	26.8	23.7	20.8	17.5	16.6	14.1	15.0	22.6
1952	13.1	13.0	9.7	8.0	6.0	6.9	6.9	5.8	4.3	5.3	7.7	6.2	7.7
1953	7.6	9.0	9.0	9.4	11.7	9.2	8.7	7.3	6.3	4.5	1.8	-1.3	6.9
1954	-3.0	-4.3	-7.7	-9.0	-9.4	-9.5	-9.1	-10.9	-9.7	-9.3	-7.2	-4.6	-7.8
1955	-3.7	-2.3	0.0	1.4	4.8	7.7	9.6	15.5	14.4	16.7	17.6	17.3	8.3
1956	17.6	17.9	16.7	18.8	17.5	16.0	14.4	13.4	12.4	10.6	8.4	6.7	14.2
1957	5.9	4.7	4.6	4.2	4.2	3.8	3.4	6.4	6.0	2.6	1.1	0.0	3.9
1958	-4.0	-7.6	-9.7	-12.9	-16.5	-16.3	-15.0	-14.5	-9.5	-6.2	-4.3	-2.0	-9.9
1959	-0.4	-1.6	4.1	7.5	10.8	14.6	15.3	15.6	18.0	16.9	14.7	14.9	11.1
1960	13.5	13.8	12.4	11.9	12.9	9.8	6.8	2.8	0.0	-1.0	-0.7	-1.7	6.7
1961	-2.7	-3.1	-4.4	-5.4	-5.5	-4.5	-4.1	-2.1	-1.1	-0.4	0.4	1.4	-2.6
1962	2.5	3.6	5.7	7.5	8.2	9.3	8.8	8.4	8.0	8.0	6.5	5.4	6.8
1963	4.4	3.7	3.3	3.3	2.6	3.3	3.6	4.3	5.6	6.6	7.5	7.8	4.7
1964	6.8	7.4	7.1	8.0	8.3	7.6	7.2	7.5	8.1	7.7	7.6	8.5	7.6
1965	9.7	9.9	11.4	11.3	12.4	11.4	12.5	11.8	11.4	11.3	10.6	13.4	11.4
1966	14.1	13.9	16.0	16.4	16.7	17.9	18.5	18.5	18.0	17.0	15.7	13.7	16.4
1967	12.1	9.1	7.1	4.3	3.6	2.7	2.2	0.4	0.2	0.2	1.8	4.2	4.0
1968	4.6	4.4	4.2	6.8	8.3	7.8	7.6	7.6	7.1	5.1	6.1	10.6	6.7
1969	11.4	11.5	11.4	10.3	10.4	11.6	11.7	11.4	10.7	9.6	8.1	7.1	10.4
1970	5.5	4.3	3.0	0.9	0.0	-1.6	-2.0	-2.7	-2.9	-4.2	-4.9	-7.2	-1.0
1971	-8.1	-8.2	-7.2	-6.3	-4.1	-3.0	-2.3	-1.0	0.6	1.0	0.6	1.4	-3.0
1972	8.4	1.4	-1.5	1.5	1.9	2.3	2.7	3.5	4.4	6.2	7.3	7.9	3.5
1973	8.4	10.1	11.4	12.9	13.1	13.6	15.0	14.4	13.3	11.9	10.4	10.8	12.1
1974	9.5	8.0	6.5	6.3	6.5	5.2	4.6	3.4	2.7	1.1	-0.2	-2.1	4.3
1975	-4.9	-8.1	-11.3	-13.8	-15.4	-16.1	-15.7	-14.3	-12.9	-10.6	-9.8	-8.4	-11.8
1976	4.1	-2.7	-1.3	0.2	1.8	3.5	3.8	3.6	4.4	3.8	3.6	4.1	1.7
1977	4.1	4.5	4.6	4.8	5.0	6.0	5.6	6.5	5.8	5.9	5.7	6.6	5.4
1978	7.4	7.7	9.1	9.3	10.3	10.7	10.2	10.1	9.3	8.9	9.8	9.3	9.3
1979	9.2	8.5	7.2	7.9	7.7	7.9	7.6	6.9	6.9	5.9	5.3	3.7	7.1
1980	2.0	1.4	1.6	1.0	-1.3	-4.5	-6.3	-6.8	-5.7	-4.3	-2.7	-0.4	-2.2
1981	-0.9	-0.9	-2.3	-1.9	0.4	1.9	3.9	4.9	5.0	4.6	3.7	3.1	1.8
1982	3.2	3.5	2.2	2.0	0.7	0.1	-1.0	-2.6	-2.3	-3.5	-5.6	-6.5	-0.8

19.0 LONG DURATION UNEMPLOYMENT, UNITED STATES (PERCENT)

YEAR	JAN	FEB	MAR	APR	MAY	JUN	JUL	AUG	SEP	OCT	NOV	DEC	AVGE
1948	0.5	0.5	0.5	0.5	0.5	0.5	0.5	0.5	0.5	0.5	0.5	0.5	0.5
1949	0.5	0.6	0.7	0.8	1.0	1.2	1.4	1.5	1.6	1.6	1.7	1.6	1.2
1950	1.5	1.5	1.5	1.5	1.4	1.4	1.2	1.0	1.0	0.9	0.8	0.8	1.2
1951	0.7	0.6	0.6	0.5	0.4	0.4	0.3	0.3	0.4	0.4	0.3	0.4	0.5
1952	0.5	0.4	0.4	0.4	0.4	0.3	0.3	0.3	0.3	0.3	0.4	0.4	0.4
1953	0.4	0.3	0.3	0.3	0.3	0.3	0.3	0.3	0.3	0.3	0.4	0.5	0.3
1954	0.6	0.8	1.2	1.2	1.4	1.4	1.5	1.6	1.6	1.6	1.5	1.3	1.3
1955	1.4	1.3	1.3	1.3	1.1	1.0	1.0	0.8	0.9	0.9	0.9	0.9	1.1
1956	0.8	0.8	0.8	0.7	0.8	0.8	0.8	0.8	0.9	0.8	0.9	0.9	0.8
1957	0.8	0.8	0.8	0.8	0.8	0.8	0.8	0.8	0.8	1.0	1.0	1.1	0.9
1958	1.3	1.5	1.7	2.1	2.2	2.5	2.6	2.8	2.6	2.5	2.3	2.2	2.2
1959	2.1	1.9	1.8	1.5	1.4	1.4	1.3	1.3	1.4	1.7	1.7	1.6	1.5
1960	1.3	1.2	1.4	1.3	1.1	1.2	1.3	1.3	1.4	1.7	2.0	1.9	1.4
1961	1.9	2.0	2.1	2.3	2.4	2.3	2.6	2.3	2.2	2.1	2.0	1.9	2.2
1962	1.8	1.8	1.7	1.6	1.6	1.5	1.5	1.6	1.5	1.4	1.5	1.4	1.6
1963	1.6	1.6	1.5	1.5	1.3	1.5	1.5	1.6	1.5	1.5	1.5	1.4	1.5
1964	1.5	1.4	1.4	1.3	1.3	1.4	1.4	1.3	1.3	1.2	1.3	1.2	1.3
1965	1.1	1.2	1.1	1.1	1.0	1.1	0.9	1.0	1.0	0.9	0.9	0.9	1.0
1966	0.8	0.8	0.8	0.8	0.7	0.6	0.6	0.6	0.6	0.6	0.6	0.6	0.7
1967	0.6	0.6	0.6	0.6	0.5	0.5	0.6	0.6	0.6	0.6	0.6	0.6	0.6
1968	0.6	0.6	0.6	0.5	0.5	0.5	0.5	0.5	0.5	0.5	0.5	0.4	0.5
1969	0.4	0.4	0.4	0.5	0.5	0.5	0.5	0.5	0.5	0.5	0.5	0.5	0.5
1970	0.5	0.6	0.6	0.7	0.7	0.8	0.8	0.9	0.9	0.9	1.0	1.3	0.8
1971	1.3	1.3	1.3	1.4	1.4	1.4	1.5	1.5	1.5	1.5	1.5	1.5	1.4
1972	1.5	1.5	1.4	1.4	1.3	1.3	1.3	1.3	1.3	1.3	1.2	1.1	1.3
1973	1.1	1.0	1.0	0.9	0.9	1.0	1.0	1.0	1.1	0.9	0.9	0.8	0.9
1974	0.9	0.9	0.9	1.0	1.0	1.0	1.0	1.0	1.1	1.2	1.2	1.4	1.0
1975	1.7	2.0	2.2	2.6	2.8	3.0	3.1	3.0	3.1	2.9	3.0	3.0	2.7
1976	2.3	2.7	2.6	2.3	2.2	2.4	2.4	2.5	2.4	2.4	2.4	2.4	2.5
1977	2.3	2.2	2.1	2.0	2.0	1.9	1.9	1.8	1.9	1.8	1.8	1.7	1.9
1978	1.6	1.6	1.3	1.5	1.2	1.3	1.3	1.2	1.1	1.3	1.2	1.2	1.2
1979	1.2	1.2	1.4	1.2	1.2	1.1	1.1	1.1	1.1	1.2	1.2	1.2	1.2
1980	1.3	1.3	1.4	1.6	1.6	1.7	1.9	2.0	2.1	2.1	2.2	2.2	1.8
1981	2.2	2.1	2.1	2.0	2.0	2.2	2.0	2.0	2.1	2.1	2.2	2.2	2.1
1982	2.2	2.5	2.7	2.8	3.0	3.2	3.2	3.3	3.5	3.8	4.1	4.3	3.2

20.0 INVESTMENT EXPENDITURES, PLANT AND EQUIPMENT, IN CONSTANT PRICES, UNITED STATES
(ANNUAL RATE, BILLION 1972 DOLLARS)

YEAR	IQ	IIQ	IIIQ	IVQ	AVGE
1948	49.57	49.21	48.00	49.12	48.97
1949	46.85	44.39	42.95	41.48	43.92
1950	42.27	43.72	47.01	49.52	45.63
1951	49.09	51.80	52.65	52.25	51.45
1952	54.14	52.49	50.12	51.13	51.97
1953	53.44	54.22	53.99	54.14	53.95
1954	53.87	53.52	53.11	52.33	53.21
1955	52.96	55.69	59.22	61.97	57.46
1956	64.36	66.67	66.92	67.32	66.32
1957	67.98	68.87	68.29	65.62	67.69
1958	63.36	58.61	57.53	57.52	59.25
1959	58.68	60.63	62.88	63.17	61.34
1960	66.37	68.08	65.65	66.68	66.69
1961	65.11	64.88	65.97	67.45	65.85
1962	68.30	69.63	72.03	70.24	70.05
1963	68.41	71.09	73.66	75.44	72.15
1964	78.80	81.91	84.05	85.96	82.68
1965	87.79	91.57	94.56	98.96	93.22
1966	102.35	104.93	107.70	108.34	105.83
1967	105.84	104.31	103.71	103.63	104.37
1968	107.30	104.77	105.16	107.83	106.26
1969	111.28	112.90	116.57	115.81	114.14
1970	115.87	116.36	112.38	112.46	115.27
1971	110.60	112.71	112.48	114.17	112.49
1972	116.87	116.69	119.20	126.95	119.93
1973	128.61	133.30	133.14	133.59	132.16
1974	135.70	137.64	135.23	132.13	135.17
1975	125.29	119.70	117.05	116.60	119.66
1976	119.99	121.27	124.51	126.67	123.11
1977	130.98	133.40	138.53	136.11	134.75
1978	139.68	146.10	146.92	153.09	146.45
1979	154.61	156.83	158.18	161.25	157.72
1980	161.54	159.78	158.16	157.00	159.12
1981	160.38	157.84	161.33	158.22	159.44
1982	157.49	152.75	149.39	***	***

21.0 BUSINESS INVENTORIES, IN CONSTANT PRICES, UNITED STATES (BILLION 1972 DOLLARS)

YEAR	JAN	FEB	MAR	APR	MAY	JUN	JUL	AUG	SEP	OCT	NOV	DEC	AVGE
1948	78.19	78.66	79.15	79.43	79.70	80.69	81.82	81.95	82.04	82.15	82.15	81.91	80.65
1949	83.20	83.50	83.52	83.16	83.12	83.16	83.30	83.32	83.63	83.11	82.31	81.28	83.05
1950	81.47	81.28	81.87	82.23	83.12	83.81	82.74	84.64	85.61	86.58	88.04	88.54	84.16
1951	90.43	91.15	92.20	93.57	95.24	96.53	97.46	98.56	98.97	99.68	100.28	100.72	96.23
1952	101.52	101.45	101.55	101.56	101.31	101.96	101.94	101.91	103.16	104.20	104.81	105.26	102.55
1953	107.67	107.90	108.39	109.38	109.72	110.18	110.99	110.94	110.99	110.26	109.52	109.18	109.59
1954	108.65	108.30	107.88	107.36	106.94	106.38	105.89	105.26	105.19	104.71	105.08	104.92	106.38
1955	105.25	105.32	106.04	105.92	106.57	107.55	108.14	108.78	108.64	109.18	109.30	109.60	107.52
1956	110.22	111.29	111.49	112.56	113.19	113.70	114.24	114.63	115.21	115.29	115.82	115.76	113.62
1957	116.00	115.81	115.77	116.05	116.04	116.20	116.43	117.05	117.46	116.37	116.10	116.16	116.29
1958	114.54	114.03	113.70	113.16	112.67	112.46	112.30	112.01	112.72	112.96	113.20	113.92	113.14
1959	114.03	114.40	114.80	116.24	116.79	117.55	118.33	118.13	117.57	117.77	117.79	119.34	116.89
1960	120.33	121.58	122.43	122.35	123.08	123.34	123.76	123.52	123.92	123.76	123.91	122.89	122.91
1961	122.35	122.29	121.67	121.68	121.96	121.81	122.21	122.62	123.20	123.34	124.01	124.22	122.61
1962	124.95	125.56	126.42	126.58	127.54	128.21	128.67	129.10	129.87	130.46	130.39	130.78	128.21
1963	131.11	131.50	132.00	132.13	132.48	133.09	133.47	134.08	134.83	135.76	136.17	136.27	133.57
1964	136.69	137.14	137.68	138.23	138.68	139.31	139.58	140.09	141.40	141.17	142.21	143.29	139.62
1965	144.22	144.69	145.98	146.63	147.27	148.00	149.17	150.08	150.41	150.82	151.41	152.13	148.40
1966	152.71	154.16	155.26	156.35	157.89	159.65	160.93	162.09	163.28	164.96	166.52	168.06	160.15
1967	170.49	171.34	172.16	172.91	173.26	173.22	173.97	174.94	175.17	175.18	176.42	177.50	173.88
1968	177.83	178.17	178.24	179.26	180.44	181.08	181.51	182.57	183.10	184.10	184.38	185.01	181.31
1969	185.29	186.45	187.06	187.79	188.58	189.35	190.35	191.14	192.13	192.96	193.10	193.70	189.82
1970	193.40	194.16	194.46	195.07	194.68	195.41	196.08	196.74	196.78	196.53	196.90	196.98	195.60
1971	197.29	197.71	198.26	198.91	199.63	200.24	200.40	200.73	201.27	201.50	201.28	201.70	199.91
1972	202.08	202.22	202.15	202.65	203.64	203.86	203.99	205.31	206.26	207.02	207.73	208.26	204.60
1973	209.47	210.32	210.86	211.27	212.14	213.23	214.26	214.62	215.42	216.51	218.02	220.24	213.86
1974	221.20	221.67	223.00	222.96	224.14	225.10	225.25	224.52	224.86	226.00	225.92	226.58	224.27
1975	225.48	223.40	221.87	220.98	219.35	218.37	218.14	218.80	218.45	218.83	217.82	216.92	219.87
1976	225.58	226.48	227.53	228.50	229.23	231.12	231.10	231.36	233.58	233.33	233.70	235.08	230.55
1977	235.70	236.44	237.08	238.13	239.07	239.78	240.70	242.13	243.78	243.97	244.92	246.18	240.66
1978	247.15	248.26	250.48	252.37	253.35	253.79	254.21	255.46	256.17	257.18	258.36	259.67	253.87
1979	261.05	261.76	262.18	263.06	264.13	264.67	266.64	266.76	265.18	266.06	265.11	264.45	264.27
1980	264.08	263.78	263.95	265.69	265.61	264.67	264.36	263.66	263.62	263.77	263.09	262.78	264.09
1981	262.33	263.33	263.10	263.41	264.70	265.92	266.53	267.56	269.42	270.47	271.17	269.85	266.48
1982	267.69	266.45	265.98	266.54	264.54	265.18	265.56	265.46	266.03	265.71	***	***	***

22.0 CHANGE IN HOURS PER UNIT OF OUTPUT, NONFARM BUSINESS, UNITED STATES
(PERCENT CHANGE FROM YEAR AGO)

YEAR	IQ	IIQ	IIIQ	IVQ	AVGE
1948	-3.1	-4.4	-3.9	-4.7	-4.0
1949	-3.2	-1.1	-3.2	-0.8	-2.1
1950	-4.5	-5.9	-5.5	-6.8	-5.7
1951	-2.3	-0.5	-1.7	-2.1	-1.6
1952	-2.9	-3.8	-1.4	-1.0	-2.3
1953	-1.7	-1.5	-2.2	-1.2	-1.6
1954	-0.7	-0.5	-1.6	-2.8	-1.4
1955	-4.3	-4.8	-3.6	-2.4	-3.8
1956	-0.5	-0.2	0.3	-0.8	-0.3
1957	-1.7	-1.3	-1.7	-1.7	-1.6
1958	-0.8	-2.2	-2.7	-4.0	-2.4
1959	-5.0	-4.7	-2.1	-0.7	-3.1
1960	-1.6	0.3	-1.2	-0.7	-0.8
1961	0.0	-2.7	-3.7	-5.2	-2.9
1962	-5.2	-2.6	-3.2	-2.8	-3.4
1963	-2.2	-3.9	-3.6	-2.8	-3.1
1964	-4.0	-3.9	-3.8	-3.6	-3.8
1965	-2.8	-2.6	-2.5	-3.8	-2.9
1966	-3.6	-2.7	-2.2	-1.2	-2.4
1967	-0.6	-2.0	-2.3	-2.6	-1.9
1968	-3.6	-3.1	-3.1	-2.3	-3.0
1969	-1.0	0.0	0.9	1.2	0.3
1970	1.5	0.0	-2.0	-1.3	-0.5
1971	-3.7	-2.8	-2.5	-3.5	-3.1
1972	-2.6	-3.5	-3.3	-4.4	-3.4
1973	-4.9	-3.2	-1.6	-0.4	-2.5
1974	2.0	2.0	2.4	2.5	2.2
1975	1.6	-1.6	-3.7	-3.3	-1.8
1976	-4.8	-3.3	-2.0	-2.2	-3.1
1977	-2.1	-1.9	-2.3	-2.4	-2.2
1978	-1.1	-0.9	0.0	-0.4	-0.6
1979	0.1	1.4	1.7	2.0	1.3
1980	1.6	1.8	0.5	-0.4	0.9
1981	-1.7	-2.4	-1.6	0.1	-1.4
1982	1.2	0.6	-0.3	***	***

161

23.0 COMMERCIAL AND INDUSTRIAL LOANS OUTSTANDING, IN CONSTANT PRICES, UNITED STATES (MILLION 1967 DOLLARS)

YEAR	JAN	FEB	MAR	APR	MAY	JUN	JUL	AUG	SEP	OCT	NOV	DEC	AVGE
1948	16303.	16317.	16333.	16371.	16810.	17001.	17229.	17175.	17054.	16909.	16677.	16571.	16729.
1949	16617.	16677.	16624.	16532.	16489.	16296.	15951.	15693.	15670.	15707.	15624.	15565.	16120.
1950	15651.	15717.	15715.	15801.	15802.	16070.	16270.	16472.	16836.	16921.	17179.	17363.	16316.
1951	17552.	18100.	18589.	19140.	19603.	19877.	20088.	20370.	20481.	20684.	20799.	21009.	19691.
1952	21298.	21307.	21514.	21595.	21746.	22000.	22217.	22164.	22321.	22670.	23116.	23200.	22096.
1953	23275.	23330.	23414.	23738.	23808.	23648.	23516.	23683.	23587.	23422.	23244.	22791.	23455.
1954	22729.	22852.	22821.	22720.	22551.	22403.	22404.	21484.	21430.	21366.	21547.	21934.	22187.
1955	22089.	22160.	22427.	22543.	22990.	23370.	23686.	23912.	24022.	24403.	24683.	24952.	23436.
1956	25229.	25376.	26038.	26451.	26947.	27334.	27718.	27751.	27992.	27951.	28140.	28213.	27095.
1957	28419.	28383.	28870.	29188.	29365.	29744.	29825.	29801.	29889.	29522.	29132.	29015.	29263.
1958	28674.	28435.	28330.	28219.	27867.	27779.	27680.	27465.	27614.	27675.	27711.	27774.	27935.
1959	27785.	27741.	27883.	28116.	28551.	29065.	28988.	29404.	29587.	29847.	29972.	30144.	28924.
1960	30252.	30705.	30919.	31112.	31532.	31938.	31142.	31772.	31952.	31957.	32108.	32012.	31515.
1961	31926.	31894.	32035.	32037.	32081.	32086.	32142.	32257.	32304.	32374.	32369.	32445.	32163.
1962	32559.	32753.	32943.	33116.	33259.	33564.	33752.	34114.	34314.	34659.	34955.	35000.	33749.
1963	35052.	35173.	35295.	35572.	35697.	35733.	35824.	35994.	36318.	36707.	37443.	37775.	36049.
1964	37625.	37921.	37966.	38308.	38626.	38955.	39155.	39553.	40114.	40146.	40530.	41089.	39166.
1965	41838.	42852.	43715.	44328.	45200.	45592.	45931.	46852.	47807.	48397.	48993.	49610.	45926.
1966	50178.	50873.	51407.	51660.	52250.	53149.	53810.	54758.	55196.	55599.	55971.	56203.	53421.
1967	56190.	56374.	56900.	57330.	57399.	57733.	58038.	57911.	58097.	58276.	58539.	59062.	57654.
1968	59286.	59231.	59340.	60273.	60489.	60861.	61177.	61716.	62125.	62560.	63338.	64074.	61206.
1969	64862.	65141.	65440.	66597.	67623.	68504.	68887.	69347.	69956.	70582.	70860.	71227.	68252.
1970	70763.	71436.	71502.	71434.	71634.	71589.	71609.	72063.	71940.	70113.	69499.	68906.	71041.
1971	68328.	68533.	68346.	67546.	67757.	67625.	66789.	67451.	68930.	68560.	68557.	67955.	68031.
1972	67159.	67444.	67511.	67737.	67968.	67774.	67660.	67959.	68199.	69537.	70339.	71006.	68358.
1973	72213.	75257.	76827.	77222.	77480.	78523.	79600.	80930.	80207.	79439.	78564.	77844.	77842.
1974	77314.	76779.	76223.	77227.	76310.	75688.	75744.	75397.	76645.	75850.	75937.	76112.	76269.
1975	75584.	74629.	73313.	72293.	70974.	69757.	69012.	67969.	67016.	66246.	65819.	65540.	69846.
1976	64399.	64221.	62435.	60434.	60173.	60115.	59409.	58551.	58847.	58246.	58987.	59264.	60493.
1977	58885.	58786.	58627.	58281.	58251.	58652.	58344.	58571.	58520.	58675.	59211.	59355.	58673.
1978	59409.	59564.	60159.	60436.	61188.	61820.	61710.	61676.	61722.	61518.	61796.	61358.	61030.
1979	62145.	62450.	62049.	62720.	63184.	63567.	63758.	63880.	64239.	63065.	62328.	61742.	62927.
1980	61209.	60989.	60633.	60227.	59009.	59323.	58612.	58809.	59460.	59551.	60548.	60531.	59884.
1981	59694.	58647.	57356.	57599.	58504.	59323.	60228.	60801.	61383.	61433.	61732.	62221.	59910.
1982	63108.	64702.	65079.	66770.	67926.	68805.	68574.	68616.	69764.	69797.	68974.	68362.	67540.

162

24.0 BANK INTEREST RATES ON BUSINESS LOANS, UNITED STATES (PERCENT)

YEAR	JAN	FEB	MAR	APR	MAY	JUN	JUL	AUG	SEP	OCT	NOV	DEC	AVGE
1948	1.75	1.75	1.75	1.75	1.75	1.75	1.75	2.00	2.00	2.00	2.00	2.00	1.85
1949	2.00	2.00	2.00	2.00	2.00	2.00	2.00	2.00	2.00	2.00	2.00	2.00	2.00
1950	2.00	2.00	2.00	2.00	2.00	2.00	2.00	2.00	2.08	2.25	2.25	2.25	2.07
1951	2.44	2.50	2.50	2.50	2.50	2.50	3.00	3.00	2.50	2.62	2.75	2.85	2.55
1952	3.00	3.00	3.00	3.00	3.00	3.00	3.00	3.00	3.00	3.00	3.00	3.00	3.00
1953	3.00	3.00	3.00	3.03	3.25	3.25	3.25	3.25	3.25	3.25	3.25	3.25	3.17
1954	3.25	3.25	3.13	3.00	3.00	3.00	3.00	3.00	3.25	3.40	3.00	3.00	3.05
1955	3.00	3.00	3.00	3.00	3.00	3.00	3.00	3.23	3.25	3.40	3.50	3.50	3.16
1956	3.50	3.50	3.50	3.65	3.75	3.75	3.75	3.84	4.00	4.00	4.00	4.00	3.77
1957	4.00	4.00	4.00	4.00	4.00	4.00	4.00	4.42	4.50	4.50	4.50	4.50	4.20
1958	4.34	4.00	4.00	3.83	3.50	3.50	3.50	3.50	3.83	4.00	4.00	4.00	3.83
1959	4.00	4.00	4.00	4.00	4.23	4.50	4.50	4.50	5.00	5.00	5.00	5.00	4.48
1960	5.00	5.00	5.00	5.00	5.00	5.00	5.00	4.85	4.50	4.50	4.50	4.50	4.82
1961	4.50	4.50	4.50	4.50	4.50	4.50	4.50	4.50	4.50	4.50	4.50	4.50	4.50
1962	4.50	4.50	4.50	4.50	4.50	4.50	4.50	4.50	4.50	4.50	4.50	4.50	4.50
1963	4.50	4.50	4.50	4.50	4.50	4.50	4.50	4.50	4.50	4.50	4.50	4.50	4.50
1964	4.50	4.50	4.50	4.50	4.50	4.50	4.50	4.50	4.50	4.50	4.50	4.50	4.50
1965	4.50	4.50	4.50	4.50	4.50	4.50	4.50	4.50	4.50	4.50	4.50	4.92	4.53
1966	5.00	5.00	5.35	5.50	5.50	5.52	5.75	5.88	6.00	6.00	6.00	6.00	5.62
1967	5.96	5.75	5.71	5.50	5.50	5.50	5.50	5.50	5.50	5.50	5.68	6.00	5.63
1968	6.00	6.00	6.00	6.20	6.50	6.50	6.50	6.50	6.40	6.00	6.15	6.60	6.28
1969	6.95	7.00	7.24	7.50	7.50	8.23	8.50	8.50	8.50	8.50	8.50	8.50	7.95
1970	8.50	8.50	8.39	8.00	8.00	8.00	8.00	8.00	7.83	7.50	7.28	6.92	7.91
1971	6.29	5.88	5.44	5.28	5.46	5.50	5.91	6.00	6.00	5.90	5.51	5.49	5.72
1972	5.18	4.75	4.75	4.97	5.00	5.04	5.25	5.27	5.50	5.73	5.75	5.79	5.25
1973	6.00	6.02	6.30	6.61	7.01	7.49	8.30	9.23	9.86	9.94	9.75	9.75	8.02
1974	9.73	9.21	8.85	10.02	11.25	11.54	11.97	12.00	12.00	11.68	10.83	10.50	10.80
1975	10.05	8.96	7.93	7.50	7.40	7.07	7.15	7.66	7.88	7.96	7.53	7.26	7.86
1976	7.00	6.75	6.75	6.75	6.75	7.20	7.25	7.01	7.00	6.77	6.50	6.35	6.84
1977	6.25	6.25	6.25	6.25	6.41	6.75	6.75	6.83	7.13	7.52	7.75	7.75	6.82
1978	7.93	8.00	8.00	8.00	8.27	8.63	9.00	9.01	9.41	9.94	10.94	11.55	9.06
1979	11.75	11.75	11.75	11.75	11.75	11.65	11.54	11.91	12.90	14.39	15.55	15.30	12.67
1980	15.25	15.63	18.31	19.77	16.57	12.63	11.48	11.12	12.23	13.79	16.06	20.35	15.27
1981	20.16	19.43	18.05	17.15	19.61	20.03	20.39	20.50	20.08	18.45	16.84	15.75	18.87
1982	15.75	16.56	16.50	16.50	16.50	16.50	16.26	14.39	13.50	12.52	11.85	11.50	14.86

CANADA

LEADING INDEX. CANADA (1980=100)

YEAR	JAN	FEB	MAR	APR	MAY	JUN	JUL	AUG	SEP	OCT	NOV	DEC	AVGE
1948	31.1	30.4	29.9	30.6	30.7	30.9	30.8	31.3	31.3	31.3	31.2	31.1	30.9
1949	30.7	30.3	30.1	29.9	29.4	29.5	29.6	29.8	29.9	30.2	30.4	30.6	30.0
1950	30.8	31.1	30.8	31.5	32.0	33.0	33.3	33.5	34.6	35.2	35.7	35.4	33.1
1951	35.6	35.7	35.3	35.1	35.0	34.2	33.8	33.2	33.1	33.2	32.8	32.7	34.1
1952	32.8	33.0	32.9	33.2	32.7	33.0	33.0	33.5	33.3	33.7	34.0	33.9	33.2
1953	34.4	34.5	34.7	34.5	35.0	34.7	34.9	34.6	34.6	34.5	34.5	34.4	34.6
1954	34.4	34.3	34.4	34.7	34.6	35.0	35.3	35.4	35.6	35.8	35.8	36.6	35.2
1955	36.9	37.1	37.4	37.9	38.0	38.5	38.9	39.4	39.5	39.7	39.7	40.1	38.6
1956	40.5	40.8	41.0	40.9	40.9	41.1	40.9	40.9	41.1	41.1	41.1	40.7	40.9
1957	40.8	40.7	40.7	40.6	40.7	40.7	40.6	40.2	39.9	39.4	39.6	39.6	40.3
1958	39.7	39.9	40.3	40.4	40.7	40.7	41.2	41.5	41.6	42.1	42.6	42.4	41.1
1959	42.9	43.0	42.9	43.2	43.2	43.5	43.8	44.0	43.8	43.9	43.4	43.8	43.4
1960	44.2	44.0	43.8	43.8	43.6	43.7	43.7	43.9	44.2	44.0	44.1	44.4	43.9
1961	44.6	44.8	45.2	45.7	45.9	46.1	46.8	46.9	47.2	47.5	47.7	47.9	46.4
1962	47.7	48.1	48.1	48.1	48.4	48.8	49.0	49.1	49.0	48.9	49.0	49.4	48.6
1963	49.6	49.9	50.0	50.4	50.8	50.9	51.1	51.1	51.7	52.1	52.9	52.8	51.1
1964	53.6	53.6	53.5	54.0	54.0	54.2	54.2	54.7	55.1	54.9	55.3	54.7	54.3
1965	55.8	56.0	56.5	56.6	56.8	57.1	57.3	57.0	57.4	58.2	58.0	58.5	57.1
1966	58.9	58.7	58.9	58.9	58.2	59.2	58.4	58.1	58.4	58.6	58.6	58.8	58.6
1967	58.9	58.8	58.7	59.3	59.2	59.8	59.9	60.1	60.3	60.1	60.0	61.0	59.7
1968	60.8	60.8	61.2	61.8	62.4	62.4	62.9	63.0	63.5	64.0	64.6	64.6	62.7
1969	64.9	65.3	65.9	65.5	65.9	65.5	65.3	65.2	65.6	64.8	65.6	65.2	65.4
1970	64.1	64.3	63.6	63.7	63.8	63.6	63.9	64.5	64.4	64.0	63.8	63.6	63.9
1971	63.9	65.0	65.7	65.9	66.1	66.9	67.3	68.1	68.4	68.7	69.0	69.5	67.0
1972	70.2	70.2	70.8	71.5	71.7	72.1	72.0	72.4	73.0	73.5	74.2	75.1	72.2
1973	76.3	77.5	77.9	77.6	77.6	77.5	79.5	80.3	79.9	80.8	81.9	82.4	79.1
1974	83.0	83.9	84.3	83.1	82.6	81.9	81.8	81.3	81.1	81.1	80.6	79.9	82.0
1975	80.0	79.4	78.7	79.1	79.3	79.0	79.8	80.4	80.1	80.6	81.4	81.3	79.9
1976	82.2	82.9	82.9	83.6	83.8	83.8	83.9	83.8	83.0	82.6	82.4	83.1	83.2
1977	84.1	84.7	85.1	84.8	84.8	85.4	85.3	85.7	85.8	86.1	86.6	87.1	85.5
1978	87.4	87.8	87.7	88.8	88.7	89.0	90.5	91.4	93.4	94.3	94.4	96.0	90.9
1979	96.7	97.0	98.2	98.2	99.3	99.0	99.1	99.9	100.0	100.0	100.1	99.3	98.9
1980	102.0	101.3	99.9	99.1	98.1	98.8	98.8	98.7	99.8	100.5	101.0	101.4	100.0
1981	102.3	102.6	103.2	103.6	103.9	102.7	103.8	102.0	100.0	99.3	97.4	98.3	101.6
1982	95.8	94.5	93.7	92.6	92.6	91.5	91.3	91.9	92.0	93.1	93.9	95.8	93.2

164

SIX MONTH SMOOTHED CHANGE IN LEADING INDEX, CANADA (ANNUAL RATE, PERCENT)

YEAR	JAN	FEB	MAR	APR	MAY	JUN	JUL	AUG	SEP	OCT	NOV	DEC	AVGE
1949	-0.8	-3.5	-4.3	-5.4	-8.2	-6.9	-5.9	-3.9	-2.8	0.0	1.6	3.3	-3.1
1950	4.9	6.7	4.2	8.5	10.3	15.3	15.3	14.6	19.7	20.5	20.5	16.2	13.1
1951	14.4	12.4	7.9	4.9	2.7	-3.2	-5.9	-9.0	-9.2	-8.4	-9.2	-8.6	-0.9
1952	-6.9	-5.1	-4.2	-1.7	-3.6	-0.5	-0.4	3.0	1.7	3.8	5.6	4.0	-0.4
1953	6.6	6.5	7.0	4.6	6.8	4.2	4.1	2.0	1.3	5.9	-0.4	-0.8	3.5
1954	-1.1	-1.7	-1.0	0.5	0.2	2.4	4.0	4.5	4.8	5.9	5.0	9.0	2.7
1955	9.4	9.4	9.3	10.8	9.7	10.7	11.3	12.2	10.9	10.2	8.7	8.9	10.1
1956	9.4	9.4	8.6	6.5	5.4	5.1	3.1	2.7	2.6	2.0	1.8	-0.7	4.7
1957	-0.4	-1.2	-1.0	-1.2	-0.8	-1.0	-1.2	-2.8	-3.7	-5.6	-5.1	-3.4	-2.3
1958	-2.4	-1.1	0.8	1.5	2.7	3.1	5.4	6.3	6.5	7.9	9.2	6.9	3.9
1959	8.1	7.6	5.9	6.1	5.1	5.5	5.6	5.6	3.9	3.4	0.7	2.2	5.0
1960	3.0	2.0	0.7	0.1	-0.6	-0.3	-0.4	0.2	1.7	0.9	0.9	2.1	0.9
1961	2.6	3.3	5.1	6.4	6.7	4.9	8.6	8.3	8.0	8.2	7.8	7.5	6.6
1962	5.3	5.8	4.8	3.7	4.3	5.2	4.7	4.4	3.5	2.6	2.4	3.3	4.1
1963	3.9	4.1	4.1	5.1	5.6	5.7	5.3	4.7	6.5	7.1	8.9	7.2	5.6
1964	9.3	7.9	6.3	7.0	6.1	5.6	4.7	5.3	5.9	4.2	4.7	2.0	5.8
1965	5.1	5.3	6.3	5.5	5.5	5.6	5.6	3.6	4.2	6.4	4.8	5.6	5.3
1966	5.7	4.3	4.2	3.7	0.6	3.4	0.6	-0.8	-0.3	0.1	0.0	0.6	1.8
1967	1.0	0.6	0.1	2.1	1.8	3.3	3.4	3.7	3.7	2.8	2.1	4.6	2.4
1968	3.6	3.1	3.8	4.8	6.0	5.1	6.3	5.8	6.5	7.1	7.9	6.7	5.6
1969	6.8	6.9	7.3	5.1	5.4	3.2	2.0	1.1	1.6	-1.2	0.9	-0.6	3.2
1970	-3.6	-3.0	-4.5	-3.8	-3.0	-3.2	-1.8	0.2	0.0	-0.9	-1.1	-1.2	-2.2
1971	-0.2	3.1	4.9	5.0	5.1	6.8	7.2	8.6	8.6	8.4	8.3	8.4	6.2
1972	9.0	7.3	7.9	8.4	7.7	7.4	5.9	5.9	6.6	8.7	7.4	8.9	7.4
1973	10.7	12.4	11.7	9.4	8.0	6.4	10.4	10.6	7.9	8.7	9.7	9.4	9.6
1974	9.4	10.0	9.6	5.6	3.2	0.6	-0.5	-2.0	-2.6	-2.7	-4.0	-5.2	1.8
1975	-4.5	-5.2	-6.0	-4.1	-3.0	-3.0	-0.8	1.2	0.5	-1.9	3.8	3.4	-1.3
1976	5.3	6.5	5.9	6.6	6.1	5.4	4.6	3.4	1.0	-0.4	-1.1	0.2	3.6
1977	2.1	3.0	3.6	2.6	2.3	3.5	3.0	3.6	3.4	3.5	3.9	4.4	3.2
1978	4.2	4.4	3.8	5.6	4.8	6.5	7.0	7.9	11.3	11.7	10.4	12.5	7.5
1979	12.2	11.1	12.0	10.0	10.5	8.1	6.6	6.8	5.5	4.6	3.7	1.3	7.7
1980	5.8	3.6	0.3	-1.4	-2.3	-1.9	-2.0	-2.0	0.1	1.5	2.4	3.0	0.6
1981	4.2	4.9	5.7	5.8	5.8	2.7	4.1	0.0	-4.1	-5.2	-8.5	-6.3	0.8
1982	-10.3	-11.7	-12.0	-12.4	-11.0	-11.4	-10.2	-7.3	-5.6	-2.1	0.3	4.8	-7.4

CANADA LEADING, COINCIDENT AND LAGGING INTERNATIONAL ECONOMIC INDICATORS

1.0 AVERAGE WORKWEEK, MANUFACTURING, CANADA (HOURS PER WEEK)

YEAR	JAN	FEB	MAR	APR	MAY	JUN	JUL	AUG	SEP	OCT	NOV	DEC	AVGE
1948	42.1	42.3	40.9	42.5	42.0	42.1	42.0	41.8	42.3	42.4	42.2	42.8	42.1
1949	42.3	42.2	42.2	41.9	41.1	41.9	41.9	42.5	42.0	42.1	42.0	42.0	42.0
1950	41.7	41.8	42.1	42.0	42.1	42.5	42.5	42.0	42.2	42.3	42.2	42.2	42.1
1951	42.4	41.7	41.5	42.0	41.9	41.7	41.5	41.5	41.4	41.1	41.1	40.1	41.5
1952	41.1	41.1	41.4	41.4	41.2	41.2	41.2	41.5	41.4	41.4	41.7	40.3	41.2
1953	41.5	41.5	41.5	41.3	41.6	41.2	41.1	40.8	40.8	40.7	40.5	40.6	41.1
1954	40.3	40.6	40.4	40.2	39.6	40.4	40.7	40.6	40.6	40.6	40.5	41.4	40.5
1955	40.7	40.7	40.6	40.8	40.8	40.7	40.8	40.8	40.8	41.0	40.8	41.1	40.8
1956	40.9	40.9	40.7	41.0	40.7	40.9	40.7	40.7	40.8	40.9	40.9	40.0	40.7
1957	40.7	40.6	40.7	40.3	40.2	40.3	40.3	40.2	40.0	39.6	39.9	39.3	40.2
1958	39.7	39.8	40.1	40.1	40.4	40.1	40.1	40.1	40.0	40.1	40.3	39.3	40.0
1959	40.4	40.7	40.0	40.4	40.7	40.6	40.6	40.5	40.5	40.6	40.1	40.6	40.5
1960	40.5	40.2	40.2	40.2	39.7	39.9	40.4	40.1	40.2	40.5	40.5	40.7	40.2
1961	40.0	40.2	40.0	40.3	40.5	40.5	40.5	40.5	40.7	40.5	40.6	40.7	40.4
1962	40.6	40.6	40.8	40.3	40.7	40.7	40.9	40.7	40.7	40.7	40.6	39.1	40.5
1963	40.6	40.5	40.6	40.7	40.8	40.6	40.6	40.6	40.6	40.7	40.9	39.7	40.6
1964	41.1	41.0	40.4	40.9	41.1	40.8	40.8	40.9	41.0	40.9	40.6	40.5	40.8
1965	40.9	40.4	41.0	40.8	40.7	40.9	40.8	40.7	40.7	40.8	40.9	41.5	40.8
1966	40.8	41.0	40.9	40.6	40.5	40.4	40.6	40.7	40.5	40.5	40.4	40.1	40.6
1967	40.1	40.0	39.8	40.1	39.9	40.3	40.2	40.1	40.0	40.1	40.1	40.3	40.1
1968	40.0	40.2	39.8	40.3	40.3	40.0	40.0	40.0	40.2	40.2	40.2	39.5	40.1
1969	40.1	40.1	40.2	39.9	40.1	39.8	40.0	39.8	39.9	39.7	39.8	38.6	39.8
1970	39.8	39.8	39.2	39.4	39.7	39.7	39.4	39.6	39.3	39.4	39.3	39.4	39.5
1971	38.9	38.8	39.6	39.4	39.3	39.5	39.6	39.6	39.6	39.6	39.7	39.4	39.5
1972	39.7	39.5	39.5	39.9	39.6	39.8	39.8	39.9	40.0	40.0	39.9	40.2	39.8
1973	39.8	39.9	39.8	39.1	39.6	39.5	39.0	39.1	39.3	39.3	39.4	39.8	39.4
1974	39.3	39.1	39.1	38.8	37.9	38.7	38.7	38.7	38.5	38.5	38.4	37.8	38.6
1975	38.5	38.3	37.9	38.4	38.5	38.2	38.4	38.3	38.4	38.5	38.4	38.6	38.4
1976	38.5	38.5	38.6	38.5	38.4	38.4	38.5	38.4	38.4	38.3	38.5	39.0	38.5
1977	38.3	38.5	38.5	38.3	38.2	38.5	38.4	38.6	38.5	38.5	38.4	38.7	38.4
1978	37.6	38.7	38.2	38.6	38.6	38.6	38.7	38.8	38.7	38.6	38.8	39.1	38.6
1979	38.8	38.7	38.7	38.7	38.7	38.6	38.7	38.6	38.6	38.4	38.5	38.2	38.6
1980	38.6	38.5	38.5	38.2	38.2	38.0	37.7	38.1	38.4	38.5	38.5	38.6	38.3
1981	38.6	38.5	38.4	38.6	38.7	38.6	38.5	38.3	38.0	38.3	37.9	37.6	38.3
1982	37.9	38.0	37.7	37.7	37.4	37.5	37.4	37.4	37.0	37.2	37.1	37.3	37.5

2.0 INITIAL CLAIMS, UNEMPLOYMENT INSURANCE, CANADA (THOUSANDS)

YEAR	JAN	FEB	MAR	APR	MAY	JUN	JUL	AUG	SEP	OCT	NOV	DEC	AVGE
1948	51.	54.	49.	56.	49.	55.	54.	47.	50.	53.	58.	66.	54.
1949	65.	66.	67.	67.	76.	76.	77.	93.	93.	95.	101.	86.	80.
1950	93.	78.	157.	92.	105.	87.	77.	115.	87.	84.	82.	82.	95.
1951	89.	81.	81.	85.	83.	99.	102.	107.	110.	112.	110.	105.	97.
1952	112.	105.	112.	114.	128.	118.	131.	111.	113.	118.	111.	127.	117.
1953	120.	130.	129.	130.	113.	125.	133.	133.	150.	166.	173.	165.	139.
1954	160.	162.	180.	171.	182.	200.	187.	200.	191.	173.	171.	170.	179.
1955	173.	182.	182.	164.	157.	160.	143.	156.	152.	129.	145.	145.	157.
1956	150.	148.	135.	143.	134.	100.	126.	131.	111.	118.	135.	134.	130.
1957	208.	157.	155.	167.	161.	158.	189.	201.	210.	221.	218.	245.	191.
1958	217.	207.	208.	221.	248.	288.	272.	247.	263.	248.	209.	230.	238.
1959	192.	196.	192.	211.	194.	198.	196.	181.	191.	193.	230.	214.	199.
1960	188.	219.	239.	219.	233.	240.	224.	269.	234.	226.	245.	218.	230.
1961	211.	218.	219.	213.	224.	211.	199.	219.	208.	200.	202.	175.	208.
1962	196.	192.	191.	181.	191.	178.	175.	180.	170.	190.	197.	159.	183.
1963	194.	175.	166.	174.	172.	157.	173.	157.	164.	159.	156.	170.	168.
1964	156.	157.	153.	172.	148.	164.	164.	143.	154.	155.	143.	157.	156.
1965	137.	144.	153.	149.	131.	133.	127.	151.	130.	108.	131.	133.	136.
1966	132.	133.	134.	119.	125.	123.	125.	149.	131.	113.	133.	131.	129.
1967	149.	149.	156.	147.	156.	155.	142.	163.	146.	150.	169.	146.	152.
1968	174.	174.	161.	164.	160.	155.	167.	152.	154.	153.	147.	153.	160.
1969	161.	151.	145.	154.	157.	142.	157.	144.	142.	155.	139.	172.	152.
1970	165.	185.	194.	211.	206.	202.	184.	167.	177.	169.	167.	212.	187.
1971	187.	198.	223.	218.	189.	196.	183.	192.	196.	185.	200.	192.	197.
1972	186.	204.	191.	190.	211.	239.	222.	233.	221.	212.	209.	180.	208.
1973	184.	163.	172.	169.	188.	195.	197.	219.	195.	195.	193.	174.	187.
1974	194.	186.	177.	180.	206.	194.	201.	200.	197.	222.	197.	232.	199.
1975	256.	245.	216.	266.	233.	236.	255.	227.	240.	239.	202.	240.	238.
1976	204.	214.	226.	221.	216.	237.	225.	219.	253.	219.	226.	223.	224.
1977	200.	226.	238.	226.	233.	242.	229.	252.	260.	234.	243.	239.	235.
1978	225.	236.	233.	245.	248.	233.	229.	260.	239.	236.	235.	212.	236.
1979	229.	220.	217.	213.	227.	212.	208.	209.	200.	219.	230.	213.	216.
1980	249.	239.	213.	239.	231.	225.	239.	232.	209.	230.	215.	237.	230.
1981	222.	227.	221.	217.	197.	223.	252.	238.	286.	225.	270.	291.	239.
1982	278.	283.	329.	318.	315.	377.	337.	359.	383.	341.	338.	302.	330.

3.0 NEW ORDERS, CONSUMER GOODS, IN CONSTANT PRICES, CANADA (MILLION 1971 CANADIAN DOLLARS)

YEAR	JAN	FEB	MAR	APR	MAY	JUN	JUL	AUG	SEP	OCT	NOV	DEC	AVGE
1952	615.6	624.7	651.5	670.2	656.7	687.9	694.4	687.7	687.9	707.4	712.8	737.0	677.8
1953	730.1	687.1	706.9	695.5	752.1	695.6	674.8	718.3	693.4	709.0	716.0	673.2	704.3
1954	719.5	733.1	714.2	710.3	737.2	742.7	712.2	710.7	723.0	700.9	730.7	737.6	722.7
1955	714.2	737.8	710.1	750.7	757.8	751.0	771.4	770.9	790.8	805.2	749.2	750.2	754.9
1956	800.8	767.2	759.5	780.6	759.9	790.0	804.2	757.8	819.7	809.2	770.2	799.2	784.9
1957	815.4	811.6	821.2	801.6	784.3	817.8	814.9	834.4	828.5	820.2	831.7	857.7	819.9
1958	831.8	854.9	892.7	881.9	890.3	882.7	876.4	908.7	856.4	901.3	909.4	873.6	880.0
1959	891.4	921.6	909.8	924.7	951.7	915.2	930.8	929.8	932.8	907.3	930.4	900.5	920.5
1960	935.0	881.5	876.2	886.1	907.5	905.9	914.7	896.9	916.4	924.6	907.1	900.6	904.4
1961	916.4	932.1	922.5	933.8	927.2	950.0	966.3	993.9	969.5	986.0	993.0	1001.8	957.7
1962	986.0	997.9	1016.7	1009.9	1028.7	1039.0	1040.5	1031.5	1043.5	1055.7	1065.7	1052.8	1030.7
1963	1074.4	1091.4	1056.4	1077.2	1098.9	1091.4	1098.5	1065.0	1136.1	1106.7	1132.4	1151.4	1098.3
1964	1163.2	1132.3	1136.4	1165.1	1152.8	1159.7	1140.4	1140.7	1194.5	1174.5	1185.3	1158.9	1158.7
1965	1194.8	1203.4	1263.3	1258.2	1262.9	1242.9	1295.4	1270.2	1241.5	1296.4	1321.7	1317.2	1264.0
1966	1319.8	1347.2	1333.6	1319.0	1319.8	1324.4	1302.8	1306.9	1301.6	1343.2	1331.8	1371.1	1326.8
1967	1343.7	1347.3	1316.4	1358.9	1353.0	1378.0	1395.8	1441.2	1393.5	1368.3	1381.9	1438.4	1376.4
1968	1422.3	1354.3	1373.1	1434.1	1463.9	1462.7	1504.0	1445.3	1521.5	1563.6	1566.6	1516.3	1469.0
1969	1542.1	1538.3	1571.0	1487.7	1553.7	1558.8	1534.1	1584.4	1613.5	1597.4	1574.7	1528.5	1557.0
1970	1265.1	1250.7	1202.5	1244.6	1249.1	1249.8	1282.3	1286.5	1315.7	1301.3	1279.0	1285.7	1267.7
1971	1285.4	1289.3	1318.6	1316.9	1329.4	1357.7	1342.9	1371.5	1384.4	1375.0	1416.8	1400.8	1349.1
1972	1411.9	1409.1	1412.4	1429.2	1443.2	1451.8	1434.6	1473.9	1483.3	1485.3	1500.8	1492.9	1452.4
1973	1493.1	1518.2	1529.8	1529.4	1500.0	1530.1	1536.4	1496.4	1545.4	1588.1	1586.2	1590.5	1537.0
1974	1653.6	1666.6	1665.7	1594.0	1630.4	1621.0	1605.8	1551.6	1587.1	1563.5	1562.7	1559.4	1605.1
1975	1492.4	1545.9	1536.1	1573.6	1558.7	1608.4	1604.7	1623.4	1624.3	1638.8	1644.3	1667.3	1593.1
1976	1677.1	1629.4	1645.2	1681.7	1674.4	1641.4	1658.0	1646.2	1644.7	1651.9	1672.7	1704.0	1660.6
1977	1691.5	1752.7	1710.8	1683.2	1704.6	1708.4	1734.9	1739.1	1722.4	1735.0	1725.9	1769.1	1723.1
1978	1769.6	1795.3	1781.2	1782.2	1829.8	1842.9	1812.8	1859.8	1894.6	1862.3	1905.1	1920.3	1838.0
1979	1912.6	1876.8	1886.4	1868.4	1857.0	1903.0	1882.3	1888.4	1880.5	1851.3	1834.7	1781.9	1868.6
1980	1802.0	1783.3	1827.3	1787.1	1827.3	1814.7	1847.3	1838.9	1817.4	1860.5	1881.0	1932.9	1835.1
1981	1959.3	1948.5	1942.9	2018.8	1968.1	1992.6	2033.2	2013.1	2023.1	1980.1	1981.0	1923.1	1982.0
1982	1939.3	1916.0	1920.0	1842.4	1936.1	1923.5	1903.3	1986.6	1915.4	1918.3	1961.1	1972.7	1927.9

168

5.1 NEW ORDERS, MACHINERY AND EQUIPMENT, IN CONSTANT PRICES, CANADA (MILLION 1971 CANADIAN DOLLARS)

YEAR	JAN	FEB	MAR	APR	MAY	JUN	JUL	AUG	SEP	OCT	NOV	DEC	AVGE
1953	76.2	178.7	169.8	270.1	34.4	212.0	155.4	252.6	184.3	291.6	167.7	269.8	188.5
1954	291.7	446.6	142.4	139.9	221.3	216.7	259.0	205.9	213.8	174.9	173.7	98.5	215.4
1955	188.9	164.6	187.6	208.2	280.0	231.1	254.6	245.5	240.9	279.8	329.4	171.0	231.8
1956	217.5	210.0	277.0	352.6	248.9	192.2	280.7	255.0	352.3	285.5	261.5	531.8	288.7
1957	211.1	307.6	219.7	236.2	188.0	270.1	230.9	251.9	228.4	255.2	208.0	139.4	228.9
1958	554.9	254.8	239.3	232.8	267.6	225.5	224.3	203.3	195.0	153.5	235.7	130.2	243.1
1959	182.4	102.0	182.8	208.1	292.5	309.1	226.8	356.5	188.8	282.7	225.2	199.9	229.7
1960	228.2	244.8	215.5	221.0	191.5	211.3	213.5	176.0	214.4	217.3	163.3	215.8	209.4
1961	200.0	203.2	218.3	213.0	187.2	168.4	198.4	206.3	212.5	217.2	269.4	238.9	211.1
1962	208.8	250.6	231.4	227.4	213.3	284.7	232.7	207.5	223.1	232.2	197.6	262.8	231.0
1963	213.4	241.4	222.3	213.6	252.0	216.2	267.1	315.2	233.8	263.3	238.9	247.3	243.7
1964	286.5	262.3	264.4	310.7	273.2	325.9	301.2	252.1	277.2	293.5	301.8	303.2	287.7
1965	284.7	315.9	350.1	318.3	294.3	308.8	310.3	336.1	344.1	372.1	341.0	319.8	324.6
1966	391.7	386.8	401.6	446.1	446.7	400.5	385.2	457.2	384.3	382.1	411.3	481.4	414.6
1967	510.4	329.6	380.6	328.1	316.5	349.6	396.3	335.2	350.6	398.0	320.1	413.2	369.0
1968	276.0	325.8	348.6	362.7	390.9	329.7	364.5	363.7	371.9	376.5	353.1	363.5	352.2
1969	398.5	468.8	363.3	402.2	420.0	429.3	440.4	375.1	510.5	255.5	499.1	428.9	416.0
1970	367.0	357.7	305.6	350.1	345.8	368.5	334.1	496.4	346.8	361.2	362.3	338.4	361.2
1971	414.3	396.9	465.1	454.0	357.1	344.1	334.5	387.4	418.6	372.8	392.3	392.6	394.1
1972	370.6	400.6	419.1	430.8	418.6	473.0	420.6	405.1	456.3	457.8	442.3	486.8	431.8
1973	512.3	503.1	459.9	510.1	496.3	376.4	677.6	589.1	560.1	608.1	621.5	672.6	548.9
1974	551.7	629.7	634.5	595.6	678.8	682.6	725.8	659.6	564.4	599.0	549.7	583.1	621.2
1975	581.1	474.9	485.8	470.2	518.8	389.0	408.4	437.6	450.7	472.3	482.4	420.0	465.9
1976	380.8	420.2	393.6	407.0	444.8	464.6	462.6	502.6	440.0	382.9	489.3	395.6	432.0
1977	609.4	643.4	621.9	590.4	508.8	605.2	415.0	486.1	514.8	577.4	528.4	444.9	545.5
1978	551.8	497.9	559.0	568.3	660.6	574.8	568.9	508.6	836.7	727.7	613.2	807.1	622.9
1979	871.4	579.5	707.3	720.5	708.2	711.3	703.0	784.0	639.7	788.5	930.7	629.4	731.1
1980	962.8	745.4	751.2	670.0	592.0	682.5	696.6	637.4	653.8	629.6	635.0	704.9	696.8
1981	738.1	676.3	777.7	680.8	736.6	653.9	729.6	621.2	782.1	662.8	577.9	616.1	687.8
1982	509.6	600.3	583.0	630.9	581.9	600.8	487.7	484.4	440.7	485.7	753.3	398.6	546.4

5.2 NONRESIDENTIAL BUILDING PERMITS, IN CONSTANT PRICES, CANADA (THOUSAND 1971 CANADIAN DOLLARS)

YEAR	JAN	FEB	MAR	APR	MAY	JUN	JUL	AUG	SEP	OCT	NOV	DEC	AVGE
1949	81548.	59771.	61797.	71511.	55323.	65930.	54484.	63792.	59636.	67395.	69234.	57990.	64034.
1950	90518.	69613.	62809.	62307.	82213.	119333.	88422.	97444.	87216.	89615.	87030.	85525.	85170.
1951	87222.	113248.	88614.	68276.	88374.	60973.	77041.	56952.	66959.	73610.	59854.	79413.	76711.
1952	54658.	67699.	65860.	90645.	59507.	77198.	82301.	75171.	70707.	79406.	83713.	114183.	76759.
1953	83425.	89183.	88562.	94193.	99919.	105115.	121854.	89452.	108220.	133904.	117278.	95620.	102227.
1954	89520.	88540.	123477.	110078.	98967.	103817.	113784.	113914.	106881.	120086.	88631.	121461.	106596.
1955	133961.	85617.	105646.	124602.	93494.	122202.	113173.	184984.	118281.	121720.	141620.	114823.	125094.
1956	171633.	155793.	130982.	128458.	156514.	137189.	123556.	130450.	128998.	137636.	145771.	103230.	137518.
1957	175706.	133207.	136915.	141036.	142408.	127150.	154275.	118927.	135732.	116885.	103354.	154217.	136651.
1958	133847.	141237.	134146.	127062.	123210.	146931.	166423.	172031.	144946.	144731.	149270.	167516.	145946.
1959	177578.	158716.	138511.	183958.	128295.	153178.	162449.	227350.	157786.	214436.	144021.	133575.	164988.
1960	146859.	137222.	151555.	159046.	154871.	168700.	125516.	147531.	161051.	195559.	166812.	134342.	153005.
1961	157712.	136117.	170351.	118808.	142681.	141694.	150120.	149861.	148780.	157843.	154269.	193135.	151781.
1962	173642.	248580.	157823.	168785.	201690.	208679.	192233.	182882.	165566.	165370.	156098.	168616.	182497.
1963	179715.	176787.	159401.	228593.	173579.	171885.	176439.	194881.	178533.	181760.	199552.	188982.	184176.
1964	197105.	197577.	180396.	201257.	168252.	185204.	195381.	192032.	306229.	222699.	300963.	209332.	213036.
1965	225644.	220462.	227186.	239622.	268349.	288239.	289193.	207002.	251010.	268870.	235702.	292868.	251179.
1966	264851.	251219.	273037.	292993.	229073.	244704.	236701.	267397.	246125.	232786.	221109.	214866.	247905.
1967	209595.	281449.	205344.	202734.	227593.	242901.	178244.	243783.	255691.	264697.	241889.	295983.	237492.
1968	261178.	278969.	246906.	231044.	250998.	251839.	286093.	263930.	189372.	229829.	267394.	203900.	246788.
1969	219636.	201649.	284923.	241705.	246071.	179806.	326974.	222387.	260765.	190692.	250250.	301631.	243874.
1970	222139.	282032.	187652.	198038.	239735.	214461.	194053.	185172.	226496.	234834.	225048.	194411.	217006.
1971	241451.	220447.	245538.	197537.	197784.	227193.	203270.	240065.	174787.	188815.	175332.	236857.	212423.
1972	216705.	200189.	217177.	196120.	212014.	196555.	211115.	208459.	242966.	228030.	259390.	234190.	218576.
1973	247198.	284179.	243774.	273781.	266684.	236286.	271888.	284355.	268210.	273186.	285012.	290656.	268767.
1974	277119.	275469.	295350.	270562.	365565.	257991.	257303.	300029.	337116.	272414.	238734.	231197.	281571.
1975	363414.	256847.	207489.	246098.	233261.	238263.	220179.	241936.	228082.	256254.	253576.	260368.	250481.
1976	229294.	280119.	243168.	259730.	237524.	290244.	240794.	197913.	184338.	217377.	248964.	231820.	238440.
1977	222680.	238383.	233333.	227128.	226223.	259066.	178296.	245321.	248397.	198505.	215949.	192807.	223007.
1978	237504.	206593.	217383.	270356.	232970.	244948.	230483.	235394.	245549.	247845.	243822.	267275.	240010.
1979	230648.	217490.	273072.	228867.	273543.	263226.	251980.	258529.	256767.	238833.	259328.	217707.	247499.
1980	365909.	286033.	244529.	245580.	247366.	250307.	252409.	233147.	275927.	308303.	304217.	396573.	284192.
1981	265459.	272773.	240711.	312168.	273461.	289841.	303711.	298155.	250266.	271956.	362073.	329980.	289213.
1982	272606.	253055.	274202.	217083.	185469.	178984.	226410.	150095.	167988.	177993.	145342.	144347.	199465.

170

6.0 RESIDENTIAL BUILDING PERMITS, CANADA (NUMBER)

YEAR	JAN	FEB	MAR	APR	MAY	JUN	JUL	AUG	SEP	OCT	NOV	DEC	AVGE
1960	6589.	6931.	6763.	6762.	7623.	7796.	7817.	7314.	9637.	8195.	8792.	8362.	7715.
1961	8816.	8900.	9849.	9683.	9285.	8965.	9607.	10266.	9363.	10103.	9348.	8629.	9401.
1962	9239.	11160.	9896.	9252.	10774.	11334.	10863.	10703.	9845.	8796.	8890.	10108.	10072.
1963	10415.	11415.	11501.	11810.	11147.	10778.	11769.	11429.	12816.	12767.	15681.	13435.	12080.
1964	14087.	12381.	12114.	12373.	11380.	12831.	13021.	15400.	14443.	16310.	17488.	11038.	13572.
1965	13332.	12206.	13730.	13838.	13353.	15548.	13855.	13251.	13169.	14237.	14848.	13897.	13772.
1966	14401.	9457.	11797.	10803.	11291.	10829.	10688.	11629.	13236.	10178.	11193.	9850.	11279.
1967	11808.	11863.	11798.	15197.	15264.	14576.	15312.	13920.	14021.	12771.	12251.	11998.	13398.
1968	15078.	17664.	19528.	15795.	16011.	13169.	15849.	16462.	17697.	17822.	18515.	22848.	17203.
1969	16391.	18365.	19528.	18584.	16040.	18920.	17512.	15985.	13909.	14416.	13344.	12512.	16292.
1970	12687.	11889.	11459.	11853.	12816.	12331.	11248.	14452.	19385.	19365.	21116.	19195.	14816.
1971	17904.	18617.	18427.	17993.	18235.	18892.	18921.	19371.	19876.	21845.	19639.	20520.	19187.
1972	21680.	21778.	20147.	22326.	18041.	22478.	20223.	20538.	20174.	19005.	19469.	19216.	20506.
1973	21738.	21197.	24561.	20615.	21923.	21292.	23444.	23695.	21561.	21642.	26507.	24376.	22713.
1974	20852.	22221.	24574.	18975.	18494.	14387.	14547.	15233.	14680.	13498.	12122.	12187.	16814.
1975	13220.	13809.	15356.	18541.	18134.	21072.	22198.	21089.	22008.	23150.	22580.	24410.	19631.
1976	23976.	24669.	22490.	22256.	20079.	22208.	22189.	21367.	21519.	21583.	21496.	19964.	21983.
1977	20116.	21157.	23724.	20662.	21941.	20835.	20771.	19775.	20349.	18885.	21466.	23958.	21137.
1978	19471.	18024.	17673.	18445.	18103.	17885.	17601.	17422.	17270.	18874.	17180.	19586.	18128.
1979	15399.	14908.	15521.	15429.	17284.	13767.	16255.	17708.	15803.	15957.	15334.	14772.	15678.
1980	14817.	13518.	11024.	10998.	9223.	11959.	12586.	13235.	15622.	14924.	14667.	15207.	13148.
1981	14632.	16738.	17802.	18414.	16185.	16194.	16954.	12609.	12540.	11048.	14832.	24801.	16062.
1982	11814.	9379.	9754.	8700.	7925.	6852.	8147.	8918.	9854.	12085.	14078.	16379.	10324.

171

7.0 CHANGE IN NONFARM BUSINESS INVENTORIES, IN CONSTANT PRICES, CANADA
(ANNUAL RATE, MILLION 1971 CANADIAN DOLLARS)

YEAR	IQ	IIQ	IIIQ	IVQ	AVGE
1948	-112.	-300.	364.	480.	108.
1949	604.	20.	196.	104.	231.
1950	276.	340.	-116.	1944.	611.
1951	980.	1628.	768.	-336.	760.
1952	-336.	136.	360.	240.	100.
1953	320.	804.	656.	492.	568.
1954	-96.	-172.	-188.	-172.	-157.
1955	144.	-104.	196.	540.	194.
1956	1224.	672.	336.	1488.	930.
1957	700.	336.	348.	-88.	329.
1958	-976.	-256.	-68.	188.	-278.
1959	528.	140.	820.	408.	474.
1960	1096.	288.	-72.	364.	419.
1961	696.	688.	44.	1088.	629.
1962	540.	188.	892.	488.	527.
1963	496.	116.	312.	1000.	481.
1964	1212.	1024.	1140.	84.	865.
1965	1936.	1352.	1116.	1404.	1452.
1966	1160.	1808.	772.	920.	1165.
1967	616.	244.	284.	-244.	225.
1968	160.	704.	760.	836.	615.
1969	1236.	912.	868.	1156.	1043.
1970	348.	956.	1032.	-1424.	228.
1971	-152.	-232.	592.	1416.	406.
1972	504.	1088.	948.	800.	835.
1973	1628.	1020.	1144.	1644.	1359.
1974	2836.	2692.	1940.	3448.	2729.
1975	1288.	-372.	-1204.	-1088.	-344.
1976	1912.	1336.	1064.	180.	1123.
1977	92.	428.	676.	180.	344.
1978	-352.	-872.	224.	988.	-3.
1979	1752.	2240.	1232.	1860.	1771.
1980	964.	568.	-2480.	-1196.	-536.
1981	1016.	468.	1328.	-476.	584.
1982	-2168.	-3536.	-3376.	-4376.	-3364.

8.0 INDUSTRIAL MATERIALS PRICE INDEX, SIX MONTH SMOOTHED CHANGE, CANADA
(ANNUAL RATE, PERCENT)

YEAR	JAN	FEB	MAR	APR	MAY	JUN	JUL	AUG	SEP	OCT	NOV	DEC	AVGE
1948	26.8	17.9	12.8	16.4	16.2	18.8	15.7	22.9	18.4	15.0	12.2	10.8	17.0
1949	8.2	4.4	0.0	-5.8	-10.3	-12.9	-14.1	-12.3	-8.6	-5.6	-3.2	-2.0	-5.2
1950	-1.2	2.5	5.0	7.2	12.8	18.4	21.8	26.0	35.0	34.3	34.8	34.5	19.3
1951	40.4	42.7	37.0	31.3	24.2	17.7	8.7	-0.6	-3.6	-2.4	-4.5	-6.8	15.3
1952	-8.9	-14.6	-16.5	-18.6	-20.9	-19.8	-17.7	-16.8	-17.3	-16.6	-13.0	-10.5	-15.9
1953	-9.0	-8.1	-6.8	-8.3	-6.2	-5.1	-5.9	-5.2	-6.3	-6.7	-7.1	-6.0	-6.7
1954	-6.1	-5.7	-5.4	-3.9	-2.7	-2.4	-1.6	-2.4	-1.6	-0.4	0.4	0.4	-2.6
1955	1.6	4.4	4.8	6.9	6.0	8.5	8.0	10.0	9.1	7.5	6.2	7.8	6.7
1956	8.1	7.3	7.6	6.4	4.5	4.1	2.6	2.9	2.6	0.7	0.4	1.8	4.1
1957	2.2	0.0	-1.1	-1.8	-4.6	-5.3	-5.4	-5.7	-6.5	-8.9	-10.4	-7.3	-4.6
1958	-6.2	-5.5	-5.2	-6.3	-6.0	-4.6	-1.9	-1.5	-1.9	-1.2	3.1	3.5	-2.8
1959	3.5	4.7	6.3	7.5	7.4	7.0	4.6	5.8	5.7	3.4	1.5	1.9	4.9
1960	2.2	0.7	-0.7	0.0	-1.1	0.4	-1.1	-0.7	-0.4	-2.6	-4.0	-4.0	-0.8
1961	-3.7	-1.1	-0.7	1.9	3.8	0.4	6.4	5.7	6.0	4.5	2.2	2.6	2.4
1962	1.5	1.5	1.8	1.8	4.8	3.7	2.9	1.4	-1.1	-1.8	-0.7	-0.4	1.3
1963	2.2	1.1	1.1	2.2	4.0	1.0	4.0	0.7	-0.4	2.9	5.4	3.9	2.7
1964	4.6	3.2	1.8	2.5	1.8	1.0	0.3	2.5	0.7	0.3	0.0	-1.7	1.4
1965	-1.0	-2.1	-1.0	-0.7	0.7	2.1	1.4	2.1	1.7	0.7	1.0	2.1	0.6
1966	-4.9	5.6	-2.4	-2.4	-2.1	0.3	0.0	-1.4	-2.7	-4.4	-0.4	-5.1	0.0
1967	-5.7	-4.8	-5.1	-4.1	-1.7	0.7	-2.1	-2.4	-2.1	-2.8	-0.4	-1.1	-2.5
1968	0.7	-0.4	0.4	-1.4	-0.7	0.0	0.7	1.4	1.1	1.0	2.8	3.6	0.8
1969	6.1	6.4	6.0	8.5	9.6	8.4	5.5	5.2	4.8	-3.3	1.3	2.0	5.4
1970	2.7	1.7	2.3	1.3	1.3	0.7	-1.0	-2.0	-2.6	-0.3	-2.6	-3.3	-0.5
1971	-2.6	-1.0	-0.7	0.0	-0.7	0.0	-0.3	-0.3	-0.6	0.7	1.8	2.4	-0.0
1972	8.5	12.0	15.8	12.9	14.2	13.7	11.5	13.5	13.3	20.9	18.9	19.3	14.5
1973	24.5	28.4	28.5	24.2	25.0	28.2	37.5	47.6	32.1	33.3	48.1	45.1	33.5
1974	38.3	37.5	34.9	31.8	25.2	19.0	15.9	17.4	15.9	13.5	9.2	5.3	22.0
1975	1.8	-1.4	-5.5	-5.1	-5.3	-10.0	-6.6	-1.3	-3.2	-2.7	-3.6	-2.4	-3.8
1976	-2.4	-0.9	0.9	3.4	4.9	5.1	6.2	3.5	1.3	-1.1	-2.7	0.0	1.5
1977	2.2	4.4	8.3	7.9	6.4	3.6	4.0	3.1	2.3	1.8	3.4	4.5	4.3
1978	6.8	7.6	6.9	10.1	10.2	12.3	10.3	13.8	16.3	24.4	22.2	19.8	13.4
1979	24.0	26.6	24.7	24.9	23.0	20.5	18.5	18.0	17.4	19.7	16.0	13.8	20.6
1980	21.3	19.2	12.5	10.4	9.0	8.3	8.8	7.7	7.2	7.6	7.1	5.7	10.4
1981	6.9	5.6	6.3	6.9	7.5	6.7	6.4	7.6	5.3	4.4	2.1	2.9	5.7
1982	3.3	3.9	2.8	3.0	2.3	2.7	1.6	0.3	1.2	-0.8	-2.9	-1.3	1.3

173

9.0 STOCK PRICE INDEX, CANADA (1975=1000)

YEAR	JAN	FEB	MAR	APR	MAY	JUN	JUL	AUG	SEP	OCT	NOV	DEC	AVGE
1948	202.3	188.4	188.4	204.5	220.5	227.0	220.5	214.1	214.1	220.5	224.8	220.5	212.1
1949	216.2	202.3	197.0	197.0	194.8	182.0	193.8	200.2	202.3	214.1	222.7	222.7	203.8
1950	224.8	222.7	222.7	238.7	245.2	249.4	236.6	263.4	276.2	283.7	283.7	285.8	252.7
1951	305.1	332.9	326.5	335.1	332.9	324.4	328.7	345.8	367.2	375.8	354.3	355.4	340.3
1952	369.3	367.2	359.7	355.4	341.5	345.8	354.3	355.4	345.8	326.5	335.1	335.1	349.3
1953	345.8	337.2	337.2	317.9	313.7	307.2	317.9	320.1	300.8	298.7	304.0	300.8	316.8
1954	309.4	322.2	326.5	345.8	357.6	355.4	357.6	371.5	379.0	379.0	401.4	415.4	360.1
1955	418.6	433.6	430.4	441.1	449.6	485.0	499.9	499.9	525.6	491.4	504.2	510.6	474.2
1956	525.6	545.2	588.9	583.6	603.8	575.4	617.7	603.8	567.0	554.0	524.6	565.0	571.2
1957	568.1	545.2	563.8	589.3	606.1	592.7	577.3	520.2	483.3	447.8	458.3	432.1	532.0
1958	449.0	444.1	457.4	454.0	472.9	484.6	508.2	514.8	531.7	537.4	540.0	547.7	495.1
1959	562.5	566.6	562.7	567.9	569.0	573.4	599.0	568.5	541.4	541.2	538.4	555.1	562.1
1960	529.8	512.2	512.0	503.1	518.0	505.1	494.1	526.5	500.3	500.2	519.4	544.7	513.8
1961	575.6	594.4	605.6	633.4	646.1	650.7	662.4	672.4	661.6	665.5	685.7	700.8	646.2
1962	682.8	686.8	686.0	667.6	612.4	572.5	586.1	600.3	571.8	580.7	626.2	629.0	625.2
1963	659.9	638.4	657.5	689.2	700.4	674.4	656.3	660.7	680.6	686.0	679.2	702.7	673.8
1964	721.4	715.4	743.2	770.5	797.1	795.6	813.8	808.8	843.6	846.7	850.1	853.5	796.6
1965	901.4	897.4	889.5	911.3	909.1	847.1	838.4	858.9	873.4	888.9	863.8	881.1	880.0
1966	917.8	895.2	883.0	891.2	861.7	856.9	842.8	780.4	761.1	775.9	770.8	789.5	835.5
1967	843.4	851.4	880.0	898.2	864.6	886.9	915.4	904.6	922.5	868.6	890.7	899.2	885.5
1968	873.6	835.3	814.8	887.5	879.1	925.4	920.1	944.0	989.1	1004.0	1041.6	1062.9	931.4
1969	1090.2	1039.0	1072.2	1102.5	1131.0	1008.6	950.8	998.5	991.8	1005.7	1031.3	1019.8	1036.8
1970	980.2	1006.4	1006.7	917.7	828.2	810.8	847.8	870.0	909.2	883.7	922.2	947.5	910.8
1971	975.1	974.5	1000.7	1017.0	973.0	986.8	983.5	976.3	962.0	881.4	885.5	990.5	967.2
1972	1078.9	1114.9	1087.7	1099.1	1129.4	1104.3	1129.9	1189.3	1167.4	1136.7	1186.7	1226.6	1137.6
1973	1246.8	1250.0	1239.0	1198.2	1153.4	1149.0	1226.4	1196.0	1250.4	1319.3	1182.6	1187.8	1216.6
1974	1196.4	1241.8	1214.9	1099.9	1031.7	1009.2	1057.0	919.9	847.2	895.7	850.4	835.4	1016.6
1975	979.6	1006.3	989.6	1008.5	1030.7	1055.3	1051.7	1038.9	976.4	930.9	980.8	953.5	1000.0
1976	1039.4	1074.4	1054.1	1075.0	1075.9	1055.6	1050.1	1048.3	1028.8	989.6	920.1	1011.5	1035.2
1977	996.6	1008.9	1022.1	994.8	981.2	1031.2	1033.5	1003.3	1000.1	970.5	1017.5	1059.6	1009.9
1978	998.4	1005.7	1063.3	1081.5	1128.8	1126.2	1193.8	1232.2	1284.7	1215.8	1269.8	1309.0	1159.1
1979	1355.4	1385.4	1466.4	1484.3	1519.7	1618.4	1558.1	1695.3	1751.9	1579.3	1699.6	1813.2	1577.2
1980	2027.7	2192.6	1797.6	1869.9	1971.7	2061.4	2197.4	2218.0	2260.0	2242.2	2402.2	2268.7	2125.8
1981	2226.7	2179.5	2333.1	2306.4	2371.2	2361.1	2253.9	2176.7	1883.4	1842.6	2012.1	1954.2	2158.4
1982	1786.9	1671.3	1587.8	1548.2	1523.7	1366.8	1411.9	1613.3	1602.0	1774.0	1838.3	1958.1	1640.2

174

10.0 CORPORATE PROFITS AFTER TAXES, IN CONSTANT PRICES, CANADA
(ANNUAL RATE, MILLION 1971 CANADIAN DOLLARS)

YEAR	IQ	IIQ	IIIQ	IVQ	AVGE
1948	2707.	2643.	2590.	2626.	2642.
1949	2370.	2430.	2391.	2420.	2403.
1950	2483.	2578.	3219.	3496.	2944.
1951	3086.	2870.	2636.	2643.	2809.
1952	2633.	2553.	2607.	2737.	2633.
1953	2898.	2821.	2663.	2617.	2750.
1954	2434.	2475.	2646.	2638.	2548.
1955	3062.	3182.	3534.	3667.	3361.
1956	3903.	3772.	3683.	3471.	3707.
1957	3367.	3290.	3135.	2926.	3180.
1958	3120.	3248.	3349.	3655.	3343.
1959	3307.	3258.	3316.	3389.	3318.
1960	3501.	3107.	3227.	2939.	3194.
1961	2847.	3369.	3607.	3642.	3366.
1962	3441.	3623.	3848.	3897.	3702.
1963	3720.	3995.	4059.	4578.	4088.
1964	4887.	4875.	4961.	4884.	4902.
1965	5149.	5109.	5245.	5385.	5222.
1966	5558.	5283.	5023.	5303.	5292.
1967	5131.	5012.	5205.	5343.	5173.
1968	5171.	5563.	5622.	5788.	5536.
1969	5765.	5797.	5151.	5249.	5491.
1970	5206.	4835.	4785.	4383.	4802.
1971	4585.	5095.	5656.	6039.	5344.
1972	6095.	6456.	6569.	7129.	6562.
1973	8233.	8592.	9376.	9860.	9015.
1974	10512.	10252.	9888.	8896.	9887.
1975	8281.	8064.	8410.	8586.	8335.
1976	8147.	8429.	8277.	7386.	8060.
1977	7714.	7621.	8012.	8535.	7971.
1978	8896.	8083.	9619.	10524.	9281.
1979	11402.	11474.	12596.	12246.	11930.
1980	11762.	10926.	11003.	9812.	10876.
1981	9755.	9176.	7616.	6193.	8185.
1982	4826.	4345.	3579.	4294.	4261.

175

11.0 RATIO. PRICE TO UNIT LABOR COST, MANUFACTURING, CANADA (INDEX, 1971=100)

YEAR	JAN	FEB	MAR	APR	MAY	JUN	JUL	AUG	SEP	OCT	NOV	DEC	AVGE
1961	95.0	94.4	94.4	96.0	95.4	96.4	95.7	95.1	97.3	96.8	96.6	96.4	95.8
1962	97.3	96.9	98.4	98.4	98.2	98.7	98.7	99.4	100.2	99.1	98.3	102.3	98.8
1963	99.2	99.2	100.9	99.0	100.1	101.7	101.0	99.0	102.6	101.6	102.1	105.0	100.9
1964	101.9	103.6	102.9	103.3	102.4	102.1	100.4	100.5	101.8	102.2	105.5	102.1	102.4
1965	101.9	102.4	101.5	101.1	102.9	102.5	104.3	101.3	101.8	102.7	102.2	102.2	102.2
1966	103.2	102.6	102.1	102.3	101.9	101.5	101.5	97.5	100.5	100.9	100.0	102.3	101.4
1967	101.4	100.3	100.4	102.2	101.5	101.0	99.3	100.5	100.7	99.5	100.7	101.3	100.7
1968	102.5	102.5	102.7	101.9	103.0	105.5	103.1	102.4	102.6	102.7	104.0	104.9	103.1
1969	103.2	103.8	105.5	104.6	104.4	104.6	105.6	104.3	103.4	101.8	101.6	105.8	104.0
1970	102.7	103.4	103.5	101.7	102.1	99.4	100.3	98.2	98.5	97.5	98.7	95.4	100.1
1971	98.0	99.8	98.7	99.8	99.5	99.4	100.1	101.3	101.3	102.1	100.2	99.5	100.0
1972	101.4	100.0	100.8	101.8	101.3	103.7	101.6	100.5	101.3	102.2	102.9	104.6	101.8
1973	105.3	107.7	109.5	109.4	109.3	109.3	113.4	113.9	111.0	111.8	113.1	113.0	110.6
1974	117.4	119.5	119.6	118.6	124.0	120.0	118.2	119.1	117.2	117.8	117.8	119.8	119.1
1975	115.6	116.5	114.9	114.9	113.3	113.5	116.1	115.8	116.1	113.5	114.6	115.4	115.0
1976	111.7	109.7	111.1	111.5	113.0	111.1	110.7	111.3	111.2	107.5	108.6	109.2	110.5
1977	112.4	110.9	112.7	112.2	112.4	112.1	111.3	110.5	109.9	110.9	111.1	110.7	111.4
1978	115.2	113.3	114.0	118.6	116.8	117.4	117.4	115.7	120.0	120.9	121.4	122.6	117.8
1979	124.8	126.9	127.5	125.1	128.9	127.2	126.0	126.4	128.2	130.4	128.1	128.0	127.3
1980	133.5	131.6	130.9	130.6	129.7	128.2	130.2	129.0	131.1	131.7	131.4	130.8	130.7
1981	130.5	131.3	132.7	132.4	132.2	133.9	137.0	129.9	128.8	126.8	124.8	124.6	130.4
1982	121.4	121.9	121.9	121.7	125.9	124.0	120.2	126.3	125.3	121.6	121.0	119.1	122.5

176

12.0 CHANGE IN CONSUMER CREDIT OUTSTANDING, IN CONSTANT PRICES, CANADA (MILLION 1981 CANADIAN DOLLARS)

YEAR	JAN	FEB	MAR	APR	MAY	JUN	JUL	AUG	SEP	OCT	NOV	DEC	AVGE
1956	63	63	84	119	126	90	59	79	86	55	92	-41	73
1957	-34	3	-47	-10	0	3	30	40	7	-7	0	7	-1
1958	20	56	79	65	59	10	16	36	55	97	117	97	59
1959	97	101	117	104	52	124	175	107	128	105	22	10	95
1960	26	38	55	80	96	86	45	48	99	98	76	110	71
1961	95	32	22	13	41	47	54	111	82	88	88	142	68
1962	145	126	129	166	147	125	97	84	31	34	46	118	104
1963	124	80	93	117	111	114	165	128	110	138	186	112	123
1964	185	176	155	166	190	227	195	171	226	199	168	155	184
1965	170	173	199	228	216	211	225	202	211	258	219	145	205
1966	182	129	152	114	20	40	105	141	118	93	107	39	103
1967	126	89	86	105	152	208	141	105	165	225	216	105	144
1968	283	201	139	178	199	92	210	228	219	237	337	362	224
1969	330	394	377	315	271	236	150	130	160	127	72	141	225
1970	-256	155	25	63	93	-41	136	189	133	102	126	170	75
1971	-796	217	169	184	188	235	311	222	275	295	369	276	162
1972	293	203	221	281	411	413	405	347	392	381	376	567	358
1973	823	346	477	734	586	133	343	393	374	436	197	277	427
1974	597	391	682	707	217	377	371	182	244	372	134	399	389
1975	481	361	214	279	470	275	469	565	94	481	742	-79	363
1976	320	416	407	479	453	581	484	494	330	541	369	236	426
1977	492	476	386	288	235	273	293	344	252	241	368	394	337
1978	380	460	470	444	364	530	395	334	483	564	136	367	411
1979	374	253	557	473	848	528	486	457	373	294	207	180	419
1980	533	554	352	381	111	163	166	349	438	701	758	482	416
1981	647	475	591	482	761	-135	863	236	17	101	-1112	329	271
1982	76	-19	-4	-262	-182	-151	-224	-152	-133	-39	-115	181	-85

177

COINCIDENT INDEX, CANADA (1980=100)

YEAR	JAN	FEB	MAR	APR	MAY	JUN	JUL	AUG	SEP	OCT	NOV	DEC	AVGE
1948	22.8	22.6	22.7	22.7	22.8	22.9	23.0	23.2	23.4	23.5	23.6	23.6	23.1
1949	23.5	23.3	23.6	23.8	23.9	23.9	24.0	24.1	24.3	24.5	24.7	24.8	24.0
1950	24.9	25.0	25.0	25.2	25.2	25.6	26.0	26.0	26.3	26.5	26.6	27.1	25.8
1951	27.5	27.8	27.7	27.8	27.7	27.5	27.4	27.4	27.3	27.2	27.3	27.7	27.5
1952	28.1	28.6	29.0	29.2	29.6	29.8	29.9	30.2	30.5	30.9	31.2	31.4	29.9
1953	31.5	31.7	32.0	32.1	32.1	31.9	31.9	31.7	31.9	31.7	31.4	31.3	31.8
1954	31.1	31.0	31.0	30.8	30.8	30.8	30.7	30.9	31.1	31.1	31.3	31.8	31.0
1955	32.1	32.3	32.5	32.9	33.3	33.6	33.7	34.3	34.4	34.8	35.0	35.3	33.7
1956	35.7	35.8	36.3	36.6	36.7	37.0	37.3	37.3	37.4	37.8	38.0	37.9	37.0
1957	37.6	37.8	37.8	37.6	37.7	37.7	37.7	37.8	37.5	37.3	37.1	37.1	37.6
1958	37.0	37.1	37.2	37.3	37.7	37.3	37.5	37.5	37.6	37.7	38.1	38.2	37.5
1959	38.5	38.9	39.1	39.5	39.3	39.7	39.8	39.7	40.0	40.2	40.0	40.0	39.6
1960	40.4	40.5	40.5	40.1	40.2	40.4	40.2	40.4	40.5	40.5	40.4	40.2	40.4
1961	39.8	39.7	39.9	40.3	40.6	41.0	41.3	41.7	41.8	41.9	42.2	42.7	41.1
1962	43.0	43.3	43.8	43.6	43.8	44.1	44.1	44.4	44.4	44.6	44.4	44.4	44.0
1963	44.9	45.1	45.3	45.5	45.8	46.0	46.1	46.6	46.8	47.4	47.9	48.0	46.3
1964	48.4	48.7	48.6	48.9	49.2	49.2	49.6	49.8	50.1	50.4	50.6	51.1	49.5
1965	51.5	51.9	52.3	52.3	52.5	52.8	53.5	53.7	54.2	55.0	55.0	55.8	53.4
1966	56.1	56.6	57.0	57.0	56.9	57.5	57.3	57.6	57.7	58.3	58.2	58.4	57.4
1967	58.7	58.6	58.9	59.2	59.5	59.5	59.5	59.7	59.9	59.5	60.2	60.1	59.4
1968	60.3	60.0	60.4	61.0	61.4	61.8	62.1	62.3	63.1	63.3	63.8	64.0	62.0
1969	64.4	64.8	65.0	64.8	64.6	64.8	65.0	65.1	65.5	65.6	65.9	66.3	65.1
1970	66.4	66.2	65.8	65.9	65.8	65.9	65.9	66.1	66.5	66.5	66.0	67.0	66.2
1971	67.7	68.3	68.6	68.6	69.6	70.0	70.4	70.9	71.5	71.7	72.0	72.5	70.1
1972	72.6	72.6	73.4	74.3	74.4	74.6	74.6	74.5	75.4	75.9	76.7	77.4	74.7
1973	78.1	79.3	80.2	80.0	80.7	80.9	81.7	80.8	81.3	82.2	83.2	83.6	81.0
1974	84.4	84.9	84.9	85.0	85.2	85.4	85.7	86.1	85.8	85.8	85.6	85.5	85.4
1975	84.7	84.9	84.9	85.1	85.3	85.7	86.1	86.0	86.4	86.4	87.0	88.1	85.9
1976	88.2	88.7	89.6	90.1	90.4	90.3	90.0	90.1	90.5	90.4	90.9	91.1	90.0
1977	91.4	90.9	91.0	90.9	91.4	91.4	91.2	91.7	91.9	91.9	92.0	92.2	91.5
1978	92.4	93.0	93.1	93.7	93.8	94.2	94.1	94.4	95.3	95.4	95.9	96.5	94.3
1979	96.9	97.2	97.6	97.4	98.1	98.2	98.9	99.2	99.4	99.6	99.6	99.7	98.5
1980	99.8	99.7	99.8	99.2	98.5	99.0	99.3	99.7	100.7	101.0	101.5	101.7	100.0
1981	102.3	103.0	103.2	103.8	103.9	104.0	103.6	103.5	102.7	102.3	102.2	101.1	103.0
1982	100.6	99.8	98.9	98.0	97.7	96.5	95.6	95.8	95.2	94.4	94.2	94.4	96.8

SIX MONTH SMOOTHED CHANGE IN COINCIDENT INDEX, CANADA (ANNUAL RATE, PERCENT)

YEAR	JAN	FEB	MAR	APR	MAY	JUN	JUL	AUG	SEP	OCT	NOV	DEC	AVGE
1949	3.5	1.5	3.3	4.1	4.5	3.8	3.6	3.6	5.1	6.3	6.8	6.7	4.4
1950	7.0	6.6	5.6	5.9	5.5	7.7	9.2	8.3	8.7	8.8	8.8	10.8	7.7
1951	12.4	13.0	10.4	9.6	7.5	4.5	2.5	1.5	0.3	-0.8	-0.8	1.3	5.1
1952	4.3	6.8	9.1	9.7	12.1	12.2	11.3	11.8	12.0	12.8	13.1	11.8	10.6
1953	10.3	10.0	10.0	8.7	7.2	4.6	3.4	1.5	1.8	-0.2	-2.0	-2.9	4.4
1954	-3.6	-4.0	-3.6	-4.6	-3.8	-3.5	-3.1	-1.8	-0.4	0.0	1.9	5.0	-1.8
1955	6.2	7.3	7.4	9.6	10.4	11.4	10.3	12.6	11.0	11.4	10.8	10.9	9.9
1956	11.2	10.2	11.2	11.2	9.9	9.8	9.8	7.9	7.1	7.8	7.4	5.6	9.1
1957	3.4	3.1	2.5	0.7	1.2	0.7	0.2	0.4	-1.2	-1.9	-3.1	-2.7	0.3
1958	-2.5	-2.0	-1.3	-0.4	-0.4	-0.3	0.8	1.0	1.8	2.3	3.8	4.2	0.7
1959	5.1	6.5	6.8	7.6	6.0	6.8	6.5	5.0	5.7	5.5	3.4	2.9	5.6
1960	4.1	3.6	2.8	0.7	0.7	1.5	0.2	0.8	1.1	1.1	0.2	-0.8	1.3
1961	-2.5	-2.8	-1.7	0.7	1.8	3.6	4.6	5.9	6.2	6.1	6.9	8.7	3.1
1962	8.7	8.9	9.6	7.2	7.2	7.1	5.8	6.0	5.2	5.0	4.6	3.4	6.6
1963	3.6	3.9	3.8	4.4	4.8	4.9	4.8	6.0	6.0	7.9	8.8	8.2	5.6
1964	8.6	8.8	7.0	6.8	6.9	5.7	6.5	6.1	6.2	5.9	6.0	6.8	6.8
1965	7.5	7.7	8.2	7.2	6.9	7.0	8.1	7.8	8.3	10.1	8.7	10.2	8.1
1966	9.5	9.9	10.0	8.6	6.8	7.3	5.5	5.1	4.6	5.5	4.3	4.0	6.8
1967	4.4	3.3	3.7	4.0	4.3	3.7	3.2	3.4	3.3	1.4	3.2	2.5	3.4
1968	2.6	1.4	2.2	3.6	4.5	5.2	5.5	5.5	7.1	7.1	7.7	7.1	5.0
1969	7.4	7.5	6.8	5.0	3.7	3.3	3.3	2.7	3.2	2.8	3.2	4.0	4.4
1970	3.4	2.4	1.0	1.1	0.5	0.6	0.3	0.8	1.7	1.4	1.7	2.4	1.4
1971	4.1	5.5	5.9	5.3	7.3	7.7	7.7	8.1	8.4	8.0	7.3	7.5	6.9
1972	6.5	5.5	6.7	7.9	6.9	6.2	5.3	4.1	5.6	6.6	7.1	7.8	6.3
1973	8.6	10.3	11.0	10.7	9.4	8.8	7.7	5.6	5.7	6.6	7.6	7.3	8.7
1974	7.8	7.8	7.4	6.0	5.5	5.1	5.0	4.9	3.3	2.4	1.4	0.7	4.7
1975	-1.5	-1.1	-1.1	-0.6	-0.1	0.7	1.5	1.1	2.1	2.6	3.1	5.4	1.0
1976	5.1	5.5	6.8	7.0	6.5	5.4	4.0	3.6	3.6	1.5	2.9	2.6	4.6
1977	2.7	1.2	1.1	0.6	1.6	1.4	0.8	1.6	4.5	4.2	4.5	1.6	1.6
1978	1.9	2.9	2.9	3.7	3.4	3.7	3.1	3.2	4.2	4.2	3.2	5.2	3.6
1979	5.1	5.0	5.1	4.0	4.6	4.2	4.8	4.7	4.2	3.8	3.4	2.7	4.3
1980	2.5	1.8	1.5	0.2	-1.4	-0.5	0.0	0.6	2.4	2.7	3.2	3.4	1.4
1981	4.2	5.2	5.1	5.6	5.1	4.4	3.9	2.0	0.0	-1.0	-1.4	-3.3	2.4
1982	-4.3	-5.3	-6.5	-7.4	-7.2	-8.4	-8.9	-7.4	-7.4	-7.7	-7.1	-5.5	-6.9

179

13.0 NONFARM EMPLOYMENT, CANADA (THOUSANDS)

YEAR	JAN	FEB	MAR	APR	MAY	JUN	JUL	AUG	SEP	OCT	NOV	DEC	AVGE
1953	4400.	4407.	4424.	4423.	4396.	4380.	4393.	4404.	4399.	4406.	4390.	4378.	4400.
1954	4420.	4384.	4395.	4365.	4386.	4384.	4362.	4363.	4399.	4360.	4397.	4430.	4387.
1955	4431.	4474.	4463.	4510.	4519.	4537.	4543.	4624.	4618.	4670.	4687.	4717.	4566.
1956	4751.	4759.	4822.	4792.	4775.	4815.	4844.	4837.	4820.	4869.	4957.	4948.	4832.
1957	4968.	4972.	4990.	4981.	5016.	5034.	5017.	5021.	5035.	5041.	5017.	4994.	5007.
1958	4960.	4967.	4976.	5001.	5018.	5013.	5015.	5011.	5030.	5040.	5062.	5061.	5013.
1959	5105.	5140.	5156.	5177.	5133.	5188.	5208.	5223.	5247.	5265.	5250.	5255.	5196.
1960	5283.	5293.	5291.	5259.	5317.	5326.	5273.	5313.	5323.	5362.	5336.	5338.	5310.
1961	5336.	5312.	5299.	5355.	5377.	5381.	5406.	5425.	5452.	5453.	5486.	5530.	5401.
1962	5512.	5510.	5563.	5572.	5599.	5630.	5621.	5615.	5600.	5632.	5642.	5624.	5593.
1963	5645.	5668.	5648.	5682.	5684.	5720.	5756.	5788.	5827.	5886.	5865.	5896.	5755.
1964	5891.	5906.	5960.	5966.	5986.	5966.	6020.	6044.	6063.	6056.	6113.	6146.	6010.
1965	6177.	6194.	6220.	6232.	6247.	6272.	6303.	6321.	6342.	6364.	6417.	6513.	6300.
1966	6515.	6549.	6589.	6637.	6589.	6595.	6634.	6687.	6701.	6759.	6719.	6742.	6643.
1967	6779.	6797.	6879.	6824.	6850.	6822.	6896.	6901.	6876.	6834.	6892.	6919.	6856.
1968	6889.	6924.	6911.	6944.	6953.	7023.	7027.	7063.	7114.	7130.	7180.	7168.	7027.
1969	7234.	7245.	7271.	7314.	7295.	7278.	7277.	7284.	7287.	7281.	7303.	7330.	7283.
1970	7343.	7329.	7336.	7376.	7409.	7406.	7369.	7407.	7502.	7472.	7483.	7433.	7405.
1971	7479.	7493.	7486.	7412.	7531.	7570.	7602.	7614.	7681.	7714.	7706.	7768.	7588.
1972	7748.	7774.	7842.	7804.	7794.	7831.	7882.	7896.	7895.	7879.	7963.	8018.	7861.
1973	8045.	8137.	8188.	8237.	8285.	8357.	8272.	8325.	8329.	8396.	8435.	8485.	8291.
1974	8524.	8534.	8537.	8596.	8601.	8603.	8674.	8760.	8711.	8720.	8764.	8786.	8651.
1975	8670.	8691.	8708.	8730.	8787.	8811.	8803.	8799.	8877.	8896.	8908.	8944.	8802.
1976	8969.	8978.	9024.	9007.	8989.	9005.	9023.	9035.	9032.	9017.	9006.	9023.	9009.
1977	9070.	9091.	9101.	9113.	9206.	9168.	9167.	9224.	9244.	9258.	9276.	9301.	9185.
1978	9286.	9361.	9404.	9442.	9481.	9488.	9544.	9551.	9556.	9575.	9616.	9678.	9499.
1979	9711.	9725.	9755.	9772.	9815.	9815.	9909.	9951.	9986.	10049.	10069.	10071.	9886.
1980	10090.	10104.	10102.	10117.	10073.	10144.	10146.	10173.	10279.	10280.	10314.	10325.	10179.
1981	10376.	10465.	10434.	10468.	10479.	10506.	10466.	10498.	10469.	10441.	10417.	10369.	10449.
1982	10337.	10305.	10281.	10227.	10175.	10103.	10064.	9984.	9996.	9966.	9938.	9964.	10112.

14.0 UNEMPLOYMENT RATE, CANADA (PERCENT)

YEAR	JAN	FEB	MAR	APR	MAY	JUN	JUL	AUG	SEP	OCT	NOV	DEC	AVGE
1953	3.0	2.8	2.6	2.6	2.6	2.7	2.9	3.1	2.8	3.5	4.1	4.0	3.1
1954	3.9	4.0	4.1	4.4	4.7	5.1	5.2	5.2	5.1	5.1	5.1	4.7	4.7
1955	4.8	4.7	4.9	4.5	4.5	4.3	4.3	3.8	4.1	4.0	3.8	3.7	4.3
1956	3.7	3.8	3.6	3.5	3.4	3.2	3.0	3.0	3.1	2.8	3.1	3.4	3.3
1957	3.8	3.9	4.1	4.2	3.9	4.3	4.6	4.8	5.1	5.3	6.2	6.5	4.7
1958	6.5	6.6	6.9	6.9	7.0	7.9	7.5	7.5	7.1	7.5	7.2	7.0	7.1
1959	6.5	6.2	6.0	5.8	6.3	5.6	5.5	5.9	5.4	5.5	5.8	6.0	5.9
1960	6.1	6.4	6.5	6.8	7.2	6.7	7.1	7.6	7.5	7.6	7.5	7.6	7.0
1961	7.6	7.7	7.6	7.6	7.6	7.4	7.2	6.8	6.9	6.5	6.1	6.0	7.1
1962	6.0	6.2	6.0	5.9	5.6	5.7	6.0	5.7	5.7	5.7	5.9	6.0	5.9
1963	5.9	5.8	5.9	5.7	5.7	5.5	5.4	5.3	5.3	5.2	5.1	5.0	5.5
1964	4.9	4.9	4.8	4.9	4.6	4.8	4.6	4.6	4.5	4.9	4.3	4.1	4.7
1965	4.2	4.1	4.3	4.4	4.0	4.1	3.9	3.8	3.6	3.1	3.6	3.5	3.9
1966	3.4	3.4	3.3	3.2	3.2	2.9	3.2	3.5	3.6	3.3	3.5	3.4	3.3
1967	3.6	3.7	3.8	3.9	3.7	3.6	3.7	3.6	3.7	4.1	4.0	4.4	3.8
1968	4.3	4.4	4.2	4.5	4.4	4.7	4.4	4.5	4.3	4.4	4.6	4.5	4.4
1969	4.5	4.3	4.6	4.3	4.4	4.4	4.3	4.5	4.4	4.7	4.6	4.5	4.4
1970	4.5	4.9	5.2	5.4	5.8	6.1	6.4	6.1	6.0	6.0	6.1	6.2	5.7
1971	6.2	6.3	6.2	6.6	6.1	6.1	6.1	6.0	6.2	6.3	6.2	5.9	6.2
1972	6.0	5.8	6.1	5.8	6.1	6.3	6.3	6.4	6.4	6.6	6.4	6.4	6.2
1973	6.1	5.9	5.5	5.5	5.3	5.4	5.3	5.3	5.6	5.7	5.5	5.4	5.5
1974	5.3	5.2	5.2	5.2	5.3	5.0	5.1	5.3	5.4	5.4	5.6	6.0	5.3
1975	6.6	6.6	6.7	6.8	6.9	7.0	6.9	7.1	7.0	7.2	7.2	7.5	6.9
1976	6.9	6.9	6.7	7.1	7.0	7.0	7.4	7.1	7.1	7.5	7.2	7.5	7.1
1977	7.6	8.0	8.0	8.1	7.8	7.9	8.3	8.2	8.3	8.3	8.4	8.5	8.1
1978	8.3	8.4	8.5	8.5	8.5	8.5	8.5	8.5	8.5	8.1	8.2	8.1	8.4
1979	7.9	7.8	7.8	7.9	7.5	7.4	7.2	7.2	7.0	7.3	7.2	7.3	7.4
1980	7.4	7.5	7.5	7.6	7.9	7.8	7.4	7.7	7.0	7.3	7.2	7.3	7.5
1981	7.2	7.2	7.4	7.0	7.2	7.4	7.4	7.1	8.2	8.3	8.3	8.6	7.6
1982	8.3	8.6	9.0	9.6	10.2	10.9	11.8	12.2	12.2	12.7	12.7	12.8	10.9

15.0 GROSS NATIONAL EXPENDITURES, IN CONSTANT PRICES, CANADA
(ANNUAL RATE, MILLION 1971 CANADIAN DOLLARS)

YEAR	IQ	IIQ	IIIQ	IVQ	AVGE
1948	29784.	29716.	30308.	31116.	30231.
1949	30272.	31036.	31520.	32724.	31388.
1950	32668.	33076.	34240.	35064.	33762.
1951	35676.	35204.	35484.	35436.	35450.
1952	37380.	38268.	38724.	40096.	38617.
1953	40460.	40648.	40452.	40860.	40605.
1954	39628.	39604.	40144.	41048.	40106.
1955	42012.	43320.	44644.	45588.	43891.
1956	46672.	47284.	47676.	48764.	47599.
1957	48748.	48548.	48976.	48600.	48718.
1958	48860.	49596.	50024.	50896.	49844.
1959	50904.	51500.	52052.	52492.	51737.
1960	53380.	52476.	53464.	53604.	53231.
1961	52780.	54548.	55372.	56264.	54741.
1962	57948.	57516.	58828.	59608.	58475.
1963	60152.	60656.	61504.	63636.	61487.
1964	64628.	64972.	66032.	66808.	65610.
1965	68428.	69256.	70316.	71924.	69981.
1966	73980.	74760.	74828.	75808.	74844.
1967	76312.	77460.	77336.	78268.	77344.
1968	79256.	81188.	82600.	84412.	81864.
1969	85496.	85124.	86416.	87864.	86225.
1970	87820.	88104.	88952.	88684.	88390.
1971	91328.	93420.	96064.	96988.	94450.
1972	97604.	100136.	100660.	102592.	100248.
1973	106248.	106736.	107708.	110556.	107812.
1974	112124.	111560.	111448.	111580.	111678.
1975	111652.	112204.	113496.	114668.	113005.
1976	118384.	120384.	119676.	120004.	119612.
1977	120803.	121268.	122396.	123480.	121988.
1978	124568.	125680.	127272.	127868.	126347.
:379	129500.	129868.	130940.	131140.	130362.
1980	131992.	130548.	131032.	133128.	131675.
1981	135760.	137240.	136292.	135760.	136263.
1982	132248.	130340.	129304.	128384.	130069.

16.0 INDUSTRIAL PRODUCTION, CANADA (INDEX, 1971=100)

YEAR	JAN	FEB	MAR	APR	MAY	JUN	JUL	AUG	SEP	OCT	NOV	DEC	AVGE
1948	27.3	27.3	27.5	28.0	27.8	27.6	27.7	28.1	28.4	28.5	28.6	28.6	27.9
1949	28.8	28.5	28.8	28.7	28.9	28.8	28.8	29.3	29.1	29.1	29.1	29.6	29.0
1950	29.3	29.6	29.6	29.7	30.0	30.9	31.6	31.1	32.2	32.7	33.1	33.5	31.1
1951	33.9	34.0	34.1	34.5	34.6	34.4	33.9	34.3	33.7	33.6	33.6	33.4	34.0
1952	34.0	33.9	34.5	34.6	35.2	35.2	35.2	36.1	36.2	36.8	37.0	37.3	35.5
1953	37.7	37.9	38.4	38.4	38.4	38.0	38.4	38.0	38.4	37.9	37.2	37.9	38.0
1954	37.9	38.4	37.9	37.5	37.5	37.5	37.3	38.0	37.7	38.1	38.4	39.1	37.9
1955	39.8	39.9	40.6	40.7	41.6	42.1	42.1	43.1	43.2	43.6	43.8	44.3	42.1
1956	44.5	44.5	45.3	46.3	45.8	46.7	47.2	47.0	47.4	47.7	48.0	48.1	46.5
1957	47.4	48.1	48.5	47.6	47.6	47.5	47.5	47.6	46.7	46.2	46.3	46.5	47.3
1958	46.1	46.5	46.5	47.0	47.4	47.0	47.4	47.2	47.0	47.2	48.1	48.5	47.2
1959	48.9	49.9	49.9	50.9	50.6	50.8	51.1	51.1	52.0	53.1	52.0	52.2	51.0
1960	53.4	53.0	53.4	51.8	52.1	52.0	51.1	51.5	52.0	52.2	52.0	51.7	52.2
1961	52.2	52.4	51.7	53.4	53.4	54.3	54.9	55.1	55.6	56.0	56.1	56.3	54.3
1962	56.5	57.0	57.9	57.6	58.8	58.9	59.8	59.7	60.1	59.5	59.7	59.3	58.7
1963	59.9	60.3	61.3	61.0	62.0	62.5	62.0	62.9	63.9	63.9	65.2	65.6	62.5
1964	66.5	67.6	66.6	68.3	68.3	68.7	68.8	69.7	69.6	69.7	71.0	70.6	68.8
1965	72.0	71.5	73.3	72.5	72.9	73.4	74.3	75.3	75.5	76.6	77.0	78.0	74.4
1966	78.3	78.8	78.8	78.8	78.8	79.2	78.3	79.2	79.8	80.5	80.2	80.2	79.2
1967	80.9	80.2	79.6	82.0	81.0	81.5	81.8	83.0	82.7	82.0	84.3	84.6	82.0
1968	83.8	83.3	83.8	85.5	86.4	87.4	86.8	86.8	87.9	88.9	89.7	89.7	86.7
1969	89.7	90.4	91.9	90.1	90.0	90.2	90.4	89.6	90.7	91.0	92.5	94.0	90.9
1970	94.2	95.0	93.2	94.0	93.3	93.8	93.3	93.2	92.5	92.4	93.8	93.3	93.5
1971	95.9	96.7	97.1	97.3	98.7	99.5	99.7	102.4	102.9	103.3	102.5	103.6	100.0
1972	104.1	102.7	103.9	106.0	105.7	107.0	107.0	107.1	109.6	111.6	112.8	113.4	107.6
1973	114.2	117.5	118.8	117.7	118.1	118.8	121.3	118.0	119.2	120.8	122.5	122.3	119.1
1974	124.4	124.7	125.2	123.0	124.8	123.4	123.0	123.0	121.5	121.6	119.8	119.6	122.8
1975	115.5	116.0	114.4	115.5	113.2	114.6	116.2	115.3	115.6	114.3	116.9	119.0	115.5
1976	118.1	118.9	121.0	122.2	124.1	122.6	122.6	123.7	123.9	120.9	123.8	124.4	122.2
1977	125.9	124.2	124.8	123.6	125.1	126.4	125.5	125.7	125.1	125.4	125.9	126.4	125.3
1978	125.8	127.0	126.4	129.2	127.6	129.8	128.6	128.8	132.3	132.3	133.9	137.0	129.9
1979	136.8	137.4	136.7	135.6	138.8	137.8	139.4	139.2	139.1	138.6	137.9	136.3	137.8
1980	138.3	136.3	138.4	135.6	132.3	132.2	132.9	132.6	135.6	136.0	137.2	137.8	135.4
1981	136.3	138.1	139.8	141.2	141.6	143.7	141.8	136.9	136.3	134.2	131.8	130.8	137.7
1982	130.0	128.7	126.9	125.2	126.3	123.1	119.2	124.4	120.2	116.5	117.2	116.2	122.8

17.0 PERSONAL INCOME, IN CONSTANT PRICES, CANADA
(ANNUAL RATE, MILLION 1981 CANADIAN DOLLARS)

YEAR	IQ	IIQ	IIIQ	IVQ	AVGE
1948	52210.	52715.	53660.	53656.	53060.
1949	53934.	54420.	54472.	55870.	54674.
1950	56016.	56355.	56790.	57180.	56585.
1951	60240.	61304.	59576.	60069.	60297.
1952	63069.	64533.	65817.	67324.	65186.
1953	68297.	69423.	69131.	69474.	69081.
1954	68056.	68947.	69524.	70434.	69240.
1955	72547.	74056.	75228.	76615.	74611.
1956	79411.	81636.	81842.	82748.	81409.
1957	83295.	83650.	85227.	85086.	84314.
1958	86007.	86824.	87451.	88078.	87090.
1959	89338.	91557.	90916.	91159.	90742.
1960	93462.	94077.	95527.	94536.	94400.
1961	92532.	94506.	96405.	97006.	95112.
1962	101572.	101643.	102592.	103703.	102378.
1963	104718.	106877.	106862.	109512.	106992.
1964	110347.	111299.	112913.	115267.	112457.
1965	118012.	118702.	122323.	124431.	120867.
1966	128253.	129721.	131537.	133843.	130839.
1967	136570.	138512.	138298.	140843.	138556.
1968	142406.	145249.	147675.	150601.	146483.
1969	153183.	153727.	156698.	158600.	155552.
1970	160649.	160137.	162751.	165718.	162314.
1971	171440.	174095.	176160.	180019.	175429.
1972	183825.	188986.	188868.	195317.	189249.
1973	201586.	205064.	204066.	211089.	205451.
1974	216143.	218769.	223821.	226505.	221310.
1975	228206.	232327.	234875.	235974.	232846.
1976	241314.	246301.	245649.	253850.	246779.
1977	251915.	252560.	253195.	253061.	252683.
1978	256594.	258284.	258053.	262703.	258909.
1979	264113.	265530.	266940.	270676.	266815.
1980	272469.	273237.	275330.	277804.	274710.
1981	282997.	286411.	289476.	290375.	287315.
1982	289773.	285324.	285279.	281967.	285586.

18.1 RETAIL TRADE, IN CONSTANT PRICES, CANADA (MILLION 1981 CANADIAN DOLLARS)

YEAR	JAN	FEB	MAR	APR	MAY	JUN	JUL	AUG	SEP	OCT	NOV	DEC	AVGE
1948	2775.3	2678.3	2735.1	2669.0	2738.3	2742.2	2681.3	2739.4	2749.0	2798.8	2783.6	2852.3	2745.2
1949	2804.1	2746.3	2867.1	2945.7	2944.9	2917.2	2919.2	2874.8	2950.4	2967.2	2900.4	2898.8	2894.2
1950	3088.2	3107.3	3066.8	3153.6	3107.7	3198.0	3269.0	3264.8	3195.3	3171.9	3164.7	3270.9	3171.5
1951	3349.2	3375.3	3247.2	3293.4	3206.2	3117.2	3151.2	3143.5	3156.1	3076.7	3116.3	3127.3	3196.6
1952	3105.9	3143.4	3243.4	3243.0	3400.4	3451.8	3396.5	3400.0	3416.2	3466.5	3541.9	3543.0	3362.7
1953	3483.5	3559.4	3614.6	3607.1	3626.1	3550.2	3582.6	3550.0	3529.6	3593.4	3634.9	3521.5	3571.1
1954	3404.6	3554.9	3595.8	3490.5	3529.3	3525.4	3532.4	3530.0	3525.9	3447.9	3506.3	3651.6	3524.5
1955	3706.0	3657.2	3623.2	3751.8	3830.2	3925.7	3810.9	3865.6	3883.9	3954.5	3896.5	3874.5	3815.0
1956	3969.2	3927.4	3975.8	4139.3	4157.5	4120.4	4188.3	4146.9	4161.6	4144.0	4120.0	4186.4	4105.6
1957	4124.7	4192.5	4223.4	4144.6	4118.9	4128.2	4140.6	4158.7	4120.5	4038.4	4073.2	4164.1	4139.1
1958	4231.1	4178.2	4235.9	4164.7	4147.4	4169.3	4190.2	4186.9	4120.5	4206.8	4280.9	4327.5	4203.3
1959	4296.1	4419.8	4421.5	4417.6	4410.4	4393.8	4422.4	4370.9	4391.3	4388.9	4342.7	4258.8	4377.8
1960	4351.3	4360.9	4355.9	4372.1	4422.8	4401.3	4370.5	4373.2	4451.0	4417.4	4344.5	4338.5	4379.9
1961	4007.6	4096.5	4174.7	4134.2	4145.3	4326.6	4282.6	4394.3	4375.3	4216.1	4235.5	4342.8	4227.6
1962	4284.9	4331.8	4608.2	4383.4	4418.5	4514.7	4374.1	4471.1	4421.8	4495.7	4569.0	4541.5	4451.2
1963	4545.5	4567.8	4581.4	4606.2	4667.0	4585.8	4576.5	4822.3	4502.1	4773.4	4864.0	4724.3	4651.4
1964	4923.4	5052.0	4755.5	4776.1	4896.4	4813.9	4954.4	4837.2	4938.9	5231.0	4754.1	4862.4	4899.6
1965	4926.8	4978.6	5067.3	5263.2	5090.5	5122.9	5286.5	5076.8	5182.4	5376.2	5318.1	5402.9	5174.3
1966	5220.5	5302.9	5483.4	5141.3	5050.4	5250.6	5257.8	5385.1	5364.8	5372.8	5386.0	5295.2	5292.6
1967	5478.2	5305.6	5354.9	5403.9	5463.9	5476.7	5351.1	5410.3	5600.0	5436.9	5503.0	5405.6	5432.5
1968	5601.1	5204.3	5432.3	5432.1	5465.5	5544.1	5705.8	5593.7	5671.5	5621.9	5743.8	5721.7	5561.5
1969	5703.9	5825.5	5720.5	5638.3	5662.5	5640.7	5604.0	5640.1	5696.8	5771.3	5667.5	5759.0	5694.2
1970	5640.9	5546.7	5497.5	5520.0	5559.0	5630.7	5738.0	5628.8	5717.2	5687.6	5676.2	5840.1	5640.2
1971	5702.9	5852.7	5869.2	6049.0	6038.1	6074.3	6046.1	5985.9	6162.4	6161.1	6232.0	6155.9	6027.5
1972	6119.2	5977.4	6257.9	6469.3	6510.5	6493.6	6348.7	6234.0	6514.9	6622.0	6566.9	6572.8	6390.6
1973	6526.3	6506.7	6779.2	6992.5	6567.6	6602.7	6681.2	6489.7	6676.4	6796.7	6891.1	6866.9	6698.1
1974	6946.5	7072.0	6998.2	7087.5	7125.5	7055.5	7117.3	7179.0	7173.7	7001.5	6925.0	6939.9	7051.8
1975	7121.8	7178.2	7146.8	7079.6	7277.2	7293.6	7339.3	7266.6	7245.1	7332.2	7483.6	7763.7	7294.0
1976	7336.0	7227.0	7426.3	7715.8	7491.8	7586.8	7557.6	7491.0	7550.6	7588.4	7520.6	7750.4	7520.2
1977	7725.1	7575.8	7570.3	7537.6	7465.9	7434.3	7403.4	7575.1	7531.3	7557.8	7628.0	7540.7	7545.4
1978	7568.9	7698.6	7677.9	7755.5	7771.5	7742.4	7628.9	7669.4	8054.1	7766.6	7768.5	7799.6	7741.8
1979	7838.9	7869.2	8131.9	7954.7	7923.2	7973.7	8039.1	8048.8	7944.3	7947.6	7847.1	7910.7	7950.2
1980	7849.3	7861.5	7799.2	7671.9	7658.7	7767.9	7771.4	7951.3	7944.3	7922.9	8071.9	7860.6	7844.2
1981	8081.2	8030.7	8062.2	8025.4	7967.7	7886.2	7795.8	7730.9	7696.9	7594.2	7859.5	7569.5	7858.3
1982	7512.6	7510.3	7323.9	7345.4	7531.0	7241.1	7257.9	7288.5	7240.7	7225.5	7177.3	7287.2	7328.4

185

LAGGING INDEX, CANADA (1980=100)

YEAR	JAN	FEB	MAR	APR	MAY	JUN	JUL	AUG	SEP	OCT	NOV	DEC	AVGE
1948	23.3	23.4	23.5	23.5	23.6	23.7	23.6	23.6	23.8	24.1	24.3	24.3	23.7
1949	24.4	24.5	24.5	24.5	24.6	24.6	24.7	24.8	24.8	24.6	24.6	24.7	24.6
1950	24.8	24.7	24.7	25.0	25.0	25.1	25.0	25.1	24.9	25.5	25.6	26.0	25.1
1951	26.2	26.3	26.4	26.8	27.1	27.5	27.9	28.2	28.4	28.5	28.5	28.7	27.5
1952	28.8	29.1	29.3	29.7	30.0	29.8	29.9	30.0	30.2	30.4	30.5	30.7	29.9
1953	31.0	31.2	31.4	31.8	31.8	31.8	32.1	32.2	32.0	31.9	31.8	31.8	31.7
1954	31.9	31.1	31.7	31.8	31.9	31.5	31.4	31.2	31.1	31.0	30.9	30.9	31.4
1955	31.0	31.1	31.4	31.7	31.9	32.1	32.6	32.8	33.0	33.8	34.0	34.4	32.5
1956	34.9	35.3	35.7	36.8	37.4	37.9	38.4	38.8	38.9	39.7	40.1	40.3	37.8
1957	40.4	40.5	40.1	40.0	40.3	40.3	40.2	40.4	40.2	40.2	39.6	39.0	40.1
1958	38.6	38.1	37.9	37.8	37.7	37.3	37.3	37.3	37.0	37.1	37.1	37.2	37.5
1959	37.4	37.5	38.3	39.0	39.4	39.6	39.8	40.2	40.3	40.3	40.3	40.4	39.4
1960	40.5	40.6	40.7	40.6	40.5	40.6	40.6	40.5	40.5	40.5	40.6	40.6	40.6
1961	40.3	40.3	40.5	40.4	40.4	40.1	40.3	40.6	40.6	40.9	41.3	41.5	40.6
1962	41.8	41.9	42.2	42.3	42.4	42.7	43.4	43.6	43.8	44.1	43.8	43.5	43.0
1963	43.7	43.8	44.0	44.1	44.2	44.3	44.4	44.6	44.9	45.2	45.3	45.9	44.5
1964	46.2	46.3	46.6	46.9	47.3	47.6	48.0	48.0	48.3	48.8	49.1	49.4	47.7
1965	49.3	49.8	50.1	50.3	50.8	51.2	51.5	52.1	52.6	53.2	53.4	54.3	51.5
1966	54.4	54.5	54.8	55.2	55.5	55.8	56.1	56.3	56.4	56.6	56.9	56.5	55.7
1967	57.3	57.4	57.3	57.0	57.0	56.8	57.0	56.9	56.9	57.3	57.4	58.2	57.2
1968	57.9	58.6	58.5	58.6	58.8	58.7	58.6	58.8	58.8	58.9	58.9	59.3	58.7
1969	59.6	59.9	60.7	61.1	61.4	62.2	62.9	63.0	63.5	64.0	64.2	64.3	62.2
1970	64.3	64.3	64.2	64.0	63.8	63.9	63.9	64.4	63.5	64.1	63.8	63.8	64.1
1971	62.7	62.7	62.4	62.3	62.7	62.8	62.9	63.0	63.4	63.3	63.5	64.0	63.0
1972	64.2	64.6	64.5	65.4	65.8	65.7	65.7	66.0	66.2	66.4	66.3	66.8	65.6
1973	67.1	67.5	67.8	69.1	70.0	71.7	71.6	72.2	73.8	74.6	75.1	76.5	71.4
1974	76.0	76.4	76.7	77.8	78.2	79.0	79.3	80.0	80.1	80.6	80.6	81.3	78.9
1975	81.0	80.0	79.6	79.5	80.0	80.0	79.8	79.9	80.7	81.1	81.3	81.5	80.4
1976	81.6	82.3	83.5	83.5	83.3	83.4	83.6	83.6	84.0	84.3	84.3	84.0	83.4
1977	83.5	83.3	83.5	83.5	83.6	83.2	83.3	83.6	83.6	83.5	83.8	83.7	83.5
1978	83.8	84.1	84.8	85.0	85.3	85.5	85.6	86.6	86.9	87.9	88.6	89.0	86.1
1979	89.8	90.0	90.7	91.4	92.0	93.1	94.4	95.3	96.3	98.0	98.8	99.6	94.1
1980	99.1	99.3	100.5	101.5	99.7	99.8	98.9	98.7	98.7	99.1	100.1	104.5	100.0
1981	105.6	106.1	106.1	107.2	107.9	108.7	109.8	111.9	111.8	111.4	110.6	110.7	109.0
1982	109.3	109.1	109.6	108.3	107.2	107.6	106.2	103.7	102.8	101.8	100.9	99.5	105.5

186

SIX MONTH SMOOTHED CHANGE IN LAGGING INDEX, CANADA (ANNUAL RATE, PERCENT)

YEAR	JAN	FEB	MAR	APR	MAY	JUN	JUL	AUG	SEP	OCT	NOV	DEC	AVGE
1949	5.3	5.7	4.9	4.2	3.9	3.5	3.8	3.5	3.0	1.0	0.6	0.5	3.3
1950	1.0	0.3	0.4	2.1	2.1	2.4	1.7	1.8	0.1	4.8	5.5	7.4	2.5
1951	8.2	7.9	7.6	9.9	10.9	12.5	13.5	14.0	13.3	11.7	10.3	9.5	10.8
1952	8.3	8.8	8.7	9.6	9.9	7.2	6.7	6.0	6.0	6.7	5.9	6.7	7.5
1953	7.2	7.4	7.2	8.5	7.4	6.6	7.1	6.9	4.6	3.2	1.8	1.0	5.7
1954	0.9	-0.2	-0.8	-0.3	-0.7	-2.0	-2.6	-3.7	-3.5	-3.9	-3.6	-3.3	-2.0
1955	-2.6	-1.5	0.5	2.5	3.9	5.0	8.0	8.5	8.8	12.8	12.2	12.8	5.9
1956	14.3	14.4	14.9	18.7	19.3	19.5	19.3	18.6	16.1	17.4	16.9	15.2	17.0
1957	13.0	10.8	6.4	4.5	4.4	3.0	1.8	0.7	-0.1	0.1	-2.8	-5.7	3.2
1958	-6.8	-8.5	-8.3	-8.1	-7.9	-8.7	-7.6	-6.7	-6.5	-4.9	-3.7	-2.5	-6.7
1959	-0.6	0.3	4.8	8.2	9.5	9.7	9.7	10.6	10.0	8.4	7.1	6.1	7.0
1960	5.4	4.5	3.6	2.3	1.5	1.2	0.8	-0.1	-0.9	0.1	0.3	0.5	1.6
1961	-1.2	-1.4	0.0	-0.4	-0.4	0.0	0.9	0.2	-0.9	2.3	3.5	4.6	0.6
1962	5.4	5.4	6.0	5.8	5.7	6.0	8.3	8.2	7.8	7.8	5.3	3.3	6.2
1963	3.2	2.9	3.1	3.0	2.9	2.3	2.5	3.0	3.6	4.6	4.3	6.6	3.5
1964	7.0	6.7	6.8	7.4	7.4	7.9	8.4	7.1	7.8	7.9	7.8	7.8	7.5
1965	6.4	7.1	7.1	6.9	7.4	7.9	8.3	9.0	9.8	10.3	9.9	11.9	8.5
1966	10.3	9.3	8.6	8.6	8.2	7.8	7.9	6.9	5.9	5.5	5.4	3.2	7.3
1967	5.4	4.8	3.6	1.7	1.2	0.4	0.6	-0.1	-0.2	1.0	1.4	3.8	2.0
1968	2.2	4.2	3.9	3.9	4.1	3.2	2.3	2.4	2.1	1.9	1.2	2.1	2.8
1969	2.9	3.2	5.4	6.0	6.4	8.2	9.7	8.8	9.2	9.3	8.7	7.6	7.1
1970	6.3	5.0	3.5	2.1	0.8	0.5	0.1	1.3	0.7	0.0	-1.1	-0.8	1.5
1971	-3.9	-3.5	-3.9	-4.0	-2.2	-1.9	-1.3	-0.8	-0.7	0.8	1.5	2.9	-1.3
1972	3.5	4.6	4.9	5.7	5.3	5.1	4.5	4.6	4.4	4.2	3.3	3.9	4.5
1973	4.3	4.4	4.9	7.6	9.7	13.2	11.2	11.7	14.7	14.8	14.3	15.9	10.5
1974	12.1	11.1	9.8	10.6	9.7	9.9	10.7	9.1	7.6	7.6	6.2	6.7	9.3
1975	5.1	1.5	6.0	-0.7	0.5	-0.2	-0.9	-0.6	-0.6	1.8	2.4	2.7	1.0
1976	2.8	4.3	6.7	6.0	4.5	4.1	4.1	3.2	3.4	3.5	3.0	1.7	3.9
1977	0.2	-0.8	-0.3	-0.5	-0.2	-1.1	-0.9	-0.1	-0.2	-0.3	0.5	0.3	-0.3
1978	0.6	1.2	2.6	2.9	3.3	3.3	3.1	4.9	5.0	6.6	7.5	7.4	4.0
1979	8.0	7.5	7.9	8.1	8.6	9.5	10.6	11.1	11.5	13.3	13.2	13.1	10.2
1980	10.0	8.7	9.6	9.9	4.3	3.5	0.6	-0.4	-1.1	-0.4	1.2	9.3	4.6
1981	10.6	10.5	9.3	10.5	10.4	11.0	11.6	13.7	11.3	8.5	5.2	3.8	9.7
1982	0.5	-0.3	0.0	-2.6	-4.1	-3.7	-6.0	-9.5	-10.0	-10.4	-10.6	-11.7	-5.7

19.0 LONG DURATION UNEMPLOYMENT, CANADA (THOUSANDS)

YEAR	JAN	FEB	MAR	APR	MAY	JUN	JUL	AUG	SEP	OCT	NOV	DEC	AVGE
1953	29.	28.	26.	29.	30.	30.	31.	30.	33.	42.	45.	48.	33.
1954	50.	56.	60.	64.	71.	79.	80.	92.	93.	101.	103.	100.	79.
1955	93.	86.	82.	75.	72.	72.	70.	66.	63.	58.	57.	53.	71.
1956	54.	54.	54.	51.	46.	39.	34.	37.	40.	32.	30.	31.	42.
1957	32.	39.	54.	60.	52.	56.	60.	64.	70.	71.	92.	102.	63.
1958	118.	125.	136.	143.	144.	168.	165.	156.	181.	167.	170.	173.	154.
1959	158.	145.	125.	123.	127.	117.	113.	116.	108.	105.	105.	111.	121.
1960	108.	119.	125.	134.	153.	145.	143.	157.	158.	172.	185.	177.	148.
1961	186.	183.	168.	178.	189.	195.	182.	177.	179.	175.	160.	151.	177.
1962	146.	142.	136.	132.	132.	132.	137.	133.	133.	127.	123.	131.	134.
1963	129.	131.	131.	129.	131.	130.	124.	121.	115.	113.	111.	99.	122.
1964	103.	106.	104.	104.	94.	96.	87.	96.	104.	90.	94.	90.	97.
1965	92.	82.	83.	87.	78.	77.	82.	81.	71.	61.	62.	62.	77.
1966	61.	63.	64.	62.	62.	61.	60.	61.	65.	70.	69.	66.	64.
1967	64.	69.	69.	71.	77.	78.	78.	74.	85.	86.	83.	96.	78.
1968	91.	97.	104.	106.	110.	109.	121.	115.	110.	114.	118.	115.	109.
1969	123.	120.	112.	116.	114.	118.	113.	127.	110.	117.	116.	118.	117.
1970	119.	129.	136.	143.	157.	169.	184.	184.	192.	188.	197.	206.	167.
1971	219.	216.	215.	221.	196.	212.	222.	214.	217.	217.	229.	209.	216.
1972	207.	192.	199.	181.	193.	211.	213.	227.	223.	225.	231.	213.	210.
1973	202.	202.	193.	175.	173.	158.	173.	176.	176.	170.	175.	168.	178.
1974	181.	174.	166.	175.	177.	164.	154.	150.	173.	158.	158.	160.	166.
1975	189.	210.	235.	249.	251.	244.	253.	256.	252.	241.	232.	244.	238.
1976	227.	223.	202.	209.	223.	232.	226.	223.	229.	256.	248.	252.	229.
1977	255.	264.	259.	257.	260.	277.	282.	301.	299.	312.	319.	332.	285.
1978	308.	307.	312.	326.	327.	329.	344.	327.	345.	314.	314.	307.	322.
1979	304.	291.	294.	290.	276.	273.	269.	253.	257.	256.	260.	258.	273.
1980	250.	271.	277.	279.	306.	286.	279.	287.	272.	279.	277.	278.	278.
1981	295.	289.	280.	272.	277.	272.	274.	286.	305.	305.	312.	328.	291.
1982	333.	351.	377.	412.	447.	497.	581.	598.	654.	672.	698.	737.	530.

20.0 PLANT AND EQUIPMENT, INVESTMENT EXPENDITURES, IN CONSTANT PRICES, CANADA
(ANNUAL RATE, MILLION 1971 CANADIAN DOLLARS)

YEAR	IQ	IIQ	IIIQ	IVQ	AVGE
1948	3908.	3984.	4028.	4292.	4053.
1949	4284.	4216.	4256.	4344.	4275.
1950	4284.	4348.	4632.	4608.	4468.
1951	4864.	4856.	4968.	4856.	4886.
1952	5116.	5492.	5436.	5504.	5387.
1953	5924.	5900.	5860.	5640.	5831.
1954	5620.	5644.	5256.	5112.	5408.
1955	5120.	5480.	5964.	6236.	5700.
1956	6568.	7212.	7676.	7996.	7363.
1957	8468.	8384.	8160.	7608.	8155.
1958	7400.	7336.	7088.	6996.	7205.
1959	6676.	7144.	7248.	7040.	7027.
1960	7196.	7120.	7012.	7052.	7095.
1961	6840.	6736.	6884.	6916.	6844.
1962	6876.	6840.	7076.	7104.	6974.
1963	7096.	7272.	7532.	7764.	7416.
1964	8288.	8524.	8664.	9248.	8681.
1965	9080.	9468.	10152.	10772.	9868.
1966	11156.	11440.	11660.	11860.	11529.
1967	11736.	11576.	11092.	10676.	11270.
1968	10988.	10696.	10804.	10876.	10841.
1969	11116.	11108.	11380.	11632.	11309.
1970	11832.	11696.	12012.	11792.	11833.
1971	11760.	12108.	12332.	12720.	12230.
1972	12696.	12860.	12740.	12708.	12751.
1973	13748.	14248.	14936.	15736.	14667.
1974	15964.	15576.	15720.	15948.	15802.
1975	16548.	16996.	17388.	17192.	17031.
1976	17020.	17372.	16480.	17020.	16973.
1977	17260.	17100.	17280.	17008.	17162.
1978	16788.	17320.	17544.	17768.	17355.
1979	18308.	18872.	20400.	20432.	19503.
1980	20972.	20628.	20996.	21208.	20951.
1981	22140.	22640.	22000.	22364.	22286.
1982	21460.	20272.	18528.	18636.	19724.

21.0 BUSINESS INVENTORIES, IN CONSTANT PRICES, CANADA (MILLION 1971 CANADIAN DOLLARS)

YEAR	JAN	FEB	MAR	APR	MAY	JUN	JUL	AUG	SEP	OCT	NOV	DEC	AVGE
1949	3376.9	3431.0	3428.1	3391.4	3411.9	3403.3	3401.7	3407.2	3390.0	3340.6	3307.0	3313.4	3383.5
1950	3297.1	3267.4	3256.3	3264.4	3253.4	3215.8	3218.8	3170.4	3080.9	3171.7	3230.4	3313.6	3228.4
1951	3260.5	3233.9	3267.5	3390.5	3501.7	3640.7	3694.0	3800.4	3890.7	3956.4	3994.2	3991.7	3635.2
1952	4038.4	4103.9	4114.0	4149.2	4193.0	4121.3	4120.4	4145.9	4190.2	4189.1	4179.8	4209.4	4146.2
1953	4186.4	4191.4	4220.2	4286.7	4299.1	4301.5	4351.8	4403.7	4377.3	4411.6	4415.3	4428.5	4322.8
1954	4428.8	4409.4	4390.9	4396.0	4398.4	4391.8	4366.8	4377.3	4360.0	4357.8	4363.4	4313.3	4379.5
1955	4323.5	4315.7	4347.5	4338.0	4342.5	4326.7	4334.5	4289.7	4297.1	4345.4	4351.3	4419.7	4336.0
1956	4479.3	4536.0	4590.7	4643.2	4680.2	4723.3	4771.1	4789.3	4817.8	4840.5	4909.1	4937.0	4726.5
1957	4929.2	4980.7	4992.1	5025.6	5049.4	5078.0	5120.3	5130.2	5152.6	5196.0	5162.6	5067.7	5073.7
1958	5020.8	4950.2	4941.9	4914.6	4886.0	4865.4	4856.0	4857.3	4856.0	4845.1	4845.6	4858.6	4891.5
1959	4877.3	4886.1	4894.0	4922.9	4921.6	4940.7	4941.9	4981.5	5004.9	5014.0	5028.0	5076.5	4957.4
1960	5099.3	5151.9	5215.6	5240.5	5270.4	5279.6	5277.1	5270.4	5249.1	5246.1	5261.3	5237.6	5233.2
1961	5118.7	5144.9	5179.6	5196.9	5225.8	5204.8	5214.5	5220.1	5234.1	5312.9	5337.7	5379.6	5230.8
1962	5414.4	5433.0	5501.8	5510.9	5485.3	5477.4	5523.6	5522.2	5565.6	5604.5	5570.4	5574.4	5515.3
1963	5582.8	5608.1	5662.5	5615.4	5671.5	5651.2	5641.5	5667.1	5695.5	5714.0	5712.7	5771.6	5670.3
1964	5826.6	5861.6	5834.1	5910.4	5949.9	6009.9	6077.2	6115.3	6178.6	6192.5	6257.3	6257.9	6039.3
1965	6304.0	6398.6	6415.6	6470.7	6510.4	6514.7	6568.4	6586.5	6684.9	6744.4	6769.6	6851.3	6568.2
1966	6848.3	6913.6	6939.8	7050.1	7093.7	7149.5	7228.6	7263.7	7342.3	7424.6	7468.7	7504.2	7185.6
1967	7641.1	7630.4	7607.4	7601.1	7646.6	7665.9	7748.8	7569.1	7657.5	7612.4	7618.7	7557.3	7641.4
1968	7548.7	7535.2	7509.7	7533.2	7537.2	7513.5	7557.1	7509.4	7639.0	7667.7	7639.6	7731.0	7581.8
1969	7664.4	7705.2	7749.1	7778.4	7841.2	7872.8	7996.6	7973.7	8018.4	8113.8	8148.0	8166.9	7919.0
1970	8173.3	8200.8	8203.7	8197.9	8234.3	8210.6	8328.8	8414.5	8458.7	8383.6	8532.6	8373.0	8309.9
1971	8305.4	8260.2	8237.6	8167.8	8201.1	8210.8	8175.4	8130.6	8161.8	8209.6	8247.1	8332.7	8220.0
1972	8270.5	8257.9	8097.1	8318.7	8327.3	8394.8	8422.4	8486.4	8530.7	8543.7	8518.4	8533.6	8391.8
1973	8432.9	8472.8	8475.4	8481.7	8439.3	8613.7	8595.4	8510.4	8659.5	8754.1	8861.7	8981.0	8606.5
1974	8928.2	9052.9	9149.2	9233.4	9314.5	9497.9	9520.5	9595.8	9676.7	9850.9	9923.5	10211.9	9496.3
1975	10207.2	10167.3	10273.2	10240.7	10202.9	10208.9	10105.7	9999.8	9958.9	9927.9	9991.2	10104.9	10115.7
1976	9977.3	10069.2	10141.1	10192.0	10141.4	10203.8	10246.6	10252.5	10278.5	10356.3	10390.5	10037.8	10215.6
1977	10229.2	10279.3	10256.3	10192.3	10214.8	10307.6	10304.4	10390.2	10354.5	10451.0	10506.4	10508.0	10332.8
1978	10497.0	10595.8	10501.4	10363.6	10363.0	10407.7	10354.0	10023.1	10393.9	10260.4	10363.5	10473.1	10418.8
1979	10369.7	10407.6	10560.1	10511.4	10723.6	10865.6	10908.7	11022.1	11120.2	11140.5	11256.0	11395.0	10857.4
1980	11110.4	11138.3	11361.8	11500.6	11560.9	11547.7	11574.9	11508.1	11429.5	11355.1	11309.7	11135.2	11396.2
1981	11339.5	11373.2	11467.8	11508.0	11546.3	11672.4	11692.7	11798.0	11916.1	11967.5	12044.7	12011.0	11694.8
1982	11998.9	12054.8	12053.8	11811.5	11712.4	11621.7	11587.1	11429.1	11295.9	11226.2	11115.1	10816.1	11560.2

22.1 CHANGE IN HOURS PER UNIT OF OUTPUT, MANUFACTURING, CANADA (PERCENT CHANGE FROM YEAR AGO)

YEAR	JAN	FEB	MAR	APR	MAY	JUN	JUL	AUG	SEP	OCT	NOV	DEC	AVGE
1962	-3.5	-4.6	-4.1	-4.9	-4.1	-4.8	-5.0	-3.1	-4.7	-3.8	-3.8	-7.9	-4.5
1963	-4.4	-3.9	-4.3	-2.4	-3.8	-4.4	-3.2	-4.1	-4.7	-4.5	-5.2	-3.7	-4.0
1964	-3.9	-5.8	-5.4	-4.7	-4.4	-3.3	-3.0	-4.9	-3.0	-3.8	-4.1	-1.0	-4.0
1965	-4.3	-2.6	-1.9	-3.3	-3.9	-3.2	-6.0	-2.7	-2.9	-4.2	-2.2	-2.3	-3.3
1966	-3.7	-3.2	-2.9	-4.0	-2.3	-2.5	-1.6	-1.0	-2.6	-1.9	-2.4	-12.7	-3.4
1967	-2.7	-2.7	-4.1	-3.3	-4.1	-4.3	-3.2	-8.0	-5.1	-3.5	-5.2	4.7	-3.5
1968	-4.9	-5.1	-4.5	-5.4	-6.4	-8.6	-7.4	-6.6	-6.2	-7.9	-7.6	-8.2	-6.6
1969	-6.2	-7.2	-7.9	-6.1	-4.9	-3.6	-6.6	-5.0	-5.0	-2.9	-2.4	-4.6	-5.2
1970	-2.8	-3.1	-2.5	-2.3	-2.7	-0.3	-0.4	-0.3	-0.3	-1.5	-2.9	2.4	-1.4
1971	-4.2	-5.3	-3.1	-4.8	-5.3	-6.9	-5.8	-8.2	-8.7	-9.8	-6.6	-7.8	-6.4
1972	-6.3	-2.6	-5.2	-5.9	-4.4	-6.2	-5.0	-3.4	-3.5	-3.3	-6.6	-7.2	-4.9
1973	-5.6	-8.6	-8.4	-6.9	-6.6	-4.5	-8.0	-5.7	-4.9	-4.8	-4.6	-2.9	-6.0
1974	-4.4	-3.4	-2.6	-1.3	-6.2	-2.8	0.4	-3.0	-1.9	-2.0	-0.8	-3.3	-2.6
1975	1.7	-0.9	0.7	-0.9	5.0	0.2	-2.6	-1.2	-2.5	-0.1	-2.2	-2.2	-0.3
1976	-3.4	-0.9	-3.4	-4.5	-7.6	-5.8	-3.4	-5.0	-4.4	-3.0	-3.2	-1.6	-3.9
1977	-6.7	-6.7	-4.8	-3.2	-2.0	-2.9	-2.7	-1.1	-1.5	-4.9	-2.9	-2.8	-3.5
1978	-2.4	-1.6	-1.6	-4.2	-2.6	-3.1	-3.2	-2.8	-5.7	-4.7	-4.9	-5.8	-3.5
1979	-3.6	-5.3	-5.3	-1.2	-5.1	-3.0	-2.4	-4.1	-1.0	-2.1	-0.3	1.2	-2.7
1980	-0.1	-1.0	0.6	-0.8	3.1	-2.0	-0.5	1.5	-0.2	0.5	-0.7	-1.4	-0.4
1981	1.4	-1.4	-1.7	-2.1	-3.4	-5.1	-4.8	-1.6	0.4	0.9	1.5	1.0	-1.3
1982	1.3	2.6	3.6	3.6	0.4	3.0	6.5	-3.8	-2.5	-0.9	-2.3	-0.7	0.9

23.0 BUSINESS LOANS OUTSTANDING, IN CONSTANT PRICES, CANADA (MILLION 1971 CANADIAN DOLLARS)

YEAR	IQ	IIQ	IIIQ	IVQ	AVGE
1948	2520.	2522.	2461.	2497.	2500.
1949	2524.	2571.	2612.	2548.	2564.
1950	2618.	2706.	2600.	2796.	2680.
1951	2909.	2969.	3045.	3029.	2988.
1952	2935.	2986.	3041.	3136.	3025.
1953	3187.	3406.	3521.	3636.	3438.
1954	3698.	3794.	3820.	3797.	3777.
1955	3739.	3787.	4003.	4382.	3978.

YEAR	JAN	FEB	MAR	APR	MAY	JUN	JUL	AUG	SEP	OCT	NOV	DEC	AVGE
1956	4631.	4722.	4794.	4847.	4933.	4971.	4991.	5008.	5006.	5011.	5066.	5080.	4922.
1957	5070.	5083.	5062.	5086.	5080.	5100.	5080.	5110.	5150.	5187.	5158.	5092.	5105.
1958	5047.	5010.	4972.	4941.	4879.	4774.	4812.	4756.	4723.	4726.	4726.	4813.	4848.
1959	4939.	4968.	5106.	5243.	5406.	5379.	5440.	5672.	5692.	5641.	5646.	5612.	5395.
1960	5560.	5570.	5571.	5533.	5531.	5497.	5511.	5502.	5504.	5591.	5653.	5729.	5563.
1961	5701.	5702.	5702.	5648.	5642.	5595.	5593.	5696.	5672.	5741.	5807.	5881.	5698.
1962	5982.	6048.	6093.	6152.	6270.	6431.	6572.	6588.	6698.	6755.	6640.	6574.	6400.
1963	6509.	6505.	6530.	6461.	6544.	6469.	6420.	6463.	6499.	6648.	6602.	6703.	6529.
1964	6782.	6753.	6899.	6996.	7046.	7103.	7160.	7210.	7241.	7295.	7378.	7484.	7112.
1965	7516.	7582.	7687.	7833.	7894.	8039.	8217.	8417.	8407.	8446.	8379.	8773.	8099.
1966	8678.	8596.	8646.	8752.	8774.	8856.	8857.	8910.	8927.	8979.	9094.	9097.	8847.
1967	9140.	9349.	9319.	9243.	9336.	9264.	9296.	9543.	9724.	9948.	10197.	10117.	9540.
1968	10031.	10182.	10336.	10544.	10653.	10566.	10656.	10581.	10594.	10741.	10734.	10831.	10537.
1969	10899.	10979.	11062.	11364.	11457.	11567.	11620.	11768.	11806.	11979.	11988.	12108.	11550.
1970	11825.	11765.	11605.	11457.	11309.	11278.	11657.	11902.	11799.	11710.	11806.	11864.	11665.
1971	11752.	11814.	11858.	11744.	11832.	11956.	12055.	12215.	12526.	12636.	12842.	13090.	12193.
1972	13298.	13439.	13789.	14173.	14725.	14701.	14555.	14802.	14836.	15027.	15159.	15166.	14473.
1973	15148.	15395.	15428.	15544.	15667.	15701.	15729.	15572.	15927.	16257.	16440.	16961.	15814.
1974	16476.	16335.	16259.	16364.	16656.	16590.	16573.	16630.	16684.	16502.	16535.	16794.	16533.
1975	16739.	16769.	16898.	16889.	16831.	16976.	17027.	17090.	17227.	17314.	17664.	17721.	17095.
1976	17992.	18429.	18991.	18857.	18877.	19035.	19212.	19454.	19670.	19821.	20189.	20333.	19238.
1977	20270.	20475.	20624.	20304.	20311.	20507.	20457.	20590.	20651.	20756.	20974.	20770.	20557.
1978	20577.	20637.	20693.	20484.	20560.	20499.	20752.	20865.	20863.	20830.	20817.	20750.	20694.
1979	20759.	20746.	21124.	21250.	21641.	21919.	22183.	22502.	22548.	22739.	23093.	23406.	21993.
1980	22957.	22974.	23500.	23753.	24406.	24870.	24646.	24046.	23922.	23881.	24025.	24873.	23988.
1981	26090.	26710.	26435.	27068.	26452.	27228.	27987.	29283.	29975.	30151.	31783.	32810.	28498.
1982	31407.	31194.	31923.	31212.	30938.	31129.	30854.	31378.	31513.	31625.	31827.	31301.	31358.

24.0 BANK INTEREST RATES, BUSINESS LOANS, CANADA (PERCENT)

YEAR	JAN	FEB	MAR	APR	MAY	JUN	JUL	AUG	SEP	OCT	NOV	DEC	AVGE
1948	4.50	4.50	4.50	4.50	4.50	4.50	4.50	4.50	4.50	4.50	4.50	4.50	4.50
1949	4.50	4.50	4.50	4.50	4.50	4.50	4.50	4.50	4.50	4.50	4.50	4.50	4.50
1950	4.50	4.50	4.50	4.50	4.50	4.50	4.50	4.50	4.50	4.50	4.50	4.50	4.50
1951	4.50	4.50	4.50	4.50	4.50	4.50	4.50	4.50	4.50	4.50	4.50	4.50	4.50
1952	4.50	4.50	4.50	4.50	4.50	4.50	4.50	4.50	4.50	4.50	4.50	4.50	4.50
1953	4.50	4.50	4.50	4.50	4.50	4.50	4.50	4.50	4.50	4.50	4.50	4.50	4.50
1954	4.50	4.50	4.50	4.50	4.50	4.50	4.50	4.50	4.50	4.50	4.50	4.50	4.50
1955	4.50	4.50	4.50	4.50	4.50	4.50	4.50	4.50	4.50	4.50	4.50	4.50	4.50
1956	4.50	4.50	4.50	5.00	5.00	5.00	5.00	5.25	5.25	5.50	5.50	5.50	5.04
1957	5.50	5.50	5.50	5.25	5.00	5.00	5.50	5.75	5.75	5.75	5.75	5.50	5.58
1958	5.50	5.25	5.25	5.75	5.25	5.75	5.25	5.25	5.25	5.25	5.25	5.25	5.27
1959	5.25	5.25	5.75	5.75	5.75	5.75	5.75	5.75	5.75	5.75	5.75	5.75	5.65
1960	5.75	5.75	5.75	5.75	5.75	5.75	5.75	5.75	5.75	5.75	5.75	5.50	5.75
1961	5.75	5.75	5.75	5.50	5.50	5.50	5.50	5.50	5.50	5.50	5.75	5.75	5.60
1962	5.50	5.50	5.50	5.75	5.75	5.75	6.00	6.00	6.00	6.00	6.00	5.75	5.71
1963	5.75	5.75	5.75	5.75	5.75	5.75	5.75	5.75	5.75	5.75	5.75	5.75	5.75
1964	5.75	5.75	5.75	5.75	5.75	5.75	5.75	5.75	5.75	5.75	5.75	5.75	5.75
1965	5.75	5.75	5.75	5.75	5.75	5.75	5.75	5.75	5.75	5.75	5.75	6.00	5.77
1966	6.00	6.00	6.00	6.00	6.00	6.00	6.00	6.00	6.00	6.00	6.00	6.00	6.00
1967	6.00	6.00	6.00	6.00	5.75	5.75	6.00	5.75	5.75	6.00	6.00	6.50	5.92
1968	6.50	7.00	7.00	7.00	7.25	7.25	7.00	7.00	6.75	6.75	6.75	6.75	6.92
1969	7.00	7.00	7.50	7.50	7.50	8.00	8.50	8.50	8.50	8.50	8.50	8.50	7.96
1970	8.50	8.50	8.50	8.50	8.50	8.50	8.00	8.00	8.00	8.00	7.50	7.50	8.17
1971	7.00	7.00	6.00	6.50	6.00	6.00	6.50	6.50	6.00	6.25	6.00	6.00	6.48
1972	6.00	6.00	6.00	6.00	6.00	6.00	6.50	6.00	6.00	6.00	6.00	6.00	6.00
1973	6.00	6.00	6.00	6.50	7.00	7.75	7.75	8.25	9.00	9.00	9.00	9.50	7.65
1974	9.50	9.50	9.50	10.50	11.00	11.00	11.50	11.50	11.50	11.50	11.00	11.00	10.75
1975	10.50	9.50	9.00	9.00	9.00	9.00	9.00	9.00	9.75	9.75	9.75	9.75	9.42
1976	9.75	9.75	10.25	10.25	10.25	10.25	10.25	10.25	10.25	10.25	9.75	9.25	10.04
1977	9.25	8.75	8.75	8.75	8.75	8.25	8.25	8.25	8.25	8.25	8.25	8.25	8.50
1978	8.25	8.25	8.75	9.25	9.25	9.25	9.25	9.75	10.25	11.00	11.50	11.50	9.69
1979	12.00	12.00	12.00	12.00	12.00	12.00	12.50	12.50	13.00	14.75	15.00	15.00	12.90
1980	15.00	15.00	15.75	16.75	13.75	13.25	12.25	12.25	12.25	12.75	13.75	18.25	14.25
1981	18.25	18.25	17.75	18.25	19.50	20.00	21.00	22.75	21.25	20.00	17.25	18.25	19.29
1982	16.50	16.50	17.00	17.00	17.00	18.25	17.25	16.00	15.00	13.75	13.00	12.50	15.81

UNITED KINGDOM

LEADING INDEX, UNITED KINGDOM (1980=100)

YEAR	JAN	FEB	MAR	APR	MAY	JUN	JUL	AUG	SEP	OCT	NOV	DEC	AVGE
1955	71.2	70.4	70.4	70.6	70.7	71.2	71.9	71.8	71.8	71.8	71.8	72.0	71.3
1956	71.8	71.4	71.7	72.1	71.7	71.8	71.5	71.5	71.6	71.8	71.8	72.1	71.7
1957	72.7	72.9	73.0	73.2	73.5	73.3	73.5	73.4	72.9	72.6	72.6	72.5	73.0
1958	72.7	72.6	72.6	72.7	72.5	72.6	73.2	73.6	73.7	74.1	74.7	74.8	73.3
1959	74.7	74.7	74.9	75.8	76.1	76.7	76.7	77.1	77.9	78.5	79.0	79.6	76.8
1960	79.9	80.4	80.4	79.8	79.6	79.4	78.9	79.3	79.1	79.0	79.2	79.1	79.5
1961	79.0	79.2	79.6	79.5	79.4	79.3	79.1	78.3	78.3	77.9	78.0	78.0	78.8
1962	77.7	77.9	77.8	77.6	77.9	78.0	78.3	78.5	78.6	78.2	78.5	78.4	78.1
1963	78.4	78.5	79.2	80.4	81.0	80.9	81.1	81.4	82.1	83.2	83.2	83.5	81.1
1964	84.2	83.9	83.9	84.0	84.0	84.1	84.3	84.5	84.8	85.0	85.2	84.9	84.4
1965	84.5	84.7	84.4	84.6	84.5	84.2	83.8	83.8	83.8	83.9	83.8	84.1	84.2
1966	84.5	84.0	84.0	84.1	84.2	84.4	83.6	83.4	82.9	82.3	82.4	82.3	83.5
1967	82.7	83.1	83.8	83.8	83.8	83.9	84.1	83.9	84.5	85.4	86.1	85.9	84.2
1968	85.4	85.9	86.8	86.6	86.6	86.8	87.4	87.5	87.5	87.5	87.4	87.8	86.9
1969	87.8	87.6	87.8	88.1	88.3	88.1	87.5	87.3	87.4	87.5	87.3	87.2	87.7
1970	87.2	87.3	87.4	87.5	87.5	87.8	87.5	88.1	88.1	88.7	88.4	89.0	87.9
1971	89.1	88.8	88.4	88.8	89.0	89.2	89.9	90.3	90.2	90.1	90.0	90.7	89.5
1972	90.9	88.6	91.0	91.5	92.2	92.0	92.6	93.2	93.4	93.6	94.3	95.2	92.4
1973	96.5	97.3	97.3	96.6	96.4	96.9	97.4	97.9	97.5	97.6	97.5	97.3	97.2
1974	95.4	95.4	96.4	97.0	96.3	95.2	94.2	93.4	92.5	92.0	92.0	90.8	94.2
1975	91.7	92.3	92.0	92.4	92.1	92.2	91.9	92.1	92.5	93.0	93.1	93.7	92.4
1976	94.4	94.8	95.6	95.9	96.3	96.4	96.7	96.6	97.1	97.5	98.2	97.9	96.4
1977	99.3	99.6	100.2	101.0	101.0	100.4	100.3	100.1	100.5	100.7	100.8	101.4	100.4
1978	101.8	101.2	101.5	101.5	101.9	101.1	101.0	100.9	101.3	100.6	100.7	101.4	101.2
1979	100.0	101.3	101.8	102.6	103.1	103.4	103.1	102.9	103.1	103.6	103.6	102.9	102.6
1980	102.3	102.0	101.4	101.0	100.5	100.4	99.7	98.8	98.6	98.4	98.4	98.6	100.0
1981	99.0	99.3	100.2	100.5	101.1	101.7	102.2	101.9	101.9	102.2	102.3	102.4	101.2
1982	102.1	102.7	103.3	102.9	103.6	103.0	103.5	102.9	103.5	103.7	104.4	105.0	103.4

SIX MONTH SMOOTHED CHANGE IN LEADING INDEX, UNITED KINGDOM (ANNUAL RATE, PERCENT)

YEAR	JAN	FEB	MAR	APR	MAY	JUN	JUL	AUG	SEP	OCT	NOV	DEC	AVGE
1956	1.3	0.1	0.8	1.5	0.2	0.2	-0.7	-0.7	-0.3	0.2	0.2	1.0	0.3
1957	2.4	2.8	2.7	3.0	3.5	2.6	2.9	2.1	0.5	-0.8	-0.9	-1.3	1.6
1958	-0.7	-1.2	-1.0	-0.8	-1.1	-0.5	1.2	2.2	2.4	3.3	4.5	4.9	1.0
1959	3.5	3.1	3.2	4.9	5.1	5.7	5.0	5.2	6.4	7.0	7.2	7.9	5.3
1960	7.5	7.7	6.3	3.9	2.5	1.4	-0.2	0.1	-0.6	-1.1	-0.8	-1.1	2.1
1961	-1.3	-0.6	0.7	0.6	0.4	0.1	-0.3	-2.1	-2.0	-2.7	-2.4	-2.0	-1.0
1962	-2.5	-1.9	-1.8	-1.9	-1.0	-0.3	0.7	1.3	1.4	0.5	1.1	0.7	-0.3
1963	0.5	0.9	2.4	4.7	5.7	4.9	4.7	4.9	5.9	7.8	6.8	6.7	4.7
1964	7.3	5.4	4.3	3.7	2.9	2.5	2.5	2.4	2.4	2.2	2.3	1.3	3.3
1965	0.1	0.6	-0.3	0.2	-0.2	-0.8	-1.7	-1.7	-1.6	-1.2	-1.2	-0.4	-0.7
1966	0.8	-0.4	-0.2	0.1	0.4	0.8	-0.2	-1.3	-2.5	-3.5	-3.0	-3.1	-1.0
1967	-1.9	-0.5	1.1	1.2	1.3	1.4	2.1	1.4	2.8	4.4	5.5	4.3	1.9
1968	2.5	3.0	4.6	3.6	3.1	3.1	3.8	3.5	2.7	2.1	1.6	2.2	3.0
1969	1.8	1.0	1.0	1.7	1.7	0.9	-0.5	-1.0	-0.6	-0.4	-0.8	-1.1	0.3
1970	-0.9	-0.7	-0.5	-0.2	0.1	0.8	0.6	-1.4	1.3	2.1	1.6	2.6	0.7
1971	2.5	1.6	0.5	1.1	1.4	1.6	2.6	3.3	2.5	2.1	1.6	2.7	2.0
1972	2.7	-2.2	2.6	3.4	4.3	3.4	4.0	4.8	4.7	4.6	5.4	6.4	3.7
1973	8.4	9.0	7.6	4.9	3.7	4.1	4.2	4.3	2.8	1.8	1.4	0.6	4.4
1974	-3.4	-3.2	-1.0	0.3	-1.1	-3.2	-4.8	-5.7	-6.8	-7.0	-6.2	-7.6	-4.1
1975	-4.8	-3.1	-3.2	-1.8	-1.5	-0.7	-0.9	-0.1	1.0	1.9	2.2	3.1	-0.7
1976	4.0	4.4	5.5	5.5	5.7	5.3	5.1	4.1	4.4	4.2	4.8	3.5	4.7
1977	5.5	5.3	5.7	6.4	5.5	3.7	2.8	1.9	2.1	1.6	1.6	2.3	3.7
1978	2.4	0.9	1.4	1.1	1.8	0.1	-0.1	-0.4	0.3	-1.2	-1.0	0.3	0.5
1979	-2.2	0.5	1.3	2.6	3.4	3.8	2.9	2.3	2.4	2.9	-2.4	0.8	1.9
1980	-0.5	-1.6	-2.7	-3.3	-3.9	-3.8	-4.6	-5.7	-5.4	-5.1	-4.2	-3.1	-3.7
1981	-1.9	-0.7	1.4	2.0	3.3	4.4	5.1	4.1	3.6	3.6	3.2	2.7	2.6
1982	1.6	2.2	2.8	1.5	2.5	0.9	1.7	0.4	1.4	1.6	2.4	3.2	1.8

UNITED KINGDOM LEADING, COINCIDENT AND LAGGING INTERNATIONAL ECONOMIC INDECATORS

1.0 AVERAGE WORKWEEK, MANUFACTURING, UNITED KINGDOM (INDEX, 1980=100)

YEAR	JAN	FEB	MAR	APR	MAY	JUN	JUL	AUG	SEP	OCT	NOV	DEC	AVGE
1956	***	114.8	***	114.9	114.8	***	***	114.4	***	114.8	114.7	***	114.7
1957	***	114.7	***	114.6	115.0	***	***	115.1	***	114.4	114.4	***	114.7
1958	***	114.3	***	113.5	113.1	***	***	113.2	***	112.9	113.2	***	113.4
1959	***	112.9	***	114.1	114.4	***	***	114.5	***	115.0	114.8	***	114.2
1960	***	115.3	***	112.9	113.2	***	***	112.7	***	112.7	112.7	***	113.3
1961	***	111.8	***	112.2	111.5	***	***	111.5	111.5	111.4	111.3	***	111.7
1962	111.1	111.5	111.1	111.1	110.7	112.2	112.2	110.7	110.5	110.2	110.1	110.1	110.7
1963	109.9	109.4	109.3	110.0	110.3	110.7	110.6	111.0	111.3	111.5	111.5	111.6	110.6
1964	111.9	111.9	112.0	111.9	110.9	110.5	110.9	111.1	111.4	111.3	111.7	111.7	111.6
1965	111.1	111.1	110.9	110.6	110.4	111.5	111.5	109.2	109.5	109.6	109.4	109.5	110.1
1966	109.3	108.6	108.9	108.9	109.0	110.3	109.6	108.3	108.0	107.3	106.8	107.0	108.3
1967	107.1	107.3	107.6	107.4	107.4	108.8	108.6	107.8	107.5	107.6	107.9	108.0	107.5
1968	107.2	108.0	108.0	108.4	108.1	107.5	107.5	108.6	108.9	108.9	108.9	109.1	108.4
1969	109.0	108.4	108.1	108.8	108.8	108.6	108.4	108.5	108.4	108.5	108.4	108.0	108.5
1970	106.5	107.4	107.0	106.8	106.8	107.6	107.4	107.2	107.1	106.9	106.9	106.5	107.0
1971	106.6	106.4	105.9	104.7	105.7	105.5	105.4	105.2	105.1	104.9	104.8	105.0	105.4
1972	105.1	97.1	105.1	105.4	105.4	105.4	105.4	105.7	105.4	105.8	105.8	106.2	104.8
1973	106.5	107.9	106.9	106.6	106.8	106.6	106.5	107.0	106.6	106.6	106.5	107.4	106.8
1974	96.4	98.7	104.3	106.0	105.9	105.8	105.5	104.9	105.1	104.7	104.7	104.9	103.9
1975	104.7	103.9	103.3	102.7	102.1	102.1	102.3	102.1	102.3	102.2	102.2	102.9	102.7
1976	102.0	102.2	102.3	102.4	102.7	102.8	102.9	103.2	103.4	103.7	103.8	103.8	102.9
1977	103.9	103.9	103.7	103.7	103.9	103.7	103.7	103.9	103.7	103.9	103.7	103.8	103.8
1978	103.9	103.8	103.8	103.7	103.5	103.2	103.4	103.2	103.5	103.5	103.5	103.5	103.5
1979	103.3	103.5	104.0	104.1	103.5	103.7	103.5	102.4	102.3	103.7	103.8	103.5	103.4
1980	103.3	103.0	102.1	101.4	101.1	100.7	99.8	99.2	98.3	97.2	96.9	96.8	100.0
1981	96.7	96.5	96.9	97.8	98.1	98.6	99.1	99.8	100.1	100.3	99.9	100.0	98.6
1982	100.2	100.6	100.6	100.1	100.6	100.3	100.3	100.4	100.4	100.8	100.9	100.8	100.5

4.1 NEW COMPANIES REGISTERED, UNITED KINGDOM (NUMBER)

YEAR	JAN	FEB	MAR	APR	MAY	JUN	JUL	AUG	SEP	OCT	NOV	DEC	AVGE
1949	1240.	1188.	1128.	1228.	1246.	1170.	1269.	1144.	1211.	1225.	1119.	1193.	1197.
1950	1161.	1216.	1103.	1162.	1139.	1185.	1106.	1165.	1209.	1046.	1156.	1128.	1148.
1951	1120.	1101.	1123.	1207.	1104.	1161.	1110.	1054.	1068.	1044.	1041.	1111.	1107.
1952	1057.	1053.	1129.	994.	1003.	975.	878.	1054.	941.	1050.	1053.	922.	1009.
1953	992.	1100.	1128.	961.	1059.	1107.	1089.	1105.	1150.	1148.	1149.	1184.	1098.
1954	1313.	1208.	1239.	1158.	1323.	1274.	1325.	1359.	1335.	1366.	1439.	1352.	1308.
1955	1413.	1352.	1398.	1463.	1491.	1417.	1524.	1451.	1491.	1435.	1424.	1543.	1450.
1956	1335.	1427.	1413.	1466.	1411.	1616.	1408.	1473.	1432.	1521.	1451.	1420.	1448.
1957	1474.	1556.	1664.	1710.	1818.	1570.	1793.	1781.	1755.	1759.	1856.	1748.	1707.
1958	1970.	1704.	1704.	1786.	1590.	1901.	1792.	1807.	1873.	2080.	1812.	2177.	1850.
1959	2193.	2209.	2040.	2431.	1977.	2442.	2652.	2394.	2671.	2616.	2641.	2807.	2423.
1960	2360.	2837.	3137.	2787.	3161.	2864.	2670.	2955.	2907.	2396.	2924.	2841.	2820.
1961	2963.	2884.	2911.	2439.	2779.	3243.	2765.	2779.	2716.	2531.	2642.	2524.	2765.
1962	2430.	2640.	2675.	2413.	2912.	2918.	3104.	3148.	2846.	2962.	3278.	3030.	2863.
1963	3357.	3372.	2925.	3451.	3397.	3216.	4045.	3459.	3506.	3884.	3494.	3767.	3489.
1964	4333.	3789.	3723.	4320.	3810.	4121.	3790.	3950.	4073.	4062.	3945.	3851.	3981.
1965	3389.	3425.	3588.	3425.	3219.	2872.	2769.	2526.	2643.	2499.	2459.	2743.	2963.
1966	2427.	2569.	2683.	2272.	2273.	2362.	2147.	2452.	2217.	2002.	2185.	2031.	2302.
1967	2219.	2450.	2534.	2453.	2476.	2474.	2475.	2556.	2521.	3963.	3191.	1304.	2551.
1968	1395.	1440.	1749.	1543.	1837.	1546.	1780.	1742.	1601.	1921.	1829.	1774.	1680.
1969	2077.	1892.	2227.	2066.	2089.	1979.	2133.	1880.	1841.	1806.	1988.	2150.	2011.
1970	2087.	2156.	2464.	2556.	2322.	2670.	2573.	2280.	2461.	2615.	2564.	2972.	2477.
1971	2684.	2323.	3136.	3210.	3088.	3569.	3142.	3483.	3139.	3490.	3950.	3748.	3247.
1972	4008.	3745.	4045.	4182.	4412.	3777.	3696.	5689.	5512.	5096.	5251.	4567.	4498.
1973	4666.	5919.	6310.	5617.	5331.	4752.	5245.	6371.	4988.	5945.	6132.	5330.	5551.
1974	4758.	2870.	3393.	3679.	3878.	3329.	3730.	3274.	3214.	3481.	3115.	3039.	3480.
1975	3648.	3442.	3478.	4944.	4245.	3465.	3752.	3267.	3781.	3879.	3739.	3450.	3758.
1976	3476.	4088.	6190.	4150.	4343.	5624.	4954.	4221.	4377.	4600.	4667.	4655.	4612.
1977	3225.	4330.	5843.	5499.	4097.	4169.	4172.	4242.	4527.	4404.	5007.	5005.	4543.
1978	4555.	4316.	6024.	5031.	5939.	5023.	5264.	5087.	5484.	5482.	6131.	4343.	5223.
1979	5421.	5142.	4828.	4828.	4829.	4829.	4829.	5709.	5010.	7211.	6184.	6256.	5423.
1980	6257.	5886.	6368.	6145.	4934.	5924.	5283.	4861.	4814.	6476.	5365.	5943.	5688.
1981	5862.	5364.	6471.	5154.	5997.	6769.	6350.	5616.	5406.	6342.	6437.	5502.	5939.
1982	4122.	7698.	8645.	6728.	6566.	8800.	8147.	5599.	7660.	6366.	8413.	6912.	7138.

4.2 BUSINESS FAILURES, UNITED KINGDOM (NUMBER)

YEAR	IQ	IIQ	IIIQ	IVQ	AVGE
1960	234.	248.	290.	301.	268.
1961	327.	316.	331.	340.	329.
1962	353.	393.	381.	407.	384.
1963	387.	371.	369.	330.	364.
1964	313.	335.	304.	303.	314.
1965	310.	296.	307.	341.	314.
1966	341.	302.	353.	358.	339.
1967	374.	385.	368.	335.	366.
1968	374.	347.	340.	372.	358.
1969	378.	365.	440.	408.	398.
1970	412.	436.	441.	406.	424.
1971	373.	409.	414.	402.	400.
1972	390.	394.	320.	342.	362.
1973	319.	314.	325.	348.	327.
1974	409.	439.	507.	552.	477.
1975	591.	598.	644.	590.	606.
1976	587.	599.	598.	618.	601.
1977	424.	364.	381.	326.	374.
1978	318.	345.	300.	338.	325.

YEAR	JAN	FEB	MAR	APR	MAY	JUN	JUL	AUG	SEP	OCT	NOV	DEC	AVGE
1979	343.	348.	299.	273.	266.	282.	305.	302.	279.	282.	290.	307.	298.
1980	285.	280.	294.	319.	331.	325.	328.	328.	344.	366.	372.	383.	330.
1981	385.	409.	415.	424.	407.	407.	404.	426.	444.	446.	449.	451.	422.
1982	446.	438.	425.	443.	462.	474.	468.	524.	551.	557.	487.	481.	480.

5.1 NEW ORDERS, ENGINEERING INDUSTRIES, VOLUME, UNITED KINGDOM (INDEX, 1980=100)

YEAR	JAN	FEB	MAR	APR	MAY	JUN	JUL	AUG	SEP	OCT	NOV	DEC	AVGE
1958	62.	59.	55.	54.	53.	42.	50.	50.	48.	54.	50.	55.	53.
1959	53.	49.	53.	55.	60.	62.	52.	61.	66.	65.	69.	69.	60.
1960	69.	73.	69.	70.	66.	69.	72.	72.	68.	69.	72.	66.	70.
1961	70.	71.	81.	73.	69.	65.	75.	61.	64.	67.	64.	69.	69.
1962	67.	67.	69.	67.	68.	73.	66.	67.	73.	88.	66.	62.	68.
1963	78.	85.	76.	81.	81.	88.	73.	91.	94.	88.	84.	88.	84.
1964	88.	81.	96.	98.	96.	95.	94.	98.	93.	96.	99.	95.	94.
1965	93.	97.	91.	84.	84.	91.	88.	92.	84.	93.	90.	95.	90.
1966	102.	91.	92.	77.	90.	90.	91.	90.	88.	95.	88.	89.	90.
1967	77.	82.	89.	92.	101.	95.	88.	90.	96.	81.	87.	90.	89.
1968	86.	94.	99.	106.	86.	96.	104.	98.	102.	95.	98.	106.	98.
1969	106.	105.	106.	108.	108.	103.	100.	102.	105.	111.	110.	100.	105.
1970	114.	112.	114.	103.	111.	109.	100.	114.	105.	107.	109.	106.	109.
1971	103.	98.	98.	102.	108.	91.	115.	105.	101.	105.	94.	107.	102.
1972	126.	106.	101.	106.	109.	106.	112.	107.	114.	120.	120.	124.	113.
1973	118.	129.	131.	140.	137.	141.	149.	143.	153.	134.	142.	160.	140.
1974	131.	129.	136.	135.	124.	139.	119.	121.	118.	118.	112.	105.	124.
1975	100.	108.	110.	106.	105.	99.	99.	100.	96.	95.	95.	93.	101.
1976	105.	104.	99.	105.	107.	106.	122.	116.	113.	124.	123.	104.	111.
1977	128.	122.	113.	121.	112.	116.	119.	122.	110.	118.	113.	123.	118.
1978	126.	119.	113.	115.	117.	113.	119.	110.	125.	111.	131.	145.	120.
1979	101.	109.	110.	116.	117.	122.	118.	114.	112.	108.	110.	127.	114.
1980	105.	108.	113.	103.	112.	110.	99.	88.	95.	87.	84.	95.	100.
1981	97.	98.	124.	101.	89.	101.	108.	108.	101.	103.	88.	100.	102.
1982	119.	96.	86.	109.	104.	83.	93.	87.	93.	107.	89.	101.	97.

5.2 NEW ORDERS. CONSTRUCTION. PRIVATE INDUSTRY, IN CONSTANT PRICES. UNITED KINGDOM (MILLION 1980 POUNDS)

YEAR	IQ	IIQ	IIIQ	IVQ	AVGE
1957	162.	159.	161.	166.	162.
1958	188.	162.	194.	159.	176.
1959	171.	195.	192.	243.	200.
1960	260.	279.	283.	298.	280.
1961	260.	250.	284.	197.	248.
1962	209.	198.	200.	186.	198.
1963	205.	216.	201.	208.	208.

YEAR	JAN	FEB	MAR	APR	MAY	JUN	JUL	AUG	SEP	OCT	NOV	DEC	AVGE
1964	306.	212.	149.	192.	186.	209.	213.	212.	242.	248.	238.	229.	220.
1965	208.	244.	218.	254.	230.	230.	230.	220.	213.	223.	233.	219.	227.
1966	248.	216.	215.	202.	222.	224.	227.	244.	189.	157.	285.	163.	216.
1967	196.	305.	247.	206.	164.	214.	303.	203.	219.	189.	190.	240.	223.
1968	226.	195.	237.	234.	236.	227.	206.	228.	238.	273.	251.	244.	233.
1969	255.	265.	240.	285.	314.	234.	262.	216.	271.	299.	220.	218.	257.
1970	225.	215.	201.	225.	219.	267.	229.	267.	242.	215.	242.	333.	240.
1971	187.	206.	181.	181.	142.	177.	155.	184.	161.	159.	167.	167.	172.
1972	193.	131.	195.	170.	185.	167.	177.	153.	168.	181.	160.	169.	171.
1973	198.	208.	213.	207.	198.	228.	235.	210.	221.	247.	224.	239.	219.
1974	192.	196.	162.	197.	194.	161.	184.	198.	177.	156.	268.	111.	183.
1975	116.	187.	125.	106.	128.	101.	118.	148.	107.	103.	64.	95.	117.
1976	119.	126.	123.	124.	126.	137.	137.	123.	133.	141.	183.	154.	136.
1977	129.	137.	174.	175.	147.	200.	169.	163.	166.	115.	180.	194.	162.
1978	206.	177.	183.	179.	192.	147.	160.	191.	171.	167.	109.	155.	170.
1979	168.	164.	157.	153.	165.	206.	164.	159.	175.	217.	172.	162.	172.
1980	144.	169.	142.	164.	139.	156.	128.	137.	137.	136.	174.	114.	145.
1981	94.	114.	125.	116.	131.	129.	198.	170.	131.	131.	133.	147.	135.
1982	104.	104.	151.	96.	116.	115.	150.	109.	98.	100.	103.	111.	113.

YEAR	JAN	FEB	MAR	APR	MAY	JUN	JUL	AUG	SEP	OCT	NOV	DEC	AVGE
1948	1.3	1.1	1.0	1.1	1.0	1.0	1.0	1.5	2.0	2.3	2.5	2.3	1.5
1949	2.3	2.6	2.4	2.6	2.7	2.6	2.7	2.7	2.3	2.7	2.7	2.6	2.6
1950	2.3	2.0	2.0	1.6	1.6	1.5	1.4	1.5	1.4	1.3	1.5	1.8	1.7
1951	2.2	2.3	2.3	2.1	2.1	2.6	2.2	1.9	2.3	2.0	2.0	3.1	2.3
1952	2.4	3.1	3.4	3.9	4.1	5.2	4.4	5.0	5.1	4.8	5.2	5.9	4.4
1953	6.0	6.1	6.5	6.5	6.3	6.5	7.0	7.0	7.8	8.0	8.2	8.6	7.0
1954	8.3	6.5	8.9	7.9	9.5	9.2	9.6	9.3	8.8	10.7	9.0	8.4	8.8
1955	8.9	8.0	9.3	10.6	11.2	10.8	11.5	11.4	11.3	12.0	11.6	10.1	10.6
1956	10.5	7.8	10.7	11.0	10.4	10.3	10.2	9.4	9.6	9.7	10.5	10.3	10.0
1957	11.1	10.0	10.1	9.9	10.7	10.7	10.4	10.7	10.8	10.6	10.4	10.2	10.5
1958	10.6	9.9	10.8	11.0	11.4	10.3	11.3	11.4	11.5	12.2	14.6	11.9	11.4
1959	12.7	14.0	13.8	13.3	13.6	13.7	13.7	15.1	15.0	14.5	15.1	14.9	14.1
1960	15.0	14.7	15.5	16.8	15.0	15.4	14.9	15.3	15.0	14.8	14.1	16.3	15.2
1961	14.2	16.7	15.5	13.7	16.1	16.6	17.0	15.3	15.2	15.6	14.9	14.6	15.8
1962	14.2	15.7	14.6	17.2	15.0	15.2	16.9	15.1	15.8	15.8	18.2	14.9	15.5
1963	7.4	8.8	18.3	16.8	16.5	19.5	17.6	19.8	19.7	19.8	18.8	19.7	16.6
1964	21.6	21.1	18.2	19.2	21.3	19.0	18.4	21.7	20.1	21.5	24.6	23.1	20.6
1965	22.5	21.6	18.0	18.6	16.7	14.8	15.4	16.2	15.2	20.2	16.2	14.9	17.6
1966	18.2	14.4	30.1	27.7	16.3	17.4	19.9	14.8	15.0	13.4	13.3	14.1	16.1
1967	16.7	18.2	20.3	15.9	18.2	17.5	18.2	16.7	17.8	16.6	17.2	18.9	19.5
1968	16.3	18.0	13.6	14.5	15.4	16.1	15.9	15.7	14.9	15.9	16.4	19.8	16.7
1969	14.8	11.0	10.9	12.6	14.7	17.5	13.9	13.9	13.5	13.8	12.9	11.8	13.9
1970	12.0	12.0	15.3	14.6	14.8	14.3	14.7	14.8	14.9	16.3	13.8	14.0	13.8
1971	16.0	14.9	17.1	17.8	15.4	15.5	17.7	16.8	19.2	19.3	18.5	24.2	17.3
1972	18.1	16.4	20.3	19.6	18.2	20.8	19.1	18.2	20.3	18.7	20.0	23.3	19.0
1973	20.8	21.5	11.4	8.4	17.8	17.5	17.6	17.1	18.1	15.3	15.2	14.9	18.0
1974	11.1	11.3	10.3	12.6	8.7	8.7	7.4	8.2	6.9	7.5	8.1	8.2	8.8
1975	10.4	12.4	15.4	13.8	11.5	13.3	12.6	12.5	12.9	13.6	13.3	13.7	12.4
1976	13.6	13.0	10.3	12.3	13.7	14.5	12.7	13.1	13.5	10.4	10.8	10.2	12.9
1977	10.1	9.5	12.3	12.9	11.2	11.2	12.2	9.8	13.3	12.3	10.8	11.8	11.2
1978	11.6	11.6	9.6	10.8	12.1	14.6	11.8	11.1	14.9	14.5	14.1	15.3	13.1
1979	7.5	10.9	9.1	8.8	11.6	13.1	12.5	11.3	14.3	14.3	14.0	14.1	12.0
1980	10.3	10.7	9.6	8.7	8.8	7.7	7.5	7.5	6.4	6.8	8.1	6.4	8.2
1981	10.5	11.4	9.6	8.7	10.3	9.3	9.7	11.0	9.8	9.1	9.4	7.5	9.7
1982	10.9	13.7	13.0	11.8	12.2	9.8	11.6	12.2	11.8	11.3	11.6	12.3	11.8

7.0 CHANGE IN STOCKS AND WORK IN PROGRESS, IN CONSTANT PRICES, UNITED KINGDOM
(MILLION 1980 POUNDS)

YEAR	IQ	IIQ	IIIQ	IVQ	AVGE
1955	506.	-98.	555.	468.	358.
1956	512.	274.	163.	165.	279.
1957	612.	364.	185.	-18.	286.
1958	301.	-35.	329.	-89.	127.
1959	128.	65.	321.	437.	238.
1960	701.	526.	781.	959.	742.
1961	742.	600.	150.	-63.	357.
1962	-96.	-4.	183.	-37.	12.
1963	150.	291.	-43.	492.	223.
1964	724.	937.	732.	1140.	883.
1965	634.	508.	673.	461.	569.
1966	484.	337.	661.	-65.	354.
1967	457.	283.	112.	262.	279.
1968	-124.	646.	825.	638.	496.
1969	671.	608.	386.	407.	518.
1970	-73.	590.	840.	274.	408.
1971	337.	-108.	150.	185.	141.
1972	-352.	177.	-116.	252.	-10.
1973	1374.	1395.	1365.	913.	1262.
1974	-37.	1303.	1440.	154.	715.
1975	-907.	-1021.	-658.	-315.	-725.
1976	-195.	-164.	409.	1031.	270.
1977	1087.	812.	71.	668.	660.
1978	383.	787.	440.	480.	523.
1979	852.	279.	1040.	319.	623.
1980	-501.	-135.	-1201.	-1399.	-809.
1981	-1010.	-1329.	-182.	-134.	-664.
1982	60.	244.	-608.	-677.	-245.

8.0 BASIC MATERIALS PRICE INDEX, SIX MONTH SMOOTHED CHANGE, UNITED KINGDOM
(ANNUAL RATE, PERCENT)

YEAR	JAN	FEB	MAR	APR	MAY	JUN	JUL	AUG	SEP	OCT	NOV	DEC	AVGE
1958	-11.9	-12.0	-7.8	-5.6	-5.7	-2.3	-2.3	-2.3	-2.3	0.0	1.2	1.2	-4.1
1959	2.4	2.4	-1.2	0.0	0.0	-1.2	-1.2	-1.2	1.2	1.2	2.4	3.6	0.9
1960	-2.3	1.2	-1.2	1.2	1.2	0.0	-2.3	-3.5	-1.2	-2.3	-2.3	-2.3	-0.7
1961	-2.3	-1.2	-1.2	0.0	0.0	0.0	0.0	0.0	-1.2	-2.4	-1.2	-1.2	-0.9
1962	1.2	2.4	1.2	1.2	0.0	-1.2	-1.2	-3.5	-3.5	-1.2	-1.2	2.4	-0.1
1963	3.6	2.4	2.4	2.4	2.3	-2.4	-1.2	-0.0	3.6	9.6	7.1	7.1	3.5
1964	7.0	7.0	4.6	4.6	2.3	-2.3	-2.3	-2.3	-1.1	3.4	3.4	1.1	3.4
1965	1.1	1.1	1.1	1.1	1.1	-1.1	-2.2	-2.2	-1.1	-1.1	0.0	-2.2	0.0
1966	3.3	4.5	4.5	7.9	6.7	5.5	5.5	2.2	-1.1	-1.1	0.0	-2.1	3.0
1967	-2.1	-2.1	-4.3	-3.2	-2.1	-2.2	-2.2	0.0	-1.1	-4.4	10.0	18.1	1.3
1968	16.7	17.7	16.4	10.7	7.4	8.4	4.1	3.1	2.0	2.0	10.0	3.0	7.9
1969	4.0	3.0	3.0	3.0	4.0	3.9	3.0	3.9	3.9	4.9	5.8	6.8	4.1
1970	4.8	4.8	5.8	4.8	3.8	2.8	2.8	0.5	3.7	2.8	4.7	2.8	3.6
1971	4.6	5.6	5.5	8.3	6.4	5.5	8.2	7.0	2.7	0.9	0.9	1.8	4.6
1972	1.8	0.9	0.9	1.7	0.9	1.7	3.5	7.0	8.8	11.5	14.1	18.5	5.9
1973	23.8	27.2	30.4	27.2	26.7	31.3	40.2	46.1	42.2	46.6	45.1	51.6	36.5
1974	139.5	125.5	110.6	93.4	70.5	50.8	41.4	32.6	23.3	21.6	21.3	17.3	62.3
1975	16.4	9.1	11.0	9.8	11.2	9.6	8.0	10.6	11.2	14.0	19.1	22.9	12.7
1976	21.8	21.2	22.7	28.1	27.6	27.8	24.8	23.0	26.7	31.3	32.2	28.7	26.3
1977	28.3	24.2	22.0	21.3	17.1	13.7	8.2	1.9	0.2	-1.9	-2.3	-0.7	11.0
1978	-0.7	0.0	0.9	4.3	6.6	7.1	6.1	4.0	5.2	7.5	9.6	11.9	5.2
1979	13.3	15.3	13.7	13.4	14.1	13.8	11.6	10.2	10.9	13.7	15.5	15.9	13.4
1980	18.8	18.3	13.7	10.5	6.4	4.8	2.7	-0.6	-1.5	-2.0	0.4	3.7	6.3
1981	6.2	7.9	8.6	10.3	12.2	14.2	12.4	11.9	12.4	12.6	14.6	16.1	11.6
1982	15.4	14.0	9.8	5.8	3.9	2.3	1.8	-0.5	-0.5	0.8	4.2	9.9	5.6

9.0 COMMON STOCK PRICE INDEX. UNITED KINGDOM (1980=100)

YEAR	JAN	FEB	MAR	APR	MAY	JUN	JUL	AUG	SEP	OCT	NOV	DEC	AVGE
1948	14.	13.	13.	14.	14.	13.	13.	13.	13.	13.	13.	13.	13.
1949	13.	13.	12.	12.	12.	11.	11.	11.	11.	11.	11.	11.	12.
1950	11.	12.	11.	11.	12.	12.	12.	12.	13.	13.	13.	13.	12.
1951	13.	13.	13.	14.	15.	15.	14.	14.	15.	15.	13.	13.	14.
1952	13.	12.	12.	13.	11.	11.	12.	13.	13.	13.	13.	13.	12.
1953	13.	13.	12.	13.	13.	13.	13.	14.	14.	15.	15.	15.	14.
1954	15.	15.	16.	17.	17.	17.	18.	19.	19.	21.	20.	21.	18.
1955	23.	21.	21.	21.	22.	23.	24.	22.	22.	21.	21.	22.	22.
1956	21.	20.	20.	21.	20.	20.	20.	21.	21.	20.	19.	20.	20.
1957	21.	21.	21.	23.	23.	23.	21.	23.	20.	19.	19.	19.	21.
1958	19.	18.	19.	20.	20.	21.	21.	22.	23.	24.	24.	26.	21.
1959	25.	26.	26.	27.	28.	28.	27.	30.	29.	33.	34.	37.	29.
1960	36.	36.	36.	34.	35.	34.	34.	34.	36.	36.	34.	35.	35.
1961	36.	38.	40.	40.	40.	37.	36.	34.	34.	33.	33.	34.	36.
1962	34.	34.	33.	35.	32.	31.	31.	38.	33.	33.	35.	35.	33.
1963	34.	35.	36.	36.	36.	36.	37.	41.	39.	39.	40.	41.	37.
1964	40.	39.	40.	40.	40.	39.	41.	35.	36.	39.	38.	37.	40.
1965	38.	39.	37.	37.	38.	36.	35.	35.	35.	39.	40.	39.	37.
1966	39.	41.	40.	40.	41.	41.	39.	40.	35.	34.	33.	34.	38.
1967	36.	36.	36.	38.	39.	39.	40.	40.	42.	45.	46.	46.	40.
1968	46.	48.	49.	54.	56.	57.	60.	62.	63.	61.	62.	64.	57.
1969	66.	64.	61.	61.	58.	54.	52.	52.	52.	51.	52.	53.	56.
1970	56.	54.	53.	52.	47.	45.	46.	48.	49.	52.	48.	49.	50.
1971	50.	49.	48.	53.	59.	59.	63.	64.	66.	64.	63.	67.	59.
1972	71.	72.	75.	77.	78.	74.	75.	79.	74.	72.	75.	77.	75.
1973	73.	68.	66.	68.	67.	69.	58.	63.	62.	64.	61.	51.	65.
1974	51.	50.	47.	45.	45.	42.	38.	33.	30.	29.	26.	23.	38.
1975	28.	40.	44.	46.	51.	51.	48.	56.	51.	53.	49.	56.	48.
1976	53.	61.	61.	62.	63.	59.	59.	64.	53.	47.	57.	53.	57.
1977	60.	63.	66.	66.	73.	72.	72.	77.	84.	85.	80.	80.	73.
1978	80.	76.	75.	77.	82.	81.	82.	89.	90.	88.	84.	86.	83.
1979	85.	85.	93.	103.	93.	97.	94.	94.	95.	96.	87.	87.	94.
1980	91.	97.	97.	92.	103.	97.	103.	103.	106.	108.	112.	108.	100.
1981	104.	108.	110.	118.	119.	116.	115.	121.	112.	104.	112.	114.	113.
1982	117.	121.	120.	122.	127.	127.	126.	129.	138.	145.	150.	147.	131.

10.0 COMPANIES' PROFITS LESS U.K. TAXES, IN CONSTANT PRICES, UNITED KINGDOM
(MILLION 1980 POUNDS)

YEAR	IQ	IIQ	IIIQ	IVQ	AVGE
1955	3200.	3177.	3244.	3236.	3214.
1956	3317.	3258.	3145.	3248.	3242.
1957	3240.	3302.	3252.	3054.	3212.
1958	2885.	2722.	2845.	3038.	2873.
1959	2702.	3228.	3480.	3976.	3347.
1960	4845.	4734.	4730.	4519.	4707.
1961	4530.	4567.	4054.	4139.	4323.
1962	3612.	3790.	4092.	4007.	3875.
1963	3576.	4714.	4874.	5318.	4621.
1964	5181.	5343.	5239.	5022.	5196.
1965	5361.	5378.	5236.	5243.	5305.
1966	5271.	4740.	4789.	4722.	4881.
1967	4158.	4591.	3985.	4874.	4402.
1968	4961.	4770.	5221.	4908.	4965.
1969	5146.	5189.	5361.	5007.	5176.
1970	4868.	4635.	4869.	5260.	4908.
1971	5392.	5160.	5479.	5421.	5363.
1972	5450.	5923.	6284.	6526.	6046.
1973	7115.	6929.	7065.	7262.	7093.
1974	7365.	7212.	6354.	6281.	6803.
1975	6062.	5409.	5323.	5942.	5684.
1976	6139.	6184.	6353.	7371.	6512.
1977	7649.	7279.	7414.	6943.	7321.
1978	7345.	7661.	7885.	7331.	7556.
1979	7476.	8551.	8334.	8291.	8163.
1980	8298.	7409.	5883.	5488.	6770.
1981	5715.	6082.	6642.	6677.	6279.
1982	5437.	5997.	6329.	6972.	6184.

11.0 RATIO, PRICE TO UNIT LABOR COST, MANUFACTURING, UNITED KINGDOM (INDEX, 1980=100)

YEAR	JAN	FEB	MAR	APR	MAY	JUN	JUL	AUG	SEP	OCT	NOV	DEC	AVGE
1963	101.8	102.5	103.7	104.1	104.6	104.6	105.2	105.9	106.3	107.6	107.3	107.8	105.1
1964	108.4	108.9	108.1	108.2	108.4	107.9	107.4	107.5	108.0	108.3	108.5	108.3	108.2
1965	107.9	106.9	106.1	107.1	107.4	106.6	105.5	105.4	105.4	104.9	104.8	104.9	106.1
1966	105.4	105.3	104.9	105.0	104.0	104.3	104.3	105.2	104.4	103.5	103.1	103.8	104.4
1967	105.0	105.5	106.0	105.9	106.0	105.3	105.5	104.8	104.4	104.6	105.6	107.0	105.5
1968	106.0	107.1	108.4	108.5	108.0	107.2	107.4	106.8	106.6	105.8	105.5	105.8	106.9
1969	105.7	105.6	105.5	105.6	106.1	106.2	105.4	104.2	103.2	102.6	102.2	101.4	104.5
1970	96.3	97.2	97.2	97.1	97.0	96.1	95.9	95.1	95.3	98.7	95.6	95.5	96.4
1971	96.9	94.9	94.6	96.7	97.1	97.0	96.9	96.6	96.2	96.2	96.1	96.9	96.3
1972	95.6	88.2	94.2	95.4	96.2	97.0	94.8	95.7	95.4	96.7	97.0	98.6	95.3
1973	101.2	99.9	99.6	95.9	96.4	97.4	97.3	98.2	98.1	98.7	98.3	97.6	98.3
1974	105.8	108.0	105.8	113.8	108.9	108.2	107.3	106.6	104.0	102.0	100.7	98.7	105.8
1975	103.2	102.3	101.2	100.6	100.2	101.5	98.7	97.1	98.7	100.0	100.9	98.9	100.3
1976	101.4	101.8	102.5	104.6	106.1	102.9	104.1	103.5	105.9	109.0	110.6	110.6	105.2
1977	114.8	114.4	114.3	114.3	118.1	113.7	115.5	115.7	115.4	114.3	111.5	113.6	114.6
1978	113.4	111.3	110.6	113.7	111.5	110.5	110.4	112.7	111.3	107.9	109.3	110.7	111.1
1979	101.7	108.0	108.1	108.5	109.1	109.9	108.9	107.1	107.4	104.8	104.7	106.3	107.0
1980	107.9	105.6	103.7	102.8	101.9	100.6	98.1	97.7	96.9	96.4	96.0	95.4	100.2
1981	95.5	96.7	98.4	100.6	99.3	100.9	101.1	99.8	101.2	101.6	101.7	100.7	99.8
1982	100.8	103.0	102.3	101.7	103.5	101.4	102.0	102.2	103.3	101.8	101.1	102.8	102.2

12.0 INCREASE IN HIRE PURCHASE DEBT, IN CONSTANT PRICES, UNITED KINGDOM (MILLION 1980 POUNDS)

YEAR	JAN	FEB	MAR	APR	MAY	JUN	JUL	AUG	SEP	OCT	NOV	DEC	AVGE
1958	14.	31.	0.	25.	25.	14.	18.	31.	31.	76.	233.	202.	58.
1959	140.	158.	132.	154.	159.	191.	179.	107.	204.	159.	158.	158.	158.
1960	146.	146.	179.	165.	39.	-14.	-17.	8.	-17.	-8.	0.	-37.	49.
1961	8.	12.	51.	18.	-8.	18.	25.	-12.	-37.	-29.	-41.	-8.	-0.
1962	-52.	-49.	-89.	-35.	-35.	-8.	0.	8.	23.	8.	0.	23.	-17.
1963	0.	8.	8.	27.	35.	47.	41.	56.	64.	68.	62.	62.	40.
1964	51.	91.	89.	78.	72.	72.	66.	78.	105.	88.	88.	54.	78.
1965	39.	64.	88.	74.	74.	74.	64.	49.	37.	21.	21.	41.	54.
1966	74.	-16.	-41.	-25.	-4.	-25.	-41.	-121.	-113.	-130.	-130.	-105.	-56.
1967	-72.	-93.	-76.	-93.	-76.	-25.	21.	16.	47.	68.	78.	4.	-17.
1968	29.	39.	95.	-14.	-10.	-14.	18.	18.	18.	27.	10.	0.	-18.
1969	-41.	-31.	0.	-10.	-10.	23.	-17.	-4.	10.	-14.	-23.	27.	-8.
1970	25.	4.	14.	25.	47.	29.	4.	60.	21.	41.	10.	74.	30.
1971	64.	43.	-72.	74.	51.	27.	62.	189.	167.	126.	113.	117.	80.
1972	89.	82.	111.	124.	167.	152.	163.	146.	124.	105.	179.	132.	131.
1973	216.	158.	208.	115.	74.	111.	119.	113.	105.	99.	99.	101.	127.
1974	-105.	-39.	-37.	-72.	-37.	-43.	-27.	-21.	-29.	-29.	-27.	-12.	-40.
1975	18.	-25.	-8.	60.	-25.	-12.	-35.	4.	10.	-23.	-10.	16.	-3.
1976	23.	25.	29.	56.	51.	53.	56.	74.	64.	82.	88.	68.	56.
1977	72.	91.	91.	105.	86.	42.	106.	131.	109.	103.	138.	141.	101.
1978	199.	187.	180.	164.	189.	143.	131.	155.	149.	151.	164.	178.	166.
1979	181.	136.	111.	134.	226.	220.	199.	139.	140.	172.	254.	163.	173.
1980	167.	162.	195.	142.	96.	114.	109.	38.	63.	69.	-12.	80.	102.
1981	29.	25.	40.	21.	46.	63.	65.	4.	52.	83.	54.	126.	51.
1982	54.	40.	114.	85.	100.	90.	91.	161.	184.	167.	171.	71.	111.

COINCIDENT INDEX, UNITED KINGDOM (1980=100)

YEAR	JAN	FEB	MAR	APR	MAY	JUN	JUL	AUG	SEP	OCT	NOV	DEC	AVGE
1952	48.4	48.1	47.7	47.2	46.7	46.3	46.0	46.0	46.2	46.4	46.7	46.8	46.9
1953	47.1	47.7	48.1	48.2	48.6	48.4	49.0	49.3	49.6	50.1	50.3	50.4	48.9
1954	51.0	50.6	51.2	51.5	51.9	52.7	53.2	53.2	53.6	54.2	54.3	54.9	52.7
1955	55.4	55.8	55.9	56.3	56.6	56.5	57.0	57.4	57.7	57.9	57.9	58.5	56.9
1956	58.4	58.5	58.5	58.7	58.6	58.7	58.6	58.4	58.6	58.7	58.9	58.8	58.6
1957	58.8	59.0	59.0	59.1	59.4	59.7	59.6	59.7	59.7	59.7	59.8	59.5	59.4
1958	59.7	59.8	59.4	58.8	58.4	58.7	58.8	58.9	58.8	58.8	58.9	59.1	59.0
1959	59.4	59.6	59.9	60.8	61.1	61.8	62.0	62.3	62.9	63.5	64.1	64.6	61.8
1960	65.4	65.8	66.1	66.3	66.7	67.0	67.4	67.8	68.4	68.8	69.0	69.3	67.3
1961	69.4	69.8	70.2	70.3	70.4	70.7	70.9	70.6	70.5	70.5	70.4	70.3	70.3
1962	70.3	70.5	70.4	70.5	70.7	70.6	70.5	70.6	70.8	70.6	70.7	70.5	70.6
1963	70.0	69.7	70.6	71.6	72.3	72.7	73.4	73.6	73.9	74.7	75.3	75.8	72.8
1964	76.5	77.1	77.5	77.8	78.0	78.6	78.6	78.9	79.6	80.2	80.6	81.2	78.7
1965	81.6	81.9	81.7	82.2	82.3	82.2	82.5	82.9	83.3	83.7	84.0	84.5	82.7
1966	85.3	85.8	85.7	85.5	85.3	84.9	85.1	85.0	84.5	84.2	83.7	83.4	84.9
1967	83.4	83.4	83.5	83.7	83.5	83.8	84.1	84.1	84.0	83.8	83.7	84.7	83.8
1968	85.1	86.0	86.3	85.7	85.1	85.9	86.0	86.4	86.0	86.8	87.6	87.6	86.3
1969	87.6	87.5	87.7	88.2	88.5	88.6	88.8	88.8	88.9	88.8	89.3	89.3	88.5
1970	89.2	89.4	89.8	90.1	90.4	90.6	90.7	90.8	90.7	90.8	90.5	90.3	90.3
1971	90.0	89.2	89.6	89.7	89.6	89.4	89.5	89.8	89.6	89.4	89.1	89.1	89.5
1972	88.9	88.2	89.7	90.8	92.0	92.2	92.0	92.1	92.7	93.5	94.5	94.6	91.8
1973	94.8	95.3	96.2	96.0	96.5	97.2	97.5	97.7	97.8	98.1	98.3	98.3	97.0
1974	96.3	96.6	96.5	97.0	97.2	98.0	98.5	99.1	98.6	98.1	97.6	97.0	97.5
1975	97.2	96.8	95.8	95.7	93.4	92.9	92.3	91.9	92.1	92.1	92.0	92.2	93.7
1976	92.7	92.7	92.4	92.6	92.2	92.6	93.2	93.5	93.8	94.1	94.4	94.0	93.2
1977	94.0	93.6	93.6	93.6	93.9	93.6	94.2	94.5	95.0	95.5	96.1	96.8	94.5
1978	96.5	96.6	97.3	98.6	99.1	99.3	99.8	100.1	100.4	100.7	101.2	101.9	99.3
1979	100.5	101.2	102.1	103.3	104.1	105.2	104.0	103.9	104.1	104.6	105.4	105.0	103.6
1980	104.1	103.2	102.6	101.7	101.1	100.1	99.9	99.1	98.1	97.4	96.5	95.7	100.0
1981	95.4	94.7	93.8	93.0	91.9	91.7	91.3	91.3	91.3	91.6	91.4	91.0	92.4
1982	90.8	90.8	90.9	90.7	90.6	90.4	90.3	90.3	90.5	90.6	90.5	90.9	90.6

SIX MONTH SMOOTHED CHANGE IN COINCIDENT INDEX, UNITED KINGDOM (ANNUAL RATE, PERCENT)

YEAR	JAN	FEB	MAR	APR	MAY	JUN	JUL	AUG	SEP	OCT	NOV	DEC	AVGE
1953	0.8	3.5	5.4	6.0	6.8	5.4	7.2	7.4	7.5	8.4	8.0	6.8	6.1
1954	8.1	5.2	6.6	6.8	7.4	9.2	9.4	8.3	8.4	9.2	8.4	9.3	8.0
1955	9.7	9.7	8.6	8.5	7.9	6.1	6.7	7.0	6.9	6.4	5.4	6.3	7.4
1956	4.9	4.4	3.7	3.6	2.6	2.5	1.3	0.4	0.8	0.9	1.2	0.6	2.2
1957	0.5	1.0	1.0	-1.1	2.1	2.6	2.1	2.3	2.0	1.7	1.6	0.6	1.5
1958	0.9	1.1	-0.4	-2.4	-3.5	-2.4	-2.0	-1.3	-1.7	-1.3	-0.7	0.2	-1.1
1959	1.2	1.8	2.9	5.8	6.2	7.5	7.4	7.5	8.5	9.2	9.6	9.8	6.4
1960	10.9	10.5	9.9	8.7	8.5	7.9	7.6	7.7	7.9	7.6	6.9	6.6	8.4
1961	5.6	5.9	6.0	5.5	4.8	4.6	4.3	2.6	1.8	1.4	0.8	0.1	3.6
1962	0.0	0.3	-0.2	0.1	0.4	0.3	0.1	0.2	0.7	0.2	0.5	-0.1	0.2
1963	-1.4	-2.3	0.3	2.8	4.6	5.4	6.5	6.6	6.8	8.1	8.8	9.0	4.6
1964	9.6	9.7	8.9	8.3	7.4	7.5	6.3	5.9	6.5	6.8	6.6	7.0	7.5
1965	6.8	6.6	5.1	4.1	4.9	3.7	3.8	3.9	4.0	4.1	4.2	4.7	4.8
1966	5.8	6.1	5.2	4.1	2.9	1.5	1.5	0.6	-0.9	-1.7	-2.7	-3.4	1.6
1967	-3.3	-2.8	-2.3	-1.4	-1.4	-0.4	0.3	0.6	-0.6	0.3	-0.1	2.1	-0.6
1968	2.9	4.6	4.7	2.8	2.4	2.6	2.5	2.8	3.0	2.9	3.8	3.4	3.2
1969	2.8	2.0	2.3	3.2	3.3	3.0	2.8	2.4	2.3	1.6	2.4	1.9	2.5
1970	1.4	1.6	2.0	2.4	2.6	2.7	2.7	2.4	2.1	1.8	0.8	0.3	1.9
1971	-0.5	-2.4	-1.4	-1.3	-1.3	-1.6	-1.3	-0.6	-0.6	-0.9	-1.4	-1.0	-1.2
1972	-1.2	-2.5	0.7	3.1	5.4	5.3	4.5	4.2	5.0	6.2	7.5	6.9	3.8
1973	6.2	6.1	6.8	5.2	5.2	6.0	5.7	5.2	4.4	4.1	3.7	3.2	5.1
1974	-1.3	-1.6	-1.3	-0.5	-0.1	1.2	2.0	2.9	1.9	0.8	-0.2	-1.2	0.3
1975	-0.7	-1.1	-3.4	-3.5	-7.6	-7.9	-8.3	-8.1	-6.7	-5.7	-4.9	-3.7	-5.2
1976	-2.0	-1.3	-1.1	-0.3	-0.4	0.5	1.8	2.3	2.5	3.0	3.0	2.0	0.8
1977	1.6	0.5	0.4	0.2	0.6	-0.1	0.9	1.3	2.1	2.9	3.9	4.9	1.6
1978	3.9	3.7	4.6	6.6	6.5	6.1	6.1	5.7	5.4	5.1	5.3	5.8	5.4
1979	2.3	2.9	3.9	5.5	6.1	7.4	4.2	3.3	3.2	3.4	4.3	2.9	4.1
1980	0.9	-1.3	-2.6	-4.2	-5.1	-5.4	-6.1	-7.0	-8.1	-8.4	-9.0	-9.0	-5.4
1981	-8.3	-8.3	-8.7	-9.0	-9.6	-8.7	-8.1	-6.9	-5.7	-4.1	-3.5	-3.6	-7.0
1982	-3.0	-2.3	-1.6	-1.5	-1.2	-1.5	-1.5	-1.3	-0.7	-0.4	-0.3	0.5	-1.2

13.1 EMPLOYMENT IN PRODUCTION INDUSTRIES, UNITED KINGDOM (THOUSANDS)

YEAR	JAN	FEB	MAR	APR	MAY	JUN	JUL	AUG	SEP	OCT	NOV	DEC	AVGE
1952	10090.8	10078.3	10060.0	10036.0	10007.5	9994.8	9973.5	9973.3	9975.8	9977.9	9990.0	10002.0	10013.3
1953	10014.3	10030.0	10048.3	10069.9	10089.2	10107.3	10122.6	10152.2	10170.1	10185.0	10200.2	10216.0	10117.1
1954	10221.6	10238.4	10256.1	10266.6	10300.1	10323.9	10352.5	10367.6	10377.6	10400.4	10421.0	10445.3	10330.9
1955	10485.0	10501.1	10514.3	10539.9	10557.3	10561.5	10577.3	10586.2	10599.5	10625.5	10637.7	10647.8	10569.4
1956	10659.9	10651.8	10670.0	10664.8	10656.4	10659.8	10658.3	10641.8	10649.0	10650.3	10648.1	10623.6	10652.8
1957	10642.6	10638.7	10628.6	10632.6	10647.3	10649.3	10651.4	10656.9	10661.5	10647.8	10632.9	10616.6	10642.2
1958	10603.7	10594.7	10575.6	10557.0	10515.1	10492.5	10477.2	10449.0	10426.7	10414.7	10414.5	10406.8	10493.9
1959	10410.6	10414.6	10432.2	10442.3	10454.8	10495.8	10497.4	10523.6	10548.5	10573.6	10598.4	10613.1	10500.4
1960	10668.1	10691.3	10716.6	10733.9	10769.6	10790.0	10796.6	10830.1	10845.6	10848.5	10850.1	10835.2	10781.3
1961	10887.3	10906.2	10924.6	10933.7	10922.7	10927.0	10923.6	10933.8	10927.5	10918.7	10921.9	10876.0	10917.0
1962	10932.4	10938.1	10913.6	10897.2	10890.3	10878.1	10869.8	10856.6	10838.7	10825.0	10795.6	10770.9	10867.2
1963	10683.4	10590.6	10692.8	10731.8	10754.2	10755.3	10759.1	10750.1	10753.5	10775.1	10785.4	10806.7	10736.5
1964	10842.8	10853.8	10867.1	10876.3	10862.7	10896.9	10912.1	10930.6	10953.5	10969.6	10988.5	11016.4	10914.2
1965	11021.9	11038.4	11036.4	11017.5	11031.0	11016.6	11019.7	11027.3	11055.1	11045.6	11041.1	11042.3	11032.7
1966	11055.2	11047.9	11036.9	11033.9	11031.3	11016.7	11008.2	10998.4	10951.5	10922.7	10956.2	10834.6	10992.2
1967	10812.8	10772.2	10745.0	10728.0	10687.6	10660.3	10632.8	10608.1	10588.3	10557.9	10538.2	10529.7	10655.1
1968	10514.7	10507.9	10500.0	10468.0	10478.5	10466.7	10459.9	10478.5	10487.9	10495.3	10512.5	10534.7	10492.0
1969	10460.0	10456.7	10452.8	10466.9	10462.5	10456.0	10459.2	10430.3	10411.3	10419.2	10406.0	10391.4	10439.4
1970	10371.4	10351.1	10341.2	10323.9	10299.0	10277.4	10246.4	10220.5	10192.3	10162.2	10126.7	10092.7	10250.4
1971	10158.1	10097.9	10095.3	10006.7	9952.2	9900.8	9871.3	9839.4	9815.9	9767.0	9716.8	9693.4	9909.6
1972	9675.0	9642.0	9624.0	9638.0	9633.0	9623.0	9617.0	9617.0	9601.0	9617.0	9646.0	9648.0	9631.7
1973	9657.0	9700.0	9718.0	9721.0	9715.0	9727.0	9738.0	9730.0	9726.0	9727.0	9756.0	9777.0	9724.3
1974	9735.0	9727.0	9704.0	9703.0	9712.0	9707.0	9701.0	9713.0	9696.0	9684.0	9634.0	9594.0	9692.5
1975	9569.0	9518.0	9478.0	9436.0	9390.0	9327.0	9281.0	9250.0	9220.0	9193.0	9172.0	9159.0	9332.7
1976	9136.0	9122.0	9110.0	9085.0	9078.0	9081.0	9076.0	9072.0	9076.0	9089.0	9090.0	9089.0	9092.0
1977	9087.0	9083.0	9087.0	9097.0	9089.0	9088.0	9083.0	9069.0	9063.0	9055.0	9053.0	9056.0	9075.8
1978	9064.0	9071.0	9066.0	9060.0	9046.0	9038.0	9033.0	9026.0	9025.0	9023.0	9029.0	9029.0	9042.5
1979	9024.0	9015.0	9005.0	8997.0	9002.0	8999.0	9008.0	8995.0	8974.0	8944.0	8935.0	8918.0	8984.7
1980	8881.0	8845.0	8803.0	8752.0	8703.0	8648.0	8570.0	8491.0	8416.0	8333.0	8238.0	8173.0	8571.1
1981	8094.0	8028.0	7961.0	7905.0	7848.0	7770.0	7718.0	7685.0	7644.0	7608.0	7567.0	7521.0	7779.1
1982	7465.0	7457.0	7438.0	7405.0	7372.0	7338.0	7300.0	7266.0	7238.0	7209.0	7172.0	7134.0	7316.2

14.1 UNEMPLOYED, UNITED KINGDOM (THOUSANDS)

YEAR	JAN	FEB	MAR	APR	MAY	JUN	JUL	AUG	SEP	OCT	NOV	DEC	AVGE
1949	350.	339.	339.	334.	343.	336.	324.	324.	327.	338.	347.	352.	338.
1950	347.	350.	345.	338.	353.	355.	356.	348.	340.	342.	324.	320.	343.
1951	305.	282.	273.	265.	244.	244.	246.	244.	254.	267.	275.	281.	265.
1952	295.	313.	335.	344.	371.	385.	394.	400.	404.	406.	407.	402.	371.
1953	394.	374.	366.	367.	369.	360.	350.	345.	346.	344.	340.	337.	358.
1954	334.	351.	332.	320.	320.	298.	288.	283.	280.	279.	274.	265.	302.
1955	256.	253.	255.	238.	234.	242.	235.	231.	228.	229.	233.	222.	238.
1956	231.	238.	242.	241.	241.	248.	261.	267.	273.	268.	270.	284.	255.
1957	316.	334.	333.	331.	331.	314.	307.	312.	315.	300.	322.	339.	321.
1958	347.	370.	397.	423.	438.	456.	461.	464.	486.	499.	506.	499.	446.
1959	499.	495.	478.	485.	485.	471.	470.	461.	454.	447.	437.	423.	467.
1960	402.	392.	387.	383.	369.	369.	363.	357.	349.	346.	347.	340.	367.
1961	330.	318.	318.	330.	322.	326.	331.	345.	346.	363.	370.	375.	340.
1962	383.	379.	400.	422.	434.	454.	474.	484.	490.	505.	520.	537.	457.
1963	567.	589.	600.	567.	555.	551.	535.	527.	517.	498.	478.	465.	537.
1964	440.	415.	402.	408.	406.	398.	395.	391.	383.	370.	352.	340.	392.
1965	329.	328.	338.	325.	343.	347.	352.	353.	353.	338.	325.	321.	338.
1966	305.	299.	302.	303.	313.	328.	338.	345.	374.	404.	454.	474.	353.
1967	499.	519.	529.	540.	547.	547.	554.	561.	565.	565.	572.	571.	547.
1968	573.	577.	571.	575.	583.	585.	580.	577.	573.	575.	569.	559.	575.
1969	560.	561.	565.	557.	555.	560.	562.	567.	571.	577.	578.	586.	567.
1970	584.	585.	592.	597.	596.	601.	604.	607.	610.	612.	614.	627.	602.
1971	636.	661.	684.	710.	753.	766.	776.	785.	803.	836.	869.	888.	764.
1972	886.	905.	917.	910.	873.	846.	835.	821.	819.	800.	782.	760.	846.
1973	726.	695.	676.	657.	639.	629.	602.	582.	557.	540.	522.	510.	611.
1974	569.	582.	580.	576.	572.	584.	598.	616.	627.	637.	650.	681.	606.
1975	704.	734.	769.	812.	862.	905.	948.	979.	1016.	1076.	1116.	1154.	923.
1976	1204.	1226.	1232.	1242.	1253.	1261.	1289.	1309.	1319.	1308.	1317.	1326.	1274.
1977	1290.	1292.	1295.	1301.	1301.	1330.	1349.	1354.	1374.	1372.	1371.	1367.	1333.
1978	1357.	1346.	1344.	1337.	1329.	1326.	1320.	1325.	1311.	1297.	1275.	1262.	1319.
1979	1271.	1294.	1289.	1253.	1254.	1233.	1227.	1214.	1212.	1222.	1216.	1224.	1242.
1980	1249.	1290.	1321.	1368.	1414.	1469.	1535.	1631.	1713.	1807.	1919.	2014.	1561.
1981	2094.	2166.	2238.	2301.	2368.	2417.	2477.	2514.	2555.	2583.	2616.	2629.	2413.
1982	2671.	2680.	2688.	2715.	2740.	2773.	2814.	2832.	2866.	2885.	2903.	2947.	2793.

15.0 GROSS DOMESTIC PRODUCT, IN CONSTANT PRICES, UNITED KINGDOM
(MILLION 1980 POUNDS)

YEAR	IQ	IIQ	IIIQ	IVQ	AVGE
1955	27737.	27219.	27907.	27991.	27714.
1956	28081.	28352.	28126.	28447.	28252.
1957	28960.	28966.	28481.	28741.	28787.
1958	28961.	28167.	28942.	28737.	28702.
1959	28872.	29252.	29967.	30651.	29686.
1960	31027.	30497.	31081.	31551.	31039.
1961	32076.	32142.	32291.	32036.	32136.
1962	32002.	32716.	32606.	32631.	32489.
1963	32831.	33991.	33877.	34761.	33865.
1964	35325.	35734.	35458.	36125.	35661.
1965	36318.	36549.	36720.	36913.	36625.
1966	36947.	37243.	37337.	37823.	37338.
1967	38505.	38369.	38645.	37955.	38369.
1968	39702.	39581.	40419.	40688.	40098.
1969	40138.	40582.	41010.	41207.	40734.
1970	40627.	41484.	41631.	42367.	41527.
1971	41465.	42408.	43083.	43140.	42524.
1972	42416.	42890.	42908.	43985.	43050.
1973	46964.	46342.	46525.	45707.	46385.
1974	45216.	46280.	46839.	45944.	46070.
1975	45757.	45703.	45181.	46217.	45715.
1976	47391.	46856.	47444.	48052.	47436.
1977	47522.	47927.	48006.	48916.	48093.
1978	48612.	50143.	49432.	49813.	49500.
1979	48828.	51153.	51016.	50388.	50346.
1980	49769.	49233.	48837.	48803.	49161.
1981	49332.	48405.	48284.	49192.	48803.
1982	49562.	49677.	49382.	50680.	49825.

16.0 INDUSTRIAL PRODUCTION, UNITED KINGDOM (INDEX, 1980=100)

YEAR	JAN	FEB	MAR	APR	MAY	JUN	JUL	AUG	SEP	OCT	NOV	DEC	AVGE
1948	45.6	45.6	47.5	46.5	45.6	45.6	46.5	46.5	47.5	46.5	47.5	49.3	46.7
1949	48.5	48.5	49.3	49.3	50.4	50.4	54.2	50.4	50.4	50.4	51.4	52.4	50.5
1950	48.5	47.7	48.5	48.5	48.5	48.5	48.5	49.3	49.3	50.9	50.9	50.9	49.2
1951	50.9	51.7	52.6	51.7	50.9	51.7	50.9	51.7	51.7	50.9	50.9	50.9	51.4
1952	50.9	50.9	50.9	49.3	49.3	48.5	47.7	47.7	48.5	49.3	50.1	50.1	49.4
1953	50.1	50.0	51.7	51.7	52.6	50.1	51.7	51.7	52.6	54.2	54.2	53.4	52.1
1954	55.8	54.2	55.0	55.0	55.8	56.6	56.6	55.8	56.6	58.2	57.4	58.2	56.3
1955	58.2	59.0	59.8	59.8	60.6	58.2	58.2	58.2	59.8	60.6	60.6	61.4	59.5
1956	60.4	60.4	59.8	60.4	59.3	60.4	59.8	59.3	60.4	59.8	60.4	59.8	60.0
1957	60.4	61.5	60.4	60.4	61.5	62.1	62.1	62.1	62.1	61.0	62.1	60.4	61.3
1958	61.0	62.2	62.8	63.4	61.0	61.0	60.4	60.4	60.4	60.4	61.0	61.6	61.0
1959	61.6	61.6	61.0	63.4	63.4	63.4	64.0	64.0	65.2	66.5	67.1	67.7	64.1
1960	68.3	68.3	68.9	69.5	68.9	68.3	68.3	68.9	68.3	69.5	68.9	68.9	68.7
1961	68.9	68.3	69.5	69.5	68.3	69.5	70.1	68.9	68.3	68.9	68.3	68.9	68.9
1962	68.3	68.9	70.4	71.1	70.1	70.1	70.1	70.1	70.7	69.5	69.5	69.5	69.6
1963	67.5	68.9	70.9	71.6	71.8	72.6	74.0	73.3	72.6	74.7	75.5	75.5	72.3
1964	76.2	76.9	79.1	80.5	77.6	79.1	77.6	77.6	79.1	79.8	79.8	80.5	78.2
1965	80.5	80.5	82.7	82.7	82.0	79.8	79.8	80.5	81.3	82.0	81.3	82.0	80.8
1966	82.0	82.0	81.3	82.7	82.7	81.3	82.7	82.0	82.0	81.3	79.8	80.5	81.8
1967	80.5	81.3	86.2	85.9	81.3	82.0	82.0	81.3	82.0	82.7	83.4	85.6	82.2
1968	84.5	85.6	88.9	90.3	86.8	86.9	87.0	87.6	87.6	86.6	87.5	88.3	86.7
1969	88.6	89.0	90.9	90.5	90.3	90.9	90.7	89.3	89.5	88.0	89.8	90.6	89.7
1970	88.4	90.0	88.4	89.8	89.6	89.9	90.3	90.3	89.9	91.2	89.8	90.7	90.1
1971	91.3	89.5	88.1	90.2	90.1	89.8	89.4	90.4	89.2	89.3	89.1	89.7	89.6
1972	87.1	80.2	88.1	90.0	92.0	92.5	91.4	92.4	93.7	94.9	95.7	96.4	91.2
1973	99.3	98.4	99.5	98.6	98.7	100.5	100.0	100.0	99.5	100.5	99.5	98.5	99.4
1974	91.4	91.4	94.6	99.5	100.7	101.1	100.7	101.0	99.2	97.3	97.0	95.5	97.4
1975	96.3	95.1	93.7	92.1	92.0	91.5	90.3	89.1	90.8	91.9	92.0	91.6	92.2
1976	92.2	93.2	93.5	94.3	95.8	93.9	94.3	94.1	95.6	97.7	98.5	99.1	95.2
1977	101.1	100.6	100.7	99.8	102.4	98.4	98.8	99.8	100.1	99.8	99.0	100.8	100.1
1978	100.9	100.6	99.5	105.4	102.3	102.3	103.2	104.8	104.5	103.1	103.8	106.8	103.1
1979	99.4	106.5	107.8	107.5	109.3	111.0	109.7	105.7	105.4	106.0	107.8	107.8	107.0
1980	106.9	104.3	104.1	101.7	101.1	101.2	99.5	97.6	96.3	96.1	95.9	95.2	100.0
1981	94.2	95.0	95.5	96.3	94.1	96.1	96.5	96.7	97.4	99.2	98.1	96.8	96.3
1982	96.6	97.0	97.4	98.3	98.8	97.7	98.1	98.7	99.2	98.5	97.1	99.2	98.0

17.0 PERSONAL DISPOSABLE INCOME, IN CONSTANT PRICES, UNITED KINGDOM
(MILLION 1980 POUNDS)

YEAR	IQ	IIQ	IIIQ	IVQ	AVGE
1955	19615.	19937.	20153.	19880.	19896.
1956	20392.	20259.	20556.	20464.	20418.
1957	20627.	20744.	20761.	20843.	20744.
1958	21063.	20954.	21101.	21110.	21057.
1959	21481.	22197.	22345.	22502.	22131.
1960	22984.	23419.	23798.	24038.	23560.
1961	24273.	24668.	24686.	24526.	24538.
1962	24474.	24482.	24873.	25258.	24772.
1963	25291.	25535.	26456.	26482.	25941.
1964	26677.	26682.	27134.	27124.	26904.
1965	27342.	27305.	27834.	27878.	27590.
1966	29134.	27930.	27808.	27974.	28212.
1967	27881.	28469.	29206.	28887.	28611.
1968	29385.	29357.	28801.	28925.	29117.
1969	29322.	29365.	29296.	29570.	29388.
1970	29744.	30782.	30959.	30638.	30531.
1971	29986.	30974.	31132.	31595.	30922.
1972	32272.	34229.	33727.	34283.	33628.
1973	35070.	36371.	36222.	36207.	35968.
1974	35601.	34896.	36227.	35989.	35678.
1975	36725.	35209.	35383.	35312.	35657.
1976	35371.	34880.	36039.	35349.	35410.
1977	34446.	33936.	34700.	36236.	34830.
1978	35855.	37079.	37970.	38698.	37401.
1979	38830.	39210.	39106.	41150.	39574.
1980	40103.	39738.	40355.	40393.	40147.
1981	40039.	38845.	38711.	38975.	39143.
1982	39174.	39028.	38557.	39130.	38972.

18.1 RETAIL SALES, VOLUME, UNITED KINGDOM (INDEX, 1980=100)

YEAR	JAN	FEB	MAR	APR	MAY	JUN	JUL	AUG	SEP	OCT	NOV	DEC	AVGE
1957	62.1	62.2	62.7	62.0	62.2	62.5	61.3	63.0	62.5	61.6	62.6	62.2	62.2
1958	62.4	62.7	62.2	62.8	62.0	63.8	63.1	63.1	63.1	64.4	64.9	64.5	63.2
1959	65.3	64.5	63.5	67.3	66.6	67.9	67.1	66.0	67.0	67.4	67.7	68.1	66.5
1960	69.1	68.7	69.4	69.8	69.6	69.3	69.3	68.8	69.8	69.4	69.0	70.1	69.4
1961	70.1	70.5	71.5	71.4	71.2	71.3	72.1	70.4	70.1	71.1	71.1	71.4	71.0
1962	70.9	71.1	70.3	72.7	71.1	71.8	71.5	71.9	72.1	71.3	72.6	71.8	71.5
1963	72.4	71.5	71.8	75.5	73.5	73.9	74.4	74.9	75.0	74.6	74.8	75.2	73.7
1964	75.4	75.4	74.0	75.5	75.5	75.4	75.2	75.5	76.7	77.3	76.1	76.9	75.8
1965	76.9	77.4	77.0	77.2	77.5	77.0	77.8	77.8	78.2	78.2	78.9	78.5	77.7
1966	79.0	78.8	79.3	79.4	80.1	78.6	79.7	78.4	77.7	78.3	77.9	78.2	78.8
1967	78.8	79.6	79.5	79.2	79.2	79.9	80.8	80.9	81.8	81.9	82.2	82.8	80.5
1968	82.7	83.9	85.5	81.9	81.0	82.8	82.8	83.1	83.0	83.3	84.9	82.4	83.1
1969	84.1	81.6	83.0	83.8	84.9	83.8	83.1	84.0	84.1	82.8	84.2	83.4	83.6
1970	84.3	85.3	84.4	85.1	85.8	86.1	85.8	86.0	86.2	85.8	85.0	85.8	85.5
1971	84.4	84.0	86.7	87.6	88.2	86.9	86.6	87.4	87.6	88.0	87.5	87.4	86.9
1972	87.1	88.1	88.9	90.1	91.4	92.2	92.8	92.3	92.3	92.4	92.9	94.5	91.2
1973	93.0	96.2	98.6	93.2	93.8	96.2	95.5	95.4	95.3	95.6	95.6	96.2	95.4
1974	92.6	94.3	95.2	93.3	92.0	94.4	94.5	95.5	96.0	95.7	95.9	93.7	94.4
1975	95.4	94.9	94.8	102.6	89.9	90.4	90.1	90.4	90.5	90.7	90.4	91.2	92.6
1976	94.1	91.2	91.1	94.2	91.9	92.3	93.3	92.8	92.5	92.4	93.2	91.6	92.5
1977	91.3	90.3	89.5	89.3	89.7	89.3	91.9	91.9	91.3	90.5	91.0	95.1	90.9
1978	92.0	93.2	94.1	94.2	94.8	95.3	97.7	97.5	96.9	96.9	96.9	100.0	95.8
1979	95.7	96.7	98.0	102.3	100.9	107.7	97.1	98.8	99.0	99.8	99.9	101.9	100.0
1980	100.4	100.4	100.0	100.2	99.7	99.7	100.5	100.6	99.0	100.2	101.6	99.5	100.0
1981	103.6	101.5	101.2	100.3	100.4	101.2	100.5	101.3	101.3	101.7	101.3	100.2	101.2
1982	102.5	101.7	102.2	101.9	102.5	102.8	103.6	104.9	104.8	104.8	105.5	107.6	103.7

215

LAGGING INDEX, UNITED KINGDOM (1970=100)

YEAR	JAN	FEB	MAR	APR	MAY	JUN	JUL	AUG	SEP	OCT	NOV	DEC	AVGE
1955	55.6	55.9	56.1	56.4	56.7	57.3	57.8	58.3	58.5	58.7	58.9	59.2	57.4
1956	59.4	59.7	58.6	57.1	55.3	57.2	58.7	59.9	60.1	60.2	60.4	60.8	58.9
1957	61.2	61.6	61.8	61.9	62.1	61.9	61.8	61.7	61.6	61.6	61.7	61.8	61.7
1958	61.9	62.0	62.0	61.7	61.5	61.5	61.5	61.6	61.6	61.6	61.6	61.6	61.7
1959	61.7	61.7	61.9	62.2	62.6	62.8	63.2	63.6	64.1	64.6	65.1	65.7	63.3
1960	66.2	66.8	67.2	67.7	68.2	69.0	69.7	70.4	71.2	72.0	72.7	73.4	69.5
1961	74.1	74.8	75.2	75.5	75.8	76.1	76.3	76.5	76.4	76.4	76.4	76.4	75.8
1962	76.2	76.1	75.9	75.8	75.7	75.5	75.2	75.0	75.0	75.0	75.0	74.9	75.4
1963	74.8	74.7	74.7	74.8	75.0	75.0	75.0	75.2	75.4	75.7	75.9	76.3	75.2
1964	76.6	77.0	77.7	78.5	79.3	79.9	80.5	81.1	81.8	82.5	83.2	83.8	80.2
1965	84.3	84.9	85.1	85.3	85.4	85.9	86.4	86.9	87.2	87.5	87.9	88.3	86.3
1966	88.8	89.2	89.3	89.5	89.6	89.9	90.5	90.6	90.6	90.6	90.6	90.4	90.0
1967	90.1	89.8	89.5	89.4	89.3	89.2	89.0	89.0	89.1	89.4	90.3	90.3	89.5
1968	90.3	90.4	90.4	90.6	90.8	91.2	91.6	91.9	92.4	93.1	93.9	93.9	91.7
1969	94.0	94.4	95.1	95.7	96.2	96.6	97.0	97.3	97.8	98.2	98.5	98.7	96.6
1970	98.8	98.8	99.0	99.1	99.7	100.0	100.4	100.6	100.7	100.9	101.0	101.0	100.0
1971	101.1	101.1	100.8	100.0	99.7	99.7	99.7	99.7	99.1	99.1	98.7	98.6	99.8
1972	98.5	98.5	98.6	98.7	99.0	100.0	100.2	100.9	101.2	101.6	101.9	102.7	100.2
1973	103.7	104.6	105.5	106.2	106.9	107.6	109.2	110.3	111.1	111.8	113.0	114.1	108.7
1974	115.3	116.5	116.5	116.3	116.1	116.5	117.0	117.4	117.6	117.9	118.1	117.2	116.9
1975	116.3	115.4	115.1	114.8	114.6	114.0	113.3	112.8	112.2	111.9	111.3	110.9	113.5
1976	110.3	109.6	109.4	109.2	109.6	109.7	110.0	110.3	111.2	112.2	112.6	112.8	110.6
1977	112.6	112.3	112.1	112.4	112.6	112.8	113.0	113.1	113.1	113.6	114.1	114.4	113.0
1978	114.7	114.8	115.3	115.8	116.6	117.2	117.2	117.3	117.7	118.2	119.4	119.9	117.0
1979	120.5	121.6	121.5	121.4	121.6	122.6	123.1	123.5	123.8	124.1	125.2	125.3	122.8
1980	125.3	125.2	125.6	125.6	125.7	125.2	125.0	124.7	124.0	123.2	121.8	121.0	124.4
1981	120.1	119.1	117.0	116.1	115.1	***	***	***	***	***	***	***	***

SIX MONTH SMOOTHED CHANGE IN LAGGING INDEX. UNITED KINGDOM (ANNUAL RATE, PERCENT)

YEAR	JAN	FEB	MAR	APR	MAY	JUN	JUL	AUG	SEP	OCT	NOV	DEC	AVGE
1956	6.4	6.2	1.5	-3.7	-9.5	-3.2	1.4	5.1	5.2	5.3	5.6	6.3	2.2
1957	7.2	7.9	8.1	7.6	6.8	4.3	2.8	1.7	1.0	0.6	0.3	0.6	4.1
1958	-0.6	0.6	0.4	-0.4	-1.1	-0.8	-0.6	-0.3	-0.4	-0.4	-0.3	-0.3	-0.2
1959	-0.1	0.2	0.8	1.8	2.7	3.2	4.0	4.6	5.9	6.7	7.4	8.2	3.8
1960	8.8	9.2	9.1	9.3	9.4	10.2	10.7	11.1	11.7	12.1	12.5	12.4	10.5
1961	12.5	12.5	11.8	10.6	9.6	8.5	7.3	6.4	4.9	3.8	2.8	2.0	7.7
1962	0.9	0.1	-0.4	-0.9	-1.3	-1.7	-2.1	-2.4	-2.2	-1.9	-1.7	-1.7	-1.3
1963	-1.6	-1.6	-1.2	-0.7	0.0	0.1	0.3	0.7	1.3	1.9	2.3	2.9	0.4
1964	3.5	4.0	5.4	6.7	7.8	8.4	8.9	9.1	9.6	9.9	10.3	10.1	7.8
1965	9.8	9.6	8.5	7.4	6.2	6.2	6.2	6.1	5.7	5.3	5.3	5.4	6.8
1966	5.4	5.4	5.1	4.7	4.1	3.8	4.5	3.9	3.3	2.7	2.0	1.3	3.8
1967	0.3	-0.6	-1.3	-1.4	-1.7	-1.9	-2.0	-1.8	-1.4	-0.6	1.5	1.6	-0.8
1968	1.6	1.7	1.7	2.0	2.2	2.7	3.1	3.3	3.9	4.8	5.7	5.2	3.2
1969	4.7	4.9	5.5	5.9	6.1	5.9	5.8	5.6	5.6	5.4	5.2	4.8	5.4
1970	4.3	3.5	3.1	2.7	3.1	3.2	3.3	3.3	3.4	2.8	2.7	2.3	3.1
1971	2.0	1.6	0.7	-0.9	-1.6	-1.6	-1.6	-1.5	-2.4	-2.3	-2.7	-2.6	-1.1
1972	-2.3	-2.0	-1.4	-0.9	-0.2	1.9	3.1	3.4	3.9	4.1	4.4	5.4	1.6
1973	6.6	7.5	8.1	8.2	8.4	8.4	10.1	10.9	10.7	10.4	10.9	11.3	9.3
1974	11.6	11.8	10.0	8.1	6.2	5.6	5.1	4.6	4.0	3.5	3.0	1.0	6.2
1975	-1.0	-2.4	-2.7	-3.0	-3.1	-4.0	-4.6	-4.9	-5.4	-5.2	-5.3	-5.1	-3.9
1976	-5.2	-5.6	-5.1	-4.7	-3.3	-2.5	-1.4	-0.5	1.4	3.2	3.9	3.9	-1.3
1977	3.4	2.6	1.9	2.0	1.8	1.8	1.7	1.3	1.0	1.6	2.2	2.5	2.0
1978	2.8	2.7	3.1	3.6	4.4	4.7	4.2	3.8	3.9	4.0	5.3	5.3	4.0
1979	5.6	6.5	5.4	4.5	4.0	5.0	4.9	4.8	4.5	4.2	5.0	4.3	4.9
1980	3.7	3.0	3.1	2.6	2.2	1.0	0.3	-0.4	-1.6	-2.7	-4.6	-5.4	0.1
1981	-6.3	-7.0	-9.4	-9.8	-10.1	***	***	***	***	***	***	***	***

19.0 LONG-DURATION UNEMPLOYMENT, UNITED KINGDOM (THOUSANDS)

YEAR	JAN	FEB	MAR	APR	MAY	JUN	JUL	AUG	SEP	OCT	NOV	DEC	AVGE
1949			29.3			26.8			24.6			25.1	27.0
1950			26.0			28.9			28.1			25.6	27.1
1951			22.7			17.4			16.9			17.5	19.3
1952			19.8			25.7			32.4			35.2	26.8
1953			34.3			32.1			28.7			27.0	31.2
1954			27.6			25.9			22.3			20.6	24.6
1955			19.9			17.6			16.8			16.8	18.1
1956			16.1			17.1			20.5			23.4	18.7
1957			25.3			29.1			29.9			28.4	27.8
1958			30.5			41.6			52.4			61.5	43.7
1959			66.3			62.2			53.4			50.0	58.9
1960			48.0			41.8			37.7			34.5	41.8
1961			29.8			30.3			33.0			33.3	31.7
1962	35.6			41.5			48.4			56.5			48.0
1963	65.3			74.7			73.0			62.3			68.0
1964	55.3			47.6			42.6			40.3			44.9
1965	37.0			33.3			34.0			35.7			34.7
1966	33.5			30.4			30.9			36.8			33.9
1967	45.3			64.6			75.6			77.6			68.5
1968	77.5			75.1			74.8			76.7			75.8
1969	74.9			69.6			69.5			70.2			70.5
1970	67.8			75.8			71.8			74.5			73.4
1971	79.4			90.0			102.9			116.5			102.0
1972	137.0			153.5			140.7			127.2			137.3
1973	109.7			96.6			79.9			68.3			85.0
1974	65.8			65.5			70.6			79.6			72.4
1975	90.6			103.8			135.2			171.1			134.4
1976	201.4			235.6			249.5			249.6			237.9
1977	248.4			241.1			249.6			258.2			250.9
1978	267.1			260.0			251.2			244.8			253.3
1979	237.7			228.4			219.5			216.0			223.6
1980	215.9			241.7			286.4			354.5			293.6
1981	443.9			537.1			***			***			***

20.0 PLANT AND EQUIPMENT INVESTMENT, IN CONSTANT PRICES, UNITED KINGDOM
(MILLION 1975 POUNDS)

YEAR	IQ	IIQ	IIIQ	IVQ	AVGE
1955	316.0	332.1	362.6	372.1	345.7
1956	383.2	382.8	386.5	421.1	393.4
1957	439.5	453.5	416.7	418.4	432.0
1958	428.0	413.4	417.6	415.0	418.5
1959	397.3	404.5	393.3	407.6	400.7
1960	428.7	436.7	471.4	495.5	458.1
1961	522.3	543.4	571.5	543.5	545.2
1962	527.8	513.7	484.8	484.7	502.7
1963	442.7	458.5	448.4	457.8	451.8
1964	472.4	499.1	508.4	535.8	503.9
1965	562.3	530.9	566.3	578.6	559.5
1966	601.9	581.8	601.6	594.4	594.9
1967	591.4	627.3	590.3	589.7	599.7
1968	611.9	599.6	626.7	730.7	642.2
1969	599.1	670.4	693.9	716.1	669.9
1970	710.9	743.9	751.2	768.2	743.5
1971	722.1	696.3	705.9	671.0	698.8
1972	650.7	596.4	582.1	591.2	605.1
1973	637.0	606.6	651.4	610.3	626.3
1974	692.5	699.3	700.9	728.6	705.3
1975	709.9	687.5	644.3	640.4	670.5
1976	622.1	642.4	654.4	665.6	646.1
1977	635.5	660.4	680.0	699.8	668.9
1978	709.0	746.3	722.8	736.6	728.7
1979	744.5	747.2	750.4	763.3	751.3
1980	750.6	710.5	689.0	623.5	693.4
1981	605.1	***	***	***	***

21.0 BUSINESS INVENTORIES. IN CONSTANT PRICES, UNITED KINGDOM
(MILLION 1980 POUNDS)

YEAR	IQ	IIQ	IIIQ	IVQ	AVGE
1955	33676.	34157.	34064.	34591.	34122.
1956	35035.	35521.	35782.	35937.	35569.
1957	36093.	36674.	37019.	37195.	36745.
1958	37178.	37464.	37431.	37744.	37454.
1959	37659.	37780.	37842.	38147.	37857.
1960	38562.	39228.	39728.	40469.	39497.
1961	41380.	42085.	42654.	42797.	42229.
1962	42737.	42646.	42642.	42816.	42710.
1963	42781.	42886.	43192.	43173.	43008.
1964	43639.	44247.	45180.	45922.	44747.
1965	47023.	47586.	48161.	48818.	47897.
1966	49258.	49702.	50127.	50770.	49964.
1967	50692.	51158.	51427.	51558.	51209.
1968	51830.	51599.	52282.	53091.	52201.
1969	53662.	54318.	54952.	55288.	54555.
1970	55691.	55628.	56243.	56933.	56124.
1971	57250.	57582.	57563.	57656.	57513.
1972	57783.	57650.	57644.	57667.	57686.
1973	57761.	59135.	60530.	61895.	59830.
1974	62808.	62771.	64074.	65514.	63792.
1975	65668.	64761.	63740.	63082.	64313.
1976	62767.	62572.	62408.	62817.	62641.
1977	63848.	64935.	65747.	65818.	65087.
1978	66486.	66869.	67656.	68096.	67277.
1979	68576.	69428.	69707.	70747.	69615.
1980	71066.	70565.	70430.	69229.	70323.
1981	67830.	66820.	65491.	65309.	66363.
1982	65175.	65231.	65460.	64840.	65177.

220

22.1 CHANGE IN EMPLOYMENT PER UNIT OF OUTPUT, PRODUCTION INDUSTRIES, UNITED KINGDOM (PERCENT CHANGE FROM YEAR AGO)

YEAR	IQ	IIQ	IIIQ	IVQ	AVGE
1961	1.6	0.1	0.3	2.1	1.0
1962	0.9	-0.3	-2.5	-2.2	-1.0
1963	-1.2	-3.1	-4.4	-7.3	-4.0
1964	-10.4	-6.4	-4.1	-4.2	-6.3
1965	-2.1	-2.1	-1.8	-1.2	-1.8
1966	-1.8	-2.2	-2.8	-0.4	-1.8
1967	-1.7	-3.3	-3.3	-6.8	-3.8
1968	-7.9	-7.6	-7.7	-5.1	-7.1
1969	-3.2	-3.4	-2.4	-2.3	-2.8
1970	-0.8	-0.5	-1.8	-3.2	-1.6
1971	-2.3	-3.1	-2.7	-2.9	-2.8
1972	-0.5	-5.1	-4.7	-6.0	-4.1
1973	-12.0	-5.2	-5.2	-1.6	-6.0
1974	8.2	0.8	1.4	3.6	3.5
1975	-3.0	5.2	4.8	-0.7	1.6
1976	-2.2	-5.2	-5.3	-6.4	-4.8
1977	-6.2	-4.3	-4.3	-1.8	-4.1
1978	-1.2	-5.0	-5.3	-3.9	-3.8
1979	-2.7	-3.8	-1.7	-2.7	-2.7
1980	-1.6	4.0	3.1	4.8	2.6

23.1 INDUSTRIAL AND AGRICULTURAL LOANS OUTSTANDING, IN CONSTANT PRICES, UNITED KINGDOM (MILLION 1975 POUNDS)

YEAR	FEB	MAY	AUG	NOV	AVGE
1948	1707.	1706.	1778.	1816.	1752.
1949	1858.	1820.	1841.	1861.	1845.
1950	1923.	1958.	1969.	1901.	1938.
1951	1896.	1876.	2023.	2161.	1989.
1952	2175.	2159.	2115.	2033.	2121.
1953	2044.	2067.	2048.	2054.	2053.
1954	2058.	2034.	2059.	2158.	2077.
1955	2186.	2246.	2310.	2267.	2252.
1956	2219.	2193.	2194.	2206.	2203.
1957	2294.	2351.	2369.	2284.	2325.
1958	2236.	2289.	2397.	2540.	2366.
1959	2680.	2845.	2975.	3147.	2912.
1960	3290.	3400.	3541.	3776.	3502.
1961	3925.	4062.	4060.	4010.	4014.
1962	4114.	4176.	4256.	4317.	4216.
1963	4436.	4514.	4599.	4603.	4538.
1964	4659.	4668.	4825.	5152.	4826.
1965	5156.	5176.	5385.	5510.	5307.
1966	5634.	5698.	5648.	5632.	5653.
1967	5521.	5600.	5694.	5960.	5694.
1968	5732.	5742.	5765.	5846.	5771.
1969	6209.	6346.	6513.	6645.	6428.
1970	6620.	6886.	7049.	7104.	6915.
1971	7246.	6948.	6811.	6939.	6986.
1972	6924.	8377.	8683.	8943.	8232.
1973	9619.	9755.	10147.	10821.	10086.
1974	10887.	11068.	11545.	11583.	11271.
1975	11235.	10735.	10280.	9926.	10544.
1976	9461.	9398.	9527.	9982.	9592.
1977	9626.	9264.	9478.	9560.	9482.
1978	9634.	9809.	9832.	10025.	9825.
1979	10206.	10368.	10207.	10417.	10300.
1980	10387.	10576.	11298.	11222.	10871.
1981	10814.	***	***	***	***

24.0 COMMERCIAL BANK LENDING RATE TO PRIME BORROWERS, UNITED KINGDOM (PERCENT)

YEAR	JAN	FEB	MAR	APR	MAY	JUN	JUL	AUG	SEP	OCT	NOV	DEC	AVGE
1966	6.5	6.5	6.5	6.5	6.5	6.5	7.5	7.5	7.5	7.5	7.5	7.5	7.0
1967	7.0	7.0	6.5	6.5	6.0	6.0	6.0	6.0	6.0	6.5	8.5	8.5	6.7
1968	8.5	8.5	8.0	8.0	8.0	8.0	8.0	8.0	7.5	7.5	7.5	7.5	7.9
1969	7.5	8.5	8.5	8.5	8.5	8.5	8.5	8.5	9.0	9.0	9.0	9.0	8.6
1970	9.0	9.0	8.5	8.0	8.0	8.0	8.0	8.0	8.0	8.0	8.0	8.0	8.2
1971	8.0	8.0	8.0	7.0	7.0	7.0	7.0	7.0	6.0	6.0	5.5	5.5	6.8
1972	5.5	5.5	5.5	5.5	5.5	7.0	8.0	8.0	8.0	8.0	8.0	8.5	6.9
1973	9.5	10.5	10.5	10.0	9.5	9.0	11.0	12.0	12.0	12.0	14.0	14.0	11.2
1974	14.0	14.0	14.0	13.5	13.0	13.0	13.0	13.0	13.0	13.0	13.0	13.0	13.3
1975	12.5	12.5	11.5	10.5	10.5	10.5	10.5	11.0	11.0	12.0	12.0	12.0	11.4
1976	11.5	10.5	10.5	10.5	12.0	11.5	11.5	11.5	13.0	15.0	15.0	15.0	12.3
1977	14.0	12.5	10.5	10.0	9.5	9.5	9.5	9.0	8.0	8.0	8.0	8.0	9.7
1978	8.0	7.5	8.0	8.8	10.3	11.5	11.5	11.5	11.5	11.5	14.0	13.5	10.6
1979	13.5	15.0	14.0	13.0	13.0	15.0	15.0	15.0	15.0	15.0	18.0	18.0	15.0
1980	18.0	18.0	19.0	18.5	18.5	17.5	17.5	17.5	17.5	17.5	15.0	15.0	17.5
1981	15.0	15.0	13.0	13.0	13.0	13.0	***	***	***	***	***	***	***

WEST GERMANY

LEADING INDEX, WEST GERMANY (1980=100)

YEAR	JAN	FEB	MAR	APR	MAY	JUN	JUL	AUG	SEP	OCT	NOV	DEC	AVGE
1957	37.6	38.2	38.3	38.4	38.4	38.3	38.4	38.5	38.6	38.8	38.7	38.9	38.4
1958	39.2	38.9	38.4	39.0	39.0	39.4	39.7	40.2	40.6	40.7	40.8	40.4	39.7
1959	40.2	39.9	41.5	42.6	44.2	44.8	45.4	45.6	46.3	46.5	46.7	46.8	44.2
1960	46.7	46.2	47.0	48.0	48.8	49.6	50.2	51.1	50.8	50.4	50.3	50.4	49.1
1961	50.8	50.8	50.8	50.5	50.1	50.2	50.0	49.6	50.3	51.0	51.8	51.8	50.6
1962	51.1	51.0	50.9	51.6	51.4	51.5	51.3	51.6	51.5	51.7	52.1	52.2	51.5
1963	52.1	51.9	52.0	52.1	52.6	53.0	53.0	53.7	53.8	54.4	54.6	54.7	53.2
1964	55.4	56.0	56.2	56.4	56.6	57.1	57.5	58.2	58.2	58.2	58.2	58.6	57.2
1965	59.1	59.3	59.1	59.6	59.6	59.2	59.0	59.6	59.3	59.1	59.1	59.4	59.3
1966	60.2	60.8	60.9	60.4	60.3	60.2	60.2	59.6	59.3	58.5	57.7	57.8	59.7
1967	57.8	57.8	58.2	58.0	58.6	58.6	59.3	59.8	60.5	61.7	62.5	63.5	59.7
1968	63.0	63.7	64.1	64.9	65.5	66.0	67.0	67.8	68.8	69.2	69.7	70.2	66.7
1969	70.5	71.1	71.6	71.9	72.4	72.8	73.2	74.1	73.5	74.0	74.3	73.6	72.7
1970	73.3	73.0	73.3	73.0	72.8	72.9	72.8	72.7	72.3	72.4	72.1	71.9	72.7
1971	72.2	72.1	72.4	72.7	72.9	72.9	73.1	72.9	73.3	73.6	73.7	73.4	72.9
1972	74.3	74.7	75.4	75.6	76.0	76.3	77.0	77.2	77.9	78.4	79.0	79.9	76.8
1973	80.8	80.4	80.2	79.8	79.7	79.1	78.6	78.0	78.3	78.4	78.9	78.5	79.2
1974	79.3	79.5	79.5	79.3	79.1	78.6	78.2	78.5	77.2	76.6	75.8	75.7	78.1
1975	75.8	76.2	76.3	76.5	77.1	78.2	77.6	77.9	79.2	80.0	81.2	81.9	78.2
1976	82.8	83.3	84.0	83.9	84.7	84.9	86.4	85.5	85.6	85.4	86.0	85.8	84.9
1977	85.8	85.6	85.7	86.4	86.3	86.6	86.8	87.4	87.6	88.1	88.0	88.8	86.9
1978	89.5	89.7	89.8	89.9	90.4	90.9	91.9	92.5	93.5	93.9	94.8	95.6	91.9
1979	95.7	96.6	97.1	98.3	98.7	99.8	99.8	100.0	100.6	100.7	100.9	101.1	99.1
1980	101.1	101.1	100.9	100.6	100.2	99.8	99.5	99.3	99.0	99.4	99.8	99.4	100.0
1981	100.2	100.6	100.4	100.5	100.1	100.5	100.8	101.2	100.7	100.4	100.2	100.2	100.5
1982	101.4	101.5	102.1	102.5	102.6	102.3	102.6	102.2	102.3	102.2	102.4	103.7	102.3

SIX MONTH SMOOTHED CHANGE IN LEADING INDEX, WEST GERMANY (ANNUAL RATE, PERCENT)

YEAR	JAN	FEB	MAR	APR	MAY	JUN	JUL	AUG	SEP	OCT	NOV	DEC	AVGE
1958	4.0	1.7	-0.9	1.7	1.4	3.4	4.4	6.3	7.3	7.0	6.5	4.0	3.9
1959	2.2	0.5	7.6	11.6	18.2	18.4	19.0	17.8	18.8	17.2	15.5	13.5	13.4
1960	10.7	6.1	7.4	9.2	10.7	12.5	13.1	15.1	11.8	8.4	6.8	6.0	9.8
1961	6.4	4.9	3.4	1.4	-0.9	-1.2	-2.0	-3.2	-0.4	2.4	5.3	4.6	1.7
1962	1.7	1.2	0.7	3.2	2.3	2.3	1.3	1.8	0.9	1.3	2.5	2.6	1.8
1963	2.1	1.0	-1.4	1.3	2.9	4.0	3.6	5.3	5.4	6.7	6.5	6.3	3.9
1964	7.9	9.1	8.4	8.0	7.4	7.7	7.9	8.9	7.7	6.6	5.2	5.6	7.5
1965	6.0	5.6	4.3	5.0	4.2	2.2	0.8	2.3	0.9	0.3	0.0	0.7	2.7
1966	2.9	4.4	4.2	2.3	1.9	1.4	1.0	-1.1	-2.1	-4.3	-6.7	-6.2	-0.2
1967	-5.7	-5.1	-3.1	-2.9	-0.5	-0.2	2.5	4.2	6.7	10.1	11.9	13.7	2.6
1968	10.5	11.3	10.7	11.7	11.9	11.5	12.3	12.7	13.7	12.8	12.1	11.7	11.9
1969	11.0	10.6	10.2	9.3	9.1	8.3	7.9	8.9	5.8	6.1	5.7	3.0	8.0
1970	-1.4	0.1	0.3	-0.7	-1.4	-1.7	-1.6	-1.7	-2.4	-1.9	-2.3	-2.3	-1.2
1971	-1.3	-1.3	-0.4	0.7	1.2	1.1	1.8	1.1	2.2	2.6	2.5	1.6	1.0
1972	3.4	4.0	5.4	5.2	5.5	5.7	6.6	6.4	7.1	7.4	7.9	8.8	6.1
1973	9.8	7.4	5.7	3.9	2.7	0.5	-1.1	-2.8	-2.3	-2.1	-1.0	-1.9	1.6
1974	0.1	1.0	1.0	0.9	0.4	-0.6	-1.5	-0.8	-3.8	-5.1	-6.5	-6.2	-1.8
1975	-5.3	-3.8	-2.9	-1.7	0.1	3.3	1.9	2.6	6.1	7.5	9.8	10.3	2.3
1976	11.1	10.9	11.2	9.2	9.5	8.6	10.7	6.8	5.5	3.9	4.2	2.9	7.9
1977	2.0	1.1	0.9	2.1	1.4	1.6	1.8	3.0	3.2	4.0	3.9	4.6	2.5
1978	5.5	5.2	4.7	4.1	4.7	4.9	6.2	6.5	7.7	7.5	8.4	8.9	6.2
1979	7.8	8.6	8.3	9.5	8.9	8.9	8.1	7.1	7.1	6.1	5.2	4.6	7.5
1980	3.7	2.9	1.8	0.7	-0.4	-1.2	-1.9	-2.3	-2.7	-1.7	-0.8	-1.3	-0.3
1981	0.4	1.3	0.9	1.3	0.5	1.2	1.7	2.2	1.0	0.2	-0.3	-0.5	0.8
1982	1.6	1.7	2.7	3.1	3.0	2.0	2.4	1.4	1.3	1.0	1.0	3.0	2.0

225

WEST GERMANY LEADING, COINCIDENT AND LAGGING INTERNATIONAL ECONOMIC INDICATORS

1.1 NUMBER WORKING SHORT HOURS, WEST GERMANY (THOUSANDS)

YEAR	JAN	FEB	MAR	APR	MAY	JUN	JUL	AUG	SEP	OCT	NOV	DEC	AVGE
1951	51	37	46	66	78	114	169	183	187	144	130	148	113
1952	96	114	115	134	150	177	112	160	133	97	86	69	120
1953	77	92	94	83	79	76	104	80	72	77	81	77	83
1954	71	69	58	51	54	60	62	48	48	43	40	39	54
1955	43	28	25	28	28	28	21	14	11	8	10	14	22
1956	17	19	26	27	22	20	19	16	50	45	37	30	27
1957	27	25	20	13	11	12	18	21	19	17	20	18	18
1958	27	32	37	48	65	78	88	82	84	94	84	66	65
1959	56	40	36	27	15	12	8	17	2	2	6	4	19
1960	3	4	3	4	4	4	3	2	2	4	4	4	3
1961	2	3	3	3	4	4	5	5	5	5	3	3	4
1962	5	3	4	4	4	4	5	4	7	5	5	5	5
1963	8	15	18	13	8	10	9	13	7	6	3	3	9
1964	3	2	2	2	4	2	2	1	1	1	2	1	2
1965	1	1	1	1	1	2	2	0	1	2	2	3	2
1966	4	3	2	4	2	3	2	19	23	44	73	85	22
1967	106	151	144	193	174	363	226	246	157	91	68	28	161
1968	15	13	16	11	9	14	5	3	2	1	2	1	8
1969	2	1	2	5	1	1	1	1	3	1	2	1	1
1970	1	1	2	5	13	8	7	9	18	8	26	35	11
1971	31	38	46	46	49	78	90	139	90	92	117	289	92
1972	162	131	79	63	58	54	52	50	29	22	18	13	61
1973	10	11	18	24	24	25	26	35	68	90	113	116	47
1974	156	210	184	177	220	256	296	298	451	451	470	527	308
1975	561	674	613	776	896	958	1214	1385	1004	831	679	592	849
1976	502	356	387	310	238	242	144	160	142	159	162	176	248
1977	190	203	202	212	299	276	351	224	238	224	223	215	238
1978	184	182	176	259	221	245	256	296	165	144	147	106	198
1979	100	121	131	106	88	68	55	56	55	69	62	67	82
1980	74	73	72	80	88	98	149	103	209	210	243	290	141
1981	290	266	308	310	333	375	398	403	402	408	402	406	358
1982	384	418	417	425	449	516	615	790	863	917	953	891	637

2.0 APPLICATIONS FOR UNEMPLOYMENT COMPENSATION, WEST GERMANY (THOUSANDS)

YEAR	JAN	FEB	MAR	APR	MAY	JUN	JUL	AUG	SEP	OCT	NOV	DEC	AVGE
1957	269.0	181.7	208.9	265.1	291.8	298.2	276.9	265.0	252.9	241.1	281.5	335.5	264.0
1958	208.6	308.2	691.0	322.5	298.3	275.2	262.8	247.7	242.2	244.8	244.7	249.7	299.6
1959	262.1	268.8	171.3	226.3	217.1	202.6	179.4	163.9	150.4	149.6	144.6	131.2	188.9
1960	118.1	120.0	108.6	92.9	117.1	110.0	98.6	94.3	90.7	89.4	81.0	77.5	99.8
1961	72.8	72.0	64.5	81.7	80.9	85.6	82.3	108.5	77.0	65.6	60.6	60.5	76.0
1962	50.4	59.5	80.7	60.7	59.7	54.3	53.5	52.7	50.9	53.8	59.3	58.8	57.9
1963	75.6	70.0	65.1	59.4	59.9	55.7	59.9	56.1	54.0	55.2	54.4	61.5	60.6
1964	53.4	47.3	53.1	52.7	49.0	52.4	49.9	49.8	50.8	49.4	46.5	49.9	50.3
1965	46.5	47.7	53.5	37.8	41.9	41.2	41.5	40.2	40.0	37.0	44.9	45.0	43.1
1966	42.0	38.5	35.3	39.3	40.9	44.1	44.0	50.4	58.7	66.4	97.6	91.7	54.1
1967	107.1	134.5	147.7	166.9	180.5	186.4	167.2	169.3	153.6	146.3	127.4	98.4	148.8
1968	95.2	81.2	90.8	85.8	82.9	71.7	73.3	66.8	62.2	61.9	57.4	58.6	74.0
1969	60.7	65.5	50.4	45.3	41.1	40.9	43.3	40.7	43.1	42.5	36.9	55.3	47.1
1970	44.3	42.1	41.6	44.5	46.1	49.8	47.8	48.0	49.2	43.3	37.7	39.5	44.5
1971	49.0	40.2	62.4	52.0	55.6	60.4	58.4	59.4	62.4	58.2	64.1	72.9	57.9
1972	55.7	79.2	57.8	66.7	67.9	73.9	66.0	72.1	68.3	61.1	59.2	45.3	64.4
1973	36.5	57.9	59.8	61.5	76.0	78.5	71.1	83.2	78.3	81.2	101.0	139.0	77.0
1974	134.2	122.8	130.9	135.3	139.8	132.0	148.0	154.0	171.6	213.0	222.6	205.3	159.1
1975	246.8	214.8	215.4	256.6	200.5	223.9	242.2	225.5	235.9	242.5	210.7	217.8	227.7
1976	208.6	220.3	209.9	212.4	196.2	203.0	208.4	204.8	204.4	196.5	197.9	210.2	206.0
1977	212.1	188.0	214.0	206.3	204.3	209.9	207.8	212.5	206.2	200.6	211.1	195.5	205.7
1978	186.5	216.1	217.6	212.9	204.4	213.9	181.5	201.3	189.0	187.6	183.7	169.1	197.0
1979	204.7	189.5	191.5	180.9	198.2	175.6	172.4	182.6	161.2	169.4	166.3	142.6	177.9
1980	193.8	177.4	171.2	188.8	187.8	185.2	197.3	189.1	205.8	203.2	200.4	228.6	194.0
1981	200.5	204.4	205.8	212.2	213.7	218.3	236.3	226.0	251.3	243.4	257.1	284.4	229.4
1982	230.7	222.4	234.0	221.0	213.1	243.0	231.9	244.4	259.1	247.2	256.9	275.3	239.9

4.1 INSOLVENT ENTERPRISES, WEST GERMANY (NUMBER)

YEAR	IQ	IIQ	IIIQ	IVQ	AVGE
1962	517.	478.	514.	495.	501.
1963	484.	518.	582.	535.	530.
1964	557.	560.	546.	543.	552.
1965	503.	438.	501.	568.	518.
1966	536.	580.	632.	780.	632.
1967	824.	853.	766.	727.	793.
1968	721.	657.	585.	643.	652.
1969	596.	648.	654.	601.	625.
1970	632.	636.	716.	732.	679.
1971	718.	754.	750.	750.	743.
1972	772.	805.	750.	772.	775.
1973	843.	872.	1066.	1217.	1000.
1974	1306.	1411.	1563.	1702.	1496.

YEAR	JAN	FEB	MAR	APR	MAY	JUN	JUL	AUG	SEP	OCT	NOV	DEC	AVGE
1975	618.	560.	566.	607.	555.	562.	725.	549.	487.	628.	583.	525.	580.
1976	528.	558.	530.	619.	528.	524.	546.	584.	578.	612.	586.	616.	567.
1977	610.	619.	607.	570.	617.	579.	525.	635.	530.	523.	556.	558.	577.
1978	523.	491.	571.	534.	513.	516.	477.	464.	492.	465.	454.	448.	496.
1979	521.	441.	444.	450.	434.	447.	491.	482.	452.	442.	448.	431.	457.
1980	480.	543.	465.	474.	524.	527.	516.	513.	562.	586.	528.	602.	527.
1981	577.	634.	633.	638.	624.	641.	763.	692.	702.	781.	893.	943.	710.
1982	831.	972.	897.	1011.	941.	985.	903.	954.	975.	1006.	1206.	1275.	996.

5.1 NEW ORDERS, INVESTMENT GOODS INDUSTRIES, VOLUME INDEX, WEST GERMANY (1980=100)

YEAR	JAN	FEB	MAR	APR	MAY	JUN	JUL	AUG	SEP	OCT	NOV	DEC	AVGE
1962	47.	44.	44.	45.	43.	43.	44.	43.	44.	43.	43.	43.	44.
1963	44.	43.	44.	46.	46.	47.	47.	50.	48.	52.	51.	47.	47.
1964	52.	55.	52.	50.	53.	53.	53.	54.	53.	54.	54.	56.	53.
1965	58.	57.	55.	56.	55.	54.	56.	54.	57.	57.	56.	57.	56.
1966	55.	56.	56.	56.	55.	56.	53.	52.	53.	55.	50.	48.	54.
1967	47.	49.	50.	49.	51.	53.	53.	55.	55.	62.	60.	63.	54.
1968	58.	60.	59.	63.	66.	65.	68.	70.	71.	75.	75.	79.	67.
1969	79.	80.	82.	85.	85.	85.	89.	94.	89.	90.	86.	83.	86.
1970	84.	88.	87.	81.	83.	80.	80.	83.	82.	78.	80.	80.	82.
1971	81.	75.	80.	78.	78.	79.	78.	73.	75.	72.	73.	69.	76.
1972	72.	74.	74.	76.	77.	79.	77.	75.	79.	83.	86.	93.	79.
1973	105.	91.	90.	93.	108.	92.	92.	88.	90.	86.	86.	87.	92.
1974	90.	95.	95.	91.	93.	91.	84.	93.	84.	86.	83.	78.	89.
1975	85.	85.	80.	82.	80.	118.	89.	79.	84.	81.	82.	81.	86.
1976	86.	84.	85.	87.	85.	88.	127.	100.	94.	92.	91.	94.	93.
1977	89.	88.	92.	89.	89.	88.	88.	92.	89.	96.	101.	100.	92.
1978	93.	88.	94.	92.	93.	93.	91.	98.	99.	96.	98.	101.	95.
1979	96.	101.	97.	105.	105.	104.	102.	100.	106.	105.	102.	100.	102.
1980	104.	104.	104.	100.	105.	99.	99.	96.	97.	101.	95.	96.	100.
1981	99.	101.	100.	112.	97.	98.	102.	101.	101.	101.	102.	103.	101.
1982	103.	97.	98.	97.	94.	95.	95.	91.	89.	89.	95.	103.	96.

6.1 RESIDENTIAL CONSTRUCTION ORDERS, IN CONSTANT PRICES, WEST GERMANY (INDEX, 1980=100)

YEAR	JAN	FEB	MAR	APR	MAY	JUN	JUL	AUG	SEP	OCT	NOV	DEC	AVGE
1971	120.	111.	118.	116.	112.	115.	118.	124.	123.	131.	113.	114.	118.
1972	131.	147.	137.	132.	124.	130.	136.	139.	138.	133.	135.	133.	135.
1973	125.	128.	126.	117.	122.	106.	97.	84.	94.	83.	81.	76.	103.
1974	74.	79.	76.	81.	88.	80.	77.	72.	70.	68.	66.	68.	75.
1975	70.	65.	66.	69.	75.	81.	80.	77.	85.	90.	88.	84.	78.
1976	80.	82.	91.	77.	82.	77.	85.	81.	73.	72.	74.	77.	79.
1977	87.	86.	77.	89.	86.	88.	87.	95.	94.	98.	105.	102.	91.
1978	109.	106.	106.	107.	110.	109.	116.	112.	122.	113.	126.	123.	113.
1979	115.	110.	109.	115.	114.	121.	112.	113.	109.	116.	111.	117.	114.
1980	108.	110.	104.	98.	94.	96.	97.	96.	101.	102.	100.	97.	100.
1981	99.	96.	96.	91.	92.	86.	83.	80.	81.	77.	72.	64.	85.
1982	72.	76.	81.	83.	80.	81.	85.	85.	84.	81.	89.	107.	84.

7.0 INVENTORY CHANGE, IN CONSTANT PRICES, WEST GERMANY
(10 MILLION 1976 DM)

YEAR	IQ	IIQ	IIIQ	IVQ	AVGE
1955	213.	93.	324.	271.	225.
1956	173.	244.	64.	124.	151.
1957	230.	220.	220.	248.	230.
1958	264.	130.	140.	164.	175.
1959	-313.	271.	343.	438.	185.
1960	-10.	327.	550.	340.	302.
1961	175.	371.	93.	303.	236.
1962	301.	127.	133.	187.	187.
1963	202.	55.	145.	83.	121.
1964	77.	246.	381.	426.	283.
1965	418.	195.	105.	-46.	168.
1966	-238.	123.	40.	-28.	93.
1967	-149.	-81.	-112.	114.	-57.
1968	90.	430.	606.	287.	353.
1969	507.	393.	540.	927.	592.
1970	658.	742.	395.	62.	464.
1971	245.	-65.	139.	166.	121.
1972	-91.	379.	137.	-30.	99.
1973	433.	108.	275.	697.	378.
1974	133.	-256.	280.	-255.	104.
1975	-102.	-246.	-369.	27.	-173.
1976	162.	273.	290.	418.	286.
1977	326.	145.	311.	11.	198.
1978	10.	230.	78.	290.	152.
1979	427.	384.	706.	655.	543.
1980	366.	426.	240.	325.	339.
1981	307.	3.	-186.	-292.	-42.
1982	65.	222.	233.	-170.	88.

231

8.0 BASIC MATERIALS PRICE INDEX, SIX MONTH SMOOTHED CHANGE, WEST GERMANY
(ANNUAL RATE, PERCENT)

YEAR	JAN	FEB	MAR	APR	MAY	JUN	JUL	AUG	SEP	OCT	NOV	DEC	AVGE
1956	2.2	1.8	2.2	1.1	0.7	0.0	0.4	0.4	0.0	2.9	4.8	5.5	1.8
1957	3.3	3.6	3.3	2.9	2.9	2.1	1.4	1.1	0.0	0.4	-0.4	1.1	1.8
1958	-1.1	-1.4	-2.1	-1.4	-1.8	-1.4	-1.1	-1.4	-0.7	-1.1	-1.1	-1.8	-1.4
1959	-1.4	-0.7	-0.7	-1.8	-0.7	-0.4	-0.4	0.0	-0.4	-0.4	0.4	0.7	-0.5
1960	1.4	1.1	0.7	-0.4	2.2	0.8	2.2	0.0	1.1	-0.7	-0.7	0.0	1.2
1961	-0.7	0.4	-0.4	0.0	-0.7	-1.1	-1.1	-0.4	-0.4	-0.4	-0.4	-0.7	-0.5
1962	-0.4	-0.7	0.0	-0.7	0.0	0.0	-0.7	0.0	-0.4	-0.4	0.0	-0.4	-0.1
1963	-0.7	-0.7	0.0	-0.7	2.2	-0.9	2.9	-0.4	-0.4	-0.4	3.9	0.4	-0.4
1964	0.7	2.5	1.4	1.8	3.5	2.9	1.0	3.2	3.6	3.6	0.7	2.8	2.5
1965	1.8	3.1	2.8	2.8	3.1	2.1	2.1	1.4	1.0	0.7	-1.4	2.1	1.9
1966	2.8	2.5	3.1	3.5	3.0	3.1	1.0	3.0	-0.7	-1.0	-0.7	-2.0	1.2
1967	-1.7	-2.4	-3.0	-5.0	-4.1	-3.4	-1.7	-0.7	-1.7	-0.3	-1.8	-1.7	-1.7
1968	-6.5	-4.5	-4.5	-6.5	-6.6	-5.6	-5.6	-4.2	-2.8	-2.5	-1.8	-1.1	-4.3
1969	0.4	0.4	0.7	1.8	2.9	3.3	3.6	5.1	5.1	5.8	6.5	7.6	3.6
1970	7.2	6.8	6.4	5.6	3.8	3.5	2.8	1.4	1.0	0.3	0.0	0.0	3.2
1971	0.3	0.3	1.7	3.1	2.4	2.7	3.1	2.4	1.7	1.3	0.7	0.3	1.7
1972	-1.3	-1.0	-0.7	-0.3	0.7	1.3	2.3	3.0	4.7	5.4	5.7	6.0	2.1
1973	7.0	7.7	8.3	8.9	9.5	10.8	12.1	12.9	12.2	14.4	22.1	24.2	12.5
1974	32.8	36.2	36.0	34.2	31.2	24.8	22.3	19.3	15.1	13.3	8.4	4.6	23.2
1975	2.9	-1.2	-3.3	-3.5	-4.2	-3.7	-2.8	-1.7	0.0	0.7	1.4	2.9	-1.0
1976	4.3	5.3	5.3	6.2	6.7	7.9	9.0	7.1	6.1	3.7	3.0	2.1	5.6
1977	-0.9	0.5	0.0	-0.7	-1.3	-1.6	-2.2	-2.2	-1.6	-1.6	-2.0	-2.5	-1.2
1978	-3.2	-4.1	-4.3	-3.4	-2.1	-1.1	-0.9	-0.9	-0.2	0.9	2.1	2.8	-1.2
1979	4.2	6.6	8.4	11.0	11.7	13.3	15.3	15.2	15.0	14.4	14.7	14.7	12.0
1980	19.8	19.2	17.6	17.0	13.3	11.3	10.0	8.1	7.0	8.3	10.0	9.5	12.6
1981	11.2	12.8	12.1	12.4	13.3	14.3	16.0	16.2	12.3	9.2	6.8	6.1	11.9
1982	5.5	5.0	3.0	2.5	-0.2	-0.2	1.1	1.1	2.3	3.4	3.4	1.3	2.3

9.0 STOCK PRICE INDEX. WEST GERMANY (1980=100)

YEAR	JAN	FEB	MAR	APR	MAY	JUN	JUL	AUG	SEP	OCT	NOV	DEC	AVGE
1955	29.1	29.9	31.5	35.5	33.9	34.7	35.5	36.3	35.5	32.3	33.1	33.1	33.4
1956	33.1	32.3	33.1	33.1	31.5	31.5	29.9	29.9	31.5	29.9	29.9	30.7	31.4
1957	29.9	29.9	30.7	30.7	29.9	29.1	30.7	31.5	32.3	31.5	32.3	32.3	30.9
1958	33.9	33.1	33.9	35.5	34.7	37.1	37.9	41.2	45.2	48.4	48.4	50.0	39.9
1959	51.7	51.7	53.3	55.7	62.1	68.6	76.7	86.4	79.9	77.5	79.9	85.5	69.1
1960	87.2	86.4	86.4	90.4	101.7	120.2	120.2	141.2	128.3	123.5	120.2	119.4	110.4
1961	117.0	117.0	115.4	117.0	106.5	110.6	107.3	102.5	102.5	112.2	121.1	125.9	112.9
1962	104.1	103.3	101.7	99.3	85.5	79.9	76.7	79.9	74.2	73.4	85.5	82.3	87.1
1963	79.9	75.9	78.3	80.7	90.4	88.0	89.6	92.8	93.6	91.2	88.8	93.6	86.9
1964	96.8	99.3	101.7	100.1	97.6	96.8	99.3	100.9	100.1	95.2	94.4	95.2	98.1
1965	96.0	93.6	90.4	90.4	90.4	85.5	87.2	88.0	87.2	83.9	81.5	80.7	87.9
1966	83.9	85.1	81.9	78.9	75.9	69.9	66.1	69.2	71.4	66.3	66.8	65.5	73.4
1967	68.9	70.6	72.6	69.4	69.8	68.0	71.8	79.3	81.5	84.4	86.8	89.7	76.1
1968	92.8	93.9	95.9	99.8	98.1	103.3	102.4	103.3	101.0	103.3	99.4	99.8	99.4
1969	104.0	102.7	103.6	103.7	111.0	107.4	104.7	110.6	108.5	113.1	119.2	113.6	108.5
1970	107.6	106.0	106.5	102.1	94.6	89.9	93.8	93.9	91.8	89.9	86.7	86.3	95.8
1971	96.0	99.6	99.7	94.3	96.9	93.4	96.2	92.2	89.0	83.0	85.0	89.9	92.9
1972	93.8	99.9	104.1	102.9	104.2	100.9	105.2	103.9	100.5	97.8	98.9	98.6	100.9
1973	104.8	103.7	110.0	106.3	97.2	95.6	89.1	89.5	87.3	93.0	83.9	82.7	95.3
1974	87.5	83.2	83.8	87.3	84.8	82.0	78.8	78.8	75.2	75.6	78.4	79.3	81.2
1975	82.8	94.0	93.7	95.3	88.4	87.8	94.0	90.6	89.0	95.5	100.7	102.3	92.8
1976	104.6	105.9	109.4	103.0	101.9	102.8	100.4	98.0	98.4	91.1	95.7	96.1	100.6
1977	97.0	95.2	97.4	104.3	102.8	99.5	100.2	101.8	102.0	103.2	104.3	103.0	100.9
1978	104.8	105.8	105.5	102.9	105.0	105.4	109.6	111.9	113.9	111.7	110.2	110.6	108.1
1979	113.3	110.0	108.3	108.4	103.7	101.9	104.1	105.9	105.8	101.1	101.2	99.1	105.2
1980	101.5	103.7	95.6	97.2	99.7	100.8	102.8	100.6	100.3	99.1	100.6	98.7	100.0
1981	97.7	98.4	100.9	104.7	104.1	108.8	111.1	108.4	101.4	101.1	103.3	101.1	100.4
1982	103.1	104.3	105.6	104.7	103.8	100.8	99.4	99.1	104.4	103.1	105.5	110.7	103.7

10.1 GROSS ENTREPRENEURIAL AND PROPERTY INCOME, IN CONSTANT PRICES, WEST GERMANY
(MILLION 1980 DM)

YEAR	IQ	IIQ	IIIQ	IVQ	AVGE
1960	56476.	54437.	58866.	57292.	56768.
1961	57550.	54717.	54830.	56016.	55778.
1962	55711.	56332.	56584.	54581.	55802.
1963	51971.	54003.	58377.	58191.	55636.
1964	58631.	61074.	60181.	59997.	59971.
1965	63041.	61560.	60871.	62511.	61996.
1966	65279.	61048.	61025.	58589.	61485.
1967	59503.	60397.	60242.	64923.	61266.
1968	63602.	68746.	69316.	73782.	68862.
1969	71341.	70850.	74056.	68536.	71196.
1970	68253.	72787.	70999.	70343.	70596.
1971	68720.	68967.	68668.	69999.	69089.
1972	70475.	69816.	69704.	75815.	71453.
1973	74222.	71165.	71205.	73495.	72522.
1974	71543.	66380.	68311.	64193.	67607.
1975	64111.	64584.	66268.	67282.	65561.
1976	72824.	74147.	71777.	72332.	72770.
1977	76052.	72066.	71443.	75389.	73738.
1978	74799.	77311.	79151.	82045.	78327.
1979	78801.	82849.	79975.	82347.	80993.
1980	81951.	78023.	76481.	71103.	76890.
1981	74111.	71485.	73908.	73216.	73180.
1982	73488.	73978.	75792.	75030.	74572.

234

11.0 RATIO. PRICE TO UNIT LABOR COST, ENTIRE ECONOMY, WEST GERMANY
(INDEX, 1980=100)

YEAR	IQ	IIQ	IIIQ	IVQ	AVGE
1958	102.6	102.5	103.7	103.6	103.1
1959	102.0	106.5	106.3	106.7	105.4
1960	106.1	106.0	106.1	106.4	106.1
1961	105.0	103.4	103.7	104.2	104.1
1962	102.4	102.3	102.5	101.8	102.2
1963	101.1	100.8	103.3	102.8	102.0
1964	103.2	103.8	104.4	103.0	103.6
1965	103.8	102.9	101.9	102.5	102.8
1966	103.4	102.0	101.9	100.2	101.9
1967	101.6	103.4	103.1	104.8	103.2
1968	103.3	104.3	104.5	105.8	104.5
1969	105.4	105.3	106.1	104.4	105.3
1970	100.3	102.7	101.1	101.1	101.4
1971	100.3	100.9	100.2	100.6	100.5
1972	100.4	100.5	100.2	101.4	100.6
1973	100.4	99.1	98.8	98.9	99.3
1974	98.3	96.2	96.9	95.8	96.8
1975	95.8	97.1	97.1	98.0	97.0
1976	99.0	99.5	98.6	99.0	99.0
1977	99.8	98.4	98.5	99.8	99.1
1978	100.4	100.3	100.6	101.2	100.6
1979	100.7	101.9	101.6	101.5	101.4
1980	101.6	100.2	99.8	98.7	100.1
1981	99.4	99.0	99.5	99.7	99.4
1982	99.7	101.2	100.5	100.4	100.4

12.0 CHANGE IN CONSUMER CREDIT, IN CONSTANT PRICES, WEST GERMANY
(MILLION 1980 DM)

YEAR	IQ	IIQ	IIIQ	IVQ	AVGE
1969	2593.	1899.	2206.	2659.	2339.
1970	1995.	1164.	1863.	1826.	1712.
1971	2316.	2761.	2652.	2657.	2597.
1972	2934.	3221.	3494.	4474.	3531.
1973	3488.	2367.	564.	-100.	1580.
1974	-174.	11.	214.	-139.	-22.
1975	1106.	550.	2445.	3545.	1912.
1976	3608.	4013.	3371.	4568.	3890.
1977	838.	5325.	3576.	2720.	3115.
1978	6063.	2554.	5555.	4353.	4631.
1979	5093.	6270.	4509.	4467.	5085.
1980	3385.	2792.	2045.	2597.	2705.
1981	1395.	1007.	1542.	1234.	1295.
1982	1645.	1930.	1758.	1071.	1601.

COINCIDENT INDEX, WEST GERMANY (1980=100)

YEAR	JAN	FEB	MAR	APR	MAY	JUN	JUL	AUG	SEP	OCT	NOV	DEC	AVGE
1950	14.6	14.6	14.8	14.8	15.1	15.5	15.7	16.0	16.1	16.2	16.3	16.4	15.5
1951	16.6	17.0	16.9	17.1	17.1	17.2	17.2	17.3	17.3	17.5	17.7	17.9	17.2
1952	18.3	18.5	18.5	18.7	18.9	18.9	19.3	19.4	19.7	19.9	19.9	20.1	19.2
1953	20.4	20.5	20.7	21.0	21.1	21.4	21.6	21.9	22.2	22.4	22.5	22.9	21.5
1954	22.7	22.8	23.2	23.3	23.6	23.9	24.2	24.3	24.8	25.1	25.6	26.0	24.1
1955	25.9	26.2	26.5	27.2	27.7	27.8	28.3	28.7	28.9	29.2	29.4	29.7	28.0
1956	30.1	30.3	30.3	30.5	30.8	31.3	31.2	31.5	31.7	32.0	32.1	32.3	31.2
1957	32.6	33.0	32.9	33.5	33.7	33.5	34.0	34.2	34.4	34.6	34.8	34.6	33.8
1958	35.4	35.4	35.1	35.5	35.5	35.8	36.5	36.3	36.6	36.9	36.7	36.9	36.0
1959	37.1	37.1	37.4	38.2	38.1	38.9	39.1	39.3	39.7	40.1	40.5	40.8	38.9
1960	41.0	41.6	42.1	42.3	42.7	43.0	43.3	44.2	44.6	44.4	45.1	45.8	43.3
1961	46.0	46.5	46.9	46.5	46.7	46.9	47.1	47.3	47.5	47.9	48.1	48.3	47.1
1962	49.3	49.5	48.9	49.1	49.3	49.8	49.9	50.3	50.4	50.6	50.6	50.6	49.9
1963	50.0	49.9	50.6	51.0	51.1	51.2	51.8	52.1	52.2	52.5	53.0	52.9	51.5
1964	53.6	53.9	54.0	54.1	54.4	54.7	55.1	55.1	55.8	56.3	57.0	57.4	55.1
1965	58.0	58.3	58.1	59.1	59.4	59.4	59.4	59.6	59.9	60.0	60.3	60.7	59.3
1966	61.3	61.5	62.2	61.3	61.6	61.6	61.5	61.7	61.2	60.5	59.8	59.5	61.1
1967	59.0	58.5	58.1	57.8	57.7	58.1	58.3	58.4	58.7	59.1	59.4	60.6	58.6
1968	59.5	60.1	60.8	61.4	62.1	62.5	63.2	64.6	64.8	65.5	66.6	66.9	63.2
1969	67.5	67.8	68.8	69.5	70.1	70.8	71.4	72.1	72.5	73.4	74.0	74.2	71.0
1970	73.7	74.4	75.0	75.5	76.0	76.6	77.3	77.5	77.9	78.3	78.7	78.7	76.6
1971	78.8	78.6	78.6	79.0	79.1	79.2	79.7	79.5	79.9	80.1	80.2	79.9	79.4
1972	80.7	80.6	81.1	80.8	81.2	81.4	81.5	82.2	82.2	82.7	83.3	84.0	81.8
1973	84.8	85.1	85.1	85.1	85.4	85.3	84.9	85.7	85.7	85.8	85.4	85.1	85.3
1974	85.1	85.0	84.8	85.0	85.0	84.6	85.1	84.7	84.3	84.3	83.4	82.9	84.5
1975	82.6	82.6	82.6	82.5	82.2	82.1	82.1	82.1	82.3	82.7	83.2	83.2	82.5
1976	83.4	83.9	83.9	84.5	84.9	85.2	85.1	86.0	86.4	86.5	87.1	87.6	85.4
1977	87.0	87.2	87.7	87.3	87.9	88.1	88.1	88.8	89.2	89.2	89.8	90.5	88.4
1978	90.8	90.3	90.5	90.7	90.8	91.8	91.7	92.7	93.2	93.3	93.5	94.0	91.9
1979	94.1	94.3	95.3	95.9	96.6	97.0	97.0	97.3	97.4	98.2	98.6	98.8	96.7
1980	99.9	100.0	100.0	99.9	99.9	99.7	100.2	100.1	100.2	100.4	100.0	99.7	100.0
1981	100.0	100.8	99.9	99.8	99.5	99.4	100.0	99.9	100.1	99.6	100.0	99.4	99.9
1982	99.4	99.3	99.3	98.9	98.5	98.2	97.9	98.2	97.5	97.0	97.3	97.4	98.2

SIX MONTH SMOOTHED CHANGE IN COINCIDENT INDEX, WEST GERMANY (ANNUAL RATE, PERCENT)

YEAR	JAN	FEB	MAR	APR	MAY	JUN	JUL	AUG	SEP	OCT	NOV	DEC	AVGE
1951	13.9	15.8	12.7	12.4	9.6	9.1	7.5	6.8	5.6	7.2	7.6	8.0	9.7
1952	11.5	12.1	11.2	11.3	12.1	10.8	12.6	12.2	13.4	13.3	11.2	11.0	11.9
1953	12.1	10.9	12.0	12.1	11.2	12.9	12.7	12.8	13.7	14.2	12.9	14.2	12.6
1954	10.2	9.3	11.1	10.0	10.9	11.2	11.9	11.3	13.5	13.5	15.8	16.9	12.1
1955	14.0	14.2	13.8	17.4	18.4	16.6	17.5	17.3	16.4	15.4	14.1	14.1	15.8
1956	14.9	13.4	11.0	10.2	10.2	11.3	8.7	9.3	8.6	9.3	8.2	8.2	10.3
1957	8.6	9.8	8.0	10.2	9.6	6.9	8.8	8.7	8.0	8.1	7.7	5.1	8.3
1958	8.9	7.2	4.7	5.7	5.1	5.4	8.2	6.2	6.7	7.2	5.2	5.5	6.3
1959	5.3	5.0	5.6	8.8	6.9	10.0	9.6	9.6	10.1	10.6	11.1	11.2	8.6
1960	10.2	11.6	12.3	11.1	11.5	10.8	10.6	13.2	12.8	10.0	11.2	12.8	11.5
1961	11.5	12.1	11.5	8.2	7.3	7.0	6.1	5.8	5.5	6.1	5.6	5.3	7.7
1962	8.7	8.2	4.9	5.1	5.0	5.8	5.3	6.2	5.5	5.0	4.5	3.5	5.6
1963	0.5	-0.3	2.4	3.3	3.2	2.8	4.7	5.3	5.0	5.8	6.7	5.7	3.8
1964	7.6	7.6	6.6	6.1	5.9	6.0	6.3	5.5	7.1	7.5	9.0	9.0	7.0
1965	9.9	9.5	7.7	9.6	9.2	7.8	6.5	5.9	5.8	5.0	4.8	5.1	7.2
1966	6.2	5.8	7.2	3.4	3.8	3.0	2.3	2.1	0.1	-2.1	-4.5	-5.2	1.8
1967	-6.4	-7.4	-7.8	-7.7	-7.2	-5.0	-3.6	-2.4	-0.5	1.2	2.7	6.6	-3.1
1968	2.8	4.6	6.2	7.4	8.7	8.9	9.7	13.1	11.8	12.4	13.9	12.9	9.4
1969	13.1	11.8	12.7	12.6	12.4	12.1	11.8	11.9	11.2	11.6	11.4	10.1	11.9
1970	7.0	7.4	7.6	7.7	7.5	7.8	8.3	7.4	7.2	7.0	7.1	6.1	7.3
1971	5.3	3.8	2.9	2.9	2.7	2.3	2.4	1.9	2.5	2.5	2.4	1.3	2.8
1972	3.0	2.5	4.1	2.0	2.6	2.7	2.4	3.7	3.1	3.9	4.7	5.7	3.4
1973	6.7	6.6	5.7	5.1	4.8	3.9	2.3	3.4	2.7	2.3	0.9	-0.3	3.7
1974	-0.3	-0.7	-1.0	-0.7	-0.5	-1.4	-0.1	-1.1	-1.7	-1.6	-3.1	-4.0	-1.3
1975	-4.1	-3.7	-3.3	-3.2	-3.4	-3.0	-2.6	-2.1	-1.1	0.2	1.5	1.5	-1.9
1976	2.0	2.9	2.8	3.9	4.3	4.5	3.8	5.1	5.3	4.6	5.4	5.6	4.2
1977	3.6	3.3	3.7	2.2	3.1	2.9	2.4	3.3	3.6	3.3	3.9	4.9	3.3
1978	5.2	3.4	3.1	3.0	2.6	4.3	3.5	5.0	5.3	4.7	4.3	4.8	4.1
1979	4.4	4.3	5.5	5.9	6.5	6.3	5.4	5.0	4.5	5.3	5.2	4.8	5.3
1980	6.2	5.4	4.4	3.4	2.8	1.9	2.5	1.7	1.5	1.5	0.4	-0.4	2.6
1981	0.1	1.5	-0.4	-0.4	-1.0	-1.2	-0.1	-0.2	0.2	-0.6	0.1	-0.9	-0.2
1982	-1.0	-0.9	-0.8	-1.3	-2.0	-2.3	-2.8	-1.9	-2.9	-3.4	-2.4	-1.8	-2.0

YEAR	JAN	FEB	MAR	APR	MAY	JUN	JUL	AUG	SEP	OCT	NOV	DEC	AVGE
1951	5658.5	5700.5	5738.5	5759.0	5771.3	5776.4	5778.5	5784.6	5780.5	5809.2	5831.8	5859.5	5770.7
1952	5882.1	5906.7	5914.9	5923.1	5926.2	5937.4	5960.0	5984.6	6020.5	6043.1	6069.7	6085.1	5971.1
1953	6118.0	6122.1	6135.4	6161.0	6187.7	6216.2	6246.2	6271.8	6306.7	6331.3	6281.0	6362.1	6228.3
1954	6371.3	6394.9	6451.3	6482.1	6532.3	6574.4	6608.2	6643.1	6675.9	6705.6	6747.7	6789.7	6581.4
1955	6830.7	6887.2	6958.2	7020.8	7079.1	7144.1	7196.2	7260.1	7314.6	7362.3	7398.6	7421.6	7156.1
1956	7464.2	7463.7	7506.1	7568.1	7598.1	7634.0	7649.2	7670.6	7675.1	7708.7	7723.0	7734.3	7616.2
1957	7701.2	7736.4	7772.9	7795.5	7830.6	7856.2	7893.8	7924.9	7960.8	7982.5	7982.1	7969.7	7867.2
1958	8138.1	8137.3	8126.8	8135.0	8130.6	8133.9	8131.2	8122.9	8129.3	8110.9	8088.1	8081.0	8122.0
1959	8049.8	8043.6	8056.8	8082.3	8095.0	8133.9	8151.1	8174.9	8217.0	8250.5	8287.9	8308.6	8154.2
1960	8327.6	8371.9	8404.4	8400.2	8425.1	8446.6	8469.6	8517.0	8562.7	8592.4	8638.3	8667.6	8485.4
1961	8707.2	8716.5	8728.7	8736.3	8752.1	8752.6	8752.6	8735.9	8729.5	8723.3	8728.5	8736.8	8732.7
1962	8759.5	8763.1	8761.9	8760.5	8759.5	8756.5	8755.1	8766.2	8752.2	8753.6	8746.0	8749.2	8756.9
1963	8727.0	8709.6	8706.1	8711.1	8685.4	8667.7	8671.7	8655.2	8649.8	8649.9	8635.2	8642.8	8675.9
1964	8648.9	8657.6	8660.2	8700.0	8691.7	8705.0	8710.9	8728.1	8741.3	8765.1	8783.2	8800.4	8716.1
1965	8824.7	8846.1	8873.2	8903.0	8900.1	8896.3	8897.1	8898.1	8893.1	8885.6	8895.0	8895.5	8884.1
1966	8887.6	8884.1	8886.3	8897.3	8884.5	8874.0	8842.9	8820.7	8762.6	8698.1	8631.5	8580.4	8804.2
1967	8488.8	8400.0	8326.1	8257.5	8226.6	8192.3	8173.1	8166.7	8162.6	8144.2	8131.8	8134.9	8233.7
1968	8142.3	8162.3	8170.1	8182.7	8219.9	8242.4	8288.2	8335.4	8382.6	8439.1	8472.8	8496.2	8294.5
1969	8533.5	8573.3	8612.9	8636.0	8661.9	8692.9	8735.9	8758.6	8806.9	8857.8	8887.5	8926.1	8723.6
1970	8799.3	8825.2	8845.7	8864.8	8874.9	8888.2	8913.1	8931.0	8928.2	8933.1	8932.2	8925.7	8888.4
1971	8908.9	8881.0	8875.8	8857.5	8841.4	8842.5	8824.8	8813.7	8808.2	8772.4	8746.7	8729.0	8825.1
1972	8690.2	8670.7	8655.9	8633.3	8635.1	8634.4	8610.4	8602.9	8589.7	8591.7	8603.2	8605.4	8626.9
1973	8634.6	8658.9	8658.1	8667.1	8673.2	8672.4	8676.1	8679.6	8666.5	8673.4	8659.7	8628.8	8662.3
1974	8608.0	8581.7	8551.1	8535.5	8512.1	8477.4	8451.0	8401.9	8355.3	8308.9	8236.4	8197.6	8434.7
1975	8141.5	8080.4	8022.9	7985.9	7940.7	7894.0	7850.3	7804.5	7769.8	7736.2	7716.1	7710.7	7887.7
1976	7685.0	7684.3	7691.8	7693.8	7697.4	7701.7	7694.5	7698.9	7710.2	7704.6	7707.3	7709.0	7698.2
1977	7635.0	7642.6	7644.3	7644.5	7636.6	7634.6	7632.8	7633.3	7629.4	7621.1	7616.6	7615.0	7632.1
1978	7617.2	7607.8	7597.6	7585.3	7577.0	7577.2	7563.7	7577.1	7569.0	7575.1	7578.7	7577.1	7583.6
1979	7578.0	7584.4	7586.2	7585.1	7595.5	7596.3	7603.0	7612.7	7614.9	7636.5	7647.7	7646.9	7607.3
1980	7668.7	7685.6	7684.5	7684.1	7679.4	7673.3	7673.5	7660.6	7651.6	7636.0	7618.2	7605.1	7660.0
1981	7593.6	7571.5	7551.1	7536.2	7517.0	7498.7	7484.4	7466.9	7450.3	7383.9	7402.4	7379.4	7486.3
1982	7353.8	7332.5	7314.4	7296.1	7276.2	7258.0	7229.7	7208.4	7175.0	7129.0	7098.2	7073.3	7228.7

14.1 UNEMPLOYMENT RATE, WEST GERMANY (PERCENT)

YEAR	JAN	FEB	MAR	APR	MAY	JUN	JUL	AUG	SEP	OCT	NOV	DEC	AVGE
1950	10.1	10.5	11.6	12.1	12.0	11.8	11.6	11.4	11.3	11.1	10.4	9.7	11.1
1951	9.8	9.0	10.2	10.4	10.7	10.9	11.1	11.3	11.3	11.3	10.6	9.7	10.5
1952	9.0	9.2	9.7	9.9	9.8	9.9	9.3	9.8	9.0	9.5	9.7	9.1	9.6
1953	8.4	8.5	8.3	8.3	8.6	8.5	8.7	8.7	9.0	8.8	8.6	7.6	8.5
1954	8.3	8.6	8.0	8.2	8.0	7.9	7.8	7.9	7.5	7.4	7.0	5.9	7.7
1955	6.6	4.1	7.4	5.8	5.4	5.3	5.0	4.9	4.8	4.8	4.6	4.4	5.5
1956	4.2	3.5	5.2	4.1	4.1	3.9	4.0	3.9	3.9	3.9	3.5	4.1	4.2
1957	3.9	3.8	3.4	3.9	3.8	3.9	3.8	3.7	3.6	3.5	3.2	4.2	3.7
1958	3.5	3.2	5.0	3.9	3.7	3.4	3.3	3.4	3.3	3.3	3.2	3.2	3.6
1959	3.2	1.5	2.8	2.7	2.5	2.3	2.0	1.9	1.9	1.8	1.7	1.6	2.3
1960	1.5	1.2	1.2	1.4	1.3	1.2	1.2	1.0	1.0	1.1	1.0	0.9	1.2
1961	0.9	0.8	0.8	0.9	0.9	0.9	0.8	0.8	0.8	0.7	0.8	0.8	0.8
1962	0.5	0.5	0.7	0.7	0.7	0.7	0.7	0.7	0.7	0.7	0.8	0.8	0.7
1963	1.0	1.0	0.8	0.8	0.8	0.8	0.8	0.8	0.7	0.8	0.7	0.7	0.8
1964	0.7	0.6	0.7	0.6	0.6	0.6	0.8	0.7	0.7	0.7	0.7	0.6	0.8
1965	0.6	0.5	0.4	0.6	0.6	0.7	0.7	0.8	0.7	0.7	0.7	0.6	0.6
1966	0.5	0.6	0.7	0.6	0.6	0.6	0.7	0.8	0.9	1.0	1.2	1.4	0.8
1967	1.8	2.0	1.8	2.4	2.5	2.4	2.4	2.3	2.3	2.2	2.1	2.1	2.2
1968	2.0	1.8	1.8	1.7	1.5	1.5	1.4	1.3	1.3	1.2	1.1	1.0	1.5
1969	0.9	1.0	0.9	0.8	0.8	0.8	0.8	0.8	0.8	0.7	0.7	0.7	0.8
1970	0.7	0.7	0.6	0.7	0.7	0.7	0.7	0.7	0.7	0.7	0.7	0.7	0.7
1971	1.0	1.1	1.0	1.1	1.2	1.2	0.9	1.2	1.0	1.2	1.0	1.1	0.9
1972	1.0	1.1	1.1	1.1	1.1	1.2	1.2	1.3	1.0	1.2	1.0	1.0	1.1
1973	1.9	2.0	2.1	1.2	1.1	1.0	1.0	1.0	1.0	1.3	1.6	1.8	1.3
1974	3.9	4.1	4.4	4.7	4.4	5.0	5.0	5.1	5.1	5.0	5.0	4.9	2.7
1975	4.8	4.9	4.8	4.5	4.6	4.6	4.6	4.5	4.5	4.5	4.4	4.1	4.8
1976	4.5	4.4	4.4	4.4	4.6	4.4	4.6	4.5	4.6	4.5	4.4	3.5	4.6
1977	4.4	4.1	4.4	4.5	4.6	4.6	4.6	4.6	4.3	4.5	4.2	4.4	4.5
1978	4.1	4.1	4.4	4.4	4.5	4.4	4.3	4.3	4.3	4.3	4.2	4.1	4.3
1979	4.1	3.5	3.9	3.9	3.8	3.8	3.7	3.7	3.7	3.6	3.6	3.5	3.8
1980	3.5	3.5	3.9	3.7	3.7	3.8	3.9	4.0	4.0	4.1	4.3	4.4	3.9
1981	4.5	4.7	4.9	5.0	5.3	5.4	5.7	5.9	6.0	6.3	6.5	6.8	5.6
1982	6.8	7.0	7.2	7.3	7.5	7.5	7.6	7.8	8.2	8.3	8.5	8.6	7.7

15.0 GROSS NATIONAL PRODUCT. IN CONSTANT PRICES, WEST GERMANY
(BILLION 1976 DM)

YEAR	IQ	IIQ	IIIQ	IVQ	AVGE
1950	66.2	67.2	72.5	75.3	70.3
1951	77.0	77.9	77.3	79.0	77.8
1952	82.3	83.1	85.9	87.3	84.6
1953	89.4	90.7	92.2	94.6	91.7
1954	93.3	96.6	100.3	103.4	98.4
1955	104.5	109.7	112.3	114.5	110.3
1956	115.5	119.5	118.4	120.6	118.5
1957	124.7	125.3	125.5	125.6	125.3
1958	126.9	127.3	131.6	133.4	129.8
1959	133.0	138.4	141.2	144.5	139.3
1960	147.7	150.3	153.0	156.4	151.8
1961	161.2	159.1	158.9	161.5	160.2
1962	165.9	167.1	168.6	170.1	167.9
1963	165.0	171.5	177.2	178.8	173.1
1964	180.5	184.2	185.1	188.6	184.6
1965	191.9	194.2	194.9	197.7	194.7
1966	201.5	200.9	199.5	197.5	199.8
1967	197.7	198.5	198.8	203.9	199.7
1968	204.2	208.7	215.8	219.1	211.9
1969	219.6	225.5	231.8	234.7	227.9
1970	230.8	240.6	241.2	244.8	239.3
1971	245.2	246.2	247.9	248.8	247.0
1972	253.7	255.6	257.2	262.6	257.3
1973	268.9	267.4	269.2	270.4	269.0
1974	272.3	270.4	271.5	266.6	270.2
1975	262.1	264.2	266.5	271.2	266.0
1976	277.0	280.5	281.0	284.4	280.7
1977	287.5	286.4	288.0	292.2	288.5
1978	293.7	297.4	300.3	302.5	298.5
1979	304.0	310.9	311.4	315.3	310.4
1980	320.0	314.5	315.3	314.5	316.1
1981	315.4	313.6	316.4	316.5	315.5
1982	313.6	313.5	311.0	310.5	312.1

16.0 INDUSTRIAL PRODUCTION, WEST GERMANY (INDEX, 1980=100)

YEAR	JAN	FEB	MAR	APR	MAY	JUN	JUL	AUG	SEP	OCT	NOV	DEC	AVGE
1948	9.	9.	9.	9.	9.	9.	11.	11.	12.	12.	13.	14.	11.
1949	15.	15.	15.	15.	15.	15.	15.	16.	16.	16.	17.	17.	16.
1950	17.	17.	18.	17.	19.	20.	20.	21.	21.	21.	22.	21.	20.
1951	22.	23.	22.	24.	23.	24.	23.	23.	22.	24.	24.	22.	23.
1952	25.	25.	24.	24.	25.	23.	25.	24.	26.	27.	25.	25.	25.
1953	26.	25.	27.	27.	26.	27.	27.	27.	28.	28.	28.	29.	27.
1954	27.	28.	30.	29.	30.	30.	31.	30.	32.	31.	33.	33.	30.
1955	32.	33.	34.	33.	35.	34.	34.	36.	36.	35.	37.	38.	35.
1956	38.	37.	37.	38.	38.	39.	38.	39.	38.	39.	39.	37.	38.
1957	39.	39.	39.	40.	42.	37.	40.	40.	39.	40.	41.	39.	40.
1958	42.	40.	40.	41.	40.	39.	42.	40.	42.	42.	40.	41.	41.
1959	41.	41.	40.	46.	40.	45.	45.	44.	45.	46.	46.	47.	44.
1960	45.	49.	50.	48.	51.	48.	48.	51.	51.	49.	51.	53.	50.
1961	52.	52.	54.	52.	51.	52.	52.	52.	52.	51.	52.	52.	52.
1962	54.	54.	53.	53.	55.	54.	54.	56.	56.	55.	56.	56.	55.
1963	54.	54.	55.	56.	56.	56.	57.	57.	57.	57.	57.	57.	56.
1964	59.	60.	59.	59.	59.	60.	61.	60.	61.	62.	62.	63.	60.
1965	64.	64.	63.	64.	64.	63.	63.	64.	65.	65.	64.	65.	64.
1966	65.	65.	67.	65.	65.	66.	65.	64.	65.	64.	63.	63.	65.
1967	61.	61.	60.	61.	60.	61.	63.	62.	63.	64.	65.	69.	63.
1968	63.	64.	65.	66.	67.	67.	67.	72.	71.	71.	73.	73.	68.
1969	74.	75.	76.	76.	77.	77.	77.	79.	79.	80.	81.	81.	78.
1970	80.	82.	82.	83.	84.	83.	84.	83.	82.	83.	82.	83.	83.
1971	85.	84.	84.	84.	83.	84.	85.	82.	84.	84.	83.	80.	84.
1972	84.	85.	86.	86.	86.	86.	86.	87.	86.	87.	88.	90.	86.
1973	90.	92.	91.	91.	92.	91.	88.	93.	92.	92.	92.	92.	91.
1974	92.	91.	91.	91.	92.	90.	92.	88.	88.	88.	87.	84.	90.
1975	84.	84.	85.	84.	83.	83.	83.	84.	84.	86.	87.	87.	85.
1976	87.	90.	88.	90.	90.	91.	90.	91.	92.	92.	92.	92.	90.
1977	93.	92.	94.	92.	92.	93.	91.	93.	94.	93.	93.	95.	93.
1978	96.	92.	91.	92.	92.	94.	94.	96.	97.	97.	97.	97.	95.
1979	96.	95.	97.	97.	99.	100.	101.	100.	99.	100.	101.	102.	99.
1980	101.	102.	101.	101.	99.	98.	99.	100.	97.	98.	97.	97.	99.
1981	97.	101.	97.	97.	97.	97.	98.	97.	97.	98.	98.	97.	99.
1982	97.	98.	98.	98.	97.	96.	94.	95.	94.	93.	93.	92.	95.

17.0 DISPOSABLE INCOME, IN CONSTANT PRICES, WEST GERMANY
(BILLION 1980 DM)

YEAR	IQ	IIQ	IIIQ	IVQ	AVGE
1950	41.8	44.1	47.0	45.7	44.6
1951	47.9	47.3	48.4	48.8	48.1
1952	50.9	53.2	55.2	55.9	53.8
1953	56.8	58.9	61.4	64.5	60.4
1954	63.6	63.9	65.2	68.4	65.3
1955	68.2	71.8	73.2	73.0	71.5
1956	76.3	74.8	76.3	78.7	76.5
1957	81.2	84.1	84.6	86.1	84.0
1958	87.7	87.0	90.7	91.8	89.3
1959	93.7	93.2	95.0	97.0	94.7
1960	97.5	100.0	104.4	105.7	101.9
1961	108.2	109.6	109.2	112.8	109.9
1962	113.1	113.7	116.9	118.7	115.6
1963	117.5	118.6	121.6	123.7	120.3
1964	125.2	126.8	127.7	133.6	128.3
1965	135.1	138.1	139.8	141.3	138.6
1966	140.0	140.7	146.2	141.5	142.1
1967	142.0	142.2	142.5	145.3	143.0
1968	145.5	148.0	152.3	155.1	150.2
1969	157.7	161.6	167.0	167.6	163.5
1970	170.5	175.4	181.7	184.5	178.0
1971	181.0	184.9	188.7	193.7	187.1
1972	195.0	196.5	198.6	201.1	197.8
1973	201.1	200.1	201.8	202.2	201.3
1974	200.5	202.6	208.0	208.8	205.0
1975	211.0	215.5	213.5	214.6	213.6
1976	213.8	214.2	218.6	220.0	216.6
1977	217.9	219.2	222.3	226.0	221.3
1978	225.9	227.2	232.8	233.1	229.7
1979	236.6	239.1	238.6	240.8	238.8
1980	241.6	242.7	244.3	243.7	243.1
1981	243.5	241.4	241.8	242.6	242.3
1982	240.3	235.0	233.5	233.3	235.5

18.1 MANUFACTURING SALES, VOLUME, WEST GERMANY (INDEX, 1980=100)

YEAR	JAN	FEB	MAR	APR	MAY	JUN	JUL	AUG	SEP	OCT	NOV	DEC	AVGE
1957	35.0	35.0	32.5	35.0	35.0	32.5	35.0	35.0	35.0	35.0	35.0	35.0	34.6
1958	34.2	34.2	34.2	34.2	34.2	34.2	36.6	34.2	34.2	36.6	34.2	35.0	34.7
1959	35.0	35.0	35.0	39.9	39.9	41.5	39.9	39.9	39.9	39.1	40.7	40.7	38.9
1960	39.1	43.1	43.1	43.1	43.1	43.1	43.1	45.6	45.6	42.3	44.7	47.2	43.6
1961	44.7	46.4	46.4	44.7	44.7	46.4	44.7	46.4	46.4	46.4	46.4	46.4	45.8
1962	50.1	49.4	48.8	47.2	48.9	50.2	50.3	50.9	50.2	50.3	50.4	48.9	49.6
1963	49.0	47.7	49.9	50.7	50.4	49.4	51.7	51.9	52.1	52.6	52.7	51.3	50.8
1964	53.6	54.7	54.6	54.3	54.1	55.0	56.9	55.6	55.9	56.4	57.8	56.8	55.5
1965	58.9	58.8	58.2	58.1	59.7	58.4	58.5	59.1	58.7	59.0	59.5	60.2	58.9
1966	61.4	60.4	62.1	60.6	61.2	61.0	60.3	60.2	60.0	58.4	57.9	58.9	60.2
1967	58.8	57.0	56.7	57.1	56.4	58.0	58.9	57.7	59.1	60.3	60.1	67.8	59.0
1968	58.9	60.0	62.6	63.7	65.4	65.0	65.6	69.7	68.3	69.7	72.7	70.8	66.0
1969	70.9	71.7	73.5	74.8	75.0	76.1	76.8	77.6	78.0	78.7	80.7	78.4	76.0
1970	78.3	80.4	80.8	81.2	80.0	80.7	82.7	81.4	82.4	81.8	83.1	83.2	81.3
1971	82.2	82.5	82.5	82.4	82.7	83.4	84.2	81.4	83.2	82.8	82.0	80.6	82.5
1972	83.7	82.3	84.1	83.6	84.6	84.3	83.2	85.7	84.9	86.9	87.2	89.9	85.0
1973	91.8	92.1	90.2	90.0	91.5	91.7	87.5	92.9	91.4	90.4	91.0	91.1	91.0
1974	91.5	92.1	90.8	91.4	91.5	87.7	91.2	88.7	87.5	87.9	86.9	84.0	89.3
1975	82.7	83.4	83.1	84.1	81.3	81.4	82.4	83.1	84.5	85.7	88.7	87.3	84.0
1976	87.5	88.3	88.0	90.2	90.9	91.0	86.1	91.2	90.7	90.7	91.4	97.9	90.3
1977	93.5	93.6	93.5	91.7	93.6	92.2	88.8	94.4	93.6	93.2	94.2	97.8	93.3
1978	99.1	93.6	92.8	92.7	92.2	96.2	91.8	96.3	99.6	97.3	96.4	96.6	95.4
1979	96.2	95.1	98.6	99.7	100.3	102.3	101.8	101.1	100.1	101.6	101.7	99.4	99.8
1980	104.0	103.6	101.7	101.9	101.5	97.5	99.1	97.7	98.4	98.8	97.6	95.2	99.7
1981	96.8	100.9	97.1	97.5	96.3	97.0	98.1	99.2	99.9	98.2	99.6	97.6	98.2
1982	96.3	97.8	98.0	97.3	96.8	96.4	95.9	96.4	93.1	90.1	93.6	94.5	95.5

244

18.2 RETAIL TRADE, VOLUME, WEST GERMANY (INDEX, 1980=100)

YEAR	JAN	FEB	MAR	APR	MAY	JUN	JUL	AUG	SEP	OCT	NOV	DEC	AVGE
1955	34.0	36.2	33.6	36.3	36.2	34.5	37.1	35.8	36.4	38.6	36.7	36.9	36.0
1956	38.0	38.6	40.3	36.0	38.4	40.3	38.7	40.5	40.2	40.0	41.2	41.4	39.5
1957	40.4	40.7	38.9	44.0	40.1	42.6	42.0	42.8	42.2	41.9	42.0	41.8	41.6
1958	42.7	42.5	42.4	42.4	42.8	41.7	43.3	43.1	42.4	43.0	42.5	43.2	42.7
1959	44.3	43.8	44.3	43.9	43.7	45.2	44.3	44.9	44.9	44.7	44.4	45.4	44.5
1960	45.9	45.3	44.3	48.7	47.7	47.8	48.0	47.9	48.5	50.2	49.3	49.0	47.7
1961	50.0	51.0	51.3	49.9	50.8	50.9	51.1	52.6	51.6	52.5	53.1	53.5	51.5
1962	50.0	50.8	49.2	53.1	50.0	53.1	50.8	52.3	52.3	52.3	53.1	53.9	51.7
1963	52.3	50.8	52.3	53.1	53.1	50.8	53.1	53.9	53.1	53.9	54.7	56.3	53.1
1964	55.5	55.5	57.0	54.7	56.3	56.3	56.3	56.3	56.3	59.4	59.4	60.9	57.0
1965	60.2	60.2	58.6	62.5	61.7	60.9	62.5	61.7	63.3	62.5	62.5	60.9	61.5
1966	63.3	64.8	64.1	63.3	64.8	63.3	64.8	64.1	64.1	63.3	63.3	61.7	63.7
1967	65.6	64.1	64.8	61.7	62.5	64.8	64.1	64.8	64.8	63.3	63.3	68.0	64.3
1968	62.5	64.1	64.8	67.2	65.6	66.4	65.6	68.8	68.0	68.0	69.5	69.5	66.7
1969	69.5	69.5	71.1	69.5	71.9	71.9	72.7	74.2	73.4	74.2	75.8	75.8	72.5
1970	73.0	75.0	77.0	76.0	77.0	79.0	80.0	78.0	79.0	80.0	82.0	81.0	78.1
1971	81.0	81.0	81.0	83.0	83.0	82.0	83.0	82.0	84.0	84.0	84.0	80.0	82.3
1972	85.0	85.0	89.0	81.0	86.0	86.0	86.0	90.0	87.0	87.0	86.0	88.0	86.3
1973	89.0	90.0	87.0	89.0	88.0	87.0	85.0	86.0	88.0	87.0	85.0	84.0	87.1
1974	86.0	85.0	85.0	86.0	86.0	84.0	86.0	86.0	86.0	88.0	85.0	84.0	85.6
1975	86.0	88.0	88.0	87.0	87.0	88.0	88.0	88.0	89.0	91.0	91.0	89.0	88.3
1976	90.0	92.0	89.0	91.0	91.0	90.0	91.0	91.0	93.0	90.0	94.0	92.0	91.2
1977	93.0	93.0	94.0	90.0	96.0	95.0	96.0	95.0	95.0	93.0	96.0	97.0	94.4
1978	97.0	96.0	97.0	96.0	95.0	98.0	97.0	98.0	99.0	98.0	97.0	99.0	97.3
1979	98.0	98.0	99.0	101.0	102.0	102.0	98.0	100.0	99.0	100.0	99.0	99.0	99.6
1980	105.0	101.0	100.0	98.0	98.0	98.0	101.0	99.0	100.0	101.0	100.0	98.0	99.9
1981	100.0	103.0	99.0	99.0	98.0	95.0	100.0	99.0	98.0	99.0	98.0	97.0	98.8
1982	98.0	97.0	98.0	96.0	94.0	93.0	92.0	94.0	93.0	93.0	94.0	94.0	94.7

LAGGING INDEX, WEST GERMANY (1970=100)

YEAR	JAN	FEB	MAR	APR	MAY	JUN	JUL	AUG	SEP	OCT	NOV	DEC	AVGE
1962	53.8	54.4	54.7	54.9	55.2	55.7	56.2	56.6	57.0	57.5	58.0	57.4	55.9
1963	56.6	55.9	57.6	59.4	61.1	61.7	62.2	62.8	63.1	63.6	64.0	64.3	61.0
1964	64.6	64.7	65.5	66.2	66.9	67.5	68.0	68.5	69.1	69.7	70.2	70.7	67.6
1965	71.1	71.7	71.7	73.4	72.6	73.9	74.3	74.2	75.0	75.3	75.6	76.4	73.8
1966	76.9	77.2	77.2	77.6	78.1	77.7	77.6	77.8	78.0	78.0	78.0	77.7	77.6
1967	77.3	77.1	77.1	76.5	76.6	76.6	76.6	77.0	77.6	77.7	78.4	77.7	77.2
1968	81.3	80.9	81.5	82.2	82.3	82.8	83.2	83.5	84.0	84.9	84.8	85.3	83.1
1969	85.0	85.5	86.3	87.3	88.3	89.2	90.4	91.5	91.8	92.5	93.2	93.9	89.6
1970	94.2	94.7	96.7	98.2	100.0	100.9	101.6	102.1	102.6	102.7	103.3	103.0	100.0
1971	102.2	102.4	102.4	102.4	102.5	102.9	103.0	103.7	103.8	104.0	104.3	105.1	103.2
1972	105.1	105.1	105.0	105.0	105.1	105.4	105.8	105.7	106.7	107.5	108.2	109.0	106.1
1973	110.3	111.1	111.7	112.3	112.6	113.5	114.1	114.7	115.0	115.8	116.2	115.6	113.6
1974	115.2	114.7	114.1	113.6	113.3	113.3	113.0	113.7	113.2	112.9	112.6	112.8	113.5
1975	112.3	111.9	111.0	110.7	110.4	109.6	109.8	108.6	108.1	108.2	108.7	108.3	109.8
1976	108.2	108.2	108.7	108.6	108.9	109.1	109.3	109.4	110.3	111.1	111.8	112.6	109.7
1977	112.5	113.1	113.0	113.6	113.6	113.8	114.0	114.4	114.5	115.2	115.5	115.5	114.1
1978	115.1	115.6	116.3	116.5	117.1	117.5	118.0	118.4	119.0	119.4	120.0	120.3	117.8
1979	120.9	120.6	121.6	123.9	125.1	126.2	127.9	129.4	130.5	131.4	133.4	134.4	127.1
1980	134.3	134.5	136.8	137.3	138.9	139.5	140.1	140.8	140.8	141.5	141.6	141.8	139.0
1981	140.9	140.7	144.3	145.5	***	***	***	***	***	***	***	***	***

SIX MONTH SMOOTHED CHANGE IN LAGGING INDEX, WEST GERMANY (ANNUAL RATE, PERCENT)

YEAR	JAN	FEB	MAR	APR	MAY	JUN	JUL	AUG	SEP	OCT	NOV	DEC	AVGE
1963	2.3	-1.0	4.3	9.7	14.1	14.3	14.1	14.4	13.6	13.4	13.0	12.2	10.4
1964	11.2	9.2	9.4	9.3	9.8	10.0	9.9	9.9	10.1	10.3	10.2	10.1	9.9
1965	9.8	9.7	7.9	11.2	7.2	9.7	9.0	7.4	8.1	7.5	7.2	7.9	8.5
1966	7.9	7.6	6.3	6.0	6.4	4.2	3.2	2.9	2.7	2.2	1.7	0.5	4.3
1967	-0.7	-1.4	-1.4	-2.8	-2.4	-1.9	-1.9	-0.7	1.0	1.2	3.1	1.2	-0.6
1968	10.0	8.2	9.0	9.6	8.6	8.8	8.3	7.7	7.4	8.3	6.6	6.6	8.3
1969	4.3	4.7	5.8	7.1	8.2	9.1	10.6	11.6	10.7	10.8	10.7	10.6	8.7
1970	9.7	9.2	11.6	12.8	14.6	14.2	13.6	12.5	11.8	10.1	9.4	7.2	11.4
1971	4.1	3.1	2.0	1.1	0.7	1.1	0.9	2.0	1.8	2.0	2.3	3.8	2.1
1972	3.4	2.9	2.3	2.0	1.8	2.0	2.3	1.6	3.2	4.1	4.8	5.7	3.0
1973	7.4	7.9	8.1	8.2	7.6	7.9	7.9	7.7	6.8	6.9	6.3	4.3	7.2
1974	2.6	1.1	-0.3	-1.4	-2.1	-2.1	-2.6	-1.3	-2.1	-2.2	-2.4	-1.6	-1.2
1975	-1.9	-2.3	-3.4	-3.4	-3.6	-4.4	-3.6	-5.1	-5.2	-4.4	-3.0	-3.2	-3.6
1976	-2.7	-2.2	-0.7	-0.7	0.2	0.7	1.2	1.4	2.9	3.9	4.6	5.6	1.2
1977	4.8	5.3	4.4	4.7	4.0	3.7	3.3	3.3	2.8	3.3	3.3	2.8	3.8
1978	1.6	2.1	2.9	2.8	3.4	3.6	3.9	4.0	4.3	4.5	4.8	4.6	3.5
1979	4.9	3.8	4.6	7.6	8.5	9.1	10.6	11.7	11.7	11.6	13.1	12.8	9.2
1980	10.7	9.3	10.8	9.7	10.2	9.4	8.6	8.1	6.6	6.4	5.3	4.6	8.3
1981	2.5	1.6	5.6	6.4	***	***	***	***	***	***	***	***	***

247

20.0 INVESTMENT EXPENDITURE, PLANT AND EQUIPMENT, IN CONSTANT PRICES, WEST GERMANY (BILLION 1970 DM)

YEAR	IQ	IIQ	IIIQ	IVQ	AVGE
1962	29.3	29.0	29.3	29.6	29.3
1963	25.3	30.9	31.9	32.0	30.0
1964	32.1	33.6	33.9	34.6	33.6
1965	34.3	35.4	35.4	35.4	35.1
1966	37.0	36.3	34.5	34.1	35.5
1967	32.6	31.4	31.9	34.0	32.5
1968	33.6	35.1	35.7	37.5	35.5
1969	36.9	38.7	40.6	40.5	39.2
1970	39.2	43.5	45.1	45.8	43.4
1971	45.8	46.4	46.2	46.5	46.2
1972	48.2	47.7	47.1	48.3	47.8
1973	50.4	48.5	46.9	46.0	47.9
1974	45.6	43.2	42.8	41.2	43.2
1975	41.1	40.8	41.1	42.3	41.3
1976	42.4	43.5	43.0	44.2	43.3
1977	45.0	44.8	44.5	45.6	45.0
1978	45.2	47.3	48.0	48.6	47.3
1979	47.2	51.8	52.6	53.5	51.3
1980	53.7	52.8	53.1	53.1	53.2
1981	51.0	***	***	***	***

21.0 BUSINESS INVENTORIES, IN CONSTANT PRICES, WEST GERMANY
(TEN MILLION 1976 DM)

YEAR	IQ	IIQ	IIIQ	IVQ	AVGE
1955	213.	306.	630.	901.	513.
1956	1074.	1318.	1382.	1506.	1320.
1957	1736.	1956.	2176.	2424.	2073.
1958	2688.	2818.	2958.	3122.	2897.
1959	2809.	3080.	3423.	3861.	3293.
1960	3851.	4178.	4728.	5068.	4456.
1961	5243.	5614.	5707.	6010.	5644.
1962	6311.	6438.	6571.	6758.	6520.
1963	6960.	7015.	7160.	7243.	7095.
1964	7320.	7566.	7947.	8373.	7802.
1965	8791.	8986.	9091.	9045.	8978.
1966	9283.	9406.	9446.	9418.	9388.
1967	9269.	9188.	9076.	9190.	9181.
1968	9280.	9710.	10316.	10603.	9977.
1969	11110.	11503.	12043.	12970.	11907.
1970	13628.	14370.	14765.	14827.	14398.
1971	15072.	15007.	15146.	15312.	15134.
1972	15221.	15600.	15737.	15707.	15566.
1973	16140.	16248.	16523.	17220.	16533.
1974	17353.	17609.	17889.	17634.	17621.
1975	17532.	17286.	16917.	16944.	17170.
1976	17106.	17379.	17669.	18087.	17560.
1977	18413.	18557.	18868.	18884.	18681.
1978	18892.	19112.	19198.	19502.	19176.
1979	19931.	20321.	21006.	21647.	20726.
1980	22047.	22480.	22747.	23108.	22596.
1981	23448.	23378.	23180.	23054.	23265.
1982	23141.	23447.	23694.	23601.	23471.

22.1 CHANGE IN HOURS PER UNIT OF OUTPUT, MINING AND MANUFACTURING, WEST GERMANY
(PERCENT CHANGE FROM YEAR AGO)

YEAR	JAN	FEB	MAR	APR	MAY	JUN	JUL	AUG	SEP	OCT	NOV	DEC	AVGE
1965	-3.6	-7.0	-3.5	-3.5	-3.5	-1.8	-1.8	-3.4	-5.1	-3.4	-1.7	-3.4	-3.5
1966	-3.4	-1.7	-1.7	-1.7	-1.7	-1.7	-1.7	-1.7	0.0	-4.9	-3.3	-4.9	-2.4
1967	-6.5	-6.5	-6.5	-9.4	-7.9	-12.1	-7.9	-9.2	-9.2	-7.6	-10.4	-9.0	-8.5
1968	-8.8	-8.8	-8.8	-5.9	-10.0	-5.7	-10.0	-7.1	-8.5	-7.0	-5.6	-6.9	-7.8
1969	-5.6	-5.6	-6.8	-5.6	-5.4	-5.4	-5.4	-5.4	-2.7	-4.1	-4.1	-2.7	-4.9
1970	-2.7	-2.7	-1.4	-2.7	0.0	-1.3	-3.9	-3.9	-3.9	-3.9	-3.9	-3.9	-2.8
1971	-5.1	-3.9	-5.1	-6.3	-6.3	-2.6	-3.7	-3.7	-6.2	-6.1	-6.1	-6.1	-5.1
1972	-4.9	-7.2	-4.9	-6.0	-7.1	-9.4	-7.0	-8.0	-6.9	-5.7	-6.8	-5.7	-6.6
1973	-5.7	-5.7	-6.8	-4.5	-3.4	-4.5	-3.4	-3.7	-2.2	-3.3	-2.2	-3.3	-3.9
1974	-5.4	-1.1	-2.2	-1.1	-1.1	1.1	1.1	-2.2	-1.1	0.0	0.0	-1.1	-0.9
1975	1.1	-2.2	-3.2	-5.3	-6.3	-9.3	-9.3	-10.1	-8.2	-9.1	-10.0	-9.0	-6.7
1976	-9.0	-9.9	-7.9	-6.9	-5.9	-4.0	-4.9	-3.9	-5.8	-2.9	-2.9	-3.8	-5.6
1977	-3.8	-2.9	-3.8	-2.9	-3.8	-4.7	-3.8	-1.0	0.0	-2.9	-1.9	-1.9	-2.8
1978	-2.8	-3.7	-3.7	-4.6	-3.7	-3.6	-0.9	-3.7	-5.5	-5.4	-6.3	-6.2	-4.2
1979	-6.1	-5.3	-3.5	-4.4	-4.4	-3.5	-5.3	-6.1	-3.5	-2.6	-0.9	0.0	-3.8
1980	0.9	1.8	0.9	1.8	1.8	2.7	0.0	-1.7	-1.7	-0.9	-2.6	***	***

23.1 BANK LOANS OUTSTANDING, IN CONSTANT PRICES, WEST GERMANY (BILLION 1975 DM)

YEAR	JAN	FEB	MAR	APR	MAY	JUN	JUL	AUG	SEP	OCT	NOV	DEC	AVGE
1960	158.9	160.0	163.1	164.8	166.9	168.3	169.8	170.9	173.3	174.8	176.1	177.9	168.7
1961	179.8	182.8	184.9	187.5	190.1	193.2	195.3	197.6	199.6	200.9	203.5	205.6	193.4
1962	207.1	209.1	211.7	213.0	215.6	217.9	220.6	222.9	224.5	227.4	229.6	232.2	219.3
1963	233.6	236.5	238.6	241.4	244.0	246.7	249.1	251.6	253.1	256.1	258.6	260.1	247.4
1964	261.3	260.8	265.1	267.7	270.4	273.4	275.7	278.3	280.0	282.5	283.9	286.4	273.8
1965	288.6	290.9	292.4	294.0	296.8	299.7	303.8	306.7	310.0	312.6	315.0	316.2	302.2
1966	316.8	317.7	321.4	323.4	326.4	329.3	332.1	335.7	339.2	340.6	341.1	341.0	330.4
1967	340.2	341.9	341.6	346.1	348.4	350.3	352.7	356.4	359.8	362.4	364.2	365.3	352.4
1968	411.7	414.4	422.1	428.8	435.4	439.4	444.4	449.5	453.2	458.8	460.5	461.4	440.4
1969	468.0	473.1	478.6	481.8	484.8	490.4	495.4	500.3	502.3	505.4	511.7	517.0	492.4
1970	515.0	518.3	519.0	523.9	530.0	536.5	542.4	545.0	548.3	550.1	551.3	553.0	536.1
1971	549.3	551.4	554.0	557.7	562.9	570.0	576.6	586.1	593.0	602.1	609.4	615.4	577.3
1972	616.2	615.2	627.9	635.8	644.8	652.3	657.6	663.1	666.0	673.5	682.2	689.3	652.0
1973	689.9	692.9	695.0	697.6	700.2	701.7	699.6	704.8	708.0	708.8	703.9	697.7	700.1
1974	686.5	672.1	665.1	664.1	661.7	665.8	666.7	667.7	669.0	667.3	669.2	671.2	668.9
1975	666.6	667.8	672.0	670.2	674.3	676.0	676.8	678.9	679.7	685.2	692.4	693.2	677.8
1976	694.0	693.4	692.8	693.5	695.2	698.7	700.6	705.4	708.4	717.0	722.4	725.9	703.9
1977	725.2	726.7	729.3	734.0	736.4	742.7	748.2	754.2	759.9	767.3	772.1	778.0	747.8
1978	777.7	784.0	788.2	793.1	797.6	803.7	811.2	817.1	825.3	831.5	835.8	843.4	809.0
1979	846.6	849.8	850.1	852.4	856.3	861.8	860.4	868.8	872.5	875.4	878.5	883.9	863.0
1980	877.8	877.4	879.7	880.5	883.7	888.3	892.1	899.0	902.5	908.3	908.7	914.3	892.7
1981	920.7	924.6	920.2	915.7	***	***	***	***	***	***	***	***	***

24.1 BANK RATES ON LARGE LOANS. WEST GERMANY (PERCENT PER ANNUM)

YEAR	JAN	FEB	MAR	APR	MAY	JUN	JUL	AUG	SEP	OCT	NOV	DEC	AVGE
1968	***	***	7.1	***	***	7.1	***	***	7.1	***	7.1	***	7.1
1969	***	7.1	***	***	7.6	***	***	8.5	***	***	9.2	***	8.1
1970	***	9.7	***	***	11.1	***	***	11.0	***	***	10.9	***	10.6
1971	10.3	10.2	***	***	9.4	***	***	9.4	***	***	9.1	***	9.5
1972	***	8.6	***	***	7.9	***	***	8.0	***	***	8.6	***	8.3
1973	***	9.6	***	***	10.9	***	12.3	12.8	***	***	13.6	***	11.7
1974	***	13.2	***	***	12.8	***	***	12.4	***	***	12.0	***	12.6
1975	**	10.8	10.1	9.8	9.5	8.9	8.8	8.2	7.7	7.6	7.7	7.7	9.0
1976	7.5	7.6	7.4	7.2	7.2	7.2	7.2	7.2	7.2	7.2	7.2	7.2	7.3
1977	7.1	7.1	7.1	7.0	6.9	6.9	6.8	6.8	6.6	6.6	6.6	6.6	6.8
1978	6.3	6.2	6.2	6.2	6.1	6.1	6.1	6.2	6.2	6.2	6.1	6.2	6.2
1979	6.2	6.3	6.3	6.9	7.0	7.2	7.9	8.2	8.3	8.5	9.4	9.6	7.6
1980	9.7	9.7	10.8	10.8	11.5	11.5	11.5	11.6	11.5	11.5	11.5	11.5	11.1
1981	11.5	11.7	13.5	14.1	14.4	14.6	***	***	***	***	***	***	***

252

FRANCE

LEADING INDEX, FRANCE (1980=100)

YEAR	JAN	FEB	MAR	APR	MAY	JUN	JUL	AUG	SEP	OCT	NOV	DEC	AVGE
1955	26.7	26.9	27.3	27.4	27.3	27.5	27.9	28.2	28.4	28.5	28.5	28.7	27.8
1956	28.6	28.6	28.8	29.1	29.2	29.6	30.0	30.1	30.1	30.3	30.3	30.6	29.6
1957	30.7	31.0	31.5	31.5	31.8	31.9	32.3	32.6	32.8	32.7	33.0	33.3	32.1
1958	33.5	33.0	32.8	32.5	32.6	32.8	32.8	32.8	33.0	33.0	33.0	33.6	32.9
1959	34.7	35.2	35.4	36.2	36.6	36.6	36.6	36.8	37.2	37.6	37.8	38.0	36.6
1960	38.0	38.3	38.6	39.0	39.2	39.3	39.8	40.0	40.1	40.1	40.5	40.6	39.5
1961	41.1	41.6	41.9	42.2	42.6	42.6	42.8	42.6	42.8	42.9	43.2	43.8	42.5
1962	43.5	44.0	44.5	44.6	43.7	43.1	42.7	43.5	44.4	45.0	45.3	45.4	44.1
1963	45.4	45.2	45.8	46.2	46.8	47.3	47.8	48.3	48.5	48.5	48.4	48.6	47.2
1964	49.1	49.0	49.2	49.5	49.5	49.4	49.7	49.5	49.5	50.0	49.6	49.4	49.4
1965	49.1	49.2	49.2	49.2	49.8	49.9	50.1	50.7	51.1	51.5	52.1	52.6	50.4
1966	53.3	53.1	53.1	53.7	53.8	54.4	54.5	54.4	54.2	54.2	54.5	54.2	53.9
1967	54.5	54.8	54.6	54.4	53.9	54.4	54.6	55.0	55.5	56.0	56.3	56.3	55.1
1968	56.8	57.5	56.8	55.5	53.9	55.4	56.4	58.2	58.9	59.7	60.7	61.7	57.6
1969	62.1	62.7	63.5	64.0	64.7	64.4	64.8	64.8	65.2	65.3	65.5	66.1	64.4
1970	66.4	66.9	67.0	67.1	66.7	66.3	65.8	66.0	66.1	65.5	65.7	66.8	66.4
1971	67.0	67.4	68.1	68.3	68.6	68.8	68.9	69.1	69.0	69.4	70.0	70.2	68.7
1972	70.7	70.9	71.3	72.0	72.4	72.0	72.4	72.9	73.6	74.6	75.1	75.3	72.8
1973	76.2	76.9	77.9	78.3	78.0	78.5	79.4	79.8	79.8	80.2	80.9	81.3	78.9
1974	82.8	83.8	84.8	85.4	85.3	83.8	83.3	81.2	79.7	78.5	77.3	75.8	81.8
1975	74.9	74.8	74.6	74.7	74.7	74.9	75.2	75.7	76.1	76.7	78.4	79.4	75.8
1976	80.1	81.2	82.4	82.9	83.4	84.0	84.6	84.8	84.8	83.9	83.5	84.6	83.3
1977	85.0	84.9	85.4	84.4	83.8	83.5	82.9	82.9	83.9	83.8	83.8	84.2	84.0
1978	84.3	85.1	86.2	87.5	88.0	88.1	88.2	88.6	90.0	90.9	91.7	91.5	88.3
1979	92.3	93.1	93.6	94.8	95.0	96.1	97.3	98.3	98.6	98.3	98.7	98.4	96.2
1980	99.7	100.4	99.6	99.6	98.6	99.6	99.9	99.8	100.3	101.1	100.8	100.6	100.0
1981	101.3	102.0	102.1	102.6	102.3	102.5	102.9	103.9	104.0	104.2	105.1	105.3	103.2
1982	105.5	106.1	104.9	105.8	107.0	105.7	105.8	106.0	106.0	106.7	107.4	107.8	106.2

SIX MONTH SMOOTHED CHANGE IN LEADING INDEX, FRANCE (ANNUAL RATE, PERCENT)

YEAR	JAN	FEB	MAR	APR	MAY	JUN	JUL	AUG	SEP	OCT	NOV	DEC	AVGE
1956	5.5	4.8	5.2	5.8	5.8	7.5	8.8	8.1	7.3	7.2	6.2	7.3	6.6
1957	6.6	7.9	9.2	8.0	8.4	7.7	9.1	9.8	9.4	7.5	8.0	8.5	8.3
1958	8.3	4.2	1.7	-0.3	-0.4	0.1	-0.4	-0.1	0.9	0.8	0.4	3.7	1.6
1959	9.8	12.4	12.5	15.7	16.2	13.7	12.0	11.4	11.8	11.5	10.8	9.6	12.3
1960	7.2	7.2	7.5	8.2	8.1	7.7	8.7	8.5	7.3	6.2	7.2	6.5	7.5
1961	7.9	8.8	9.2	9.2	9.4	8.4	7.8	5.8	5.8	4.9	5.1	7.0	7.4
1962	4.4	5.5	6.9	6.2	1.4	-1.4	-3.1	0.4	4.0	5.6	6.5	5.8	3.5
1963	5.3	4.0	6.0	7.1	9.1	9.9	10.6	10.9	10.1	8.5	6.9	6.6	7.9
1964	7.4	5.7	5.1	5.1	4.0	2.8	3.4	2.0	1.7	3.0	1.1	0.1	3.4
1965	-1.1	-1.0	-1.1	-0.9	1.3	1.6	2.1	4.3	5.4	6.7	8.2	9.5	2.9
1966	11.0	9.0	7.5	8.6	7.4	8.5	7.4	5.4	3.9	2.9	3.1	1.3	6.3
1967	2.0	2.5	1.3	0.2	0.8	0.0	0.6	2.0	4.2	4.8	5.0	4.5	2.3
1968	5.6	7.4	4.3	-0.6	-6.1	-1.2	1.9	7.5	9.0	10.6	13.0	15.0	5.5
1969	14.8	15.3	16.4	15.9	15.7	11.8	10.3	8.2	7.7	6.4	5.5	5.9	11.2
1970	5.8	6.2	5.3	4.9	2.8	1.2	-0.6	-0.2	-0.3	-2.2	-1.6	1.4	1.9
1971	1.8	2.9	4.7	4.8	5.4	5.5	5.2	5.2	4.2	4.4	5.1	4.8	4.5
1972	5.3	4.9	5.3	6.4	6.8	4.7	5.2	5.5	6.7	8.3	8.3	7.8	6.3
1973	9.0	9.4	10.6	10.3	8.1	8.1	8.9	8.5	6.9	6.6	7.1	6.8	8.4
1974	9.3	10.2	11.2	11.0	9.4	4.4	2.3	-3.0	-6.6	-9.2	-11.4	-14.1	-1.1
1975	-15.0	-14.0	-13.0	-10.9	-9.2	-6.8	-4.4	-1.7	0.4	2.8	7.4	9.6	-4.6
1976	10.6	12.4	14.0	13.5	12.9	12.2	11.8	10.3	8.4	4.6	2.3	3.8	9.7
1977	3.6	2.6	2.8	0.2	-1.4	-2.2	-3.4	-3.1	-0.5	-0.5	-0.5	0.4	-0.2
1978	0.6	2.4	4.8	7.8	8.2	7.7	6.9	6.7	8.9	9.8	10.1	8.1	6.8
1979	8.5	8.8	8.3	9.3	8.4	9.5	10.6	11.0	9.8	7.7	7.1	5.4	8.7
1980	6.8	6.9	4.1	3.1	0.5	1.9	1.9	1.3	1.9	3.1	2.2	1.4	2.9
1981	2.4	3.5	3.5	3.9	3.0	2.6	2.9	4.4	4.0	3.8	4.9	4.5	3.6
1982	4.2	4.5	1.8	3.0	4.6	1.7	1.3	1.3	1.0	1.9	2.9	3.2	2.6

FRANCE LEADING, COINCIDENT AND LAGGING INTERNATIONAL ECONOMIC INDICATORS

1.0 AVERAGE WORKWEEK, INDUSTRY, FRANCE (HOURS PER WEEK)

YEAR	JAN	APR	JUL	OCT	AVGE
1960	45.5	45.7	45.8	45.8	45.7
1961	45.6	46.0	46.2	46.0	46.0
1962	46.2	46.3	44.9	46.2	45.9
1963	46.3	46.3	46.3	46.4	46.3
1964	46.4	46.2	46.2	45.9	46.2
1965	45.5	45.1	45.6	45.8	45.5
1966	46.0	45.7	46.1	45.9	45.9
1967	45.8	45.6	45.3	45.3	45.4
1968	45.0	45.4	45.2	45.5	45.3
1969	45.5	45.6	45.5	45.2	45.4
1970	45.1	45.0	44.7	44.6	44.8
1971	44.6	44.7	44.4	44.4	44.5
1972	44.3	44.2	43.9	43.9	44.0
1973	43.8	43.9	43.6	43.4	43.6
1974	43.1	43.3	42.9	42.7	42.9
1975	42.0	41.9	41.7	41.4	41.7
1976	41.5	41.9	41.7	41.5	41.6
1977	41.4	41.5	41.3	41.1	41.3
1978	40.9	41.2	41.0	40.8	41.0
1979	40.8	41.0	40.7	40.7	40.8
1980	40.6	40.5	40.5	40.4	40.5
1981	40.3	40.3	40.3	40.2	40.3
1982	40.1	39.3	39.2	39.1	39.3

2.0 NEW UNEMPLOYMENT CLAIMS, FRANCE (THOUSANDS)

YEAR	JAN	FEB	MAR	APR	MAY	JUN	JUL	AUG	SEP	OCT	NOV	DEC	AVGE
1975	219.5	223.3	229.5	228.7	215.7	214.8	208.6	204.9	222.8	213.2	211.1	212.2	217.0
1976	213.0	210.5	201.2	208.2	208.2	214.9	212.8	218.3	223.3	227.2	232.0	217.8	215.6
1977	225.8	230.3	225.1	236.1	232.9	243.8	250.5	249.4	230.4	231.9	234.0	227.5	234.8
1978	225.2	233.7	244.0	242.3	248.2	249.6	264.3	256.1	250.2	244.8	236.6	254.7	245.8
1979	253.9	248.3	255.2	257.5	275.7	261.6	252.6	256.6	259.6	253.1	249.3	256.6	256.7
1980	262.6	255.1	276.0	262.9	284.4	264.0	266.0	274.0	264.4	245.6	276.9	280.1	267.7
1981	279.2	283.2	293.5	280.6	287.4	295.6	299.5	292.3	287.0	295.9	296.8	285.5	289.7
1982	297.9	290.5	294.0	303.4	297.2	315.7	303.9	296.8	305.0	301.0	304.6	303.1	301.1

256

3.1 CHANGE IN UNFILLED ORDERS, TOTAL, FRANCE (PERCENT)

YEAR	JAN	FEB	MAR	APR	MAY	JUN	JUL	AUG	SEP	OCT	NOV	DEC	AVGE
1968	6.	7.	9.	11.	9.	9.	5.	6.	11.	8.	12.	13.	9.
1969	7.	9.	6.	3.	2.	7.	11.	-1.	-7.	-7.	-6.	-1.	2.
1970	-6.	-7.	-4.	-5.	-7.	-10.	-12.	-8.	-3.	-10.	-11.	-3.	-7.
1971	7.	5.	-4.	-2.	4.	0.	0.	3.	-3.	-2.	-3.	-1.	0.
1972	3.	1.	1.	4.	4.	1.	4.	7.	5.	3.	1.	5.	3.
1973	4.	3.	8.	9.	3.	4.	7.	0.	-4.	-2.	5.	1.	3.
1974	-4.	1.	1.	-5.	-4.	-2.	-6.	-8.	-14.	-22.	-20.	-19.	-9.
1975	-21.	-14.	-11.	-14.	-8.	-3.	-7.	-6.	1.	6.	19.	20.	-3.
1976	11.	13.	9.	6.	12.	10.	1.	-1.	3.	-5.	-11.	1.	4.
1977	3.	-4.	1.	-2.	-16.	-10.	-5.	-7.	0.	2.	-3.	-2.	-4.
1978	0.	4.	5.	6.	7.	3.	2.	-3.	3.	9.	7.	4.	4.
1979	8.	3.	-2.	4.	7.	3.	4.	2.	-3.	3.	3.	3.	3.
1980	1.	-6.	5.	-3.	-14.	-6.	-8.	-11.	-11.	-11.	-5.	-12.	-7.
1981	-7.	1.	-6.	-4.	-3.	-3.	2.	10.	11.	3.	8.	9.	2.
1982	-2.	3.	-4.	5.	3.	-4.	-2.	-3.	-6.	2.	8.	1.	0.

257

6.0 BUILDING PERMITS, RESIDENTIAL, FRANCE (THOUSANDS)

YEAR	JAN	FEB	MAR	APR	MAY	JUN	JUL	AUG	SEP	OCT	NOV	DEC	AVGE
1955	21.5	22.4	22.6	23.5	23.2	22.3	23.4	24.8	24.9	28.3	27.4	28.1	24.4
1956	29.3	33.5	28.1	28.7	28.1	30.0	29.7	31.7	29.2	28.8	30.0	26.7	29.5
1957	27.4	29.3	29.8	28.9	27.8	26.6	28.7	28.0	31.9	25.8	22.2	29.9	28.0
1958	33.0	25.7	26.3	25.1	28.2	31.3	28.2	27.3	29.6	32.6	29.6	29.0	28.8
1959	29.6	31.7	28.1	34.0	28.9	30.4	25.5	25.7	27.6	27.1	26.7	28.4	28.6
1960	28.1	26.1	33.9	31.9	32.5	26.6	33.6	32.2	30.6	27.6	32.9	28.4	30.4
1961	36.8	32.7	29.3	30.5	31.8	30.7	30.1	24.3	28.1	30.3	27.6	41.1	31.1
1962	29.4	31.7	36.9	34.4	33.9	33.5	36.4	38.7	39.0	36.1	38.2	37.0	35.4
1963	39.4	40.3	38.9	36.7	39.1	44.4	46.1	49.5	54.6	49.2	43.7	41.7	43.6
1964	45.6	44.6	44.4	49.2	44.6	45.5	46.0	38.3	44.8	65.1	45.2	52.7	47.2
1965	47.0	52.0	46.7	46.2	49.7	47.3	40.0	49.0	50.3	51.2	54.7	57.4	49.3
1966	50.9	43.0	42.9	53.1	40.2	45.8	42.7	43.1	39.3	41.2	40.8	33.3	43.0
1967	38.5	43.8	40.6	43.0	45.4	37.3	40.8	37.6	39.0	35.9	36.6	32.8	39.3
1968	41.4	36.0	43.9	40.6	38.8	42.6	44.2	51.2	42.8	51.3	55.8	59.1	45.6
1969	48.3	44.7	46.1	45.7	48.8	47.5	54.3	49.6	60.5	49.7	43.3	46.4	48.7
1970	43.9	52.9	49.5	51.6	46.8	51.9	43.0	47.6	51.6	38.0	42.6	65.7	48.8
1971	46.3	53.2	67.1	52.7	53.5	59.2	53.4	52.6	50.9	52.0	58.9	61.0	55.1
1972	57.4	48.8	47.9	51.5	55.7	50.6	53.2	48.9	51.0	59.0	63.8	53.6	53.4
1973	57.0	59.5	57.5	54.0	51.0	50.0	56.5	61.0	60.0	57.5	57.0	58.5	56.6
1974	56.6	56.6	58.0	43.2	58.4	58.5	71.4	46.4	50.8	47.2	48.7	44.0	53.3
1975	35.3	54.1	42.4	44.8	47.3	44.9	41.4	51.0	45.7	45.1	47.2	44.5	45.3
1976	52.9	43.2	51.4	55.8	48.1	44.7	48.6	46.7	46.1	45.1	40.8	47.4	48.0
1977	45.4	43.3	50.5	40.3	42.4	40.6	36.8	42.5	42.5	41.1	39.0	40.7	42.1
1978	40.1	40.2	36.5	44.2	36.3	38.8	36.9	38.0	37.6	43.5	40.6	38.3	39.2
1979	35.5	39.8	38.0	37.6	40.6	39.2	42.6	35.1	39.1	36.3	44.4	36.6	38.7
1980	38.6	40.8	42.0	42.0	39.1	42.1	42.5	40.0	42.7	43.0	43.8	43.7	41.7
1981	46.1	40.5	44.3	42.7	42.2	40.6	39.1	43.1	38.2	41.4	38.8	34.2	40.9
1982	36.6	43.2	37.0	29.7	30.8	34.6	29.7	34.8	38.7	35.3	33.9	39.9	35.3

7.0 CHANGE IN STOCKS, FRANCE
(BILLION 1970 FRANCS)

YEAR	IQ	IIQ	IIIQ	IVQ	AVGE
1963	-0.2	1.5	2.9	2.9	1.8
1964	2.8	4.1	3.7	2.6	3.3
1965	2.0	2.1	2.1	2.4	2.1
1966	3.0	2.7	3.7	3.4	3.2
1967	3.4	2.7	2.5	2.5	2.8
1968	5.7	-1.7	4.1	4.4	3.1
1969	5.2	5.7	4.6	5.0	5.1
1970	5.4	5.5	5.7	4.5	5.3
1971	3.0	3.2	3.2	3.6	3.3
1972	4.5	3.9	3.8	5.3	4.4
1973	4.6	4.9	7.0	5.6	5.5
1974	5.5	7.3	6.6	3.5	5.7
1975	-0.1	-1.2	-1.9	0.3	-0.7
1976	2.5	1.5	4.7	4.0	3.2
1977	5.3	3.2	0.4	1.4	2.6
1978	1.7	1.9	2.1	3.2	2.2
1979	2.8	3.2	7.1	4.8	4.5
1980	6.7	5.9	6.6	3.1	5.6
1981	1.2	-2.3	-1.5	2.6	0.0
1982	3.0	6.7	2.7	2.1	3.6

8.0 RAW MATERIALS PRICE INDEX, SIX MONTH SMOOTHED CHANGE, FRANCE
(ANNUAL RATE, PERCENT)

YEAR	JAN	FEB	MAR	APR	MAY	JUN	JUL	AUG	SEP	OCT	NOV	DEC	AVGE
1955	-1.3	-0.7	0.7	0.7	0.7	2.1	7.6	8.3	6.2	5.5	6.8	7.5	3.7
1956	6.1	5.4	6.7	5.3	2.0	3.9	3.9	0.0	0.0	1.3	4.5	6.5	3.8
1957	4.5	4.5	5.1	4.5	4.4	1.9	1.9	3.8	3.1	6.9	10.7	9.4	5.1
1958	8.1	5.5	4.3	0.6	-0.6	0.6	0.0	-1.2	-2.4	-4.7	-4.1	0.0	0.5
1959	8.5	9.1	11.0	12.2	15.2	10.8	10.1	9.4	11.1	9.2	6.8	5.6	9.9
1960	7.9	6.7	3.8	3.8	2.7	0.0	-1.6	-3.2	-2.1	-1.6	0.0	1.6	1.5
1961	1.1	2.7	4.3	4.3	6.0	5.4	4.8	4.8	4.3	3.2	1.6	2.1	3.7
1962	0.5	0.0	-0.5	0.5	0.5	-0.5	-1.6	-2.1	-2.6	-2.6	-1.6	0.0	-0.8
1963	2.1	3.2	3.7	2.6	3.1	4.7	4.7	4.7	4.7	4.1	5.7	6.2	4.1
1964	7.7	9.2	9.2	9.1	8.6	7.5	6.9	7.9	7.3	7.8	6.8	2.9	7.6
1965	0.0	1.4	1.4	1.4	0.9	-0.5	-0.9	-1.4	-0.5	0.0	0.5	0.9	0.2
1966	4.2	3.8	2.3	10.0	10.9	9.9	6.0	-0.5	-0.5	-0.5	-1.3	-1.8	3.5
1967	-0.9	-2.7	-4.4	-6.6	-4.5	-5.4	-4.5	-3.2	-1.8	-0.3	2.3	0.0	-2.6
1968	-4.6	-0.5	-2.8	-7.3	-5.5	-3.7	-4.2	-2.8	-1.4	0.3	3.3	9.7	-1.8
1969	11.7	11.1	12.6	14.9	15.3	14.1	14.0	22.6	25.1	23.3	23.3	21.1	17.4
1970	20.7	20.0	18.8	17.2	11.6	5.0	1.5	-1.5	-4.1	-8.1	-7.7	-7.0	5.5
1971	-5.2	-5.6	-1.5	-0.4	-3.0	-1.5	-0.8	-1.2	-2.7	-0.8	-1.2	-1.2	-2.1
1972	-1.2	0.0	1.6	2.3	0.8	0.8	1.6	2.7	4.7	8.7	8.2	13.8	3.8
1973	19.4	25.0	25.8	26.3	21.1	23.9	29.7	33.4	29.9	34.0	45.4	42.2	29.7
1974	61.0	57.3	62.6	64.2	44.9	30.5	21.1	11.6	3.6	-3.7	-9.8	-16.8	27.2
1975	-19.5	-25.5	-23.9	-24.3	-26.1	-24.5	-17.4	-12.2	-10.2	-13.4	-6.6	-2.4	-17.2
1976	-1.4	4.8	9.9	16.0	21.0	22.9	29.1	29.5	25.2	21.2	19.7	14.3	17.9
1977	15.1	14.9	14.6	11.7	7.7	0.7	-1.4	-2.0	-0.9	-4.5	-2.9	-2.7	4.2
1978	-3.6	-2.2	-1.6	-0.5	4.1	2.8	3.2	6.0	7.9	9.5	10.6	8.7	3.7
1979	10.9	16.0	17.4	17.3	16.1	14.8	13.3	13.4	12.8	8.6	7.9	5.2	12.8
1980	11.7	11.0	7.9	6.6	2.7	1.7	1.5	0.4	4.6	6.1	7.4	5.2	5.7
1981	11.6	11.9	13.0	14.6	18.5	22.6	17.3	16.7	8.9	7.0	1.7	1.0	12.1
1982	2.2	2.7	3.5	4.3	4.1	4.9	10.3	9.5	9.0	7.3	6.8	4.9	5.8

9.0 INDEX OF STOCK PRICES (INDUSTRIALS), FRANCE (1980=100)

YEAR	JAN	FEB	MAR	APR	MAY	JUN	JUL	AUG	SEP	OCT	NOV	DEC	AVGE
1948	12.5	11.8	11.8	11.8	11.2	10.5	11.8	11.8	13.1	13.8	12.5	12.5	12.1
1949	12.5	11.2	10.5	11.2	10.5	10.5	11.2	11.2	11.2	11.2	10.5	11.2	11.1
1950	10.4	9.9	10.4	9.9	9.9	10.4	9.5	10.4	10.9	10.4	10.4	9.5	10.2
1951	10.4	11.8	11.8	11.8	11.8	12.3	12.3	13.7	14.7	14.7	14.2	14.7	12.8
1952	16.6	17.5	16.6	16.6	15.6	17.1	17.1	17.1	16.6	16.6	16.1	16.6	16.7
1953	17.5	17.5	17.1	17.1	17.1	17.5	18.0	18.0	18.5	18.5	18.5	18.5	17.8
1954	19.9	19.4	20.4	21.3	22.7	22.3	24.2	26.5	27.9	28.9	32.2	34.6	25.0
1955	35.1	35.1	39.1	39.6	34.8	35.3	36.7	36.7	38.9	36.7	35.0	35.8	36.6
1956	34.7	33.9	35.9	37.4	37.8	39.6	43.2	41.8	41.7	41.6	36.7	40.2	38.7
1957	40.2	43.5	48.3	49.4	53.7	55.9	60.6	60.7	57.1	52.7	53.6	51.2	52.2
1958	51.3	45.9	42.8	43.4	43.8	41.6	41.1	41.7	43.4	42.5	42.1	42.1	43.5
1959	46.5	46.7	46.7	49.7	53.4	52.7	54.1	57.7	57.6	62.0	65.4	65.6	54.8
1960	59.3	61.9	60.5	64.2	65.5	68.1	70.3	73.7	69.5	67.1	70.2	68.3	66.5
1961	73.7	77.9	81.0	81.7	82.1	79.4	75.2	75.7	73.3	73.6	78.5	80.8	77.7
1962	78.1	86.4	90.8	90.9	82.8	78.4	80.9	80.2	80.8	76.7	81.2	78.6	82.1
1963	77.0	74.5	74.7	71.9	70.0	68.1	71.4	74.2	70.6	68.7	65.9	66.1	71.1
1964	69.9	65.4	62.4	62.6	59.4	55.7	63.3	63.5	59.9	61.1	62.4	62.3	62.3
1965	60.8	59.0	61.6	60.7	59.9	57.1	55.4	57.4	57.0	55.3	54.8	57.0	58.0
1966	62.2	59.9	57.4	55.7	54.0	53.7	52.7	53.0	49.6	49.1	52.5	50.7	54.2
1967	48.5	50.1	47.9	46.7	48.5	47.7	45.9	48.5	53.8	53.3	52.0	50.2	49.4
1968	52.1	51.0	55.3	57.4	54.3	52.3	50.1	51.5	51.4	50.6	51.5	53.1	52.5
1969	58.4	62.3	67.1	66.4	70.2	64.1	62.6	65.7	65.8	70.2	69.1	71.8	66.1
1970	75.5	73.4	72.0	69.3	67.1	65.4	67.5	68.3	66.7	67.6	66.2	67.0	68.8
1971	67.0	68.8	67.6	67.7	69.6	69.1	69.8	66.8	63.3	58.5	61.3	61.2	65.9
1972	63.1	64.3	69.3	72.6	76.8	72.7	76.9	80.1	80.6	80.9	75.6	73.8	73.9
1973	78.5	78.1	83.4	86.4	88.6	85.6	82.4	81.0	81.3	82.6	75.1	74.9	81.5
1974	78.1	75.2	68.9	67.7	65.4	60.8	61.0	56.3	47.8	51.3	51.0	52.7	61.3
1975	61.6	60.7	64.8	70.1	64.3	62.5	64.9	67.6	66.2	67.1	69.7	69.0	65.7
1976	70.9	74.5	72.4	69.2	68.3	66.9	64.1	64.5	62.6	55.6	53.5	56.9	64.9
1977	57.3	54.2	50.2	46.4	48.0	51.4	49.3	52.1	54.2	55.2	55.0	52.1	52.1
1978	48.5	49.6	59.3	64.5	65.9	67.0	74.0	74.4	81.6	78.4	76.8	77.7	68.1
1979	79.5	74.0	77.6	81.3	80.0	84.8	85.8	93.1	102.4	92.6	93.4	92.3	86.4
1980	100.7	102.4	91.6	93.4	99.3	99.5	98.2	98.8	100.3	107.7	106.3	102.1	100.0
1981	94.4	99.3	103.4	97.6	80.3	75.2	83.5	87.7	87.2	81.0	83.6	84.3	88.1
1982	91.8	95.4	72.1	92.0	91.2	82.9	80.2	83.6	83.2	84.7	85.8	86.0	85.7

261

11.O RATIO. PRICE TO UNIT LABOR COST. MANUFACTURING. FRANCE
(INDEX, 1980=100)

YEAR	IQ	IIQ	IIIQ	IVQ	AVGE
1955	114.1	114.0	114.0	114.9	114.2
1956	111.3	113.4	115.8	115.4	114.0
1957	115.4	113.8	115.2	116.4	115.2
1958	117.4	112.1	111.9	109.9	112.8
1959	116.2	119.3	118.6	120.8	118.7
1960	120.5	121.3	122.7	123.0	121.9
1961	124.2	120.9	121.1	120.1	121.6
1962	117.9	115.6	116.3	114.8	116.1
1963	108.1	114.0	115.2	112.6	112.5
1964	111.7	110.8	107.7	107.8	109.5
1965	106.8	107.2	106.5	108.4	107.2
1966	108.8	109.9	108.4	106.8	108.5
1967	106.3	104.4	106.0	107.4	106.0
1968	106.8	86.2	99.8	105.2	99.5
1969	108.4	111.1	109.5	111.0	110.0
1970	111.8	113.1	109.1	109.0	110.8
1971	110.1	109.9	110.1	110.7	110.2
1972	108.9	110.3	109.0	111.7	110.0
1973	112.2	112.8	113.1	115.1	113.3
1974	124.4	131.7	126.8	116.7	124.9
1975	107.2	102.8	98.7	101.1	102.4
1976	102.3	103.6	104.4	102.6	103.2
1977	102.8	100.9	97.5	94.8	99.0
1978	95.0	97.4	95.8	98.9	96.8
1979	100.4	102.6	107.5	105.5	104.0
1980	104.8	100.1	97.7	98.0	100.1
1981	101.3	104.9	101.3	101.6	102.3
1982	100.1	100.6	98.4	99.7	99.7

COINCIDENT INDEX, FRANCE (1980=100)

YEAR	JAN	FEB	MAR	APR	MAY	JUN	JUL	AUG	SEP	OCT	NOV	DEC	AVGE
1955	22.8	23.0	23.1	23.3	23.4	23.7	23.9	24.1	24.3	24.6	24.9	24.9	23.8
1956	25.8	25.8	26.5	26.6	27.1	27.4	27.7	28.0	28.3	28.8	29.2	29.5	27.6
1957	29.9	30.4	30.8	31.0	31.4	31.7	32.1	32.4	32.6	32.7	33.2	33.2	31.8
1958	33.3	33.4	33.3	33.3	33.3	33.2	33.3	33.1	32.7	32.8	32.4	32.1	33.0
1959	31.9	31.5	31.7	31.8	32.0	32.2	32.3	32.2	32.6	32.8	33.1	33.2	32.3
1960	33.4	33.3	34.0	34.3	34.4	34.8	35.0	35.2	35.7	36.0	36.0	36.3	34.9
1961	36.5	36.6	37.3	37.1	37.4	37.9	37.9	38.1	38.4	39.1	39.4	39.7	37.9
1962	39.8	40.6	40.5	40.9	41.1	41.3	41.3	42.0	42.4	42.6	43.1	43.6	41.6
1963	43.7	43.8	43.9	45.2	45.9	46.4	47.0	47.6	47.8	48.3	48.6	49.2	46.4
1964	50.0	50.5	50.6	50.6	50.8	50.8	50.9	51.1	51.6	52.1	51.9	51.7	51.0
1965	51.8	51.7	51.5	52.2	52.3	52.5	52.8	52.9	53.3	53.6	53.9	54.1	52.7
1966	54.3	54.8	55.1	55.3	55.9	56.4	56.6	56.7	56.7	56.8	57.0	57.1	56.1
1967	57.4	57.3	57.6	57.4	57.5	57.8	57.8	57.8	58.0	57.7	57.6	57.9	57.6
1968	58.0	58.2	57.9	57.3	53.3	55.9	58.5	59.5	59.7	60.5	61.5	61.7	58.5
1969	62.2	62.5	63.2	63.9	65.2	65.6	66.1	66.8	67.1	67.8	68.1	68.4	65.6
1970	69.1	69.3	69.6	69.8	70.2	70.1	70.4	70.6	70.9	71.4	71.2	71.7	70.4
1971	71.8	72.0	72.4	72.9	72.8	73.4	73.8	74.0	74.8	74.9	75.5	75.7	73.7
1972	76.1	76.4	76.8	76.9	77.2	77.8	78.4	78.8	79.5	79.8	80.8	81.5	78.3
1973	82.2	83.1	83.8	84.0	84.8	85.2	85.3	85.6	85.5	86.3	86.9	87.2	85.0
1974	88.5	89.0	89.0	89.7	90.4	90.3	90.7	90.4	89.2	88.4	86.8	86.4	89.1
1975	85.9	85.5	84.9	84.6	84.2	83.9	83.7	83.8	83.7	84.2	84.3	85.2	84.5
1976	85.7	86.1	86.7	87.5	88.0	88.4	89.2	89.4	90.4	90.3	91.1	91.5	88.7
1977	92.0	92.2	92.3	92.0	91.6	92.3	91.8	92.1	92.0	91.9	92.4	92.3	92.1
1978	93.3	93.5	93.9	94.3	94.6	94.5	94.5	94.6	95.0	95.4	96.0	96.1	94.6
1979	96.2	96.5	96.9	96.6	97.3	97.8	98.3	99.1	98.8	99.1	99.3	99.5	97.9
1980	99.8	100.2	100.2	100.4	99.9	99.9	100.4	100.3	99.9	100.1	99.5	99.5	100.0
1981	98.7	98.6	98.1	98.2	98.1	98.1	97.9	97.7	98.1	98.1	98.2	98.5	98.2
1982	98.3	98.6	99.0	99.1	99.4	99.9	99.9	99.8	99.9	100.5	100.5	100.5	99.6

SIX MONTH SMOOTHED CHANGE IN COINCIDENT INDEX, FRANCE (ANNUAL RATE, PERCENT)

YEAR	JAN	FEB	MAR	APR	MAY	JUN	JUL	AUG	SEP	OCT	NOV	DEC	AVGE
1956	15.9	13.3	17.2	15.5	17.0	17.1	16.2	16.5	15.9	16.5	17.1	16.1	16.2
1957	16.5	17.0	16.8	16.0	15.6	15.4	15.1	14.7	13.7	9.7	12.4	10.4	14.4
1958	9.0	8.0	5.9	4.7	3.6	2.0	2.0	0.4	-2.2	-2.4	-4.1	-5.6	1.8
1959	-6.4	-7.9	-5.8	-4.7	-3.0	-1.1	-0.1	0.1	2.7	4.2	5.8	6.1	-0.8
1960	6.4	5.5	8.6	8.8	8.6	9.2	9.3	8.9	10.5	10.3	9.2	9.2	8.7
1961	9.0	8.0	10.1	7.6	7.9	8.8	7.5	7.3	7.8	10.0	9.9	10.2	8.7
1962	9.4	11.5	9.6	10.2	9.5	8.8	7.2	9.4	8.7	8.7	9.7	10.8	9.5
1963	9.7	8.6	7.4	12.1	13.5	14.0	14.4	14.8	13.7	13.6	12.7	13.2	12.3
1964	14.6	14.3	12.3	10.0	8.9	7.2	6.1	5.6	6.3	6.8	4.8	3.1	8.3
1965	2.8	1.7	0.8	3.1	2.7	3.0	3.7	3.6	4.2	5.0	5.4	5.5	3.5
1966	5.7	6.7	6.8	6.4	7.5	8.1	7.6	6.8	6.0	5.2	4.9	4.3	6.3
1967	4.3	3.4	3.4	2.3	1.9	2.6	2.0	1.7	2.3	0.9	0.3	1.1	2.2
1968	0.9	1.4	0.3	-1.7	-13.7	-4.8	3.9	7.0	7.3	9.5	12.0	11.5	2.8
1969	11.8	11.8	12.6	13.7	15.7	13.6	12.5	12.8	11.6	11.7	10.7	9.8	12.4
1970	10.1	9.1	8.2	7.1	6.7	5.3	5.0	4.7	4.5	5.1	3.7	4.4	6.2
1971	3.8	3.8	4.1	4.8	3.9	4.9	5.3	5.0	6.3	5.7	6.6	6.0	5.0
1972	6.2	6.1	6.1	5.2	5.3	5.7	6.5	6.4	7.0	6.7	8.1	8.9	6.5
1973	9.2	10.2	10.5	9.5	9.9	9.4	7.9	7.2	5.6	6.3	6.5	5.9	8.2
1974	7.7	7.6	6.6	7.1	7.4	6.4	6.3	4.5	1.0	-1.2	-4.9	-5.5	3.6
1975	-6.5	-6.9	-7.4	-7.4	-7.5	-6.9	-6.3	-5.0	-4.0	-2.0	-1.2	1.3	-5.0
1976	2.7	3.6	4.7	6.2	6.8	6.9	7.9	7.4	8.4	6.8	7.6	7.2	6.3
1977	6.9	6.3	5.3	3.8	2.1	2.9	1.3	1.3	0.7	0.2	1.0	0.6	2.7
1978	2.5	2.6	3.3	3.8	4.0	3.2	3.0	2.7	3.0	3.2	3.9	3.5	3.2
1979	3.1	3.1	3.4	2.5	3.4	3.9	4.3	5.3	4.0	4.0	3.6	3.5	3.7
1980	3.5	3.7	3.0	2.8	1.4	-0.9	1.6	1.1	0.2	-0.3	-1.0	-1.0	1.4
1981	-2.4	-2.4	-3.0	-2.5	-2.5	-2.1	-2.3	-2.2	-1.1	-0.9	-0.4	0.3	-1.8
1982	0.3	0.8	1.5	1.7	2.0	2.8	2.4	1.9	1.8	2.7	2.4	1.9	1.8

13.0 EMPLOYMENT, NONFARM, FRANCE (1980=100)

YEAR	JAN	APR	JUL	OCT	AVGE
1951	94.7	92.6	92.6	93.6	93.3
1952	93.6	93.6	92.6	92.6	92.9
1953	91.5	91.5	92.2	92.6	92.0
1954	92.6	93.6	93.6	93.6	93.5
1955	94.9	95.2	95.5	95.7	95.4
1956	95.9	96.4	96.6	97.0	96.6
1957	98.0	98.6	99.4	100.0	99.2
1958	100.4	100.5	100.3	99.8	100.1
1959	98.9	98.5	98.7	98.7	98.7
1960	98.8	99.1	99.2	99.4	99.2
1961	99.6	99.5	99.9	100.3	99.9
1962	100.4	100.8	101.2	101.7	101.2
1963	102.7	103.3	103.8	104.2	103.7
1964	104.8	105.0	105.3	105.6	105.2
1965	105.2	104.9	104.8	104.7	104.8
1966	104.6	104.7	105.1	104.9	104.8
1967	104.8	104.7	104.3	103.9	104.3
1968	103.3	103.0	102.4	102.4	102.7
1969	102.9	103.4	104.1	104.7	103.9
1970	105.0	105.1	105.4	105.4	105.2
1971	105.3	105.1	105.5	105.6	105.4
1972	105.4	105.3	105.4	105.5	105.4
1973	106.0	106.4	106.5	106.8	106.5
1974	107.1	107.3	107.4	107.0	107.1
1975	106.4	105.4	104.6	103.9	104.8
1976	103.7	103.8	104.0	104.1	103.9
1977	104.2	104.1	103.5	103.1	103.6
1978	102.7	102.0	101.9	101.8	102.0
1979	101.6	101.4	101.1	100.9	101.2
1980	100.7	100.6	100.3	99.7	100.2
1981	98.9	98.1	97.4	96.9	97.6
1982	96.5	96.3	96.6	96.0	96.3

14.1 REGISTERED UNEMPLOYED, FRANCE (THOUSANDS)

YEAR	JAN	FEB	MAR	APR	MAY	JUN	JUL	AUG	SEP	OCT	NOV	DEC	AVGE
1955	168.0	168.0	171.0	168.0	167.0	164.0	159.0	155.0	151.0	148.0	143.0	136.0	158.2
1956	132.0	130.0	124.0	120.0	114.0	108.0	107.0	103.0	98.0	92.0	90.0	90.0	109.0
1957	86.0	83.0	80.0	78.0	79.0	79.0	78.0	79.0	79.0	81.0	80.0	80.0	80.2
1958	80.0	80.0	85.0	87.0	88.0	92.0	94.0	97.0	101.0	107.0	114.0	122.0	95.6
1959	134.0	142.0	142.0	143.0	143.0	141.0	140.0	140.0	141.0	142.0	140.0	141.0	140.7
1960	140.0	137.0	135.0	135.0	135.0	129.0	130.0	127.0	126.0	121.0	122.0	120.0	129.7
1961	121.0	119.0	114.0	113.0	113.0	112.0	111.0	110.0	108.0	106.0	103.0	101.0	110.9
1962	99.0	95.0	97.0	97.0	97.0	99.0	109.0	101.0	98.0	97.0	97.0	96.0	98.5
1963	98.0	101.0	100.0	98.0	99.0	97.0	97.0	96.0	97.0	93.0	92.0	91.0	96.6
1964	83.0	83.0	87.0	93.0	95.0	99.0	102.0	105.0	103.0	106.0	109.0	113.0	98.2
1965	115.0	121.0	127.0	128.0	132.0	135.0	135.0	138.0	140.0	139.0	139.0	138.0	132.2
1966	135.0	134.0	134.0	136.0	136.0	139.0	141.0	143.0	145.0	149.0	152.0	156.0	141.7
1967	160.0	164.0	170.0	181.0	183.0	186.0	190.0	195.0	203.0	214.0	226.0	235.0	192.2
1968	243.0	249.0	250.0	252.0	265.0	277.5	269.3	266.9	260.6	252.0	244.8	241.0	255.9
1969	238.7	236.7	233.7	238.0	226.2	221.0	220.1	216.0	211.0	210.1	210.6	215.9	223.2
1970	221.7	230.0	237.7	246.6	253.2	261.5	268.7	273.4	277.3	283.7	294.7	297.9	262.2
1971	308.9	311.7	316.8	319.1	326.6	336.1	340.0	345.3	347.3	355.4	361.8	364.8	336.1
1972	366.9	371.7	374.9	382.9	387.6	383.1	379.6	384.2	388.7	385.6	378.9	375.5	380.0
1973	371.0	364.7	365.4	372.8	374.5	376.3	395.9	405.0	420.1	421.5	416.9	424.1	392.3
1974	428.4	428.3	427.4	426.2	424.8	432.4	455.2	475.3	528.5	578.0	630.1	664.8	491.6
1975	694.0	722.8	747.8	783.3	804.5	842.7	870.1	880.8	916.2	922.7	922.4	927.1	836.2
1976	927.0	925.1	933.7	929.5	926.2	928.0	918.5	929.8	925.2	931.3	941.4	952.0	930.6
1977	984.2	1006.8	1018.7	1036.0	1051.0	1068.0	1083.0	1104.0	1114.0	1117.0	1116.0	1110.0	1067.4
1978	1073.0	1077.0	1094.0	1103.0	1115.0	1146.0	1180.0	1203.0	1223.0	1244.0	1253.0	1274.0	1165.4
1979	1288.0	1306.0	1318.0	1334.0	1348.0	1356.0	1354.0	1360.0	1363.0	1375.0	1387.0	1403.0	1349.3
1980	1409.0	1410.0	1417.0	1421.0	1430.0	1424.0	1433.0	1437.0	1458.0	1476.0	1518.0	1552.0	1448.7
1981	1591.0	1619.0	1655.0	1693.0	1733.0	1771.0	1807.0	1833.0	1859.0	1880.0	1903.0	1917.0	1771.7
1982	1928.0	1946.0	1962.0	1982.0	2000.0	2027.0	2039.0	2046.0	2045.0	2046.0	2039.0	2028.0	2007.3

15.0 GROSS DOMESTIC PRODUCT, IN CONSTANT PRICES, FRANCE
(BILLION 1970 FRANCS)

YEAR	IQ	IIQ	IIIQ	IVQ	AVGE
1963	128.6	134.1	138.3	138.7	134.9
1964	141.5	142.9	144.7	145.9	143.7
1965	146.2	149.8	152.1	154.3	150.6
1966	155.6	157.9	159.7	160.6	158.4
1967	163.3	165.1	166.7	168.4	165.9
1968	173.2	160.1	178.4	180.2	173.0
1969	180.5	184.9	186.6	188.1	185.0
1970	191.9	195.0	196.4	199.3	195.6
1971	201.6	204.8	207.6	210.9	206.2
1972	214.2	216.3	219.7	223.4	218.4
1973	227.2	229.4	231.0	232.9	230.1
1974	236.9	237.6	240.0	235.8	237.6
1975	235.2	236.5	238.5	241.8	238.0
1976	246.3	249.5	251.4	254.0	250.3
1977	257.6	256.7	258.2	259.2	257.9
1978	263.4	268.1	267.7	271.7	267.7
1979	272.6	274.4	279.2	279.9	276.5
1980	281.4	279.0	279.3	278.5	279.5
1981	276.9	279.8	281.2	283.4	280.3
1982	283.8	286.1	284.6	287.1	285.4

16.0 INDUSTRIAL PRODUCTION, FRANCE (1980=100)

YEAR	JAN	FEB	MAR	APR	MAY	JUN	JUL	AUG	SEP	OCT	NOV	DEC	AVGE
1951	23.	23.	23.	23.	24.	24.	25.	25.	25.	25.	24.	24.	24.
1952	25.	25.	25.	25.	23.	24.	24.	25.	24.	24.	25.	23.	24.
1953	23.	23.	24.	24.	25.	25.	25.	23.	25.	25.	26.	27.	25.
1954	26.	25.	26.	26.	28.	28.	27.	26.	28.	28.	28.	28.	27.
1955	28.	28.	29.	29.	29.	29.	29.	29.	29.	30.	31.	30.	29.
1956	34.	33.	34.	35.	36.	36.	36.	36.	37.	37.	37.	37.	36.
1957	38.	38.	38.	38.	39.	38.	39.	39.	40.	39.	40.	41.	39.
1958	41.	41.	41.	41.	40.	41.	40.	40.	40.	40.	40.	39.	40.
1959	39.	40.	40.	41.	40.	41.	41.	41.	42.	42.	43.	43.	41.
1960	43.	43.	43.	44.	44.	44.	45.	45.	46.	46.	46.	46.	45.
1961	46.	47.	47.	47.	47.	47.	48.	48.	48.	48.	48.	49.	48.
1962	49.	49.	50.	49.	50.	49.	50.	50.	51.	51.	51.	51.	50.
1963	51.	50.	45.	51.	53.	53.	55.	55.	54.	54.	54.	55.	53.
1964	56.	56.	56.	57.	56.	56.	55.	55.	56.	56.	56.	55.	56.
1965	55.	56.	56.	56.	56.	57.	57.	57.	57.	59.	59.	59.	57.
1966	58.	59.	60.	59.	60.	61.	61.	61.	61.	61.	61.	61.	60.
1967	61.	61.	61.	60.	61.	62.	62.	62.	63.	62.	63.	64.	62.
1968	64.	64.	65.	65.	44.	56.	68.	68.	66.	69.	70.	70.	64.
1969	70.	69.	69.	71.	73.	72.	72.	72.	71.	74.	72.	72.	71.
1970	74.	75.	75.	76.	75.	75.	75.	75.	76.	76.	76.	77.	75.
1971	76.	78.	78.	78.	77.	78.	79.	79.	81.	81.	82.	81.	79.
1972	82.	81.	83.	83.	84.	83.	85.	85.	86.	87.	87.	89.	85.
1973	88.	89.	90.	88.	93.	91.	93.	93.	91.	92.	93.	90.	91.
1974	94.	95.	93.	94.	96.	94.	97.	97.	92.	92.	89.	87.	93.
1975	86.	86.	84.	85.	82.	84.	83.	83.	84.	86.	85.	90.	85.
1976	90.	90.	91.	92.	92.	92.	93.	93.	97.	93.	96.	95.	93.
1977	97.	96.	96.	94.	93.	97.	94.	94.	95.	93.	95.	93.	95.
1978	95.	94.	96.	99.	97.	96.	96.	96.	97.	99.	99.	99.	97.
1979	98.	99.	100.	99.	101.	102.	105.	105.	102.	102.	102.	102.	97.
1980	102.	102.	102.	102.	99.	99.	101.	101.	97.	99.	98.	99.	101.
1981	96.	99.	97.	96.	97.	99.	97.	97.	99.	98.	98.	99.	100.
1982	97.	96.	96.	97.	97.	97.	95.	95.	95.	96.	97.	95.	96.

18.1 RETAIL SALES, VOLUME, FRANCE (1980=100)

YEAR	JAN	FEB	MAR	APR	MAY	JUN	JUL	AUG	SEP	OCT	NOV	DEC	AVGE
1955	38.	39.	38.	40.	39.	40.	41.	38.	39.	42.	40.	40.	40.
1956	44.	40.	45.	41.	45.	46.	45.	47.	46.	46.	48.	47.	45.
1957	48.	48.	48.	48.	51.	52.	52.	55.	53.	47.	55.	49.	51.
1958	48.	46.	47.	47.	47.	47.	50.	48.	45.	48.	48.	50.	48.
1959	54.	50.	51.	50.	52.	52.	51.	48.	50.	52.	54.	53.	51.
1960	52.	47.	56.	56.	56.	56.	56.	55.	60.	60.	58.	58.	56.
1961	60.	55.	65.	58.	61.	64.	58.	57.	59.	67.	65.	64.	61.
1962	60.	67.	62.	68.	66.	68.	70.	71.	70.	66.	68.	68.	67.
1963	71.	71.	71.	73.	73.	72.	73.	76.	76.	77.	75.	77.	74.
1964	75.	77.	77.	76.	78.	75.	75.	75.	76.	82.	77.	76.	77.
1965	79.	78.	74.	83.	79.	79.	81.	79.	82.	81.	80.	80.	80.
1966	80.	81.	79.	81.	81.	84.	83.	81.	80.	83.	83.	82.	82.
1967	84.	81.	84.	84.	83.	84.	84.	82.	87.	83.	84.	86.	84.
1968	84.	84.	86.	87.	71.	83.	91.	89.	89.	89.	95.	90.	87.
1969	92.	92.	91.	91.	95.	91.	91.	94.	89.	86.	89.	86.	91.
1970	90.	89.	89.	88.	90.	87.	88.	90.	87.	91.	86.	89.	89.
1971	86.	83.	86.	90.	87.	88.	87.	89.	89.	87.	88.	92.	88.
1972	89.	90.	90.	87.	90.	92.	91.	92.	93.	90.	93.	89.	91.
1973	88.	92.	90.	93.	92.	94.	95.	92.	89.	94.	97.	95.	93.
1974	98.	95.	93.	95.	96.	94.	94.	95.	98.	96.	89.	94.	95.
1975	93.	94.	93.	92.	94.	89.	93.	93.	94.	97.	94.	95.	93.
1976	95.	93.	93.	97.	96.	95.	96.	95.	97.	95.	96.	99.	96.
1977	98.	97.	97.	96.	92.	99.	96.	98.	95.	94.	95.	95.	96.
1978	95.	96.	99.	97.	98.	99.	99.	99.	99.	96.	100.	98.	98.
1979	99.	100.	101.	99.	101.	102.	98.	104.	99.	101.	101.	98.	100.
1980	100.	102.	99.	99.	100.	97.	100.	98.	100.	101.	100.	101.	100.
1981	101.	99.	99.	101.	99.	101.	102.	100.	101.	102.	101.	102.	101.
1982	101.	104.	104.	104.	99.	105.	102.	102.	99.	104.	102.	105.	103.

269

LAGGING INDEX, FRANCE (1970=100)

YEAR	JAN	FEB	MAR	APR	MAY	JUN	JUL	AUG	SEP	OCT	NOV	DEC	AVGE
1964	66.9	67.5	68.3	69.1	69.9	70.5	71.2	71.8	71.9	72.1	72.2	72.5	70.3
1965	72.9	73.2	73.5	73.7	74.0	74.2	74.4	74.6	74.9	75.3	75.7	76.0	74.4
1966	76.4	76.7	77.1	77.4	77.8	78.2	78.6	79.1	79.3	79.6	79.7	79.9	78.3
1967	80.2	80.5	80.8	81.1	81.4	81.6	81.9	82.1	82.4	82.6	82.9	83.2	81.7
1968	83.6	83.9	84.2	84.5	84.8	85.2	87.1	87.4	87.8	88.2	89.9	90.3	86.4
1969	90.8	91.2	90.9	90.6	90.9	93.4	94.6	96.0	96.3	97.7	98.0	98.2	94.0
1970	98.3	98.5	99.0	99.5	100.0	100.3	100.7	101.0	100.8	100.4	100.5	101.0	100.0
1971	101.1	101.5	101.7	101.7	102.5	103.0	103.5	103.9	104.2	104.5	104.8	104.5	103.1
1972	104.8	105.1	104.7	105.1	105.5	105.9	106.3	106.7	107.4	107.8	109.3	109.8	106.5
1973	110.2	110.7	111.0	111.7	112.0	112.9	114.1	115.8	117.3	117.6	117.8	118.3	114.1
1974	119.7	120.2	120.5	121.3	121.6	122.3	122.5	122.8	123.0	123.3	123.5	123.6	122.0
1975	123.2	123.3	122.4	122.2	122.5	122.1	122.4	122.6	121.6	121.8	121.9	122.2	122.3
1976	122.2	122.5	123.2	123.7	124.2	125.0	125.2	125.4	126.4	127.0	127.5	128.0	125.0
1977	128.6	129.2	129.4	129.6	129.8	130.3	130.9	131.1	131.1	131.2	131.3	131.8	130.4
1978	132.2	132.7	132.9	133.0	133.2	133.8	133.3	133.2	134.7	134.9	135.1	135.3	133.7
1979	135.5	135.3	135.3	135.2	135.7	136.1	137.2	137.4	138.1	138.6	139.7	139.6	137.0
1980	139.5	140.3	140.7	140.8	140.9	141.4	141.8	141.9	142.5	142.9	143.2	143.0	141.6
1981	142.8	143.2	143.4	143.0	142.3	141.8	141.7	141.7	141.7	141.6	141.7	142.0	142.2
1982	142.0	141.9	***	***	***	***	***	***	***	***	***	***	***

SIX MONTH SMOOTHED CHANGE IN LAGGING INDEX, FRANCE (ANNUAL RATE, PERCENT)

YEAR	JAN	FEB	MAR	APR	MAY	JUN	JUL	AUG	SEP	OCT	NOV	DEC	AVGE
1965	6.9	6.3	5.8	5.2	4.9	4.4	4.1	4.1	4.1	4.6	4.8	4.8	5.0
1966	5.0	5.0	5.5	5.5	5.4	5.7	5.9	6.1	5.8	5.6	4.8	4.5	5.4
1967	4.5	4.5	4.5	4.2	4.2	4.0	4.2	3.9	3.9	3.9	3.9	4.1	4.1
1968	4.3	4.3	4.3	4.3	4.3	4.7	8.3	7.8	7.8	7.5	10.4	9.9	6.5
1969	9.6	9.1	7.1	5.1	4.6	8.9	9.9	11.5	10.6	12.0	10.8	9.7	9.1
1970	8.6	7.5	7.3	6.8	6.4	5.4	5.1	4.7	3.4	2.1	1.7	2.2	5.1
1971	2.0	2.4	2.2	1.8	2.9	3.5	4.0	4.2	4.4	4.4	4.4	3.1	3.3
1972	3.1	3.1	1.8	2.1	2.3	2.5	2.8	3.2	3.9	4.2	6.4	6.5	3.5
1973	6.5	6.5	6.3	6.4	6.0	6.5	7.7	9.4	10.5	9.6	8.5	8.1	7.7
1974	9.2	8.7	7.8	7.7	6.9	6.7	5.7	5.0	4.3	4.2	3.7	3.1	6.1
1975	1.8	1.5	-0.3	-0.8	-0.5	-1.2	-0.7	-0.5	-1.8	-1.3	-1.1	-0.5	-0.5
1976	-0.2	0.3	1.5	2.1	2.7	3.8	3.6	3.6	4.8	5.1	5.1	5.3	3.1
1977	5.4	5.4	4.9	4.4	4.0	3.9	4.2	3.8	3.0	2.6	2.3	2.6	3.9
1978	2.6	2.8	2.8	2.5	2.4	2.8	1.7	1.3	3.1	2.9	2.8	2.6	2.5
1979	2.5	1.8	1.5	1.1	1.5	1.8	3.0	2.9	3.4	3.7	4.8	4.1	2.7
1980	3.4	4.1	4.1	3.5	3.1	3.1	3.1	2.7	2.9	3.0	2.9	2.2	3.2
1981	1.6	1.8	1.7	0.9	-0.3	-1.0	-1.2	-1.2	-1.2	-1.3	-0.9	-0.4	-0.1
1982	-0.3	-0.4	***	***	***	***	***	***	***	***	***	***	***

19.0 LONG-DURATION UNEMPLOYMENT, FRANCE (THOUSANDS)

YEAR	JAN	FEB	MAR	APR	MAY	JUN	JUL	AUG	SEP	OCT	NOV	DEC	AVGE
1979	786.	804.	816.	836.	840.	856.	850.	866.	864.	865.	871.	880.	845.
1980	892.	895.	897.	897.	917.	918.	916.	918.	920.	931.	950.	976.	919.
1981	1002.	1026.	1050.	1077.	1121.	1168.	1187.	1202.	1215.	1235.	1242.	1253.	1148.
1982	1288.	1325.	1334.	1328.	1351.	1374.	1380.	***	***	***	***	***	***

20.0 INVESTMENT EXPENDITURES, PLANT AND EQUIPMENT, IN CONSTANT PRICES, FRANCE
(MILLION 1970 FRANCS)

YEAR	IQ	IIQ	IIIQ	IVQ	AVGE
1963	15853.	16739.	17668.	17594.	16964.
1964	17987.	18172.	18558.	18492.	18302.
1965	18376.	18869.	18898.	19406.	18887.
1966	19882.	20192.	20760.	20651.	20371.
1967	21197.	21382.	21493.	21955.	21507.
1968	22616.	20082.	23917.	24400.	22754.
1969	24046.	25512.	25585.	25398.	25135.
1970	25356.	26107.	26394.	26378.	26059.
1971	27062.	27549.	28762.	28936.	28077.
1972	29074.	29487.	29964.	30475.	29750.
1973	31154.	31028.	31610.	31331.	31281.
1974	31502.	31439.	31187.	29636.	30941.
1975	28546.	28904.	28836.	30065.	29088.
1976	30687.	31017.	30702.	30718.	30781.
1977	31226.	30217.	30930.	29964.	30584.
1978	30489.	31071.	31816.	32312.	31422.
1979	31325.	31458.	33764.	33836.	32596.
1980	34720.	34670.	34650.	35010.	34763.
1981	33930.	33820.	33440.	33520.	33678.
1982	33600.	***	***	***	***

21.0 BUSINESS INVENTORIES, IN CONSTANT PRICES, FRANCE
(BILLION 1970 FRANCS)

YEAR	IQ	IIQ	IIIQ	IVQ	AVGE
1963	-0.2	1.3	4.2	7.1	3.1
1964	9.9	14.0	17.7	20.3	15.5
1965	22.3	24.4	26.5	28.9	25.5
1966	31.9	34.6	38.3	41.7	36.6
1967	45.1	47.8	50.3	52.8	49.0
1968	58.4	56.7	60.8	65.3	60.3
1969	70.5	76.2	80.8	85.8	78.3
1970	91.2	96.7	102.4	106.9	99.3
1971	109.3	112.5	115.9	119.8	114.4
1972	124.5	128.2	132.1	137.3	130.5
1973	141.9	146.8	153.7	159.4	150.4
1974	165.1	172.4	178.7	182.2	174.6
1975	182.6	181.2	179.0	179.2	180.5
1976	181.5	183.1	187.6	191.8	186.0
1977	196.9	200.0	200.5	202.0	199.8
1978	203.7	205.6	207.8	211.0	207.0
1979	213.6	216.9	223.8	228.8	220.8
1980	235.4	241.3	247.9	251.1	243.9
1981	252.0	249.7	248.2	251.1	250.2
1982	253.6	259.9	262.4	264.1	260.0

22. Ò CHANGE IN HOURS PER UNIT OF OUTPUT, NONFARM BUSINESS, FRANCE
(PERCENT CHANGE FROM YEAR AGO)

YEAR	IQ	IIQ	IIIQ	IVQ	AVGE
1964	-6.	-3.	-1.	-3.	-3.
1965	-1.	-3.	-3.	-4.	-3.
1966	-5.	-4.	-4.	-3.	-4.
1967	-3.	-3.	-3.	-4.	-3.
1968	-5.	4.	-6.	-6.	-3.
1969	-4.	-14.	-3.	-2.	-6.
1970	-3.	-3.	-3.	-5.	-3.
1971	-5.	-4.	-5.	-5.	-5.
1972	-6.	-6.	-6.	-6.	-6.
1973	-6.	-5.	-5.	-4.	-5.
1974	-4.	-4.	-4.	-1.	-3.
1975	0.	-1.	-1.	-5.	-1.
1976	-6.	-5.	-5.	-4.	-5.
1977	-3.	-2.	-2.	-1.	-2.
1978	-1.	-4.	-3.	-5.	-3.
1979	-4.	-3.	-5.	-3.	-4.
1980	-5.	-4.	-1.	-1.	-3.
1981	1.	-2.	-2.	-4.	-2.
1982	-4.	***	***	***	***

23.0 BUSINESS LOANS OUTSTANDING, IN CONSTANT PRICES, FRANCE
(BILLION 1970 FRANCS)

YEAR	IQ	IIQ	IIIQ	IVQ	AVGE
1979	477.	473.	471.	469.	473.
1980	465.	465.	464.	466.	465.
1981	464.	464.	464.	464.	464.
1982	466.	***	***	***	***

24.0 COMMERCIAL BANK LENDING RATE TO PRIME BORROWERS, FRANCE (PERCENT)

YEAR	JAN	FEB	MAR	APR	MAY	JUN	JUL	AUG	SEP	OCT	NOV	DEC	AVGE
1966	6.10	6.10	6.10	6.10	6.10	6.10	6.10	6.10	6.10	6.10	5.95	5.85	6.07
1967	5.85	5.85	5.85	5.85	5.85	5.85	5.85	5.85	5.85	5.85	5.85	5.85	5.85
1968	5.85	5.85	5.85	5.85	5.85	5.85	6.85	6.85	6.85	6.85	7.85	7.85	6.52
1969	7.85	7.85	7.85	7.85	8.35	9.35	9.35	9.35	9.35	10.35	10.35	10.35	9.02
1970	10.35	10.35	10.35	10.35	10.35	10.35	10.35	10.35	10.05	9.65	9.65	9.65	10.15
1971	9.40	9.40	9.15	8.75	9.05	9.05	9.05	9.05	9.05	9.05	9.05	8.65	9.06
1972	8.65	8.65	8.15	8.15	8.15	8.15	8.15	8.15	8.35	8.35	9.15	9.15	8.43
1973	9.15	9.15	9.15	9.45	9.45	9.75	10.25	11.25	12.45	12.45	12.45	12.45	10.62
1974	13.45	13.95	13.45	13.95	13.95	14.45	14.45	14.45	14.45	14.45	14.45	14.45	14.12
1975	13.95	13.95	12.85	12.35	12.35	11.85	11.85	11.85	10.85	10.85	10.85	10.85	12.03
1976	10.65	10.65	10.85	10.85	10.85	11.25	11.25	11.25	11.65	11.65	11.65	11.65	11.18
1977	11.65	11.65	11.65	11.65	11.65	11.35	11.65	11.35	11.35	11.35	11.35	11.35	11.52
1978	11.35	11.35	11.35	11.35	11.35	11.35	10.50	10.95	10.95	10.95	10.95	10.95	11.04
1979	10.95	10.95	10.95	10.95	11.30	11.60	12.20	12.20	12.50	12.65	13.65	13.65	11.96
1980	13.65	14.65	14.65	14.15	14.15	14.15	13.90	13.40	13.40	13.40	13.40	13.40	13.86
1981	13.40	14.15	14.90	14.15	14.15	14.15	***	***	***	***	***	***	***

ITALY

LEADING INDEX, ITALY (1980=100)

YEAR	JAN	FEB	MAR	APR	MAY	JUN	JUL	AUG	SEP	OCT	NOV	DEC	AVGE
1955	36.0	36.0	35.8	35.9	36.2	36.5	37.0	37.4	37.5	37.8	37.8	38.2	36.8
1956	37.3	37.5	37.4	37.4	37.8	37.3	37.9	38.1	38.3	38.3	38.5	39.3	37.9
1957	39.2	39.3	39.6	39.5	39.6	40.1	40.0	40.2	40.4	40.2	40.3	40.4	39.9
1958	40.5	40.7	40.9	40.7	41.0	41.0	40.6	41.4	41.5	41.8	42.2	41.8	41.2
1959	42.7	43.2	43.5	44.4	44.9	44.8	45.5	46.4	45.9	45.9	46.5	47.8	45.1
1960	47.4	47.2	47.5	47.6	48.2	48.9	49.4	50.7	51.5	51.4	50.6	49.7	49.2
1961	51.2	51.6	51.8	52.5	53.3	53.8	53.7	54.3	54.3	55.0	55.0	54.2	53.4
1962	54.4	54.3	54.9	54.8	54.8	54.5	54.3	54.1	54.1	53.8	54.2	54.8	54.4
1963	54.7	54.4	54.1	54.0	54.0	54.4	54.0	54.0	54.2	54.0	54.9	55.3	54.4
1964	54.5	53.8	54.3	53.6	54.5	54.2	54.0	54.1	54.6	54.4	54.9	55.0	54.3
1965	54.9	55.5	56.2	56.6	56.6	56.8	56.9	57.9	58.0	58.0	58.1	59.2	57.1
1966	60.4	61.1	60.9	60.6	60.5	61.1	61.2	61.0	61.1	61.7	61.9	61.8	61.1
1967	61.7	61.3	60.8	63.0	61.9	61.9	61.8	62.0	62.5	62.2	62.5	63.3	62.1
1968	63.1	63.0	63.6	64.4	64.6	64.6	65.1	67.7	65.3	65.3	66.5	67.3	65.0
1969	67.6	67.2	67.3	67.6	67.6	68.1	67.9	68.0	67.5	67.5	67.6	68.1	67.7
1970	68.7	69.5	69.7	69.3	68.9	68.6	68.2	68.6	69.1	69.4	69.8	69.7	69.1
1971	69.5	70.3	70.1	69.6	69.4	69.3	69.8	69.7	69.8	70.0	70.4	72.4	70.0
1972	71.3	70.8	71.6	72.2	73.2	72.9	73.1	73.0	73.3	74.1	74.5	75.3	72.9
1973	74.8	74.8	75.2	76.7	77.3	78.5	79.1	78.6	78.6	80.1	79.9	80.1	77.8
1974	79.5	80.0	81.1	80.9	80.7	81.1	81.3	80.9	80.3	79.9	80.2	79.2	80.4
1975	79.1	80.7	81.2	80.9	80.1	80.5	78.9	78.8	79.8	80.6	80.2	80.4	80.1
1976	80.5	82.7	82.6	82.6	83.3	82.8	83.5	83.7	84.5	84.6	84.6	85.7	83.4
1977	86.4	85.1	84.4	84.4	84.6	83.6	85.2	85.1	85.7	85.2	84.6	84.6	84.9
1978	85.4	85.3	85.6	85.7	86.9	87.8	88.2	88.4	90.1	90.1	90.4	91.2	87.9
1979	90.6	92.1	92.6	92.0	92.1	92.5	92.8	93.9	94.0	95.2	96.1	96.0	93.3
1980	97.0	97.6	98.2	99.2	99.4	99.7	99.8	100.2	101.6	102.4	103.0	101.8	100.0
1981	103.6	104.0	104.6	104.9	105.7	104.7	103.9	104.3	105.1	105.2	105.3	104.4	104.6
1982	105.4	106.1	106.5	106.9	106.1	104.4	105.1	105.8	105.8	106.0	105.5	106.7	105.9

SIX MONTH SMOOTHED CHANGE IN LEADING INDEX, ITALY (ANNUAL RATE, PERCENT)

YEAR	JAN	FEB	MAR	APR	MAY	JUN	JUL	AUG	SEP	OCT	NOV	DEC	AVGE
1956	2.5	2.6	1.5	1.2	2.5	-0.6	1.6	2.2	3.2	2.6	3.5	7.3	2.5
1957	6.3	5.9	7.0	5.4	4.7	6.8	4.9	4.9	5.0	3.4	3.2	2.7	5.0
1958	2.8	3.2	3.7	2.4	2.9	2.4	0.5	3.6	3.7	4.8	5.9	3.3	3.3
1959	7.2	8.5	8.8	11.9	12.8	10.6	12.4	14.4	10.2	8.3	9.6	13.7	10.7
1960	9.4	6.7	6.9	5.5	7.2	8.6	9.5	13.1	15.1	12.6	7.5	2.4	8.7
1961	7.6	8.1	7.3	8.6	9.8	10.4	8.4	9.1	7.8	9.5	8.4	4.3	8.3
1962	3.6	2.3	3.4	2.2	1.5	0.0	-0.7	-1.1	-1.7	-2.6	-0.9	3.2	0.6
1963	1.1	-0.1	-1.2	-1.4	-1.1	0.7	0.5	-1.0	0.0	-0.7	2.2	3.2	0.2
1964	0.5	-1.7	0.1	-2.6	0.8	-0.3	-1.0	-0.5	1.2	0.2	1.8	2.3	0.1
1965	1.9	3.8	5.7	6.5	5.8	5.8	5.5	8.0	7.0	6.3	5.6	8.1	5.8
1966	11.2	11.8	9.6	7.2	5.7	6.4	5.6	3.8	3.5	4.4	4.2	2.7	6.3
1967	1.8	0.4	-1.4	5.3	1.5	1.0	0.7	1.0	2.3	1.1	1.7	4.2	1.6
1968	3.1	2.4	3.9	5.4	5.7	5.0	5.8	12.9	4.0	3.3	6.1	7.4	5.4
1969	7.3	5.1	4.5	4.5	3.5	4.2	2.8	2.3	1.1	0.6	0.4	1.3	3.1
1970	2.9	4.7	4.9	3.0	1.6	0.5	-0.7	0.5	1.6	1.9	2.7	2.0	2.1
1971	0.9	3.1	2.3	0.8	0.2	-0.1	-1.1	0.4	0.5	0.8	1.7	7.0	1.6
1972	3.4	1.7	3.7	5.0	6.9	5.2	4.9	4.0	4.2	5.5	5.6	6.7	4.7
1973	4.8	3.9	4.0	7.3	7.8	9.9	10.2	7.5	6.2	8.9	7.1	6.5	7.0
1974	4.0	4.4	5.8	4.3	2.9	3.2	-3.0	1.8	0.0	-1.5	-0.6	-3.0	2.0
1975	-3.1	0.8	1.7	1.1	-0.9	0.2	-3.4	-3.2	-0.4	-1.5	-0.3	1.0	-0.4
1976	1.0	5.7	5.1	4.9	6.3	4.4	5.5	5.1	5.9	5.2	4.5	6.1	5.0
1977	6.7	2.6	0.6	0.3	0.4	-2.0	1.3	0.9	2.0	0.6	-0.8	-0.9	1.0
1978	1.2	1.0	1.5	1.6	4.1	5.5	5.7	5.5	8.6	7.8	7.7	8.2	4.9
1979	5.6	8.0	7.7	5.2	4.3	4.2	3.9	5.5	4.7	6.4	7.5	6.1	5.8
1980	7.4	7.5	7.9	8.9	7.9	7.2	6.3	5.9	7.4	7.8	7.8	4.3	7.2
1981	6.8	6.4	6.6	6.0	6.7	3.8	1.5	1.6	2.4	2.1	1.9	0.0	3.8
1982	1.4	2.4	2.7	3.2	1.5	-1.6	-0.4	0.7	0.5	0.7	-0.3	1.9	1.1

ITALY LEADING, COINCIDENT AND LAGGING INTERNATIONAL ECONOMIC INDICATORS

1.1 HOURS PER MONTH PER WORKER IN INDUSTRY, ITALY (INDEX, 1980=100)

YEAR	JAN	FEB	MAR	APR	MAY	JUN	JUL	AUG	SEP	OCT	NOV	DEC	AVGE
1972	114.1	115.0	121.1	107.4	108.3	102.5	106.1	101.9	107.5	105.0	101.8	103.2	107.8
1973	98.4	99.4	99.8	102.1	103.3	105.2	104.5	106.8	105.1	106.4	108.7	106.3	103.8
1974	109.7	104.5	104.8	104.0	100.4	101.7	100.4	103.2	99.4	97.0	97.4	95.5	101.5
1975	95.4	104.4	93.2	100.6	88.5	95.8	96.5	85.3	96.9	99.2	96.5	97.6	95.8
1976	94.0	96.5	99.4	99.1	100.9	94.5	103.0	99.3	102.9	101.3	101.9	113.0	100.5
1977	107.4	104.8	105.3	101.3	103.6	101.4	98.7	100.3	100.1	99.9	99.6	101.6	102.0
1978	105.5	100.7	100.7	99.2	102.6	104.7	97.7	101.8	99.9	101.5	103.3	99.6	101.4
1979	102.0	100.2	98.2	94.8	96.5	94.2	92.8	103.7	98.3	104.7	104.8	96.7	98.9
1980	102.6	105.9	101.0	103.1	100.9	100.7	102.3	92.6	93.0	96.2	98.7	100.6	99.8
1981	98.1	96.0	97.1	100.7	96.2	99.8	99.0	84.9	98.1	95.9	95.3	95.5	96.4
1982	94.2	95.3	99.2	99.4	94.4	95.1	94.4	93.4	94.5	92.0	91.5	97.4	95.1

3.1 CHANGE IN UNFILLED ORDERS, TOTAL, ITALY (PERCENT)

YEAR	JAN	FEB	MAR	APR	MAY	JUN	JUL	AUG	SEP	OCT	NOV	DEC	AVGE
1963	3.	-8.	-12.	-13.	-2.	6.	4.	1.	-1.	-8.	1.	11.	-2.
1964	-7.	-18.	-18.	-28.	-18.	-8.	-12.	4.	1.	-12.	-1.	7.	-9.
1965	3.	-11.	-9.	8.	13.	9.	3.	9.	10.	0.	4.	8.	4.
1966	8.	10.	1.	5.	12.	7.	1.	4.	3.	-1.	-2.	2.	5.
1967	4.	4.	-10.	-1.	-1.	-1.	1.	1.	15.	-10.	-22.	1.	-2.
1968	3.	3.	-2.	-1.	3.	4.	1.	2.	4.	3.	6.	16.	4.
1969	10.	0.	4.	6.	4.	10.	9.	5.	-4.	-13.	-8.	-6.	1.
1970	-8.	1.	4.	-4.	-6.	-12.	-15.	-14.	-8.	-4.	-4.	-12.	-7.
1971	11.	-2.	-8.	-5.	-8.	-9.	-2.	-1.	3.	-7.	-6.	16.	-3.
1972	12.	1.	-2.	4.	8.	6.	9.	7.	2.	7.	15.	17.	7.
1973	-8.	-7.	-10.	5.	9.	12.	20.	17.	-2.	-4.	9.	2.	5.
1974	-21.	-4.	1.	-16.	-17.	-5.	-18.	-22.	-13.	-16.	-25.	-23.	-14.
1975	4.	-11.	-4.	-7.	-7.	-2.	1.	1.	3.	9.	11.	3.	-2.
1976	2.	12.	17.	25.	19.	5.	4.	6.	11.	7.	-5.	-8.	8.
1977	-1.	-4.	-14.	-7.	-5.	-12.	-9.	-6.	-3.	-3.	-11.	-3.	-6.
1978	4.	4.	-3.	-2.	7.	12.	2.	5.	14.	2.	17.	18.	7.
1979	2.	6.	17.	6.	-10.	1.	12.	0.	-7.	-5.	7.	5.	3.
1980	5.	0.	-2.	-3.	-14.	-21.	-25.	-4.	-3.	-9.	-7.	-13.	-8.
1981	-1.	4.	-8.	-2.	4.	-8.	2.	9.	-4.	7.	2.	-9.	-0.
1982	-1.	-1.	-6.	5.	9.	-5.	-3.	-6.	-2.	3.	-11.	-2.	-2.

4.1 DECLARED BANKRUPTCIES, ITALY (NUMBER)

YEAR	JAN	FEB	MAR	APR	MAY	JUN	JUL	AUG	SEP	OCT	NOV	DEC	AVGE
1952	545.	642.	598.	565.	594.	589.	679.	576.	607.	423.	466.	443.	561.
1953	443.	453.	477.	404.	551.	390.	529.	432.	509.	390.	481.	404.	455.
1954	537.	419.	504.	455.	468.	475.	534.	476.	506.	448.	486.	490.	483.
1955	548.	550.	612.	594.	599.	596.	615.	611.	655.	546.	563.	591.	590.
1956	610.	585.	634.	575.	544.	646.	567.	649.	601.	676.	698.	505.	608.
1957	611.	654.	593.	611.	692.	610.	654.	674.	622.	684.	700.	671.	648.
1958	691.	655.	586.	691.	632.	658.	828.	648.	702.	676.	654.	784.	684.
1959	730.	732.	722.	718.	561.	713.	668.	553.	613.	634.	645.	515.	650.
1960	591.	631.	607.	641.	577.	606.	569.	570.	526.	438.	500.	668.	577.
1961	472.	469.	547.	499.	487.	482.	550.	566.	548.	447.	486.	551.	509.
1962	518.	544.	499.	421.	544.	513.	473.	492.	519.	542.	543.	484.	508.
1963	517.	474.	434.	426.	484.	436.	465.	549.	447.	491.	459.	455.	470.
1964	479.	504.	392.	651.	502.	607.	573.	576.	597.	611.	529.	644.	555.
1965	690.	645.	670.	694.	651.	649.	658.	582.	632.	618.	658.	650.	650.
1966	619.	608.	626.	589.	717.	566.	550.	628.	594.	550.	552.	557.	596.
1967	535.	519.	577.	195.	741.	686.	640.	597.	631.	614.	629.	616.	582.
1968	615.	700.	584.	601.	560.	652.	729.	618.	569.	648.	591.	579.	621.
1969	631.	617.	630.	614.	668.	541.	590.	588.	621.	638.	629.	660.	619.
1970	690.	686.	538.	677.	554.	560.	589.	538.	546.	538.	520.	614.	588.
1971	505.	476.	501.	556.	569.	563.	560.	526.	527.	604.	572.	523.	540.
1972	489.	520.	558.	504.	485.	556.	494.	488.	499.	403.	474.	439.	492.
1973	437.	481.	455.	321.	440.	392.	350.	398.	368.	201.	349.	374.	381.
1974	358.	325.	298.	316.	278.	314.	291.	387.	375.	383.	309.	331.	330.
1975	356.	298.	233.	342.	373.	359.	499.	377.	383.	393.	401.	408.	369.
1976	398.	450.	423.	429.	366.	312.	427.	413.	406.	368.	402.	420.	401.
1977	392.	376.	433.	381.	455.	542.	288.	444.	442.	447.	445.	459.	425.
1978	422.	468.	415.	493.	471.	524.	344.	458.	413.	422.	470.	448.	446.
1979	531.	469.	510.	470.	473.	429.	489.	463.	520.	511.	501.	453.	485.
1980	469.	464.	461.	421.	457.	459.	467.	441.	438.	452.	417.	471.	451.
1981	473.	474.	428.	496.	415.	580.	501.	462.	468.	523.	525.	625.	498.
1982	533.	566.	660.	618.	684.	804.	545.	494.	608.	647.	718.	771.	637.

6.0 BUILDING PERMITS, RESIDENTIAL, ITALY (MILLION CUBIC METERS)

YEAR	JAN	FEB	MAR	APR	MAY	JUN	JUL	AUG	SEP	OCT	NOV	DEC	AVGE
1955	16.3	14.7	15.4	15.6	16.5	15.2	16.1	16.0	16.2	16.4	16.5	24.8	16.6
1956	14.7	13.8	14.5	14.7	15.3	14.3	14.6	15.3	16.1	16.5	17.5	17.9	15.4
1957	17.2	17.3	17.7	16.1	16.4	17.9	17.9	17.2	16.3	16.0	17.2	17.1	17.0
1958	17.2	16.8	16.1	17.3	16.0	16.7	15.9	15.9	16.3	16.0	15.3	12.7	16.1
1959	16.0	17.5	16.4	19.1	17.2	17.5	17.8	17.0	16.5	15.6	17.1	22.1	17.5
1960	16.4	15.2	17.4	15.6	15.6	15.3	15.5	16.3	17.1	16.6	16.5	16.2	16.1
1961	16.3	15.8	17.0	18.1	18.2	17.7	17.7	18.7	18.3	18.2	17.5	16.2	17.5
1962	19.5	20.9	22.9	18.4	21.4	21.6	20.2	19.7	21.1	22.5	22.6	21.6	21.0
1963	23.2	22.9	21.5	20.6	22.8	21.5	24.1	23.1	21.5	21.1	22.3	22.7	22.3
1964	23.4	21.6	20.0	21.7	16.6	19.1	18.5	16.7	17.9	17.5	17.3	15.3	18.8
1965	11.5	11.5	14.2	15.2	14.8	15.1	14.6	14.2	14.3	15.5	14.7	16.4	14.3
1966	20.7	20.3	20.6	17.5	17.5	16.9	15.2	11.4	12.9	17.1	20.2	21.4	17.6
1967	22.0	19.5	19.5	20.4	21.5	19.3	16.8	15.3	15.0	16.9	25.7	30.6	20.2
1968	25.6	28.5	28.7	34.0	27.3	31.0	43.6	191.3	8.7	8.4	12.3	12.3	37.6
1969	15.2	13.0	13.4	11.5	12.9	11.9	11.6	10.6	11.7	13.8	15.2	15.3	13.0
1970	16.3	14.4	13.4	15.1	13.7	12.9	10.8	9.7	11.7	11.7	15.4	19.3	13.7
1971	12.5	14.5	14.9	12.9	13.9	14.0	15.9	14.0	12.8	15.3	16.0	27.8	15.4
1972	14.7	14.3	15.6	15.3	15.3	18.6	14.1	15.2	15.9	16.9	18.1	20.8	16.2
1973	17.7	20.1	16.6	16.6	18.1	16.9	18.7	17.7	18.9	19.1	18.3	31.7	19.2
1974	13.7	15.3	16.6	16.3	14.7	15.0	16.7	13.6	13.4	13.1	12.1	10.3	14.2
1975	11.0	11.6	13.4	14.5	14.5	14.8	9.8	11.5	12.2	17.5	13.9	12.7	13.1
1976	11.8	25.3	15.5	12.9	11.7	10.1	10.6	12.7	12.5	13.2	12.3	12.7	13.5
1977	17.9	11.5	11.4	12.0	16.6	13.0	14.0	15.2	14.3	13.3	12.3	11.0	13.5
1978	10.4	8.8	8.0	9.0	8.6	10.2	10.5	9.0	8.2	7.4	7.6	9.6	8.9
1979	7.9	10.0	8.9	8.7	8.6	7.0	6.6	7.0	7.9	8.0	8.9	9.8	8.3
1980	9.1	9.1	10.2	9.6	9.7	10.4	10.3	7.8	9.6	9.5	8.1	6.2	9.1
1981	9.1	8.8	9.6	7.5	7.8	8.4	6.6	7.4	8.3	8.9	8.0	5.8	8.0

7.O CHANGE IN INVENTORIES, IN CONSTANT PRICES, ITALY
(BILLION 1970 LIRE)

YEAR	IQ	IIQ	IIIQ	IVQ	AVGE
1970	398.	235.	183.	261.	269.
1971	181.	107.	-57.	167.	100.
1972	13.	-256.	58.	598.	103.
1973	565.	255.	883.	466.	542.
1974	685.	719.	626.	156.	547.
1975	-160.	-66.	-133.	216.	-36.
1976	268.	463.	337.	797.	466.
1977	884.	21.	-202.	200.	226.
1978	35.	79.	259.	314.	172.
1979	59.	136.	567.	586.	337.
1980	1023.	948.	547.	587.	776.
1981	425.	248.	-237.	38.	119.
1982	370.	181.	121.	15.	172.

8.O PRODUCERS' MATERIALS PRICE INDEX, SIX MONTH SMOOTHED CHANGE, ITALY
(ANNUAL RATE, PERCENT)

YEAR	JAN	FEB	MAR	APR	MAY	JUN	JUL	AUG	SEP	OCT	NOV	DEC	AVGE
1977	20.2	18.4	15.3	13.7	12.0	9.6	8.0	7.3	6.9	5.6	4.4	4.7	10.5
1978	5.5	5.8	5.8	6.6	6.9	6.9	6.3	6.5	7.1	7.3	8.4	9.5	6.9
1979	12.3	15.6	18.6	21.2	22.6	22.6	22.0	24.7	25.8	26.4	25.9	25.9	22.0
1980	29.2	30.0	28.1	26.3	23.5	21.7	17.1	15.8	14.5	12.2	14.3	14.5	20.6
1981	14.3	15.9	16.6	18.8	20.6	20.9	20.6	19.8	19.3	17.0	17.5	16.2	18.1
1982	16.1	15.1	13.4	12.4	10.7	8.9	9.9	10.7	10.5	10.2	11.2	10.2	11.6

9.0 STOCK PRICE INDEX, ITALY (1980=100)

YEAR	JAN	FEB	MAR	APR	MAY	JUN	JUL	AUG	SEP	OCT	NOV	DEC	AVGE
1949	35.7	37.9	37.0	36.0	32.3	29.8	31.0	32.2	32.0	32.0	31.7	32.0	33.3
1950	33.9	32.5	31.2	32.5	31.2	29.9	29.9	31.2	32.5	35.3	35.3	33.9	32.4
1951	33.9	35.3	36.6	35.3	35.3	33.9	35.3	35.3	36.6	36.6	36.6	36.6	35.6
1952	38.0	40.7	40.7	39.3	38.0	39.3	40.7	42.0	43.4	46.1	48.8	48.8	42.1
1953	52.9	51.6	50.1	47.5	48.8	47.5	48.8	51.6	51.6	51.6	50.1	50.1	50.2
1954	50.1	51.6	51.6	48.8	50.1	51.6	54.2	57.0	58.3	59.6	62.4	65.1	55.0
1955	71.4	72.2	68.8	68.4	70.3	75.7	81.0	86.2	88.0	86.1	84.2	79.7	77.7
1956	77.6	78.4	76.0	72.3	74.1	70.7	73.2	77.2	76.1	76.1	76.9	78.8	75.6
1957	81.9	83.1	83.8	83.4	85.4	87.1	85.2	87.5	88.0	86.8	85.5	83.1	85.1
1958	83.7	84.0	82.6	81.4	82.5	80.7	81.4	83.9	85.8	88.8	93.8	96.3	85.4
1959	102.1	106.0	111.2	121.8	123.8	128.2	138.8	150.4	141.3	141.0	151.2	156.4	131.0
1960	164.7	162.3	159.5	165.3	174.7	194.9	203.2	239.4	256.9	232.3	209.2	194.8	196.4
1961	213.9	226.8	222.7	223.5	237.2	242.7	224.8	225.7	215.4	222.7	224.7	211.6	224.3
1962	206.7	205.6	208.6	200.6	202.3	188.1	185.2	186.0	178.5	163.3	172.9	185.5	190.3
1963	178.0	164.6	161.7	167.9	168.1	174.4	168.8	163.8	157.2	151.4	157.6	160.3	164.5
1964	150.3	141.9	134.0	121.5	129.6	117.6	115.0	114.1	126.1	126.1	122.0	116.3	126.2
1965	112.0	119.7	133.5	131.9	129.4	123.0	120.0	125.9	124.1	123.5	123.4	133.4	125.0
1966	148.0	154.1	156.7	144.6	143.6	144.2	146.5	147.9	146.3	150.0	148.0	145.5	147.9
1967	143.5	142.4	128.5	129.7	133.5	131.3	130.2	134.2	139.8	144.1	140.4	136.0	136.1
1968	134.6	131.4	133.9	136.7	135.7	133.4	136.0	137.9	136.6	131.4	127.1	133.9	134.0
1969	135.0	133.6	136.3	152.3	153.7	150.7	146.7	152.3	153.0	162.8	163.7	156.2	149.7
1970	157.0	156.8	157.2	162.7	151.8	144.2	139.9	145.2	139.5	137.2	130.1	128.1	145.8
1971	123.5	127.2	126.6	120.2	114.9	112.7	112.7	111.2	105.8	106.0	101.9	104.4	113.9
1972	106.0	102.7	100.0	106.9	107.9	105.8	109.0	109.1	107.2	109.3	116.2	116.1	108.0
1973	112.2	114.4	126.1	131.2	148.1	169.5	160.2	142.7	144.5	147.8	146.0	131.3	139.5
1974	144.7	147.7	152.4	158.7	144.4	131.4	123.1	119.8	103.9	100.3	108.0	98.4	127.7
1975	97.2	108.1	111.3	106.7	105.5	99.3	89.9	87.5	87.3	81.9	80.2	83.1	94.8
1976	81.7	85.2	79.3	72.0	73.0	77.1	87.6	87.0	81.1	70.3	68.5	75.8	78.2
1977	72.0	68.1	66.4	62.9	60.4	59.1	59.9	61.7	68.6	62.9	59.4	54.4	63.0
1978	55.4	59.2	58.3	56.3	58.8	60.4	61.1	65.1	78.1	78.8	70.3	69.8	64.3
1979	71.2	74.6	78.9	73.6	77.3	79.0	80.1	84.0	85.7	85.2	79.6	75.4	78.7
1980	81.4	83.1	83.2	83.0	83.7	88.1	89.8	101.2	112.6	127.8	135.0	130.7	100.0
1981	149.7	166.3	171.1	180.2	185.0	168.2	134.8	146.5	134.9	124.2	127.8	131.9	151.7
1982	129.4	134.5	141.9	131.6	123.9	113.2	106.8	117.2	116.8	117.6	120.8	124.2	123.2

11.0 RATIO, PRICE TO UNIT LABOR COST, MANUFACTURING, ITALY
(INDEX, 1980=100)

YEAR	IQ	IIQ	IIIQ	IVQ	AVGE
1961	90.9	93.3	97.2	97.2	94.6
1962	94.2	94.2	91.5	90.9	92.7
1963	90.9	86.3	85.0	86.5	87.2
1964	84.6	88.3	85.1	85.0	85.8
1965	90.6	87.8	91.4	91.6	90.3
1966	94.4	92.8	94.7	92.2	93.5
1967	88.1	91.0	89.5	88.1	89.2
1968	86.5	88.6	87.7	90.6	88.3
1969	90.7	88.0	87.5	83.3	87.4
1970	87.0	83.8	84.3	84.0	84.8
1971	83.5	82.3	80.9	82.8	82.4
1972	80.6	86.0	84.0	84.6	83.8
1973	85.5	85.6	86.6	87.9	86.4
1974	88.3	90.2	94.2	91.4	91.0
1975	87.3	86.0	83.7	83.1	85.0
1976	85.7	89.4	87.1	91.8	88.5
1977	89.9	87.0	87.3	85.6	87.4
1978	85.9	88.3	88.9	90.6	88.4
1979	92.3	92.5	92.8	95.8	93.3
1980	97.2	102.5	101.1	99.3	100.0
1981	96.1	95.8	96.6	97.1	96.4
1982	98.2	97.4	95.7	97.9	97.3

COINCIDENT INDEX, ITALY (1980=100)

YEAR	JAN	FEB	MAR	APR	MAY	JUN	JUL	AUG	SEP	OCT	NOV	DEC	AVGE
1956	33.6	33.5	34.1	34.5	34.9	35.1	35.4	35.6	36.1	36.5	36.5	36.5	35.2
1957	36.8	37.3	37.3	37.8	37.7	38.0	38.1	38.2	38.2	37.8	38.1	38.5	37.8
1958	38.7	38.8	39.2	39.1	39.9	39.5	40.1	40.3	40.4	40.7	40.6	41.2	39.9
1959	41.5	41.5	41.5	41.3	41.4	41.6	41.9	42.4	43.2	43.7	43.9	44.0	42.3
1960	44.2	44.7	45.0	45.4	46.2	46.6	47.1	47.6	47.9	47.6	47.7	48.3	46.5
1961	49.1	49.8	50.6	51.2	51.3	51.6	52.0	51.7	51.2	55.1	52.2	53.2	51.3
1962	54.0	53.9	53.5	53.7	54.1	54.3	54.8	54.8	55.0	55.1	55.6	55.7	54.5
1963	55.7	56.2	56.9	57.9	58.3	58.9	59.3	59.7	60.0	60.0	60.2	60.3	58.6
1964	60.5	59.9	59.5	58.7	58.6	58.7	58.7	58.1	58.1	57.9	57.0	56.7	58.5
1965	55.9	55.4	54.8	54.9	55.3	55.5	55.4	56.1	56.8	57.1	56.8	56.5	55.9
1966	56.1	56.4	56.7	56.8	57.1	57.3	57.4	58.1	58.6	59.1	59.8	60.1	57.8
1967	60.8	61.2	61.3	61.5	62.2	62.9	63.6	63.4	63.5	63.3	64.2	64.7	62.7
1968	64.7	65.0	65.2	65.5	65.5	65.8	65.8	65.7	66.4	66.6	66.8	67.2	65.8
1969	67.5	67.6	68.3	68.6	68.9	69.2	69.4	69.8	69.3	68.9	69.0	70.2	68.9
1970	72.7	73.6	74.1	74.4	73.5	74.2	74.7	74.5	74.6	75.1	75.3	75.3	74.3
1971	75.5	75.1	74.7	74.8	74.5	75.0	74.7	74.3	74.7	74.1	74.3	74.6	74.7
1972	74.1	73.9	74.3	73.7	74.3	74.0	73.8	74.6	74.9	76.2	76.7	76.8	74.8
1973	75.6	75.1	75.4	76.0	78.2	80.3	82.7	83.6	84.6	85.7	86.5	86.9	80.9
1974	87.8	88.2	88.8	90.1	89.3	88.9	88.3	88.0	87.6	87.0	85.4	85.3	87.9
1975	85.0	84.4	83.5	82.5	82.2	83.1	83.8	83.4	83.5	84.5	83.7	83.8	83.6
1976	83.6	84.6	85.4	85.8	86.9	87.2	87.1	87.8	88.0	87.8	88.8	89.6	86.9
1977	90.0	89.6	89.9	89.2	89.1	88.1	87.4	87.8	88.0	87.3	88.0	88.0	88.5
1978	89.1	89.3	89.5	89.8	90.3	90.6	90.8	90.7	91.2	91.8	92.4	92.7	90.7
1979	92.6	93.1	93.3	92.9	93.2	93.1	94.2	95.5	97.1	98.2	97.9	98.7	95.0
1980	98.7	99.7	100.1	100.5	99.8	100.2	100.3	100.1	99.6	100.4	100.7	100.0	100.0
1981	100.5	100.6	99.5	98.9	98.3	98.6	99.1	99.2	98.9	98.5	99.6	98.7	99.2
1982	99.4	100.4	100.7	100.7	99.9	98.9	98.4	97.8	96.8	96.6	96.8	96.4	98.6

SIX MONTH SMOOTHED CHANGE IN COINCIDENT INDEX, ITALY (ANNUAL RATE, PERCENT)

YEAR	JAN	FEB	MAR	APR	MAY	JUN	JUL	AUG	SEP	OCT	NOV	DEC	AVGE
1957	8.9	9.9	8.0	9.2	7.1	7.4	6.7	6.1	4.7	2.1	2.7	4.3	6.4
1958	4.6	4.1	5.5	3.9	7.6	4.5	7.1	6.9	6.5	7.0	5.3	7.2	5.8
1959	7.9	6.7	5.7	3.4	3.3	3.8	3.9	5.8	8.8	9.6	9.6	8.6	6.4
1960	8.3	9.5	9.5	9.8	12.1	11.9	12.1	12.3	11.3	8.6	7.6	8.9	10.2
1961	10.4	11.7	13.2	13.4	11.9	11.1	11.0	8.2	4.7	3.7	6.3	8.6	9.5
1962	10.0	8.2	5.3	5.0	5.8	5.6	6.5	5.8	5.8	4.7	5.4	4.8	6.1
1963	3.9	5.2	6.8	9.5	9.7	10.2	10.4	10.3	9.7	9.9	7.4	6.6	8.3
1964	5.8	2.7	0.4	-2.7	-3.1	-2.9	-2.9	-4.5	-4.3	-4.5	-6.5	-6.7	-2.4
1965	-8.0	-8.7	-9.2	-7.9	-5.7	-4.3	-3.5	-0.5	2.4	3.9	3.0	1.9	-3.0
1966	0.8	1.7	2.3	2.2	2.7	3.0	2.5	4.5	5.6	6.5	8.5	8.6	4.1
1967	9.8	9.9	8.7	8.2	9.1	9.6	10.3	8.1	7.1	5.2	6.8	7.0	8.3
1968	6.0	5.7	5.5	5.2	4.3	3.6	3.6	4.5	4.2	4.3	4.1	4.4	4.5
1969	4.9	4.3	5.9	5.7	6.0	5.9	5.7	2.9	3.4	1.7	1.4	4.2	4.6
1970	10.4	11.7	11.5	11.1	7.3	8.1	8.2	5.7	5.7	5.7	4.8	3.5	7.9
1971	2.9	-1.4	-0.1	-0.1	-0.6	0.4	-0.6	-1.6	-0.4	-1.9	-1.3	-0.4	-0.2
1972	-1.5	-1.7	-0.5	-1.7	-0.1	-0.9	-1.1	-1.1	-0.8	5.0	5.8	5.4	1.0
1973	2.2	0.4	0.9	2.4	7.4	11.7	16.4	16.7	17.3	17.9	17.5	16.5	10.6
1974	16.3	14.7	13.4	13.6	8.9	5.9	2.9	1.2	-0.3	-2.2	-5.6	-5.7	5.3
1975	-6.0	-6.7	-8.0	-9.2	-8.6	-5.4	-3.0	-3.0	-2.1	-0.9	-0.3	0.2	-4.3
1976	-0.1	2.4	4.1	4.8	6.7	6.2	5.4	6.2	5.9	4.7	6.2	7.0	5.0
1977	6.6	4.8	4.4	2.1	1.2	-1.3	-2.8	-2.0	-1.7	-3.0	-1.6	-1.5	0.4
1978	1.3	1.8	2.3	2.9	3.9	4.4	4.4	3.5	4.0	4.6	5.1	5.0	3.6
1979	3.9	4.3	4.0	2.6	2.7	2.0	3.7	5.9	8.2	9.5	7.8	8.4	5.2
1980	7.3	8.4	7.9	7.6	4.8	4.6	3.6	2.2	0.7	1.7	1.9	0.3	4.2
1981	1.0	0.9	-1.4	-2.4	-3.2	-2.5	-1.2	-0.8	-1.3	-2.0	0.3	-1.2	-1.1
1982	0.5	2.4	3.1	2.8	1.0	-1.1	-2.1	-3.1	-4.7	-4.6	-4.0	-4.4	-1.2

13.0 NONFARM EMPLOYMENT, ITALY (100 THOUSAND PERSONS)

YEAR	JAN	APR	JUL	OCT	AVGE
1959	144.0	143.6	143.7	143.8	143.8
1960	142.2	143.3	145.4	146.2	144.3
1961	147.9	149.1	147.2	146.7	147.7
1962	148.9	148.5	147.9	147.6	148.2
1963	147.8	148.3	148.7	149.8	148.7
1964	151.0	150.0	149.8	147.6	149.6
1965	144.8	144.6	145.7	145.7	145.2
1966	143.6	144.2	145.3	146.6	144.9
1967	147.4	147.3	148.2	149.4	148.1
1968	150.6	150.9	150.3	150.1	150.5
1969	150.0	150.5	151.5	153.3	151.3
1970	155.0	156.1	156.8	156.8	156.2
1971	156.7	155.9	155.2	154.7	155.6
1972	155.0	155.4	155.8	156.0	155.6
1973	156.1	157.8	160.3	161.3	158.9
1974	162.6	163.4	163.6	164.7	163.6
1975	164.5	163.8	164.6	164.5	164.3
1976	164.2	166.7	167.6	167.7	166.5
1977	169.3	169.9	168.5	169.0	169.2
1978	170.1	170.8	171.1	171.4	170.9
1979	172.1	173.1	174.7	175.7	173.9
1980	176.1	177.3	178.5	179.4	177.8
1981	179.6	179.6	180.1	180.9	180.0
1982	181.8	182.1	180.5	181.0	181.4

14.0 UNEMPLOYMENT RATE, ITALY (PERCENT)

YEAR	JAN	APR	JUL	OCT	AVGE
1959	7.0	7.4	7.1	6.5	7.0
1960	5.9	5.6	5.4	5.5	5.6
1961	5.3	5.0	4.9	5.0	5.1
1962	4.7	4.8	4.4	4.3	4.5
1963	4.1	3.8	3.6	3.7	3.8
1964	4.2	4.4	4.4	4.6	4.4
1965	5.0	5.6	5.7	5.7	5.5
1966	5.7	5.8	6.1	5.7	5.8
1967	5.5	5.3	5.1	5.5	5.3
1968	5.5	5.8	5.9	5.8	5.7
1969	5.7	5.7	5.7	5.5	5.6
1970	5.4	5.4	5.5	5.4	5.4
1971	5.3	5.4	5.4	5.9	5.5
1972	6.2	6.4	6.5	6.4	6.4
1973	6.8	7.0	5.9	5.6	6.3
1974	5.3	5.1	5.4	5.5	5.3
1975	5.7	5.9	5.9	6.3	5.9
1976	6.5	6.7	6.8	6.9	6.7
1977	7.0	7.2	7.3	7.2	7.2
1978	7.2	7.2	7.3	7.5	7.3
1979	7.7	7.8	7.8	7.6	7.7
1980	7.7	7.5	7.6	7.6	7.6
1981	8.0	8.6	8.6	9.1	8.6
1982	9.3	9.1	8.9	9.3	9.1

15.0 GROSS DOMESTIC PRODUCT, IN CONSTANT PRICES, ITALY
(BILLION 1970 LIRE)

YEAR	IQ	IIQ	IIIQ	IVQ	AVGE
1952	5684.	5785.	5831.	5861.	5790.
1953	5995.	6139.	6287.	6486.	6227.
1954	6340.	6373.	6493.	6596.	6451.
1955	6765.	6882.	6943.	6930.	6880.
1956	7009.	7151.	7287.	7379.	7206.
1957	7502.	7596.	7642.	7645.	7596.
1958	7823.	7939.	8063.	8042.	7967.
1959	8292.	8372.	8555.	8759.	8495.
1960	8858.	8988.	9120.	9127.	9023.
1961	9454.	9654.	9879.	10068.	9764.
1962	10217.	10327.	10389.	10545.	10370.
1963	10615.	10906.	11085.	11199.	10951.
1964	11365.	11250.	11231.	11184.	11258.
1965	11335.	11561.	11715.	11891.	11626.
1966	12006.	12177.	12521.	12581.	12321.
1967	12832.	13108.	13310.	13573.	13206.
1968	13606.	13891.	14225.	14558.	14070.
1969	14786.	15053.	15089.	14784.	14928.
1970	15627.	15639.	15736.	15881.	15721.
1971	15870.	15839.	15964.	16243.	15979.
1972	16301.	16291.	16352.	17019.	16491.
1973	16821.	17399.	18013.	18368.	17650.
1974	18550.	18615.	18443.	17917.	18381.
1975	17721.	17520.	17650.	17960.	17713.
1976	18357.	18661.	18796.	19197.	18753.
1977	19354.	19025.	19016.	19040.	19109.
1978	19352.	19437.	19585.	20114.	19622.
1979	20271.	20206.	20626.	21234.	20584.
1980	21636.	21498.	21099.	21325.	21390.
1981	21517.	21403.	21240.	21518.	21420.
1982	21830.	21518.	21035.	20996.	21345.

16.0 INDUSTRIAL PRODUCTION, ITALY (INDEX, 1980=100)

YEAR	JAN	FEB	MAR	APR	MAY	JUN	JUL	AUG	SEP	OCT	NOV	DEC	AVGE
1948	11.7	12.3	12.4	12.4	13.4	12.7	12.7	14.4	14.0	13.9	14.2	13.9	13.2
1949	13.9	13.9	13.2	13.4	14.4	15.0	14.4	14.8	14.4	14.4	14.4	14.2	14.2
1950	14.4	15.0	15.0	15.6	15.6	15.6	15.6	16.2	16.2	16.2	16.8	17.4	15.8
1951	17.4	17.4	18.0	18.0	18.0	18.0	18.0	18.0	18.0	17.4	16.8	17.4	17.7
1952	17.4	17.4	17.4	18.0	18.0	18.0	18.0	18.6	18.6	18.6	18.6	18.6	18.1
1953	18.6	18.6	19.2	19.2	18.6	19.2	19.2	19.8	19.2	19.8	21.0	21.0	19.4
1954	20.4	21.0	21.0	21.0	21.0	20.4	21.0	21.6	21.6	21.6	21.6	22.2	21.2
1955	22.5	22.8	23.1	22.9	23.2	23.8	23.8	23.6	23.8	23.8	24.0	23.9	23.4
1956	24.2	23.4	24.4	25.1	25.4	25.4	25.8	25.5	26.1	26.2	25.8	26.3	25.3
1957	26.4	26.9	26.9	27.3	27.0	27.3	27.5	27.7	28.0	26.9	27.2	27.5	27.2
1958	27.9	27.4	27.3	27.2	27.3	28.0	28.2	28.1	28.6	28.8	29.0	29.0	28.1
1959	29.1	30.1	30.1	30.2	30.2	30.1	30.3	31.4	32.1	32.7	33.4	33.8	31.1
1960	33.7	34.7	35.2	35.3	35.7	36.5	36.4	36.6	37.0	36.6	36.7	36.8	35.9
1961	37.4	38.3	38.2	38.6	39.0	39.6	40.3	40.3	40.7	41.5	42.0	42.3	39.8
1962	43.0	43.2	42.8	43.1	43.6	42.5	44.0	44.1	43.3	43.9	44.9	45.9	43.7
1963	45.9	44.8	46.0	47.2	47.1	47.9	47.5	48.2	49.2	49.2	49.0	48.6	47.5
1964	49.9	48.3	49.3	48.7	48.2	47.3	48.2	45.2	47.8	47.6	48.0	48.2	48.1
1965	48.0	48.5	47.9	48.6	50.3	50.8	51.2	50.5	51.2	51.4	52.7	52.5	50.3
1966	53.7	53.5	54.8	53.7	55.7	55.9	56.4	57.9	58.1	57.4	57.7	58.9	56.1
1967	59.1	60.0	59.1	60.3	60.7	60.4	60.5	60.7	60.4	61.1	61.5	61.4	60.4
1968	61.9	62.0	62.0	63.0	63.9	63.7	64.3	64.0	66.0	66.4	64.0	66.9	64.0
1969	68.2	66.2	68.2	68.6	67.3	69.2	69.5	68.4	64.6	61.7	60.4	63.0	66.3
1970	70.6	71.5	71.2	70.6	69.5	69.6	71.5	69.6	71.8	70.1	71.0	71.2	70.7
1971	70.2	69.4	70.2	68.2	69.9	69.9	69.2	70.6	72.2	70.2	72.1	75.1	70.6
1972	73.2	71.3	71.6	70.9	73.5	73.3	71.6	74.2	71.6	77.5	76.8	78.7	73.7
1973	74.1	72.5	73.4	78.3	80.8	82.5	84.6	83.7	83.7	85.4	85.0	85.7	80.8
1974	88.0	83.8	85.3	87.7	87.0	88.0	86.4	84.7	86.7	81.8	77.2	76.6	84.4
1975	77.5	77.4	74.5	75.7	72.6	76.4	77.7	76.5	76.9	78.0	78.6	78.5	76.7
1976	79.0	81.3	82.3	83.0	87.7	86.3	87.5	86.2	89.4	87.3	90.4	94.2	86.2
1977	91.3	88.8	90.0	85.1	89.8	85.7	86.2	87.2	88.2	84.9	85.2	83.5	87.2
1978	86.7	86.3	86.7	85.4	87.7	88.8	88.6	90.0	88.7	92.6	92.5	91.9	88.8
1979	92.3	94.7	92.6	93.0	92.4	88.3	92.3	95.6	96.4	100.1	99.8	99.5	94.7
1980	102.3	104.2	103.8	104.7	98.6	101.8	101.5	101.5	96.5	97.4	100.8	96.2	100.8
1981	96.1	100.8	100.6	100.2	96.1	97.2	100.7	100.7	98.7	95.7	101.6	96.9	98.8
1982	97.9	102.6	100.2	99.5	98.3	93.6	96.5	96.5	93.1	90.5	93.9	91.7	96.2

18.1 RETAIL SALES, IN CONSTANT PRICES, ITALY (INDEX, 1980=100)

YEAR	JAN	FEB	MAR	APR	MAY	JUN	JUL	AUG	SEP	OCT	NOV	DEC	AVGE
1956	30.	30.	30.	30.	31.	31.	31.	32.	33.	35.	34.	33.	32.
1957	34.	35.	34.	36.	35.	36.	35.	35.	35.	34.	36.	36.	35.
1958	35.	35.	37.	36.	39.	34.	37.	37.	37.	38.	38.	39.	37.
1959	39.	39.	40.	40.	40.	42.	42.	42.	45.	43.	43.	42.	41.
1960	43.	45.	44.	45.	48.	45.	44.	47.	49.	47.	47.	47.	46.
1961	49.	48.	51.	49.	48.	48.	50.	50.	49.	51.	51.	51.	50.
1962	49.	49.	48.	51.	51.	51.	50.	51.	52.	51.	53.	52.	51.
1963	52.	53.	53.	53.	55.	54.	57.	56.	55.	56.	54.	55.	54.
1964	55.	55.	54.	53.	54.	55.	54.	55.	55.	55.	54.	55.	55.
1965	54.	52.	51.	54.	54.	55.	53.	55.	58.	55.	55.	56.	54.
1966	57.	57.	57.	55.	56.	57.	56.	56.	56.	57.	61.	56.	57.
1967	58.	59.	60.	59.	59.	59.	60.	58.	61.	57.	62.	62.	60.
1968	59.	62.	63.	63.	63.	62.	64.	62.	63.	63.	65.	64.	63.
1969	63.	63.	66.	65.	68.	67.	67.	69.	68.	68.	67.	66.	66.
1970	68.	68.	69.	73.	65.	72.	73.	71.	69.	72.	72.	70.	70.
1971	73.	72.	70.	76.	73.	76.	74.	70.	77.	74.	75.	75.	74.
1972	76.	75.	81.	75.	79.	76.	78.	81.	81.	78.	80.	83.	79.
1973	80.	81.	84.	84.	84.	83.	83.	86.	89.	92.	95.	92.	86.
1974	93.	96.	91.	92.	90.	90.	94.	91.	89.	90.	84.	85.	90.
1975	82.	85.	87.	83.	83.	84.	85.	83.	83.	91.	85.	87.	85.
1976	86.	87.	88.	86.	85.	88.	81.	91.	89.	88.	87.	87.	87.
1977	91.	89.	89.	90.	91.	92.	90.	93.	91.	87.	91.	89.	90.
1978	92.	91.	90.	93.	93.	93.	94.	91.	94.	92.	96.	97.	93.
1979	95.	97.	101.	97.	99.	99.	98.	100.	103.	100.	95.	102.	99.
1980	98.	98.	99.	99.	98.	101.	103.	102.	98.	102.	99.	97.	100.
1981	103.	103.	100.	101.	100.	101.	101.	104.	104.	103.	105.	100.	102.
1982	106.	104.	107.	107.	107.	109.	107.	106.	100.	104.	104.	106.	106.

LAGGING INDEX, ITALY (1970=100)

YEAR	JAN	FEB	MAR	APR	MAY	JUN	JUL	AUG	SEP	OCT	NOV	DEC	AVGE
1970	92.3	92.2	95.6	97.2	99.0	100.5	101.5	102.1	103.4	104.5	105.6	106.1	100.0
1971	105.8	106.2	105.8	105.4	105.3	104.7	104.4	104.1	104.4	105.0	104.8	104.6	105.0
1972	104.1	104.0	102.7	101.4	100.5	100.5	100.9	101.3	103.2	104.8	105.8	106.3	103.0
1973	106.8	107.1	108.9	110.6	112.3	114.2	118.2	122.4	125.2	125.8	126.3	126.5	117.0
1974	127.2	129.6	133.9	135.7	138.0	142.1	143.4	143.5	141.8	141.2	140.0	139.5	138.0
1975	138.4	136.9	134.6	132.3	128.8	127.0	126.5	126.0	123.3	123.4	121.9	122.6	128.5
1976	123.4	127.0	133.7	134.3	135.0	137.9	137.9	138.3	138.9	141.4	142.4	143.1	136.1
1977	143.8	143.5	143.2	141.4	140.6	138.7	137.8	136.9	135.1	136.6	134.8	133.8	138.8
1978	133.9	134.0	134.0	134.0	134.0	134.4	134.8	135.3	135.1	136.2	137.3	136.8	135.0
1979	136.3	135.8	135.9	135.9	135.9	136.6	137.3	138.1	139.9	143.7	145.5	149.8	139.2
1980	150.5	151.2	151.9	152.5	153.2	152.4	151.5	150.7	152.2	153.7	156.8	155.9	152.7
1981	155.9	156.7	157.3	***	***	***	***	***	***	***	***	***	***

SIX MONTH SMOOTHED CHANGE IN LAGGING INDEX, ITALY (ANNUAL RATE, PERCENT)

YEAR	JAN	FEB	MAR	APR	MAY	JUN	JUL	AUG	SEP	OCT	NOV	DEC	AVGE
1971	11.0	9.5	6.4	4.2	2.7	0.7	-0.5	-1.4	-1.2	-0.4	-0.7	-1.1	2.4
1972	-1.6	-1.6	-3.5	-5.4	-6.3	-5.6	-4.4	-3.2	0.7	3.8	5.6	6.4	-1.3
1973	6.9	7.1	10.0	12.0	13.8	15.3	20.6	25.4	27.0	24.1	21.6	18.7	16.9
1974	16.7	17.6	21.3	20.4	20.4	23.2	21.2	17.8	12.4	9.4	5.8	3.5	15.8
1975	0.5	-2.6	-6.4	-9.4	-13.5	-14.8	-14.0	-13.0	-14.7	-12.8	-12.9	-10.1	-10.3
1976	-7.2	-0.3	10.9	12.0	12.8	16.4	14.9	13.9	13.2	14.8	13.9	12.3	10.6
1977	10.7	7.8	5.4	1.9	0.0	-3.0	-4.3	-5.4	-7.6	-5.3	-7.1	-7.5	-1.2
1978	-6.4	-5.3	-4.3	-3.4	-2.4	-1.2	-0.1	0.8	0.7	2.2	3.9	2.9	-1.0
1979	1.8	0.8	0.8	0.5	0.4	1.1	1.8	2.6	4.8	9.5	11.0	16.2	4.3
1980	15.5	14.7	13.7	12.6	11.5	8.5	5.5	3.0	3.5	4.1	6.8	4.5	8.7
1981	3.9	4.3	4.5	***	***	***	***	***	***	***	***	***	***

20.1 INVESTMENT EXPENDITURES, PLANT AND EQUIPMENT, IN CONSTANT PRICES, ITALY
(BILLION 1970 LIRE)

YEAR	IQ	IIQ	IIIQ	IVQ	AVGE
1970	2606.	2618.	2586.	2617.	2607.
1971	2602.	2555.	2548.	2590.	2574.
1972	2575.	2561.	2620.	2675.	2608.
1973	2585.	2833.	2956.	3042.	2854.
1974	3044.	3052.	3003.	2825.	2981.
1975	2707.	2553.	2506.	2500.	2567.
1976	2589.	2645.	2684.	2763.	2670.
1977	2799.	2698.	2602.	2578.	2669.
1978	2604.	2608.	2657.	2801.	2668.
1979	2732.	2734.	2819.	3064.	2837.
1980	3108.	3153.	3019.	3213.	3123.
1981	3218.	3062.	3013.	3172.	3116.
1982	3125.	***	***	***	***

21.0 BUSINESS INVENTORIES, IN CONSTANT PRICES, ITALY
(BILLION 1970 LIRE)

YEAR	IQ	IIQ	IIIQ	IVQ	AVGE
1970	398.	633.	816.	1077.	731.
1971	1258.	1365.	1308.	1475.	1352.
1972	1488.	1232.	1290.	1888.	1475.
1973	2453.	2708.	3591.	4057.	3202.
1974	4742.	5461.	6087.	6243.	5633.
1975	6083.	6017.	5884.	6100.	6021.
1976	6368.	6831.	7168.	7965.	7083.
1977	8849.	8870.	8668.	8868.	8814.
1978	8903.	8982.	9241.	9555.	9170.
1979	9614.	9750.	10317.	10903.	10146.
1980	11926.	12874.	13421.	14008.	13057.
1981	14433.	14681.	14444.	14482.	14510.
1982	14852.	15033.	15154.	15169.	15052.

24.0 COMMERCIAL BANK LENDING RATE TO PRIME BORROWERS, ITALY (PERCENT)

YEAR	JAN	FEB	MAR	APR	MAY	JUN	JUL	AUG	SEP	OCT	NOV	DEC	AVGE
1966	7.50	7.50	7.50	7.50	7.50	7.50	7.50	7.50	7.50	7.50	7.50	7.50	7.50
1967	7.50	7.50	7.50	7.50	7.50	7.50	7.50	7.50	7.50	7.50	7.50	6.75	7.44
1968	6.75	6.75	6.75	6.75	6.75	6.75	6.75	6.75	6.50	6.50	6.50	6.50	6.67
1969	6.50	6.50	6.50	6.50	6.50	7.25	7.25	7.75	7.75	7.75	8.25	8.25	7.23
1970	8.25	8.25	9.25	9.25	9.50	10.00	10.25	10.25	10.25	10.25	10.25	10.25	9.67
1971	9.75	9.75	9.50	9.25	9.25	9.00	9.00	9.00	8.75	8.75	8.25	8.25	9.04
1972	8.00	8.00	7.75	7.50	7.50	7.25	7.25	7.25	7.25	7.25	7.00	7.00	7.42
1973	7.00	7.00	7.00	7.00	7.00	7.00	8.00	9.25	10.25	10.00	9.50	9.50	8.23
1974	9.50	10.50	12.75	13.50	14.75	18.00	19.00	19.00	18.50	19.00	19.00	19.50	16.08
1975	19.50	19.00	18.00	17.00	15.00	14.00	14.00	14.00	12.00	12.00	11.00	11.00	14.71
1976	11.00	13.00	18.00	18.00	18.00	20.50	20.00	20.00	19.50	21.00	21.00	21.00	18.42
1977	21.00	20.00	20.50	19.50	19.50	18.50	18.50	18.50	17.00	18.50	17.00	16.00	18.71
1978	16.00	16.00	16.00	16.00	16.00	16.00	16.00	16.00	15.00	15.00	15.00	15.00	15.67
1979	15.00	15.00	15.00	15.00	15.00	15.00	15.00	15.00	15.00	16.50	16.50	19.50	15.63
1980	19.50	19.50	19.50	19.50	19.50	19.50	19.50	19.50	19.50	19.50	21.00	20.50	19.71
1981	20.50	21.00	22.50	***	***	***	***	***	***	***	***	***	***

294

JAPAN

LEADING INDEX, JAPAN (1980=100)

YEAR	JAN	FEB	MAR	APR	MAY	JUN	JUL	AUG	SEP	OCT	NOV	DEC	AVGE
1953	17.9	18.5	18.6	18.5	18.9	18.8	18.9	19.9	20.2	20.3	20.1	20.3	19.2
1954	20.0	19.8	19.3	18.8	18.1	17.7	17.5	17.3	17.5	17.6	17.7	17.9	18.3
1955	18.3	18.7	18.8	19.0	18.8	18.9	19.2	19.7	20.1	20.5	20.8	21.2	19.5
1956	21.7	22.1	22.5	22.8	23.6	24.2	24.6	24.9	25.4	25.5	26.0	26.5	24.1
1957	26.7	26.6	26.3	26.8	26.6	26.3	25.5	25.1	25.1	25.0	24.5	23.8	25.7
1958	24.0	23.4	23.5	23.7	23.9	23.9	24.3	24.6	24.6	25.1	25.4	25.9	24.4
1959	26.5	27.4	27.9	28.6	29.2	29.7	30.6	30.8	31.3	31.9	32.3	33.4	30.0
1960	32.1	32.9	32.9	32.9	32.7	32.9	33.1	33.4	33.8	34.2	34.7	35.0	33.4
1961	35.3	36.1	35.9	36.1	36.7	36.7	36.9	37.0	36.3	36.1	35.9	35.2	36.2
1962	35.2	34.9	35.2	34.7	34.4	34.0	33.6	33.6	33.5	33.3	33.7	34.1	34.2
1963	34.8	35.1	36.0	37.0	37.0	37.6	38.1	38.0	38.3	38.6	38.6	38.6	37.3
1964	38.8	39.1	38.8	38.4	38.9	39.0	39.0	38.8	38.9	38.5	38.2	38.3	38.7
1965	38.4	38.4	38.0	37.3	37.2	37.1	36.9	37.1	37.6	37.9	38.4	38.8	37.8
1966	39.4	40.3	40.9	40.9	41.5	42.1	42.6	42.6	42.8	43.2	43.7	44.2	42.0
1967	45.0	45.1	45.3	45.6	46.0	46.2	46.5	46.9	46.8	47.1	47.8	47.8	46.3
1968	47.9	48.0	48.4	48.8	49.5	49.3	49.2	50.0	50.9	51.3	51.7	51.9	49.7
1969	52.3	52.8	52.7	53.8	54.6	55.4	55.8	56.5	57.3	58.3	58.7	59.3	55.6
1970	59.7	60.4	60.3	60.5	59.7	59.0	58.7	58.2	57.5	57.3	56.7	56.4	58.7
1971	57.0	55.9	56.5	56.3	55.9	56.6	57.1	57.2	57.3	56.8	57.0	57.2	56.7
1972	57.7	57.8	60.6	61.8	63.3	64.2	65.2	67.2	68.8	70.5	72.7	75.8	65.5
1973	79.1	81.2	81.3	81.4	81.2	81.2	81.9	82.3	82.1	82.4	83.3	83.9	81.8
1974	84.2	86.4	83.4	80.3	77.4	75.8	74.5	72.8	70.1	67.3	65.2	63.7	75.1
1975	62.1	61.2	61.8	62.8	63.4	64.3	64.7	65.6	65.9	66.7	67.1	68.3	64.5
1976	69.1	70.7	71.9	72.4	73.5	75.1	75.9	76.4	76.3	75.9	75.8	76.0	74.1
1977	76.4	75.6	74.9	74.6	74.2	73.8	73.7	74.7	75.2	76.0	76.8	76.5	75.2
1978	76.8	77.1	78.2	79.3	80.6	81.4	81.2	81.1	82.3	83.4	85.4	86.2	81.1
1979	86.7	88.2	90.2	92.7	94.1	95.5	96.2	96.3	97.0	97.0	97.4	99.3	94.3
1980	102.3	104.9	104.2	105.8	104.6	101.4	99.6	97.2	95.9	95.6	94.1	94.5	100.0
1981	93.8	94.0	93.8	94.1	94.7	95.5	96.2	98.0	98.9	99.4	99.9	99.4	96.5
1982	98.8	99.2	97.5	95.4	95.1	95.9	96.8	98.3	98.4	97.8	98.3	96.0	97.3

SIX MONTH SMOOTHED CHANGE IN LEADING INDEX, JAPAN (ANNUAL RATE, PERCENT)

YEAR	JAN	FEB	MAR	APR	MAY	JUN	JUL	AUG	SEP	OCT	NOV	DEC	AVGE
1954	7.4	3.2	-2.1	-7.2	-14.0	-16.4	-17.4	-18.7	-14.7	-12.2	-9.0	-5.4	-8.9
1955	-0.1	5.9	7.9	10.0	8.4	8.5	10.8	14.8	16.6	18.5	18.5	19.4	11.6
1956	21.7	22.8	24.0	23.1	27.5	28.5	27.4	25.9	25.6	22.8	22.8	22.7	24.6
1957	20.3	15.8	10.6	11.5	7.4	3.5	-3.8	-6.7	-7.3	-7.3	-10.7	-14.7	1.5
1958	-11.9	-14.5	-12.2	-9.2	-6.0	-4.4	0.3	3.3	3.8	7.5	10.1	13.5	-1.6
1959	16.8	22.1	23.6	25.5	26.7	26.7	29.7	26.3	25.5	25.4	24.2	26.8	24.9
1960	13.6	15.3	12.6	9.7	6.3	5.5	4.8	5.4	6.9	7.6	9.6	9.8	8.9
1961	11.0	13.6	11.2	10.5	12.5	10.3	9.9	8.3	3.2	0.8	-0.6	-4.6	7.2
1962	-5.1	-6.3	-4.5	-6.7	-7.4	-8.8	-9.7	-8.1	-7.2	-7.0	-3.8	-0.7	-6.3
1963	3.2	5.4	9.9	15.6	14.3	16.1	17.0	14.6	13.8	13.1	10.6	8.7	11.9
1964	7.4	7.5	3.8	1.0	2.8	2.4	2.0	0.8	0.7	-1.4	-3.0	-2.0	1.8
1965	-1.6	-1.5	-3.2	-5.8	-5.9	-5.7	-6.2	-4.2	-1.4	0.8	3.3	5.4	-2.2
1966	8.4	12.3	14.6	13.2	14.8	15.7	15.8	13.2	12.0	11.9	12.1	11.9	13.0
1967	13.4	11.8	10.6	10.3	9.9	9.3	9.0	9.3	7.5	7.2	8.5	7.0	9.5
1968	6.1	5.5	6.4	7.0	8.4	6.6	5.3	7.4	9.7	10.0	10.3	9.7	7.7
1969	9.8	10.2	8.2	10.9	12.2	13.4	13.1	13.5	14.3	15.9	14.9	14.9	12.6
1970	13.8	14.0	11.2	9.7	5.1	1.5	-0.4	-2.5	-5.0	-5.7	-7.5	-7.9	2.2
1971	-5.4	-7.8	-5.0	-4.6	-4.7	-1.7	0.7	1.4	1.9	0.4	1.1	1.8	-1.8
1972	3.0	3.3	12.2	15.1	18.4	19.2	20.4	24.4	26.8	28.9	31.9	36.9	20.0
1973	41.8	41.5	34.6	29.0	23.1	18.5	16.2	13.4	9.7	7.5	7.1	6.5	20.7
1974	5.6	9.6	1.8	-5.6	-11.5	-14.2	-16.1	-18.4	-22.6	-26.5	-28.7	-29.2	-13.0
1975	-29.5	-28.2	-23.0	-16.7	-11.8	-6.7	-3.0	1.7	4.3	8.0	9.1	12.3	-7.0
1976	13.6	16.7	17.6	16.5	17.1	19.0	18.3	16.9	14.0	10.4	7.9	6.4	14.5
1977	5.8	2.2	-0.5	-1.7	-3.3	-4.4	-4.4	-1.5	0.2	2.3	4.3	3.3	0.2
1978	3.9	4.6	7.2	9.1	11.5	12.1	9.7	7.9	9.6	10.7	14.0	14.1	9.5
1979	13.2	14.6	16.9	20.4	22.3	21.1	19.6	16.7	15.3	12.4	10.8	12.5	16.3
1980	16.2	18.7	14.3	14.9	10.2	2.5	-1.8	-6.6	-9.0	-9.3	-11.8	-10.5	2.3
1981	-11.1	-9.7	-8.4	-6.4	-3.5	-0.4	1.9	6.1	7.6	8.3	8.4	6.4	-0.1
1982	4.6	4.4	0.4	-4.2	-4.9	-3.6	-1.8	0.9	0.9	-0.2	1.2	-2.9	-0.4

JAPAN LEADING, COINCIDENT AND LAGGING INTERNATIONAL ECONOMIC INDICATORS

1.1 INDEX OF OVERTIME WORKED, MANUFACTURING, JAPAN (1980=100)

YEAR	JAN	FEB	MAR	APR	MAY	JUN	JUL	AUG	SEP	OCT	NOV	DEC	AVGE
1954	125.2	122.2	120.1	115.8	114.4	109.3	105.4	102.8	98.5	101.0	100.9	100.1	109.6
1955	103.7	105.0	105.6	108.4	107.8	107.6	109.8	112.5	115.9	119.9	124.9	125.7	112.2
1956	125.6	127.8	132.2	131.3	133.3	136.4	138.0	139.6	142.4	141.4	143.5	144.1	136.3
1957	147.0	146.3	145.0	145.8	147.7	145.5	143.8	140.3	135.3	133.3	124.6	125.7	140.0
1958	125.0	123.1	121.8	121.1	119.6	119.8	121.9	123.3	124.7	126.1	126.9	130.5	123.6
1959	133.3	135.7	137.4	140.8	142.9	146.3	147.3	149.3	149.6	150.7	155.3	155.4	145.3
1960	155.3	156.6	155.4	151.3	152.5	152.1	152.8	149.0	151.7	151.9	153.0	150.8	152.7
1961	146.6	148.9	148.3	148.1	149.7	148.6	146.7	147.1	143.2	147.6	144.0	139.9	146.6
1962	135.1	132.1	129.5	126.8	125.2	119.5	115.6	112.3	110.8	109.4	108.8	108.9	119.5
1963	107.5	109.3	112.1	114.0	117.0	117.5	119.7	121.3	122.0	121.5	121.2	122.4	117.1
1964	124.2	123.9	124.8	119.9	120.7	120.8	119.7	118.6	118.0	117.3	116.1	113.7	119.8
1965	111.4	108.4	106.4	103.7	102.1	101.7	99.6	98.5	94.8	97.2	98.6	97.3	101.6
1966	100.9	102.3	104.9	106.5	108.4	110.0	112.5	114.2	116.9	118.6	117.9	118.9	111.0
1967	118.6	121.1	120.6	122.3	124.7	121.6	121.5	121.5	122.4	121.7	124.4	125.2	122.1
1968	124.5	123.4	125.5	122.1	121.9	120.9	120.2	119.8	120.6	120.2	120.4	119.7	121.6
1969	120.3	120.3	119.0	121.3	124.0	122.7	122.0	121.9	120.6	120.1	120.3	119.8	121.0
1970	118.0	122.4	120.9	119.9	118.8	117.9	115.7	113.3	111.5	112.1	109.9	107.7	115.7
1971	106.4	105.6	102.0	99.7	95.7	95.6	96.6	96.5	95.5	92.2	90.4	89.6	97.1
1972	89.8	90.2	92.2	94.3	93.5	94.0	94.6	95.6	96.8	97.4	99.1	101.8	94.9
1973	103.7	106.0	104.9	105.5	105.2	105.7	103.8	99.7	100.0	99.5	100.4	97.4	102.6
1974	88.3	88.7	87.0	82.2	79.9	76.4	71.8	69.9	66.8	65.2	61.7	58.0	74.7
1975	55.9	51.6	50.3	51.2	50.8	53.7	56.5	58.3	59.7	61.0	62.0	63.9	56.2
1976	64.4	68.5	70.8	71.3	73.8	74.7	75.9	76.6	77.1	78.3	79.1	78.4	74.1
1977	78.7	79.4	79.4	79.3	78.6	78.6	77.4	77.1	77.2	77.9	78.7	80.0	78.5
1978	79.2	79.4	80.5	81.9	80.8	80.6	81.9	82.9	84.2	83.7	86.1	86.4	82.3
1979	87.8	88.8	88.4	92.1	93.8	94.0	94.5	94.7	95.8	96.3	97.5	99.5	93.6
1980	98.8	101.3	102.0	101.9	103.2	101.8	101.3	100.7	99.1	97.1	96.6	96.4	100.0
1981	98.0	97.5	96.7	97.6	97.4	97.7	97.0	97.8	99.2	101.2	100.1	100.5	98.4
1982	101.3	98.0	97.1	95.3	94.2	93.4	93.9	93.4	92.1	92.3	92.4	90.8	94.5

4.1 BUSINESS FAILURES, JAPAN (NUMBER)

YEAR	JAN	FEB	MAR	APR	MAY	JUN	JUL	AUG	SEP	OCT	NOV	DEC	AVGE
1956	214.	170.	170.	178.	180.	155.	128.	141.	136.	146.	161.	119.	158.
1957	163.	177.	230.	190.	259.	236.	373.	289.	244.	220.	222.	316.	243.
1958	185.	264.	232.	246.	175.	217.	183.	183.	209.	215.	173.	187.	206.
1959	195.	190.	160.	182.	175.	158.	103.	143.	178.	153.	183.	140.	163.
1960	197.	148.	160.	151.	173.	185.	195.	175.	151.	163.	151.	136.	165.
1961	113.	114.	126.	150.	106.	131.	143.	167.	155.	202.	175.	246.	152.
1962	266.	274.	244.	212.	252.	251.	286.	239.	267.	237.	252.	224.	250.
1963	182.	215.	197.	180.	276.	234.	237.	267.	256.	254.	318.	288.	242.
1964	412.	375.	481.	525.	484.	493.	513.	634.	681.	848.	862.	847.	596.
1965	862.	756.	825.	856.	863.	865.	880.	870.	850.	846.	846.	838.	846.
1966	771.	807.	753.	878.	838.	882.	861.	1026.	1010.	1019.	1072.	1091.	917.
1967	1075.	1100.	1135.	1081.	1151.	1150.	1145.	1141.	1182.	1157.	1172.	1175.	1139.
1968	1233.	1375.	1258.	1212.	1177.	1127.	1137.	1017.	976.	1018.	928.	870.	1111.
1969	946.	927.	900.	971.	915.	830.	852.	894.	871.	878.	846.	844.	890.
1970	951.	901.	863.	947.	888.	972.	976.	1008.	1017.	1013.	1002.	1035.	964.
1971	970.	936.	972.	941.	980.	964.	1046.	968.	929.	882.	956.	945.	957.
1972	842.	894.	894.	704.	800.	827.	778.	728.	797.	761.	786.	741.	796.
1973	797.	733.	802.	810.	881.	916.	885.	991.	947.	1031.	963.	1021.	898.
1974	1209.	1163.	1150.	1151.	1131.	985.	1096.	1168.	1133.	1121.	1121.	1172.	1133.
1975	1114.	1186.	1089.	1155.	1176.	1048.	1204.	1146.	1246.	1278.	1263.	1462.	1197.
1976	1359.	1327.	1258.	1304.	1305.	1275.	1431.	1373.	1446.	1469.	1608.	1585.	1395.
1977	1526.	1572.	1801.	1664.	1594.	1650.	1545.	1583.	1513.	1458.	1421.	1438.	1564.
1978	1378.	1362.	1511.	1313.	1351.	1354.	1283.	1274.	1229.	1213.	1231.	1095.	1300.
1979	1130.	1125.	1200.	1168.	1146.	1164.	1270.	1334.	1252.	1345.	1412.	1306.	1238.
1980	1396.	1499.	1334.	1374.	1440.	1402.	1351.	1385.	1441.	1378.	1308.	1368.	1390.
1981	1399.	1375.	1324.	1349.	1351.	1296.	1322.	1272.	1262.	1269.	1231.	1285.	1311.
1982	1271.	1277.	1285.	1344.	1247.	1301.	1245.	1137.	1213.	1179.	1174.	1187.	1238.

5.0 NEW ORDERS, MACHINERY AND CONSTRUCTION WORKS, IN CONSTANT PRICES, JAPAN (100 MILLION 1980 YEN)

YEAR	JAN	FEB	MAR	APR	MAY	JUN	JUL	AUG	SEP	OCT	NOV	DEC	AVGE
1960	2310.	2125.	2011.	2181.	2175.	2622.	2307.	2520.	2273.	2862.	2785.	3244.	2451.
1961	3289.	3529.	3000.	3361.	3560.	3607.	4010.	3732.	3191.	3249.	2853.	2661.	3337.
1962	2349.	2209.	2665.	2468.	2153.	2321.	1974.	2122.	2392.	2244.	2214.	2367.	2290.
1963	2298.	2653.	2538.	2806.	2613.	2975.	2967.	3037.	3323.	3171.	3655.	3200.	2936.
1964	3559.	3588.	3488.	3854.	3811.	3401.	3452.	3507.	3416.	3415.	3318.	3278.	3507.
1965	3222.	3203.	3295.	2722.	3176.	3068.	3177.	3024.	3245.	3146.	2841.	3117.	3103.
1966	2934.	3082.	3359.	2894.	3103.	3478.	3376.	3479.	3595.	3618.	3873.	4923.	3476.
1967	4804.	4838.	4632.	5271.	5071.	5821.	5513.	5597.	5248.	6038.	6382.	5739.	5413.
1968	5739.	5383.	5197.	6105.	6068.	6027.	5897.	6436.	6386.	6814.	7126.	6972.	6179.
1969	6979.	7140.	6520.	7616.	7785.	7744.	7584.	7583.	6901.	9734.	8846.	8394.	7736.
1970	8599.	9699.	7595.	9932.	9619.	8517.	9303.	8599.	8597.	9248.	8285.	8254.	8854.
1971	9041.	8175.	9681.	7639.	7662.	9049.	8908.	8792.	9330.	7801.	8468.	9139.	8640.
1972	8384.	8088.	9322.	8728.	9289.	8154.	8355.	9397.	9854.	9656.	10482.	10864.	9214.
1973	12002.	11855.	10557.	12318.	12489.	12365.	12466.	11715.	10671.	14162.	14171.	9779.	12046.
1974	7889.	7308.	7103.	9358.	9164.	9365.	10159.	9076.	9026.	8451.	8150.	7986.	8586.
1975	8154.	8283.	7513.	6745.	6943.	7164.	6360.	7490.	7273.	7012.	6840.	6907.	7224.
1976	6678.	7434.	7639.	6911.	6939.	7362.	7683.	6855.	8396.	7586.	7849.	7809.	7428.
1977	8233.	7387.	7495.	7665.	7617.	6897.	7370.	7733.	7108.	8037.	7729.	8134.	7617.
1978	7920.	8279.	8537.	7852.	8547.	8781.	8664.	9964.	9196.	8835.	9843.	9364.	8815.
1979	9019.	9633.	11126.	10997.	9443.	9767.	9828.	9185.	9910.	9231.	9385.	9109.	9719.
1980	10010.	9977.	7933.	9447.	9468.	9396.	10046.	9159.	8689.	12037.	9409.	12292.	9822.
1981	9792.	8890.	10469.	9721.	10559.	9296.	8641.	9258.	9746.	9920.	9565.	10203.	9672.
1982	9171.	11723.	10028.	8023.	10502.	8868.	8765.	9219.	9888.	8536.	9683.	10555.	9580.

6.1 DWELLING UNITS STARTED, JAPAN (NUMBER)

YEAR	JAN	FEB	MAR	APR	MAY	JUN	JUL	AUG	SEP	OCT	NOV	DEC	AVGE
1953	15682.	17208.	17812.	18581.	19134.	19155.	17844.	19370.	21297.	21254.	21871.	23668.	19406.
1954	22933.	21291.	20902.	22094.	19827.	18827.	18533.	17411.	18042.	17328.	18607.	18674.	19539.
1955	18066.	19395.	19856.	20715.	20651.	19260.	18753.	20059.	22040.	23789.	23334.	24006.	20827.
1956	26934.	26099.	28006.	24736.	26750.	26414.	26505.	25973.	25630.	23773.	23481.	24644.	25745.
1957	25855.	26280.	26008.	26941.	26353.	28495.	27323.	25348.	26007.	28523.	28498.	25122.	26729.
1958	28684.	25693.	25723.	27169.	27197.	28534.	28701.	30563.	28701.	29149.	29602.	27988.	28142.
1959	28945.	32133.	28775.	28934.	29378.	28723.	31601.	31041.	33214.	30518.	31484.	44190.	31578.
1960	24984.	30270.	37954.	33937.	34173.	34523.	36214.	37042.	36757.	35147.	40208.	40591.	35150.
1961	38071.	44492.	44173.	45939.	45249.	45009.	42963.	45997.	44598.	45685.	46176.	46206.	44547.
1962	46863.	42103.	46465.	45488.	49271.	49065.	50943.	50083.	51533.	50083.	50752.	51706.	48696.
1963	51802.	48960.	53553.	56341.	55210.	56609.	62313.	60356.	60882.	61335.	57840.	60202.	57117.
1964	61497.	65476.	61964.	57948.	63742.	62402.	60152.	62304.	63740.	65236.	62366.	65098.	62660.
1965	66292.	69816.	66981.	69405.	66370.	69004.	67578.	67819.	70311.	76143.	76945.	74367.	70086.
1966	65024.	70601.	69669.	66063.	70260.	74592.	77326.	72632.	70509.	71615.	75494.	70515.	71192.
1967	77598.	73590.	82112.	85394.	79724.	74548.	78459.	91143.	83447.	84182.	88145.	91224.	82464.
1968	97377.	97931.	95554.	100155.	104145.	93663.	88370.	97459.	107045.	104979.	107339.	108069.	100174.
1969	102261.	103011.	98085.	107937.	111491.	120186.	116486.	120226.	121356.	110894.	112249.	116828.	111751.
1970	119665.	125102.	125518.	126552.	123223.	130191.	125775.	127760.	116276.	117385.	120999.	124255.	123558.
1971	154410.	105550.	119368.	113827.	117807.	114728.	122939.	122842.	120680.	128327.	122505.	122800.	122149.
1972	123983.	125513.	197537.	138852.	147588.	150286.	139359.	142804.	149124.	157057.	165136.	163090.	150027.
1973	172979.	168515.	177414.	168856.	161569.	153219.	141209.	147235.	162135.	155030.	155382.	150379.	159494.
1974	130151.	124049.	108697.	96646.	106233.	104881.	116810.	122957.	115250.	104160.	98082.	93085.	110083.
1975	85384.	99202.	112140.	109783.	112155.	112827.	117399.	116548.	110744.	119427.	114475.	139129.	112434.
1976	129617.	129105.	121958.	121526.	130315.	133710.	130249.	124580.	122193.	125049.	124506.	134359.	127264.
1977	142305.	127039.	118895.	129044.	124457.	113759.	115369.	132031.	124127.	124180.	136753.	128402.	126363.
1978	136274.	141004.	135255.	120832.	122337.	146474.	126993.	107293.	113583.	128248.	149427.	129587.	129776.
1979	109395.	115560.	126628.	132113.	123402.	131168.	134386.	126571.	126603.	122518.	122125.	115326.	123816.
1980	117846.	111864.	117574.	116151.	110604.	105638.	99944.	99467.	100295.	97819.	94509.	98992.	105892.
1981	91102.	103353.	91776.	98719.	122678.	97188.	84168.	91573.	94215.	91254.	92826.	94991.	96154.
1982	89920.	93543.	92269.	86994.	94755.	94877.	91434.	96743.	100315.	104985.	105562.	97409.	95734.

7.0 CHANGE IN INVENTORIES, IN CONSTANT PRICES, JAPAN
(100 MILLION 1975 YEN)

YEAR	IQ	IIQ	IIIQ	IVQ	AVGE
1952	3879.	-697.	-262.	2504.	1356.
1953	-2028.	5127.	2971.	2222.	2073.
1954	2347.	883.	-717.	-665.	462.
1955	961.	-1602.	1262.	1819.	610.
1956	2413.	3067.	4271.	5292.	3761.
1957	5746.	5464.	2799.	1207.	3804.
1958	-1695.	288.	-147.	-807.	-590.
1959	-144.	5327.	4108.	4960.	3563.
1960	5434.	-1133.	2760.	3335.	2599.
1961	8309.	5135.	8841.	7801.	7523.
1962	6503.	3205.	-1980.	2959.	2672.
1963	-1002.	5110.	6196.	5611.	3979.
1964	5922.	6147.	6100.	6348.	6129.
1965	2901.	1046.	-25.	2837.	1690.
1966	4124.	3175.	5847.	5017.	4541.
1967	10238.	10939.	10404.	9042.	10156.
1968	7290.	13859.	7769.	10093.	9753.
1969	9280.	3984.	13259.	14046.	10142.
1970	15221.	18600.	14163.	11720.	14926.
1971	7558.	2383.	6703.	8046.	6173.
1972	5050.	19119.	14426.	19460.	14514.
1973	29598.	33643.	37589.	35976.	34202.
1974	62567.	43716.	25255.	10788.	35582.
1975	4312.	7227.	2372.	6357.	5067.
1976	1525.	4270.	14359.	9084.	7310.
1977	6353.	100.	-769.	2797.	2120.
1978	-7793.	3829.	1666.	5653.	839.
1979	6853.	12269.	20737.	24529.	16097.
1980	29746.	50852.	22392.	9924.	28229.
1981	9791.	-687.	5432.	11895.	6608.
1982	5097.	-2883.	4298.	6731.	3311.

8.0 RAW MATERIALS PRICE INDEX, SIX MONTH SMOOTHED CHANGE, JAPAN
(ANNUAL RATE, PERCENT)

YEAR	JAN	FEB	MAR	APR	MAY	JUN	JUL	AUG	SEP	OCT	NOV	DEC	AVGE
1953	5.1	8.0	6.2	4.5	5.6	2.8	3.3	11.8	10.6	10.0	8.8	9.3	7.2
1954	9.8	7.5	7.4	3.1	-4.1	-6.1	-5.6	-5.6	-3.1	-1.6	0.0	-0.5	0.1
1955	-2.1	-0.5	0.0	0.5	0.0	-1.0	-1.6	-2.6	-2.6	0.0	-2.1	-1.6	-1.1
1956	-0.5	-0.5	1.1	2.1	4.3	5.9	6.4	9.1	11.8	11.7	15.5	14.2	6.8
1957	15.7	13.4	11.2	11.1	9.9	7.8	4.3	0.5	-2.3	-2.8	-5.6	-7.4	4.6
1958	-9.2	-12.0	-12.5	-12.1	-13.1	-13.3	-10.6	-8.8	-8.4	-7.0	-6.1	-5.1	-9.8
1959	-2.6	0.5	1.1	6.4	5.3	1.6	2.1	3.7	4.8	4.7	5.8	6.3	3.3
1960	5.7	4.1	3.6	2.0	1.5	0.0	-1.0	-2.5	-3.0	-3.5	-4.0	-4.0	-0.1
1961	-4.0	-3.5	-2.0	-0.5	1.0	0.0	1.0	1.0	1.0	1.0	0.0	-0.5	-0.4
1962	-2.5	-2.6	-3.1	-4.1	-5.1	-7.6	-6.2	-7.2	-6.7	-7.3	-6.3	-6.3	-5.4
1963	-4.3	-3.2	-2.2	-0.5	0.5	1.6	2.2	2.2	1.6	2.2	2.7	2.2	0.5
1964	2.7	2.7	1.1	1.6	1.1	0.5	1.6	2.7	3.8	3.8	3.8	3.7	2.5
1965	4.3	2.7	1.4	0.5	1.6	0.0	-1.6	0.0	0.5	0.0	0.5	2.1	1.0
1966	5.8	10.7	9.0	9.5	10.0	11.0	10.4	7.2	3.0	4.0	4.5	3.5	7.4
1967	8.5	6.4	1.5	-2.9	-4.1	-4.3	-3.8	-4.3	-3.9	-3.4	-0.5	0.0	-0.9
1968	-0.5	1.0	1.5	-2.0	-5.4	-3.9	-4.4	-3.9	-2.0	-0.5	-1.0	-0.5	-1.8
1969	0.5	1.5	1.5	5.1	7.4	6.5	7.6	9.6	13.6	13.0	12.9	14.3	7.8
1970	14.7	13.0	12.4	10.8	7.3	1.4	-0.9	-2.2	-4.8	-7.0	-8.7	-9.6	2.2
1971	-8.8	-8.9	-7.6	-4.1	-3.2	-3.7	-2.3	-0.9	-3.7	-6.1	-7.0	-6.1	-5.2
1972	-5.2	-4.3	-3.3	-1.0	0.1	0.5	0.5	2.0	3.9	5.4	6.4	9.4	1.2
1973	14.3	14.7	13.6	12.5	13.4	17.2	25.4	33.0	35.3	34.6	41.5	52.6	25.7
1974	62.1	75.3	69.8	60.9	54.1	46.4	41.9	39.7	27.2	17.3	10.0	4.4	42.4
1975	0.5	-5.0	-7.9	-5.8	-6.8	-7.9	-7.4	-3.5	-1.9	-0.5	0.3	2.2	-3.6
1976	3.9	7.0	8.7	9.5	10.0	10.5	10.7	9.8	7.3	6.1	5.6	3.4	7.7
1977	2.6	2.8	1.5	-0.8	-1.0	-3.0	-5.0	-3.3	-2.5	-4.1	-6.8	-7.6	-2.3
1978	-6.1	-3.9	-3.9	-5.2	-3.1	-3.9	-8.1	-10.2	-8.7	-8.0	-5.4	-1.4	-5.7
1979	1.9	7.0	10.4	15.9	22.0	24.5	27.8	30.3	31.2	32.9	36.0	40.2	23.3
1980	48.8	54.7	46.5	42.7	27.1	16.8	14.0	13.3	6.6	0.9	-0.6	-3.7	22.3
1981	-6.7	-5.7	-3.7	-0.6	3.4	5.7	7.2	8.2	6.4	5.8	3.2	-0.4	2.0
1982	0.9	3.7	4.1	4.2	0.5	2.2	4.7	5.5	6.2	8.0	5.6	-2.3	3.6

9.0 STOCK PRICE INDEX, JAPAN (JANUARY 4, 1968=100)

YEAR	JAN	FEB	MAR	APR	MAY	JUN	JUL	AUG	SEP	OCT	NOV	DEC	AVGE
1953	37.4	39.2	33.8	30.6	31.5	30.5	32.0	34.9	37.5	37.9	36.5	35.5	34.8
1954	31.9	31.6	29.5	28.8	28.4	28.8	29.1	29.1	30.0	28.5	27.4	28.7	29.3
1955	31.3	32.1	30.8	30.5	30.4	30.9	31.3	33.7	34.5	36.1	36.6	37.5	33.0
1956	39.4	39.5	40.8	43.0	44.2	46.4	45.8	46.5	45.1	46.1	49.8	51.7	44.9
1957	53.6	53.4	52.5	53.8	50.6	48.4	45.9	47.0	48.4	46.9	45.9	44.7	49.3
1958	46.0	48.0	47.8	49.0	50.2	51.8	51.2	52.2	52.8	55.2	56.8	59.1	51.7
1959	62.0	64.5	67.8	69.3	71.4	74.5	76.7	78.1	81.9	86.1	87.1	84.8	75.3
1960	84.4	86.7	89.6	95.9	93.7	92.4	97.2	99.8	104.3	108.0	109.8	106.1	97.3
1961	113.4	118.9	115.4	119.3	118.9	118.3	124.1	117.7	107.5	97.3	98.2	94.7	112.0
1962	103.5	108.1	102.8	95.9	97.6	98.7	100.4	98.5	94.2	87.2	96.9	100.6	98.7
1963	102.8	107.3	112.6	121.0	120.5	119.3	113.4	104.4	103.8	101.7	97.2	93.0	108.1
1964	97.1	97.5	97.9	92.4	97.5	100.6	101.7	98.7	95.3	91.0	89.1	89.7	95.7
1965	95.3	95.3	90.6	87.8	87.1	84.3	82.8	90.7	96.3	93.2	97.3	101.1	91.8
1966	106.3	108.8	112.7	111.7	113.2	110.3	109.7	111.1	109.9	108.7	108.5	107.3	109.8
1967	111.3	114.0	113.7	111.5	115.1	116.2	116.3	109.4	106.0	106.7	104.3	100.4	110.4
1968	102.4	104.5	104.7	108.6	112.4	115.8	120.2	125.7	136.3	135.6	130.0	130.7	118.9
1969	137.0	138.6	139.9	145.3	151.0	152.9	149.9	147.1	155.4	159.5	165.0	171.1	151.1
1970	177.2	174.7	182.2	181.6	156.9	157.8	158.7	159.6	156.6	154.2	154.1	148.2	163.5
1971	154.0	160.1	170.6	181.0	182.6	192.9	201.6	189.9	180.2	175.9	177.6	188.9	179.6
1972	206.5	216.1	227.4	244.0	256.2	272.4	289.7	307.6	318.3	328.0	347.6	375.2	282.4
1973	410.9	386.3	385.5	365.4	360.1	358.9	376.7	372.6	353.4	344.8	332.3	302.5	362.4
1974	311.4	326.9	322.1	323.4	334.7	337.7	326.0	298.9	288.4	264.5	270.4	282.1	307.2
1975	276.1	299.8	313.5	320.6	329.7	327.7	323.5	309.8	299.1	308.6	315.8	315.9	311.7
1976	337.3	336.9	341.6	334.4	341.2	352.5	351.4	355.2	354.9	351.6	346.9	364.9	347.4
1977	379.5	380.6	376.9	374.0	378.9	376.0	375.1	381.0	387.7	381.0	367.2	362.7	376.8
1978	374.3	384.5	397.0	410.5	409.7	412.1	422.6	419.9	428.0	436.1	440.3	446.9	415.2
1979	459.5	452.7	447.8	444.7	453.7	444.3	442.4	450.3	455.3	450.7	445.5	453.5	450.0
1980	463.8	469.7	455.9	461.0	466.9	467.9	469.2	473.6	483.2	494.1	494.3	489.7	474.1
1981	505.7	505.9	515.8	546.0	555.0	568.7	590.0	596.7	564.6	545.0	558.1	566.1	551.5
1982	572.8	570.7	536.9	535.0	555.7	540.6	530.8	523.5	531.7	541.4	566.0	583.1	549.0

303

10.0 OPERATING PROFITS, ALL INDUSTRIES, IN CONSTANT PRICES, JAPAN
(100 MILLION 1975 YEN)

YEAR	IQ	IIQ	IIIQ	IVQ	AVGE
1954	4505.	3602.	3418.	3601.	3782.
1955	3849.	3896.	4184.	4315.	4061.
1956	4777.	5589.	5885.	6529.	5695.
1957	6697.	6765.	6162.	5721.	6336.
1958	5092.	5164.	5421.	5778.	5364.
1959	6792.	7691.	8854.	10397.	8434.
1960	10434.	10601.	10781.	11385.	10800.
1961	11363.	11829.	12379.	12275.	11962.
1962	12155.	12100.	11915.	11700.	11968.
1963	12969.	13648.	14547.	15618.	14196.
1964	15933.	16017.	16441.	15841.	16058.
1965	16344.	15184.	14777.	15723.	15507.
1966	17085.	18219.	18928.	20706.	18735.
1967	21083.	22394.	24064.	24028.	22892.
1968	24821.	25677.	26172.	27039.	25927.
1969	28525.	30351.	31904.	33176.	30989.
1970	34599.	33445.	34978.	32538.	33890.
1971	29638.	29527.	28905.	29801.	29468.
1972	29898.	31880.	33645.	38143.	33392.
1973	44525.	46347.	51119.	54351.	49086.
1974	52888.	40613.	39788.	31366.	41164.
1975	27052.	29418.	31112.	32022.	29901.
1976	33642.	34980.	37116.	36090.	35457.
1977	34751.	34225.	33056.	33176.	33802.
1978	34702.	34775.	35436.	39896.	36202.
1979	41065.	46844.	50004.	51792.	47426.
1980	54804.	56185.	52362.	51061.	53603.
1981	49391.	46385.	49894.	52210.	49470.
1982	51332.	45860.	46740.	45761.	47423.

11.0 RATIO, PRICE TO UNIT LABOR COST, MANUFACTURING, JAPAN (INDEX, 1980=100)

YEAR	JAN	FEB	MAR	APR	MAY	JUN	JUL	AUG	SEP	OCT	NOV	DEC	AVGE
1953	105.8	110.7	115.2	114.5	115.0	117.8	118.8	122.8	121.9	123.6	121.5	122.9	117.5
1954	121.4	121.0	119.1	117.7	113.2	111.2	109.2	106.7	110.1	109.4	109.1	109.0	113.1
1955	108.9	110.9	112.9	112.5	109.3	108.6	110.8	112.6	113.6	111.4	112.6	113.9	111.5
1956	115.4	116.6	113.3	114.9	122.6	123.9	125.1	127.9	130.6	133.2	132.4	132.0	124.0
1957	133.5	132.1	133.2	135.3	138.3	135.0	133.3	127.8	127.3	126.7	124.9	121.3	130.7
1958	116.3	115.2	113.6	114.6	110.7	109.0	109.6	108.6	107.9	110.3	107.6	109.4	111.1
1959	109.6	112.7	112.7	113.4	115.1	116.8	116.7	117.7	118.5	119.7	119.9	122.8	116.3
1960	120.1	123.5	120.8	120.8	120.3	119.2	118.3	118.3	119.8	119.2	120.2	118.8	119.6
1961	118.7	118.7	120.1	117.9	118.2	117.6	117.0	117.8	114.5	114.2	113.0	111.7	116.6
1962	112.5	112.0	112.3	108.2	107.8	104.2	102.8	104.2	101.5	100.2	100.2	98.7	105.4
1963	101.7	102.3	102.5	104.4	104.8	103.4	105.5	106.0	104.1	106.6	107.6	107.1	104.7
1964	106.1	106.6	104.1	104.6	103.9	104.1	103.0	101.9	103.9	102.3	100.2	101.7	103.6
1965	100.2	98.7	99.5	97.7	96.1	96.5	95.3	95.1	95.5	94.7	95.3	94.9	96.6
1966	95.0	95.6	96.9	98.3	98.9	100.1	101.0	100.8	101.4	102.0	104.2	104.5	99.9
1967	104.6	102.7	103.3	102.5	104.0	104.4	104.0	104.9	106.7	105.6	107.6	106.7	104.7
1968	104.6	104.6	103.3	101.8	104.2	102.0	101.8	103.3	101.8	102.9	103.7	102.0	103.0
1969	102.4	102.9	102.0	103.3	103.1	102.0	102.4	102.4	103.4	105.6	104.0	105.5	103.2
1970	106.5	105.4	105.4	104.3	103.7	102.5	101.1	99.8	99.2	97.9	95.3	96.0	101.4
1971	94.5	92.6	92.9	92.3	90.3	90.2	89.1	87.7	88.0	86.0	86.3	85.3	89.6
1972	84.9	84.6	85.2	85.0	85.4	84.8	83.6	85.2	85.2	85.7	87.5	88.9	85.5
1973	90.5	91.5	94.0	93.9	92.4	91.8	92.2	96.1	94.9	96.4	98.6	104.3	94.7
1974	111.0	111.2	108.1	102.2	94.3	91.3	91.5	90.3	88.4	86.5	85.2	83.7	95.3
1975	80.1	79.1	77.8	80.3	79.5	78.8	79.2	77.9	78.0	77.7	75.6	77.2	78.4
1976	77.9	79.7	80.7	82.7	82.0	83.8	84.0	83.7	83.0	82.2	82.8	82.9	82.1
1977	82.6	81.1	82.2	81.2	80.5	81.0	79.0	80.3	80.0	78.8	79.7	79.3	80.5
1978	82.3	81.7	82.8	82.9	84.0	84.4	83.8	83.6	83.7	83.3	83.1	83.7	83.3
1979	83.5	83.7	84.4	85.4	88.2	89.3	90.5	91.0	91.7	94.2	95.4	95.6	89.4
1980	98.8	103.1	100.9	103.9	102.4	100.9	100.7	97.8	98.6	98.6	96.9	97.5	100.0
1981	96.8	95.3	95.3	94.3	93.0	95.0	95.8	95.5	96.6	96.4	95.8	95.0	95.4
1982	93.9	93.2	94.6	91.7	89.5	91.9	91.3	90.7	92.0	88.7	90.7	88.8	91.4

12.1 CHANGE IN CONSUMER AND HOUSING CREDIT, IN CONSTANT PRICES, JAPAN
(100 MILLION 1980 YEN)

YEAR	IQ	IIQ	IIIQ	IVQ	AVGE
1966	278.	297.	382.	401.	340.
1967	438.	571.	644.	711.	591.
1968	848.	989.	1051.	1145.	1008.
1969	1286.	1492.	1825.	2336.	1735.
1970	2250.	2045.	1697.	1581.	1893.
1971	1955.	1957.	2077.	2341.	2083.
1972	1998.	3247.	5522.	6877.	4411.
1973	8882.	8224.	6272.	5097.	7119.
1974	3897.	3907.	4167.	4383.	4089.
1975	4423.	5031.	5420.	5422.	5074.
1976	5878.	6062.	5963.	5796.	5925.
1977	5499.	4796.	5112.	6009.	5354.
1978	5597.	6271.	6243.	6082.	6048.
1979	6368.	6780.	5005.	3432.	5396.
1980	4190.	2998.	2651.	2557.	3099.
1981	2402.	2337.	2604.	2496.	2460.
1982	2102.	1640.	2153.	940.	1709.

COINCIDENT INDEX, JAPAN (1980=100)

YEAR	JAN	FEB	MAR	APR	MAY	JUN	JUL	AUG	SEP	OCT	NOV	DEC	AVGE
1954	6.5	6.6	6.6	6.5	6.4	6.4	6.5	6.5	6.5	6.5	6.6	6.7	6.5
1955	6.8	7.0	7.0	6.9	7.0	7.0	7.1	7.3	7.4	7.5	7.7	7.8	7.2
1956	7.9	8.0	7.9	8.2	8.3	8.4	8.7	8.7	8.9	9.0	9.1	9.2	8.5
1957	9.4	9.6	9.7	9.9	10.2	10.2	10.4	10.3	10.4	10.4	10.6	10.7	10.1
1958	10.6	10.8	10.8	10.9	10.9	10.8	11.1	11.2	11.3	11.4	11.5	11.8	11.1
1959	11.8	12.1	12.2	12.6	12.9	13.2	13.3	13.6	14.1	14.2	14.5	14.9	13.3
1960	15.2	15.7	15.9	16.1	16.1	16.5	16.9	17.1	17.5	18.0	18.4	18.7	16.8
1961	19.2	19.3	20.0	20.1	20.4	20.8	21.1	21.5	21.8	22.0	22.3	22.5	20.9
1962	23.0	23.2	23.3	23.6	24.2	24.2	24.2	24.7	24.8	24.7	25.0	25.1	24.2
1963	25.2	25.5	25.8	26.8	26.9	27.4	28.0	28.5	28.4	29.4	29.8	30.1	27.6
1964	30.4	31.0	30.9	31.5	32.0	32.3	32.7	33.0	33.4	33.2	33.6	34.0	32.3
1965	33.6	33.7	34.2	33.7	33.9	34.4	34.7	34.9	34.8	34.9	35.3	35.6	34.5
1966	35.7	36.1	36.1	37.2	37.6	38.0	38.6	39.0	39.0	39.5	40.1	40.7	38.1
1967	40.7	41.4	40.9	42.1	43.0	43.7	44.6	45.0	45.7	45.7	45.9	46.5	43.8
1968	46.8	47.3	47.9	48.7	49.3	50.0	50.1	50.8	51.5	52.3	53.4	53.8	50.2
1969	54.0	54.1	54.6	55.5	56.3	56.3	56.8	57.5	58.3	59.3	60.5	60.8	57.0
1970	60.7	61.4	62.6	62.8	64.0	64.9	65.1	65.1	65.6	65.7	65.7	66.5	64.2
1971	67.3	67.7	68.5	68.9	68.9	69.4	69.8	69.9	70.5	70.4	70.8	70.9	69.4
1972	71.3	72.1	72.7	73.0	73.5	73.8	74.4	75.2	75.8	76.6	77.6	78.8	74.6
1973	80.8	81.9	82.0	82.3	82.2	82.8	82.9	83.6	82.8	84.6	84.6	83.4	82.8
1974	82.0	80.0	79.6	80.5	82.7	82.6	82.3	81.3	82.3	80.1	80.0	79.4	81.1
1975	78.6	78.4	78.9	79.1	79.3	79.7	80.1	80.2	80.2	80.2	80.1	81.0	79.6
1976	81.2	82.3	82.1	81.5	81.7	82.4	82.4	83.3	83.2	83.7	84.3	85.0	82.8
1977	85.6	85.4	85.9	86.4	86.0	86.2	86.2	87.3	87.1	87.7	88.1	88.5	86.7
1978	88.9	89.0	89.6	89.8	89.9	90.3	91.0	90.7	91.4	92.1	92.7	93.3	90.7
1979	94.0	94.8	94.8	95.0	96.3	96.6	96.1	97.3	97.9	97.9	98.7	98.9	96.5
1980	99.1	101.0	100.1	100.4	100.2	100.0	99.3	99.2	100.0	100.4	99.9	100.3	100.0
1981	101.4	101.0	101.7	102.0	101.5	102.2	102.9	103.2	103.3	103.6	103.3	103.4	102.5
1982	103.7	103.3	103.7	104.2	104.7	104.8	105.1	104.8	105.0	104.3	105.4	105.1	104.5

SIX MONTH SMOOTHED CHANGE IN COINCIDENT INDEX, JAPAN (ANNUAL RATE, PERCENT)

YEAR	JAN	FEB	MAR	APR	MAY	JUN	JUL	AUG	SEP	OCT	NOV	DEC	AVGE
1955	8.8	11.5	10.8	8.5	9.6	8.7	10.8	12.8	15.4	14.8	17.6	18.3	12.3
1956	17.2	17.8	14.2	18.1	19.5	19.4	21.7	20.0	19.4	18.8	19.9	19.2	18.8
1957	19.7	20.1	21.1	20.4	23.0	20.7	20.1	16.5	14.2	12.7	13.2	12.0	17.8
1958	8.3	9.7	8.2	8.0	6.1	4.9	9.3	8.5	9.7	10.2	10.1	14.3	8.9
1959	12.2	15.7	15.9	19.4	22.2	23.6	22.9	24.4	27.7	26.5	25.5	27.9	22.0
1960	27.5	31.1	28.3	26.0	22.5	23.5	25.0	23.0	24.0	25.9	26.5	25.2	25.7
1961	27.0	24.5	28.2	24.4	24.6	24.2	23.3	23.2	21.4	20.2	18.7	17.4	23.1
1962	19.4	17.7	15.5	15.6	17.8	15.2	12.7	13.8	12.8	9.7	10.0	9.3	14.1
1963	7.7	8.6	9.8	15.9	14.5	16.0	18.8	19.6	16.7	21.5	21.3	20.3	15.9
1964	19.5	19.9	15.6	16.5	17.1	16.3	16.0	15.0	15.4	11.4	11.2	11.8	15.5
1965	7.4	6.1	8.1	3.6	3.7	5.0	5.8	6.1	4.7	4.5	5.8	7.1	5.7
1966	6.8	7.9	6.9	11.9	12.2	13.0	14.3	14.6	12.7	13.5	14.2	15.3	11.9
1967	12.7	14.2	8.9	13.0	15.2	16.1	18.0	17.5	18.5	15.2	13.9	14.3	14.8
1968	13.0	13.2	13.3	14.2	14.0	14.7	12.6	13.8	14.4	15.3	17.7	16.3	14.4
1969	14.5	12.3	12.2	13.3	13.9	11.7	11.5	11.9	12.5	14.1	16.1	14.8	13.2
1970	12.2	12.7	14.4	12.7	14.5	15.4	13.3	11.1	10.6	9.1	7.2	8.3	11.8
1971	10.1	8.5	9.3	8.9	7.4	7.7	7.8	6.9	7.2	5.8	5.9	4.8	7.5
1972	5.0	6.4	6.9	6.7	7.0	6.9	7.6	8.5	9.0	9.7	11.1	12.5	8.1
1973	15.9	16.7	14.7	13.1	10.8	10.4	8.9	8.6	5.0	7.8	6.4	2.1	10.0
1974	-1.9	-6.5	-6.9	-4.5	0.6	0.4	-0.4	-2.5	0.2	-4.5	-3.9	-4.6	-2.9
1975	-5.5	-5.3	-4.0	-3.4	-2.6	-1.0	0.3	1.1	1.1	1.6	1.4	3.6	-1.1
1976	3.7	5.7	4.4	2.3	2.5	3.4	2.9	4.6	3.8	4.5	5.0	5.8	4.0
1977	6.4	5.1	5.7	6.1	4.2	3.8	3.2	4.8	3.6	4.7	4.3	4.6	4.7
1978	4.6	4.4	4.9	4.8	3.9	4.6	5.3	3.7	4.6	5.3	5.7	6.3	4.8
1979	6.8	7.5	6.5	6.0	7.6	7.1	5.1	6.6	6.7	5.6	6.2	5.5	6.4
1980	5.1	7.9	5.0	4.7	3.4	2.4	0.6	0.0	1.1	1.5	0.3	0.8	2.7
1981	2.6	1.5	2.9	3.1	2.0	3.1	3.9	4.0	3.5	3.5	2.5	2.3	2.9
1982	2.2	1.1	1.5	2.1	2.6	2.5	2.5	1.8	1.9	0.4	2.1	1.3	1.8

13.0 REGULAR WORKERS' EMPLOYMENT, ALL INDUSTRIES, JAPAN (INDEX, 1980=100)

YEAR	JAN	FEB	MAR	APR	MAY	JUN	JUL	AUG	SEP	OCT	NOV	DEC	AVGE
1954	35.2	35.2	35.2	35.2	35.3	35.2	35.4	35.4	35.5	35.6	35.7	35.9	35.4
1955	36.1	36.2	36.0	35.9	36.0	36.0	36.3	36.4	36.6	36.8	36.9	37.1	36.4
1956	37.4	37.6	37.8	38.1	38.4	38.8	39.1	39.4	39.7	39.9	40.2	40.7	38.9
1957	41.1	41.4	42.0	42.3	42.7	42.9	43.2	43.4	43.6	43.8	44.1	44.3	42.9
1958	44.5	44.8	44.9	45.1	45.2	45.5	45.6	45.8	46.1	46.4	46.6	47.1	45.6
1959	47.4	48.0	48.3	48.9	49.4	49.8	50.4	51.1	51.7	52.4	53.0	53.5	50.3
1960	54.1	54.6	55.2	55.9	56.5	57.1	57.6	58.1	58.7	59.3	59.7	60.1	57.2
1961	61.1	61.5	62.1	62.6	62.9	63.4	64.1	64.4	65.0	65.5	65.8	66.4	63.7
1962	66.8	67.4	67.3	68.3	68.9	69.2	69.5	69.9	70.1	70.2	70.6	70.9	69.1
1963	71.1	71.3	71.5	72.2	72.5	72.9	73.2	73.6	73.9	74.5	74.7	75.2	73.0
1964	75.4	75.9	75.1	76.3	76.6	77.0	77.3	77.7	77.9	78.1	78.4	78.6	77.0
1965	78.8	79.0	78.9	79.3	79.3	79.4	79.6	79.7	79.9	80.2	80.3	80.5	79.6
1966	80.7	80.8	79.9	81.1	81.3	81.4	81.7	81.7	81.8	82.0	82.2	82.3	81.4
1967	82.4	82.9	82.4	83.4	83.7	84.1	84.3	84.6	84.9	85.1	85.2	85.4	84.0
1968	85.8	85.9	86.0	86.5	86.7	87.0	87.2	87.6	87.9	88.2	88.4	88.7	87.2
1969	88.7	88.8	89.0	89.3	89.6	89.8	90.1	90.2	90.4	90.7	91.0	91.3	89.9
1970	91.5	92.0	92.6	93.1	93.4	93.9	93.9	93.3	94.1	94.3	94.4	94.5	93.4
1971	94.8	94.8	95.1	95.3	95.5	95.5	95.6	95.6	95.8	95.8	96.0	96.0	95.5
1972	95.9	96.1	96.1	96.1	96.1	96.1	96.2	96.4	96.4	96.3	96.5	96.5	96.2
1973	96.7	96.6	96.4	96.7	96.9	96.8	97.0	96.9	96.8	97.0	97.2	97.1	96.8
1974	97.1	97.0	97.2	97.3	97.4	97.5	97.3	97.0	97.0	96.7	96.4	96.2	97.0
1975	95.9	95.7	95.3	95.0	95.0	95.2	95.2	95.3	95.3	95.4	95.5	95.8	95.4
1976	95.6	95.6	95.3	95.1	95.0	95.1	95.1	95.3	95.5	95.7	95.8	96.0	95.4
1977	96.2	96.3	96.5	96.8	96.9	96.8	96.7	96.8	96.8	96.8	96.9	96.8	96.7
1978	96.9	97.1	97.1	97.0	97.1	97.2	97.3	97.3	97.4	97.3	97.4	97.6	97.2
1979	97.7	98.0	98.0	98.1	98.3	98.4	98.6	98.7	98.8	99.0	99.1	99.2	98.5
1980	99.1	99.5	99.6	99.7	99.8	99.8	99.9	100.2	100.3	100.4	100.6	100.6	100.0
1981	101.1	101.2	101.4	101.7	101.8	102.3	102.0	102.1	102.2	102.3	102.3	102.4	101.9
1982	102.5	102.5	102.4	103.1	103.2	103.3	103.3	103.4	103.5	103.5	103.6	103.5	103.1

14.0 UNEMPLOYMENT RATE, JAPAN (PERCENT)

YEAR	JAN	FEB	MAR	APR	MAY	JUN	JUL	AUG	SEP	OCT	NOV	DEC	AVGE
1953	2.0	2.0	1.9	2.0	2.0	1.9	1.8	1.8	1.7	1.7	1.8	1.6	1.8
1954	1.8	1.8	1.9	2.0	2.2	2.2	2.4	2.6	2.5	2.6	2.6	2.7	2.3
1955	2.5	2.4	2.2	2.4	2.5	2.6	2.7	2.7	2.6	2.7	2.5	2.4	2.5
1956	2.5	2.5	2.5	2.4	2.4	2.2	2.2	2.1	2.2	2.0	2.2	2.3	2.3
1957	2.0	2.0	2.0	2.0	1.9	1.8	1.8	1.8	2.2	2.0	1.9	1.8	1.9
1958	1.9	1.9	2.0	2.0	2.0	2.2	2.1	2.2	2.0	2.1	2.1	2.1	2.1
1959	2.4	2.4	2.4	2.2	2.2	2.3	2.3	2.3	2.2	1.9	2.0	2.0	2.2
1960	1.8	1.6	1.7	1.7	1.7	1.6	1.5	1.4	1.6	1.4	1.5	1.4	1.6
1961	1.4	1.5	1.3	1.4	1.5	1.5	1.5	1.4	1.4	1.4	1.3	1.3	1.4
1962	1.3	1.3	1.4	1.2	1.2	1.3	1.3	1.2	1.2	1.2	1.2	1.2	1.3
1963	1.4	1.4	1.4	1.2	1.3	1.1	1.1	1.2	1.3	1.3	1.1	1.3	1.2
1964	1.2	1.3	1.0	1.2	1.1	1.3	1.2	1.2	1.1	1.3	1.3	1.2	1.2
1965	1.1	1.2	1.4	1.3	1.4	1.3	1.3	1.3	1.4	1.2	1.3	1.3	1.3
1966	1.4	1.3	1.6	1.3	1.2	1.3	1.3	1.2	1.1	1.1	1.0	1.2	1.3
1967	1.2	1.3	1.1	1.2	1.2	1.3	1.3	1.1	1.3	1.3	1.3	1.3	1.3
1968	1.3	1.3	1.1	1.1	1.2	1.1	1.2	1.2	1.1	1.2	1.0	1.1	1.2
1969	1.2	1.2	1.0	1.2	1.2	1.3	1.3	1.1	1.1	1.1	1.0	1.1	1.1
1970	1.1	1.1	1.1	1.1	1.1	1.1	1.2	1.2	1.3	1.3	1.3	1.2	1.2
1971	1.1	1.2	1.2	1.2	1.4	1.3	1.2	1.4	1.5	1.2	1.4	1.4	1.2
1972	1.4	1.4	1.4	1.4	1.4	1.4	1.4	1.4	1.4	1.4	1.2	1.1	1.4
1973	1.3	1.2	1.2	1.3	1.2	1.3	1.3	1.2	1.3	1.1	1.5	1.7	1.3
1974	1.2	1.3	1.4	1.8	1.8	1.8	1.8	1.5	1.4	1.6	2.1	1.8	1.4
1975	1.7	1.8	1.8	1.8	1.8	1.8	1.8	1.9	2.0	2.1	2.1	2.1	1.9
1976	2.1	2.0	2.0	2.1	2.1	2.0	2.1	2.0	2.0	2.1	2.0	2.1	2.0
1977	1.9	2.0	2.0	1.9	2.3	2.3	2.2	2.3	2.4	2.9	2.0	2.1	2.0
1978	2.1	2.2	2.2	2.1	2.0	2.0	2.2	2.1	2.0	2.1	2.1	2.2	2.2
1979	2.0	1.9	1.9	2.0	2.0	1.9	2.0	2.1	2.0	2.1	2.2	2.0	2.1
1980	2.0	2.3	2.2	2.2	2.0	2.3	2.0	2.3	2.2	2.2	2.2	2.2	2.0
1981	2.1	2.3	2.2	2.2	2.3	1.9	2.2	2.1	2.2	2.2	2.2	2.2	2.2
1982	2.2	2.3	2.3	2.3	2.3	2.4	2.4	2.4	2.4	2.5	2.4	2.4	2.4

15.0 GROSS NATIONAL EXPENDITURES, AT CONSTANT PRICES, JAPAN
(BILLION 1975 YEN)

YEAR	IQ	IIQ	IIIQ	IVQ	AVGE
1952	21806.	23328.	22899.	24675.	23177.
1953	23705.	24510.	25319.	25257.	24698.
1954	26833.	25420.	26145.	26049.	26112.
1955	27144.	27659.	28689.	29772.	28316.
1956	29956.	30203.	30258.	31188.	30401.
1957	31654.	32620.	33225.	33420.	32730.
1958	33511.	34330.	34974.	35625.	34610.
1959	35806.	37301.	38815.	38828.	37688.
1960	41578.	41265.	42891.	44855.	42647.
1961	46821.	48135.	49063.	51170.	48797.
1962	51121.	52104.	52674.	53013.	52228.
1963	54601.	56553.	58460.	60917.	57633.
1964	63267.	64740.	65917.	66929.	65213.
1965	66929.	68251.	69930.	69853.	68741.
1966	72944.	75921.	77701.	78668.	76308.
1967	80937.	82856.	86166.	88006.	84491.
1968	90369.	93260.	95617.	101531.	95194.
1969	102155.	105731.	107332.	112277.	106874.
1970	114397.	116274.	119324.	119978.	117493.
1971	120524.	122305.	124066.	125225.	123030.
1972	130068.	132116.	135029.	138572.	133946.
1973	144848.	146306.	146129.	146214.	145874.
1974	141620.	143992.	145714.	145073.	144100.
1975	143984.	147122.	148623.	150719.	147612.
1976	153179.	154984.	156592.	157134.	155472.
1977	161488.	163116.	164079.	166364.	163762.
1978	169514.	170866.	172816.	175250.	172112.
1979	177498.	180102.	182079.	184249.	180982.
1980	187049.	188110.	190658.	192849.	189667.
1981	194593.	196856.	198535.	198009.	196998.
1982	198755.	202624.	204512.	205426.	202829.

16.0 INDUSTRIAL PRODUCTION, JAPAN (INDEX, 1980=100)

YEAR	JAN	FEB	MAR	APR	MAY	JUN	JUL	AUG	SEP	OCT	NOV	DEC	AVGE
1953	6.6	6.8	7.2	7.3	7.5	7.6	7.7	7.8	7.9	8.2	8.2	8.3	7.6
1954	8.3	8.3	8.4	8.4	8.3	8.3	8.2	8.0	8.1	8.2	8.3	8.3	8.3
1955	8.3	8.5	8.5	8.5	8.5	8.5	8.8	9.0	9.2	9.2	9.3	9.6	8.8
1956	9.8	10.1	9.8	10.2	10.4	10.7	11.0	11.1	11.4	11.8	11.9	11.9	10.8
1957	12.0	12.2	12.8	12.8	13.5	13.2	13.4	12.9	12.9	12.8	12.8	12.6	12.8
1958	12.4	12.5	12.4	12.4	12.1	12.0	12.4	12.6	12.6	12.9	12.8	13.2	12.5
1959	13.3	13.8	13.8	14.1	14.6	15.0	15.2	15.4	15.9	16.1	16.4	17.1	15.1
1960	17.1	17.9	18.0	18.2	18.3	18.5	18.8	19.1	19.5	19.7	20.1	20.3	18.8
1961	20.8	20.9	21.5	21.5	22.0	22.4	22.7	23.2	23.0	23.5	23.7	24.0	22.4
1962	24.5	24.4	24.8	24.5	24.8	24.4	24.0	24.4	24.0	24.0	24.0	24.0	24.3
1963	24.5	25.1	25.3	26.2	26.6	26.3	27.4	27.9	27.9	28.8	29.2	29.5	27.1
1964	29.7	30.4	30.1	30.5	30.9	31.5	31.5	31.5	32.4	32.4	32.1	32.8	31.3
1965	32.5	32.2	32.5	32.2	31.8	32.4	32.4	32.4	32.6	32.6	33.2	33.2	32.5
1966	33.7	33.8	34.7	35.4	35.8	36.4	37.1	37.6	38.1	38.8	39.7	40.5	36.8
1967	40.8	40.4	41.5	41.8	42.8	43.5	43.9	44.7	46.0	46.4	47.5	47.9	43.9
1968	47.7	48.4	48.8	49.0	50.6	49.8	50.3	51.6	51.4	52.6	54.1	53.9	50.7
1969	54.6	55.4	55.5	57.1	58.4	57.9	58.7	59.2	60.5	62.2	62.2	63.4	58.8
1970	64.2	64.9	65.4	66.0	66.8	67.8	67.8	67.5	67.8	68.0	67.3	68.7	66.8
1971	68.6	68.2	68.9	68.6	66.8	68.2	68.5	68.7	69.6	68.7	69.5	69.1	68.6
1972	69.5	70.2	71.6	71.2	72.3	72.6	72.5	74.4	75.2	76.0	77.5	79.3	73.5
1973	81.4	82.1	83.4	83.2	84.0	84.8	83.8	86.3	85.0	86.4	87.2	87.2	84.6
1974	87.6	87.4	85.4	83.6	83.7	81.6	80.8	79.7	78.8	77.1	75.8	74.4	81.3
1975	71.4	70.8	69.8	71.5	71.5	72.2	73.0	72.9	73.6	73.9	72.6	74.2	72.3
1976	75.5	77.3	78.5	79.5	79.2	80.8	81.5	81.7	81.6	81.6	82.8	83.2	80.3
1977	83.8	82.7	83.9	83.4	83.0	83.7	82.1	83.9	83.8	83.2	84.8	85.4	83.6
1978	86.3	85.7	87.5	87.6	87.8	88.3	88.9	90.0	90.7	90.9	91.3	92.2	88.9
1979	92.0	91.9	92.8	93.0	95.1	95.5	96.2	97.6	95.8	97.9	99.0	98.7	95.5
1980	99.4	103.1	100.3	102.0	101.4	100.3	100.2	97.2	98.8	99.4	98.1	99.5	100.0
1981	99.7	99.3	99.6	99.6	98.1	100.6	101.4	101.1	102.7	103.2	103.3	102.9	101.0
1982	102.3	101.4	103.2	101.0	99.3	101.7	101.5	101.0	102.4	98.9	101.9	100.9	101.3

17.1 WAGE AND SALARY INCOME, IN CONSTANT PRICES, JAPAN (INDEX, 1980=100)

YEAR	JAN	FEB	MAR	APR	MAY	JUN	JUL	AUG	SEP	OCT	NOV	DEC	AVGE
1954	12.1	12.1	12.2	12.1	12.2	12.2	12.3	12.5	12.6	12.5	12.9	13.0	12.4
1955	13.0	13.2	13.1	12.9	13.2	13.2	13.6	13.6	13.9	13.8	14.2	14.4	13.5
1956	14.4	14.5	14.4	14.6	14.9	14.8	15.4	15.4	15.4	15.4	15.7	15.8	15.1
1957	15.8	16.0	16.3	16.5	16.3	16.5	16.6	16.6	16.7	16.8	17.2	17.4	16.6
1958	17.6	17.8	18.0	17.9	18.0	17.8	18.3	18.1	18.3	18.0	18.3	18.8	18.1
1959	18.9	19.4	19.4	19.8	20.3	20.5	20.7	20.6	21.1	21.3	21.7	21.9	20.5
1960	22.0	22.4	23.0	23.0	23.1	23.5	23.8	23.8	24.0	24.3	25.0	25.1	23.6
1961	25.3	25.5	26.1	26.1	26.9	27.5	27.7	28.7	28.4	28.4	28.7	28.8	27.3
1962	29.1	29.4	29.5	29.8	30.3	30.7	30.6	31.0	31.3	31.2	31.1	31.4	30.5
1963	30.9	31.3	31.5	32.3	32.2	32.2	33.1	33.8	33.3	34.2	34.7	34.8	32.9
1964	35.3	36.1	35.7	36.1	36.5	37.2	37.8	38.0	37.9	37.7	38.4	38.7	37.1
1965	38.2	38.6	38.7	38.1	38.5	39.1	39.3	39.7	39.2	39.2	40.2	40.3	39.1
1966	40.5	40.4	40.2	40.5	41.5	41.6	42.1	42.9	42.8	43.0	43.6	43.9	41.9
1967	43.8	44.4	44.2	45.2	46.0	47.0	47.6	47.8	47.7	47.6	48.0	48.3	46.5
1968	48.6	49.0	49.4	50.1	50.7	51.6	52.2	52.4	51.9	52.4	53.1	54.1	51.3
1969	54.5	55.1	55.0	55.6	56.5	57.2	57.1	57.5	58.0	58.5	59.7	60.3	57.1
1970	59.9	60.8	61.8	63.1	64.4	65.4	65.6	65.5	66.6	66.9	66.8	67.6	64.5
1971	68.0	68.9	70.3	70.3	70.3	71.0	71.6	72.3	71.9	72.9	74.2	74.9	71.4
1972	76.0	76.8	77.7	78.6	78.4	78.9	79.4	79.4	81.3	82.0	82.7	83.5	79.6
1973	84.6	84.8	83.5	84.3	84.5	86.0	85.5	85.1	84.6	86.5	87.1	84.5	85.1
1974	82.0	79.9	80.8	82.7	87.9	89.0	88.0	87.4	88.1	86.9	86.5	86.4	85.5
1975	87.7	87.7	88.0	87.3	87.7	88.3	88.7	89.7	90.2	90.0	90.6	91.5	88.9
1976	91.4	91.7	92.3	91.0	90.9	90.8	90.7	91.8	91.5	92.3	92.4	92.1	91.6
1977	93.0	92.7	92.8	93.3	93.1	93.2	93.7	93.9	94.0	94.7	95.4	96.0	93.8
1978	97.0	96.8	96.5	96.7	96.6	96.7	97.0	96.7	97.6	98.0	98.9	99.3	97.3
1979	100.2	100.8	100.6	100.7	100.5	100.4	99.8	100.6	101.5	101.1	101.0	100.7	100.7
1980	100.4	100.4	100.5	100.1	100.1	99.5	99.5	99.8	99.7	100.1	99.6	100.1	100.0
1981	100.7	100.8	101.0	101.8	101.9	102.2	102.2	102.6	102.9	103.3	102.8	103.0	102.1
1982	103.9	104.0	104.1	105.3	106.1	106.3	107.4	106.3	106.4	106.6	107.5	107.3	105.9

18.1 RETAIL SALES, IN CONSTANT PRICES, JAPAN (INDEX, 1980=100)

YEAR	JAN	FEB	MAR	APR	MAY	JUN	JUL	AUG	SEP	OCT	NOV	DEC	AVGE
1954	15.8	16.1	16.1	16.1	16.1	15.7	16.4	16.7	16.7	16.7	16.7	17.0	16.3
1955	17.8	17.8	17.8	18.0	18.3	18.3	17.9	18.7	18.9	19.3	19.8	19.8	18.5
1956	19.8	20.1	19.8	20.9	21.5	21.4	22.0	21.9	22.1	21.6	22.5	22.8	21.4
1957	22.7	23.2	23.2	22.6	23.7	23.6	23.9	23.9	24.3	24.6	24.7	24.7	23.8
1958	23.8	24.8	24.7	25.1	24.7	25.0	26.1	26.0	26.5	26.6	26.5	27.5	25.6
1959	27.2	27.7	28.0	28.0	28.1	29.0	28.3	29.4	30.0	29.5	29.7	30.5	28.8
1960	29.8	30.3	30.1	30.5	29.9	30.2	31.1	31.3	32.2	32.7	33.6	34.0	31.3
1961	34.1	34.1	35.1	34.8	35.7	35.9	36.2	35.4	36.2	35.9	36.2	35.6	35.4
1962	37.6	37.6	37.5	38.5	38.7	39.0	39.1	39.3	40.3	40.9	40.6	41.1	39.2
1963	41.1	40.8	41.9	43.3	43.2	43.7	44.2	45.2	45.0	46.6	46.8	46.5	44.0
1964	46.6	47.3	47.7	47.7	48.0	48.3	49.2	49.5	50.0	47.8	48.4	49.8	48.4
1965	47.5	48.4	49.4	48.0	48.9	50.3	51.2	50.0	50.6	50.6	50.8	51.5	49.7
1966	50.3	50.6	51.6	51.9	52.8	53.2	52.9	54.2	54.2	54.8	55.8	56.4	53.2
1967	54.6	55.9	56.7	57.1	58.0	59.0	60.7	60.2	61.0	60.1	60.3	62.0	58.8
1968	61.3	62.5	62.3	64.1	63.1	64.2	64.4	64.3	65.2	64.6	64.7	66.1	63.9
1969	65.7	65.3	65.5	66.1	67.5	67.5	67.0	67.6	67.7	68.8	69.4	69.4	67.3
1970	66.9	67.1	67.7	67.8	68.9	69.5	70.5	71.7	71.9	71.2	71.3	71.2	69.6
1971	74.5	75.5	75.9	77.4	78.1	77.9	78.2	78.5	78.6	78.8	77.5	76.9	77.3
1972	75.9	76.3	76.1	76.1	77.2	77.1	78.7	79.2	79.7	79.6	81.2	82.2	78.3
1973	85.3	86.9	88.2	88.9	87.8	88.7	89.0	88.9	89.0	89.9	90.1	86.4	88.2
1974	85.6	81.4	80.2	79.6	83.0	84.4	84.5	84.5	89.0	84.4	85.6	87.4	84.1
1975	85.9	88.0	91.1	91.8	91.1	91.0	90.9	91.0	89.4	89.6	88.6	89.1	89.8
1976	88.5	90.3	87.0	85.3	87.0	86.9	85.7	87.9	87.2	88.3	89.4	88.6	87.7
1977	89.1	89.0	89.4	89.3	89.1	89.3	90.6	92.5	90.4	91.3	91.1	92.7	90.3
1978	90.6	91.9	93.1	94.0	93.6	95.5	96.1	93.9	96.0	96.3	96.6	97.2	94.6
1979	98.7	97.9	97.9	97.5	99.7	100.0	98.7	101.6	102.0	100.0	102.4	101.3	99.8
1980	101.7	104.6	101.4	102.7	101.6	99.9	96.5	98.0	98.2	99.2	98.7	97.6	100.0
1981	98.4	97.8	99.0	97.8	97.1	96.0	97.4	96.8	96.0	96.0	95.2	95.1	96.9
1982	95.1	93.1	94.3	91.7	94.9	93.9	91.1	92.2	92.1	92.9	92.5	92.6	93.0

LAGGING INDEX, JAPAN (1980=100)

YEAR	JAN	FEB	MAR	APR	MAY	JUN	JUL	AUG	SEP	OCT	NOV	DEC	AVGE
1953	4.8	4.8	5.2	5.5	5.9	6.1	6.3	6.5	6.6	6.9	7.0	7.2	6.1
1954	7.4	7.5	7.6	7.6	7.6	7.6	7.6	7.4	7.4	7.4	7.4	7.4	7.5
1955	7.5	7.5	7.4	7.5	7.5	7.6	7.6	7.6	7.8	7.9	8.1	8.2	7.7
1956	8.3	8.5	8.6	8.7	8.8	9.0	9.2	9.4	9.7	9.9	10.2	10.5	9.2
1957	10.7	10.9	11.3	11.6	12.0	12.3	12.5	12.8	12.8	12.8	12.8	12.9	12.1
1958	13.0	13.1	13.1	13.2	13.2	13.3	13.4	13.5	13.5	13.4	13.4	13.5	13.3
1959	13.5	13.6	13.8	14.1	14.3	14.5	14.7	14.8	15.2	15.5	15.8	16.3	14.7
1960	16.9	17.4	17.5	17.5	17.6	18.0	18.4	18.7	19.0	19.3	19.6	20.2	18.3
1961	20.7	21.1	21.3	21.7	21.9	22.3	22.7	23.1	23.4	23.9	24.3	24.5	22.6
1962	24.7	24.9	25.1	25.5	25.7	25.8	26.0	26.1	26.2	26.6	26.7	26.6	25.8
1963	26.5	26.8	26.5	26.7	26.7	27.0	26.8	27.1	27.3	27.7	28.1	28.2	27.1
1964	28.8	28.9	29.5	30.1	30.6	30.9	31.4	31.8	31.9	32.2	32.6	32.6	30.9
1965	32.8	32.9	32.4	32.5	32.2	32.1	32.2	32.2	32.2	32.4	32.3	32.6	32.4
1966	32.4	32.6	33.0	33.2	33.5	33.8	34.0	34.2	34.5	34.6	34.8	35.1	33.8
1967	35.5	35.9	36.3	37.1	37.5	37.9	38.4	38.8	39.2	39.8	40.2	40.6	38.1
1968	41.2	41.6	42.5	42.9	43.2	43.7	43.9	44.3	44.7	45.0	45.9	46.3	43.8
1969	46.3	46.5	47.3	47.7	48.6	49.1	49.7	50.3	50.8	51.8	52.6	53.3	49.5
1970	53.7	54.5	54.8	55.5	56.2	56.4	57.2	57.8	58.3	59.2	59.6	59.7	56.9
1971	60.5	60.8	60.9	61.1	61.6	61.9	62.2	62.0	62.3	62.9	62.7	63.7	61.9
1972	63.4	63.5	63.9	64.3	64.0	64.6	64.6	64.2	64.8	64.9	65.4	65.6	64.4
1973	66.0	66.6	66.6	67.7	68.9	70.4	71.7	73.2	74.6	76.1	77.1	76.9	71.3
1974	78.0	80.1	82.4	83.6	84.6	85.4	85.6	86.5	86.8	87.0	88.9	89.4	84.9
1975	90.5	90.6	90.4	89.8	89.4	88.9	88.6	87.8	87.4	87.0	86.3	84.7	88.4
1976	83.6	83.0	83.1	82.8	83.1	82.9	83.1	83.5	83.8	84.1	83.8	84.3	83.4
1977	85.1	85.5	85.7	86.1	85.4	84.4	84.3	83.8	83.6	83.2	82.5	82.2	84.3
1978	81.6	81.5	81.7	81.3	80.2	80.3	79.9	79.6	80.1	80.3	81.0	80.9	80.7
1979	80.8	80.7	80.7	81.0	81.6	82.7	82.8	84.4	86.1	87.1	88.4	89.6	83.8
1980	90.3	91.3	94.5	97.6	100.9	102.3	103.9	105.3	103.6	104.0	103.9	102.4	100.0
1981	102.9	103.7	103.5	103.4	103.0	101.9	101.9	101.7	101.8	102.6	102.5	103.0	102.7
1982	103.1	102.3	102.1	102.5	102.6	102.7	103.0	103.2	103.8	104.6	104.7	104.9	103.3

SIX MONTH SMOOTHED CHANGE IN LAGGING INDEX, JAPAN (ANNUAL RATE, PERCENT)

YEAR	JAN	FEB	MAR	APR	MAY	JUN	JUL	AUG	SEP	OCT	NOV	DEC	AVGE
1954	43.3	39.4	32.0	26.5	21.9	16.5	10.7	4.7	1.7	0.4	-1.4	-0.7	16.2
1955	-0.8	-0.7	-1.2	-0.8	0.1	2.3	3.5	4.4	7.3	10.3	13.2	15.4	4.4
1956	16.6	17.4	19.2	19.1	19.3	21.3	22.9	23.3	25.3	27.5	30.2	31.1	22.8
1957	30.9	31.1	33.6	34.8	37.3	36.0	34.7	33.6	28.0	22.3	18.1	15.8	29.7
1958	13.9	12.1	9.6	7.8	6.5	6.6	6.4	6.2	5.2	4.2	3.0	2.9	7.0
1959	3.4	3.7	6.1	8.5	11.2	12.3	13.6	14.1	17.1	19.1	21.4	25.7	13.0
1960	29.3	31.7	27.9	24.4	21.3	22.4	22.8	22.7	21.8	21.3	21.8	23.8	24.2
1961	25.4	25.3	23.5	24.0	22.7	22.2	21.9	22.2	21.5	22.0	21.8	19.4	22.7
1962	18.4	16.4	15.2	15.7	14.6	12.8	12.1	10.4	9.6	10.2	9.1	7.1	12.6
1963	4.7	5.7	2.8	3.4	2.4	4.3	2.2	3.3	4.6	6.3	8.5	8.6	4.7
1964	12.0	11.4	14.2	16.1	17.5	17.1	18.6	18.4	15.8	15.2	14.9	12.4	15.3
1965	11.1	10.0	4.9	3.7	0.9	-0.4	-0.3	-0.6	-0.9	-0.1	-0.6	0.9	2.4
1966	0.2	1.3	3.7	4.5	5.9	7.3	7.4	7.4	8.7	8.0	7.8	8.6	5.9
1967	9.6	10.2	10.9	13.3	14.0	14.1	14.8	14.6	14.9	15.9	15.5	15.1	13.6
1968	15.4	14.9	16.7	16.0	15.2	14.7	13.3	12.8	12.6	11.6	13.6	13.4	14.2
1969	11.1	10.0	11.3	11.5	13.2	13.6	13.8	14.6	14.0	15.9	16.9	17.1	13.6
1970	16.3	16.7	15.3	15.3	15.2	13.5	13.8	13.7	13.0	13.8	12.9	11.2	14.2
1971	12.0	10.8	9.4	8.4	8.4	7.7	7.2	5.3	5.2	5.8	4.3	6.4	7.6
1972	4.6	4.1	4.7	4.9	3.3	4.6	3.8	2.0	5.4	3.0	4.0	3.9	3.9
1973	4.5	5.8	4.9	7.5	9.9	13.3	15.5	18.1	19.7	21.6	21.4	17.7	13.3
1974	18.0	20.7	23.6	22.8	21.7	19.8	17.0	16.0	13.9	13.5	13.7	12.5	17.8
1975	12.4	10.1	7.6	4.8	3.0	1.0	-0.2	-2.3	-3.5	-4.3	-5.6	-8.4	1.2
1976	-9.9	-10.0	-8.5	-7.9	-6.1	-5.6	-4.1	-2.3	-0.8	0.4	0.3	1.8	-4.4
1977	3.8	4.2	4.3	4.8	2.4	-0.1	-0.6	-1.8	-2.4	-3.3	-4.5	-4.9	-0.2
1978	-6.0	-5.5	-4.4	-4.6	-6.0	-5.0	-5.0	-4.9	-3.1	-2.0	0.2	-0.3	-3.8
1979	-0.4	-0.2	-0.3	1.2	2.7	4.9	4.7	7.7	10.9	11.9	13.6	15.0	6.1
1980	14.7	15.1	20.2	24.5	28.7	27.7	27.0	25.6	17.8	15.5	12.2	6.6	19.6
1981	5.5	4.9	2.5	1.1	-0.6	-2.8	-2.7	-2.8	-2.1	-0.4	-0.3	0.7	0.2
1982	0.8	-0.7	-0.9	0.0	0.4	0.6	1.1	1.3	2.1	3.2	3.2	3.1	1.2

20.0 NEW PLANT AND EQUIPMENT EXPENDITURE, IN CONSTANT PRICES, JAPAN
(BILLION 1975 YEN)

YEAR	IQ	IIQ	IIIQ	IVQ	AVGE
1952	1645.	1789.	1779.	1714.	1732.
1953	1776.	1926.	2052.	2228.	1996.
1954	2316.	2164.	1978.	1928.	2097.
1955	1880.	1911.	2011.	2256.	2015.
1956	2475.	2684.	2849.	3179.	2797.
1957	3275.	3656.	3756.	3368.	3514.
1958	3378.	3280.	3381.	3375.	3354.
1959	3504.	3796.	3929.	4402.	3908.
1960	5090.	5080.	5665.	6162.	5499.
1961	6954.	7361.	7795.	7986.	7524.
1962	7712.	7864.	7807.	7792.	7794.
1963	7774.	8008.	8098.	8880.	8190.
1964	9363.	9693.	10162.	10133.	9838.
1965	9826.	8662.	8523.	8343.	8839.
1966	8578.	9668.	10316.	10760.	9831.
1967	11390.	12214.	12933.	13836.	12593.
1968	14413.	14998.	15438.	16962.	15453.
1969	16792.	18883.	20062.	21201.	19235.
1970	22378.	22850.	23413.	23402.	23011.
1971	23160.	22771.	22300.	21894.	22531.
1972	22543.	22860.	23123.	24286.	23203.
1973	25078.	26010.	27732.	28701.	26880.
1974	26589.	25915.	25043.	24823.	25593.
1975	24327.	24279.	24190.	23935.	24183.
1976	24004.	24300.	24534.	24521.	24340.
1977	24737.	24820.	25000.	25225.	24946.
1978	25267.	25954.	26506.	28528.	26564.
1979	28917.	29371.	30027.	30596.	29728.
1980	31324.	31934.	32391.	32842.	32123.
1981	33523.	33985.	33884.	34295.	33922.
1982	34320.	34504.	34725.	34611.	34540.

21.0 BUSINESS INVENTORIES, IN CONSTANT PRICES, JAPAN

YEAR	IQ	IIQ	IIIQ	IVQ	AVGE
1952	1334.3	1264.6	1238.4	1488.8	1331.5
1953	1286.0	1798.7	2095.8	2318.0	1874.6
1954	2552.7	2641.0	2569.3	2502.8	2566.4
1955	2598.9	2438.7	2564.9	2746.8	2587.3
1956	2988.1	3294.8	3721.9	4251.1	3564.0
1957	4825.7	5372.1	5652.0	5772.7	5405.6
1958	5603.2	5632.0	5617.3	5536.6	5597.3
1959	5522.2	6054.9	6465.7	6961.7	6251.1
1960	7505.1	7391.8	7667.8	8001.3	7641.5
1961	8832.2	9346.1	10230.2	11010.3	9854.7
1962	11660.6	11981.1	11783.1	12079.0	11875.9
1963	11978.8	12489.8	13109.4	13670.5	12812.1
1964	14262.7	14877.4	15487.4	16122.2	15187.4
1965	16412.3	16516.9	16514.4	16798.1	16560.4
1966	17528.0	17528.0	18112.7	18614.4	17866.4
1967	19638.2	20732.1	21772.5	22676.7	21204.9
1968	23405.7	24791.6	25568.5	26577.8	25085.9
1969	27505.8	27904.2	29230.1	30634.7	28818.7
1970	32156.8	34016.8	35433.1	36605.1	34552.9
1971	37360.9	37599.2	38269.5	39074.1	38075.9
1972	39579.1	41491.0	42933.6	44879.6	42220.8
1973	47839.4	51203.7	54962.6	58560.2	53141.5
1974	64816.9	69188.5	71714.0	72782.7	69625.5
1975	73224.0	73946.7	74183.9	74819.6	74043.5
1976	74972.1	75399.1	76835.0	77743.4	76237.4
1977	78378.7	78388.7	78311.7	78591.5	78417.6
1978	77812.2	78195.1	78361.7	78927.0	78324.0
1979	79612.2	80839.2	82912.9	85365.7	82182.4
1980	88340.4	93425.6	95664.7	96657.2	93521.9
1981	97636.2	97567.6	98110.7	99300.2	98153.6
1982	99810.0	99521.7	99951.5	100625.	99977.0

22.1 CHANGE IN HOURS PER UNIT OF OUTPUT, INDUSTRY, JAPAN (PERCENT CHANGE FROM YEAR AGO)

YEAR	JAN	FEB	MAR	APR	MAY	JUN	JUL	AUG	SEP	OCT	NOV	DEC	AVGE
1961	-12.5	-12.5	-12.5	-9.6	-9.6	-9.6	-9.9	-9.9	-9.9	-9.1	-9.1	-9.1	-10.3
1962	-6.6	-6.6	-6.6	-4.0	-4.0	-4.0	-1.0	-1.0	-1.0	1.3	1.3	1.3	-2.6
1963	-0.6	2.3	-5.7	-5.0	-7.9	-5.0	-11.4	-11.7	-13.7	-14.4	-14.4	-17.6	-8.8
1964	-13.3	-16.2	-13.6	-13.3	-13.0	-14.7	-11.7	-10.7	-12.5	-11.0	-9.0	-9.3	-12.4
1965	-7.5	-6.1	-8.9	-5.6	-5.5	-6.0	-4.3	-3.6	-3.7	-2.2	-3.5	-2.6	-5.0
1966	-5.7	-5.5	-5.9	-8.5	-9.7	-9.3	-11.5	-13.4	-12.5	-14.1	-15.1	-15.6	-10.6
1967	-14.2	-14.7	-15.9	-13.2	-13.0	-13.8	-13.4	-14.2	-14.5	-13.6	-14.4	-13.6	-14.0
1968	-12.9	-14.1	-10.9	-12.8	-13.4	-12.2	-13.2	-12.0	-11.6	-14.2	-11.0	-10.5	-12.4
1969	-12.4	-12.5	-11.9	-13.3	-11.7	-11.6	-12.0	-11.2	-12.5	-11.5	-11.3	-11.4	-11.9
1970	-11.8	-10.3	-11.3	-10.0	-9.3	-11.8	-10.4	-9.6	-9.3	-6.2	-6.3	-7.6	-9.5
1971	-4.6	-5.1	-5.4	-4.9	-3.4	-3.6	-3.0	-5.1	-4.7	-3.1	-5.6	-2.6	-4.3
1972	-5.9	-6.6	-6.2	-6.8	-10.7	-8.5	-9.3	-11.3	-10.0	-13.5	-13.1	-15.5	-9.8
1973	-16.0	-15.0	-18.3	-17.6	-18.2	-17.4	-17.9	-16.6	-17.2	-16.5	-15.4	-12.9	-16.6
1974	-12.5	-10.5	-7.5	-5.8	-3.4	-1.0	-0.2	3.5	3.7	6.7	10.1	11.3	-0.5
1975	15.5	14.4	11.4	8.0	6.4	5.0	4.4	1.5	1.2	0.6	-1.2	-4.9	5.2
1976	-8.2	-10.7	-9.7	-11.7	-10.8	-13.2	-12.9	-12.0	-11.7	-11.9	-14.0	-12.8	-11.6
1977	-9.9	-9.5	-8.8	-5.5	-5.2	-4.8	-3.0	-3.2	-1.9	-1.0	-1.9	-1.7	-4.7
1978	-4.1	-4.3	-3.7	-5.3	-5.7	-3.8	-5.1	-7.8	-8.2	-9.6	-8.4	-9.0	-6.2
1979	-9.0	-9.5	-9.8	-10.2	-10.5	-9.7	-12.8	-12.7	-11.2	-10.9	-10.7	-11.1	-10.7
1980	-12.7	-12.4	-11.0	-10.5	-8.6	-9.4	-6.5	-2.9	-6.6	-5.9	-5.5	-6.6	-8.2
1981	-4.2	-2.3	-2.9	-1.0	-1.1	-2.9	-3.0	-4.0	-5.1	-3.9	-5.9	-4.0	-3.4
1982	-2.8	-3.6	-3.2	-1.4	-1.6	-2.3	-1.7	-1.9	-1.3	0.6	0.3	0.3	-1.5

23.1 TOTAL LOANS OUTSTANDING, IN CONSTANT PRICES, JAPAN (100 BILLION 1975 YEN)

YEAR	JAN	FEB	MAR	APR	MAY	JUN	JUL.	AUG	SEP	OCT	NOV	DEC	AVGE
1953	33.5	34.1	35.7	36.3	37.2	37.5	37.9	38.1	38.2	39.1	39.5	39.8	37.2
1954	40.3	40.5	41.4	42.4	43.4	44.5	45.1	45.1	45.3	46.1	46.4	47.0	44.0
1955	47.1	47.2	47.3	48.0	49.2	49.7	49.8	49.6	49.5	49.8	50.7	51.1	49.1
1956	51.0	51.1	51.8	51.5	51.7	53.4	54.8	55.3	55.9	56.6	58.1	59.8	54.2
1957	60.9	62.2	64.1	65.3	67.1	68.5	70.0	71.5	72.8	73.7	75.9	78.1	69.2
1958	80.2	82.5	83.6	84.7	86.2	88.1	90.0	91.6	93.2	94.6	95.1	95.6	88.8
1959	96.5	97.0	98.0	98.7	100.2	101.3	102.5	102.8	103.7	104.0	105.3	107.2	101.4
1960	109.2	110.6	112.4	114.2	116.2	118.6	120.4	122.3	124.6	126.7	129.4	132.1	119.7
1961	134.0	136.1	138.0	139.6	141.8	144.3	146.8	148.4	150.6	153.0	155.5	157.4	145.5
1962	159.3	161.1	163.3	166.7	169.4	172.5	174.5	177.0	179.8	182.8	186.0	188.8	173.4
1963	192.4	197.4	202.3	204.6	208.0	211.3	215.7	220.0	223.9	226.4	229.8	234.1	213.8
1964	237.2	240.4	243.7	247.1	251.0	254.6	257.7	260.6	263.0	266.4	269.7	271.5	255.2
1965	273.9	277.3	279.7	283.8	287.5	290.3	294.2	297.4	300.7	303.8	306.4	309.7	292.1
1966	310.9	311.9	315.4	316.8	320.0	322.7	326.4	330.0	336.8	338.0	341.3	346.0	326.3
1967	346.4	351.2	357.9	363.2	367.6	372.4	376.9	382.1	386.0	389.8	392.4	394.8	373.4
1968	399.2	403.5	407.1	413.7	417.0	419.7	424.2	428.3	430.7	436.4	441.0	452.4	422.8
1969	457.0	462.7	467.8	471.7	477.0	482.7	488.1	493.0	496.1	500.9	506.0	506.8	484.1
1970	506.6	511.5	515.2	520.2	527.2	535.3	542.0	549.2	557.3	565.8	575.3	585.3	540.9
1971	596.5	608.0	618.3	627.3	640.4	654.0	666.4	676.8	690.5	706.1	718.7	735.0	661.5
1972	744.7	756.6	770.6	782.1	792.7	806.0	823.8	832.1	849.4	862.3	868.1	878.2	813.9
1973	876.6	876.9	873.8	883.1	884.7	886.4	882.0	875.5	871.0	862.7	844.9	793.7	867.6
1974	762.6	752.1	754.1	755.8	760.5	763.5	762.7	763.3	770.1	773.3	777.6	782.4	764.8
1975	787.8	800.7	811.3	817.9	825.9	834.2	842.2	849.0	853.8	859.9	868.0	872.1	835.2
1976	871.9	876.0	877.2	879.8	883.3	889.0	889.0	890.3	898.7	908.5	911.9	917.8	891.1
1977	925.0	931.0	939.7	946.4	950.9	960.6	973.0	975.4	981.8	988.5	1001.1	1013.6	965.6
1978	1019.8	1026.6	1038.7	1052.6	1046.2	1061.7	1074.0	1089.3	1104.2	1110.7	1125.0	1138.2	1073.9
1979	1132.9	1132.2	1129.8	1131.9	1118.4	1113.4	1101.7	1096.5	1092.6	1080.1	1077.1	1064.6	1105.9
1980	1057.2	1042.8	1027.1	1014.7	1017.7	1020.1	1024.6	1031.6	1024.9	1042.9	1055.1	1056.5	1034.5
1981	1074.2	1087.4	1094.3	1099.1	1104.2	1100.5	1108.7	1113.6	1121.1	1133.0	1143.3	1158.7	1111.5
1982	1176.4	1179.7	1187.2	1189.5	1202.4	1214.5	1224.9	1229.8	1241.5	1253.3	1263.8	1284.0	1220.6

24.1 BANK RATES ON LOANS, JAPAN (PERCENT)

YEAR	JAN	FEB	MAR	APR	MAY	JUN	JUL	AUG	SEP	OCT	NOV	DEC	AVGE
1955	9.11	9.10	9.10	9.10	9.09	9.03	8.95	8.90	8.89	8.87	8.81	8.77	8.98
1956	8.73	8.67	8.61	8.56	8.49	8.41	8.35	8.32	8.29	8.29	8.27	8.25	8.44
1957	8.23	8.23	8.22	8.22	8.28	8.36	8.43	8.51	8.57	8.61	8.62	8.62	8.41
1958	8.63	8.63	8.63	8.64	8.64	8.61	8.54	8.48	8.41	8.34	8.30	8.27	8.51
1959	8.26	8.25	8.18	8.14	8.10	8.08	8.07	8.06	8.06	8.06	8.06	8.11	8.12
1960	8.16	8.20	8.21	8.22	8.22	8.22	8.22	8.20	8.14	8.11	8.09	8.08	8.17
1961	8.06	7.99	7.92	7.91	7.89	7.88	7.89	7.96	8.00	8.09	8.17	8.20	8.00
1962	8.20	8.21	8.22	8.27	8.22	8.23	8.23	8.24	8.24	8.24	8.19	8.09	8.21
1963	8.00	7.96	7.92	7.87	7.80	7.75	7.72	7.70	7.68	7.68	7.68	7.67	7.79
1964	7.67	7.67	7.73	7.85	7.94	7.98	7.99	7.99	7.99	7.99	7.99	7.99	7.90
1965	7.98	7.97	7.94	7.92	7.88	7.83	7.78	7.73	7.68	7.66	7.64	7.61	7.80
1966	7.58	7.57	7.54	7.53	7.51	7.49	7.48	7.45	7.42	7.41	7.39	7.37	7.48
1967	7.35	7.34	7.32	7.31	7.30	7.29	7.29	7.28	7.29	7.32	7.34	7.35	7.31
1968	7.39	7.45	7.49	7.52	7.52	7.52	7.52	7.49	7.43	7.40	7.38	7.38	7.46
1969	7.37	7.36	7.36	7.36	7.36	7.35	7.35	7.36	7.38	7.47	7.55	7.61	7.41
1970	7.62	7.62	7.63	7.64	7.65	7.66	7.67	7.68	7.69	7.70	7.70	7.69	7.66
1971	7.69	7.68	7.66	7.65	7.64	7.62	7.60	7.57	7.54	7.52	7.49	7.46	7.59
1972	7.41	7.34	7.27	7.24	7.19	7.13	7.01	6.90	6.81	6.78	6.75	6.72	7.05
1973	6.71	6.71	6.71	6.76	6.89	7.02	7.16	7.30	7.50	7.71	7.84	7.93	7.19
1974	8.31	8.72	9.03	9.15	9.19	9.22	9.24	9.25	9.26	9.29	9.33	9.37	9.11
1975	9.39	9.39	9.40	9.37	9.30	9.20	9.11	9.03	8.92	8.83	8.72	8.51	9.10
1976	8.40	8.35	8.30	8.28	8.26	8.24	8.23	8.22	8.21	8.20	8.19	8.18	8.25
1977	8.17	8.16	8.13	8.04	7.85	7.60	7.45	7.35	7.21	7.06	6.91	6.81	7.56
1978	6.76	6.73	6.66	6.56	6.38	6.25	6.17	6.13	6.08	6.05	6.00	5.94	6.31
1979	5.92	5.89	5.87	5.89	6.00	6.10	6.20	6.40	6.58	6.71	6.87	7.06	6.29
1980	7.18	7.32	7.76	8.22	8.61	8.82	8.89	8.88	8.74	8.66	8.53	8.27	8.32
1981	8.14	8.09	8.02	7.90	7.79	7.70	7.67	7.65	7.64	7.64	7.63	7.56	7.79
1982	7.46	7.34	7.26	7.24	7.21	7.19	7.17	7.17	7.18	7.18	7.17	7.15	7.23

MULTICOUNTRY INDEXES

LEADING INDEX, FOUR EUROPEAN COUNTRIES (1980=100)

YEAR	JAN	FEB	MAR	APR	MAY	JUN	JUL	AUG	SEP	OCT	NOV	DEC	AVGE
1955	41.3	41.4	41.5	41.8	41.7	42.1	42.6	43.0	43.1	43.1	43.1	43.2	42.3
1956	43.0	42.8	43.0	43.1	43.2	43.2	43.3	43.4	43.4	43.6	43.8	44.2	43.3
1957	44.3	44.7	44.9	45.0	45.1	45.2	45.3	45.5	45.5	45.4	45.5	45.6	45.2
1958	45.8	45.6	45.4	45.5	45.5	45.7	45.9	46.3	46.5	46.7	47.0	46.9	46.1
1959	47.3	47.4	48.1	49.0	49.8	50.1	50.5	50.8	51.3	51.6	51.9	52.4	50.0
1960	52.3	52.3	52.7	53.0	53.4	53.8	54.1	54.7	54.7	54.6	54.6	54.4	53.7
1961	54.9	55.2	55.4	55.5	55.5	55.6	55.5	55.3	55.6	55.8	56.2	56.2	55.6
1962	55.9	56.0	56.2	56.4	56.1	56.0	55.9	56.2	56.4	56.5	56.9	57.0	56.3
1963	56.9	56.8	57.1	57.5	58.0	58.3	58.5	58.9	59.1	59.6	59.8	60.0	58.4
1964	60.4	60.4	60.6	60.6	60.8	61.0	61.2	61.4	61.6	61.7	61.7	61.8	61.1
1965	61.7	62.0	62.0	62.2	62.4	62.2	62.1	62.7	62.7	62.7	62.9	63.4	62.4
1966	64.1	64.3	64.3	64.2	64.2	64.5	64.4	64.1	63.8	63.5	63.4	63.3	64.0
1967	63.4	63.5	63.7	63.9	64.0	64.0	64.3	64.6	65.2	65.9	66.4	66.8	64.6
1968	66.7	67.2	67.4	67.4	67.2	67.8	68.7	69.9	70.0	70.3	71.0	71.6	68.8
1969	71.9	72.1	72.6	72.9	73.3	73.4	73.5	73.7	73.6	73.8	73.9	73.9	73.2
1970	74.0	74.2	74.4	74.3	74.0	73.9	73.7	73.9	73.9	73.9	73.9	74.2	74.0
1971	74.4	74.5	74.7	74.8	75.0	75.1	75.4	75.5	75.6	75.8	76.0	76.5	75.3
1972	76.8	76.3	77.4	77.9	78.4	78.3	78.8	79.2	79.7	80.3	80.9	81.5	78.8
1973	82.3	82.6	82.8	82.9	82.8	83.1	83.4	83.3	83.3	83.7	84.0	84.0	83.2
1974	84.1	84.5	85.2	85.4	85.1	84.3	83.9	83.1	82.0	81.3	80.7	79.9	83.3
1975	79.9	80.4	80.3	80.5	80.5	81.0	80.5	80.8	81.6	82.3	83.1	83.8	81.2
1976	84.5	85.4	86.1	86.3	86.9	87.0	87.9	87.7	87.9	87.7	88.0	88.3	87.0
1977	88.9	88.6	88.8	89.0	88.8	88.6	88.7	88.8	89.4	89.5	89.5	89.9	89.0
1978	90.4	90.5	90.9	91.3	91.9	92.1	92.5	92.8	93.9	94.1	94.7	95.2	92.5
1979	95.0	96.0	96.5	97.4	97.7	98.4	98.8	99.3	99.6	99.9	100.2	100.0	98.2
1980	100.4	100.6	100.2	100.2	99.7	99.9	99.7	99.5	99.7	100.1	100.3	99.9	100.0
1981	100.8	101.2	101.5	101.8	101.8	102.0	102.2	102.6	102.6	102.6	102.8	102.8	102.1
1982	103.3	103.8	103.8	104.2	104.6	103.7	104.1	104.0	104.1	104.4	104.7	105.6	104.2

SIX MONTH SMOOTHED CHANGE IN LEADING INDEX, FOUR EUROPEAN COUNTRIES (ANNUAL RATE, PERCENT)

YEAR	JAN	FEB	MAR	APR	MAY	JUN	JUL	AUG	SEP	OCT	NOV	DEC	AVGE
1956	2.8	1.6	1.7	1.9	1.5	1.2	1.1	1.1	1.1	1.9	2.5	4.1	1.9
1957	4.2	5.2	5.6	5.2	5.2	4.6	4.7	4.4	3.7	2.7	2.3	2.3	4.2
1958	2.7	1.3	0.2	0.5	0.4	1.1	1.6	3.0	3.7	4.0	4.5	4.0	2.3
1959	4.9	4.9	7.0	9.9	11.9	11.7	11.4	11.2	11.4	11.0	10.7	10.7	9.7
1960	8.7	7.1	6.9	6.6	6.7	6.9	6.8	8.1	6.9	5.2	4.3	3.1	6.4
1961	4.2	4.3	4.1	3.6	3.2	2.9	2.1	1.7	1.5	1.3	3.1	2.8	2.9
1962	1.1	1.2	1.6	2.0	1.0	0.3	-0.3	0.8	1.3	1.3	2.3	2.5	1.3
1963	2.2	1.4	2.2	3.3	4.5	5.0	5.0	5.5	5.7	6.3	6.1	6.0	4.4
1964	6.5	5.5	5.1	4.4	4.2	3.8	3.8	3.8	3.6	3.5	3.0	2.5	4.1
1965	2.0	2.3	1.8	2.3	2.3	1.5	0.9	2.2	2.0	1.9	2.1	3.3	2.0
1966	5.1	4.9	4.3	3.7	3.2	3.5	2.7	1.0	-0.1	-1.2	-1.8	-2.1	1.9
1967	-1.6	-1.2	-0.5	0.3	0.6	0.6	1.6	2.4	4.2	5.7	6.8	7.2	2.2
1968	5.8	6.5	6.3	5.4	4.0	5.0	6.4	8.7	7.8	7.6	8.2	8.9	6.7
1969	8.5	7.9	8.0	7.7	7.5	6.3	5.2	4.9	3.6	3.4	2.9	2.3	5.7
1970	2.0	2.0	2.0	1.3	0.5	0.0	-0.6	-0.2	-0.3	-0.2	-0.3	0.6	0.6
1971	0.9	1.1	1.5	1.8	2.1	2.1	2.7	2.5	2.4	2.6	2.8	3.5	2.2
1972	3.7	2.1	4.3	4.9	5.7	4.7	5.3	5.4	5.9	6.5	6.9	7.6	5.2
1973	8.4	7.9	7.2	6.2	5.0	4.7	4.5	3.5	2.7	2.9	2.9	2.2	4.8
1974	2.0	2.6	3.8	4.1	2.7	0.6	-0.7	-2.4	-4.8	-6.1	-6.8	-8.2	-1.1
1975	-7.5	-5.7	-5.0	-3.8	-2.9	-0.9	-1.3	-0.1	2.2	3.9	5.6	6.7	-0.7
1976	7.5	8.7	9.4	8.6	8.8	7.9	8.7	6.7	6.0	4.4	3.9	3.7	7.0
1977	4.1	2.8	2.6	2.4	1.6	0.7	0.7	0.8	1.7	1.7	1.4	2.0	1.9
1978	2.8	2.8	3.4	3.8	4.7	4.4	4.6	4.6	6.2	5.8	6.2	6.3	4.6
1979	5.0	6.4	6.4	7.1	6.7	7.1	6.8	6.6	6.2	5.0	5.4	4.1	6.1
1980	4.0	3.6	2.6	1.6	0.2	0.2	-0.3	-0.9	-0.6	0.2	0.5	-0.2	0.9
1981	1.4	2.2	2.6	2.9	2.8	2.8	2.8	3.1	2.6	2.3	2.3	1.7	2.5
1982	2.3	2.7	2.5	2.7	3.1	1.1	1.5	1.0	1.1	1.3	1.6	2.9	2.0

COINCIDENT INDEX, FOUR EUROPEAN COUNTRIES (1980=100)

YEAR	JAN	FEB	MAR	APR	MAY	JUN	JUL	AUG	SEP	OCT	NOV	DEC	AVGE
1955	32.9	33.2	33.4	33.9	34.2	34.3	34.7	35.0	35.2	35.4	35.5	35.8	34.5
1956	36.2	36.3	36.6	36.8	37.0	37.3	37.4	37.6	37.9	38.2	38.4	38.5	37.3
1957	38.8	39.1	39.2	39.6	39.8	39.9	40.2	40.4	40.5	40.5	40.8	40.7	40.0
1958	41.1	41.2	41.0	41.0	41.0	41.1	41.5	41.4	41.4	41.6	41.4	41.6	41.3
1959	41.7	41.6	41.8	42.3	42.4	43.0	43.1	43.3	43.8	44.3	44.6	44.9	43.1
1960	45.2	45.6	46.1	46.3	46.7	47.0	47.4	47.9	48.4	48.4	48.7	49.2	47.2
1961	49.5	49.9	50.4	50.4	50.5	50.9	51.0	51.0	51.1	51.4	51.7	52.0	50.8
1962	52.5	52.8	52.5	52.7	52.9	53.2	53.2	53.6	53.8	53.9	54.1	54.2	53.3
1963	54.0	54.0	54.5	55.4	55.5	56.2	56.8	57.2	57.4	57.9	58.2	58.5	56.3
1964	59.2	59.4	59.5	59.5	59.7	60.0	60.1	60.1	60.7	61.1	61.2	61.4	60.2
1965	61.6	61.6	61.4	62.0	62.3	62.3	62.5	62.8	63.2	63.4	63.6	63.9	62.5
1966	64.3	64.6	65.0	64.7	65.0	65.0	65.1	65.3	65.1	64.9	64.7	64.6	64.9
1967	64.6	64.5	64.5	64.4	64.5	64.9	65.1	65.1	65.1	65.2	65.2	66.2	65.0
1968	66.0	66.5	66.8	66.7	65.9	66.7	67.8	68.6	68.8	69.4	70.2	70.4	67.8
1969	70.8	71.0	71.7	72.3	72.9	73.4	73.8	74.3	74.4	74.8	75.2	75.6	73.3
1970	76.0	76.4	76.9	77.2	77.4	77.8	78.2	78.3	78.5	78.9	78.9	79.0	77.8
1971	79.0	78.8	78.9	79.2	79.2	79.4	79.6	79.6	80.0	79.9	80.1	80.1	79.5
1972	80.3	80.2	81.0	81.0	81.6	81.8	81.9	82.4	82.8	83.4	84.2	84.7	82.1
1973	85.0	85.4	85.8	85.9	86.7	87.3	87.6	88.2	88.3	88.8	89.0	89.1	87.3
1974	89.1	89.3	89.3	89.9	90.0	90.0	90.3	90.2	89.5	89.1	88.0	87.6	89.4
1975	87.3	87.0	86.2	86.2	85.4	85.3	85.2	85.1	85.2	85.6	85.7	86.0	85.9
1976	86.3	86.7	86.9	87.4	87.8	88.1	88.4	89.0	89.5	89.5	90.2	90.5	88.4
1977	90.5	90.5	90.7	90.4	90.5	90.5	90.4	90.9	91.1	91.1	91.7	92.1	90.9
1978	92.6	92.5	92.9	93.4	93.7	94.1	94.2	94.6	95.1	95.1	95.8	96.2	94.2
1979	95.9	96.3	97.0	97.4	98.0	98.5	98.6	99.1	99.3	100.0	100.3	100.4	98.4
1980	100.7	100.8	100.7	100.6	100.2	100.1	100.2	99.9	99.5	99.6	99.1	98.7	100.0
1981	98.6	98.7	97.9	97.6	97.1	97.1	97.2	97.2	97.3	97.1	97.4	97.1	97.5
1982	97.1	97.3	97.5	97.3	97.1	96.9	96.7	96.7	96.4	96.4	96.5	96.5	96.9

SIX MONTH SMOOTHED CHANGE IN COINCIDENT INDEX, FOUR EUROPEAN COUNTRIES (ANNUAL RATE, PERCENT)

YEAR	JAN	FEB	MAR	APR	MAY	JUN	JUL	AUG	SEP	OCT	NOV	DEC	AVGE
1956	9.5	8.3	8.5	8.1	8.2	8.5	7.5	7.1	7.4	7.8	7.6	6.9	7.9
1957	7.1	8.0	7.1	7.7	7.7	7.1	7.3	7.1	6.5	5.1	5.9	4.5	6.8
1958	5.4	4.7	3.2	2.4	2.0	1.9	3.2	2.4	1.9	2.2	1.2	1.5	2.7
1959	1.8	1.3	2.2	4.0	4.0	5.8	5.9	6.2	7.7	8.6	9.3	9.2	5.5
1960	9.5	9.6	10.2	9.7	9.8	9.7	9.6	10.2	10.5	9.1	8.8	9.3	9.7
1961	8.9	9.0	9.7	7.9	7.3	7.2	6.6	5.4	4.6	4.9	5.0	5.1	6.8
1962	6.1	6.3	4.2	4.4	4.5	4.6	4.2	4.8	4.8	4.3	4.4	4.0	4.7
1963	2.3	1.9	3.6	6.1	6.8	7.2	8.3	8.6	8.2	8.8	8.8	8.5	6.6
1964	9.4	8.9	7.6	6.1	5.5	5.3	4.8	4.0	4.9	5.3	4.8	4.6	5.9
1965	4.4	4.0	2.6	4.1	4.1	3.6	3.4	3.7	4.3	4.5	4.5	4.6	4.0
1966	5.1	5.6	5.8	4.1	4.2	3.7	3.3	3.1	1.9	0.9	0.0	-0.5	3.1
1967	-0.6	-1.1	-1.1	-1.2	-0.9	0.3	1.0	1.0	1.5	1.4	1.9	4.0	0.5
1968	2.9	4.0	4.3	3.6	0.6	2.8	5.2	6.9	6.8	7.5	8.8	8.3	5.1
1969	8.4	7.7	8.5	8.9	9.4	8.9	8.4	8.3	7.4	7.2	7.1	6.8	8.1
1970	6.7	6.8	6.8	6.5	5.9	5.8	5.9	5.2	4.8	4.9	4.1	3.6	5.6
1971	2.9	1.7	1.6	1.9	1.3	1.5	1.8	1.5	2.1	1.7	1.9	1.6	1.8
1972	2.0	1.4	3.0	2.5	3.6	3.6	3.4	4.1	4.4	5.4	6.5	6.8	3.9
1973	6.6	6.5	6.5	5.8	6.6	6.9	6.7	6.8	6.0	6.0	5.5	4.7	6.2
1974	3.9	3.7	3.0	3.6	3.1	2.4	2.6	1.8	0.2	-0.9	-3.2	-3.9	1.4
1975	-4.2	-4.5	-5.2	-5.3	-6.4	-5.8	-5.2	-4.6	-3.5	-1.9	-1.2	-0.1	-4.0
1976	0.8	2.0	2.5	3.6	4.2	4.4	4.6	5.1	5.5	4.8	5.5	5.3	4.0
1977	4.5	3.6	3.5	2.1	1.9	1.5	0.9	1.4	1.6	1.3	2.3	2.8	2.3
1978	3.5	3.0	3.4	4.1	4.2	4.5	4.1	4.3	4.5	4.4	4.6	4.7	4.1
1979	3.4	3.6	4.3	4.3	5.0	5.2	4.5	4.8	4.6	5.1	5.0	4.5	4.5
1980	4.3	3.7	2.8	2.0	0.8	0.3	0.3	-0.5	-1.3	-1.2	-2.0	-2.6	0.5
1981	-2.5	-2.0	-3.2	-3.4	-3.8	-3.4	-2.7	-2.4	-1.7	-1.7	-0.8	-1.2	-2.4
1982	-0.9	-0.2	0.3	0.1	-0.2	-0.5	-0.9	-0.9	-1.4	-1.3	-1.0	-0.7	-0.6

LAGGING INDEX, FOUR EUROPEAN COUNTRIES (1970=100)

YEAR	JAN	FEB	MAR	APR	MAY	JUN	JUL	AUG	SEP	OCT	NOV	DEC	AVGE
1966	81.8	82.1	82.2	82.4	82.7	82.8	83.0	83.2	83.3	83.4	83.4	83.3	82.8
1967	83.1	83.1	83.1	82.9	83.0	83.0	83.0	83.2	83.5	83.7	84.2	83.3	83.3
1968	84.7	84.6	84.9	85.3	85.4	85.8	86.5	86.7	86.9	87.4	88.0	88.3	86.2
1969	88.4	88.7	89.1	89.4	90.0	91.7	92.5	93.7	94.0	94.7	95.5	95.8	92.0
1970	96.0	96.2	97.6	98.6	99.8	100.5	101.1	101.5	101.8	102.0	102.4	102.6	100.0
1971	102.3	102.5	102.4	102.2	102.4	102.5	102.6	102.9	103.0	103.2	103.3	103.4	102.7
1972	103.4	103.5	103.1	103.0	103.1	103.5	104.0	104.2	105.1	105.8	106.7	107.4	104.4
1973	108.2	108.9	109.7	110.5	111.1	112.2	113.7	115.3	116.5	117.1	117.6	117.8	113.2
1974	118.5	119.1	119.7	120.0	120.3	121.3	121.6	122.0	121.6	121.6	121.4	121.2	120.7
1975	120.5	120.0	118.9	118.3	117.7	116.9	116.8	116.2	115.2	115.2	115.0	115.0	117.1
1976	115.0	115.5	117.0	117.1	117.6	118.4	118.5	118.8	119.6	120.7	121.4	121.9	118.5
1977	122.1	122.4	122.3	122.3	122.3	122.2	122.3	122.4	122.1	122.7	122.7	122.7	122.4
1978	122.8	123.1	123.5	123.7	124.1	124.6	124.7	125.0	125.6	126.1	126.8	127.0	124.7
1979	127.3	127.3	127.7	128.4	129.0	129.8	130.9	131.7	132.6	133.8	135.3	136.4	130.8
1980	136.5	136.8	137.9	138.2	139.0	139.1	139.2	139.2	139.5	139.9	140.3	139.9	138.8
1981	139.4	139.3	***	***	***	***	***	***	***	***	***	***	***

SIX MONTH SMOOTHED CHANGE IN LAGGING INDEX, FOUR EUROPEAN COUNTRIES (ANNUAL RATE, PERCENT)

YEAR	JAN	FEB	MAR	APR	MAY	JUN	JUL	AUG	SEP	OCT	NOV	DEC	AVGE
1967	0.7	0.4	0.2	-0.4	-0.2	-0.2	-0.2	0.2	0.9	1.1	2.2	0.0	0.4
1968	3.1	2.7	3.1	3.6	3.3	3.8	4.9	4.6	4.4	4.8	5.5	5.4	4.1
1969	4.8	4.7	4.7	4.7	5.3	8.1	8.7	10.2	9.5	9.6	10.0	9.3	7.5
1970	8.2	7.3	8.9	9.4	10.2	9.9	9.6	8.7	8.1	7.1	6.6	6.0	8.3
1971	4.3	3.7	2.4	1.3	1.1	0.9	0.9	1.1	1.1	1.3	1.3	1.3	1.7
1972	1.3	1.3	0.4	0.0	0.2	0.7	1.4	1.6	3.1	4.0	5.2	5.9	2.1
1973	6.8	7.3	8.0	8.4	8.3	9.0	10.3	11.7	12.1	11.3	10.5	9.2	9.4
1974	8.8	8.2	7.8	6.8	6.1	6.4	5.5	5.2	3.6	3.0	2.0	1.2	5.4
1975	-0.3	-1.4	-3.0	-3.9	-4.5	-5.4	-5.0	-5.3	-6.3	-5.4	-4.9	-4.2	-4.1
1976	-3.3	-1.9	1.1	1.6	2.6	3.9	3.7	4.0	5.0	6.1	6.5	6.4	3.0
1977	5.7	5.3	4.2	3.4	2.8	2.0	1.7	1.4	0.5	1.1	0.8	0.6	2.5
1978	0.6	1.1	1.5	1.7	2.1	2.6	2.4	2.6	3.2	3.5	4.2	3.9	2.4
1979	3.9	3.3	3.3	3.8	4.1	4.7	5.6	6.0	6.6	7.4	8.6	9.1	5.5
1980	8.2	7.4	7.8	6.9	6.8	5.8	4.8	3.8	3.4	3.1	3.0	1.9	5.2
1981	0.8	0.4	***	***	***	***	***	***	***	***	***	***	***

327

LEADING INDEX, THREE COUNTRIES, EXCLUDING EUROPE (1980=100)

YEAR	JAN	FEB	MAR	APR	MAY	JUN	JUL	AUG	SEP	OCT	NOV	DEC	AVGE
1953	35.2	35.4	35.5	35.4	35.4	35.0	35.1	35.0	34.4	34.3	33.8	34.0	34.9
1954	34.0	34.2	34.1	34.3	34.3	34.6	34.8	34.9	35.3	35.8	36.4	37.0	35.0
1955	37.7	38.4	38.7	38.9	39.0	39.2	39.5	39.7	40.1	40.0	40.4	40.5	39.3
1956	40.4	40.2	40.5	40.6	40.5	40.6	40.6	40.8	40.9	41.2	41.5	41.5	40.8
1957	41.2	41.1	41.2	41.2	41.3	41.4	41.0	40.9	40.4	40.0	39.5	38.9	40.7
1958	38.8	38.2	38.4	38.6	39.2	39.7	40.4	41.1	41.7	42.3	43.1	43.3	40.4
1959	44.0	44.7	45.5	45.9	46.3	46.1	46.1	45.6	45.9	46.0	45.9	46.9	45.7
1960	46.8	46.9	46.3	46.3	45.9	45.5	46.0	46.0	45.9	45.7	45.6	45.5	46.1
1961	45.9	46.3	46.8	47.4	47.9	48.4	48.7	49.3	48.9	49.4	49.8	49.8	48.2
1962	49.8	50.2	50.1	50.0	49.5	49.3	49.4	49.7	49.9	49.9	50.4	50.6	49.9
1963	51.0	51.3	51.8	52.4	52.9	53.1	53.3	53.4	53.8	54.1	54.2	54.5	53.0
1964	54.9	55.3	55.5	55.6	56.0	56.1	56.3	56.5	56.7	56.6	56.7	57.3	56.1
1965	57.9	58.4	58.3	58.1	58.4	58.4	58.5	58.5	58.8	59.4	60.0	60.5	58.8
1966	61.0	61.5	61.9	61.6	61.3	61.4	61.4	61.0	60.9	61.1	61.3	61.3	61.3
1967	61.9	61.4	61.5	61.7	62.1	62.8	63.1	63.9	64.1	64.2	65.0	65.3	63.1
1968	65.0	65.3	66.1	65.8	66.5	66.7	67.0	67.1	67.9	68.7	68.6	68.9	67.0
1969	69.3	69.7	69.3	69.9	70.1	70.0	69.9	70.1	70.4	70.2	69.8	69.6	69.9
1970	69.3	69.1	68.8	68.6	68.4	68.4	68.4	68.2	67.9	67.5	67.3	68.5	68.4
1971	69.9	69.7	70.2	70.5	70.7	71.3	71.7	71.7	72.0	72.2	72.6	73.3	71.3
1972	73.8	74.1	75.9	76.7	77.3	77.7	78.2	79.4	80.3	81.2	82.4	84.0	78.4
1973	86.0	87.0	87.0	86.3	86.8	86.3	86.6	86.5	86.4	86.9	87.4	86.5	86.6
1974	86.6	87.1	86.2	84.7	83.8	83.1	82.6	81.0	79.2	77.5	76.0	74.6	81.9
1975	73.3	72.7	72.8	74.5	75.6	77.1	78.8	79.9	80.2	80.7	81.2	82.4	77.4
1976	84.0	84.7	86.3	85.9	86.4	87.3	88.0	87.5	87.5	87.2	87.5	88.4	86.7
1977	89.0	89.4	90.2	90.3	90.5	90.9	90.8	91.8	91.5	91.7	92.0	92.3	90.9
1978	91.9	92.5	93.8	95.3	96.3	96.8	96.5	96.7	97.6	98.6	99.3	99.2	96.2
1979	99.4	100.2	101.4	100.8	102.0	101.8	101.5	101.3	101.7	100.8	100.4	100.9	101.0
1980	102.8	102.7	101.9	99.6	98.2	97.8	98.5	98.8	99.3	99.9	100.2	100.5	100.0
1981	100.7	101.0	101.1	101.8	101.6	101.5	102.1	102.9	102.0	100.8	100.5	99.5	101.3
1982	98.6	98.2	97.3	97.2	97.4	97.2	97.6	97.6	97.7	97.6	98.0	98.6	97.7

SIX MONTH SMOOTHED CHANGE IN LEADING INDEX, THREE COUNTRIES, EXCLUDING EUROPE (ANNUAL RATE, PERCENT)

YEAR	JAN	FEB	MAR	APR	MAY	JUN	JUL	AUG	SEP	OCT	NOV	DEC	AVGE
1954	-4.4	-2.9	-3.1	-1.4	-0.7	1.0	2.4	3.0	5.6	7.9	10.6	12.4	2.5
1955	14.9	17.1	16.7	15.2	13.4	12.5	12.0	10.7	10.5	8.0	7.9	6.6	12.1
1956	4.8	3.1	3.6	3.6	2.4	2.1	1.7	2.3	2.3	3.3	4.1	3.6	3.1
1957	2.0	1.2	1.1	0.8	1.0	1.2	-0.7	-1.2	-3.6	-5.1	-7.0	-8.8	-1.6
1958	-8.2	-10.1	-8.3	-6.4	-2.7	0.5	4.6	7.8	10.7	13.2	16.3	15.7	2.8
1959	17.3	18.2	19.1	18.0	16.9	12.9	10.2	6.1	5.8	4.5	2.7	6.1	11.5
1960	4.2	3.9	0.7	0.1	-1.3	-1.2	-0.9	-1.0	-1.3	-2.0	-2.6	-2.6	-0.3
1961	-0.7	1.1	3.6	5.6	7.6	8.8	9.4	10.5	8.0	8.9	9.2	7.8	6.6
1962	6.0	6.2	4.7	3.1	0.6	-0.8	-0.4	0.3	1.0	0.5	2.2	2.8	2.2
1963	4.1	4.9	6.2	8.1	9.1	8.7	8.3	7.7	7.9	7.8	6.6	6.6	7.2
1964	6.9	7.2	6.5	5.8	6.2	5.4	5.4	5.1	5.1	3.8	3.3	4.5	5.4
1965	6.0	6.5	5.6	4.1	4.2	3.5	3.2	2.7	3.6	4.7	5.6	6.4	4.7
1966	7.0	7.8	8.1	6.3	4.4	3.9	3.2	1.2	0.4	0.4	0.7	0.2	3.6
1967	1.7	0.2	0.3	1.0	2.3	4.1	4.9	6.8	6.6	6.2	7.7	7.7	4.1
1968	5.6	5.6	7.2	5.1	6.1	5.6	5.4	4.9	6.3	7.6	6.4	6.4	6.0
1969	6.7	6.6	4.5	5.4	5.0	3.8	2.8	2.5	2.6	1.7	0.2	-0.5	3.4
1970	-1.6	-2.0	-2.6	-3.0	-3.3	-3.0	-2.6	-2.8	-3.2	-3.6	-3.7	-0.1	-2.6
1971	4.2	3.4	4.7	5.2	5.4	6.4	6.7	6.2	6.0	5.6	5.8	6.3	5.5
1972	6.6	6.5	10.3	11.0	11.1	10.7	10.4	12.0	12.7	13.2	14.2	15.8	11.2
1973	18.6	18.2	15.4	11.3	10.4	7.4	6.3	4.6	3.0	2.9	3.1	0.2	8.4
1974	-0.1	0.9	-1.1	-4.1	-5.6	-6.7	-7.1	-9.8	-12.7	-14.9	-16.5	-17.7	-7.9
1975	-18.5	-17.6	-15.1	-9.0	-4.6	0.5	5.9	9.4	10.4	11.5	12.0	13.8	-0.1
1976	16.3	15.4	16.8	12.9	11.7	11.6	11.0	8.1	6.4	4.6	3.8	4.7	10.3
1977	4.8	4.9	5.6	5.2	4.9	4.9	4.1	5.7	4.6	3.9	3.7	3.6	4.7
1978	2.1	2.8	5.0	7.4	8.5	8.6	6.8	6.3	7.3	8.2	8.4	7.1	6.5
1979	6.2	6.5	7.6	5.2	6.5	5.1	3.7	2.6	2.6	0.3	-0.8	0.1	3.8
1980	3.3	2.6	0.6	-3.5	-5.8	-6.0	-4.1	-3.2	-2.0	-0.4	-0.8	0.8	-1.5
1981	1.3	2.2	2.7	4.0	3.4	2.7	3.2	4.0	1.7	-0.9	-1.6	-3.3	1.6
1982	-4.9	-5.3	-6.5	-6.0	-5.0	-4.8	-3.4	-2.7	-1.7	-1.4	0.0	1.4	-3.4

COINCIDENT INDEX, THREE COUNTRIES, EXCLUDING EUROPE (1980=100)

YEAR	JAN	FEB	MAR	APR	MAY	JUN	JUL	AUG	SEP	OCT	NOV	DEC	AVGE
1954	29.4	29.3	29.1	28.9	28.8	28.9	28.9	28.9	29.1	29.3	29.8	30.2	29.2
1955	30.5	30.9	31.3	31.5	32.0	32.2	32.5	32.6	32.9	33.1	33.3	33.5	32.2
1956	33.6	33.6	33.5	33.8	33.7	33.8	33.2	33.9	34.3	34.5	34.4	34.6	33.9
1957	34.7	35.0	35.1	34.9	34.9	34.9	35.0	35.0	34.6	34.4	33.9	33.5	34.7
1958	33.0	32.5	32.3	32.0	32.0	32.3	32.8	33.1	33.4	33.7	34.3	34.4	33.0
1959	34.8	35.3	35.5	36.3	36.1	36.9	36.1	36.2	36.2	36.2	36.4	37.5	36.2
1960	37.9	38.2	37.9	38.1	37.9	37.9	37.9	37.8	37.8	37.8	37.6	37.4	37.8
1961	37.4	37.4	37.8	38.0	38.4	38.9	39.1	39.5	39.7	40.1	40.7	41.0	39.0
1962	41.1	41.5	41.8	42.1	42.3	42.3	42.5	42.7	42.8	42.9	43.0	43.0	42.3
1963	43.1	43.3	43.7	44.2	44.3	44.7	45.0	45.4	45.5	46.0	46.1	46.5	44.8
1964	46.8	47.2	47.3	47.9	48.3	48.4	49.0	49.2	49.5	49.2	49.9	50.5	48.6
1965	50.7	50.9	51.5	51.6	51.9	52.3	52.9	53.1	53.6	54.0	54.5	55.1	52.7
1966	55.4	56.0	56.3	56.6	56.9	57.4	57.7	58.0	58.2	58.5	58.8	59.0	57.4
1967	59.2	59.3	59.2	59.7	60.0	60.2	60.7	61.2	61.5	61.4	62.1	62.7	60.6
1968	62.8	63.1	63.7	64.3	64.8	65.2	65.6	66.0	66.4	66.8	67.4	67.8	65.3
1969	68.0	68.4	68.7	69.1	69.3	69.4	69.7	70.1	70.3	70.6	70.8	70.9	69.6
1970	70.3	70.3	70.5	70.6	70.7	70.9	70.9	70.9	70.9	70.2	69.7	70.6	70.5
1971	71.4	71.6	72.0	72.3	72.5	73.0	73.0	73.0	73.5	73.6	74.0	74.4	72.9
1972	75.3	75.8	76.5	77.0	77.5	77.6	78.1	78.9	79.4	80.5	81.5	82.4	78.4
1973	83.8	84.7	84.9	84.9	85.0	85.4	85.7	85.7	85.8	86.9	87.1	86.4	85.5
1974	85.7	84.8	84.7	85.0	85.8	85.6	85.4	84.9	84.7	83.6	82.4	80.9	84.5
1975	79.6	79.0	78.7	78.9	79.2	80.1	80.5	81.1	81.4	81.6	81.8	82.5	80.4
1976	83.3	84.3	84.6	84.6	85.0	85.2	85.3	85.7	85.9	85.9	86.6	87.3	85.3
1977	87.7	88.1	88.9	89.3	89.7	90.1	90.6	91.2	91.5	91.9	92.2	92.9	90.3
1978	92.8	93.3	94.1	95.4	95.7	96.3	96.7	97.0	97.4	98.2	98.8	99.2	96.2
1979	99.4	99.7	100.2	99.7	100.6	100.7	101.0	101.2	101.4	101.3	101.6	101.7	100.7
1980	101.9	102.2	101.3	100.1	98.9	98.5	98.3	98.4	99.3	100.0	100.2	100.8	100.0
1981	101.5	101.6	102.0	102.2	101.9	102.4	103.0	103.1	102.5	101.8	101.0	100.0	101.9
1982	99.3	99.3	99.1	98.8	99.1	98.5	98.2	97.8	97.5	96.7	97.0	96.9	98.2

SIX MONTH SMOOTHED CHANGE IN COINCIDENT INDEX, THREE COUNTRIES, EXCLUDING EUROPE (ANNUAL RATE, PERCENT)

YEAR	JAN	FEB	MAR	APR	MAY	JUN	JUL	AUG	SEP	OCT	NOV	DEC	AVGE
1955	8.6	10.6	12.3	12.2	14.0	13.1	13.5	11.6	11.4	10.5	10.1	9.3	11.4
1956	7.9	6.5	4.8	5.5	3.8	3.3	-0.9	3.2	4.4	5.1	3.9	4.6	4.3
1957	4.2	5.5	5.4	.3	2.8	2.2	2.4	1.5	-0.7	-1.9	-4.7	-6.4	1.1
1958	-8.4	-10.4	-10.7	-11.1	-9.5	-6.8	-3.4	-0.8	2.1	4.3	8.4	8.7	-3.1
1959	10.6	12.3	13.3	15.0	15.1	13.7	10.2	5.5	4.3	3.3	3.2	7.7	9.5
1960	8.6	8.7	6.0	5.8	4.4	3.9	3.0	2.2	1.8	0.8	-0.9	-2.2	3.5
1961	-2.0	-2.0	0.3	1.3	3.1	5.6	6.0	7.8	7.8	9.3	11.1	11.2	5.0
1962	10.4	10.8	10.2	9.8	9.3	7.8	7.0	6.7	5.9	5.2	4.5	3.8	7.6
1963	3.5	3.4	4.4	6.2	5.8	6.9	7.1	7.7	7.2	8.5	7.7	8.3	6.4
1964	8.3	8.9	7.8	8.7	9.1	8.3	9.2	8.7	8.7	6.0	7.5	8.8	8.3
1965	8.1	7.5	8.7	7.5	7.5	8.0	8.9	8.4	9.0	9.0	9.5	10.0	8.5
1966	9.6	10.3	10.0	9.6	8.9	9.3	8.7	8.2	7.4	7.4	7.0	6.4	8.6
1967	5.8	5.1	4.0	4.6	4.9	4.6	5.5	6.2	6.2	5.0	6.4	7.5	5.5
1968	6.8	6.8	7.6	8.3	8.6	8.6	8.4	8.2	8.3	8.3	8.7	8.3	8.1
1969	7.6	7.4	7.1	7.0	6.4	5.7	5.5	5.6	5.0	5.1	4.6	4.2	5.9
1970	1.8	1.3	1.5	1.3	1.3	1.4	1.2	0.8	0.6	-1.4	-2.4	0.0	0.6
1971	2.2	2.6	3.3	3.7	3.8	4.9	4.3	3.8	4.7	4.4	4.7	4.9	3.9
1972	6.2	6.8	7.5	7.8	8.0	7.3	7.6	8.3	8.4	9.7	10.9	11.5	8.3
1973	13.1	13.4	12.0	10.4	9.0	8.1	7.3	5.9	4.7	6.0	5.2	2.7	8.1
1974	-0.3	-1.9	-2.1	-1.4	0.3	-0.3	-0.7	-1.7	-2.1	-4.3	-6.3	-8.6	-2.4
1975	-10.4	-10.6	-10.3	-8.9	-7.1	-4.1	-2.2	0.1	1.7	2.7	3.6	5.2	-3.4
1976	6.9	8.5	8.0	6.9	6.4	5.9	5.3	5.2	4.6	3.8	4.6	5.3	6.0
1977	5.3	5.2	6.3	6.5	6.4	6.4	6.6	6.9	6.6	6.3	5.9	6.3	6.2
1978	5.0	5.5	6.0	7.6	7.2	7.3	7.0	6.8	6.5	7.1	7.1	6.9	6.6
1979	6.3	5.6	5.6	3.5	4.6	4.0	3.7	3.5	3.1	2.4	2.4	2.2	3.9
1980	2.1	2.3	0.4	-2.0	-4.2	-4.7	-4.8	-2.2	-2.2	-0.6	0.0	1.4	-1.4
1981	2.8	3.1	3.9	4.1	3.3	3.8	4.2	3.6	1.8	0.0	-1.7	-3.6	2.1
1982	-4.7	-4.3	-4.4	-4.5	-3.5	-4.1	-4.1	-4.1	-3.9	-4.5	-3.3	-2.9	-4.0

LAGGING INDEX, THREE COUNTRIES, EXCLUDING EUROPE (1970=100).

YEAR	JAN	FEB	MAR	APR	MAY	JUN	JUL	AUG	SEP	OCT	NOV	DEC	AVGE
1953	32.5	32.8	33.2	33.7	34.4	34.4	34.6	34.7	34.9	35.0	34.8	34.6	34.1
1954	34.5	34.4	33.9	33.7	33.5	33.3	33.1	32.6	32.5	32.4	32.4	32.7	33.2
1955	32.6	32.7	32.9	33.1	33.5	34.0	34.4	35.3	35.4	36.1	36.6	37.1	34.5
1956	37.6	38.0	38.4	39.2	39.7	40.1	40.4	40.8	41.1	41.4	41.7	41.8	40.0
1957	42.1	42.2	42.6	42.9	43.3	43.5	43.7	44.4	44.5	44.0	43.8	43.7	43.4
1958	43.0	42.4	41.9	41.2	40.4	40.0	40.2	40.0	40.5	40.8	40.8	41.0	41.0
1959	41.1	41.2	41.7	42.4	43.1	44.0	44.5	45.0	45.9	46.2	46.5	47.2	44.1
1960	47.7	48.4	48.6	49.0	49.6	49.7	49.7	49.4	49.2	49.3	49.6	49.8	49.2
1961	49.9	50.0	49.9	49.8	49.8	50.1	50.1	50.7	50.9	51.2	51.6	51.9	50.5
1962	52.2	52.5	53.0	53.6	54.1	54.4	54.8	55.0	55.2	55.6	55.6	55.6	54.3
1963	55.5	55.7	55.7	55.9	55.9	56.4	56.5	56.8	57.3	57.9	58.4	58.8	56.7
1964	59.1	59.4	60.0	60.7	61.3	61.6	62.1	62.6	63.0	63.4	63.8	64.3	61.8
1965	64.9	65.3	65.7	66.1	66.6	66.7	67.4	67.7	68.0	68.5	68.8	70.1	67.1
1966	70.7	71.2	72.4	73.2	74.1	75.1	76.0	76.8	77.6	78.1	78.6	79.0	75.2
1967	79.5	79.5	79.6	79.7	80.1	80.3	80.7	80.6	80.9	81.3	82.0	83.1	80.6
1968	83.5	83.8	84.3	85.4	86.3	86.7	86.9	87.4	87.8	87.7	88.8	90.8	86.6
1969	91.4	92.1	92.9	93.4	94.4	95.5	96.4	97.2	97.8	98.6	99.1	99.7	95.7
1970	99.8	100.2	100.2	100.0	100.2	99.9	100.2	100.3	100.1	100.2	100.0	99.0	100.0
1971	98.6	98.4	98.4	98.4	99.1	99.3	99.5	99.6	100.1	100.3	100.0	100.6	99.4
1972	100.5	100.6	100.9	101.2	101.4	101.8	102.0	102.2	103.0	103.7	104.6	105.1	102.2
1973	105.8	107.1	107.9	109.6	110.9	112.6	114.3	115.7	116.8	117.9	118.6	119.4	113.0
1974	120.1	121.3	122.4	123.5	124.6	125.0	125.3	125.6	125.7	125.8	126.0	125.6	124.2
1975	124.8	123.2	121.4	119.7	118.3	117.1	116.4	115.8	115.5	115.5	114.7	113.7	118.0
1976	113.8	113.7	113.9	114.0	114.5	114.8	115.1	115.3	115.9	115.9	115.9	116.4	114.9
1977	117.0	117.4	117.8	118.3	118.2	118.4	118.5	118.9	118.8	118.9	118.8	119.3	118.4
1978	119.7	120.1	121.2	121.6	122.0	122.7	122.9	123.4	123.8	124.5	125.6	126.2	122.8
1979	126.8	127.1	127.2	128.2	129.0	130.2	130.7	131.7	133.0	133.7	134.6	134.8	130.6
1980	134.7	135.1	136.9	138.3	138.7	137.9	137.5	137.1	137.1	137.6	138.1	138.6	137.3
1981	138.6	138.7	137.8	137.8	138.3	138.4	139.4	140.1	140.4	140.8	140.5	140.6	139.3
1982	140.7	140.5	140.1	140.3	139.8	139.8	139.4	138.5	138.7	138.2	137.0	136.2	139.1

SIX MONTH SMOOTHED CHANGE IN LAGGING INDEX, THREE COUNTRIES, EXCLUDING EUROPE (ANNUAL RATE, PERCENT)

YEAR	JAN	FEB	MAR	APR	MAY	JUN	JUL	AUG	SEP	OCT	NOV	DEC	AVGE
1954	1.9	0.4	-3.0	-4.4	-5.3	-5.9	-6.4	-8.2	-7.9	-7.6	-6.4	-4.1	-4.7
1955	-3.6	-2.3	-0.3	1.1	3.7	6.8	8.6	13.2	12.8	15.3	16.2	16.6	7.3
1956	17.2	17.4	16.8	18.5	17.9	16.8	15.8	14.9	14.2	13.2	11.9	10.5	15.4
1957	9.7	8.5	8.5	8.2	8.5	8.1	7.6	9.8	8.7	5.2	3.2	1.8	7.3
1958	-1.6	-4.6	-6.6	-9.2	-12.0	-11.8	-10.9	-10.5	-6.9	-4.5	-3.1	-1.3	-6.9
1959	0.2	1.7	4.2	7.4	10.5	13.6	14.3	14.6	16.8	16.2	15.2	16.0	10.9
1960	15.7	16.1	14.3	13.2	13.3	11.3	9.3	6.3	4.0	3.2	3.5	3.5	9.5
1961	2.9	2.6	1.5	0.9	0.6	1.4	1.6	3.5	4.0	4.6	5.5	5.7	2.9
1962	6.3	6.7	7.8	9.0	9.5	9.5	9.3	8.7	8.2	8.2	6.9	5.4	8.0
1963	4.1	3.9	2.9	2.9	2.2	3.2	3.0	3.6	4.8	6.0	7.2	7.7	4.3
1964	7.9	8.0	8.7	9.8	10.3	9.7	9.9	10.1	9.8	9.4	9.1	9.2	9.3
1965	9.6	9.3	8.9	8.5	8.5	7.6	8.3	7.8	7.6	7.8	7.1	9.7	8.4
1966	9.8	9.9	11.9	12.4	13.1	14.2	14.5	14.6	14.6	13.6	12.8	11.4	12.7
1967	10.7	8.8	7.4	5.9	5.6	4.9	4.7	3.5	3.4	3.7	4.8	6.5	5.8
1968	6.8	6.7	7.0	8.6	9.4	9.0	8.4	8.2	7.7	6.3	7.5	10.5	8.0
1969	10.5	10.3	10.7	10.0	10.6	11.6	11.8	11.8	11.1	10.9	10.1	9.3	10.7
1970	8.0	7.3	5.9	4.4	3.7	2.2	2.0	1.6	1.3	0.6	-0.1	-2.0	2.9
1971	-2.6	-2.8	-2.5	-2.3	-0.7	-0.1	0.2	0.6	1.7	2.0	1.4	2.6	-0.2
1972	2.1	2.0	2.5	2.5	2.3	2.8	2.0	2.8	3.8	4.7	5.6	5.9	3.3
1973	6.5	8.0	8.6	10.4	11.5	13.1	14.6	15.0	15.0	14.6	13.6	12.8	12.0
1974	11.8	11.7	11.5	11.2	10.9	9.7	8.4	7.3	6.2	5.1	4.4	2.8	8.4
1975	-0.9	-2.1	-4.9	-7.2	-8.8	-9.8	-9.9	-9.8	-9.1	-8.0	-7.9	-8.1	-7.1
1976	-6.5	-5.3	-3.8	-2.7	-1.2	-0.1	-0.7	1.1	2.1	2.2	2.0	2.8	-0.7
1977	3.3	3.5	3.8	4.0	3.3	3.0	2.7	2.8	2.2	2.0	1.5	1.8	2.8
1978	2.0	2.4	3.7	3.9	4.1	4.8	4.4	4.6	4.7	5.0	6.4	6.0	4.3
1979	6.1	5.5	4.8	5.5	6.0	6.8	6.6	7.1	8.0	7.8	7.9	7.2	6.6
1980	5.8	5.5	7.1	8.0	7.3	4.9	3.5	2.8	1.4	1.6	1.8	2.1	4.3
1981	1.7	1.4	-0.3	-0.4	0.4	0.6	1.8	2.7	2.8	2.9	2.1	1.9	1.5
1982	1.8	1.4	0.6	0.6	-0.2	-0.4	-1.1	-2.3	-1.9	-2.4	-3.6	-4.2	-1.0

LEADING INDEX, SIX COUNTRIES, EXCLUDING U.S. (1980=100)

YEAR	JAN	FEB	MAR	APR	MAY	JUN	JUL	AUG	SEP	OCT	NOV	DEC	AVGE
1955	33.7	33.9	34.1	34.3	34.2	34.6	35.0	35.4	35.6	35.7	35.8	36.1	34.9
1956	36.1	36.1	36.4	36.6	36.8	37.1	37.2	37.4	37.5	37.7	38.0	38.4	37.1
1957	38.5	38.7	38.7	38.9	39.0	38.9	38.7	38.7	38.7	38.5	38.4	38.3	38.7
1958	38.5	38.2	38.1	38.3	38.4	38.5	38.8	39.1	39.3	39.6	39.9	40.0	38.9
1959	40.4	40.8	41.4	42.2	42.9	43.2	43.7	44.0	44.5	44.9	45.2	45.8	43.2
1960	45.4	45.6	45.9	46.1	46.2	46.5	46.8	47.3	47.4	47.4	47.6	47.6	46.6
1961	48.0	48.5	48.5	48.7	48.9	49.0	49.1	48.9	48.9	49.0	49.2	49.0	48.8
1962	48.8	48.8	49.0	49.0	48.8	48.6	48.4	48.6	48.7	48.7	49.0	49.3	48.8
1963	49.5	49.5	50.0	50.6	50.9	51.3	51.6	51.8	52.1	52.4	52.6	52.7	51.2
1964	53.1	53.2	53.2	53.2	53.5	53.6	53.7	53.8	54.0	53.9	53.9	53.9	53.6
1965	54.0	54.1	54.0	54.0	54.1	54.0	53.9	54.2	54.4	54.6	54.8	55.3	54.3
1966	56.0	56.3	56.5	56.5	56.7	57.1	57.1	56.9	56.8	56.8	56.8	57.0	56.7
1967	57.3	57.4	57.6	57.8	58.0	58.1	58.4	58.7	59.1	59.6	60.1	60.4	58.5
1968	60.3	60.7	61.0	61.2	61.3	61.6	62.1	63.1	63.5	63.9	64.5	64.9	62.3
1969	65.2	65.6	65.9	66.4	66.9	67.2	67.3	67.7	67.9	68.3	68.6	68.7	67.1
1970	68.8	69.2	69.2	69.2	68.8	68.5	68.3	68.3	68.1	68.0	67.8	67.9	68.5
1971	68.2	68.0	68.3	68.4	68.4	68.7	69.1	69.2	69.3	69.3	69.6	69.9	68.9
1972	70.3	70.1	71.6	72.4	73.2	73.4	74.1	74.9	75.8	76.7	77.8	79.3	74.1
1973	80.9	81.8	82.0	82.1	81.9	82.1	82.6	82.8	82.7	83.1	83.6	83.8	82.4
1974	84.0	85.1	84.6	83.6	82.5	81.5	80.8	79.8	78.2	76.9	75.8	74.8	80.6
1975	74.3	74.3	74.4	74.8	75.0	75.6	75.5	76.0	76.6	77.3	77.9	78.7	75.9
1976	79.5	80.6	81.4	81.7	82.4	83.1	83.8	83.8	83.9	83.7	83.8	84.1	82.6
1977	84.6	84.3	84.2	84.2	83.9	83.7	83.7	84.2	84.7	85.0	85.3	85.5	84.4
1978	85.9	86.1	86.7	87.4	88.1	88.6	88.8	89.0	90.2	90.7	91.7	92.4	88.8
1979	92.5	93.6	94.7	95.9	96.9	97.5	98.0	98.4	98.8	99.0	99.3	99.7	97.0
1980	101.1	102.0	101.5	101.9	101.2	100.3	99.6	98.7	98.5	98.7	98.4	98.3	100.0
1981	98.7	99.0	99.2	99.5	99.7	100.0	100.4	101.1	101.2	101.4	101.5	101.4	100.3
1982	101.4	101.7	101.2	100.6	100.8	100.4	100.9	101.4	101.5	101.6	102.0	101.9	101.3

SIX MONTH SMOOTHED CHANGE IN LEADING INDEX, SIX COUNTRIES, EXCLUDING U.S. (ANNUAL RATE, PERCENT)

YEAR	JAN	FEB	MAR	APR	MAY	JUN	JUL	AUG.	SEP	OCT	NOV	DEC	AVGE
1956	6.5	5.8	6.0	6.0	6.4	6.4	6.1	5.8	5.9	5.8	6.4	7.4	6.2
1957	7.1	6.9	6.1	6.0	5.2	3.9	2.4	1.4	0.8	-0.1	-1.0	-1.8	3.1
1958	-0.8	-2.3	-2.4	-1.5	-0.7	0.1	1.6	3.3	3.8	5.0	5.9	6.0	1.5
1959	7.5	8.4	10.1	12.8	14.4	14.3	14.6	13.9	13.8	13.5	12.7	13.5	12.5
1960	9.4	8.5	7.7	6.9	6.1	6.1	6.0	7.0	6.5	5.5	5.2	4.6	6.6
1961	5.6	6.4	5.7	5.4	5.5	4.8	4.2	2.9	2.3	2.3	2.5	1.2	4.1
1962	-0.1	-0.3	0.4	0.1	-0.8	-1.5	-2.1	-1.1	-0.6	-0.6	0.9	1.8	-0.3
1963	-2.5	2.4	4.0	6.0	6.7	7.5	7.7	7.4	7.6	7.9	7.3	6.6	6.1
1964	6.9	6.0	5.0	3.8	4.0	3.6	3.4	3.2	3.1	2.4	1.7	1.4	3.7
1965	1.4	1.7	1.0	0.7	0.6	0.1	-0.3	0.9	1.4	1.0	2.6	3.9	1.3
1966	5.8	6.5	6.5	5.7	5.5	6.2	5.4	3.6	2.6	1.8	1.4	1.3	4.4
1967	2.0	1.9	2.1	2.8	2.9	2.8	3.5	4.2	4.9	5.9	6.9	7.0	3.9
1968	5.8	6.1	6.1	5.7	5.3	5.4	6.0	8.1	8.2	8.2	8.7	8.9	6.9
1969	8.7	8.4	8.0	8.3	8.6	7.9	7.0	6.8	6.2	6.2	5.9	5.3	7.3
1970	4.7	4.8	4.0	3.2	1.5	0.2	-0.6	-0.8	-1.6	-1.8	-2.3	-1.8	0.8
1971	-0.9	-1.2	-0.1	0.3	0.4	1.4	2.5	2.6	2.7	2.4	2.7	3.3	1.3
1972	3.9	-2.8	6.6	7.7	9.1	8.6	9.2	10.3	11.3	12.3	13.5	15.4	9.2
1973	17.5	17.3	15.1	12.8	10.4	8.9	8.3	6.9	5.1	4.7	4.7	4.0	9.6
1974	3.6	5.3	3.5	1.0	-1.8	-4.2	-5.6	-7.5	-10.3	-12.3	-13.5	-14.5	-4.7
1975	-14.1	-12.5	-10.3	-7.5	-5.4	-2.6	-1.7	0.5	2.7	4.8	6.4	8.0	-2.6
1976	8.9	10.6	11.3	10.5	10.8	10.7	11.0	9.3	7.8	5.7	4.7	4.3	8.8
1977	4.5	2.7	1.8	1.2	0.3	-0.6	-0.6	0.4	1.4	2.0	2.4	2.5	1.5
1978	3.2	3.4	4.4	5.4	6.5	6.7	6.2	5.8	7.5	7.6	8.7	8.9	6.2
1979	7.8	9.1	9.8	11.1	11.4	11.2	10.5	9.6	8.8	7.7	6.9	6.4	9.2
1980	7.8	8.2	5.8	5.5	3.2	0.8	-0.9	-2.8	-3.2	-2.8	-3.4	-3.3	1.2
1981	-2.5	-1.4	-0.7	0.2	1.0	1.8	2.6	3.8	3.7	3.5	3.4	2.6	1.5
1982	2.1	2.2	0.8	-0.4	-0.3	-1.1	-0.3	0.4	0.6	0.7	1.4	1.2	0.6

COINCIDENT INDEX, SIX COUNTRIES, EXCLUDING U.S. (1980=100)

YEAR	JAN	FEB	MAR	APR	MAY	JUN	JUL	AUG	SEP	OCT	NOV	DEC	AVGE
1955	24.6	24.9	25.0	25.3	25.5	25.7	25.9	26.2	26.4	26.6	26.7	26.9	25.8
1956	27.2	27.3	27.5	27.7	28.0	28.2	28.4	28.5	28.7	29.0	29.1	29.2	28.2
1957	29.4	29.7	29.8	30.1	30.3	30.4	30.6	30.7	30.8	30.8	31.0	31.0	30.4
1958	31.2	31.1	31.2	31.3	31.3	31.3	31.6	31.6	31.7	31.8	31.8	31.1	31.5
1959	32.0	32.1	32.3	32.8	32.9	33.3	33.5	33.7	34.2	34.5	34.8	35.1	33.4
1960	35.4	35.8	36.2	36.4	36.6	37.0	37.3	37.7	38.1	38.3	38.6	39.0	37.2
1961	39.3	39.6	40.1	40.1	40.4	40.7	40.9	41.1	41.2	41.5	41.8	42.1	40.7
1962	42.5	42.8	42.7	42.9	43.3	43.4	43.5	43.9	44.0	44.1	44.3	44.4	43.5
1963	44.3	44.4	44.9	45.7	46.1	46.5	47.0	47.4	47.5	48.2	48.6	48.8	46.6
1964	49.4	49.8	49.8	50.0	50.3	50.5	50.8	50.9	51.4	51.6	51.8	52.1	50.7
1965	52.1	52.2	52.2	52.4	52.7	52.9	53.1	53.4	53.6	53.9	54.1	54.4	53.1
1966	54.7	55.1	55.3	55.5	55.8	56.0	56.2	56.5	56.4	56.4	56.5	56.7	55.9
1967	56.7	56.8	56.7	57.0	57.4	57.8	58.3	58.4	58.7	58.7	58.9	59.6	57.9
1968	59.6	60.0	60.4	60.6	60.3	61.1	61.8	62.5	63.0	63.6	64.5	64.8	61.8
1969	65.1	65.3	65.8	66.5	67.1	67.4	67.8	68.4	68.7	69.3	70.0	70.3	67.6
1970	70.5	71.0	71.6	71.9	72.4	72.9	73.2	73.3	73.6	73.9	73.9	74.3	72.7
1971	74.7	74.6	74.9	75.2	75.3	75.6	75.9	76.0	76.4	76.4	76.6	76.7	75.7
1972	77.0	77.1	77.9	78.0	78.5	78.8	79.1	79.6	80.1	80.8	81.6	82.3	79.2
1973	83.2	83.9	84.2	84.4	84.9	85.4	85.7	86.2	86.1	87.1	87.2	86.9	85.4
1974	86.5	86.1	86.0	86.6	87.4	87.4	87.5	87.1	87.0	86.0	85.3	84.9	86.5
1975	84.4	84.2	84.0	83.9	83.5	83.6	83.7	83.6	83.7	84.0	84.0	84.5	83.9
1976	84.8	85.4	85.6	85.7	86.1	86.5	86.6	87.3	87.6	87.8	88.4	88.8	86.7
1977	89.0	88.9	89.2	89.2	89.1	89.2	89.1	89.8	89.9	90.1	90.6	91.0	89.6
1978	91.4	91.4	91.9	92.3	92.5	92.9	93.2	93.4	93.9	94.3	94.8	95.3	93.1
1979	95.4	95.9	96.4	96.6	97.5	97.9	97.8	98.5	98.9	99.3	99.7	99.9	97.8
1980	100.1	100.8	100.4	100.4	100.1	100.0	99.9	99.7	99.8	100.0	99.5	99.4	100.0
1981	99.8	99.7	99.5	99.4	99.0	99.2	99.4	99.5	99.5	99.5	99.6	99.3	99.4
1982	99.4	99.3	99.5	99.5	99.5	99.4	99.3	99.2	99.0	98.7	99.1	99.1	99.2

SIX MONTH SMOOTHED CHANGE IN COINCIDENT INDEX, SIX COUNTRIES, EXCLUDING U.S. (ANNUAL RATE, PERCENT)

YEAR	JAN	FEB	MAR	APR	MAY	JUN	JUL	AUG	SEP	OCT	NOV	DEC	AVGE
1956	10.5	9.4	9.1	9.3	9.3	9.5	9.0	8.3	8.6	8.9	8.6	7.9	9.0
1957	7.9	8.8	7.9	8.4	8.6	7.8	8.0	7.4	6.6	5.2	5.9	4.8	7.3
1958	5.0	4.7	3.4	2.8	2.3	1.9	3.5	3.0	2.7	3.0	2.3	3.0	3.1
1959	3.2	3.3	4.0	6.1	6.2	8.0	7.8	8.1	9.9	10.4	10.6	11.0	7.4
1960	11.3	11.7	11.9	11.1	10.7	10.8	10.8	11.2	11.5	10.7	10.6	10.8	11.1
1961	10.6	10.2	11.5	9.8	9.3	9.4	8.9	8.1	7.3	7.3	7.4	7.3	8.9
1962	8.3	8.3	6.4	6.4	6.9	6.5	5.7	6.5	6.2	5.3	5.4	4.9	6.4
1963	3.4	3.2	4.7	7.7	8.0	8.7	9.9	10.4	9.6	11.0	11.1	10.6	8.2
1964	11.2	10.9	9.0	8.1	7.8	7.4	7.0	6.2	6.9	6.5	6.2	6.2	7.8
1965	5.2	4.7	4.0	4.2	4.2	4.2	4.3	4.5	4.7	4.9	5.1	5.5	4.6
1966	5.7	6.3	6.3	5.9	6.0	5.8	5.7	5.6	4.3	4.6	3.2	3.0	5.1
1967	2.5	2.4	1.5	2.2	2.1	2.1	5.0	4.9	5.4	4.6	4.7	6.2	3.9
1968	5.3	6.0	6.3	6.1	4.1	5.8	7.1	8.4	8.7	9.4	10.9	10.3	7.4
1969	9.9	8.9	9.3	9.8	10.2	9.2	8.9	8.9	8.5	8.7	9.1	8.7	9.2
1970	8.0	8.1	8.4	7.8	7.9	8.0	7.5	6.5	6.2	5.8	4.8	4.8	7.0
1971	5.0	3.8	4.4	4.1	3.4	3.6	3.8	3.4	4.0	3.3	3.3	2.9	3.7
1972	3.1	3.1	4.4	4.1	4.8	4.7	4.7	5.4	5.8	6.7	7.9	8.5	5.3
1973	9.4	9.7	9.2	8.3	8.1	8.1	7.4	7.3	5.7	6.6	5.9	4.1	7.5
1974	2.4	0.8	0.1	1.2	2.5	2.0	1.8	0.7	0.4	-1.8	-3.2	-3.8	-0.3
1975	-4.4	-4.5	-4.6	-4.5	-4.9	-4.0	-3.1	-2.6	-1.7	-0.6	-0.1	-1.3	-2.8
1976	1.9	3.3	3.4	3.5	3.8	4.2	4.1	4.9	4.9	4.5	5.2	5.3	4.1
1977	5.0	3.9	4.0	3.2	2.6	2.2	1.5	2.0	2.2	4.7	2.8	3.2	2.9
1978	3.7	3.4	3.8	4.3	4.4	4.4	4.4	5.0	4.5	4.7	4.9	5.2	4.3
1979	4.6	4.9	5.1	4.8	5.8	5.8	4.7	5.3	5.2	5.2	5.2	4.7	5.1
1980	-0.5	-0.4	-0.8	-0.7	-1.4	-0.8	-0.2	-0.3	-0.3	-0.1	-0.9	-1.1	1.3
1981	-0.1	-0.4	-0.8	-0.7	-1.4	-0.8	-0.2	-0.1	0.1	0.0	0.3	-0.2	-0.4
1982	-0.1	-0.1	0.2	0.2	0.2	-0.1	-0.3	-0.5	-0.8	-1.2	-0.3	-0.4	-0.3

337

LAGGING INDEX, SIX COUNTRIES, EXCLUDING UNITED STATES (1970=100)

YEAR	JAN	FEB	MAR	APR	MAY	JUN	JUL	AUG	SEP	OCT	NOV	DEC	AVGE
1966	76.3	76.5	76.8	77.0	77.4	77.5	77.8	78.1	78.2	78.5	78.6	78.7	77.6
1967	78.8	78.9	79.1	79.2	79.4	79.6	79.9	80.1	80.6	81.0	81.5	81.3	79.9
1968	82.4	82.9	83.4	83.7	84.2	84.6	85.1	85.3	85.5	86.1	86.7	87.1	84.7
1969	87.3	87.7	88.3	88.8	89.4	90.9	91.7	92.9	93.3	94.3	95.3	95.6	91.3
1970	96.0	96.4	97.5	98.5	99.5	100.2	101.0	101.5	101.9	102.1	102.6	102.8	100.0
1971	102.7	102.9	102.8	102.8	102.9	103.3	103.2	103.4	103.6	103.8	103.7	104.2	103.3
1972	104.2	104.2	104.1	104.1	104.3	104.5	104.6	104.7	105.2	106.0	106.7	107.6	105.0
1973	108.4	109.4	110.1	111.3	112.6	114.4	116.1	118.0	120.0	121.3	122.2	122.5	115.5
1974	123.6	125.5	126.8	127.9	128.6	129.6	130.3	130.4	129.9	129.6	129.3	129.0	128.4
1975	128.3	127.3	126.6	126.1	125.5	124.3	123.7	122.9	122.2	121.8	121.5	120.8	124.2
1976	120.5	120.7	121.9	121.9	122.0	122.6	123.0	123.2	124.0	125.1	125.6	125.9	123.0
1977	126.2	126.3	126.2	125.9	125.3	124.4	124.0	123.7	123.2	123.0	122.6	122.5	124.0
1978	122.3	122.2	122.5	122.4	122.3	122.3	122.2	122.5	123.1	123.7	124.3	124.6	122.9
1979	124.7	124.7	125.1	125.8	126.6	127.7	128.8	130.2	131.7	133.4	135.3	136.7	129.2
1980	137.4	138.5	140.5	142.4	143.8	144.5	144.9	145.2	144.9	145.3	145.4	145.4	143.2
1981	144.9	144.9	***	***	***	***	***	***	***	***	***	***	***

SIX MONTH SMOOTHED CHANGE IN LAGGING INDEX, SIX COUNTRIES, EXCLUDING UNITED STATES (ANNUAL RATE, PERCENT)

YEAR	JAN	FEB	MAR	APR	MAY	JUN	JUL	AUG	SEP	OCT	NOV	DEC	AVGE
1967	2.9	2.6	2.6	2.4	2.4	2.4	2.8	2.8	3.5	4.0	4.7	3.7	3.1
1968	5.9	6.3	6.5	6.5	6.7	6.7	6.9	6.1	5.6	6.1	6.5	6.2	6.3
1969	5.7	5.5	5.9	6.1	6.5	8.9	9.5	10.8	10.2	10.8	11.4	10.4	8.5
1970	9.7	9.0	9.8	10.1	10.4	9.9	10.0	9.4	8.7	7.7	7.2	6.4	9.0
1971	5.0	4.3	3.1	2.1	1.8	2.0	1.4	1.4	1.4	1.6	1.1	1.8	2.3
1972	1.6	1.4	1.1	0.9	1.1	1.2	1.2	1.1	1.8	3.0	3.9	5.2	2.0
1973	6.1	7.1	7.6	8.9	10.1	12.0	13.5	15.0	16.4	16.4	15.5	13.6	11.8
1974	13.3	14.2	14.0	13.4	12.1	11.5	10.4	8.6	6.3	4.6	3.1	1.7	9.4
1975	-0.1	-2.1	-3.3	-4.0	-4.5	-6.0	-6.1	-6.6	-6.7	-6.3	-5.9	-6.0	-4.8
1976	-5.4	-4.0	-1.8	-1.2	-0.5	0.9	1.7	2.1	3.2	4.7	5.0	5.0	-0.8
1977	4.9	4.2	3.3	2.4	0.9	-0.7	-1.6	-2.2	-2.9	-3.1	-3.5	-3.2	-0.1
1978	-3.1	-2.8	-1.9	-1.6	-1.3	-0.9	-0.8	-0.7	0.9	1.8	2.7	2.9	-0.4
1979	-2.7	2.4	2.7	3.5	4.2	5.4	6.3	7.7	8.8	10.3	11.9	12.6	6.5
1980	12.0	11.9	13.2	13.9	13.8	12.6	11.1	9.4	7.3	6.3	5.0	3.8	10.0
1981	2.2	1.4	***	***	***	***	***	***	***	***	***	***	***

LEADING INDEX, SEVEN COUNTRIES (1980=100)

YEAR	JAN	FEB	MAR	APR	MAY	JUN	JUL	AUG	SEP	OCT	NOV	DEC	AVGE
1955	39.0	39.5	39.7	39.9	40.0	40.3	40.6	40.9	41.1	41.1	41.3	41.4	40.4
1956	41.3	41.1	41.4	41.5	41.5	41.5	41.6	41.7	41.8	42.1	42.3	42.4	41.7
1957	42.3	42.4	42.5	42.5	42.6	42.7	42.5	42.5	42.2	41.9	41.6	41.3	42.2
1958	41.3	40.8	40.9	41.1	41.5	41.9	42.4	42.9	43.4	43.9	44.5	44.6	42.4
1959	45.2	45.7	46.4	47.0	47.6	47.5	47.6	47.5	47.8	48.0	48.0	48.9	47.3
1960	48.8	48.9	48.6	48.7	48.6	48.7	48.9	49.1	49.1	48.9	48.8	48.7	48.8
1961	49.1	49.5	49.9	50.3	50.7	51.0	51.2	51.4	51.3	51.7	52.1	52.1	50.9
1962	52.0	52.3	52.3	52.3	51.9	51.7	51.7	52.0	52.3	52.3	52.7	52.9	52.2
1963	53.1	53.3	53.7	54.2	54.7	54.9	55.1	55.4	55.7	56.1	56.2	56.5	54.9
1964	56.9	57.1	57.3	57.4	57.7	57.8	58.1	58.3	58.5	58.4	58.5	58.9	57.9
1965	59.1	59.6	59.6	59.6	59.8	59.7	59.8	60.0	60.3	60.6	61.0	61.5	60.1
1966	62.1	62.5	62.7	62.5	62.8	62.5	62.5	62.1	62.0	62.0	62.1	62.0	62.3
1967	62.4	62.2	62.3	62.5	62.8	63.2	63.5	64.1	64.5	64.8	65.5	65.9	63.6
1968	65.6	65.9	66.6	66.4	66.7	67.1	67.6	68.1	68.6	69.3	69.5	69.9	67.6
1969	70.2	70.6	70.5	71.0	71.3	71.4	71.2	71.4	71.5	71.5	71.3	71.1	71.1
1970	71.0	70.9	70.8	70.7	70.4	70.4	70.3	70.3	70.0	69.8	69.7	70.5	70.4
1971	71.5	71.4	71.8	72.0	72.2	72.6	73.0	73.1	73.3	73.5	73.9	74.4	72.7
1972	74.9	74.9	76.4	77.1	77.7	77.9	78.4	79.3	80.1	80.9	81.8	83.1	78.5
1973	84.7	85.4	85.5	85.1	85.3	85.1	85.4	85.4	85.3	85.7	86.2	85.6	85.4
1974	85.7	86.2	85.8	84.9	84.3	83.5	83.1	81.8	80.2	78.9	77.7	76.5	82.4
1975	75.6	75.5	75.5	76.7	77.4	78.5	79.4	80.2	80.7	81.3	81.9	82.9	78.8
1976	84.2	84.9	86.2	86.0	86.6	87.2	87.9	87.6	87.6	87.4	87.6	88.4	86.8
1977	88.9	89.1	89.7	89.8	89.9	90.1	90.0	90.7	90.8	90.9	91.1	91.4	90.2
1978	91.3	91.8	92.8	93.9	94.7	95.1	95.0	95.3	96.3	96.9	97.8	97.8	94.9
1979	97.8	98.7	99.7	99.6	100.4	100.5	100.5	100.5	100.9	100.4	100.3	100.6	100.0
1980	101.9	101.9	101.3	99.8	98.7	98.5	98.9	99.0	99.4	100.0	100.2	100.3	100.0
1981	100.7	101.1	101.3	101.8	101.7	101.7	102.2	102.8	102.2	101.4	101.3	100.7	101.6
1982	100.3	100.2	99.6	99.8	100.0	99.6	100.0	99.9	100.1	100.0	100.0	101.1	100.1

SIX MONTH SMOOTHED CHANGE IN LEADING INDEX, SEVEN COUNTRIES (ANNUAL RATE, PERCENT)

YEAR	JAN	FEB	MAR	APR	MAY	JUN	JUL	AUG	SEP	OCT	NOV	DEC	AVGE
1956	4.0	2.5	2.9	3.0	2.1	1.8	1.5	1.9	1.8	2.8	3.5	3.8	2.6
1957	2.8	2.7	2.8	2.5	2.6	2.5	1.3	0.9	-0.9	-2.2	-3.5	-4.6	0.6
1958	-4.1	-5.8	-5.0	-3.8	-1.5	0.7	3.4	5.9	7.9	9.5	11.6	11.0	2.5
1959	12.4	12.9	14.4	14.9	15.0	12.5	10.6	8.0	7.9	6.9	5.7	7.8	10.7
1960	5.9	5.1	3.1	2.6	1.8	1.9	2.1	2.5	1.8	0.8	0.1	-0.3	2.3
1961	1.2	2.4	3.8	4.8	5.8	6.4	6.3	6.5	5.4	6.2	6.8	5.8	5.1
1962	4.0	4.3	3.5	2.7	0.7	-0.4	-0.4	0.5	1.0	0.8	2.3	2.7	1.8
1963	3.4	3.5	4.7	6.2	7.3	7.3	7.0	6.8	7.0	7.2	6.4	6.3	6.1
1964	6.7	6.5	6.0	5.2	5.4	4.8	4.8	4.6	4.5	3.7	3.2	3.8	4.9
1965	4.5	4.9	4.2	3.4	3.5	2.8	2.3	2.5	3.0	3.6	4.3	5.2	3.7
1966	6.3	6.7	6.7	5.3	3.9	3.8	3.6	1.1	0.2	-0.2	-0.2	-0.7	3.0
1967	0.5	-0.3	0.0	0.7	1.7	2.8	3.0	5.2	5.7	6.0	7.4	7.5	3.4
1968	5.6	5.9	6.9	5.2	5.3	5.4	5.7	6.3	6.8	7.6	7.1	7.4	6.3
1969	7.3	7.1	5.8	6.3	5.9	4.7	3.7	3.3	3.0	2.3	1.2	0.5	4.3
1970	-0.3	-0.5	-0.9	-1.4	-1.9	-1.9	-1.9	-1.8	-2.1	-2.3	-2.4	0.3	-1.4
1971	3.0	2.5	3.5	3.9	4.1	4.8	5.2	4.8	4.7	4.5	4.7	5.3	4.2
1972	5.5	4.9	8.1	8.7	9.1	8.4	8.5	9.6	10.2	10.7	11.5	12.8	9.0
1973	14.9	14.4	12.4	9.5	8.5	6.5	5.7	4.2	2.9	2.9	3.0	0.9	7.1
1974	0.7	1.5	0.6	-1.3	-2.7	-4.2	-4.8	-7.2	-9.9	-11.8	-13.0	-14.3	-5.5
1975	-14.6	-13.3	-11.4	-7.1	-4.0	-0.1	3.2	5.8	7.3	8.6	9.6	11.1	-0.4
1976	13.0	12.9	14.1	11.3	10.7	10.3	10.1	7.6	6.3	4.5	3.9	4.4	9.1
1977	4.6	4.1	4.5	4.2	3.7	3.4	2.9	4.0	3.6	3.1	2.9	3.0	3.7
1978	2.3	2.8	4.4	6.1	7.1	7.1	6.1	5.7	6.9	7.4	7.7	6.8	5.9
1979	5.8	6.4	7.2	5.9	6.6	5.8	4.8	4.0	3.9	2.2	1.4	1.5	4.6
1980	3.6	3.0	1.2	-1.7	-3.7	-3.8	-2.8	-2.4	-1.5	-0.1	-0.3	0.4	-0.6
1981	1.3	2.2	2.7	3.6	3.2	2.7	3.0	3.7	2.0	-0.2	-0.2	-1.5	1.9
1982	-2.3	-2.4	-3.3	-2.8	-2.1	-2.7	-1.6	-1.3	-0.7	-0.4	0.6	2.0	-1.4

COINCIDENT INDEX, SEVEN COUNTRIES (1980=100)

YEAR	JAN	FEB	MAR	APR	MAY	JUN	JUL	AUG	SEP	OCT	NOV	DEC	AVGE
1955	31.4	31.8	32.1	32.4	32.8	32.9	33.3	33.4	33.7	33.9	34.1	34.3	33.0
1956	34.5	34.5	34.6	34.9	34.9	35.1	34.7	35.2	35.6	35.8	35.8	36.0	35.1
1957	36.1	36.5	36.6	36.6	36.6	36.7	36.9	36.9	36.8	36.6	36.4	36.1	36.6
1958	35.9	35.6	35.4	35.2	35.3	35.5	35.9	36.1	36.3	36.5	36.9	37.0	36.0
1959	37.3	37.6	37.9	38.5	38.8	39.1	39.0	38.7	38.9	39.1	39.4	40.1	38.7
1960	40.5	40.8	40.8	41.0	41.1	41.2	41.3	41.4	41.6	41.6	41.6	41.6	41.2
1961	41.8	41.9	42.3	42.4	42.7	43.2	43.4	43.7	43.8	44.2	44.7	44.9	43.2
1962	45.2	45.6	45.6	45.9	46.1	46.2	46.3	46.6	46.8	46.9	47.0	47.1	46.3
1963	47.0	47.1	47.6	48.2	48.5	48.9	49.2	49.6	49.8	50.3	50.5	50.8	49.0
1964	51.2	51.6	51.7	52.1	52.4	52.6	53.0	53.1	53.5	53.5	54.0	54.4	52.8
1965	54.6	54.8	55.1	55.3	55.6	55.9	56.3	56.6	57.1	57.4	57.8	58.2	56.2
1966	58.6	59.1	59.4	59.5	59.8	60.1	60.4	60.6	60.7	60.8	60.9	61.0	60.1
1967	61.1	61.2	61.1	61.4	61.6	61.9	62.3	62.6	62.8	62.8	63.3	64.0	62.2
1968	63.9	64.3	64.8	65.2	65.2	65.8	66.4	66.9	67.3	67.7	68.4	68.7	66.2
1969	69.0	69.3	69.8	70.2	70.6	70.8	71.2	71.6	71.7	72.1	72.4	72.6	70.9
1970	72.3	72.5	72.8	73.0	73.2	73.4	73.5	73.6	73.6	73.3	73.0	73.6	73.1
1971	74.1	74.2	74.5	74.8	74.9	75.3	75.4	75.4	75.8	75.9	76.2	76.5	75.2
1972	77.1	77.4	78.1	78.4	78.9	79.1	79.5	80.1	80.6	81.5	82.5	83.2	79.7
1973	84.2	84.9	85.2	85.3	85.6	86.0	86.4	86.6	86.7	87.6	87.8	87.4	86.1
1974	86.9	86.4	86.4	86.8	87.3	87.2	87.2	86.8	86.4	85.6	84.4	83.3	86.2
1975	82.4	81.9	81.5	81.5	81.4	82.0	82.2	82.5	82.8	83.1	83.2	83.7	82.3
1976	84.4	85.2	85.4	85.6	86.0	86.2	86.5	86.9	87.2	87.2	87.9	88.5	86.4
1977	88.7	88.9	89.5	89.7	90.0	90.3	90.5	91.1	91.4	91.6	92.0	92.6	90.5
1978	92.7	93.0	93.7	94.7	95.0	95.5	95.8	96.2	96.6	97.2	97.7	98.1	95.5
1979	98.2	98.5	99.1	98.9	99.7	99.9	100.1	100.4	100.6	100.8	101.1	101.2	99.9
1980	101.4	101.7	101.1	100.3	99.4	99.5	99.0	99.0	99.4	99.8	99.8	100.1	100.0
1981	100.5	100.6	100.5	100.5	100.2	100.5	100.9	100.9	100.6	100.1	99.7	98.9	100.3
1982	98.5	98.6	98.5	98.3	98.4	97.9	97.7	97.4	97.1	96.6	96.8	96.8	97.7

SIX MONTH SMOOTHED CHANGE IN COINCIDENT INDEX, SEVEN COUNTRIES (ANNUAL RATE, PERCENT)

YEAR	JAN	FEB	MAR	APR	MAY	JUN	JUL	AUG	SEP	OCT	NOV	DEC	AVGE
1956	8.5	7.2	6.2	6.5	5.5	5.3	2.3	4.7	5.5	6.1	5.3	5.5	5.7
1957	5.3	6.5	6.0	5.1	4.6	4.1	4.3	3.6	2.1	0.8	-0.6	-2.1	3.3
1958	-3.1	-4.5	-5.3	-5.8	-4.9	-3.3	-0.8	0.5	2.0	3.5	5.4	5.7	-0.9
1959	6.9	7.7	8.7	10.4	10.5	10.4	8.4	5.8	5.7	5.4	5.6	8.3	7.8
1960	8.9	9.1	7.7	7.4	6.6	6.2	5.6	5.4	5.3	4.2	3.0	2.4	6.0
1961	2.5	2.5	4.2	4.0	4.8	6.3	6.3	6.8	6.5	7.4	8.5	8.6	5.7
1962	8.6	8.9	7.7	7.5	7.3	6.5	5.8	5.9	5.4	4.8	4.5	3.9	6.4
1963	3.0	2.8	4.1	6.1	6.3	7.0	7.6	8.1	7.6	8.6	8.1	8.4	6.5
1964	8.8	8.9	7.7	7.6	7.6	7.0	7.3	6.7	7.1	5.7	6.4	7.1	7.3
1965	6.6	6.0	6.2	6.1	6.1	6.2	6.7	6.5	7.1	7.1	7.5	7.8	6.7
1966	7.8	8.4	8.3	7.4	7.0	7.1	6.6	6.2	5.3	4.8	4.3	3.7	6.4
1967	3.3	2.7	2.0	2.4	2.6	3.0	3.8	4.2	4.4	3.6	4.7	6.1	3.6
1968	5.3	5.8	6.3	6.5	5.6	6.4	7.2	7.7	7.8	8.0	8.8	8.3	7.0
1969	7.9	7.5	7.6	7.7	7.5	6.9	6.6	6.6	5.9	5.9	5.5	5.2	6.7
1970	3.6	3.3	3.5	3.2	3.0	3.6	3.0	2.5	2.2	1.0	0.1	1.4	2.5
1971	2.5	2.3	2.7	3.0	2.9	3.6	3.3	2.9	3.7	3.4	3.6	3.7	3.1
1972	4.6	4.7	5.8	5.8	6.3	5.9	6.0	6.7	6.9	8.1	9.2	9.7	6.6
1973	10.6	10.9	10.0	8.7	8.1	7.7	7.1	6.2	5.2	6.0	5.3	3.4	7.4
1974	1.6	0.1	-0.3	0.4	1.3	0.7	0.5	-0.4	-1.3	-3.0	-5.1	-6.9	-1.0
1975	-8.1	-8.3	-8.4	-7.6	-6.8	-4.7	-3.3	-1.7	-0.3	1.0	1.8	3.2	-3.6
1976	4.6	6.0	5.9	5.7	5.7	5.3	5.0	5.2	5.0	4.2	4.9	5.3	5.2
1977	5.0	4.7	5.3	4.9	4.8	4.6	4.4	4.9	4.8	4.5	4.6	5.0	4.8
1978	4.4	4.4	5.0	6.4	6.1	6.3	6.0	5.9	5.8	6.1	6.2	6.1	5.7
1979	5.2	4.9	5.2	3.8	4.4	4.4	4.0	3.9	3.7	3.4	3.3	3.0	4.1
1980	2.9	2.8	1.2	-0.5	-2.4	-2.9	-3.0	-2.8	-1.9	-0.8	-0.7	0.0	-0.7
1981	0.9	1.3	1.3	1.4	0.7	1.2	1.7	1.5	0.5	-0.6	-1.4	-2.7	0.5
1982	-3.4	-2.9	-2.7	-2.9	-2.4	-2.9	-3.0	-3.0	-3.0	-3.4	-2.5	-2.1	-2.8

LAGGING INDEX, SEVEN COUNTRIES (1970=100)

YEAR	JAN	FEB	MAR	APR	MAY	JUN	JUL	AUG	SEP	OCT	NOV	DEC	AVGE
1966	75.3	75.8	76.6	77.2	77.9	78.6	79.3	80.0	80.4	80.9	81.3	81.6	78.7
1967	81.8	81.8	82.0	81.9	82.1	82.3	82.5	82.5	82.7	82.9	83.5	83.9	82.5
1968	84.6	84.9	85.1	85.9	86.5	86.9	87.3	87.6	87.9	88.2	89.0	90.3	87.0
1969	91.1	91.7	92.5	93.0	93.7	95.4	96.3	97.2	97.7	98.4	98.9	99.3	95.4
1970	99.4	99.5	100.0	99.9	100.2	100.3	100.5	100.6	100.6	100.1	99.9	99.0	100.0
1971	98.2	97.7	97.5	97.4	97.8	98.2	98.3	98.7	99.1	99.0	98.6	99.0	98.3
1972	98.8	98.6	98.6	98.9	99.2	99.4	99.9	100.2	101.0	102.0	102.9	103.7	100.3
1973	104.6	105.8	107.1	108.5	110.0	111.7	113.7	115.6	117.0	117.9	118.4	119.2	112.5
1974	119.9	120.7	121.2	122.6	123.8	124.4	125.0	125.0	124.8	124.2	123.5	122.7	123.1
1975	121.2	119.0	117.0	115.4	114.1	112.6	112.0	111.7	111.4	111.3	110.7	110.1	113.9
1976	110.4	110.6	111.1	111.3	111.6	112.6	112.9	112.9	113.7	114.2	114.5	114.5	112.5
1977	114.8	115.1	115.5	115.6	115.7	116.0	115.9	116.3	116.3	116.7	116.9	117.4	116.0
1978	118.0	118.5	119.4	119.8	120.6	121.4	121.8	122.3	123.0	124.0	125.5	126.0	121.7
1979	126.6	126.8	127.0	128.1	128.8	129.8	130.6	131.6	133.0	134.4	135.8	136.0	130.7
1980	136.1	136.6	138.5	139.7	138.6	136.7	135.7	135.4	136.0	137.1	138.4	140.0	137.4
1981	139.7	139.3	***	***	***	***	***	***	***	***	***	***	***

Appendix A

Current Sources of International Economic Indicators

INTERNATIONAL

Main Economic Indicators, Organization for Economic Cooperation and Development, Paris

United Nations Monthly Bulletin of Statistics and its *Supplement*, United Nations, New York

Statistical Indicators of Short Term Economic Changes in ECE Countries, United Nations Economic Commission for Europe, Geneva

European Economy, Commission of the European Communities, Luxembourg

International Economic Scoreboard, The Conference Board, New York

International Financial Statistics, International Monetary Fund, Washington

International Economic Indicators, Center for International Business Cycle Research, New York, and Citicorp Information Services, New York

World Financial Markets, Morgan Guaranty Trust Company of New York

CANADA

Current Economic Analysis, Statistics Canada, Ottawa

Canadian Statistical Review, Statistics Canada, Ottawa

Bank of Canada Review, Bank of Canada, Ottawa

FRANCE

Bulletin Mensuel de Statistique, Institut National de la Statistique et des Études Économiques, Paris

Tendances de la Conjoncture, Institut National de la Statistique et des Études Économiques, Paris

Informations Rapides, Institut National de la Statistique et des Études Économiques, Paris

ITALY

Congiuntura Italiana, Istituto Nazionale per lo Studio Della Congiuntura, Rome

Bollettino Mensile di Statistica, Istituto Centrale di Statistica, Rome

Indicatori Mensile, Istituto Centrale di Statistica, Rome

JAPAN

Japanese Economic Indicators, Economic Planning Agency, Tokyo

Economic Statistics Monthly, Bank of Japan, Tokyo

Monthly Statistics of Japan, Statistics Bureau, Prime Minister's Office, Tokyo

UNITED KINGDOM

Monthly Digest of Statistics, Central Statistical Office, London

British Business, Department of Trade and Industry, London

Economic Trends, Central Statistical Office, London

UNITED STATES

Business Conditions Digest and its supplement, *Handbook of Cyclical Indicators*, U.S. Department of Commerce, Washington

Survey of Current Business, U.S. Department of Commerce, Washington

Federal Reserve Bulletin, Board of Governors of the Federal Reserve System, Washington

Economic Indicators, Joint Economic Committee, Washington

WEST GERMANY

Wirtschaft und Statistik, Statistisches Bundesamt, Wiesbaden

Statistische Beihefte zu den Monatsberichten der Deutschen Bundesbank, Deutsche Bundesbank, Frankfurt am Main

Monthly Report of the Deutsche Bundesbank, Frankfurt am Main

Statistischer Wochendienst, Statistisches Bundesamt, Wiesbaden, W. Kohlhammer GMBH Stuttgart und Mainz

Chronologies of Growth Cycles in Thirteen Countries, 1948–83

The historical growth-cycle turning points for thirteen countries given in table B.1 have been designated by the Center for International Business Cycle Research (CIBCR). They mark the approximate dates when aggregate economic activity was farthest above its long-run trend level (peak) or farthest below its long-run trend level (trough). Growth-cycle turning points are not to be confused with business-cycle turning points, which mark the dates when the actual "level" of economic activity reached a peak or trough, regardless of the long-run trend.

These historical growth-cycle turning dates are subject to periodic review by CIBCR and on occasion are changed as a result of significant revisions in the economic time series used in their determination. The dates shown in table B.1 are based upon a 1984 review. The absence of a recent turning date, however, does not necessarily mean that one has not occurred, since dates for some countries are not kept up to date on a regular basis. Also, the chronologies begin at different dates because suitable data are not available for all countries back to 1948.

Growth-cycle chronologies are important for two basic reasons. First, growth-cycle peaks tend to precede business-cycle peaks while their troughs tend to be coincident with business cycle troughs. Thus, growth-cycle analysis offers an "early warning system" for cyclical episodes which ultimately may become actual recessions. Second, growth-cycle analysis provides a means of identifying mild setbacks in economic activity which do not actually become declines in the level of activity but merely declines in its rate of growth. As a result, there are usually more growth cycles than business cycles in a given country.

In dating growth cycles, selection of turning points is based upon visually inspected computer-selected turns in a variety of economic series. The methodology for turning point selection, as described here briefly, involves the following basic steps:

1. Coincident series such as industrial production, gross national product (GNP), personal income, employment, and retail sales are first deflated, seasonally adjusted, and their trend removed.

2. For each of these series final, computer-selected turning points are then derived from the deviations of the seasonally adjusted data from the final trend.[1]

3. These computer-selected turning points in the deviations are then visually inspected and, in some cases, amended; if, for example, the cycle involves too small an amplitude, or if there were identifiable "exogenous" factors upsetting the cycle.

4. Median dates of peaks (or of troughs) of all the coincident series considered above are then computed.

5. These median dates are then compared with the turning points in the composite coincident index, and a decision made on the final growth-cycle dates based on the consensus of the evidence.

---

1. For a description of the trend-fitting procedure see "The Phase-Average Trend: A New Way of Measuring Economic Growth," by Charlotte Boschan and Walter W. Ebanks, *Proceedings of the Business and Economics Statistics Section*, American Statistical Association, 1978, p. 332.

Table B.1
Growth Cycle Peak and Trough Dates, Thirteen Countries, 1948-83

Peak or Trough	United States	Australia	Belgium	Canada	France	Italy	Japan	South Korea	Netherlands	Sweden	Switzerland	United Kingdom	West Germany	Three Countries	Four Countries	Six Countries	Seven Countries
P	7/48								7/50		2/50						
T	10/49			5/50					6/52				2/51				
P	3/51	4/51		4/51							3/51	3/51					
T	7/52	11/52		12/51							2/53	8/52					
P	3/53			3/53			12/53										
T	8/54			10/54			6/55						2/56	8/54			
P	2/57	8/55		11/56	8/57	10/56	5/57		10/56		6/57	12/55	10/55	2/57	5/57	2/57	2/57
T	4/58	1/58		8/58	8/59	7/59	1/59		5/58		9/58	11/58	4/59	4/58	2/59	2/59	5/58
P	2/60	8/60		10/59										2/60			2/60
T	2/61	9/61		3/61										2/61			2/61
P	5/62			3/62	2/64	9/63	1/62		3/61		4/64	3/61	2/61	4/62	3/61	3/61	2/62
T	10/64			5/63	6/65	3/65	1/63		2/63			2/63	2/63	2/63	2/63	2/63	2/63
P							7/64									7/64	
T							2/66										
P	6/66	4/65	10/64	3/66	6/66				11/65	2/65		2/66	5/65	2/66	3/66		3/66
T	10/67	1/68	7/68	2/68	5/68			8/66	8/67	7/67	5/68	8/67	8/67	3/67	5/68	5/68	10/67
P	3/69	5/70	9/70	2/69	11/69	8/69	6/70	1/69	11/70	7/70	5/70	6/69	5/70	5/69	5/70	6/70	8/69
T	11/70	3/72	7/71	12/70	11/71	9/72	1/72	3/72	8/72	7/72	1/71	2/72	12/71	11/70	2/72	2/72	8/71
P	3/73	2/74	7/74	2/74	5/74	4/74	11/73	2/74	8/74	6/74	4/74	6/73	8/73	10/73	7/74	11/73	11/73
T	3/75		10/75	10/75	6/75	5/75	3/75	6/75	7/75		8/75	8/75	5/75	3/75	8/75	9/75	5/75
P				5/76	5/76	12/76		7/76	9/76								
T		10/77		12/77	12/77	10/77			11/77	7/78							
P	12/78		6/79	10/79	8/79			12/79	12/79		6/79	6/79		9/79			
T				5/80		2/80	2/80						2/80	8/80	2/80	2/80	2/80
P	12/82	6/81		6/81										8/81			
T		5/83		11/82		6/83	6/83				6/83	6/83	7/83	10/82		4/83	2/83

Note: The three, four, six and seven country chronologies are based on composite indexes of output, income, employment and trade, weighted by each country's GNP in 1980, expressed in U.S. dollars. The three countries include the United States, Canada and Japan. The four countries are the United Kingdom, West Germany, France and Italy. The six countries include these four plus Canada and Japan, and the seven countries include the United States as well. The chronologies begin at different dates because appropriate data are not available earlier. The absence of a recent date does not necessarily mean that a turn has not occurred.

Source: For the United States, National Bureau of Economic Research. For other countries, Center for International Business Cycle Research.

The Record of the Leading Economic Indicators, Seven Countries

The median lead time, in months, of each of the leading indicators that form the composite leading indexes is shown in table C.1. A minus sign— say, −3—means that in the past the indicator has reached its turning point, on the average, three months before the turning point in the economy. Where there is a plus sign, as in the case of the average workweek in Italy, the indicator lagged behind the economy more often than not.

The vast majority of the entries in the table are minuses, that is, leads. There are three zeroes, meaning coincident behavior; six pluses, or lags; and seventy-nine minuses, or leads. The composite indexes themselves all lead, and the entries for the seven countries taken together show that every single indicator leads, on average.

The reader may wonder why, if the indicators are selected because of their tendency to lead the economy into and out of recession, there are any entries showing lags. Why aren't such indicators rejected? The answer is that the indicators were originally selected on the basis of their behavior in the United States, in studies completed a number of years ago. This left open the possibility, however, that in some countries they might not perform the same way, and when the international indicator system was set up one objective was to see whether they did or not. By and large, the indicators performed as expected, and consequently the entire set was left as it was prepared originally. This had the advantage of preserving comparability across countries, to the degree that is attainable from available statistics. Moreover, it is not always easy to ascertain whether deviant behavior is systematic or simply a temporary aberration. At any rate, the overall record is quite good—90 percent of the entries in the table are leads.

Some observations on cyclical behavior suggested by the table are:

1. Stock prices, profits, and the ratio of prices to unit labor costs all lead the business cycle, and are obviously related to one another. Stock prices are influenced by earnings and earnings are influenced by margins, for which the price/labor-cost ratio is a good proxy.

Table C.1
Median Leads and Lags of Leading Indicators at Growth Cycle Peaks and Troughs, Seven Countries

Indicators: U.S. Classification and U.S. Title[a]	United States	Canada	United Kingdom	West Germany	France	Italy	Japan	Seven Countries
	lead (−) or lag (+), in months							
Average workweek, manufacturing	−2	−4	−2	−2	−3	+2	−4	−2
New unemployment claims[b]	−2	−2	NA	−2	−41[d]	NA	NA	−2
New orders, consumer goods[c]	−2	−1	NA	NA	−11	−8	NA	−5
Formation of business enterprises	−4	NA	−8	−8	NA	−6	−13	−8
Contracts and orders, plant and equipment[c]	−2	+2	−3	−4	NA	NA	−4	−3
Building permits, housing	−7	−5	−11	+8	−8	−2	−9	−7
Change in business inventories[c]	−1	0	−5	−4	+2	NA	−2	−2
Change in industrial materials prices	−4	−3	+3	0	−1	NA	−7	−2
Stock price index	−4	−4	−8	−7	−8	−8	−6	−7
Profits[c]	−2	−3	−3	−9	NA	NA	−10	−3
Ratio, price to unit labor cost	−7	0	−12	−9	−4	+1	−2	−4
Change in consumer debt[c]	−6	−7	−16	−18	NA	NA	−9	−9
Composite Leading Index	−2	−2	−6	−6	−4	−5	−4	−4

Note: NA = Indicator not available.

[a]The indicator available for each country is sometimes only roughly equivalent in content to the U.S. indicator. In some cases two indicators are used to match the U.S. indicator and the median covers all observations for both indicators. The periods covered vary for each indicator and each country, but all are within the years 1948-1981. The growth cycle peaks and troughs are based upon turning points in output, employment, real income and sales after long-run growth trends are eliminated.
[b]Inverted.
[c]In constant prices.
[d]One observation.

2. Changes in inventories and the rate of change in materials prices both show leads in most instances. The accumulation of inventories of materials often goes hand in hand with a firming of prices, while liquidation makes for a softening of prices.

3. Commitments for new investment—represented by the formation of business enterprises, contracts and orders for plant and equipment, and building permits for new housing—show leads for the most part, evidencing their close connection with the indicators of profitability. But actual investment expenditures are not in the leading group. They follow the commitments, and are represented among the lagging indicators.

4. Only two series relating directly to consumption are in the table—new orders for consumer goods and change in consumer debt. They anticipate the movement of total retail sales, which move with the business cycle but seldom before it.

5. The two leading indicators pertaining directly to employment and unemployment are the average workweek and initial claims for unemployment insurance. Shorter or longer workweeks are a management device to give quick effect to decisions to change labor input. Putting in a claim for unemployment insurance benefits is one of the first steps a newly unemployed worker takes. Hence, these are early warning indicators of developments that show up later in the employment and unemployment numbers.

Construction of Composite Indexes

Leading, coincident, and lagging composite indexes have been constructed by the Center for International Business Cycle Research (CIBCR) for the United States, Canada, United Kingdom, West Germany, France, Italy, and Japan, as well as for other countries. In addition, composite indexes are compiled for several groups of countries, all weighted by the respective countries' gross national product (GNP) in current U.S. dollars in 1980. The method used in constructing the indexes corresponds to that used by the U.S. Department of Commerce in *Business Conditions Digest*, with some differences in the method of amplitude and trend adjustment as described below.[1]

Historical data for the indexes and their components are shown in chapter 3. Data are also available on magnetic tape from the Center for International Business Cycle Research.

The starting dates for the composite indexes, beginning in January of the year shown are as follows:

	Leading	Coincident	Lagging
United States	1948	1948	1948
Canada	1948	1948	1948
United Kingdom	1955	1952	1955
West Germany	1957	1950	1962
France	1955	1955	1964
Italy	1955	1956	1970
Japan	1953	1954	1953
3 countries excl. Europe	1953	1954	1953
4 European countries	1955	1955	1966
6 countries excl. U.S.	1955	1955	1966
7 countries	1955	1955	1966

1. See *Handbook of Cyclical Indicators*, U.S. Department of Commerce, Bureau of Economic Analysis, 1984, pp. 65-70.

The weights for the multicountry indexes, expressed as percentages of GNP in 1980, are:

	US	Can	UK	WG	FR	IT	JA	Total
3 countries excl. Europe	65.1	6.1					28.8	100.0%
4 European countries			23.7	33.3	27.0	16.0		100.0%
6 countries excl. U.S.		6.7	14.6	20.6	16.7	9.9	31.5	100.0%
7 countries	41.6	3.9	8.5	12.0	9.8	5.8	18.4	100.0%

The method of constructing the indexes can be explained by reference to the printout in Table D.1, using the U.S. coincident index as an example. Starting at the top the country is identified followed by the title of the composite index. The word "deflated" in the title signifies that each of the component indicators either represents a physical quantity or an aggregate value deflated by an appropriate price index.

Line 1. Each of the component series is identified by a code (for example, component series USGM) the first two letters of which represent the country. Monthly series are distinguished from quarterly. Quarterly series are interpolated to obtain monthly values, with the quarterly figure centered in the middle month of the quarter. If a moving average were applied to the series the span of the moving average would be indicated on this line, but in these indexes no moving averages are used. Also, the component indicators are unweighted. A brief title of the series is given on the next line, together with the unit, whether it is monthly (M) or quarterly (Q), and whether it is treated invertedly. In the case of bankruptcies, for example, an increase is treated as a decline and vice versa (see line 2 below). All series are used in seasonally adjusted form unless otherwise specified after the title (NSA = not seasonally adjusted). Annual averages are computed from seasonally adjusted data and hence may not correspond to those published in the source, which are usually based upon raw data. Also, for quarterly series the annual averages are computed from monthly interpolations rather than from the quarterly figures.

Line 2. The "weighted changes" are the month-to-month changes in the series, either in percentage form ("percents") or differences, with signs either inverted (that is, reversed) or not inverted as indicated. The next line gives the average month-to-month change without regard to sign, together with the period for which the average was computed (i.e., the entire length of the series). The words "imposed standardization" followed by a figure mean that the latter figure was used to standardize the changes. The alternative would be to use the average covering the entire period, but since this would change as more data are included, an average ending at an earlier, fixed date was "imposed." The percentage changes are not computed in the usual fashion, with the initial figure as the base, but rather the base is the average of the two adjacent figures. That is, $(a_2 - a_1) \div (a_1 + a_2) / 2 \times 100$. This has the effect of equalizing the range of percentage increases and percentage decreases (the limits are $+200$ and -200) so that they may be averaged without the upward bias that applies to the usual percentage changes. The standardization is performed by dividing the percent changes calculated in the above manner by the "imposed standardization" factor.

Line 3. The "average weighted changes" are the means for each month of the standardized percent changes (or differences) for all the series listed. The weights in this instance are unity, but standardization is, of course, itself a form of weighting. Its purpose is to equalize the month-to-month variations in the different series so that those that usually move in wide swings do not have a larger influence on the average than those that have a smaller amplitude of variation.

Line 4. Count of component series is the number of series included in the average change. It diminishes toward the most recent months because not all series are equally up to date. Hence the averages for the recent months are less representative and most subject to revision. The CIBCR does not, as a rule, use averages based upon less than half the total number of series regularly included in an index.

Line 5. "Standardized average weighted changes" are the average changes in line 3 divided first by a standardization factor, namely the "average change without regard to sign" shown on the line immediately below line 5, and then by a "weight applied" given on the next line. The first divisor is designed to adjust the "average weighted changes" (line 3) so that they will average unity. The divisor is computed for a fixed period, January 1953 to November 1975. The second divisor is designed to make the average of the final, standardized changes equal to the average percent change per month in the "trend-cycle component" of the industrial production index in the country concerned (the latter average is the reciprocal of the "weight applied" figure). In this way both the leading and coincident indexes for a given country have the same average percent change, equal to that of the cyclical movements in industrial production in that country. The second step in the procedure seemed preferable to the alternative of letting the indexes for all countries have the same average percent change, namely unity. Using industrial production as the standard also seemed preferable to using real GNP for this purpose, since industrial production typically has a larger cyclical amplitude than real GNP. The trend-cycle component is a smooth moving average of the index. The average percent changes, 1953-75, in this component of industrial production are:

United States	.72
Canada	.53
United Kingdom	.41
West Germany	.62
France	.65
Italy	.77
Japan	1.16

Line 6.0. The composite index, 1980 = 100, is derived by first cumulating the standardized percent changes (line 5) with the initial month of the historical series as 100 and then rebasing the resulting index so that 1980 = 100. The method of cumulation takes account of the method by which the changes were calculated. That is, if p is the percent change from month 1 to month 2 (calculated as explained in line 2), and y is the index for month 1, then the index for month 2 is y times $(200 + p)/(200 - p)$.

Line 6.1. This line shows the composite index adjusted each month so that its rate of growth, 1969 to 1979, is equal to that in real GNP for the country concerned during 1969 to 1979, and rebased so that 1980 = 100. Hence line 6.0 contains the composite index without adjustment to the GNP trend, while line 6.1 contains the index with adjustment to the GNP trend. For most purposes the latter index is the most useful. The GNP trend rates, 1969-79 at annual rate, in percentages, are:

United States	3.1
Canada	4.2
United Kingdom	1.6
West Germany	3.1
France	4.1
Italy	3.3
Japan	5.4
3 countries, excluding Europe	3.7
4 European countries	3.0
6 countries, excluding U.S.	3.8
7 countries	3.5

Line 6.2. This is the percentage change in the GNP trended index (line 6.1) over moving 6-month intervals (for example, June to December, July to January) compounded at an annual rate, and placed in the terminal month of the interval.

Line 6.3. This is the percentage change in the GNP trended index (line 6.1) obtained by dividing the current month by the average of the 12 preceding months. For example, if June is the current month, the rate is based upon the ratio of June to the average of the 12 months ending May. The interval from June to the middle of this 12-month average is 6.5 months. Hence the ratio is raised to the 12/6.5 power to put it on an annual rate basis. The result, expressed as a percentage change at annual rate, is placed in June. It is called a 6-month smoothed rate.

Since the 12-month moving average used as the base for this rate is smoother than the individual monthly figures, the rate is smoother than the ordinary 6-month rate (line 6.2) but has approximately the same cyclical timing characteristics. It will usually reach highs and lows earlier than the 12-month rate (line 6.4) but may not show cyclical movements so clearly.

The new rate is analogous to what would be obtained by taking a weighted, 12-month moving average of the index itself, giving a weight of 12 to the current month, 11 to the preceding month, 10 to the month before that, and so on down to 1, and then taking the month-to-month changes in this smoothed index.

Line 6.4. This is the percentage change in the GNP trended index (line 6.1) obtained by dividing the current month by the average of the 12 months ending 6 months before the current month. For example, the December figure is divided by the average for the year ending the preceding June; the January figure is divided by the average for the year ending the preceding July; and so on. The result is similar to the ordinary change from the same month of the preceding year except that the year-ago figure is replaced by an average for the year of which it is (approximately) the central month. This has the effect of eliminating erratic movements in the year-ago figure and producing a smoother percentage change. These rates are decidedly less erratic than the 6-month rates (line 6.2) but tend to reach cyclical turning points about 3 months later. They are somewhat less erratic than the 6-month, smoothed rates (line 6.3) but also reach turning points later.

Line 10. The summary measures pertain to the smoothness of the index without adjustment for GNP trend (line 6.0). CI-bar is the average percentage change in the index without regard to sign over spans of 1, 2, 3 months, and so on. For the 1-month span it is equal (approximately) to the average month-to-month change in the "trend-cycle component" of the industrial production index for the country concerned, which was used to adjust the average changes on line 5. That is, the CI-bar figure for 1-month span is approximately equal to the reciprocal of the "weight applied" factor on line 5. I-bar and C-bar are the average percentage changes without regard to sign in the "irregular" component and the "trend-cycle" component of the index, respectively, and the I/C ratio is the ratio between these two averages. Months for cyclical dominance (MCD) is the number of months' span required to reduce the I/C ratio to less than unity. Average duration of run is the average number of consecutive months the index (CI), or its components (I and C), or its moving average with span equal to MCD, moves in one direction. For further explanation of these measures see *Business Conditions Digest*, U.S. Department of Commerce, Appendix A.

Table D.1
Sample Printout: Coincident Index, United States

COMPOSITE INDEX-   UNITED STATES DEFLATED COMPOSITE INDEX OF COINCIDENT INDICATORS (6)
4. COMPONENT SERIES USGM   MONTHLY,   0-MONTH MOVING AVGE APPLIED, WEIGHT SERIES-

PERSONAL INCOME, BILLION 1972$, ANNUAL RATE (M)

YEAR	JAN	FEB	MAR	APR	MAY	JUN	JUL	AUG	SEP	OCT	NOV	DEC	AVGE
1981	1233.0	1236.2	1240.9	1241.6	1242.5	1251.6	1266.0	1274.7	1274.4	1268.1	1263.8	1257.5	1254.2
1982	1249.1	1255.7	1256.0	1258.1	1263.8	1254.3	1256.0	1250.8	1251.2	1253.7	1259.9	1264.9	1256.1
1983	1264.3	1262.1	1269.1	1267.8	1278.5	1285.3	1286.3	1283.8	1289.6	1302.7	1311.8	1320.8	1285.2
1984	1336.4	1345.6	1348.9	...	...	...	...	...	...	...	...	...	...

2. WEIGHTED CHANGES   PERCENTS, 1-MONTH SPAN, SIGNS NOT INVERTED; SERIES USGM
   AVERAGE CHANGE W/O REGARD TO SIGN   0.518 COMPUTED FROM 48 1 TO 84 3 . IMPOSED STANDARDIZATION 0.519
   WEIGHT APPLIED   1.000

	JAN	FEB	MAR	APR	MAY	JUN	JUL	AUG	SEP	OCT	NOV	DEC
1981	0.8	0.5	0.7	0.1	0.1	1.4	2.2	1.3	-0.0	-1.0	-0.7	-1.0
1982	-1.3	1.0	0.0	0.3	0.9	-1.5	0.3	-0.8	0.1	0.4	1.0	0.8
1983	-0.1	-0.3	1.1	-0.2	1.6	1.0	0.1	-0.4	0.9	1.9	1.3	1.3
1984	2.3	1.3	0.5	...	...	...	...	...	...	...	...	...

1. COMPONENT SERIES USGN   QURTRLY,   0-MONTH MOVING AVGE APPLIED, WEIGHT SERIES-

GROSS NATIONAL PRODUCT, BILLION 1972$, ANNUAL RATE (Q)

	JAN	FEB	MAR	APR	MAY	JUN	JUL	AUG	SEP	OCT	NOV	DEC	AVGE
1981	1499.4	1510.1	1510.9	1511.7	1512.5	1516.9	1521.4	1525.8	1519.5	1513.2	1506.9	1499.9	1512.3
1982	1492.8	1485.8	1487.0	1488.1	1489.3	1488.1	1486.9	1485.7	1484.0	1482.4	1480.7	1483.8	1486.2
1983	1487.0	1490.1	1501.8	1513.4	1525.1	1534.5	1544.0	1553.1	1559.8	1566.1	1572.5	1583.1	1535.9
1984	1593.7	1604.3	...										...

2. WEIGHTED CHANGES   PERCENTS, 1-MONTH SPAN, SIGNS NOT INVERTED; SERIES USGN
   AVERAGE CHANGE W/O REGARD TO SIGN   0.391 COMPUTED FROM 48 2 TO 84 2 . IMPOSED STANDARDIZATION 0.392
   WEIGHT APPLIED   1.000

	JAN	FEB	MAR	APR	MAY	JUN	JUL	AUG	SEP	OCT	NOV	DEC
1981	1.8	1.8	0.1	0.1	0.1	0.7	0.7	0.7	-1.1	-1.1	-1.1	-1.2
1982	-1.2	-1.2	0.2	0.2	0.2	-0.2	-0.2	-0.3	-0.3	-0.3	-0.3	0.5
1983	0.5	0.5	2.0	2.0	2.0	1.6	1.6	1.6	1.0	1.0	1.0	1.7
1984	1.7	1.7	...									

362

1. COMPONENT SERIES USIP   MONTHLY,   0-MONTH MOVING AVGE APPLIED, WEIGHT SERIES—

INDUSTRIAL PRODUCTION, 1967=100 (M)

1981	151.4	151.8	152.1	152.7	152.9	153.9	153.6	151.6	149.1	146.3	143.4	150.9
1982	140.7	142.9	141.7	139.2	138.7	138.8	138.8	137.3	135.7	134.9	135.2	138.6
1983	137.4	138.1	140.0	144.4	146.4	149.7	151.8	153.8	155.0	155.3	156.2	147.6
1984	158.4	160.0	160.7	...	...	...	...	...	...	...	...	...

2. WEIGHTED CHANGES   PERCENTS,   1-MONTH SPAN, SIGNS NOT INVERTED, SERIES USIP

AVERAGE CHANGE W/O REGARD TO SIGN   0.928 COMPUTED FROM 48   1 TO 84   3 . IMPOSED STANDARDIZATION   0.922
WEIGHT APPLIED

1981	0.7	0.3	0.2	-0.1	0.6	0.1	0.7	-0.2	-1.4	-1.8	-2.1	-2.2
1982	-2.1	1.7	-0.9	-1.2	-0.8	-0.4	0.1	-0.3	-0.9	-1.3	-0.6	0.2
1983	1.8	0.6	1.5	2.0	1.4	1.5	2.4	1.5	1.4	0.8	0.2	0.6
1984	1.5	1.1	0.5	...	...	...	...	...	...	...	...	...

1. COMPONENT SERIES USMT   MONTHLY,   0-MONTH MOVING AVGE APPLIED, WEIGHT SERIES—

MANUFACTURING AND TRADE SALES, TEN MILLION 1972$ (M)

1981	16213.2	16164.5	16166.1	16225.2	16159.4	16237.1	16126.2	16090.2	15903.2	15638.9	15555.8	15335.4
1982	15087.1	15372.3	15418.8	15261.9	15586.6	15340.9	15295.7	15177.0	15118.4	14845.6	14987.7	14995.9
1983	15388.4	15207.9	15441.6	15508.6	16062.7	16440.5	16271.9	16310.1	16447.4	16488.3	16753.2	17076.9
1984	17284.2	17186.9	...	...	...	...	...	...	...	...	...	...

2. WEIGHTED CHANGES   PERCENTS,   1-MONTH SPAN, SIGNS NOT INVERTED, SERIES USMT
AVERAGE CHANGE W/O REGARD TO SIGN   1.027 COMPUTED FROM 48   1 TO 84   2 . IMPOSED STANDARDIZATION   1.018
WEIGHT APPLIED

1981	0.9	-0.3	0.0	0.4	-0.4	0.5	-0.7	-0.2	-1.1	-1.6	-0.5	-1.4
1982	-1.6	1.8	0.3	-1.0	2.1	-1.6	-0.3	-0.8	-0.4	-1.8	0.9	0.1
1983	2.5	-1.2	1.5	0.4	3.4	2.3	-1.0	0.2	0.8	0.2	1.6	1.9
1984	1.2	-0.6	...	...	...	...	...	...	...	...	...	...

1. COMPONENT SERIES USLP   MONTHLY,   0-MONTH MOVING AVGE APPLIED, WEIGHT SERIES—

EMPLOYEES ON NONFARM PAYROLLS, THOUSANDS (M)

1981	90920.0	90990.0	91030.0	91128.0	91131.0	91322.0	91484.0	91424.0	91411.0	91295.0	91041.0	90730.0
1982	90396.0	90417.0	90207.0	90024.0	90016.0	89775.0	89450.0	89264.0	89235.0	88938.0	88785.0	88665.0
1983	88885.0	88746.0	88814.0	89090.0	89421.0	89844.0	89152.0	89748.0	90851.0	91084.0	91355.0	91599.0
1984	91930.0	92357.0	92506.0	...	...	...	...	...	...	...	...	...

2. WEIGHTED CHANGES   PERCENTS,   1-MONTH SPAN, SIGNS NOT INVERTED, SERIES USLP
AVERAGE CHANGE W/O REGARD TO SIGN   0.320 COMPUTED FROM 48   1 TO 84   4 . IMPOSED STANDARDIZATION   0.321
WEIGHT APPLIED

1981	0.4	0.2	0.1	0.1	0.0	0.0	0.7	0.6	-0.0	-0.2	-0.4	-1.1
1982	-1.1	0.1	-0.7	-0.6	-0.0	-0.8	-1.1	-0.6	-0.1	-1.0	-0.5	-0.4
1983	0.8	-0.5	0.2	1.0	1.2	1.5	1.1	1.1	3.8	0.9	0.9	0.8
1984	1.1	1.4	...	...	...	...	...	...	...	...	...	...

Table D.1 (*continued*)

1. COMPONENT SERIES USLH   MONTHLY, 0-MONTH MOVING AVGE APPLIED, WEIGHT SERIES-

UNEMPLOYMENT RATE, PERCENT (M) - INVERTED

	JAN	FEB	MAR	APR	MAY	JUN	JUL	AUG	SEP	OCT	NOV	DEC	AVGE
1981	7.4	7.3	7.2	7.1	7.3	7.3	7.2	7.3	7.5	7.8	8.1	8.4	7.5
1982	8.5	8.7	8.9	9.2	9.4	9.2	9.7	9.7	10.0	10.3	10.6	10.6	9.6
1983	10.3	10.2	10.2	10.1	9.8	9.9	9.3	9.3	9.1	8.7	8.3	8.1	9.4
1984	7.9	7.7	7.7	7.7	...	...	...	...	...	...	...	...	...

2. WEIGHTED CHANGES PERCENTS, 1-MONTH SPAN, SIGNS INVERTED; SERIES USLH

AVERAGE CHANGE W/O REGARD TO SIGN   3.232 COMPUTED FROM 48 1 TO 84 4 . IMPOSED STANDARDIZATION   3.416
WEIGHT APPLIED   1.000

	JAN	FEB	MAR	APR	MAY	JUN	JUL	AUG	SEP	OCT	NOV	DEC
1981	-1.2	0.4	0.4	0.4	-0.8	0.0	0.4	-0.4	-0.8	-1.1	-1.1	-1.1
1982	-0.3	-0.7	-0.7	-1.0	-0.6	-0.9	0.0	0.2	-0.9	-0.9	-0.8	0.0
1983	0.8	0.3	0.0	0.3	0.6	1.5	0.0	0.0	0.6	1.3	1.4	0.7
1984	0.7	0.8	0.0	0.0	...	...	...	...	...	...	...	...

3. AVERAGE WEIGHTED CHANGES   COMPOSITE INDEX- UNITED STATES DEFLATED COMPOSITE INDEX OF COINCIDENT INDICATORS (6)

YEAR	JAN	FEB	MAR	APR	MAY	JUN	JUL	AUG	SEP	OCT	NOV	DEC
1981	0.6	0.5	0.3	0.2	-0.1	0.6	0.7	0.2	-0.8	-1.2	-1.0	-1.3
1982	-1.3	0.5	-0.3	-0.5	0.4	-0.8	-0.4	-0.5	-0.4	-0.8	-0.1	0.2
1983	1.1	-0.1	-0.3	0.9	1.7	1.4	1.0	0.3	1.4	1.0	1.1	1.2
1984	1.4	1.0	0.4	...	...	...	...	...	...	...	...	...

4. COUNT OF COMPONENT SERIES

YEAR	JAN	FEB	MAR	APR	MAY	JUN	JUL	AUG	SEP	OCT	NOV	DEC
1981	6.0	6.0	6.0	6.0	6.0	6.0	6.0	6.0	6.0	6.0	6.0	6.0
1982	6.0	6.0	6.0	6.0	6.0	6.0	6.0	6.0	6.0	6.0	6.0	6.0
1983	6.0	6.0	6.0	6.0	6.0	6.0	6.0	6.0	6.0	6.0	6.0	6.0
1984	6.0	6.0	4.0	2.0	...	...	...	...	...	...	...	...

5. STANDARDIZED AVERAGE WEIGHTED CHANGES

AVERAGE CHANGE W/O REGARD TO SIGN   0.755 COMPUTED FROM 53 1 TO 75 11
WEIGHT APPLIED   1.389

YEAR	JAN	FEB	MAR	APR	MAY	JUN	JUL	AUG	SEP	OCT	NOV	DEC
1981	0.5	0.5	0.3	0.2	-0.1	0.5	0.6	0.2	-0.7	-1.1	-1.0	-1.2
1982	-1.2	0.4	-0.3	-0.5	0.4	-0.8	-0.4	-0.4	-0.4	-0.8	-0.1	0.2
1983	1.0	1.0	1.0	0.9	1.6	1.3	0.9	0.2	1.4	1.0	1.0	1.1
1984	1.4	0.9	0.3	...	...	...	...	...	...	...	...	...

6.0 COMPOSITE INDEX 1980=100

YEAR	JAN	FEB	MAR	APR	MAY	JUN	JUL	AUG	SEP	OCT	NOV	DEC	AVGE
1981	102.2	102.6	102.9	103.1	103.0	103.6	104.3	104.4	103.7	102.5	101.5	100.3	102.8
1982	99.0	99.5	99.2	98.7	99.1	98.3	97.9	97.5	97.1	96.4	96.3	96.5	97.9
1983	97.5	97.4	98.3	99.2	100.8	102.1	103.0	103.3	104.7	105.7	106.8	108.0	102.2
1984	109.5	110.5	110.9	...	...	...	...	...	...	...	...	...	...

6.1 COMPOSITE INDEX ADJUSTED TO GNP TREND, 1980 = 100

YEAR	JAN	FEB	MAR	APR	MAY	JUN	JUL	AUG	SEP	OCT	NOV	DEC	AVGE
1981	101.5	101.8	102.0	102.1	101.9	102.4	102.9	103.0	102.1	100.9	99.8	98.4	101.6
1982	97.2	97.5	97.1	96.5	96.8	95.9	95.4	94.9	94.5	93.6	93.5	93.6	95.5
1983	94.4	94.2	95.1	95.8	97.2	98.4	99.2	99.3	100.6	101.5	102.4	103.5	98.5
1984	104.8	105.6	105.9	...	...	...	...	...	...	...	...	...	...

6.2 SIX MONTH CHANGE IN ADJUSTED INDEX, ANNUAL RATE, PERCENT

YEAR	JAN	FEB	MAR	APR	MAY	JUN	JUL	AUG	SEP	OCT	NOV	DEC
1981	7.9	8.0	6.6	4.9	3.3	2.7	2.9	2.2	0.2	-2.3	-4.2	-7.5
1982	-10.9	-10.4	-9.6	-8.5	-6.0	-5.1	-3.5	-5.1	-5.4	-5.8	-6.7	-4.8
1983	-2.2	-1.5	1.3	4.6	8.2	10.6	10.4	11.2	12.0	12.2	10.9	10.6
1984	11.6	13.1	10.8	...	...	...	...	...	...	...	...	...

6.3 SIX MONTH SMOOTHED CHANGE IN ADJUSTED INDEX, ANNUAL RATE, PERCENT

YEAR	JAN	FEB	MAR	APR	MAY	JUN	JUL	AUG	SEP	OCT	NOV	DEC
1981	2.7	3.7	4.2	4.4	3.7	4.0	4.3	3.6	1.2	-1.5	-3.7	-6.0
1982	-7.9	-6.7	-6.7	-7.1	-5.9	-6.7	-6.5	-6.4	-6.0	-6.4	-5.6	-4.5
1983	-2.2	-2.1	0.1	1.8	4.8	7.0	8.2	7.8	9.6	10.3	10.8	11.3
1984	12.1	12.0	10.5	...	...	...	...	...	...	...	...	...

6.4 TWELVE MONTH SMOOTHED CHANGE IN ADJUSTED INDEX, PERCENT

YEAR	JAN	FEB	MAR	APR	MAY	JUN	JUL	AUG	SEP	OCT	NOV	DEC
1981	0.0	0.8	1.3	1.7	1.7	2.4	3.1	3.2	2.4	1.0	-0.4	-2.1
1982	-3.8	-3.9	-4.5	-5.2	-4.9	-5.6	-5.7	-5.9	-5.9	-6.3	-6.1	-5.5
1983	-4.0	-3.6	-2.1	-0.7	1.4	3.0	4.1	4.5	6.0	7.0	8.0	8.9
1984	9.9	10.3	10.0	...	...	...	...	...	...	...	...	...

10. SUMMARY MEASURES OF COMPOSITE INDEX (NOT ADJUSTED FOR GNP TREND)

CI-BAR, I-BAR, C-BAR AND I/C RATIO FOR 1-5, 7, 9 AND 11 MONTHS SPAN

	MONTHS SPAN							
	1	2	3	4	5	7	9	11
CI-BAR	0.75	1.39	2.01	2.62	3.20	4.30	5.33	6.27
I-BAR	0.35	0.42	0.46	0.42	0.41	0.39	0.39	0.37
C-BAR	0.64	1.28	1.91	2.52	3.11	4.24	5.28	6.22
I/C RATIO	0.55	0.33	0.24	0.17	0.13	0.09	0.07	0.06

MONTHS FOR CYCLICAL DOMINANCE

	CI	I	C	MCD
AVERAGE DURATION OF RUN	4.5	1.7	18.9	4.5

Indicator Series Finding Guide

Note: numbers after the decimal, other than 0, indicate some variation from U.S. definition.

UNITED STATES

	Source & Description	Data
Composite Leading Index, 1948–	357	134–35
1.0 Average Workweek, Mfg., 1948–	27	136
2.0 Initial Claims, Unemployment Insurance, 1948–	28	137
3.0 New Orders, Consumer Goods and Materials*, 1948–	29	138
4.0 Net Business Formation, 1948–	30	139
5.0 Contracts and Orders, Plant and Equipment*, 1948–	31	140
6.0 New Building Permits, Private Housing, 1948–	32	141
7.0 Change in Business Inventories*, 1948–	32	142
8.0 Change in Industrial Materials Price Index, 1948–	33	143
9.0 Stock Price Index, 500 S and P Common, 1948–	34	144
10.0 Corporate Profits after Taxes*, 1948–	35	145
11.0 Ratio, Price to Unit Labor Cost, Nonfarm Business, 1948–	36	146
12.0 Change in Consumer Installment Credit*, 1948–	36	147

*In constant prices.

CANADA

		Source & Description	Data
15.0	Gross National Expenditures*, 1948–	58	182
16.0	Industrial Production, 1948–	59	183
17.0	Personal Income*, 1948–	60	184
18.1	Retail Trade*, 1948–	60	185
Composite Lagging Index, 1948–		357	186–87
19.0	Long Duration unemployment, 1953–	61	188
20.0	Plant and Equipment, Investment Expenditures*, 1948–	62	189
21.0	Business Inventories*, 1949–	62	190
22.1	Change in Hours per Unit of Output, Manufacturing, 1962–	63	191
23.0	Business Loans Outstanding*, 1948–	64	192
24.0	Bank Interest Rates, Business Loans, 1948–	65	193

UNITED KINGDOM

Composite Leading Index, 1955–		357	194–95
1.0	Average Workweek, Manufacturing, 1956–	65	196
4.1	New Companies Registered, 1949–	66	197
4.2	Business Failures, 1960–	67	198
5.1	New Orders, Engineering Industries, Volume, 1958–	67	199
5.2	New Orders, Construction*, 1957–	68	200
6.1	Housing Starts, 1948–	69	201
7.0	Change in Stocks and Work in Progress*, 1955–	70	202
8.0	Change in Basic Materials Price Index, 1958–	71	203
9.0	Common Stock Price Index, 1948–	71	204
10.0	Companies' Profits less Taxes*, 1955–	72	205
11.0	Ratio, Price to Labor Cost, Manufacturing, 1963–	73	206
12.0	Increase in Hire Purchase Debt*, 1958–	74	207
Composite Coincident Index, 1952–		357	208–9
13.1	Employment in Production Industries, 1952–	75	210
14.1	Unemployed, 1949–	76	211
15.0	Gross Domestic Product*, 1955–	77	212
16.0	Industrial Production, 1948–	77	213
17.0	Personal Disposable Income*, 1955–	78	214
18.1	Retail Sales, Volume, 1957–	79	215

WEST GERMANY

		Source & Description	Data
23.1	Bank Loans Outstanding*, 1960–	97	251
24.1	Bank Rates on Large Loans, 1968–	98	252

FRANCE

Composite Leading Index, 1955–		357	253–54
1.0	Average Workweek, Industry, 1960–	98	255
2.0	New Unemployment Claims, 1975–	99	256
3.1	Change in Unfilled Orders†, 1968–	99	257
6.0	Building Permits, Residential, 1955–	100	258
7.0	Change in Stocks*, 1963–	101	259
8.0	Change in Wholesale Price Index, Raw Materials, 1955–	101	260
9.0	Index of Stock Prices (Industrials), 1948–	102	261
11.0	Ratio, Price to Unit Labor Cost, Manufacturing, 1955–	102	262
Composite Coincident Index, 1955–		357	263–64
13.0	Employment, Nonfarm, 1951–	103	265
14.1	Registered Unemployed, 1955–	104	266
15.0	Gross Domestic Product*, 1963–	105	267
16.0	Industrial Production, 1951–	106	268
18.1	Retail Sales, Volume, 1955–	106	269
Composite Lagging Index, 1964–		357	270–71
19.0	Long Duration Unemployment, 1979–	107	271
20.0	Investment Expenditures, Plant and Equipment*, 1963–	108	272
21.0	Business Inventories*, 1963–	108	273
22.0	Change in Hours per Unit of Output, Nonfarm Business, 1964–	109	274
23.0	Business Loans Outstanding*, 1979–	109	274
24.0	Commercial Bank Lending Rate to Prime Borrowers, 1966–	110	275

ITALY

Composite Leading Index, 1955–		357	276–77
1.1	Hours per Month per Worker in Industry, 1972–	110	278
3.1	Change in Unfilled Orders†, 1963–	110	279
4.1	Declared Bankruptcies, 1952–	111	280
6.0	Building Permits, Residential, 1955–	111	281

†Change in net balance of survey responses.

About the Authors

Geoffrey H. Moore is Director of the Center for International Business Cycle Research at Columbia University Business School. He previously served as Director and Vice President of the National Bureau of Economic Research and as U.S. Commissioner of Labor Statistics. His other books include *Business Cycle Indicators* and *Business Cycles, Inflation and Forecasting*.

Melita H. Moore was for many years Chief of the Research and Analysis Section in the Statistical Office of the United Nations.